RAPID DEVELOPMENT

Taming Wild Software Schedules

Steve McConnell

PUBLISHED BY
Microsoft Press
A Division of Microsoft Corporation
One Microsoft Way
Redmond, Washington 98052-6399

Library of Congress Cataloging-in-Publication Data
McConnell, Steve.
    Rapid development : taming wild software schedules / Steve
McConnell.
        p.   cm.
    Includes index.
    ISBN 1-55615-900-5
    1. Computer software--Development.   I. Title.
QA76.76.D47M393   1996
005.1'068--dc20   96-21517
                                                                             CIP

Printed and bound in the United States of America.

    3 4 5 6 7 8 9 MLML 4 9 8 7

Distributed to the book trade in Canada by Macmillan of Canada, a division of Canada Publishing Corporation.

A CIP catalogue record for this book is available from the British Library.

Microsoft Press books are available through booksellers and distributors worldwide. For further information about international editions, contact your local Microsoft Corporation office. Or contact Microsoft Press International directly at fax (206) 936-7329.

Acquisitions Editor: David J. Clark
Project Editor: Jack Litewka

Contents

PART III   BEST PRACTICES

Case Studies

Reference Tables

Preface

Software developers are caught on the horns of a dilemma. One horn of the dilemma is that developers are working too hard to have time to learn about effective practices that can solve most development-time problems; the other horn is that they won't get the time until they do learn more about rapid development.

Other problems in our industry can wait. It's hard to justify taking time to learn more about quality when you're under intense schedule pressure to "just ship it." It's hard to learn more about usability when you've worked 20 days in a row and haven't had time to see a movie, go shopping, work out, read the paper, mow your lawn, or play with your kids. Until we as an industry learn to control our schedules and free up time for developers and managers to learn more about their professions, we will never have enough time to put the rest of our house in order.

The development-time problem is pervasive. Several surveys have found that about two-thirds of all projects substantially overrun their estimates (Lederer and Prasad 1992, Gibbs 1994, Standish Group 1994). The average large project misses its planned delivery date by 25 to 50 percent, and the size of the average schedule slip increases with the size of the project (Jones 1994). Year after year, development-speed issues have appeared at the tops of lists of the most critical issues facing the software-development community (Symons 1991).

Although the slow-development problem is pervasive, some organizations are developing rapidly. Researchers have found 10-to-1 differences in productivity between companies within the same industries, and some researchers have found even greater variations (Jones 1994).

The purpose of this book is to provide the groups that are currently on the "1" side of that 10-to-1 ratio with the information they need to move toward the "10" side of the ratio. This book will help you bring your projects under control. It will help you deliver more functionality to your users in less time. You don't have to read the whole book to learn something useful; no matter what state your project is in, you will find practices that will enable you to improve its condition.

Who Should Read This Book?

Slow development affects everyone involved with software development, including developers, managers, clients, and end-users—even their families and friends. Each of these groups has a stake in solving the slow-development problem, and there is something in this book for each of them.

This book is intended to help developers and managers know what's possible, to help managers and clients know what's realistic, and to serve as an avenue of communication between developers, managers, and clients so that they can tailor the best possible approach to meet their schedule, cost, quality, and other goals.

Technical Leads

This book is written primarily with technical leads or team leads in mind. If that's your role, you usually bear primary responsibility for increasing the speed of software development, and this book explains how to do that. It also describes the development-speed limits so that you'll have a firm foundation for distinguishing between realistic improvement programs and wishful-thinking fantasies.

Some of the practices this book describes are wholly technical. As a technical lead, you should have no problem implementing those. Other practices are more management oriented, and you might wonder why they are included here. In writing the book, I have made the simplifying assumption that you are Technical Super Lead—faster than a speeding hacker; more powerful than a loco-manager; able to leap both technical problems and management problems in a single bound. That is somewhat unrealistic, I know, but it saves both of us from the distraction of my constantly saying, "If you're a manager, do this, and if you're a developer, do that." Moreover, assuming that technical leads are responsible for both technical and management practices is not as far-fetched as it might sound. Technical leads are often called upon to make recommendations to upper management about technically oriented management issues, and this book will help prepare you to do that.

Individual Programmers

Many software projects are run by individual programmers or self-managed teams, and that puts individual technical participants into de facto technical-lead roles. If you're in that role, this book will help you improve your development speed for the same reasons that it will help bona fide technical leads.

Managers

Managers sometimes think that achieving rapid software development is primarily a technical job. If you're a manager, however, you can usually do as much to improve development speed as your developers can. This book describes many management-level rapid-development practices. Of course, you can also read the technically oriented practices to understand what your developers can do at their level.

Key Benefits of This Book

I conceived of this book as a *Common Sense* for software developers. Like Thomas Paine's original *Common Sense*, which laid out in pragmatic terms why America should secede from Mother England, this book lays out in pragmatic terms why many of our most common views about rapid development are fundamentally broken. These are the times that try developers' souls, and, for that reason, this book advocates its own small revolution in software-development practices.

My view of software development is that software projects can be optimized for any of several goals—lowest defect rate, fastest execution speed, greatest user acceptance, best maintainability, lowest cost, or shortest development schedule. Part of an engineering approach to software is to balance trade-offs: Can you optimize for development time by cutting quality? By cutting usability? By requiring developers to work overtime? When crunch time comes, how much schedule reduction can you ultimately achieve? This book helps answer such key trade-off questions as well as other questions.

Improved development speed. You can use the strategy and best practices described in this book to achieve the maximum possible development speed in your specific circumstances. Over time, most people can realize dramatic improvements in development speed by applying the strategies and practices described in this book. Some best practices won't work on some kinds of projects, but for virtually any kind of project, you'll find other best practices that will. Depending on your circumstances, "maximum development speed" might not be as fast as you'd like, but you'll never be completely out of luck just because you can't use a rapid-development language, are maintaining legacy code, or work in a noisy, unproductive environment.

Rapid-development slant on traditional topics. Some of the practices described in this book aren't typically thought of as rapid-development practices. Practices such as risk management, software-development fundamentals, and lifecycle planning are more commonly thought of as "good software-development practices" than as rapid-development methodologies.

These practices, however, have profound development-speed implications that in many cases dwarf those of the so-called rapid-development methods. This book puts the development-speed benefits of these practices into context with other practices.

Practical focus. To some people, "practical" means "code," and to those people I have to admit that this book might not seem very practical. I've avoided code-focused practices for two reasons. First, I've already written 800 pages about effective coding practices in *Code Complete* (Microsoft Press, 1993). I don't have much more to say about them. Second, it turns out that many of the critical insights about rapid development are not code-focused; they're strategic and philosophical. Sometimes, there is nothing more practical than a good theory.

Quick-reading organization. I've done all I can to present this book's rapid-development information in the most practical way possible. The first 400 pages of the book (Parts I and II) describe a strategy and philosophy of rapid development. About 50 pages of case studies are integrated into that discussion so that you can see how the strategy and philosophy play out in practice. If you don't like case studies, they've been formatted so that you can easily skip them. The rest of the book consists of a set of rapid-development *best practices*. The practices are described in quick-reference format so that you can skim to find the practices that will work best on your projects. The book describes how to use each practice, how much schedule reduction to expect, and what risks to watch out for.

The book also makes extensive use of marginal icons and text to help you quickly find additional information related to the topic you're reading about, avoid classic mistakes, zero in on best practices, and find quantitative support for many of the claims made in this book.

A new way to think about the topic of rapid development. In no other area of software development has there been as much disinformation as in the area of rapid development. Nearly useless development practices have been relentlessly hyped as "rapid-development practices," which has caused many developers to become cynical about claims made for any development practices whatsoever. Other practices are genuinely useful, but they have been hyped so far beyond their real capabilities that they too have contributed to developers' cynicism.

Each tool vendor and each methodology vendor want to convince you that their new silver bullet will be the answer to your development needs. In no other software area do you have to work as hard to separate the wheat from the chaff. This book provides guidelines for analyzing rapid-development information and finding the few grains of truth.

This book provides ready-made mental models that will allow you to assess what the silver-bullet vendors tell you and will also allow you to incorporate new ideas of your own. When someone comes into your office and says, "I just heard about a great new tool from the GigaCorp Silver Bullet Company that will cut our development time by 80 percent!" you will know how to react. It doesn't matter that I haven't said anything specifically about the GigaCorp Silver Bullet Company or their new tool. By the time you finish this book, you'll know what questions to ask, how seriously to take GigaCorp's claims, and how to incorporate their new tool into your development environment, if you decide to do that.

Unlike other books on rapid development, I'm not asking you to put all of your eggs into a single, one-size-fits-all basket. I recognize that different projects have different needs, and that one magic method is usually not enough to solve even one project's schedule problems. I have tried to be skeptical without being cynical—to be critical of practices' effectiveness but to stop short of *assuming* that they don't work. I revisit those old, overhyped practices and salvage some that are still genuinely useful—even if they aren't as useful as they were originally promised to be.

Why is this book about rapid development so big? Developers in the IS, shrink-wrap, military, and software-engineering fields have all discovered valuable rapid-development practices, but the people from these different fields rarely talk to one another. This book collects the most valuable practices from each field, bringing together rapid-development information from a wide variety of sources for the first time.

Does anyone who needs to know about rapid development really have time to read 650 pages about it? Possibly not, but a book half as long would have had to be oversimplified to the point of uselessness. To compensate, I've organized the book so that it can be read quickly and selectively—you can read short snippets while you're traveling or waiting. Chapters 1 and 2 contain the material that you *must* read to understand how to develop products more quickly. After you read those chapters, you can read whatever interests you most.

Why This Book Was Written

Clients' and managers' first response to the problem of slow development is usually to increase the amount of schedule pressure and overtime they heap on developers. Excessive schedule pressure occurs in about 75 percent of all large projects and in close to 100 percent of all very large projects (Jones 1994). Nearly 60 percent of developers report that the level of stress they feel is increasing (Glass 1994c). The average developer in the U.S. works from 48 to 50 hours per week (Krantz 1995). Many work considerably more.

In this environment, it isn't surprising that general job satisfaction of software developers has dropped significantly in the last 15 years (Zawacki 1993), and at a time when the industry desperately needs to be recruiting additional programmers to ease the schedule pressure, developers are spreading the word to their younger sisters, brothers, and children that our field is no fun anymore.

Clearly our field can be fun. Many of us got into it originally because we couldn't believe that people would actually pay us to write software. But something not-so-funny happened on the way to the forum, and that something is intimately bound up with the topic of rapid development.

It's time to start shoring up the dike that separates software developers from the sea of scheduling madness. This book is my attempt to stick a few fingers into that dike, holding the madness at bay long enough to get the job started.

Acknowledgments

Heartfelt thanks go first to Jack Litewka, the project editor, for making the creation of this book a thoroughly constructive and enjoyable experience. Thanks also go to Peggy Herman and Kim Eggleston for the book's design, to Michael Victor for the diagrams, and to Mark Monlux for the terrific illustrations. Sally Brunsman, David Clark, Susanne Freet, Dean Holmes, Wendy Maier, and Heidi Saastamoinen also helped this project go smoothly. Literally dozens of other people contributed to this book in one way or another; I didn't have personal contact with any of them, but I appreciate their contributions, too. (Chief among these, I am told, are layout artist Jeannie McGivern and production manager Jean Trenary of ArtSource and Microsoft Press's proof/copy-edit platoon supervised by Brenda Morris: Richard Carey, Roger LeBlanc, Patrick Forgette, Ron Drummond, Patricia Masserman, Paula Thurman, Jocelyn Elliott, Deborah Long, and Devon Musgrave.)

Microsoft Corporation's technical library provided invaluable aid in digging up the hundreds of books and articles that laid the foundation for this book. Keith Barland spearheaded that effort, making my research efforts much less arduous and time-consuming than they otherwise might have been. Other people at the library who helped included Janelle Jones, Christine Shannon, Linda Shaw, Amy Victor, Kyle Wagner, Amy Westfall, and Eilidh Zuvich.

I expound on the virtue of reviews in several places in this book, and this book has benefited greatly from extensive peer reviews. Al Corwin, Pat Forman, Tony Garland, Hank Meuret, and Matt Peloquin stuck with the project from beginning to end. Thanks to them for seeing that the book you hold in your hands doesn't look very much like the book I originally set out to write! I also received valuable comments from Wayne Beardsley, Duane Bedard, Ray Bernard, Bob Glass, Sharon Graham, Greg Hitchcock, Dave Moore, Tony Pisculli, Steve Rinn, and Bob Stacy—constructive critics, all. David Sommer (age 11) came up with the idea for the last panel of Figure 14-3. Thanks, David. And, finally, I'd like to thank my wife, Tammy, for her moral support and good humor. I have to start working on my third book immediately so that she will stop elbowing me in the ribs and calling me a Two-Time Author!

Bellevue, Washington
June 1996

EFFICIENT
DEVELOPMENT

1

Welcome to Rapid Development

Contents

Related Topics

THE PRODUCT MANAGER TOLD ME he wanted to build a product right for a change. He wanted to pay attention to quality, prevent feature creep, control the schedule, and have a predictable ship date.

When the time came to actually do the project, it became clear that getting the product to market quickly was the only real priority. Usability? *We don't have time.* Performance? *It can wait.* Maintainability? *Next project.* Testing? *Our users want the product now. Just get it out the door.*

This particular product manager wasn't the manager on just one product. He could have been almost any product manager I've worked for. This pattern is repeated day after day, state by state, all across the country. Development time has become such an important priority that it has blinded people to other important considerations, even to considerations that ultimately affect development time.

1.1 What Is Rapid Development?

To some people, rapid development consists of the application of a single pet tool or method. To the hacker, rapid development is coding for 36 hours at a stretch. To the information engineer, it's RAD—a combination of CASE tools, intensive user involvement, and tight timeboxes. To the vertical-market programmer, it's rapid prototyping using the latest version of Microsoft Visual Basic or Delphi. To the manager desperate to shorten a schedule, it's whatever practice was highlighted in the most recent issue of *Business Week*.

Each one of these tools and methods is fine as far as it goes, and each can contribute to increased development speed. But to provide full benefit, each must be orchestrated as part of a full-fledged strategy. No one of them applies to all cases. And no one of them can measure up to certain other practices that are not commonly thought of as rapid-development practices but that nonetheless have profound development-speed implications.

Rather than identifying a specific tool or method, for purposes of this book "rapid development" is merely a descriptive phrase that contrasts with "slow and typical development." It isn't *Rapid Development*™—a magic phrase or buzzword. It isn't a glitzy *Blaze-O-Matic®* or *Gung-HO-OO*™ rapid-development methodology. Rapid development is a generic term that means the same thing as "speedy development" or "shorter schedules." It means developing software faster than you do now.

A "rapid-development project," then, is any project that needs to emphasize development speed. In today's climate, that description fits a lot of projects.

1.2 Attaining Rapid Development

The road mapped out in this book is clearly the road less traveled in today's industry. Switching to the road less traveled might seem risky. But the road *more* traveled is the road that is currently resulting in massive cost and schedule overruns; low quality; canceled projects; high turnover; friction between managers, developers, and customers; and all the rest of the problems we're trying to get rid of.

If you work in a typical organization and follow the practices in this book, you'll be able to cut your development time significantly, perhaps by as much as half, and boost your productivity significantly, too. You'll be able to do that without harming quality, cost, performance, or maintainability. But the improvement won't come instantly, you won't attain it from any single new tool or method, and you won't attain it merely by taking the shrink-wrap off the box. It will take time and effort.

For every complex problem, there is an answer that is short, simple, and wrong.

H. L. Mencken

I wish I had a simple solution to the development-speed problem. I also wish I had five million dollars. But simple solutions tend to work only for simple problems, and software development isn't a simple problem. Rapid development of software is even less simple.

As Figure 1-1 suggests, the set of all available software practices is huge. Within that set, the subset of effective practices is also quite large. You use only a small sub-subset of those practices on any particular project. At an executive-overview level, success at rapid development consists of two elements:

- Choosing effective practices rather than ineffective practices
- Choosing practices that are oriented specifically toward achieving your schedule objectives

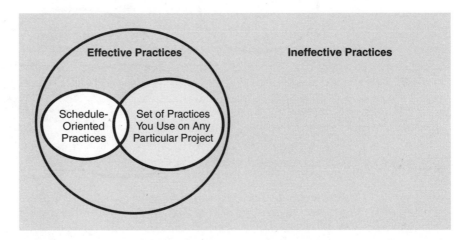

Figure 1-1. *Set of all software-development practices. Development speed depends on the choice of development practices. How rapidly you develop any particular program depends on the extent to which you choose effective practices and on the extent to which you choose schedule-oriented practices.*

You might think this is obvious, but, as Chapter 3 explains, organizations routinely choose ineffective practices. They choose practices that are proven failures or that fail more often than they succeed. When they need maximum scheduling certainty, they choose high-risk practices that reduce the chance of meeting their schedule goals. When they need to reduce costs, they choose speed-oriented practices that drive costs up. The first step toward improving development speed for those organizations is to admit that they're choosing ineffective practices and then to begin choosing effective ones.

All of the effective schedule-oriented practices are lumped into one category in Figure 1-1, but, as Figure 1-2 suggests, you actually have a choice among three kinds of schedule-oriented practices:

- Practices that improve development speed, allowing you to deliver software faster
- Practices that reduce schedule risk, allowing you to avoid huge schedule overruns
- Practices that make progress visible, allowing you to dispel the appearance of slow development

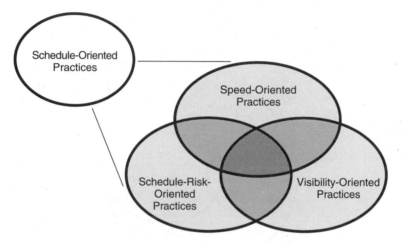

Figure 1-2. *Schedule-oriented practices come in three kinds: practices that enable you to develop faster, reduce schedule risk, and make your progress visible.*

The specific kinds of schedule-oriented practices you choose will be determined by your specific concerns about development speed. If you think you genuinely need to develop faster, you should focus on speed-oriented practices. If you think that your development speed is OK and that your customer's perception of your development speed is the problem, you should focus on visibility-oriented practices.

When you put effective schedule-oriented practices together with a plan for using them, you'll find that the whole package provides for dramatic, real improvements in development speed. That's better than using a *Magic-Beans™* software cure-all that doesn't really work. Of course, choosing effective practices and avoiding ineffective practices is easier said than done, and that's what the rest of the book is about.

2

Rapid-Development Strategy

Contents

Related Topics

IF YOU TOOK 100 WORLD-CLASS MUSICIANS and put them into an orchestra without a conductor, they wouldn't sound like a world-class orchestra. The string section's timing wouldn't match that of the woodwind or brass section. Instructing the musicians to "do their best" wouldn't help them know whether they should play louder or softer. Such a musical event would be a waste of talent.

A similar waste of talent is commonplace in software development. Teams of smart, dedicated developers employ the latest best practices and still fail to meet their schedule goals.

One of the most tempting traps that people who want faster development fall into is the trap of focusing too much on a single schedule-oriented development practice. You might execute rapid prototyping perfectly, but if you make a mistake somewhere else—"Oops! We forgot to include time in the schedule for the printing subsystem!"—you will not achieve rapid development. Individual schedule-oriented practices are only part of what's needed to achieve the shortest possible schedule. A general framework that allows those practices to be used to maximum advantage is also needed.

This chapter puts forth an orchestrated strategy for achieving rapid development.

Case Study 2-1. Rapid Development Without a Clear Strategy

Mickey was ready to lead his second project at Square-Tech, a giant in the PC spreadsheet world. His previous project had been tough. The original schedule had called for his team to deliver Square-Calc version 2.0 in 12 months, but it had taken 18. The team had known at the outset that the date was aggressive, so for almost the entire 18 months they were on a death march, working 12-hour days and 6- or 7-day weeks. At the end of the project, two of the six team members quit, and Bob, the strongest developer on the team, set out from Seattle on his bicycle for parts unknown. Bob said he wasn't quitting, and he sent Mickey a postcard from Ottumwa, South Dakota—a picture of himself riding a giant jackalope—but no one knew when he would be back.

Square-Calc 3.0 needed to be released 12 months after version 2.0, so after two months of project cleanup, post mortems, and vacations, Mickey was ready to try again. He had 10 months to deliver version 3.0. Mickey met with Kim, his manager, to discuss the project plan. Kim was known for being able to eke out every possible bit of work from the developers she managed. John, from user documentation, and Helen, from QA, were also present.

"Version 3.0 needs to leapfrog the competition," Kim said. "So we need a strong effort on this project. I know that your team didn't feel that the company was fully behind them last time, so this time the company is ready to provide all the support it can. I've approved individual private offices, new state-of-the-art computers, and free soda pop for the whole project. How does that sound?"

"That sounds great," Mickey said. "All these developers are experienced, so I mainly want to provide lots of motivation and support and then get out of the way. I don't want to micro-manage them. I'd like to have each developer sign up for a part of the system. We had a lot of interface problems last time, so I also want to spend some time designing the interfaces between the parts, and then turn them loose."

"If this is a 10-month project, we're going to need visually frozen software by the 8-month mark to get the user documentation ready on time," John said. "Last time the developers kept making changes right up until the end. The README file was 20 pages long, which was embarrassing. Our user manuals are getting killed in the reviews. As long as you agree to a visual freeze, your development approach sounds fine."

"We need visual freeze by about the same time to write our automated test scripts," Helen added. Mickey agreed to the visual freeze. Kim approved Mickey's overall approach and told him to keep her posted.

(continued)

As the project began, the developers were happy about their private offices, new computers, and soda pop, so they got off to a strong start. It wasn't long before they were voluntarily working well into the evening.

Months went by, and they made steady progress. They produced an early prototype, and continued to produce a steady stream of code. Management kept the pressure on. John reminded Mickey several times of his commitment to a visual freeze at the 8-month mark, which Mickey found irritating, but everything seemed to be progressing nicely.

Bob returned from his bike trip during the project's fourth month, refreshed, and jumped into the project with some new thoughts he'd had while riding. Mickey worried about whether Bob could implement as much functionality as he wanted to in the time allowed, but Bob was committed to his ideas and guaranteed on-time delivery no matter how much work it took.

The team members worked independently on their parts, and as visual freeze approached, they began to integrate their code. They started at 2:00 in the afternoon the day before the visual freeze deadline and soon discovered that the program wouldn't compile, much less run. The combined code had several dozen syntax errors, and it seemed like each one they fixed generated 10 more. At midnight, they decided to call it a night.

The next morning, Kim met with the team. "Is the program ready to hand over to documentation and testing?"

"Not yet," Mickey said. "We're having some integration problems. We might be ready by this afternoon." The team worked that afternoon and evening, but couldn't fix all of the bugs they were discovering. At the end of the day they conceded that they had no idea how much longer integration would take.

It took two full weeks to fix all the syntax errors and get the system to run at all. When the team turned over the frozen build two weeks late, testing and documentation rejected it immediately. "This is too unstable to document," John said. "It crashes every few minutes, and there are lots of paths we can't even exercise."

Helen agreed. "There's no point in having testers write defect reports when the system is so unstable that it crashes practically every time you make a menu selection."

Mickey agreed with them and said he'd focus his team's efforts on bug fixes. Kim reminded them of the 10-month deadline and said that this product couldn't be late like the last one.

It took a month to make the system reliable enough to begin documenting and testing it. By then they were only two weeks from the 10-month mark, and they worked even harder.

(continued)

Case Study 2-1. Rapid Development Without a Clear Strategy, *continued*

But testing began finding defects faster than the developers could correct them. Fixes to one part of the system frequently caused problems in other parts. There was no chance of making the 10-month ship date. Kim called an emergency meeting. "I can see that you're all working hard," she said, "but that's not good enough. I need results. I've given you every kind of support I know how, and I don't have any software to show for it. If you don't finish this product soon, the company could go under."

As the pressure mounted, morale faded fast. More months went by, the product began to stabilize, and Kim kept the pressure on. Some of the interfaces turned out to be extremely inefficient, and that called for several more weeks of performance work.

Bob, despite working virtually around the clock, delivered his software later than the rest of the team. His code was virtually bug-free, but he had changed some of the user-interface components, and testing and user documentation threw fits.

Mickey met with John and Helen. "You won't like it, but our options are as follows: We can keep Bob's code the way it is and rev the test scripts and user documentation, or we can throw out Bob's code and write it all again. Bob won't rewrite his code, and no one else on the team will either. Looks like you'll have to change the user documentation and test scripts." After putting up token resistance, John and Helen begrudgingly agreed.

In the end, it took the developers 15 months to complete the software. Because of the visual changes, the user documentation missed its slot in the printer's schedule, so after the developers cut the master disks there was a two-week shipping delay while Square-Tech waited for documents to come back from the printer. After release, user response to Square-Calc version 3.0 was lukewarm, and within months it slipped from second place in market share to fourth. Mickey realized that he had delivered his second project 50 percent over schedule, just like the first.

2.1 General Strategy for Rapid Development

The pattern described in Case Study 2-1 is common. Avoidance of the pattern takes effort but is within reach of anyone who is willing to throw out their bad habits. You can achieve rapid development by following a four-part strategy:

1. Avoid classic mistakes.
2. Apply development fundamentals.

3. Manage risks to avoid catastrophic setbacks.

4. Apply schedule-oriented practices such as the three kinds of practices shown in Figure 1-2 in Chapter 1.

As Figure 2-1 suggests, these four practices provide support for the best possible schedule.

Figure 2-1. *The four pillars of rapid development. The best possible schedule depends on classic-mistake avoidance, development fundamentals, and risk management in addition to the use of schedule-oriented practices.*

> **Rapid product development is not a quick fix for getting one product—which is probably already late—to market faster. Instead, it is a strategic capability that must be built from the ground up.**
>
> *Preston G. Smith and Donald G. Reinertsen,* Developing Products in Half the Time

Pictures with pillars have become kind of hokey, but the pillars in this picture illustrate several important points.

The optimum support for the best possible schedule is to have all four pillars in place and to make each of them as strong as possible. Without the support of the first three pillars, your ability to achieve the best possible schedule will be in jeopardy. You can use the strongest schedule-oriented practices, but if you make the classic mistake of shortchanging product quality early in the project, you'll waste time correcting defects when it's most expensive to do so. Your project will be late. If you skip the development fundamental of creating a good design before you begin coding, your program can fall apart when the product concept changes partway through development, and your project will be late. And if you don't manage risks, you can find out just before your release date that a key subcontractor is three months behind schedule. You'll be late again.

The illustration also suggests that the first three pillars provide most of the support needed for the best possible schedule. Not ideal support, perhaps, but most of what's needed. You might be able to achieve an optimal schedule without schedule-oriented practices.

Can you achieve the best possible schedule by focusing only on schedule-oriented practices? You might just be able to pull it off. People have pulled off stunts like that before. But as Figure 2-2 illustrates, it's a difficult balancing act. I can balance a chair on my chin, and my dog can balance a biscuit on his nose. But running a software project isn't a parlor trick, and if you rely on schedule-oriented practices to do all the work, you probably won't get all the support you need. If you do manage to pull it off once, you can't count on being able to do so again.

Schedule-
Oriented
Practices

Figure 2-2. *Result of focusing solely on schedule-oriented practices. Even the finest schedule-oriented practices aren't strong enough to support the best possible schedule by themselves.*

The first three pillars shown in Figure 2-1 are critical to the success of rapid development, so I intend to lay out in very clear terms what I mean by classic-mistake avoidance, development fundamentals, and risk management. Chapter 3 will introduce classic mistakes. In most cases, simply being aware of a mistake will be enough to prevent it, so I will present a list of classic mistakes in that chapter. I'll take up the topic of development fundamentals in Chapter 4 and the topic of risk management in Chapter 5.

The rest of this book discusses specific schedule-oriented practices, including speed-oriented, schedule-risk-oriented, and visibility-oriented practices. The best-practice summaries in Part III of this book list the effect that each practice has on development speed, schedule risk, and visibility. If you'd rather read about rapid development itself before reading about the three steps needed to lay the groundwork for rapid development, you might skip ahead to Chapter 6, "Core Issues in Rapid Development," and to other chapters.

2.2   Four Dimensions of Development Speed

Whether you're bogged down trying to avoid mistakes or cruising at top speed with highly effective schedule-oriented practices, your software project operates along four important dimensions: people, process, product, and technology. People perform quickly, or they perform slowly. The process leverages people's time, or it throws up one stumbling block after another. The product is defined in such a way that it almost builds itself, or it is defined in a way that stymies the best efforts of the people who are building it. Technology assists the development effort, or it thwarts developers' best attempts.

You can leverage each of these four dimensions for maximum development speed. Figure 2-3 illustrates the point.

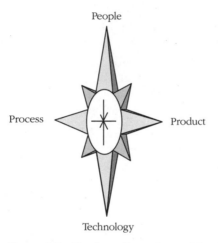

Figure 2-3. *The four dimensions of development speed—shown here in two dimensions. You can focus on all four dimensions at the same time.*

In response to this diagram, I can almost hear some engineers saying, "Hey! That's not four *dimensions*. It's four *directions*. You can't even draw in four dimensions!" Well, you're right. I can't draw in four dimensions, which is why I've shown this illustration in two dimensions. But the concept I want to get across is very much one of dimension rather than direction.

Software development books tend to emphasize one dimension and downplay the others, but there isn't necessarily a trade-off between emphases on people, process, product, and technology. If these were directions, a focus on people would detract from a focus on technology. A focus on product would detract from a focus on process. But because they're dimensions, you can focus on people, process, product, and technology all at the same time.

Software organizations tend to view the dimensions they don't focus on as fixed, and I think that's one reason that project planning can be so frustrating, especially schedule planning. When you focus on a single dimension, it can be nearly impossible to satisfy everyone's objectives. Truly rapid development requires you to incorporate a variety of kinds of practices (Boehm et al. 1984, Jones 1991). The organizations that are the most effective at achieving rapid development optimize all four rapid-development dimensions simultaneously.

Once you realize that each of the four dimensions can potentially provide tremendous leverage over a software schedule, your planning can become fuller, more creative, more effective, and better able to satisfy you and the other concerned parties.

The following subsections introduce the four dimensions and discuss the synergy among them.

People

Results of individual experiments on peopleware issues are well known. You might be familiar with the claim that there is at least a 10-to-1 difference in productivity among different developers. Or you might be familiar with the positive contribution that an explicit motivational improvement program can have.

What is less familiar to most developers, indeed to most people in the industry, is that the research on peopleware issues has been steadily accumulating over the past 15 to 20 years. It is now possible to step beyond the many individual-study conclusions and synthesize some general conclusions from trends in the research.

HARD DATA

The first conclusion is that we now know with certainty that peopleware issues have more impact on software productivity and software quality than any other factor. Since the late 1960s, study after study has found that the productivity of individual programmers with similar levels of experience does indeed vary by a factor of at least 10 to 1 (Sackman, Erikson, and Grant 1968, Curtis 1981, Mills 1983, DeMarco and Lister 1985, Curtis et al. 1986, Card 1987, Valett and McGarry 1989).

HARD DATA

Studies have also found variations in the performance of entire teams on the order of 3, 4, or 5 to 1 (Weinberg and Schulman 1974; Boehm 1981; Mills 1983; Boehm, Gray, and Seewaldt 1984). After 20 years of experimentation on live projects, researchers at NASA's Software Engineering Laboratory have concluded that technology is not the answer; the most effective practices are those that leverage the human potential of their developers (Basili et al. 1995).

Because it is so clear that peopleware issues strongly influence productivity, it is also now crystal clear that any organization that's serious about improving productivity should look first to the peopleware issues of motivation, teamwork, staff selection, and training. There are other ways to improve productivity, but peopleware offers the greatest potential benefit. If you are serious about rapid development, you have to be serious about peopleware issues. Taken collectively, peopleware issues matter more than process, product, or technology. You have to address them if you want to succeed.

This conclusion is a strong one, but it should not be taken as support for any peopleware initiative whatsoever. The research results simply say that the effects of individual ability, individual motivation, team ability, and team motivation dwarf other productivity factors. They do not say specifically that team T-shirts, free soda pop, windowed offices, productivity bonuses, or Friday afternoon beer busts improve motivation, but the implication is clear: any organization that wants to improve its productivity should be actively trying all these things.

This book deals with several ways that you can maximize human potential to reduce software schedules.

CROSS-REFERENCE
For more on job matching and career progression, see "Work Itself" in Section 11.2. For more on team balance and problem personnel, see Chapter 12, "Teamwork," and Chapter 13, "Team Structure."

Staff selection for team projects. In his landmark book, *Software Engineering Economics*, Barry Boehm presents five principles of software staffing (Boehm 1981):

- *Top talent*—Use better and fewer people.
- *Job matching*—Fit the tasks to the skills and motivation of the people available.
- *Career progression*—Help people to self-actualize rather than forcing them to work where they have the most experience or where they are most needed.
- *Team balance*—Select people who will complement and harmonize with each other.
- *Misfit elimination*—Eliminate and replace problem team members as quickly as possible.

Other factors that can make a difference include people's design ability, programming ability, programming-language experience, machine and environment experience, and applications-area experience.

Team organization. The way that people are organized has a great effect on how efficiently they can work. Software shops can benefit from tailoring their teams to match project size, product attributes, and schedule goals. A specific software project can also benefit from appropriate specialization.

Motivation. A person who lacks motivation is unlikely to work hard and is more likely to coast. No factor other than motivation will cause a person to forsake evenings and weekends without being asked to do so. Few other factors can be applied to so many people on so many teams in so many organizations. Motivation is potentially the strongest ally you have on a rapid-development project.

Variations in Productivity

I refer to several ratios related to variations in productivity in this book, and keeping them straight can get confusing. Here's a summary of the variations that researchers have found:

- Greater than 10-to-1 differences in productivity among individuals with different depths and breadths of experience.

- 10-to-1 differences in productivity among individuals with the same levels of experience.

- 5-to-1 differences in productivity among groups with different levels of experience.

- 2.5-to-1 differences in productivity among groups with similar levels of experience.

Process

Process, as it applies to software development, includes both management and technical methodologies. The effect that process has on a development schedule is easier to assess than the effect that people have, and a great deal of work is being done by the Software Engineering Institute and other organizations to document and publicize effective software processes.

HARD DATA

Process represents an area of high leverage in improving your development speed—almost as much as people. Ten years ago it might have been reasonable to debate the value of a focus on process, but, as with peopleware, today the pile of evidence in favor of paying attention to process has become overwhelming. Organizations such as Hughes Aircraft, Lockheed, Motorola, NASA, Raytheon, and Xerox that have explicitly focused on improving their development processes have, over several years, cut their times-to-market by about one-half and have reduced cost and defects by factors of 3 to 10 (Pietrasanta 1991a, Myers 1992, Putnam and Myers 1992, Gibbs 1994, Putnam 1994, Basili et al. 1995, Raytheon 1995, Saiedian and Hamilton 1995).

Some people think that attention to process is stifling, and there's no doubt that some processes are overly rigid or overly bureaucratic. A few people have created process standards primarily to make themselves feel powerful. But that's an abuse of power—and the fact that a process focus can be abused should not be allowed to detract from the benefits a process focus can offer. The most common form of process abuse is neglect, and the effect of that is that intelligent, conscientious developers find themselves working inefficiently and at cross-purposes when there's no need for them to work that way. A focus on process can help.

Rework avoidance. If requirements change in the late stages of project, you might have to redesign, recode, and retest. If you have design problems that you didn't find until system testing, you might have to throw away detailed design and code and then start over. One of the most straightforward ways to save time on a software project is to orient your process so that you avoid doing things twice.

Raytheon won the IEEE Computer Society's Software Process Achievement Award in 1995 for reducing their rework costs from 41 percent to less than 10 percent and simultaneously tripling their productivity (Raytheon 1995). The relationship between those two feats is no coincidence.

CROSS-REFERENCE
For more on quality assurance, see Section 4.3, "Quality-Assurance Fundamentals."

Quality assurance. Quality assurance has two main purposes. The first purpose is to assure that the product you release has an acceptable level of quality. Although that is an important purpose, it is outside the scope of this book. The second function of quality assurance is to detect errors at the stage when they are least time-consuming (and least costly) to correct. This nearly always means catching errors as close as possible to the time that they are introduced. The longer an error remains in the product, the more time-consuming (and more costly) it will be to remove. Quality assurance is thus an indispensable part of any serious rapid-development program.

CROSS-REFERENCE
For more on development fundamentals, see Section 4.2, "Technical Fundamentals."

Development fundamentals. Much of the work that has been done in the software-engineering field during the last 20 years has been related to developing software rapidly. A lot of that work has focused on "productivity" rather than on rapid development per se, and, as such, some of it has been oriented toward getting the same work done with fewer people rather than getting a project done faster. You can, however, interpret the underlying principles from a rapid-development viewpoint. The lessons learned from 20 years of hard knocks can help your project to proceed smoothly. Although standard software-engineering practices for analysis, design, construction, integration, and testing won't produce lightning-fast schedules by themselves, they can prevent projects from spinning out of control. Half of the challenge of rapid development is avoiding disaster, and that is an area in which standard software-engineering principles excel.

CROSS-REFERENCE
For more on risk management, see Chapter 5, "Risk Management."

Risk management. One of the specific practices that's focused on avoiding disaster is risk management. Developing rapidly isn't good enough if you get your feet knocked out from under you two weeks before you're scheduled to ship. Managing schedule-related risks is a necessary component of a rapid-development program.

Resource targeting. Resources can be focused effectively and contribute to overall productivity, or they can be misdirected and used ineffectively. On a rapid-development project, it is even more important than usual that you get the maximum bang for your schedule buck. Best practices such as productivity offices, timebox development, accurate scheduling, and voluntary overtime help to make sure that you get as much work done each day as possible.

CROSS-REFERENCE
For more on lifecycle planning, see Chapter 7, "Lifecycle Planning."

Lifecycle planning. One of the keys to targeting resources effectively is to apply them within a lifecycle framework that makes sense for your specific project. Without an overall lifecycle model, you can make decisions that are individually on target but collectively misdirected. A lifecycle model is useful because it describes a basic management plan. For example, if you have a risky project, a risk-oriented lifecycle model will suit you; and if you have vague requirements, an incremental lifecycle model may work best. Lifecycle models make it easy to identify and organize the many activities required by a software project so that you can do them with the utmost efficiency.

CROSS-REFERENCE
For more on customer orientation, see Chapter 10, "Customer-Oriented Development."

Customer orientation. One of the gestalt shifts between traditional, mainframe software development and more modern development styles has been the switch to a strong focus on customers' needs and desires. Developers have learned that developing software to specification is only half the job. The other half is helping the customer figure out what the product should be, and most of the time that requires an approach other than a traditional paper-specification approach. Putting yourself on the same side as the customer is one of the best ways to avoid the massive rework caused by the customer deciding that the product you just spent 12 months on is not the right product after all. The best practices of staged releases, evolutionary delivery, evolutionary prototyping, throwaway prototyping, and principled negotiation can all give you leverage in this area.

Who Is "The Customer"?

In this book, when I refer to "customers," I'm referring to the people who pay to have the software developed and the people who are responsible for accepting or rejecting the product. On some projects, those will be the same person or group; on others, they'll be different. On some projects, the customer is a real flesh-and-blood client who pays your project's development costs directly. On other projects, it's another internal group within your organization. On still other projects, the customer is the person who plunks down $200 for a shrink-wrap software package. In that case, the real customer is remote, and there is usually a manager or marketer who represents the customer to you.

Depending on your situation, you might understand the term "customer" to mean "client," "marketer," "end-user," or "boss."

Product

The most tangible dimension of the people/process/product/technology compass is the product dimension, and a focus on product size and product characteristics presents enormous opportunities for schedule reduction. If you can reduce a product's feature set, you can reduce the product's schedule. If the feature set is flexible, you might be able to use the 80/20 rule and develop the 80 percent of the product that takes only 20 percent of the time. You can develop the other 20 percent later. If you can keep the product's look and feel, performance characteristics, and quality characteristics flexible, you can assemble the product from preexisting components and write a minimum amount of custom code. The exact amount of schedule reduction made possible by focusing on product size and product characteristics is limited only by your customer's product concept and your team's creativity.

Both product size and product characteristics offer opportunities to cut development time.

CROSS-REFERENCE
For more on manipulating product size to support development speed, see Chapter 14, "Feature-Set Control." For more on the effect that product size has on a development schedule, see Chapter 8, "Estimation."

Product size. Product size is the largest single contributor to a development schedule. Large products take a long time. Smaller products take less time. Additional features require additional specification, design, construction, testing, and integration. They require additional coordination with other features, and they require that you coordinate other features with them. Because the effort required to build software increases disproportionately faster than the size of the software, a reduction in size will improve development speed disproportionately. Cutting the size of a medium-size program by one-half will typically cut the effort required by almost *two-thirds*.

You can reduce product size outright by striving to develop only the most essential features, or you can reduce it temporarily by developing a product in stages. You can also reduce it by developing in a higher-level language or tool set so that each feature requires less code.

CROSS-REFERENCE
For more on the effect that goals can have on a development schedule, see "Goal Setting" in Section 11.2.

Product characteristics. Although not as influential as product size, other product characteristics do have an effect on software schedules. A product with ambitious goals for performance, memory use, robustness, and reliability will take longer to develop than a product without any goals for those characteristics. Choose your battles. If rapid development is truly top priority, don't shackle your developers by insisting on too many priorities at once.

Technology

CROSS-REFERENCE
For more on productivity tools, see Chapter 15, "Productivity Tools."

Changing from less effective tools to more effective tools can also be a fast way to improve your development speed. The change from low-level languages like assembler to high-level languages like C and Pascal was one of the most influential changes in software-development history. The current move toward componentware (VBXs and OCXs) might eventually produce similarly dramatic results. Choosing tools effectively and managing the risks involved are key aspects of a rapid-development initiative.

Synergy

HARD DATA

There is a point at which your focus on people, process, product, and technology becomes synergistic. Neil Olsen conducted a study in which he found that going from low spending to medium spending on staffing, training, and work environment produced proportionate gains: additional spending was justified on roughly a 1-to-1 payback basis. But when spending on staffing, training, and work environment went from medium to high, productivity skyrocketed, paying back 2 to 1 or 3 to 1 (Olsen 1995).

Software-engineering practices can also be synergistic. For example, an organizationwide coding standard helps an individual project, but it also makes it easier for one project to reuse components from another project. At the same time, a reusable-components group can help to enforce a coding standard and ensure that it's meaningful across projects. Design and code reviews help to disseminate knowledge about both the coding standard and existing reusable components, and they promote the level of quality needed for reuse to succeed. Good practices tend to support one another.

2.3 General Kinds of Fast Development

Different situations call for different levels of commitment to development speed. In some cases, you'd like to increase development speed if you can do it easily and without additional cost or product degradation. In other cases, circumstances call for you to increase development speed at all costs. Table 2-1 describes some trade-offs among different development approaches.

Table 2-1. Characteristics of Standard Approaches to Schedule-Oriented Development

Development Approach	Effect of Development Approach On...		
	...Schedule	...Cost	...Product
Average practice	Average	Average	Average
Efficient development (balancing cost, schedule, and functionality)	Better than average	Better than average	Better than average
Efficient development (tilted toward best schedule)	Much better than average	Somewhat better than average	Somewhat better than average
All-out rapid development	Fastest possible	Worse than average	Worse than average

Efficient Development

CROSS-REFERENCE
For an example of the benefits of efficient development, see Section 4.2, "Technical Fundamentals" and Chapter 4, "Software Development Fundamentals," generally.

As you can see from Table 2-1, average practice is...average. The second approach listed in the table is what I call "efficient development," which is the combination of the first three pillars of maximum development speed as shown in Figure 2-4. That approach produces better than average results in each of the three categories. Many people achieve their schedule goals after they put the first three pillars into place. Some people discover that they didn't need rapid development after all; they just needed to get organized! For many projects, efficient development represents a sensible optimization of cost, schedule, and product characteristics.

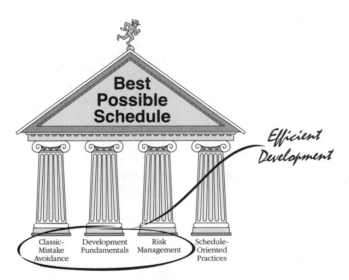

Figure 2-4. *Efficient development. The first three steps in achieving the best possible schedule make up "efficient development." Many project teams find that efficient development provides all the development speed they need.*

Can you achieve shorter schedules without first attaining efficient development? Maybe. You can choose effective, schedule-oriented practices and avoid slow or ineffective practices without focusing on efficient development per se. Until you attain efficient development, however, your chances of success in using schedule-oriented practices will be uncertain. If you choose specific schedule-oriented practices without a general strategy, you'll have a harder time improving your overall development capability. Of course, only you can know whether it's more important to improve your overall development capabilities or to try completing a specific project faster.

CROSS-REFERENCE
For more on the relationship
between quality and
development speed, see
Section 4.3, "Quality-
Assurance Fundamentals."

Another reason to focus on efficient development is that for most organizations the paths to efficient development and shorter schedules are the same. For that matter, until you get to a certain point, the paths to shorter schedules, lower defects, and lower cost are all the same, too. As Figure 2-5 shows, once you get to efficient development the roads begin to diverge, but from where they are now, most development groups would benefit by setting a course for efficient development first.

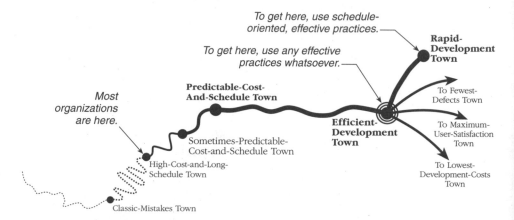

Figure 2-5. *The road to rapid development. From where most organizations are now, the route to rapid development follows the same road as the route to fewest defects, maximum user satisfaction, and lowest development costs. After you reach efficient development, the routes begin to diverge.*

Efficient Development Tilted Toward Best Schedule

CROSS-REFERENCE
For more on deciding
between speed-oriented and
schedule-risk–oriented
practices, see Section 1.2,
"Attaining Rapid Develop-
ment," and Section 6.2,
"What Kind of Rapid
Development Do You Need?"

The third development approach listed in Table 2-1 is a variation of efficient development. If you are practicing efficient development and find that you still need better schedule performance, you can choose development practices that are tilted toward increasing development speed, reducing schedule risk, or improving progress visibility. You'll have to make small trade-offs in cost and product characteristics to gain that speed or predictability; if you start from a base of efficient development, however, you'll still be much better off than average.

All-Out Rapid Development

CROSS-REFERENCE
For more on nominal schedules,
see "Nominal Schedules" in
Section 8.6. For more on the
costs of schedule compression,
see "Two Facts of Life"
in Section 8.6.

The final schedule-oriented development approach is what I call "all-out rapid development"—the combination of efficient and *in*efficient schedule-oriented practices. There comes a point when you're working as smart as you can and as hard as you can, and the only thing left to do at that point is to pay more, reduce the feature set, or reduce the product's polish.

Here's an example of what I mean by an "inefficient" practice: you can compress a project's nominal development schedule by 25 percent simply by adding more people to it. Because of increased communications and management overhead, however, you have to increase your team size by about 75 percent to achieve that 25-percent schedule reduction. The net effect of a shorter schedule and larger team size is a project that costs 33 percent more than the nominal project.

CROSS-REFERENCE
For more on whether you need all-out rapid development, see Section 6.2, "What Kind of Rapid Development Do You Need?"

The move to all-out rapid development is a big step and requires that you accept increased schedule risk or large trade-offs between cost and product characteristic—or both. Few projects welcome such trade-offs, and most projects are better off just choosing some form of efficient development.

2.4 Which Dimension Matters the Most?

CROSS-REFERENCE
For more on customizing software processes to the needs of specific projects, see Section 6.1, "Does One Size Fit All?"

Boeing, Microsoft, NASA, Raytheon, and other companies have all learned how to develop software in ways that meet their needs. At the strategy level, these different organizations have a lot in common. They have learned how to avoid classic mistakes. They apply development fundamentals. And they practice active risk management. At the tactical level, there is a world of difference in the ways that each of these successful organizations emphasize people, process, product, and technology.

Different projects have different needs, but the key in all cases is to accept the limitations on the dimensions you can't change and then to emphasize the other dimensions to get the rest of the schedule benefit you need.

If you're developing a fuel-injection system for a car, you can't use 4GLs or a visual programming environment to develop the real-time, embedded software; you need greater performance and better low-level control than these tools can provide. You're prevented from exercising the technology dimension to the utmost. Instead, you have to emphasize technology as much as you can—and then get your real leverage from the people, process, and product dimensions.

If you're working on an in-house business program, perhaps you can use a 4GL, a visual programming environment, or a CASE tool. You're able to exercise technology to the utmost. But you might work for a stodgy corporation that prevents you from doing much in the people dimension. Emphasize people as much as the company allows, and then get the remaining leverage you need from the product and process dimensions.

If you're working in a feature-driven shrink-wrap market, you might not be able to shrink your feature set much to meet a tight schedule. Shrink it as much as you can, and then emphasize people, process, and technology to give you the rest of what you need to meet your schedule.

Kinds of Projects—Systems, Business, and Shrink-Wrap

This book describes three general kinds of projects: *systems*, *business*, and *shrink-wrap*.

Systems software includes operating system software, device drivers, compilers, and code libraries. For purposes of this book (and despite their differences), *embedded software, firmware, real-time systems,* and *scientific software* share many characteristics with systems software.

Business software refers to in-house systems that are used by a single organization. They run on a limited set of hardware, perhaps only a single computer. Payroll systems, accounting systems, and inventory control systems are typical examples. In this book, I treat *IS, IT,* and *MIS* software as belonging to the general category of business software.

Shrink-wrap software is software that is packaged and sold commercially. It includes both horizontal-market products like word-processors and spreadsheets and vertical-market products like financial-analysis, screenplay-writing, and legal case-management programs.

I use a few other terms to refer to kinds of software that aren't described by these three general labels. *Commercial* software is any kind of software developed for commercial sale. *In-house* software is software that is developed solely for in-house use and is not for commercial sale. *Military* software is written for use by the military. *Interactive* software is any software with which a user can interact directly, which includes most of the software being written today.

To summarize: analyze your project to determine which of the four dimensions are limited and which you can leverage to maximum advantage. Then stretch each to the utmost. That, in a nutshell, is the key to successful rapid development.

2.5 An Alternative Rapid-Development Strategy

CROSS-REFERENCE
For more on commitment-based approaches, see "Commitment-Based Scheduling" in Section 8.5 and Chapter 34, "Signing Up."

The approach to rapid development that I lay out in this book is not the only approach that has ever been known to work. There is a different road that some projects have traveled successfully. That road is characterized by hiring the best possible people, asking for a total commitment to the project, granting them nearly total autonomy, motivating them to an extreme degree, and then seeing that they work 60, 80, or even 100 hours a week until either they or the project are finished. Rapid development with this commitment-based approach is achieved through grit, sweat, and determination.

This approach has produced notable successes, including Microsoft NT 3.0 and the Data General Eagle Computer, and it is unquestionably the most popular approach to rapid development in use today. For a start-up company with cash-flow concerns, it has the advantage of extracting two months' work from an employee for one month's pay. That can mean the difference between finishing a killer product in time to meet a marketing window that allows the company to make a fortune and running out of money before the team even finishes the product. By keeping team size small, it also reduces communications, coordination, and management overhead. If practiced with a keen awareness of the risks involved and with some restraint, the approach can be successful.

Unfortunately, this approach is hardly ever practiced that carefully. It usually devolves to a code-like-hell approach, which produces drawn-out projects that seem to last forever. The approach is a quick fix, and it shares many problems with other quick fixes. I criticize aspects of the approach throughout the book. Here's a summary.

The approach is hit-or-miss. Sometimes it works; sometimes it doesn't. The factors that make it work or not work are largely impossible to control. When you do manage to complete a project, sometimes you get the functionality you planned for; sometimes you're surprised. Sometimes you hit your quality targets; sometimes you don't. The approach makes specific product characteristics difficult to control.

It causes long-term motivation problems. On commitment-based projects, developers start out enthusiastically and put in ever-increasing overtime as they begin to fully realize what it will take to meet their commitments. Eventually, long hours aren't enough, and they fail to meet their schedule commitments. Their morale fades as, one by one, they are forced to admit defeat.

Once developers have put their hearts and souls into trying to meet their commitments and have failed, they become reluctant to make additional strong commitments. They start to resent the overtime. They make additional commitments with their mouths but not with their hearts, and the project loses any semblance of planning or control. It is not uncommon for a project that has reached this state to stay "three weeks from completion" for six months or more.

It's unrepeatable. Even if the code-like-hell approach succeeds once, it doesn't lay the groundwork for succeeding next time. Because it burns people out, it more likely lays the groundwork for future failures. A company cannot easily repair the human damage inflicted by such a project, and accounts of such projects invariably report that massive staff turnover accompanies them (see, for example, Kidder 1981, Carroll 1990, Zachary 1994).

It's hard on nonsoftware organizations. Because it's based on individual heroics rather than on coordination, cooperation, and planning, the code-like-hell approach provides little visibility or control to other stakeholders in the project. Even when you succeed in developing the software faster than average, you have no way of knowing how long the project will take. You don't know when you'll be done until you're actually done.

Some of the speed benefit arising from the commitment-based approach is neutralized because other groups that must coordinate with software developers—including testing, user documentation, and marketing—can't plan. In a code-like-hell project, frustration about the inability to get reliable schedule information from developers causes tempers to flare, and people within the development team are set against people outside the team. What's good for the software part of the project isn't necessarily good for the project overall.

It wastes human resources extravagantly. Developers who participate in this kind of project forego families, friends, hobbies, and even their own health to make a project successful. Severe personality conflicts are the rule rather than the exception. This level of sacrifice might be justifiable to win a war or put a man on the moon, but it isn't needed to develop business software. With few exceptions, the sacrifices aren't necessary: the same results can be achieved through careful, thoughtful, knowledgeable management and technical planning—with much less effort.

Table 2-2 summarizes some of the differences between the code-like-hell approach and the approach this book describes.

Table 2-2. Code-Like-Hell Approach Compared to This Book's Approach

Code-Like-Hell	This Book's Approach
Proponents claim incredible, instant improvement in development time.	Proponents claim modest instant improvement followed by greater, long-term improvement.
Requires little technical expertise beyond coding knowledge.	Requires significant technical expertise beyond coding knowledge.
High risk: frequently fails even when done as effectively as possible.	Low risk: seldom fails when done effectively.
Others will see you as "radical, dude." You'll look like you're giving your all.	Others will see you as conservative, boring, even old-fashioned. You won't look like you're working as hard.
Wastes human resources extravagantly.	Uses human resources efficiently and humanely.
Provides little progress visibility or control. You know you're done when you're done.	Permits tailoring the approach to provide as much visibility and control as you want.
Approach is as old as software itself.	Key parts of the approach used successfully for 15 years or more.

Source: Inspired by "Rewards of Taking the Path Less Traveled" (Davis 1994).

The approach this book describes achieves rapid development through careful planning, efficient use of available time, and the application of schedule-oriented development practices. Overtime is not uncommon with this kind of rapid development, but it does not begin to approach the mountain of overtime commonly found when the code-like-hell approach is used. Efficient development commonly produces a shorter-than-average schedule. When it fails, it fails because people lose their resolve to continue using it, not because the practice itself fails.

In short, the code-like-hell approach guarantees extraordinary sacrifice but not extraordinary results. If the goal is maximum development speed rather than maximum after-hours hustle, any betting person has to favor efficient development.

If you read between the lines in this book, you'll find all the information you need to conduct a code-like-hell project as successfully as possible. A person could certainly transform this book's Dr. Jekyll into code-like-hell's Mr. Hyde. But I personally have had more than my fill of that kind of development, and I'm not going to spell out how to do it!

Case Study 2-2. Rapid Development with a Clear Strategy

Across the company from the Square-Calc 3.0 project, Sarah was ramping up the Square-Plan 2.0 project. Square-Plan was Square-Tech's project-management package. Sarah was the technical lead.

At the first team meeting, she introduced the team members and got right down to business. "I've gone all over the company collecting project postmortems," she said. "I've got a list a mile long of all the mistakes that other projects in this company have made. I'm posting the list here in the conference room, and I'd like you to raise a flag if we start to make any of them. I'd also like you to add any other potential mistakes you already know about or learn about as we go along. There's no point in repeating history if we don't have to.

"I selected you for this team because each one of you is strong in development fundamentals. You know what it means to do a good job of requirements gathering and design so that we won't waste time on needless rework downstream. I want everybody on this project to work smart instead of working hard. People who work too hard make too many mistakes, and we don't have time for that.

"I've also put together a risk-management plan. We've got an aggressive schedule, so we can't afford to be caught off guard by risks we could have prevented. The top risk on this list is that the schedule might be unachievable. I want us to reassess the schedule at the end of the week, and if it's unachievable, we'll come up with something more realistic."

(continued)

Case Study 2-2. Rapid Development with a Clear Strategy, *continued*

Everybody on the team nodded. To the people who had been through death-march projects, Sarah's talk felt like a breath of fresh air.

Later that week, Sarah met with her boss, Eddie. "The team has taken a hard look at the project's schedule, Eddie, and we've concluded that we have only about a five-percent chance of making our current deadline with the current feature set. That's assuming nothing changes, and of course a few things always change."

"That's no good," Eddie said. Eddie had a reputation for delivering what he promised. "I want at least a 50/50 chance of delivering the software on time. And I want to be able to respond to changes in the marketplace over the next 12 months. What do you recommend?"

"We haven't completely specified the product yet, so there's some flexibility there," Sarah said. "But we think the current set of requirements will take 10 to 30 months. I know that's a broad range, but that's the best we can do before we know more about what we're building. We need to have a product in 12 months, right? Considering that, I think we should add another developer and then set up an evolutionary delivery plan where we plan to build a shippable version of the software every two months, with our first delivery at the 8-month mark."

"That sounds good to me," Eddie said. "Besides, I think that functionality might be more important than schedule on this project. Let me talk with some people and get back to you."

When Eddie got back to Sarah, he told her that the company was willing to stretch the software schedule to 14 months to get the features it wanted but that she should still use the evolutionary-delivery plan to be safe. Sarah was relieved and said that she thought that was a more realistic target.

Over the first few weeks of the project, her team built a detailed, Hollywood-facade user-interface prototype. The "mistakes list" warned that sometimes a prototyping effort could take on a life of its own, so they set rigid timeboxes for prototyping work to avoid gold-plating the prototype. They used the prototype to interview potential customers about the candidate features and revised the prototype several times in response to user feedback.

Sarah continued to maintain the risks list and determined that the three key risks to the project were low quality that would cause excessive rework and lengthen the schedule, aggressiveness of the schedule, and features added by the competition between now and the end of the project. Sarah felt that the quality risk was addressed by the evolutionary-delivery plan. They would hand the first version of their software to QA at the 8-month mark, and QA could evolve their test cases along with the software.

The team addressed the schedule risk by creating a prioritized list of features. They would develop as much as they could in 14 months, but by bringing the

(continued)

26

Case Study 2-2. Rapid Development with a Clear Strategy, *continued*

product to a shippable state every two months, they would be guaranteed to have something to ship when they were supposed to. They also made design decisions for several features that were specifically intended to save implementation time. The less time-consuming implementations of the features would not be as slick, but they would be acceptable, and they made for a significant reduction in schedule risk.

The team addressed the competitive-features risk in two ways. They spent about five months developing a design that included a framework capable of supporting all the features they'd prototyped and a few more features that they thought they would include in version 3.0. Their design was intended to accommodate changes with little difficulty. They also allocated time at the 12-month mark to review competitor's products, revise the prototype, and implement competitively necessary features in the final two months.

At the 6-month mark, with the design complete, the team mapped out a set of miniature milestones that marked a path they would follow to release their first shippable version to testing at the 8-month mark. The 8-month version didn't do much, but its quality was good, and it provided a good foundation for further work. When that was behind them, the team mapped out another set of miniature milestones to get to the 10-month mark. The team used the same approach to get to the 12-month mark.

At the 12-month mark, the team reviewed competing products as planned. A competitor had released a good product at the 10-month mark, and it contained some features that Square-Plan 2.0 needed to include to be competitive. The team added the new features to their prioritized list, reprioritized, and mapped out miniature milestones for the final two months.

At about the same time, José, one of the junior developers, discovered a slightly better organization of one of the product's dialog boxes and brought the issue up at a staff meeting. George, one of the more senior developers, responded. "Your idea is great. I think we should change it, but we can't change it now, José. It's a 1-day change for you, but it would affect the documentation schedule by a week or more. How about putting it on the list for version 3.0?"

"I hadn't thought about the effect on the documentation schedule," José said. "That's a good point. I'll just submit it as a to-be-done-later change request."

At the 14-month mark, the team delivered its final software as planned. Square-Plan's quality was excellent because it had been in testing since Month 8. Documentation had been able to base its efforts on the detailed user-interface prototype while they waited for the live software, and the documentation was ready at the same time as the software. The developers had not had time to implement several low-priority features, but they had implemented all of the important ones. Square-Plan 2.0 was a success.

Further Reading

I know of no general books that discuss the topics of product or technology as they have been described in this chapter. This book discusses the topics further in Chapter 14, "Feature-Set Control," Chapter 15, "Productivity Tools," and Chapter 31, "Rapid-Development Languages."

The next three books provide general information on peopleware approaches to software development. The first is the classic.

DeMarco, Tom, and Timothy Lister. *Peopleware: Productive Projects and Teams.* New York: Dorset House, 1987.

Constantine, Larry L. *Constantine on Peopleware.* Englewood Cliffs, N.J.: Yourdon Press, 1995.

Plauger, P. J. *Programming on Purpose II: Essays on Software People.* Englewood Cliffs, N.J.: PTR Prentice Hall, 1993.

The following books provide information on software processes, the first at an organizational level, the second at a team level, and the third at an individual level.

Carnegie Mellon University/Software Engineering Institute. *The Capability Maturity Model: Guidelines for Improving the Software Process.* Reading, Mass.: Addison-Wesley, 1995. This book is a summary of the Software Engineering Institute's latest work on software process improvement. It fully describes the five-level process maturity model, benefits of attaining each level, and practices that characterize each level. It also contains a detailed case study of an organization that has achieved the highest levels of maturity, quality, and productivity.

Maguire, Steve. *Debugging the Development Process.* Redmond, Wash.: Microsoft Press, 1994. Maguire's book presents a set of folksy maxims that project leads can use to keep their teams productive, and it provides interesting glimpses inside some of Microsoft's projects.

Humphrey, Watts S. *A Discipline for Software Engineering.* Reading, Mass.: Addison-Wesley, 1995. Humphrey lays out a personal software process that you can adopt at an individual level regardless of whether your organization supports process improvement.

3

Classic Mistakes

Contents

Related Topics

SOFTWARE DEVELOPMENT IS A COMPLICATED ACTIVITY. A typical software project can present more opportunities to learn from mistakes than some people get in a lifetime. This chapter examines some of the classic mistakes that people make when they try to develop software rapidly.

3.1   Case Study in Classic Mistakes

The following case study is a little bit like the children's picture puzzles in which you try to find all the objects whose names begin with the letter "M". How many classic mistakes can you find in the following case study?

Case Study 3-1. Classic Mistakes

Mike, a technical lead for Giga Safe, was eating lunch in his office and looking out his window on a bright April morning.

"Mike, you got the funding for the Giga-Quote program! Congratulations!" It was Bill, Mike's boss at Giga, a medical insurance company. "The executive committee loved the idea of automating our medical insurance quotes. It also

(continued)

Case Study 3-1. Classic Mistakes, *continued*

loved the idea of uploading the day's quotes to the head office every night so that we always have the latest sales leads online. I've got a meeting now, but we can discuss the details later. Good job on that proposal!"

Mike had written the proposal for the Giga-Quote program months earlier, but his proposal had been for a stand-alone PC program without any ability to communicate with the head office. Oh well. This would give him a chance to lead a client-server project in a modern GUI environment—something he had wanted to do. They had almost a year to do the project, and that should give them plenty of time to add a new feature. Mike picked up the phone and dialed his wife's number. "Honey, let's go out to dinner tonight to celebrate…"

The next morning, Mike met with Bill to discuss the project. "OK, Bill. What's up? This doesn't sound like quite the same proposal I worked on."

Bill felt uneasy. Mike hadn't participated in the revisions to the proposal, but there hadn't been time to involve him. Once the executive committee heard about the Giga-Quote program, they'd taken over. "The executive committee loves the idea of building software to automate medical insurance quotes. But they want to be able to transfer the field quotes into the mainframe computer automatically. And they want to have the system done before our new rates take effect January 1. They moved the software-complete date you proposed up from March 1 to November 1, which shrinks your schedule to 6 months."

Mike had estimated the job would take 12 months. He didn't think they had much chance of finishing in 6 months, and he told Bill so. "Let me get this straight," Mike said. "It sounds like you're saying that the committee added a big communications requirement and chopped the schedule from 12 months to 6?"

Bill shrugged. "I know it will be a challenge, but you're creative, and I think you can pull it off. They approved the budget you wanted, and adding the communications link can't be that hard. You asked for 36 staff-months, and you got it. You can recruit anyone you like to work on the project and increase the team size, too." Bill told him to go talk with some other developers and figure out a way to deliver the software on time.

Mike got together with Carl, another technical lead, and they looked for ways to shorten the schedule. "Why don't you use C++ and object-oriented design?" Carl asked. "You'll be more productive than with C, and that should shave a month or two off the schedule." Mike thought that sounded good. Carl also knew of a report-building tool that was supposed to cut development time in half. The project had a lot of reports, so those two changes would get them down to about 9 months. They were due for newer, faster hardware, too, and that could shave off a couple weeks. If he could recruit really top-notch developers, that might bring them down to about 7 months. That should be close enough. Mike took his findings back to Bill.

(continued)

"Look," Bill said. "Getting the schedule down to 7 months is good, but it isn't good enough. The committee was very clear about the 6-month deadline. They didn't give me a choice. I can get you the new hardware you want, but you and your team are going to have to find some way to get the schedule down to 6 months or work some overtime to make up the difference."

Mike considered the fact that his initial estimate had just been a ballpark guess and thought maybe he could pull it off in 6 months. "OK, Bill. I'll hire a couple of sharp contractors for the project. Maybe we can find some people with communications experience to help with uploading data from the PC to the mainframe."

By May 1, Mike had put a team together. Jill, Sue, and Tomas were solid, in-house developers, and they happened to be unassigned. He rounded out the team with Keiko and Chip, two contractors. Keiko had experience both on PCs and the kind of mainframe they would interface with. Jill and Tomas had interviewed Chip and recommended against hiring him, but Mike was impressed. He had communications experience and was available immediately, so Mike hired him anyway.

At the first team meeting, Bill told the team that the Giga-Quote program was strategically important to the Giga Safe Corporation. Some of the top people in the company would be watching them. If they succeeded, there would be rewards all around. He said he was sure that they could pull it off.

After Bill's pep talk, Mike sat down with the team and laid out the schedule. The executive committee had more or less handed them a specification, and they would spend the next 2 weeks filling in the gaps. Then they'd spend 6 weeks on design, which would leave them 4 months for construction and testing. His seat-of-the-pants estimate was that the final product would consist of about 30,000 lines of code in C++. Everyone around the table nodded agreement. It was ambitious, but they'd known that when they signed up for the project.

The next week, Mike met with Stacy, the testing lead. She explained that they should begin handing product builds over to testing no later than September 1, and they should aim to hand over a feature-complete build by October 1. Mike agreed.

The team finished the requirements specification quickly, and dove into design. They came up with a design that seemed to make good use of C++'s features.

They finished the design by June 15, ahead of schedule, and began coding like crazy to meet their goal of a first-release-to-testing by September 1. Work on the project wasn't entirely smooth. Neither Jill nor Tomas liked Chip, and Sue had also complained that he wouldn't let anyone near his code. Mike

(continued)

Case Study 3-1. Classic Mistakes, *continued*

attributed the personality clashes to the long hours everyone was working. Nevertheless, by early August, they reported that they were between 85-percent and 90-percent done.

In mid-August, the actuarial department released the rates for the next year, and the team discovered that they had to accommodate an entirely new rate structure. The new rating method required them to ask questions about exercise habits, drinking habits, smoking habits, recreational activities, and other factors that hadn't been included in the rating formulas before. C++, they thought, was supposed to shield them from the effects of such changes. They had been counting on just plugging some new numbers into a ratings table. But they had to change the input dialogs, database design, database access, and communications objects to accommodate the new structure. As the team scrambled to retrofit their design, Mike told Stacy that they might be a few days late releasing the first build to testing.

The team didn't have a build ready by September 1, and Mike assured Stacy that the build was only a day or two away.

Days turned into weeks. The October 1 deadline for handing over the feature-complete build to testing came and went. Development still hadn't handed over the first build to testing. Stacy called a meeting with Bill to discuss the schedule. "We haven't gotten a build from development yet," she said. "We were supposed to get our first build on September 1, and since we haven't gotten one yet, they've got to be at least a full month behind schedule. I think they're in trouble."

"They're in trouble, all right," Bill said. "Let me talk to the team. I've promised 600 agents that they would have this program by November 1. We have to get that program out in time for the rate change."

Bill called a team meeting. "This is a fantastic team, and you should be meeting your commitments," he told them. "I don't know what's gone wrong here, but I expect everyone to work hard and deliver this software on time. You can still earn your bonuses, but now you're going to have to work for them. As of now, I'm putting all of you on a 6-day-per-week, 10-hour-per-day schedule until this software is done." After the meeting, Jill and Tomas grumbled to Mike about not needing to be treated like children, but they agreed to work the hours Bill wanted.

The team slipped the schedule two weeks, promising a feature-complete build by November 15. That allowed for 6 weeks of testing before the new rates went into effect in January.

The team released its first build to testing 4 weeks later on November 1 and met to discuss a few remaining problem areas.

(continued)

Case Study 3-1. Classic Mistakes, *continued*

Tomas was working on report generation and had run into a roadblock. "The quote summary page includes a simple bar chart. I'm using a report generator that's supposed to generate bar charts, but the only way it will generate them is on pages by themselves. We have a requirement from the sales group to put the text and bar charts on the same page. I've figured out that I can hack up a report with a bar chart by passing in the report text as a legend to the bar-chart object. It's definitely a hack, but I can always go back and reimplement it more cleanly after the first release."

Mike responded, "I don't see where the issue is. We have to get the product out, and we don't have time to make the code perfect. Bill has made it crystal clear that there can't be any more slips. Do the hack."

Chip reported that his communications code was 95-percent done and that it worked, but he still had a few more tests to run. Mike caught Jill and Tomas rolling their eyes, but he decided to ignore it.

The team worked hard through November 15, including working almost all the way through the nights of the 14th and 15th, but they still didn't make their November 15 release date. The team was exhausted, but on the morning of the 16th, it was Bill who felt sick. Stacy had called to tell him that development hadn't released its feature-complete build the day before. Last week he had told the executive committee that the project was on track. Another project manager, Claire, had probed into the team's progress, saying that she had heard that they weren't making their scheduled releases to testing. Bill thought Claire was uptight, and he didn't like her. He had assured her that his team was definitely on track to make their scheduled releases.

Bill told Mike to get the team together, and when he did, they looked defeated. A month and a half of 60-hour weeks had taken their toll. Mike asked what time today they would have the build ready, but the only response he got was silence. "What are you telling me?" he said. "We are going to have the feature-complete build today, aren't we?"

"Look, Mike," Tomas said. "I can hand off my code today and call it 'feature complete', but I've probably got 3 weeks of cleanup work to do once I hand it off." Mike asked what Tomas meant by "cleanup." "I haven't gotten the company logo to show up on every page, and I haven't gotten the agent's name and phone number to print on the bottom of every page. It's little stuff like that. All of the important stuff works fine. I'm 99-percent done."

"I'm not exactly 100-percent done either," Jill admitted. "My old group has been calling me for technical support a lot, and I've been spending a couple hours a day working for them. Plus, I had forgotten until just now that we were supposed to give the agents the ability to put their names and phone numbers on the reports. I haven't implemented the dialogs to input that data yet, and I still have to do some of the other housekeeping dialogs, too. I didn't think we needed them to make our 'feature-complete' milestone."

(continued)

Case Study 3-1. Classic Mistakes, *continued*

Now Mike started to feel sick, too. "If I'm hearing what I think I'm hearing, you're telling me that we're 3 weeks away from having feature-complete software. Is that right?"

"Three weeks *at least*," Jill said. The rest of the developers agreed. Mike went around the table one by one and asked the developers if they could completely finish their assignments in 3 weeks. One by one, the developers said that if they worked hard, they thought they could make it.

Later that day, after a long, uncomfortable discussion, Mike and Bill agreed to slip the schedule 3 weeks to December 5, as long as the team promised to work 12-hour days instead of 10. Bill said he needed to show his boss that he was holding the development team's feet to the fire. The revised schedule meant that they would have to test the code and train the field agents concurrently, but that was the only way they could hope to release the software by January 1. Stacy complained that that wouldn't give QA enough time to test the software, but Bill overruled her.

On December 5, the Giga-Quote team handed off the feature-complete Giga-Quote program to testing before noon and left work early to take a long-awaited break. They had worked almost constantly since September 1.

Two days later, Stacy released the first bug list, and all hell broke loose. In two days, the testing group had identified more than 200 defects in the Giga-Quote program, including 23 that were classified as Severity 1—"Must Fix"—errors. "I don't see any way that the software will be ready to release to the field agents by January 1," she said. "It will probably take the test group that long just to write the regression test cases for the defects we've already discovered, and we're finding new defects every hour."

Mike called a staff meeting for 8 o'clock the next morning. The developers were touchy. They said that although there were a few serious problems, a lot of the reported bugs weren't really bugs at all but were misinterpretations of how the program was supposed to operate. Tomas pointed to bug #143 as an example. "The test report for bug #143 says that on the quote summary page, the bar chart is required to be on the right side of the page rather than the left. That's hardly a Sev-1 error. This is typical of the way that testing overreacts to problems."

Mike distributed copies of the bug reports. He tasked the developers to review the bugs that testing had assigned to them and to estimate how much time it would take to fix each one.

When the team met again that afternoon, the news wasn't good. "Realistically, I would estimate that I have 2 weeks' worth of work just to fix the bugs that have already been reported," Sue said. "Plus I still have to finish the referential integrity checks in the database. I've got 4 weeks of work right now, total."

(continued)

Tomas had assigned bug #143 back to testing, changing its priority from Sev-1 to Sev-3—"Cosmetic Change." Testing had responded that Giga-Quote's summary reports had to match similar reports generated by the mainframe policy-renewal program, which were also similar to preprinted marketing materials that the company had used for many years. The company's 600 agents were accustomed to giving their sales pitches with the bar chart on the right, and it had to stay on the right. The bug stayed at Sev-1, and that created a problem.

"Remember the hack I used to get the bar chart and the report to print on the same page in the first place?" Tomas asked. "To put the bar chart on the right, I will have to rewrite this particular report from scratch, which means that I will have to write my own low-level code to do the report formatting and graphics." Mike cringed, and asked for a ballpark estimate of how long all that would take. Tomas said it would take at least 10 days, but he would have to look into it more before he would know for sure.

Before he went home for the day, Mike told Stacy and Bill that the team would work through the holidays and have all the reported defects fixed by January 7. Bill said he had almost been expecting this one and approved a 4-week schedule slip before leaving for a monthlong Caribbean cruise he had been planning since the previous summer.

Mike spent the next month holding the troops together. For 4 months, they had been working as hard as it was possible to work, and he didn't think he could push them any harder. They were at the office 12 hours a day, but they were spending a lot of time reading magazines, paying bills, and talking on the phone. They seemed to make a point of getting irritable whenever he asked how long it would take to get the bug count down. For every bug they fixed, testing discovered two new ones. Bugs that should have taken minutes to fix had projectwide implications and took days instead. They soon realized there was no way they could fix all the defects by January 7.

On January 7, Bill returned from his vacation, and Mike told him that the development team would need another 4 weeks. "Get serious," Bill said. "I've got 600 field agents who are tired of getting jerked around by a bunch of computer guys. The executive committee is talking about canceling the project. You have to find a way to deliver the software within the next 2 weeks, no matter what."

Mike called a team meeting to discuss their options. He told them about Bill's ultimatum and asked for a ballpark estimate of when they could release the product, first just in weeks, then in months. The team was silent. No one would hazard a guess about when they might finally release the product. Mike didn't know what to tell Bill.

(continued)

Case Study 3-1. Classic Mistakes, *continued*

After the meeting, Chip told Mike that he had accepted a contract with a different company that started February 3. Mike began to feel that it would be a relief if the project were canceled.

Mike got Kip, the programmer who had been responsible for the mainframe side of the PC-to-mainframe communications, reassigned to help out on the project and assigned him to fix bugs in the PC communications code. After struggling with Chip's code for a week, Kip realized that it contained some deep conceptual flaws that meant it could never work correctly. Kip was forced to redesign and reimplement the PC side of the PC-to-mainframe communications link.

As Bill rambled on at an executive meeting in the middle of February, Claire finally decided that she had heard enough and called a "stop work" on the Giga-Quote program. She met with Mike on Friday. "This project is out of control," she said. "I haven't gotten a reliable schedule estimate from Bill for months. This was a 6-month project, and it's now more than 3 months late with no end in sight. I've looked over the bug statistics, and the team isn't closing the gap. You're all working such long hours that you're not even making progress anymore. I want you all to take the weekend off; then I want you to develop a detailed, step-by-step report that includes everything—and I do mean *everything*—that remains to be done on that project. I don't want you to force-fit the project into an artificial schedule. If it's going to take another 9 months, I want to know that. I want that report by end-of-work Wednesday. It doesn't have to be fancy, but it does have to be complete."

The development team was glad to have the weekend off, and during the next week they attacked the detailed report with renewed energy. It was on Claire's desk Wednesday. She had the report reviewed by Charles, a software engineering consultant who also reviewed the project's bug statistics. Charles recommended that the team focus its efforts on a handful of error-prone modules, that it immediately institute design and code reviews for all bug fixes, and that the team start working regular hours so that they could get an accurate measure of how much effort was being expended on the project and how much would be needed to finish.

Three weeks later, in the first week in March, the open-bug count had ticked down a notch for the first time. Team morale had ticked up a notch, and based on the steady progress being made, the consultant projected that the software could be delivered—fully tested and reliable—by May 15. Since Giga Safe's semi-annual rate increase would go into effect July 1, Claire set the official launch date for June 1.

Epilogue

The Giga-Quote program was released to the field agents according to plan on June 1. Giga Safe's field agents greeted it with a warm if somewhat skeptical reception.

(continued)

Case Study 3-1. Classic Mistakes, *continued*

> The Giga Safe Corporation showed its appreciation for the development team's hard work by presenting each of the developers with a $250 bonus. A few weeks later, Tomas asked for an extended leave of absence, and Jill went to work for another company.
>
> The final Giga-Quote product was delivered in 13 months rather than 6, a schedule overrun of more than 100 percent. The developer effort, including overtime, consisted of 98 staff-months, which was a 170-percent overrun of the planned 36 staff-months.
>
> The final product was determined to consist of about 40,000 nonblank, noncomment lines of code in C++, which was about 33 percent more than Mike's seat-of-the-pants guess. As a product that was distributed to 600 in-house sites, Giga-Quote was a hybrid between a business product and a shrink-wrap product. A product of its size and type should normally have been completed in 11.5 months with 71 staff-months of effort. The project had overshot both of those nominals.

CROSS-REFERENCE
For a table of ballpark estimates such as these for projects of various sizes, see Section 8.6, "Ballpark Schedule Estimates."

3.2 Effect of Mistakes on a Development Schedule

Michael Jackson (the singer, not the computer scientist) sang that "One bad apple don't spoil the whole bunch, baby." That might be true for apples, but it isn't true for software. One bad apple *can* spoil your whole project.

A group of ITT researchers reviewed 44 projects in 9 countries to examine the impact of 13 productivity factors on productivity (Vosburgh et al. 1984). The factors included the use of modern programming practices, code difficulty, performance requirements, level of client participation in requirements specification, personnel experience, and several others. They divided each of the factors into categories that you would expect to be associated with low, medium, and high performance. For example, they divided the "modern programming practices" factor into low use, medium use, and high use. Figure 3-1 on the next page shows what the researchers found for the "use of modern programming practices" factor.

The longer you study Figure 3-1, the more interesting it becomes. The general pattern it shows is representative of the findings for each of the productivity factors studied. The ITT researchers found that projects in the categories that they expected to have poor productivity did in fact have poor productivity, such as the narrow range shown in the Low category in Figure 3-1. But productivity in the high-performance categories varied greatly, such as the wide range shown in the High category in Figure 3-1. Productivity of projects in the High category varied from poor to excellent.

CROSS-REFERENCE
For more discussion of
this specific graph, see
Section 4.2, "Technical
Fundamentals."

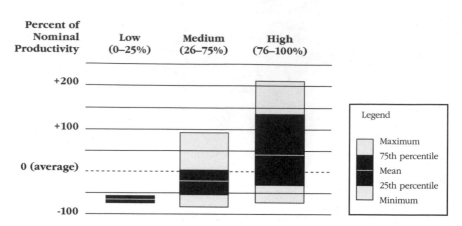

Figure 3-1. *Findings for "Use of Modern Programming Practices" factor (Vosburgh et al. 1984). Doing a few things right doesn't guarantee rapid development. You also have to avoid doing anything wrong.*

CROSS-REFERENCE
For more on the role that
mistakes play in rapid
development, see Section
2.1, "General Strategy for
Rapid Development."

That projects that were expected to have poor productivity do in fact have poor productivity shouldn't surprise you. But the finding that many of the projects expected to have excellent productivity actually have poor productivity just might be a surprise. What this graph and other graphs like it throughout the book show is that the use of any specific best practice is necessary but not sufficient for achieving maximum development speed. Even if you do a few things right, such as making high use of modern programming practices, you might still make a mistake that nullifies your productivity gains.

When thinking about rapid development, it's tempting to think that all you have to do is identify the root causes of slow development and eliminate them—and then you'll have rapid development. The problem is that there aren't just a handful of root causes of slow development, and in the end trying to identify the root causes of slow development isn't very useful. It's like asking, 'What is the root cause of my not being able to run a 4-minute mile?' Well, I'm too old. I weigh too much. I'm too out of shape. I'm not willing to train that hard. I don't have a world-class coach or athletic facility. I wasn't all that fast even when I was younger. The list goes on and on.

When you talk about exceptional achievements, the reasons that people don't rise to the top are simply too numerous to list. The Giga-Quote team in Case Study 3-1 made many of the mistakes that have plagued software developers since the earliest days of computing. The software-development road is mined with potholes, and the potholes you fall into partially determine how quickly or slowly you develop software.

In software, one bad apple can spoil the whole bunch, baby. To slip into slow development, all you need to do is make one really big mistake; to achieve rapid development you need to avoid making *any* big mistakes. The next section lists the most common of those big mistakes.

3.3 Classic Mistakes Enumerated

CLASSIC MISTAKE

Some ineffective development practices have been chosen so often, by so many people, with such predictable, bad results that they deserve to be called "classic mistakes." Most of the mistakes have a seductive appeal. Do you need to rescue a project that's behind schedule? Add more people! Do you want to reduce your schedule? Schedule more aggressively! Is one of your key contributors aggravating the rest of the team? Wait until the end of the project to fire him! Do you have a rush project to complete? Take whatever developers are available right now and get started as soon as possible!

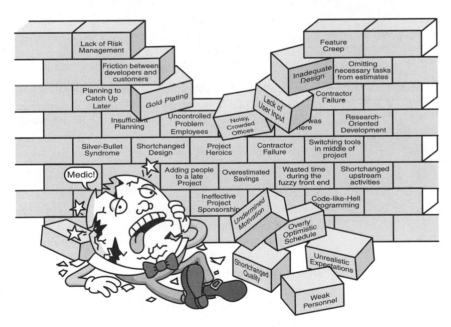

Figure 3-2. *The software project was riddled with mistakes, and all the king's managers and technical leads couldn't rescue the project for anyone's sake.*

Developers, managers, and customers usually have good reasons for making the decisions they do, and the seductive appeal of the classic mistakes is part of the reason these mistakes have been made so often. But because they have been made so many times, their consequences have become easy to predict. And classic mistakes rarely produce the results that people hope for.

This section enumerates three dozen classic mistakes. I have personally seen each of these mistakes made at least once, and I've made more than a few of them myself. Many of them crop up in Case Study 3-1. The common denominator of these mistakes is that you won't necessarily get rapid development if you avoid these mistakes, but you will definitely get slow development if you don't avoid them.

If some of these mistakes sound familiar, take heart—many other people have made them too. Once you understand their effect on development speed you can use this list to help with your project planning and risk management.

Some of the more significant mistakes are discussed in their own sections in other parts of this book. Others are not discussed further. For ease of reference, the list has been divided along the development-speed dimensions of people, process, product, and technology.

People

Here are some of the people-related classic mistakes.

CROSS-REFERENCE
For more on the uses and misuses of motivation, see Chapter 11, "Motivation."

1: Undermined motivation. Study after study has shown that motivation probably has a larger effect on productivity and quality than any other factor (Boehm 1981). In Case Study 3-1, management took steps that undermined morale throughout the project—from giving a hokey pep talk at the beginning to requiring overtime in the middle, from going on a long vacation while the team worked through the holidays to providing end-of-project bonuses that worked out to less than a dollar per overtime hour at the end.

2: Weak personnel. After motivation, either the individual capabilities of the team members or their relationship as a team probably has the greatest influence on productivity (Boehm 1981, Lakhanpal 1993). Hiring from the bottom of the barrel will threaten a rapid-development effort. In the case study, personnel selections were made with an eye toward who could be hired fastest instead of who would get the most work done over the life of the project. That practice gets the project off to a quick start but doesn't set it up for rapid completion.

CROSS-REFERENCE
For more on creating effective teams, see Chapter 12, "Teamwork."

3: Uncontrolled problem employees. Failure to deal with problem personnel also threatens development speed. This is a common problem and has been well-understood at least since Gerald Weinberg published *Psychology of Computer Programming* in 1971. Failure to take action to deal with a problem employee is the most common complaint that team members have about their leaders (Larson and LaFasto 1989). In Case Study 3-1, the team knew that Chip was a bad apple, but the team lead didn't do anything about it. The result—redoing all of Chip's work—was predictable.

CROSS-REFERENCE
For more on heroics and commitment-based projects, see Section 2.5, "An Alternative Rapid-Development Strategy," "Commitment-Based Scheduling" in Section 8.5, and Chapter 34, "Signing Up."

4: Heroics. Some software developers place a high emphasis on project heroics, thinking that certain kinds of heroics can be beneficial (Bach 1995). But I think that emphasizing heroics in any form usually does more harm than good. In the case study, mid-level management placed a higher premium on can-do attitudes than on steady and consistent progress and meaningful progress reporting. The result was a pattern of scheduling brinkmanship in which impending schedule slips weren't detected, acknowledged, or reported up the management chain until the last minute. A small development team and its immediate management held an entire company hostage because they wouldn't admit that they were having trouble meeting their schedule. An emphasis on heroics encourages extreme risk taking and discourages cooperation among the many stakeholders in the software-development process.

Some managers encourage heroic behavior when they focus too strongly on can-do attitudes. By elevating can-do attitudes above accurate-and-sometimes-gloomy status reporting, such project managers undercut their ability to take corrective action. They don't even know they need to take corrective action until the damage has been done. As Tom DeMarco says, can-do attitudes escalate minor setbacks into true disasters (DeMarco 1995).

CROSS-REFERENCE
For alternative means of rescuing a late project, see Chapter 16, "Project Recovery."

5: Adding people to a late project. This is perhaps the most classic of the classic mistakes. When a project is behind, adding people can take more productivity away from existing team members than it adds through new ones. Fred Brooks likened adding people to a late project to pouring gasoline on a fire (Brooks 1975).

CROSS-REFERENCE
For more on the effects of the physical environment on productivity, see Chapter 30, "Productivity Environments."

6: Noisy, crowded offices. Most developers rate their working conditions as unsatisfactory. About 60 percent report that they are neither sufficiently quiet nor sufficiently private (DeMarco and Lister 1987). Workers who occupy quiet, private offices tend to perform significantly better than workers who occupy noisy, crowded work bays or cubicles. Noisy, crowded work environments lengthen development schedules.

CROSS-REFERENCE
For more on effective customer relations, see Chapter 10, "Customer-Oriented Development."

7: Friction between developers and customers. Friction between developers and customers can arise in several ways. Customers may feel that developers are not cooperative when they refuse to sign up for the development schedule that the customers want or when they fail to deliver on their promises. Developers may feel that customers are unreasonably insisting on unrealistic schedules or requirements changes after the requirements have been baselined. There might simply be personality conflicts between the two groups.

The primary effect of this friction is poor communication, and the secondary effects of poor communication include poorly understood requirements, poor user-interface design, and, in the worst case, customers' refusing to accept the completed product. On average, friction between customers and software developers becomes so severe that both parties consider canceling the project (Jones 1994). Such friction is time-consuming to overcome, and it distracts both customers and developers from the real work of the project.

CROSS-REFERENCE
For more on setting expectations, see Section 10.3, "Managing Customer Expectations."

8: Unrealistic expectations. One of the most common causes of friction between developers and their customers or managers is unrealistic expectations. In Case Study 3-1, Bill had no sound reason to think that the Giga-Quote program could be developed in 6 months, but that's when the company's executive committee wanted it done. Mike's inability to correct that unrealistic expectation was a major source of problems.

In other cases, project managers or developers ask for trouble by getting funding based on overly optimistic schedule estimates. Sometimes they promise a pie-in-the-sky feature set.

Although unrealistic expectations do not in themselves lengthen development schedules, they contribute to the perception that development schedules are too long, and that can be almost as bad. A Standish Group survey listed realistic expectations as one of the top five factors needed to ensure the success of an in-house business-software project (Standish Group 1994).

9: Lack of effective project sponsorship. High-level project sponsorship is necessary to support many aspects of rapid development, including realistic planning, change control, and the introduction of new development practices. Without an effective executive sponsor, other high-level personnel in your organization can force you to accept unrealistic deadlines or make changes that undermine your project. Australian consultant Rob Thomsett argues that lack of an effective executive sponsor virtually guarantees project failure (Thomsett 1995).

10: Lack of stakeholder buy-in. All the major players in a software-development effort must buy in to the project. That includes the executive sponsor, team leader, team members, marketing staff, end-users, customers, and anyone else who has a stake in it. The close cooperation that occurs only when you have complete buy-in from all stakeholders allows for precise coordination of a rapid-development effort that is impossible to attain without good buy-in.

11: Lack of user input. The Standish Group survey found that the number one reason that IS projects succeed is because of user involvement (Standish Group 1994). Projects without early end-user involvement risk misunderstanding the projects' requirements and are vulnerable to time-consuming feature creep later in the project.

CROSS-REFERENCE
For more on healthy politics,
see Section 10.3, "Managing
Customer Expectations."

12: Politics placed over substance. Larry Constantine reported on four teams that had four different kinds of political orientations (Constantine 1995a). "Politicians" specialized in "managing up," concentrating on relationships with their managers. "Researchers" concentrated on scouting out and gathering information. "Isolationists" kept to themselves, creating project boundaries that they kept closed to non-team members. "Generalists" did a little bit of everything: they tended their relationships with their managers, performed research and scouting activities, and coordinated with other teams through the course of their normal workflow. Constantine reported that initially the political and generalist teams were both well regarded by top management. But after a year and a half, the political team was ranked dead last. Putting politics over results is fatal to speed-oriented development.

13: Wishful thinking. I am amazed at how many problems in software development boil down to wishful thinking. How many times have you heard statements like these from different people:

> "None of the team members really believed that they could complete the project according to the schedule they were given, but they thought that maybe if everyone worked hard, and nothing went wrong, and they got a few lucky breaks, they just might be able to pull it off."

> "Our team hasn't done very much work to coordinate the interfaces among the different parts of the product, but we've all been in good communication about other things, and the interfaces are relatively simple, so it'll probably take only a day or two to shake out the bugs."

> "We know that we went with the low-ball contractor on the database subsystem, and it was hard to see how they were going to complete the work with the staffing levels they specified in their proposal. They didn't have as much experience as some of the other contractors, but maybe they can make up in energy what they lack in experience. They'll probably deliver on time."

> "We don't need to show the final round of changes to the prototype to the customer. I'm sure we know what they want by now."

> "The team is saying that it will take an extraordinary effort to meet the deadline, and they missed their first milestone by a few days, but I think they can bring this one in on time."

Wishful thinking isn't just optimism. It's closing your eyes and hoping something works when you have no reasonable basis for thinking it will. Wishful thinking at the beginning of a project leads to big blowups at the end of a project. It undermines meaningful planning and may be at the root of more software problems than all other causes combined.

Process

Process-related mistakes slow down projects because they squander people's talents and efforts. Here are some of the worst process-related mistakes.

CROSS-REFERENCE
For more on unrealistic schedules, see Section 9.1, "Overly Optimistic Scheduling."

14: Overly optimistic schedules. The challenges faced by someone building a 3-month application are quite different from the challenges faced by someone building a 1-year application. Setting an overly optimistic schedule sets a project up for failure by underscoping the project, undermining effective planning, and abbreviating critical upstream development activities such as requirements analysis and design. It also puts excessive pressure on developers, which hurts long-term developer morale and productivity. This was a major source of problems in Case Study 3-1.

CROSS-REFERENCE
For more on risk management, see Chapter 5, "Risk Management."

15: Insufficient risk management. Some mistakes are not common enough to be considered classic. Those are called "risks." As with the classic mistakes, if you don't actively manage risks, only one thing has to go wrong to change your project from a rapid-development project to a slow-development one. The failure to manage such unique risks is a classic mistake.

CROSS-REFERENCE
For more on contractors, see Chapter 28, "Outsourcing."

16: Contractor failure. Companies sometimes contract out pieces of a project when they are too rushed to do the work in-house. But contractors frequently deliver work that's late, that's of unacceptably low quality, or that fails to meet specifications (Boehm 1989). Risks such as unstable requirements or ill-defined interfaces can be magnified when you bring a contractor into the picture. If the contractor relationship isn't managed carefully, the use of contractors can slow a project down rather than speed it up.

CROSS-REFERENCE
For more on planning, see "Planning" in Section 4.1.

17: Insufficient planning. If you don't plan to achieve rapid development, you can't expect to achieve it.

CROSS-REFERENCE
For more on planning under pressure, see Section 9.2, "Beating Schedule Pressure," and Chapter 16, "Project Recovery."

18: Abandonment of planning under pressure. Project teams make plans and then routinely abandon them when they run into schedule trouble (Humphrey 1989). The problem isn't so much in abandoning the plan as in failing to create a substitute, and then falling into code-and-fix mode instead. In Case Study 3-1, the team abandoned its plan after it missed its first delivery, and that's typical. The work after that point was uncoordinated and awkward—to the point that Jill even started working on a project for her old group part of the time and no one even knew it.

19: Wasted time during the fuzzy front end. The "fuzzy front end" is the time before the project starts, the time normally spent in the approval and budgeting process. It's not uncommon for a project to spend months or years in the fuzzy front end and then to come out of the gates with an aggressive schedule. It's much easier and cheaper and less risky to save a few weeks or months in the fuzzy front end than it is to compress a development schedule by the same amount.

CROSS-REFERENCE
For more on shortchanging upstream activities, see "Effects of Overly Optimistic Schedules" in Section 9.1.

HARD DATA

20: Shortchanged upstream activities. Projects that are in a hurry try to cut out nonessential activities, and since requirements analysis, architecture, and design don't directly produce code, they are easy targets. On one disastrous project that I took over, I asked to see the design. The team lead told me, "We didn't have time to do a design."

The results of this mistake—also known as "jumping into coding"—are all too predictable. In the case study, a design hack in the bar-chart report was substituted for quality design work. Before the product could be released, the hack work had to be thrown out and the higher-quality work had to be done anyway. Projects that skimp on upstream activities typically have to do the same work downstream at anywhere from 10 to 100 times the cost of doing it properly in the first place (Fagan 1976; Boehm and Papaccio 1988). If you can't find the 5 hours to do the job right the first time, where are you going to find the 50 hours to do it right later?

21: Inadequate design. A special case of shortchanging upstream activities is inadequate design. Rush projects undermine design by not allocating enough time for it and by creating a pressure cooker environment that makes thoughtful consideration of design alternatives difficult. The design emphasis is on expediency rather than quality, so you tend to need several ultimately time-consuming design cycles before you can finally complete the system.

CROSS-REFERENCE
For more on quality assurance, see Section 4.3, "Quality-Assurance Fundamentals."

HARD DATA

22: Shortchanged quality assurance. Projects that are in a hurry often cut corners by eliminating design and code reviews, eliminating test planning, and performing only perfunctory testing. In the case study, design reviews and code reviews were given short shrift in order to achieve a perceived schedule advantage. As it turned out, when the project reached its feature-complete milestone it was still too buggy to release for 5 more months. This result is typical. Shortcutting 1 day of QA activity early in the project is likely to cost you from 3 to 10 days of activity downstream (Jones 1994). This short-cut undermines development speed.

CROSS-REFERENCE
For more on management controls, see "Tracking" in Section 4.1 and Chapter 27, "Miniature Milestones."

23: Insufficient management controls. In the case study, few management controls were in place to provide timely warnings of impending schedule slips, and the few controls that were in place at the beginning were abandoned once the project ran into trouble. Before you can keep a project on track, you have to be able to tell whether it's on track in the first place.

CROSS-REFERENCE
For more on premature convergence, see "Premature convergence" in Section 9.1.

24: Premature or overly frequent convergence. Shortly before a product is scheduled to be released, there is a push to prepare the product for release—improve the product's performance, print final documentation, incorporate final help-system hooks, polish the installation program, stub out functionality that's not going to be ready on time, and so on. On rush projects, there is a tendency to force convergence early. Since it's not possible to force the product to converge when desired, some rapid-development projects try to force convergence a half dozen times or more before they finally succeed. The extra convergence attempts don't benefit the product. They just waste time and prolong the schedule.

CROSS-REFERENCE
For a list of commonly omitted tasks, see "Don't omit common tasks" in Section 8.3.

25: Omitting necessary tasks from estimates. If people don't keep careful records of previous projects, they forget about the less visible tasks, but those tasks add up. Omitted effort often adds about 20 to 30 percent to a development schedule (van Genuchten 1991).

26: Planning to catch up later. One kind of reestimation is responding inappropriately to a schedule slip. If you're working on a 6-month project, and it takes you 3 months to meet your 2-month milestone, what do you do? Many projects simply plan to catch up later, but they never do. You learn more about the product as you build it, including more about what it will take to build it. That learning needs to be reflected in the reestimated schedule.

CROSS-REFERENCE
For more on reestimation, see "Recalibration" in Section 8.7.

Another kind of reestimation mistake arises from product changes. If the product you're building changes, the amount of time you need to build it changes too. In Case Study 3-1, major requirements changed between the original proposal and the project start without any corresponding reestimation of schedule or resources. Piling on new features without adjusting the schedule guarantees that you will miss your deadline.

CROSS-REFERENCE
For more on the Code-and-Fix approach, see Section 7.2, "Code-and-Fix."

27: Code-like-hell programming. Some organizations think that fast, loose, all-as-you-go coding is a route to rapid development. If the developers are sufficiently motivated, they reason, they can overcome any obstacles. For reasons that will become clear throughout this book, this is far from the truth. This approach is sometimes presented as an "entrepreneurial" approach to software development, but it is really just a cover for the old Code-and-Fix paradigm combined with an ambitious schedule, and that combination almost never works. It's an example of two wrongs not making a right.

Product

Here are classic mistakes related to the way the product is defined.

28: Requirements gold-plating. Some projects have more requirements than they need, right from the beginning. Performance is stated as a requirement more often than it needs to be, and that can unnecessarily lengthen a software schedule. Users tend to be less interested in complex features than marketing and development are, and complex features add disproportionately to a development schedule.

CROSS-REFERENCE
For more on feature creep, see Chapter 14, "Feature-Set Control."

29: Feature creep. Even if you're successful at avoiding requirements gold-plating, the average project experiences about a 25-percent change in requirements over its lifetime (Jones 1994). Such a change can produce at least a 25-percent addition to the software schedule, which can be fatal to a rapid-development project.

CROSS-REFERENCE
For an example of the way
that developer gold-plating
can occur even accidentally,
see "Unclear or Impossible
Goals" in Section 14.2.

30: Developer gold-plating. Developers are fascinated by new technology and are sometimes anxious to try out new features of their language or environment or to create their own implementation of a slick feature they saw in another product—whether or not it's required in their product. The effort required to design, implement, test, document, and support features that are not required lengthens the schedule.

31: Push-me, pull-me negotiation. One bizarre negotiating ploy occurs when a manager approves a schedule slip on a project that's progressing slower than expected and then adds completely new tasks after the schedule change. The underlying reason for this is hard to fathom, because the manager who approves the schedule slip is implicitly acknowledging that the schedule was in error. But once the schedule has been corrected, the same person takes explicit action to make it wrong again. This can't help but undermine the schedule.

32: Research-oriented development. Seymour Cray, the designer of the Cray supercomputers, says that he does not attempt to exceed engineering limits in more than two areas at a time because the risk of failure is too high (Gilb 1988). Many software projects could learn a lesson from Cray. If your project strains the limits of computer science by requiring the creation of new algorithms or new computing practices, you're not doing software development; you're doing software research. Software-development schedules are reasonably predictable; software research schedules are not even theoretically predictable.

If you have product goals that push the state of the art—algorithms, speed, memory usage, and so on—you should assume that your scheduling is highly speculative. If you're pushing the state of the art and you have any other weaknesses in your project—personnel shortages, personnel weaknesses, vague requirements, unstable interfaces with outside contractors—you can throw predictable scheduling out the window. If you want to advance the state of the art, by all means, do it. But don't expect to do it rapidly!

Technology

The remaining classic mistakes have to do with the use and misuse of modern technology.

CROSS-REFERENCE
For more on the silver-bullet
syndrome, see Section 15.5,
"Silver-Bullet Syndrome."

33: Silver-bullet syndrome. In the case study, there was too much reliance on the advertised benefits of previously unused technologies (report generator, object-oriented design, and C++) and too little information about how well they would do in this particular development environment. When project teams latch onto a single new practice, new technology, or rigid process and expect it to solve their schedule problems, they are inevitably disappointed (Jones 1994).

CROSS-REFERENCE
For more on estimating savings from productivity tools, see "How Much Schedule Reduction to Expect" in Section 15.4.

34: Overestimated savings from new tools or methods. Organizations seldom improve their productivity in giant leaps, no matter how many new tools or methods they adopt or how good they are. Benefits of new practices are partially offset by the learning curves associated with them, and learning to use new practices to their maximum advantage takes time. New practices also entail new risks, which you're likely to discover only by using them. You are more likely to experience slow, steady improvement on the order of a few percent per project than you are to experience dramatic gains. The team in Case Study 3-1 should have planned on, at most, a 10-percent gain in productivity from the use of the new technologies instead of assuming that they would nearly double their productivity.

CROSS-REFERENCE
For more on reuse, see Chapter 33, "Reuse."

A special case of overestimated savings arises when projects reuse code from previous projects. This kind of reuse can be a very effective approach, but the time savings is rarely as dramatic as expected.

35: Switching tools in the middle of a project. This is an old standby that hardly ever works. Sometimes it can make sense to upgrade incrementally within the same product line, from version 3 to version 3.1 or sometimes even to version 4. But the learning curve, rework, and inevitable mistakes made with a totally new tool usually cancel out any benefit when you're in the middle of a project.

CROSS-REFERENCE
For more on source-code control, see "Software Configuration Management" in Section 4.2.

36: Lack of automated source-code control. Failure to use automated source-code control exposes projects to needless risks. Without it, if two developers are working on the same part of the program, they have to coordinate their work manually. They might agree to put the latest versions of each file into a master directory and to check with each other before copying files into that directory. But someone invariably overwrites someone else's work. People develop new code to out-of-date interfaces and then have to redesign their code when they discover that they were using the wrong version of the interface. Users report defects that you can't reproduce because you have no way to re-create the build they were using. On average, source code changes at a rate of about 10 percent per month, and manual source-code control can't keep up (Jones 1994).

Table 3-1 contains a complete list of classic mistakes.

Table 3-1. Summary of Classic Mistakes

People-Related Mistakes	Process-Related Mistakes	Product-Related Mistakes	Technology-Related Mistakes
1. Undermined motivation	14. Overly optimistic schedules	28. Requirements gold-plating	33. Silver-bullet syndrome
2. Weak personnel	15. Insufficient risk management	29. Feature creep	34. Overestimated savings from new tools or methods
3. Uncontrolled problem employees	16. Contractor failure	30. Developer gold-plating	
4. Heroics	17. Insufficient planning	31. Push-me, pull-me negotiation	35. Switching tools in the middle of a project
5. Adding people to a late project	18. Abandonment of planning under pressure	32. Research-oriented development	
6. Noisy, crowded offices	19. Wasted time during the fuzzy front end		36. Lack of automated source-code control
7. Friction between developers and customers	20. Shortchanged upstream activities		
8. Unrealistic expectations	21. Inadequate design		
9. Lack of effective project sponsorship	22. Shortchanged quality assurance		
10. Lack of stakeholder buy-in	23. Insufficient management controls		
11. Lack of user input	24. Premature or overly frequent convergence		
12. Politics placed over substance	25. Omitting necessary tasks from estimates		
13. Wishful thinking	26. Planning to catch up later		
	27. Code-like-hell programming		

3.4   Escape from *Gilligan's Island*

A complete list of classic mistakes would go on for pages more, but those presented are the most common and the most serious. As Seattle University's David Umphress points out, watching most organizations attempt to avoid these classic mistakes seems like watching reruns of *Gilligan's Island*. At the beginning of each episode, Gilligan, the Skipper, or the Professor comes up with a cockamamie scheme to get off the island. The scheme seems as though it's going to work for a while, but as the episode unfolds, something goes wrong, and by the end of the episode the castaways find themselves right back where they started—stuck on the island.

Similarly, most companies at the end of each project find that they have made yet another classic mistake and that they have delivered yet another project behind schedule or over budget or both.

Your Own List of Worst Practices

Be aware of the classic mistakes. Create lists of "worst practices" to avoid on future projects. Start with the list in this chapter. Add to the list by conducting project postmortems to learn from your team's mistakes. Encourage other projects within your organization to conduct postmortems so that you can learn from their mistakes. Exchange war stories with your colleagues in other organizations, and learn from their experiences. Display your list of mistakes prominently so that people will see it and learn not to make the same mistakes yet another time.

Further Reading

Although a few books discuss coding mistakes, there are no books that I know of that describe classic mistakes related to development schedules. Further reading on related topics is provided throughout the rest of this book.

4

Software-Development Fundamentals

Contents

Related Topics

RED AUERBACH, THE LONG-TIME COACH of the Boston Celtics and until recently the winningest coach in the history of professional basketball, created a videotape called "Red on Roundball." Auerbach drives home the point that the key to success in professional basketball is fundamentals. He says at least 20 times that a pass is only a successful pass *if someone catches it.* The key to successful rebounding is *getting the ball.* Auerbach's roadmap to eight consecutive NBA championships relied on fundamentals.

In software, one path to success is paying attention to fundamentals. You might be the Bob Cousy, Kareem Abdul Jabbar, or Michael Jordan of your software organization. You might have a battery of schedule-oriented practices at your disposal. But if you don't put fundamental development practices at the heart of your development effort, you will seriously risk failing to meet your schedule goals.

People often tell you to use good software engineering practices because they're "right" or because they'll promote high quality. Their admonitions take on religious tones. But I don't think this is a religious issue. If the practices work—use them. If they don't—don't! My contention is that you should use the fundamental software-engineering practices described in this chapter not because they're "right," but because they reduce cost and time to market.

This position is less theoretical than you might think. In a review of 10 software projects that organizations had selected as their "best projects," Bill Hetzel concluded that "If there was one high-level finding that stood out, it is that best projects get to be best based on fundamentals. All of us know the fundamentals for good software—the difference is that most projects don't do them nearly so well and then get into trouble" (Hetzel 1993).

The best place to start looking for information on software-development fundamentals is a general software-engineering textbook. This book is not a software-engineering textbook, so this chapter confines itself to identifying the development fundamentals, explaining how they affect development schedules, quantifying how large their effect is (whenever possible), and providing pointers to more information.

The practices in this chapter are divided into management, technical, and quality-assurance practices. Some of the practices don't fit neatly into one category, so you may want to browse all the categories even if you're most interested in a particular one. But first, you might want to read Case Study 4-1 to put you in an appropriate frame of mind.

Case Study 4-1. Lack of Fundamentals

"We thought we had figured out what we were doing," Bill told Charles. "We did pretty well on version 3 of our Sales Bonus Program, SBP, which is the program we use to pay our field agents their commissions. But on version 4, everything fell apart." Bill had been the manager of SBP versions 1 through 4, and Charles was a consultant Giga-Safe had called in to help figure out why version 4 had been so problematic.

"What were the differences between versions 3 and 4?" Charles asked.

"We had problems with versions 1 and 2," Bill responded, "but by version 3 we felt that we had put our problems behind us. Development proceeded with hardly any problems at all. Our estimates were accurate, partly because we've learned to pad them with a 30-percent safety margin. The developers had almost no problems with forgotten tasks, tools, or design elements. Everything went great."

"So what happened on version 4?" Charles prompted.

"That was a different story. Version 3 was an evolutionary upgrade, but version 4 was a completely new product developed from scratch.

"The team members tried to apply the lessons they'd learned on SBP versions 1 through 3. But partway through the project, the schedule began to slip. Technical tasks turned out to be more complicated than anticipated. Tasks that the developers had estimated would take 2 days instead took 2 to 3 weeks. There were problems with some new development tools, and the team lost

(continued)

ground fighting with them. The new team members didn't know all the team's rules, and they lost work and time because new team members kept overwriting each other's working files. In the end no one could predict when the product would be ready until the day it actually was ready. Version 4 was almost 100 percent late."

"That does sound pretty bad," Charles agreed. "You mentioned that you had had some problems with versions 1 and 2. Can you tell me about those projects?"

"Sure," Bill replied. "On version 1 of SBP, the project was complete chaos. Total-project estimates and task scheduling seemed almost random. Technical problems turned out to be harder than expected. Development tools that were supposed to save time actually added time to the schedule. The development team took one schedule slip after another, and no one knew when the product would be ready to release until a day or two before it actually was ready. In the end, the SBP team delivered the product about 100 percent over schedule."

"That sounds a lot like what happened on version 4," Charles said.

"That's right," Bill shook his head. "I thought we had learned our lesson a long time ago."

"What about version 2?" Charles asked.

"On version 2, development proceeded more smoothly than on version 1. The project estimates and task schedules seemed more realistic, and the technical work seemed to be more under control. There were fewer problems with development tools, and the development team's work took about as long as they had estimated. They made up the estimation errors they did have through increased overtime.

"But toward the end of the project, the team discovered several tasks that they hadn't included in their original estimates. They also discovered fundamental design flaws, which meant they had to rework 10 to 15 percent of the system. They took one big schedule slip to include the forgotten tasks and the rework. They finished that work, found a few more problems, took another schedule slip, and finally delivered the product about 30 percent late. That's when we learned to add a 30-percent safety margin to our schedules."

"And then version 3 went smoothly?" Charles asked.

"Right," Bill agreed.

"I take it that versions 1 through 3 used the same code base?" Charles asked.

"Yes."

"Did versions 1 through 3 use the same team members?"

(continued)

Case Study 4-1. Lack of Fundamentals, *continued*

"Yes, but several developers quit after version 3, so most of the version 4 team hadn't worked on the project before."

"Thanks," Charles said. "That's all helpful."

Charles spent the rest of the day talking with the development team and then met with Bill again that night. "What I've got to tell you might not be easy for you to hear," Charles said. "As a consultant, I see dozens of projects a year, and throughout my career I've seen hundreds of projects in more than a hundred organizations. The pattern you experienced with SBP versions 1 through 4 is actually fairly common.

"Earlier, you implied that the developers weren't using automated source-code control, and I confirmed that this afternoon in my talks with your developers. I also confirmed that the development team doesn't use design or code reviews. The organization relies on seat-of-the-pants estimates even though more effective estimation methods are available."

"OK," Bill said. "Those things are all true. But what do we need to do so that we never experience another project like version 4 again?"

"That's the part that's going to be hard for you to hear," Charles said. "There isn't any one thing you need to do. You need to improve on the software development fundamentals or you'll see this same pattern again and again. You need to strengthen your foundation. On the management side, you need more effective scheduling, planning, tracking, and measurement. On the technical side, you need more effective requirements management, design, construction, and configuration management. And you need much stronger quality assurance."

"But we did fine on version 3," Bill objected.

"That's right," Charles agreed. "You will do fine once in awhile—when you're working on a familiar product with team members who have worked on the same product before. Most of the version 3 team had also worked on versions 1 and 2. One of the reasons that organizations think they don't need to master software-development fundamentals is that they do have a few successes. They can get pretty good at estimating and planning for a specific product. They think they're doing well, and they don't think that anyone else is doing any better.

"But their development capability is built on a fragile foundation. They really only know how to develop one specific product in one specific way. When they are confronted with major changes in personnel, development tools, development environment, or product concept, that fragile development capability breaks down. Suddenly they find themselves back at square 1. That's what happened on SBP 4 when you had to rewrite the product from scratch with new developers. That's why your experiences on version 1 and version 4 were so similar."

(continued)

Case Study 4-1. Lack of Fundamentals, *continued*

"I hadn't thought about it that way before, but maybe you're right," Bill said quietly. "That sounds like a lot of work, though. I don't know if we can justify it."

"If you don't master the fundamentals, you'll do OK on the easy projects, but your hard projects will fall apart," Charles said, "and those are usually the ones you really care about."

4.1 Management Fundamentals

FURTHER READING
This chapter's description of development fundamentals is similar to what the Software Engineering Institute calls a "repeatable" process. For details, see *The Capability Maturity Model: Guidelines for Improving the Software Process* (Carnegie Mellon University/Software Engineering Institute, 1995).

Management fundamentals have at least as large an influence on development schedules as technical fundamentals do. The Software Engineering Institute has repeatedly observed that organizations that attempt to put software-engineering discipline in place before putting project-management discipline in place are doomed to fail (Burlton 1992). Management often controls all three corners of the classic trade-off triangle—schedule, cost, and product—although sometimes the marketing department controls the product specification and sometimes the development department controls the schedule. (Actually, development always controls the real schedule; sometimes development also controls the planned schedule.)

Management fundamentals consist of determining the size of the product (which includes functionality, complexity, and other product characteristics), allocating resources appropriate for a product of that size, creating a plan for applying the resources, and then monitoring and directing the resources to keep the project from heading into the weeds. In many cases, upper management delegates these management tasks to technical leads explicitly, and in other cases it simply leaves a vacuum that a motivated lead or developer can fill.

Estimation and Scheduling

CROSS-REFERENCE
For more on estimation, see Chapter 8, "Estimation." For more on scheduling, see Chapter 9, "Scheduling."

Well-run projects go through three basic steps to create a software schedule. They first estimate the size of the project, then they estimate the effort needed to build a product of that size, and then they estimate a schedule based on the effort estimate.

Estimation and scheduling are development fundamentals because creating an inaccurate estimate reduces development efficiency. Accurate estimation is essential input for effective planning, which is essential for efficient development.

Planning

As Philip W. Metzger points out in his classic *Managing a Programming Project*, poor planning boils to the surface as a source of problems more often than any other problem (Metzger 1981). His list of software-development problems looks like this:

CLASSIC MISTAKE

- Poor planning
- Ill-defined contract
- Poor planning
- Unstable problem definition
- Poor planning
- Inexperienced management
- Poor planning
- Political pressures
- Poor planning
- Ineffective change control
- Poor planning
- Unrealistic deadlines
- Poor planning

In his review of best projects, Bill Hetzel found that the industry's best projects are characterized by strong up-front planning to define tasks and schedules (Hetzel 1993). Planning a software project includes these activities:

CROSS-REFERENCE
For more on these topics, see Chapter 12, "Teamwork"; Chapter 13, "Team Structure"; Chapter 7, "Lifecycle Planning"; Chapter 5, "Risk Management"; and Chapter 14, "Feature-Set Control."

- Estimation and scheduling
- Determining how many people to have on the project team, what technical skills are needed, when to add people, and who the people will be
- Deciding how to organize the team
- Choosing which lifecycle model to use
- Managing risks
- Making strategic decisions such as how to control the product's feature set and whether to buy or build pieces of the product

Tracking

CROSS-REFERENCE
For details on one project-tracking practice, see Chapter 27, "Miniature Milestones."

Once you've planned a project, you track it to check that it's following the plan—that it's meeting its schedule, cost, and quality targets. Typical management-level tracking controls include task lists, status meetings, status reports, milestone reviews, budget reports, and management by walking around. Typical technical-level tracking controls include technical audits, technical reviews, and quality gates that control whether you consider milestones to be complete.

Bill Hetzel found that strong measurement and tracking of project status was evident in every "best project." Status measurement to support project management appears as a natural by-product of the good planning work and is a critical success factor (Hetzel 1993).

As Figure 4-1 suggests, on a typical project, project management is almost a black-box function. You rarely know what's going on during the project, and you just have to take whatever comes out at the end. On an ideal project, you have 100 percent visibility at all times. On an efficient project, you always have at least some visibility and you have good visibility more often than not.

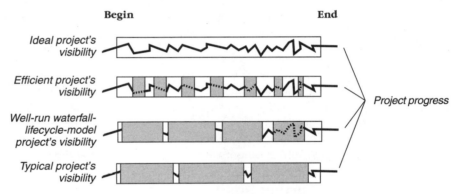

Figure 4-1. *Progress visibility for different kinds of projects. Efficient development provides much better visibility than typical development.*

HARD DATA

Capers Jones reports that "software progress monitoring is so poor that several well-known software disasters were not anticipated until the very day of expected deployment" (Jones 1995b). After assessing 59 sites between 1987 and 1993, the Software Engineering Institute found that 75 percent of the sites needed to improve their project tracking and oversight (Kitson and Masters 1993). When organizations have been assessed, tried to improve, and then been reassessed, the biggest problems for the organizations that failed to improve lay in the project planning and tracking-and-oversight areas (Baumert 1995).

Tracking is a fundamental software management activity. If you don't track a project, you can't manage it. You have no way of knowing whether your plans are being carried out and no way of knowing what you should do next. You have no way of monitoring risks to your project. Effective tracking enables you to detect schedule problems early, while there's still time to do something about them. If you don't track a project, you can't do rapid development.

Measurement

CROSS-REFERENCE
For more on measurement, see Chapter 26, "Measurement."

One key to long-term progress in a software organization is collecting metrics data to analyze software quality and productivity. Virtually all projects collect data on costs and schedules. But this limited data doesn't provide much insight into how to reduce the costs or shorten the schedules.

Collecting a little more data can go a long way. If, in addition to cost and schedule data, you collect historical data on how large your programs are in lines of code or some other measurement, you will have a basis for planning future projects that's better than gut instinct. When your boss says, "Can we develop this product in 9 months?" You can say, "Our organization has never developed a product of this size in less than 11 months, and the average time for such a product is 13 months."

You need to have a basic knowledge of software measurement to develop efficiently. You need to understand the issues involved in collecting metrics, including how much or how little data to collect and how to collect it. You should have a knowledge of specific metrics you can use to analyze status, quality, and productivity. An organization that wants to develop rapidly needs to collect basic metrics in order to know what its development speed is and whether it's improving or degrading over time.

Further Reading on Management Fundamentals

The first four volumes listed below discuss far-ranging software topics, including pragmatic issues such as what to do with a problem team member, theoretical issues such as how to model a software project as a system, and esoteric issues such as the importance of observation to software development. Weinberg's writing is entertaining and full of insights.

Weinberg, Gerald M. *Quality Software Management, Vol. 1: Systems Thinking.* New York: Dorset House, 1992.

Weinberg, Gerald M. *Quality Software Management, Vol. 2: First-Order Measurement.* New York: Dorset House, 1993.

Weinberg, Gerald M. *Quality Software Management, Vol. 3: Congruent Action.* New York: Dorset House, 1994.

Weinberg, Gerald M. *Quality Software Management, Vol. 4: Anticipating Change,* New York: Dorset House, 1996.

Pressman, Roger S. *A Manager's Guide to Software Engineering*. New York: McGraw-Hill, 1993. This might be the best overview available on general aspects of software project management. It includes introductory sections on estimation, risk analysis, scheduling and tracking, and the human element. Its only drawback is its use of a question-and-answer format that might come across as disjointed to some readers. (It does to me.)

Carnegie Mellon University/Software Engineering Institute. *The Capability Maturity Model: Guidelines for Improving the Software Process*. Reading, Mass.: Addison-Wesley, 1995. This book describes a management-level framework for understanding, managing, and improving software development.

Thayer, Richard H., ed. *Tutorial: Software Engineering Project Management*. Los Alamitos, Calif.: IEEE Computer Society Press, 1990. This is a collection of about 45 papers on the topic of managing software projects. The papers are some of the best discussions available on the topics of planning, organizing, staffing, directing, and controlling a software project. Thayer provides an introduction to the topics and comments briefly on each paper.

Gilb, Tom. *Principles of Software Engineering Management*. Wokingham, England: Addison-Wesley, 1988. Gilb's thesis is that project managers generally do not want to predict what will happen on their projects; they want to control it. Gilb's focus is on development practices that contribute to controlling software schedules, and several of the practices he describes in his book have been included as best practices in this book.

DeMarco, Tom. *Controlling Software Projects*. New York: Yourdon Press, 1982. Although now in its second decade, DeMarco's book doesn't seem the least bit dated. He deals with problems that are the same today as they were in 1982—managers who want it all and customers who want it all *now*. He lays out project-management strategies, with a heavy emphasis on measurement.

Metzger, Philip W. *Managing a Programming Project, 2d Ed*. Englewood Cliffs, N.J.: Prentice Hall, 1981. This little book is the classic introductory project-management textbook. It's fairly dated now because of its emphasis on the waterfall lifecycle model and on document-driven development practices. But anyone who's willing to read it critically will find that Metzger still has some important things to say about today's projects and says them well.

The following book is not specifically about software projects, but it is applicable nonetheless.

Grove, Andrew S. *High Output Management*. New York: Random House, 1983. Andy Grove is one of the founders of Intel Corporation and has strong opinions about how to manage a company in a competitive technical industry. Grove takes a strongly quantitative approach to management.

4.2   Technical Fundamentals

A 1984 study of "modern programming practices"—technical fundamentals—found that you can't achieve high productivity without using them. Figure 4-2 illustrates the study's results.

CROSS-REFERENCE
For general comments on this kind of graph, see Section 3.2, "Effect of Mistakes on a Development Schedule."

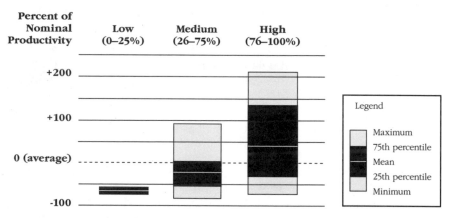

Figure 4-2. *Findings for "Use of Modern Programming Practices" factor (Vosburgh et al. 1984). You can't achieve top productivity without making extensive use of "modern programming practices"—what this chapter calls "technical fundamentals."*

This is the same kind of chart that I presented in the "Classic Mistakes" chapter, and it describes the same lesson. Application of technical fundamentals, by itself, is not enough to create high productivity. Some projects used modern programming practices a great deal and still had productivity about as low as other projects that didn't use them at all. Thus attention to development fundamentals is necessary but not sufficient for achieving rapid development.

Larry Constantine tells a story about the Australian Computer Society Software Challenge (Constantine 1995b). The challenge called for three-person teams to develop and deliver a 200 function-point application in 6 hours.

The team from Ernst and Young decided to follow a formal development methodology—a scaled-down version of their regular methodology—complete with staged activities and intermediate deliverables. Their approach included careful analysis and design—part of what this chapter describes as technical fundamentals. Many of their competitors dived straight into coding, and for the first few hours, the team from Ernst and Young lagged behind.

By midday, however, the Ernst and Young team had developed a commanding lead. At the end of the day, the team from Ernst and Young lost, but not because of their formal methodology. They lost because they accidentally overwrote some of their working files, delivering less functionality at the end of the day than they had demonstrated at lunchtime. Ironically, what would have saved their bacon was not less formality, but more—namely, formal configuration management including periodic backups. They got bitten by the classic mistake of not using effective source-code control.

The moral of this story seems clear enough, but some skeptics, including me, were left wondering: Would the team from Ernst and Young really have won without the configuration-management snafu? The answer is "yes." They reappeared a few months later at another rapid-development face-off—this time with version control and backup—and they won (Constantine 1996).

In this case, formal methodologies paid off within a single day. If attention to technical fundamentals can make this much difference in that amount of time, imagine how much of a difference they can make over a 6- to 12-month project.

Requirements Management

CROSS-REFERENCE
For more on traditional requirements-management practices, see Chapter 14, "Feature-Set Control."

Requirements management is the process of gathering requirements; recording them in a document, email, user-interface storyboard, executable prototype, or some other form; tracking the design and code against them; and then managing changes to them for the rest of the project.

HARD DATA

It's not uncommon for developers to complain about the problems associated with traditional requirements-management practices, the most common being that they are too rigid. Some practices can be overly rigid, but the alternative is often worse. A survey of more than 8000 projects found that the top three reasons that projects were delivered late, over budget, and with less functionality than desired all had to do with requirements-management practices: lack of user input, incomplete requirements, and changing requirements (Standish Group 1994). A survey of projects by the Software Engineering

Institute reached essentially the same conclusion: more than half the projects surveyed suffered from inadequate requirements management (Kitson and Masters 1993).

CROSS-REFERENCE
For more on controlling feature creep, see Section 14.2, "Mid-Project: Feature-Creep Control."

Success at requirements management depends on knowing enough different practices to be able to choose the ones that are appropriate for a specific project. Here are the fundamentals of requirements management:

- Requirements-analysis methodologies including structured analysis, data structured analysis, and object-oriented analysis
- System-modeling practices such as class diagrams, dataflow diagrams, entity-relationship diagrams, data-dictionary notation, and state-transition diagrams
- Communication practices such as Joint Application Development (JAD), user-interface prototyping, and general interview practices
- The relationships between requirements management and the different lifecycle models including evolutionary prototyping, staged releases, spiral, waterfall, and code-and-fix

CROSS-REFERENCE
For more on speeding up requirements gathering, see "Requirements specification" in Section 6.5.

Requirements management provides great development-speed leverage in two ways. First, requirements gathering tends to be done at a leisurely pace compared with other software-development activities. If you can pick up the pace without hurting quality, you can shorten overall development time.

HARD DATA

Second, getting a requirement right in the first place typically costs 50 to 200 times less than waiting until construction or maintenance to get it right (Boehm and Papaccio 1988). The typical project experiences a 25-percent change in requirements. Some fundamental requirements-management practices allow you to reduce the number of requirements changes. Other fundamental development practices allow you to reduce the cost of each requirements change. Imagine what the combined effect would be if you could reduce the number of changes from 25 percent to 10 percent and simultaneously reduce the cost of each change by a factor of 5 or 10. Rapid development would be within your grasp.

Design

HARD DATA

Just as it makes sense to create a set of blueprints before you begin building a house, it makes sense to create an architecture and design before you begin building a software system. A design error left undetected until system testing typically takes 10 times as long to fix as it would if it were detected at design time (Dunn 1984).

CLASSIC MISTAKE

Doesn't everyone already do good design? No. My impression is that good design receives more lip service than any other activity in software development and that few developers really do design at all. A design architect who works for Microsoft said that in 6 years of interviewing more than 200 candidates for software-development positions, he had interviewed only 5 who could accurately describe the concepts of "modularity" and "information hiding" (Kohen 1995).

The ideas of modularity and information hiding are design fundamentals. They are part of the foundation of both structured design and object design. A developer who can't discuss modularity and information hiding is like a basketball player who can't dribble. When you consider that Microsoft screens its candidates rigorously before they are even interviewed, you come to the somewhat frightening conclusion that the situation throughout most of the software-development world is considerably worse than 195 out of 200 developers who have major gaps in their knowledge of design fundamentals.

Here are the fundamental topics in architecture and design:

- Major design styles (such as object design, structured design, and data-structure design)
- Foundational design concepts (such as information hiding, modularity, abstraction, encapsulation, cohesion, coupling, hierarchy, inheritance, polymorphism, basic algorithms, and basic data structures)
- Standard design approaches to typically challenging areas (including exception handling, internationalization and localization, portability, string storage, input/output, memory management, data storage, floating-point arithmetic, database design, performance, and reuse)
- Design considerations unique to the application domain you're working in (financial applications, scientific applications, embedded systems, real-time systems, safety-critical software, or something else)
- Architectural schemes (such as subsystem organization, layering, subsystem communication styles, and typical system architectures)
- Use of design tools

CROSS-REFERENCE
For details on a kind of design well suited to rapid-development projects, see Chapter 19, "Designing for Change."

It is possible to develop a system without designing it first. Major systems have been implemented through sheer coding and debugging prowess, high enthusiasm, and massive overtime—and without systematic design. However, design serves as the foundation for construction, project scheduling, project tracking, and project control, and as such effective design is essential to achieving maximum development speed.

Construction

By the time you get to construction, most of the groundwork for your project's success or failure has already been laid. Both requirements management and design offer greater leverage on your development schedule than construction does. In those activities, small changes can make a big difference in your schedule.

Construction might not offer many opportunities for large reductions in schedule, but construction work is so detailed and labor intensive that it's important to do a good job of it. If your code quality isn't good to start with, it's nearly impossible to go back and make it better. It certainly isn't time-effective to do it twice.

Although construction is a low-level activity, it does present many occasions to use time inefficiently or to become sidetracked on noncritical but time-consuming tasks. You can, for example, waste time gold-plating functions that do not need to be gold-plated, debugging needlessly sloppy code, or performance-tuning small sections of the system before you know whether they need to be tuned.

Poor design practices can force you to rewrite major parts of your system; poor construction practices won't force you to do that. Poor construction practices can, however, introduce subtle errors that take days or weeks to find and fix. It can sometimes take as long to find an off-by-one array declaration error as it can to redesign and reimplement a poorly designed module. The total work you have to show for your debugging is a "+1" rather than several pages of new code, but the schedule penalty is just as real.

Construction fundamentals include the following topics:

- Coding practices (including variable and function naming, layout, and documentation)
- Data-related concepts (including scope, persistence, and binding time)
- Guidelines for using specific types of data (including numbers in general, integers, floating-point numbers, characters, strings, Booleans, enumerated types, named constants, arrays, and pointers)
- Control-related concepts (including organizing straight-line code, using conditionals, controlling loops, using Boolean expressions, controlling complexity, and using unusual control structures such as *goto*, *return*, and recursive procedures)
- Assertions and other code-centered error-detection practices
- Rules for packaging code into routines, modules, classes, and files
- Unit-testing and debugging practices

- Integration strategies (such as incremental integration, big-bang integration, and evolutionary development)
- Code-tuning strategies and practices
- The ins and outs of the particular programming language you're using
- Use of construction tools (including programming environments, groupwork support such as email and source-code control, code libraries, and code generators)

Adherence to some of these fundamentals takes time, but it saves time over the life of a project. Toward the end of a project, a product manager told a friend of mine, "You're slower than some of the other programmers on the team, but you're more careful. There's a place for that on this team because we have a lot of modules that have too many bugs and will need to be re-written." That statement reveals a person who doesn't yet understand what makes software projects take as long as they do.

When all is said and done, paying attention to construction fundamentals is as much a risk-management practice as a time-savings practice. Good construction practices prevent the creation of a rat's nest of indecipherable code that causes your project to grind to a halt when a key person gets sick, when a critical bug is discovered, or when a simple change needs to be made. Such practices improve the predictability and control you have over your project and increase the chance of delivering on time.

Software Configuration Management

Software configuration management (SCM) is the practice of managing project artifacts so that the project stays in a consistent state over time. SCM includes practices for evaluating proposed changes, tracking changes, handling multiple versions, and keeping copies of project artifacts as they existed at various times. The project artifact managed the most often is source code, but you can apply SCM to requirements, plans, designs, test cases, problem reports, user documentation, data, and any other work you use to build your product. I even used SCM in writing this book because not using it on my last book caused too many problems.

Most software-development books treat SCM as a quality-assurance practice—and it does have a strong effect on quality. But treating it as a QA practice could imply that it has either a neutral or negative effect on the development schedule. SCM is sometimes implemented in a way that hurts project efficiency, but it is critical if you want to achieve maximum development speed. Without configuration management, your teammates can change part of the design and forget to tell you. You can then implement code that's incompatible with the design changes, which eventually will require either you or your teammates to redo your work.

CLASSIC MISTAKE

Lack of automated source-code control is a common and irksome inefficiency. Of sites surveyed between 1987 and 1993, the Software Engineering Institute found that more than 50 percent needed to improve their software configuration management (Kitson and Masters 1993). On small projects, lack of configuration management adds a few percentage points to the overall project cost. On large projects, configuration management is a critical-path item (Jones 1994).

Further Reading on Development Fundamentals

Many training organizations offer workshops on requirements analysis and design. Workshops on construction and configuration management may be more difficult to find. The most readily available source of information on any of the topics will probably be books, so I've listed the best books on each topic here.

Requirements management

Yourdon, Edward. *Modern Structured Analysis*, New York: Yourdon Press, 1989. Yourdon's book contains a survey of requirements specification and analysis circa 1989 including modeling tools, the requirements-gathering process, and related issues. Note that one of the most useful sections is hidden in an appendix: "Interviewing and Data Gathering Techniques."

Hatley, Derek J., and Imtiaz A. Pirbhai. *Strategies for Real-Time System Specification*. New York: Dorset House Publishing, 1988. Hatley and Pirbhai emphasize real-time systems and extend the graphical notation used by Yourdon to real-time environments.

Gause, Donald C., and Gerald Weinberg. *Exploring Requirements: Quality Before Design*. New York: Dorset House, 1989. Gause and Weinberg chart an untraditional course through the requirements-management terrain. They discuss ambiguity, meetings, conflict resolution, constraints, expectations, reasons that methodologies aren't enough, and quite a few other topics. They mostly avoid the topics that other requirements books include and include the topics that the other books leave out.

Design

Plauger, P. J. *Programming on Purpose: Essays on Software Design*. Englewood Cliffs, N.J.: PTR Prentice Hall, 1993. This is a refreshing collection of essays that were originally published in *Computer Language* magazine. Plauger is a master designer and takes up a variety of topics having as much to do with being a designer as with design in the abstract. What makes the essays refreshing is that Plauger ranges freely over the entire landscape of design topics rather than restricting himself to a discussion of any one design style. The result is uniquely insightful and thought provoking.

McConnell, Steve. *Code Complete.* Redmond, Wash.: Microsoft Press, 1993. This book contains several sections about design, particularly design as it relates to construction. Like the Plauger book, it describes several design styles.

Yourdon, Edward, and Larry L. Constantine. *Structured Design: Fundamentals of a Discipline of Computer Program and Systems Design,* Englewood Cliffs, N.J.: Yourdon Press, 1979. This is the classic text on structured design by one of the co-authors (Constantine) of the original paper on structured design. The book is written with obvious care. It contains full discussions of coupling, cohesion, graphical notations, and other relevant concepts. Some people have characterized the book as "technically difficult," but it's hard to beat learning about a practice from its original inventor.

Page-Jones, Meilir. *The Practical Guide to Structured Systems Design, 2d Ed.* Englewood Cliffs, N.J.: Yourdon Press, 1988. This is a popular textbook presentation of the same basic structured-design content as Yourdon and Constantine's book and is written with considerable enthusiasm. Some people have found Page-Jones's book to be more accessible than Yourdon and Constantine's.

Booch, Grady. *Object Oriented Analysis and Design: With Applications, 2d Ed.* Redwood City, Calif.: Benjamin/Cummings, 1994. Booch's book discusses the theoretical and practical foundations of object-oriented design for about 300 pages and then has 175 more pages of object-oriented application development in C++. No one has been a more active advocate of object-oriented design than Grady Booch, and this is the definitive volume on the topic.

Coad, Peter, and Edward Yourdon. *Object-Oriented Design.* Englewood Cliffs, N.J.: Yourdon Press, 1991. This is a slimmer alternative to Booch's book, and some readers might find it to be an easier introduction to object-oriented design.

Construction

McConnell, Steve. *Code Complete.* Redmond, Wash.: Microsoft Press, 1993. This is the only book I know of that contains thorough discussions of all the key construction issues identified in the "Construction" section. It contains useful checklists on many aspects of construction as well as hard data on the most effective construction practices. The book contains several hundred coding examples in C, Pascal, Basic, Fortran, and Ada.

Marcotty, Michael. *Software Implementation*. New York: Prentice Hall, 1991. Marcotty discusses the general issues involved in constructing software by focusing on abstraction, complexity, readability, and correctness. The first part of the book discusses the history of programming, programming subculture, programming teams, and how typical programmers spend their time. The book is written with wit and style, and the first 100 pages on the "business of programming" are especially well done.

The two Bentley books below discuss programming energetically, and they clearly articulate the reasons that some of us find programming so interesting. The fact that the information isn't comprehensive or rigidly organized doesn't prevent the books from conveying powerful insights that you'll read in a few minutes and use for years.

Bentley, Jon. *Programming Pearls*. Reading, Mass.: Addison-Wesley, 1986.

Bentley, Jon. *More Programming Pearls: Confessions of a Coder*. Reading, Mass.: Addison-Wesley, 1988.

Maguire, Steve. *Writing Solid Code*. Redmond, Wash.: Microsoft Press, 1993. This book describes key software-construction practices used at Microsoft. It explains how to minimize defects by using compiler warnings, protecting your code with assertion statements, fortifying subsystems with integrity checks, designing unambiguous function interfaces, checking code in a debugger, and avoiding risky programming practices.

Software configuration management (SCM)

These Bersoff and Babich books thoroughly cover the SCM topic.

Bersoff, Edward H. et al. *Software Configuration Management*. Englewood Cliffs, N.J.: Prentice Hall, 1980.

Babich, W. *Software Configuration Management*. Reading, Mass.: Addison-Wesley, 1986.

Bersoff, Edward H., and Alan M. Davis. "Impacts of Life Cycle Models on Software Configuration Management," *Communications of the ACM* 34, no. 8 (August 1991): 104–118. This article describes how SCM is affected by newer approaches to software development, especially by prototyping approaches.

4.3   Quality-Assurance Fundamentals

Like management and technical fundamentals, quality-assurance fundamentals provide critical support for maximum development speed. When a software product has too many defects, developers spend more time fixing the software than they spend writing it. Most organizations have found that they are better off not installing the defects in the first place. The key to not installing defects is to pay attention to quality-assurance fundamentals from Day 1 on.

CLASSIC MISTAKE

Some projects try to save time by reducing the time spent on quality-assurance practices such as design and code reviews. Other projects—running late—try to make up for lost time by compressing the testing schedule, which is vulnerable to reduction because it's usually the critical-path item at the end of the project. These are some of the worst decisions a person who wants to maximize development speed can make because higher quality (in the form of lower defect rates) and reduced development time go hand in hand. Figure 4-3 illustrates the relationship between defect rate and development time.

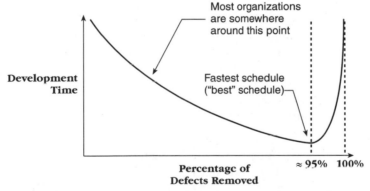

Source: Derived from data in *Applied Software Measurement* (Jones 1991).

Figure 4-3.   *Relationship between defect rate and development time. In most cases, the projects that achieve the lowest defect rates also achieve the shortest schedules.*

A few organizations have achieved extremely low defect rates (shown on the far right of the curve in Figure 4-3), at which point, further reducing the number of defects will increase the amount of development time. It's worth the extra time when it's applied to life-critical systems such as the life-support systems on the Space Shuttle—but not when it applies to non-life-critical software development.

IBM was the first company to discover that software quality and software schedules were related. They found that the products with the lowest defect counts were also the products with the shortest schedules (Jones 1991).

HARD DATA

Many organizations currently develop software with a level of defects that gives them longer schedules than necessary. After surveying about 4000 software projects, Capers Jones reports that poor quality is one of the most common reasons for schedule overruns (Jones 1994). He also reports that poor quality is implicated in close to half of all canceled projects. A Software Engineering Institute survey found that more than 60 percent of organizations assessed suffered from inadequate quality assurance (Kitson and Masters 1993). On the curve in Figure 4-3, those organizations are to the left of the 95-percent-removal line.

HARD DATA

Some point in the neighborhood of the 95 percent is significant because that level of prerelease defect removal appears to be the point at which projects generally achieve the shortest schedules, least effort, and highest level of user satisfaction (Jones 1991). If you're finding more than 5 percent of your defects after your product has been released, you're vulnerable to the problems associated with low quality, and you're probably taking longer to develop your software than you need to.

CLASSIC MISTAKE

Projects that are in a hurry are particularly vulnerable to shortchanging quality assurance at the individual-developer level. When you're in a hurry, you cut corners because "we're only 30 days from shipping." Rather than writing a separate, completely clean printing module, you piggyback printing onto the screen-display module. You might know that that's a bad design, that it isn't extendible or maintainable, but you don't have time to do it right. You're being pressured to get the product done, so you feel compelled to take the shortcut.

Three months later, the product still hasn't shipped, and those cut corners come back to haunt you. You find that users are unhappy with printing, and the only way to satisfy their requests is to significantly extend the printing functionality. Unfortunately, in the 3 months since you piggybacked printing onto the screen display module, the printing functionality and the screen display functionality have become thoroughly intertwined. Redesigning printing and separating it from the screen display is now a tough, time-consuming, error-prone operation.

The upshot is that a project that was supposed to place a strong emphasis on achieving the shortest possible schedule instead wasted time in the following ways:

- The original time spent designing and implementing the printing hack was completely wasted because most of that code will be thrown away. The time spent unit-testing and debugging the printing-hack code was wasted too.

- Additional time must be spent to strip the printing-specific code out of the display module.

- Additional testing and debugging time must be spent to ensure that the modified display code still works after the printing code has been stripped out.

- The new printing module, which should have been designed as an integral part of the system, has to be designed onto and around the existing system, which was not designed with it in mind.

All this happens, when the only necessary cost—if the right decision had been made at the right time—was to design and implement one version of the printing module.

HARD DATA

This example is not uncommon. Up to four times the normal number of defects are reported for released products that were developed under excessive schedule pressure (Jones 1994). Projects that are in schedule trouble often become obsessed with working harder rather than working smarter. Attention to quality is seen as a luxury. The result is that projects often work dumber, which gets them into even deeper schedule trouble.

A decision early in a project not to focus on defect detection amounts to a decision to postpone defect detection until later in the project, when it will be much more expensive and time-consuming. That's not a rational decision when time is at a premium.

HARD DATA

If you can prevent defects or detect and remove them early, you can realize a significant schedule benefit. Studies have found that reworking defective requirements, design, and code typically consumes 40 to 50 percent of the total cost of software development (Jones 1986b; Boehm 1987a). As a rule of thumb, every hour you spend on defect prevention will reduce your repair time 3 to 10 hours (Jones 1994). In the worst case, reworking a software-requirements problem once the software is in operation typically costs 50 to 200 times what it would take to rework the problem in the requirements stage (Boehm and Papaccio 1988). Given that about 60 percent of all defects usually exist at design time (Gilb 1988), you can save enormous amounts of time by detecting defects earlier than system testing.

How Much Does It Cost Not to Find a Defect?

I refer to several cost ratios in this book, and since some of the numbers are similar, the differences can seem confusing. Here is a summary:

- Each hour spent on quality-assurance activities such as design reviews saves from 3 to 10 hours in downstream costs.

- A requirements defect that is left undetected until construction or maintenance will cost 50 to 200 times as much to fix as it would have cost to fix at requirements time.

- More generally, a defect that isn't detected upstream (during requirements or design) will cost from 10 to 100 times as much to fix downstream (during testing) as it would have cost to fix at its origin. The further from its origin that a defect is detected, the more it will cost to fix.

Error-Prone Modules

HARD DATA

One aspect of quality assurance that's particularly important to rapid development is the existence of error-prone modules. An error-prone module is a module that's responsible for a disproportionate number of defects. On its IMS project, for example, IBM found that 57 percent of the errors were clumped in 7 percent of the modules (Jones 1991). Barry Boehm reports that about 20 percent of the modules in a program are typically responsible for about 80 percent of the errors (Boehm 1987b).

HARD DATA

Modules with such high defect rates are more expensive and time-consuming to deliver than less error-prone modules. Normal modules cost about $500 to $1,000 per function point to develop. Error-prone modules cost about $2,000 to $4,000 per function point (Jones 1994). Error-prone modules tend to be more complex than other modules in the system, less structured, and unusually large. They often were developed under excessive schedule pressure and were not fully tested.

If development speed is important, make identification and redesign of error-prone modules a priority. If a module's error rate hits about 10 defects per 1000 lines of code, review it to determine whether it should be redesigned or reimplemented. If it's poorly structured, excessively complex, or excessively long, redesign the module and reimplement it from the ground up. You'll save time and improve the quality of your product.

Testing

The most common quality-assurance practice is undoubtedly execution testing, finding errors by executing a program and seeing what it does. The two basic kinds of execution testing are unit tests, in which the developer checks his or her own code to verify that it works correctly, and system tests, in which an independent tester checks to see whether the system operates as expected.

HARD DATA

Testing's effectiveness varies enormously. Unit testing can find anywhere from 10 to 50 percent of the defects in a program. System testing can find from 20 to 60 percent of a program's defects. Together, their cumulative defect-detection rate is often less than 60 percent (Jones 1986a). The remaining errors are found either by other error-detecting techniques such as reviews or by end-users after the software has been put into production.

Testing is the black sheep of QA practices as far as development speed is concerned. It can certainly be done so clumsily that it slows down the development schedule, but most often its effect on the schedule is only indirect. Testing discovers that the product's quality is too low for it to be released, and the product has to be delayed until it can be improved. Testing thus becomes the messenger that delivers bad news that affects the schedule.

The best way to leverage testing from a rapid-development viewpoint is to plan ahead for bad news—set up testing so that if there's bad news to deliver, testing can deliver it as early as possible.

Technical Reviews

Technical reviews include all kinds of reviews that are used to detect defects in requirements, design, code, test cases, or other project artifacts. Reviews vary in level of formality and in effectiveness, and they play a more critical role in development speed than testing does. The following sections summarize the most common kinds of reviews.

Walkthroughs

HARD DATA

The most common kind of review is probably the informal walkthrough. The term "walkthrough" is loosely defined and refers to any meeting at which two or more developers review technical work with the purpose of improving its quality. Walkthroughs are useful to rapid development because you can use them to detect defects well before testing. The earliest time that testing can detect a requirements defect, for example, is after the requirement has been specified, designed, and coded. A walkthrough can detect a requirements defect at specification time, before any design or code work is done. Walkthroughs can find between 30 and 70 percent of the errors in a program (Myers 1979, Boehm 1987b, Yourdon 1989b).

Code reading

HARD DATA

Code reading is a somewhat more formal review process than a walkthrough but nominally applies only to code. In code reading, the author of the code hands out source listings to two or more reviewers. The reviewers read the code and report any errors to the author of the code. A study at NASA's Software Engineering Laboratory found that code reading detected about twice as many defects per hour of effort as testing (Card 1987). That suggests that, on a rapid-development project, some combination of code reading and testing would be more schedule-effective than testing alone.

Inspections

CROSS-REFERENCE
For a summary of the
schedule benefits
of inspections, see
Chapter 23, "Inspections."

Inspections are a kind of formal technical review that has been shown to be extremely effective in detecting defects throughout a project. With inspections, developers receive special training in inspections and play specific roles during the inspection. The "moderator" hands out the work product to be inspected before the inspection meeting. The "reviewers" examine the work product before the meeting and use checklists to stimulate their review. During the inspection meeting, the "author" usually paraphrases the material being inspected, the reviewers identify errors, and the "scribe" records the errors. After the meeting, the moderator produces an inspection report that describes each defect and indicates what will be done about it. Throughout the inspection process you gather data on defects, hours spent correcting defects, and hours spent on inspections so that you can analyze the effectiveness of your software-development process and improve it.

HARD DATA

As with walkthroughs, you can use inspections to detect defects earlier than you can with testing. You can use them to detect errors in requirements, user-interface prototypes, design, code, and other project artifacts. Inspections find from 60 to 90 percent of the defects in a program, which is considerably better than walkthroughs or testing. Because they can be used early in the development cycle, inspections have been found to produce net schedule savings of from 10 to 30 percent (Gilb and Graham 1993). One study of large programs even found that each hour spent on inspections avoided an average of 33 hours of maintenance, and inspections were up to 20 times more efficient than testing (Russell 1991).

Comment on technical reviews

Technical reviews are a useful and important supplement to testing. Reviews tend to find different kinds of errors than testing does (Myers 1978; Basili, Selby, and Hutchens 1986). They find defects earlier, which is good for the schedule. Reviews are more cost effective on a per-defect-found basis because they detect both the symptom of the defect and the underlying cause of the defect at the same time. Testing detects only the symptom of the defect; the developer still has to find the cause by debugging. Reviews tend to find a higher percentage of defects. And reviews provide a forum for developers to share their knowledge of best practices with each other, which increases their rapid-development capabilities over time. Technical reviews are a critical component of any development effort that is trying to achieve the shortest possible schedule.

Figure 4-4. *Don't let this happen to you! The longer defects remain undetected, the longer they take to fix. Correct defects when they're young and easy to control.*

Further Reading on QA Fundamentals

Several of the books referenced elsewhere in this chapter contain sections on general aspects of software quality, reviews, inspections, and testing. Those books include *A Manager's Guide to Software Engineering* (Pressman 1993), *Software Engineering: A Practitioner's Approach* (Pressman 1992), *Software Engineering* (Sommerville 1996), and *Code Complete* (McConnell 1993). Here are additional sources of information on specific topics:

General software quality

Glass, Robert L. *Building Quality Software*. Englewood Cliffs, N.J.: Prentice Hall, 1992. This book examines quality considerations during all phases of software development including requirements, design, implementation, maintenance, and management. It describes and evaluates a wide variety of methods and has numerous capsule descriptions of other books and articles on software quality.

Chow, Tsun S., ed. *Tutorial: Software Quality Assurance: A Practical Approach*. Silver Spring, Md.: IEEE Computer Society Press, 1985. This book is a collection of about 45 papers clustered around the topic of software quality. Sections include software-quality definitions, measurements, and applications; managerial issues of planning, organization, standards, and conventions; technical issues of requirements, design, programming, testing, and validation; and implementation of a software-quality-assurance program. It contains many of the classic papers on this subject, and its breadth makes it especially valuable.

Testing

Myers, Glenford J. *The Art of Software Testing*. New York: John Wiley & Sons, 1979. This is the classic book on software testing and is still one of the best available. The contents are straightforward: the psychology and economics of program testing; test-case design; module testing; higher-order testing; debugging; test tools; and other techniques. The book is short (177 pages) and readable. The quiz at the beginning gets you started thinking like a tester and demonstrates just how many ways a piece of code can be broken.

Hetzel, Bill. *The Complete Guide to Software Testing, 2d Ed*. Wellesley, Mass.: QED Information Systems, 1988. A good alternative to Myers's book, Hetzel's is a more modern treatment of the same territory. In addition to what Myers covers, Hetzel discusses testing of requirements and designs, regression testing, purchased software, and management considerations. At 284 pages, it's also relatively short, and the author has a knack for lucidly presenting powerful technical concepts.

Reviews and inspections

Gilb, Tom, and Dorothy Graham. *Software Inspection*. Wokingham, England: Addison-Wesley, 1993. This book contains the most thorough discussion of inspections available. It has a practical focus and includes case studies that describe the experiences of several organizations who set up inspection programs.

Freedman, Daniel P., and Gerald M. Weinberg. *Handbook of Walkthroughs, Inspections and Technical Reviews, 3d Ed.* New York: Dorset House, 1990. This is an excellent sourcebook on reviews of all kinds, including walkthroughs and inspections. Weinberg is the original proponent of "egoless programming," the idea upon which most review practices are based. It's enormously practical and includes many useful checklists, reports about the success of reviews in various companies, and entertaining anecdotes. It's presented in a question-and-answer format.

The next two articles are written by the developer of inspections. They contain the meat of what you need to know to run an inspection, including the standard inspection forms.

Fagan, Michael E. "Design and Code Inspections to Reduce Errors in Program Development," *IBM Systems Journal*, vol. 15, no. 3, 1976, pp. 182–211.

Fagan, Michael E. "Advances in Software Inspections," *IEEE Transactions on Software Engineering*, July 1986, pp. 744–751.

4.4 Following the Instructions

When I was in seventh grade, my art teacher stressed that any student who followed his instructions would get at least a B—no artistic talent required. He was a 220-pound ex-Marine, and considering that he drove that advice home at least once a week, I was amazed at how many 98-pound seventh-graders didn't follow his instructions and didn't get at least a B. Judging from their work, it wasn't because they were tormented by glorious, conflicting artistic visions, either. They just felt like doing something different.

As an adult, I often see software projects that fail merely because the developers and managers who work on them don't follow the instructions—the software-development fundamentals described in this chapter. It's true that you can develop software without mastering the fundamentals—sometimes even rapidly. But judging from most people's results, if you don't master the fundamentals first, you'll lack the project control needed to develop rapidly. You often won't even know whether you're succeeding or failing until late in the project.

Suppose you're starting a painting project, and you read the following instructions on the paint can:

1. Prepare the surface: strip it down to the wood or metal; sand it smooth; remove residue with a solvent.
2. Prime the surface using an appropriate primer.

3. After the surface is completely dry (at least 6 hours), apply one thin coat. The air temperature must be between 55 and 80 degrees Fahrenheit. Let dry for 2 hours.

4. Apply a second thin coat and let dry for 24 hours before using.

What happens if you don't follow the instructions? If you're painting a doghouse on a hot Tuesday night after work, you might have only 2 hours to do the job, and Fido needs a place to sleep that night. You don't have time to follow the instructions. You might decide that you can skip steps 1 through 3, and apply a thick coat instead of a thin one in step 4. If the weather's right and Fido's house is made of wood and isn't too dirty, your approach will probably work fine.

Over the next few months, the paint might crack from being too thick or it might flake off from the metal surfaces of the nails where you didn't prime them, and you might have to repaint it again next year, but it really doesn't matter.

What if, instead of a doghouse, you're painting a Boeing 747? In that case, you had better follow the instructions to the letter. If you don't strip off the previous coat, you'll incur significant fuel-efficiency and safety penalties: a coat of paint on a 747 weighs 400 to 800 pounds. If you don't prepare the surface adequately, wind and rain attacking the paint at 600 miles per hour will take their toll much quicker than a gentle wind and rain will on Fido's doghouse.

What if you're painting something between a doghouse and a 747, say a house? In that case, the penalty for doing a bad job is less severe than for a 747, but a lot more severe than for a doghouse. You don't want to have to repaint a whole house every 2 years, and therefore you hold the results to a higher standard than you do with a doghouse.

Most of the software projects that have schedule problems are house-sized projects or larger, and those projects are the primary concern of this book. On such projects, the development fundamentals save time. Far from being as rigid as the steps on the paint can, if you know enough about them, they also provide all the flexibility anyone ever needs. Ignore the instructions if you wish, but do so at your peril.

Further General Reading

This chapter's final further-reading section lists software-engineering books. The point of reading a general book on software engineering is not to acquire deep knowledge about any specific subject but to see the big issues of software development in context. The following two books each provide an overview of the practices that this chapter describes as software-development fundamentals.

Sommerville, Ian. *Software Engineering, 6th Ed*. Reading, Mass.: Addison-Wesley, 1996. The sixth edition of this book is a balanced treatment of requirements, design, quality validation, and management. It contains helpful diagrams and each subject has an annotated further-reading section. At 700 pages, it isn't necessarily a book you'll read cover to cover, but if you want a thumbnail description of a topic, it's probably in here. It has a good index.

Pressman, Roger S. *Software Engineering: A Practitioner's Approach, 3d Ed*. New York: McGraw-Hill, 1992. This is an excellent alternative to Sommerville's book and is similar in scope and size. Don't be misled by the *Practitioner's Approach* in the title; excellent as it is, this book is better suited to provide an overview of important issues than to serve as a practitioner's handbook.

5

Risk Management

Contents

Related Topics

IF YOU WANT A SAFE BET, GO TO LAS VEGAS and play the slot machines. The casinos have figured the odds carefully and determined that they can make a profit even when the slots pay out 97 percent of the money they take in. Odds are that if you spend a day pumping $1000 in quarters into the slot machines, you'll get back $970. If you don't like slot machines, you can play blackjack and count cards to tilt the odds slightly in your favor. (Just don't get caught counting!)

If Las Vegas sounds too tame for you, software might be just the right gamble. Software projects include a glut of risks that would give Vegas oddsmakers nightmares—shifting user requirements, poor schedule estimates, unreliable contractors, management inexperience, personnel problems, bleeding-edge technology failures, changing government regulations, and performance shortfalls—just to name a few. The odds of a large project finishing on time are close to zero. The odds of a large project being canceled are an even-money bet (Jones 1991).

HARD DATA

In 1988, Peat Marwick found that about 35 percent of 600 firms surveyed had at least one runaway software project (Rothfeder 1988). The damage done by runaway projects makes the Las Vegas prize fights look as tame as having high tea with the queen. Allstate set out in 1982 to automate all of its office operations. They set a 5-year timetable and an $8 million budget. Six years and $15 million later, Allstate set a new deadline and readjusted its sights on a new budget of $100 million. In 1988, Westpac Banking Corporation decided to redefine its information systems. It set out on a 5-year, $85 million project. Three years later, after spending $150 million with little to show for it, Westpac cut its losses, canceled the project, and eliminated 500 development jobs (Glass 1992). Even Vegas prize fights don't get this bloody.

There are a multitude of risk-management practices that can prevent disasters such as these, and you can learn most of them more easily than you could learn to count cards at blackjack. Of course many people who play blackjack don't bother learning to count cards, and many people who manage software projects don't bother learning much about risk management. But the unalterable fact is this: if you don't manage risks, you will not achieve rapid development. As Tom Gilb says, "If you don't actively attack the risks, they will actively attack you."

Risk management does involve a few disadvantages. Projects that manage risks effectively are a lot less exciting to work on than projects that don't. You'll miss the adrenaline rush of telling your boss the day that the project is due that it's going to be 3 months late because of a problem that you've never mentioned before. You won't get to be a hero for working nights and weekends 6 months in a row. For a lot of us, those are disadvantages we can live with.

Risk management in software is a fairly new topic, but already too much information exists to cover it thoroughly in one chapter. The discussion in this chapter focuses on schedule risks and ignores cost and product risks except when they affect the schedule. This chapter also focuses on practical aspects of schedule risk management. Risk-management theory is interesting and important, but it's less directly useful so I have mostly ignored it, instead describing where to find more information in the further-reading section at the end of the chapter.

Case Study 5-1. Lack of Contractor Risk Management

"I got approval to do Square-Plan 2.5," Kim told Eddie. Kim and Eddie were project managers at Square-Tech, a shrink-wrap software company. "I've got 4 months to deliver the update, and I think it's going to be a blast." Kim had delivered her last project, Square-Calc 3.0, very late. Eddie had done well on his last one, Square-Plan 2.0, and Kim was eager to demonstrate that the difference had just been that her product was a lot more complicated than Eddie's.

(continued)

Case Study 5-1. Lack of Contractor Risk Management, *continued*

"I wouldn't get too excited just yet," Eddie told her. "I've seen the specification for 2.5, and I think you've got at least 6 months of work with the current team. Are you still planning to use the 2.0 team?"

"Yeah, I am. And I've got a plan to shrink the schedule to 4 months. I read an article on outsourcing last week, and I've found a contractor who will handle the graphics updates at his site. That will reduce the schedule by 2 months."

"Well, I hope you know what you're doing," Eddie said. "I've seen a lot of people get burned by contractors. What's your risk-management plan?"

"I've picked a reputable contractor," Kim said. "I checked his references, and I'm sure he'll do a good job. I'll just keep an eye on him. This is a risky business, and some risk is inescapable. When I've got this much work to do, I'm not going to waste my time on useless management overhead."

Eddie thought she should be more careful, but he and Kim had been over this ground before. He had learned not to argue with her when she had already decided what to do. "Good luck," he said.

Kim met with the contractor right away and gave him the specification for the graphics updates. The contractor, Chip, said that the specifications all made sense and that he would get on it right away.

Six weeks later, Kim called Chip to check on his progress. "Everything's going great," he said. "I've been working on a high-priority project for another company, so I haven't made as much progress as I'd like. But I've still got 3 1/2 months to do 2 months of work, so I don't see any problems."

"That sounds fine," Kim responded. "Let me know if you need anything. I'll be back in touch in another 6 weeks, and then we can talk about integration."

Six weeks later, Kim called again to check on progress. "The last project took me longer than I expected," Chip said. "I've gotten into the graphics updates, and I've been working like crazy, but now that I've taken a closer look at it, I think there's at least a good 3 months of work on this job."

Kim almost choked. That would make the total development time 6 months instead of 4 months. "Three months? Are you kidding? I need to have that code in 2 weeks to begin integration. You were supposed to be almost done by now!"

"I'm sorry," Chip said. "But it's not my fault. There's more work here than you guys estimated. I'll finish it as fast as I can."

Chip delivered the software in 3 months, but the project took another month after that because of integration problems with the in-house team's code. In the end, the development time totaled 7 months rather than the planned 4 months. Kim concluded that Eddie had sandbagged her by palming off a project that he wouldn't have been able to handle.

5.1   Elements of Risk Management

The job of software risk management is to identify, address, and eliminate sources of risk before they become threats to successful completion of a software project. You can address risks at any of several levels. Table 5-1 describes some different levels of risk management.

Table 5-1. Levels of Risk Management

1. *Crisis management*—Fire fighting; address risks only after they have become problems.
2. *Fix on failure*—Detect and react to risks quickly, but only after they have occurred.
3. *Risk mitigation*—Plan ahead of time to provide resources to cover risks if they occur, but do nothing to eliminate them in the first place.
4. *Prevention*—Implement and execute a plan as part of the software project to identify risks and prevent them from becoming problems.
5. *Elimination of root causes*—Identify and eliminate factors that make it possible for risks to exist at all.

Source: Adapted from *A Manager's Guide to Software Engineering* (Pressman 1993).

The purpose of this chapter is to describe how to address software schedule risks at levels 4 and 5 rather than at levels 1 through 3. If you're addressing risks at level 1, 2, or 3, you've already lost the schedule battle.

Generally, risk management is made up of risk assessment and risk control. These, in turn, are made up of several subcategories as shown in Figure 5-1. These are outlined in the following subsections.

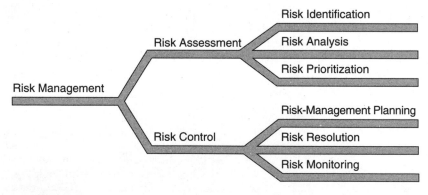

Figure 5-1. *Risk management is composed of risk assessment and control. Source:* Software Risk Management *(Boehm 1989).*

Risk Assessment

Risk assessment is made up of risk identification, risk analysis, and risk prioritization:

- *Risk identification* produces a list of risks that have the potential to disrupt the project's schedule.
- *Risk analysis* assesses the likelihood and impact of each risk and the risk levels of alternative practices.
- *Risk prioritization* produces a list of risks prioritized by impact. This list serves as a basis for risk control.

Risk Control

Risk control is made up of risk-management planning, risk resolution, and risk monitoring:

- *Risk-management planning* produces a plan for dealing with each significant risk. It also makes sure that the risk-management plans for each of the individual risks are consistent with each other and with the overall project plan.
- *Risk resolution* is the execution of the plan for dealing with each significant risk.
- *Risk monitoring* is the activity of monitoring progress toward resolving each risk item. Risk monitoring can also include the ongoing activity of identifying new risks and feeding them back into the risk-management process.

The subsections in the following section explain each of these aspects of risk management as they apply to managing software schedule risks.

5.2   Risk Identification

If you don't ask for risk information, you are asking for trouble.
Tom Gilb

The first step in managing risks is to identify the factors that pose a risk to your schedule. Three general risks to any rapid-development project are overlooking the first three pillars of rapid development, which were described in Chapter 2, "Rapid-Development Strategy":

- Making one of the classic mistakes described in Chapter 3, "Classic Mistakes"
- Ignoring the development basics described in Chapter 4, "Software-Development Fundamentals"
- Failing to actively manage risks as described in this chapter

Once you get past these general risks, you'll find almost as many different risks as there are software projects. Some risks appear again and again, however, and one of the easiest ways to identify risks is to check your project against a list of schedule risks. The next subsection describes the most common schedule risks. The subsection after that provides an exhaustive list of possible schedule risks.

Most Common Schedule Risks

Table 5-2 lists the most common schedule risks.

CLASSIC MISTAKE

Table 5-2. Most Common Schedule Risks

1. Feature creep
2. Requirements or developer gold-plating
3. Shortchanged quality
4. Overly optimistic schedules
5. Inadequate design
6. Silver-bullet syndrome
7. Research-oriented development
8. Weak personnel
9. Contractor failure
10. Friction between developers and customers

Sources: Adapted from *Software Risk Management* (Boehm 1989) and *Assessment and Control of Software Risks* (Jones 1994).

If you think the risks in this table look familiar, it's because each of them were also presented as classic mistakes in Chapter 3. The only difference between a classic mistake and a risk is that the classic mistake has been made more often. Risks can be less common or unique to your project. Each of the risks listed in Table 5-2 is described in more detail in Section 3.3, "Classic Mistakes Enumerated," and means of controlling them are described later in this chapter, in Table 5-6.

Complete List of Schedule Risks

Table 5-3 contains an exhaustive list of risks that can adversely affect a software schedule. Only a few of the risks will apply to most projects. The risks are organized by loose categories but otherwise are in no particular order. If the list seems overwhelming, you can concentrate on the most common risks, listed in the preceding subsection.

In addition to the lists presented in this table, most projects have risks that are unique to the specific project: "Joe's going to quit unless he can start bringing his dog to work, and management hasn't decided yet whether to let Bowser come to the office." You'll have to identify those risks yourself.

Table 5-3. Potential Schedule Risks

Schedule creation

Schedule, resources, and product definition have all been dictated by the customer or upper management and are not in balance

Schedule is optimistic, "best case" (rather than realistic, "expected case")

Schedule omits necessary tasks

Schedule was based on the use of specific team members, but those team members were not available

Cannot build a product of the size specified in the time allocated

Product is larger than estimated (in lines of code, function points, or percentage of previous project's size)

Effort is greater than estimated (per line of code, function point, module, etc.)

Reestimation in response to schedule slips is overly optimistic or ignores project history

Excessive schedule pressure reduces productivity

Target date is moved up with no corresponding adjustment to the product scope or available resources

A delay in one task causes cascading delays in dependent tasks

Unfamiliar areas of the product take more time than expected to design and implement

Organization and management

Project lacks an effective top-management sponsor

Project languishes too long in fuzzy front end

Layoffs and cutbacks reduce team's capacity

Management or marketing insists on technical decisions that lengthen the schedule

Inefficient team structure reduces productivity

Management review/decision cycle is slower than expected

Budget cuts upset project plans

Management makes decisions that reduce the development team's motivation

Nontechnical third-party tasks take longer than expected (budget approval, equipment purchase approval, legal reviews, security clearances, etc.)

Planning is too poor to support the desired development speed

Sources: *Principles of Software Engineering Management* (Gilb 1988), *Software Risk Management* (Boehm 1989), *A Manager's Guide to Software Engineering* (Pressman 1993), *Third Wave Project Management* (Thomsett 1993), and *Assessment and Control of Software Risks* (Jones 1994).

(continued)

Table 5-3. Potential Schedule Risks, *continued*

Project plans are abandoned under pressure, resulting in chaotic, inefficient development

Management places more emphasis on heroics than accurate status reporting, which undercuts its ability to detect and correct problems

Development environment

Facilities are not available on time

Facilities are available but inadequate (e.g., no phones, network wiring, furniture, office supplies, etc.)

Facilities are crowded, noisy, or disruptive

Development tools are not in place by the desired time

Development tools do not work as expected; developers need time to create workarounds or to switch to new tools

Development tools are not chosen based on their technical merits and do not provide the planned productivity

Learning curve for new development tool is longer or steeper than expected

End-users

End-user insists on new requirements

End-user ultimately finds product to be unsatisfactory, requiring redesign and rework

End-user does not buy into the project and consequently does not provide needed support

End-user input is not solicited, so product ultimately fails to meet user expectations and must be reworked

Customer

Customer insists on new requirements

Customer review/decision cycles for plans, prototypes, and specifications are slower than expected

Customer will not participate in review cycles for plans, prototypes, and specifications or is incapable of doing so—resulting in unstable requirements and time-consuming changes

Customer communication time (e.g., time to answer requirements-clarification questions) is slower than expected

Customer insists on technical decisions that lengthen the schedule

Customer micro-manages the development process, resulting in slower progress than planned

Customer-furnished components are a poor match for the product under development, resulting in extra design and integration work

Customer-furnished components are poor quality, resulting in extra testing, design, and integration work and in extra customer-relationship management

Customer-mandated support tools and environments are incompatible, have poor performance, or have inadequate functionality, resulting in reduced productivity

(continued)

Table 5-3. Potential Schedule Risks, *continued*

Customer will not accept the software as delivered even though it meets all specifications

Customer has expectations for development speed that developers cannot meet

Contractors

Contractor does not deliver components when promised

Contractor delivers components of unacceptably low quality, and time must be added to improve quality

Contractor does not buy into the project and consequently does not provide the level of performance needed

Requirements

Requirements have been baselined but continue to change

Requirements are poorly defined, and further definition expands the scope of the project

Additional requirements are added

Vaguely specified areas of the product are more time-consuming than expected

Product

Error-prone modules require more testing, design, and implementation work than expected

Unacceptably low quality requires more testing, design, and implementation work to correct than expected

Pushing the computer science state-of-the-art in one or more areas lengthens the schedule unpredictably

Development of the wrong software functions requires redesign and implementation

Development of the wrong user interface results in redesign and implementation

Development of extra software functions that are not required (gold-plating) extends the schedule

Meeting product's size or speed constraints requires more time than expected, including time for redesign and reimplementation

Strict requirements for compatibility with existing system require more testing, design, and implementation than expected

Requirements for interfacing with other systems, other complex systems, or other systems that are not under the team's control result in unforeseen design, implementation, and testing

Requirement to operate under multiple operating systems takes longer to satisfy than expected

Operation in an unfamiliar or unproved software environment causes unforeseen problems

Operation in an unfamiliar or unproved hardware environment causes unforeseen problems

Development of a kind of component that is brand new to the organization takes longer than expected

(continued)

Table 5-3. Potential Schedule Risks, *continued*

Dependency on a technology that is still under development lengthens the schedule

External environment

Product depends on government regulations, which change unexpectedly

Product depends on draft technical standards, which change unexpectedly

Personnel

Hiring takes longer than expected

Task prerequisites (e.g., training, completion of other projects, acquisition of work permit) cannot be completed on time

Poor relationships between developers and management slow decision making and follow through

Team members do not buy into the project and consequently do not provide the level of performance needed

Low motivation and morale reduce productivity

Lack of needed specialization increases defects and rework

Personnel need extra time to learn unfamiliar software tools or environment

Personnel need extra time to learn unfamiliar hardware environment

Personnel need extra time to learn unfamiliar programming language

Contract personnel leave before project is complete

Permanent employees leave before project is complete

New development personnel are added late in the project, and additional training and communications overhead reduces existing team members' effectiveness

Team members do not work together efficiently

Conflicts between team members result in poor communication, poor designs, interface errors, and extra rework

Problem team members are not removed from the team, damaging overall team motivation

The personnel most qualified to work on the project are not available for the project

The personnel most qualified to work on the project are available for the project but are not used for political or other reasons

Personnel with critical skills needed for the project cannot be found

Key personnel are available only part time

Not enough personnel are available for the project

People's assignments do not match their strengths

Personnel work slower than expected

Sabotage by project management results in inefficient scheduling and ineffective planning

Sabotage by technical personnel results in lost work or poor quality and requires rework

(continued)

Table 5-3. Potential Schedule Risks, *continued*

Design and Implementation

Overly simple design fails to address major issues and leads to redesign and reimplementation

Overly complicated design requires unnecessary and unproductive implementation overhead

Poor design leads to redesign and reimplementation

Use of unfamiliar methodology results in extra training time and in rework to fix first-time misuses of the methodology

Product is implemented in a low-level language (e.g., assembler), and productivity is lower than expected

Necessary functionality cannot be implemented using the selected code or class libraries; developers must switch to new libraries or custom-build the necessary functionality

Code or class libraries have poor quality, causing extra testing, defect correction, and rework

Schedule savings from productivity enhancing tools are overestimated

Components developed separately cannot be integrated easily, requiring redesign and rework

Process

Amount of paperwork results in slower progress than expected

Inaccurate progress tracking results in not knowing the project is behind schedule until late in the project

Upstream quality-assurance activities are shortchanged, resulting in time-consuming rework downstream

Inaccurate quality tracking results in not knowing about quality problems that affect the schedule until late in the project

Too little formality (lack of adherence to software policies and standards) results in miscommunications, quality problems, and rework

Too much formality (bureaucratic adherence to software policies and standards) results in unnecessary, time-consuming overhead

Management-level progress reporting takes more developer time than expected

Half-hearted risk management fails to detect major project risks

Software project risk management takes more time than expected

5.3   Risk Analysis

After you've identified the schedule risks to your project, the next step is to analyze each risk to determine its impact. You can use risk analysis to help choose among several development options, or you can use it to manage the risks associated with an option you've already chosen. With risks in general, this can be a tricky business, but when you're primarily concerned with schedule risks, assessment is simpler.

Risk Exposure

A useful risk-analysis practice is to determine the "risk exposure" of each of the risks you've identified. Risk exposure is often abbreviated as "RE." (Sometimes it's called "risk impact.") One definition of risk is "unexpected loss." Risk exposure is equal to the probability of the unexpected loss multiplied by the size of the loss. For example, if you think there's about a 25-percent chance that it will take 4 weeks longer than expected to get your project approved, the risk exposure would be 25 percent multiplied by 4 weeks—which equals 1 week.

Because you're concerned only with schedule risks, you can express all the losses in weeks or months or some other unit of time that makes them easy to compare.

Table 5-4 is an example of a risk assessment table you could create using the risk, the probability of loss, the size of the loss, and the risk exposure.

Table 5-4. Example of a Risk-Assessment Table

Risk	Probability of Loss	Size of Loss (weeks)	Risk Exposure (weeks)
Overly optimistic schedule	50%	5	2.5
Addition of requirement to fully support automated updates from the mainframe	5%	20	1.0
Additional features added by marketing (specific features unknown)	35%	8	2.8
Unstable graphics-formatting subsystem interface	25%	4	1.0
Inadequate design—redesign required	15%	15	2.25
Project approval takes longer than expected	25%	4	1.0
Facilities not ready on time	10%	2	0.2
Management-level progress reporting takes more developer time than expected	10%	1	0.1
Late delivery of graphics-formatting subsystem by contractor	10–20%	4	0.4–0.8
New programming tools do not produce the promised savings	30%	5	1.5

In the sample risk-assessment table shown in Table 5-4, a theoretical project has identified several risks that range in potential severity from 1 week to 20 weeks. The probabilities that the risks will occur range from 5 percent to 50 percent. On a real project, you might identify many more risks than I've shown in this table.

How do you come up with the probability and size of the loss? You have to estimate both numbers, so you can't expect either to be exact.

Estimating Size of Loss

The size of the loss is often easier to pin down than the probability. In the example above, you might have a precise estimate of 20 months for the time it would take to fully support automated updates from the mainframe. Or you might know that the project will be approved either February 1 or March 1, depending on which month the executive committee reviews the proposal for the project. If you assumed that it would be approved February 1, the size of the risk that the project approval will take longer than expected would be exactly 1 month.

In cases in which the size of the loss is not easy to estimate directly, sometimes you can break down the loss into smaller losses, estimate those, and then combine the individual estimates into an aggregate estimate. For example, if you're using three new programming tools, you could estimate the loss resulting from each tool not producing its expected productivity gain. You could then add the losses together, which might be easier than estimating the combined loss.

Estimating Probability of Loss

Estimating the probability of the loss is usually more subjective than estimating the size of the loss, and there are many practices available to improve the accuracy of this subjective estimate. Here are a few ideas:

- Have the person most familiar with the system estimate the probability of each risk, and then hold a risk-estimate review.

- Use Delphi or group-consensus practices. In the Delphi approach, you have each person estimate each risk individually, and then discuss (verbally or in writing) the rationale behind each estimate, especially the very high and low ones. Continue the process in successive rounds until the estimates converge.

- Use betting analogies with personally significant amounts of money: "Would you take this bet? If the facilities will be ready on time, you win $125. If they're not ready on time, I win $100." Refine the bet until you'd be just as happy being on either side of it. The risk probability is the dollar amount on the downside divided by the total dollar amount at stake. In the example, the probability of the facilities not being ready on time would be $100 / ($100 + $125) = 44 percent.

- Use "adjective calibration." First have each person choose the risk level from a verbal scale of phrases like highly likely, very good chance, probable, likely, improbable, unlikely, and highly unlikely. Then convert the verbal assessments to quantitative assessments (Boehm 1989).

Total Project Overrun and Buffers

An interesting side effect of computing risk-exposure numbers as illustrated in Table 5-4 arises from the fact that in statistical terms these risk exposures are "expected values." The risk of an inadequate design would cost you 15 weeks if it actually occurred. Since it's not 100 percent likely to occur, you don't actually expect to lose 15 weeks. But it's not 0 percent likely either, so you don't expect to lose 0 weeks. In a statistical sense, the amount you expect to lose is the probability times the size, or 15 percent times 15 weeks. In this example, you "expect" to lose 2.25 weeks. Since we're talking only about schedule risks, you can add up all the risk exposures to get the total expected overrun for your project. The expected overrun for this project is 12.8 to 13.2 weeks. That's the overrun before doing any risk management.

The size of the expected overrun provides insight into the overall risk level of your project. If the project in the example is a 25-week project, an expected overrun of 12.8 to 13.2 weeks clearly calls for active risk management.

CROSS-REFERENCE
For more on plus-or-minus schedule qualifiers, see "Estimate Presentation Styles" in Section 8.3.

Should you change your schedule to reflect the expected overrun? Yes, I think so. Recompute the total risk exposure after you've done your risk-management plan, and then add it to your schedule as a buffer. That will give you a more meaningful buffer than the rule-of-thumb buffers that people sometimes use to pad their schedules. Alternatively, you can simply publish a schedule with plus-or-minus qualifiers for each risk and adjust the schedule whenever a risk materializes.

5.4 Risk Prioritization

While it is futile to try to eliminate risk, and questionable to try to minimize it, it is essential that the risks taken be the *right risks*.

Peter Drucker

Once you've created the list of schedule risks, the next step is to prioritize the risks so that you know where to focus your risk-management efforts. Projects typically spend 80 percent of their money fixing 20 percent of their problems, so it's useful to be able to focus on the most important 20 percent (Boehm 1989).

Once again, the job is easier if you're focusing solely on schedule risks than if you're concerned with all kinds of risks. After you've computed the risk exposure by multiplying the probability of the loss by the size of the loss, sort the risks in your risk-assessment table by the risk exposure and see what you've got. Table 5-5 is an example of a risk-assessment table sorted by risk exposure.

Table 5-5. Example of a Prioritized Risk-Assessment Table

Risk	Probability of Loss	Size of Loss (weeks)	Risk Exposure (weeks)
Additional features added by marketing (specific features unknown)	35%	8	2.8
Overly optimistic schedule	50%	5	2.5
Inadequate design— redesign required	15%	15	2.25
New programming tools do not produce the promised savings	30%	5	1.5
Addition of requirement to fully support automated updates from the mainframe	5%	20	1.0
Unstable graphics-formatting subsystem interface	25%	4	1.0
Project approval takes longer than expected	25%	4	1.0
Late delivery of graphics-formatting subsystem by contractor	10–20%	4	0.4–0.8
Facilities not ready on time	10%	2	0.2
Management-level progress reporting takes more developer time than expected	10%	1	0.1

Sorting the table in this way produces a list of risks that are ordered roughly by priority. If you were to successfully address the top five risks in the table, you would expect to avoid 9.8 weeks of expected schedule overruns. If you were to successfully address the bottom five risks, you would avoid only 2.7 to 3.1 weeks of expected schedule overruns. On average, your time is better spent addressing the risks toward the top of the list.

The reason that the list is ordered only "roughly" is that you might want to prioritize some of the larger-loss risks higher than their position in the rough ordering implies. In Table 5-5, the risk "Addition of requirement to fully support automated updates from the mainframe" is only 5 percent likely, but the 20-week impact if it occurs is larger than any other risk. If a 20-week loss would be catastrophic to your project, you should manage risks of that size to ensure that none of them occur even if they have low probabilities.

Likewise, you might want to prioritize a pair of synergistic risks higher than you would prioritize either risk individually. In the example, the instability of the interface to the graphics-formatting subsystem is a risk, and so is the contractor's schedule for its delivery. The combined risk of using a contractor and having the contractor develop code to an unstable interface is likely to be larger than either of the risks individually.

The priority ordering is only approximate for another reason: the numbers that you used to create it were all *estimates*. The accuracy of the risk-exposure numbers and the priority ordering that comes from them is limited by the accuracy of the probability and size estimates. Converting the estimates into a hard risk-exposure number can make it seem as though the prioritization is precise. But the prioritization can only be as accurate as the input, and because the input is subjective, the prioritization is subjective too. Your judgment is a necessary part of every aspect of risk management.

After you've identified the high-risk items, risk prioritization is also useful for the risks it tells you to ignore. There's no point in managing a low-loss risk that also has a low likelihood of becoming a problem. In the example, you could easily spend more time managing the risk of facilities not being ready on time than you would expect to lose by not managing it at all. Risk prioritization is critical to not becoming overwhelmed by the risk-management activity itself.

5.5 Risk Control

After you've identified your project's risks, analyzed their probabilities and magnitudes, and prioritized them, you're ready to control them. This section describes the three aspects of controlling risks: risk-management planning, risk resolution, and risk monitoring.

Risk-Management Planning

The focus of risk-management planning is to develop a plan to handle each of the high-priority risks identified during the previous activities. The risk-management plan can be as simple as a paragraph for each risk that describes the who, what, when, where, why, and how of each risk's management. It should also contain general provisions for monitoring the risks, closing out risks that have been resolved, and identifying emerging risks.

Risk Resolution

FURTHER READING
Effective risk resolution often hinges on finding a creative solution to the specific risk. One good source of ideas on how to resolve many software project risks is *Assessment and Control of Software Risks* (Jones 1994).

The resolution of any particular risk depends a lot on the specific risk. Practices that address the risk of an inadequate design don't transfer well to the risk of your group being bumped out of its office space.

Suppose you're a contractor and you're concerned about both the risk of creating an inadequate design in a product area that's new to you and of getting bumped from your office space by another group within your company. Here are a few generic methods of addressing risks with examples related to both the design and office-space risks:

Avoid the risk. Don't do the risky activity. For example, take responsibility for most of the system design, but not for the unfamiliar part of the system. Have the client design the unfamiliar area. On the office-space problem, negotiate with the group that's bumping you out of your office space and convince them not to bump you.

Transfer the risk from one part of a system to another. Sometimes a risk in one part of the project isn't as risky in another part of the project, and you can move it to the other area. For example, trade design areas with the client: say that you will design a part of the system they were scheduled to design if they will design the part that's unfamiliar to you. Or you could have them review and approve your design, effectively transferring responsibility for some of the risk onto their shoulders. On the office-space issue, have another group whose schedule is less critical change office space instead of your group, or wait until the system has been delivered to move.

In general, get the risk off the critical path. Orient the rest of your project so that even if the risk occurs, the project as a whole isn't delayed.

Buy information about the risk. If you don't know exactly how serious the risk is, investigate it. For example, develop a design prototype to test the feasibility of your design approach. Bring in an outside consultant to evaluate your design. Work with facilities planning to put you into office space you can stay in for the duration of the project.

Eliminate the root cause of the risk. If the design for part of the system is exceptionally challenging, recast that part of the system as a research project and eliminate it from the version you're building. Try to interest the group that's bumping you from your office space in different office space altogether. Or get a commitment from the space-planning group to keep you in your office space for the duration of the project.

Assume the risk. Accept that the risk might occur, but don't do anything special to handle it. If the consequences are small and the effort required to avoid them is large, rolling with the punches might be the most efficient approach. Simply accept the consequences of an inadequate design or of getting bumped from your office space.

Publicize the risk. Let upper management, marketing, and customers know about the risk and its consequences. Minimize the surprise they'll feel if it occurs.

Control the risk. Accept that the risk might occur, and develop contingency plans to handle it if you can't resolve it. Allocate extra resources to test the part of the system whose design you're worried about, and plan for extra time to fix defects. Get your space planning group on board far enough ahead of time to make the move go smoothly; schedule the move for a weekend night to minimize the disruption; and bring in temporary personnel to help with packing and unpacking.

Remember the risk. Build up a collection of risk-management plans that you can use on future projects.

To further illustrate the way that you can control some risks, Table 5-6 lists means of controlling the most common schedule risks.

Table 5-6. Means of Controlling the Most Common Schedule Risks

Risk	Means of Control	Where to Find More Information
1. Feature creep	Use customer-oriented practices	Chapter 10, "Customer-Oriented Development"
	Use incremental development practices	Chapter 7, "Lifecycle Planning"
	Control the feature set	Chapter 14, "Feature-Set Control"
	Design for change	Chapter 19, "Designing for Change"
2. Requirements gold-plating or developer gold-plating	Scrub requirements	"Requirements Scrubbing" in Section 14.1
	Timebox development	Chapter 39, "Timebox Development"
	Control the feature set	Chapter 14, "Feature-Set Control"
	Use staged delivery	Chapter 36, "Staged Delivery" and Section 7.6, "Staged Delivery"

(continued)

Table 5-6. Means of Controlling the Most Common Schedule Risks, *continued*

Risk	Means of Control	Where to Find More Information
2. *(continued)*	Use throwaway prototyping	Chapter 38, "Throwaway Prototyping"
	Design to schedule	Section 7.7, "Design-to-Schedule"
3. Shortchanged quality	Allow time for QA activities and pay attention to quality-assurance fundamentals	Section 4.3, "Quality-Assurance Fundamentals"
4. Overly optimistic schedules	Use multiple estimation practices, multiple estimators, and automated estimation tools	Chapter 8, "Estimation"
	Use principled negotiation	Section 9.2, "Beating Schedule Pressure"
	Design to schedule	Section 7.7, "Design-to-Schedule"
	Use incremental development practices	Chapter 7, "Lifecycle Planning"
5. Inadequate design	Have an explicit design activity and schedule enough time for design	"Design" in Section 4.2
	Hold design inspections	"Inspections" in Section 4.3 and summary in Chapter 23, "Inspections"
6. Silver-bullet syndrome	Be skeptical of productivity claims	Section 15.5, "Silver-Bullet Syndrome"
	Set up a software measurement program	Chapter 26, "Measurement"
	Set up a software tools group	Chapter 15, "Productivity Tools"
7. Research-oriented development	Don't try to do research and maximize development speed at the same time	"Research-oriented development" in Section 3.3
	Use a risk-oriented lifecycle	Chapter 7, "Lifecycle Planning"
	Manage risks vigilantly	This chapter
8. Weak personnel	Staffing with top talent	Chapter 12, "Teamwork," and Chapter 13, "Team Structure"

(continued)

Table 5-6. Means of Controlling the Most Common Schedule Risks, *continued*

Risk	Means of Control	Where to Find More Information
8. *(continued)*	Recruiting and scheduling key team members long before the project starts	Chapter 12, "Teamwork," and Chapter 13, "Team Structure"
	Training	Chapter 12, "Teamwork," and Chapter 13, "Team Structure"
	Teambuilding	Chapter 12, "Teamwork," and Chapter 13, "Team Structure"
9. Contractor failure	Check references	Chapter 28, "Outsourcing"
	Assess the contractor's ability before hiring it	Chapter 28, "Outsourcing"
	Actively manage the relationship with the contractor	Chapter 28, "Outsourcing"
10. Friction between developers and customers	Use customer-oriented practices	Chapter 10, "Customer-Oriented Development"

Risk Monitoring

Life in the software world would be easier if the risks would stand still after we developed plans for dealing with them. But risks wax and wane as a project progresses, so you need risk monitoring to check progress toward resolving each risk and to identify new risks as they emerge.

Top-10 Risks List

One of the most potent risk-monitoring tools is the use of a "Top-10 Risks" list that you create. The Top-10 list contains each risk's current rank, its previous rank, the number of times it has been on the list, and a summary of steps taken to resolve the risk since the previous review. Table 5-7 on the facing page shows a sample list.

It isn't important that the Top-10 list contain exactly 10 risks. As shown by the last item on the list, the list should also contain any risks that have moved off the list since the last review.

Table 5-7. Example of a "Top-10 Risks List"

This Week	Last Week	Weeks on List	Risk	Risk Resolution Progress
1	1	5	Feature creep	Staged delivery approach adopted; need to explain approach to marketing and end-users
2	5	5	Inadequate design— redesign required	Design under way Identification and selection of expert reviewers under way
3	2	4	Test lead not yet on board	Top candidate has been offered job; awaiting acceptance of offer
4	7	5	Unstable graphics-formatting subsystem interface	Graphics-formatting interface design moved to front of schedule; design not yet complete
5	8	5	Late delivery of graphics-formatting subsystem by contractor	Appointed experienced contract liaison Requested contractor to designate official liaison; haven't responded yet
6	4	2	Development tools delivered late	5 of 7 tools delivered OK Tool acquisition group notified that acquiring remaining tools is high priority
7	–	1	Slow manager review cycle	Evaluation under way
8	–	1	Slow customer review cycle	Evaluation under way
9	3	5	Overly optimistic schedule	Completed first milestone on time
10	9	5	Addition of requirement to fully support automated updates from the mainframe	Investigating feasibility of manual update See feature-creep risk
–	6	5	Design lead's time drained by ongoing requests to support former project	Former project has been moved to Anchorage office

On a rapid-development project, the project manager and the project manager's boss should review the Top-10 list once a week. The most useful aspects of the Top-10 list are that it forces you to look at risks regularly, to think about them regularly, and to be alert to changes in importance.

Interim Postmortems

Although the Top-10 list is probably the most useful risk-monitoring practice, a fast-track project should also include postmortems conducted throughout the project. Many project managers wait until the end to do a postmortem. That produces a nice benefit for the next project, but it doesn't help you when you really need it—on your current project! For maximum effectiveness, conduct a small-scale postmortem after you complete each major milestone.

Risk Officer

Some organizations have found appointing a risk officer to be useful. The job of the risk officer is to be alert to risks to the project and to keep managers and developers from ignoring them in their planning. As with testing and peer reviews, it turns out that for psychological reasons it's beneficial to have a person whose job it is to play devil's advocate—to look for all of the reasons that the project might fail. On large projects (50 persons or more), the job of risk officer might be full time. On smaller projects, you can assign someone with other project duties to play the role when needed. For the psychological reasons mentioned, the person assigned shouldn't be the project manager.

5.6 Risk, High Risk, and Gambling

It is not only the magnitude of the risk that we need to be able to appraise in entrepreneurial decisions. It is above all the character of the risk. Is it, for instance, the kind of risk we can afford to take, or the kind of risk we cannot afford to take? Or is it that rare but singularly important risk, the risk we cannot afford not to take— sometimes regardless of the odds?

Peter Drucker

For purposes of rapid development, some projects are risks, some are high risks, and some are gambles. It's hard to find a software project that doesn't involve some risk, and projects that are merely "risks" are the kind best-suited to achieving maximum development speed. They allow you to move in an efficient, straight line from the beginning of the project to the end. Fast development, while not necessarily easy to achieve, is well within the grasp of the person who understands the strategies and practices described in this book.

High risk and rapid development make a less compatible combination. Risks tend to extend development schedules, and high risks tend to extend them a lot. But business realities sometimes require you to commit to an ambitious development schedule even when a project involves many risks—vague requirements, untrained personnel, unfamiliar product areas, strong research elements, or all of the above.

If you find yourself forced to commit to an ambitious schedule in such circumstances, be aware of the nature of the commitment. With two or three high-risk areas, even your best schedule projections will be nearly meaningless. Be careful to explain to the people who depend on you that you are willing to take calculated risks, even high risks, but more likely than not you won't be able to deliver what everyone is hoping for. In such cases, not just active but vigorous risk management will help you to make the best of a difficult situation.

CROSS-REFERENCE
For more on projects that have their schedules, feature sets, and resources dictated to them, see Section 6.6, "Development-Speed Trade-Offs." For more on code and fix, see Section 7.2, "Code-and-Fix."

At the extreme end of the risk scale, some projects are scheduled so aggressively that they become out-and-out gambles—they are more like the purchase of a lottery ticket than a calculated business decision. About one-third of all projects have an impossible combination of schedules, feature sets, and resources dictated to them before they start. In such circumstances, there is no incentive to practice risk management because the project starts out with a 100-percent chance of failure. With no chance of meeting their schedules through the use of any known development practices, it becomes rational to gamble on 1000-to-1 long shots such as code-and-fix development. These projects, which know they need maximum development speed, ironically become the projects that are most likely to throw effective, proven speed-oriented practices out the window.

CLASSIC MISTAKE

The results are inevitable. The long shot doesn't pay off, and the project is delivered late—much later than it would have been if the project had been set up to take calculated risks rather than desperate gambles.

Do one-third of the projects in the industry really need to take desperate gambles? Do one-third of the projects have business cases for taking 1000-to-1 long shots? I don't think so. Beware of the risk level on your project, and try to keep it in the "risk" or "high-risk" category.

Case Study 5-2. Systematic Risk Management

Square-Calc version 3.0 had been a disaster, overrunning its schedule by 50 percent. Eddie agreed to take over the project with version 3.5, and he hoped to do better than the last manager had done.

"As you know, Square-Calc 3.0 didn't do very well compared to its planned schedule," he told the team at the first planning meeting. "It was scheduled to take 10 months, and it took 15. We need to do better. We've got 4 months to complete a medium-sized upgrade, and I think that's a reasonable amount of time for this work. Risk management is going to be a top priority. The first thing I want to do is appoint a risk officer, someone who will look for all of the things that might go wrong on this project. Is anyone interested?"

(continued)

Case Study 5-2. Systematic Risk Management, *continued*

Jill had worked a lot harder than she wanted to on the last project and was willing to help prevent that from happening again so she said, "Sure, I'm interested. What do I need to do?"

"The first thing you need to do is create a list of known risks," replied Eddie. "I want you to get together with each of the developers this morning and find out what risks they're aware of, and then I want to get together with you this afternoon. We'll look at the risks and go from there."

That afternoon, Eddie and Jill met in Eddie's office. "Everyone, including me, thinks that the biggest risk is the Square-Calc 3.0 code base. It really sucks," Jill said. "None of us wants to make any major changes to it, and there are certain modules we don't even want to touch.

"The next most important risk is the user-documentation schedule. We shipped late last time partly because we didn't coordinate well enough with user documentation. We've got to make sure that doesn't happen again.

"The last big risk is creeping requirements. There were a lot of features that didn't make the cutoff for version 3.5, and I'm afraid that marketing will try to shoehorn them in." Jill went on to note a dozen smaller risks, but the first three were the big ones.

"OK, I want us to come up with a risk-management plan for the major risks," Eddie said. He explained the idea of the Top-10 Risks list to her and said that he wanted to review the top 10 risks with the team every week.

To manage the code-base risk, they decided to analyze their bug database to see whether any modules in the system were truly error prone. They allocated 1 month of their 4-month schedule to focus on rewriting the most error-prone modules.

For the user-documentation risk, they decided to develop a throwaway user-interface prototype that exactly matched the appearance of the new code they'd be writing. They would not allow visual deviations from the prototype. They would also include a rep from user documentation in their weekly risk-management meetings, which would help them to stay in synch with the documentation effort.

For the feature-creep risk, Eddie promised to talk with someone in the marketing department. "I know their number-one goal is to get the product out on time," he said. "We need to restore customer confidence after the schedule problems on 3.0. I'll explain the importance of setting crystal-clear goals to them, and I think that will cut down on the feature requests." They also

(continued)

Case Study 5-2. Systematic Risk Management, *continued*

invited Carlos from marketing to attend their risk meetings, reasoning that if someone from marketing understood all the other risks they faced, marketing might be less inclined to pile on new risks themselves.

During the next 4 weeks, identification and replacement of the error-prone modules went about as planned. It turned out that about 5 percent of the modules accounted for about 50 percent of the errors. They were able to redesign and reimplement those at a careful pace. They subjected each module to a thorough review at each stage, and by the time they were done, they felt comfortable that the code base could sustain the rest of the modifications they needed to make for version 3.5.

At the weekly risk meeting 6 weeks into the schedule, Jill raised a new issue. "As you know, I've been monitoring some lower-priority risks in addition to the bigger ones, and one of them has become more important. Bob has been working on speeding up some of the scientific functions, and he told me a few weeks ago that he wasn't sure he could meet the revised spec. Apparently he researched the best available algorithms, implemented them, and that only made the functions about 50 percent faster. The spec calls for a 100-percent speedup, so Bob's been trying to come up with faster algorithms. I told him that I wanted to set a red-alert point in the schedule so that if he wasn't done at that point I could raise a warning flag. Yesterday we hit the red-alert point, and Bob says he is nowhere near being done. Basically, I think he's doing software research, and there's no way to predict how long he's going to take."

Carlos from marketing spoke up. "I was one of the people who pushed for the speed improvement, and I think that '100 percent' number is flexible. It's more important to me to get the product out on time than it is to meet that performance requirement to the letter. At least we'll be able to show our customers that we're responsive."

"That sounds good," Eddie said. "I think the 50-percent improvement we've already reached is good enough, so I'll redirect Bob to some other tasks. That's one less risk to worry about."

After that, there were few surprises. Minor issues arose and were addressed while they were still minor. Compared to the last project, this one seemed a little boring, but no one minded. A few marketing people tried to add features, but Carlos understood the importance of the schedule goal, and he fended off most of the requests before development even heard about them. The team performed well, and they delivered Square-Calc 3.5 by the 4-month due date.

Further Reading

Boehm, Barry W., ed. *Software Risk Management*. Washington, DC: IEEE Computer Society Press, 1989. This collection of papers is based on the premise that successful project managers are good risk managers. Boehm has collected a nicely balanced set of papers from both technical and business sources. One of the best features of the book is that Boehm contributed about 70 pages of original writing himself. That 70 pages is a good introduction to software risk management. You might think that a tutorial published in 1989 would seem dated by now, but it actually presents a more forward-looking view of software project management than you'll find most other places.

Boehm, Barry W. "Software Risk Management: Principles and Practices." *IEEE Software*, January 1991, pp. 32–41. This article hits the high points of the comments Boehm wrote for *Software Risk Management* and contains many practical suggestions.

Jones, Capers. *Assessment and Control of Software Risks*. Englewood Cliffs, N.J.: Yourdon Press, 1994. Jones's book is an excellent complement to Boehm's risk-management tutorial. It says almost nothing about how to manage software risks in general; instead, it describes 60 of the most common and most serious software risks in detail. Jones uses a standard format for each risk that describes the severity of the risk, frequency of occurrence, root causes, associated problems, methods of prevention and control, and support available through education, books, periodicals, consulting, and professional associations. Much of the risk analysis in the book is supported by information from Jones's database of more than 4000 software projects.

Gilb, Tom. *Principles of Software Engineering Management*. Wokingham, England: Addison-Wesley, 1988. This book has one chapter that is specifically devoted to the topic of risk estimation. The software development method that Gilb describes in the rest of the book puts a strong emphasis on risk management.

Thomsett, Rob. *Third Wave Project Management*. Englewood Cliffs, N.J.: Yourdon Press, 1993. The book contains a 43-question risk-assessment questionnaire that you can use to obtain a rough idea of whether your project's risk level is low, medium, or high.

RAPID DEVELOPMENT

6

Core Issues in Rapid Development

Contents

Related Topics

ONCE YOU'VE LEARNED HOW TO AVOID the classic mistakes and mastered development fundamentals and risk management, you're ready to focus on schedule-oriented development practices. The first step in that direction is to understand several issues that lie at the heart of maximum development speed.

6.1 Does One Size Fit All?

You will use different practices to develop a heart-pacemaker control than you will to develop an inventory tracking system that tracks videotapes. If a software malfunction causes you to lose 1 video out of 1000, it might affect your profits by a fraction of a percent, but it doesn't really matter. But if a malfunction causes you to lose 1 pacemaker out of 1000, you've got real problems.

Different projects have different rapid-development needs, even when they all need to be developed "as fast as possible." Generally speaking, products that are widely distributed need to be developed more carefully than products that are narrowly distributed. Products whose reliability is important need to be developed more carefully than products whose reliability doesn't much matter. Figure 6-1 illustrates some of the variations in distribution and reliability.

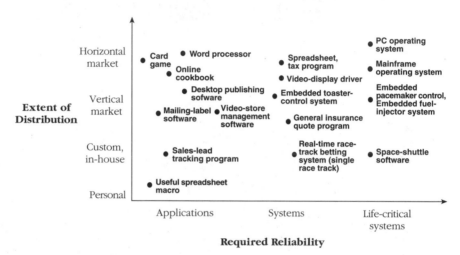

Figure 6-1. *Different kinds of software require different kinds of solutions. Practices that would be considered to be quick and dirty for an embedded heart-pacemaker control might be overly rigorous for an online cookbook.*

CROSS-REFERENCE
For more on customizing software processes to the needs of specific projects, see Section 2.4, "Which Dimension Matters the Most?"

The specific entries in the grid are intended to serve only as illustrations. You could argue about whether a video-display driver or a tax program needs to be more reliable or whether desktop-publishing software or spreadsheet programs are more widely distributed. The point is that both the extent of distribution and the required reliability vary greatly among different kinds of software. A software failure can cause a loss of time, work, money, or human life. Some schedule-oriented development practices that are perfectly acceptable when only time is at stake would be unconscionably reckless when human life is at stake.

On the other hand, practices that would be considered quick and dirty in a life-critical system might be overly rigorous for a custom business-software application. Rapid development of limited-distribution custom software could conceivably consist of what we think of as "workarounds" in more widely distributed software. Glue together some pieces that solve today's problem today, not tomorrow. Tomorrow might be too late—a late solution might be worthless.

As a result of this tremendous variation in development objectives, it's impossible to say, "Here's the rapid-development solution for you" without knowing your specific circumstances. The right solution for you depends on where you would place yourself on Figure 6-1's grid. Many products don't fit neatly into the grid's categories, and products vary in many ways other than degree of reliability and extent of distribution. That means that most people will need to customize a solution for their situation. As Figure 6-2 suggests, one size does not fit all.

Figure 6-2. *One size does not fit all.*

6.2   What Kind of Rapid Development Do You Need?

The most central issue to the topic of rapid development is determining what kind of rapid development you need. Do you need a slight speed edge, more predictability, better progress visibility, lower costs, or more speed at all costs?

One of the most surprising things I've discovered while doing the background research for this book is that many people who initially say they need faster development find that what they really need is lower cost or more predictability—or simply a way to avoid a catastrophic failure.

You can ask several questions to help determine what kind of rapid development you need:

- How strong is the product's schedule constraint?
- Does the project's emphasis on schedule arise because it is really one of the common "rapid-development look-alikes"?
- Is your project limited by any weaknesses that would prevent a rapid-development success?

The following sections describe how to answer these questions.

Products with Strong Schedule Constraints

Products that truly need to focus on all-out development speed rather than cost or predictability have a different time-value curve than typical products have. As the value line for a typical product in Figure 6-3 shows, the value of a typical product declines gradually as time goes by. But with a product that has a strong schedule constraint, there is a point at which the value of the product declines precipitously.

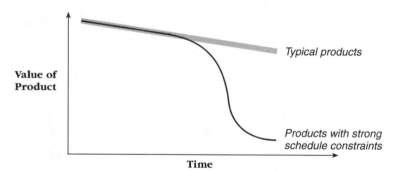

Figure 6-3. *Depiction of value over time for typical products and products with strong schedule constraints. There isn't as much urgency to complete a typical product by any particular date as there is for a product that has a strong schedule constraint.*

For a typical product, efficient development usually provides the best combination of development cost and schedule performance. But maybe your product must be ready in time for the Christmas sales season or you'll have to wait another year. Maybe you need to make a payroll-system change in time to comply with a new tax law. Maybe your company is about to go under financially, and you need the revenue from the product to save the company. Or maybe you need to leapfrog a competitive product, and you stand to double your revenue if you can beat your competitor to market by 6 weeks instead of releasing your product 2 weeks after they do.

As the graph suggests, on these projects there may be a point by which, if you haven't released your product, you might as well not have developed it at all. In these cases, a focus on all-out development speed can be appropriate.

Rapid-Development Look-Alikes

In some instances the demand for "rapid development" comes via a circuitous path from users or customers or upper management. They can apply an incredible amount of pressure to get a product done fast, but sometimes they really want lower cost or less risk instead. They just don't know how to ask for those things—or don't know that those things do not go hand in hand with all-out development speed.

Before you orient your project toward the shortest schedule rather than the least cost, lowest risk, or best functionality, find out what's really needed. Several rapid-development look-alikes appear to call for all-out development speed but really call for something else; these are discussed in the following subsections.

Runaway prevention. If the software organization has a history of overshooting its planned schedules and budgets, the customer might ask for "rapid development." But in this case, what the customer really wants is assurance that the project will be completed close to its target schedule and budget.

You can distinguish this rapid-development look-alike from a need for all-out development speed either by realizing that there's no specific schedule goal other than "as soon as possible" or, if there is a specific goal, by finding that no one can explain why it matters. A history of runaway projects can be another tip-off. The solution in this case is not the use of schedule-oriented practices but rather the use of better risk management, project estimation, and management control.

Predictability. In many instances, customers want to coordinate the software-development part of a project with revenue projections, marketing, personnel planning, and other software projects. Although they might call for "rapid development," they're really calling for predictability good enough to let them coordinate related efforts. If your customers emphasize the need to complete the software "on time" and don't have an external constraint such as a trade show, they are probably more concerned about predictability than out-and-out development speed. In that case, focus on efficient development, and emphasize practices that reduce schedule risk.

Lowest cost. It isn't uncommon for customers to want to minimize the cost of a software-development project. In such cases, they will talk about getting the software done quickly, but they will emphasize their budget concerns more than their schedule concerns.

CROSS-REFERENCE
For more on schedule compression, see "Costs increase rapidly when you shorten the schedule below nominal" in Section 8.6.

If the customers' primary concern is the cost of a project, a focus on development schedule is particularly unfortunate. Although it's logical to assume that the shortest development schedule is also the cheapest, in actuality the practices that minimize cost and schedule are different. Lengthening the schedule somewhat beyond the nominal schedule and shrinking the team size can actually reduce the total cost of a project. Some rapid-development practices increase the total cost.

Fixed drop-dead date. As shown in Figure 6-3, sometimes the value of a product declines steadily over time, and sometimes it declines precipitously after a certain point. If there is a point at which it declines precipitously, it seems logical to say that: "We need all-out development speed so that we can be sure to release the product by that point."

But whether you need rapid development really depends on how much time you have to do the project and how much time it would take to develop the project using efficient-development methods. Figure 6-4 shows two possibilities.

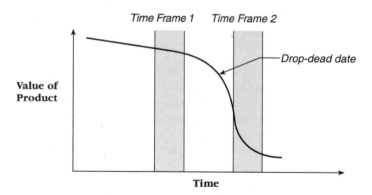

Figure 6-4. *Whether you need to use rapid-development practices depends on how soon you need the software. If you can develop it in Time Frame 1 by using efficient-development practices, you should do that and keep risks low instead of focusing on speed-oriented practices that can increase risk.*

If you can complete the project in Time Frame 1 (before the drop-dead date) by using efficient-development practices, then do that—and focus on risk-reduction rather than development speed. That will provide the greatest likelihood of completing the project on time. Some rapid-development practices reduce development time but also increase schedule uncertainty, and it would be a mistake to use practices that increase schedule risk in this situation.

If efficient-development practices alone aren't capable of completing the project before the drop-dead date—for example if they are capable only of completing the project in Time Frame 2—then you'll need to use speed-oriented practices to have any chance of completing the project on time.

Desire for free overtime. In a few instances, the customer's (or manager's) interest in rapid development masks a desire to improve rapid development's bottom line by eking out as much unpaid overtime as possible. The sense of urgency created by an ambitious schedule helps to do that.

This look-alike is easy to distinguish from true rapid development because the customer will stress the importance of the schedule and simultaneously refuse to provide the support needed to improve development speed through any means other than unpaid overtime. The customer won't kick in for more developers, improved hardware tools, improved software tools, or other kinds of support. The customer won't be willing to make feature-set trade-offs to achieve schedule goals. On a true rapid-development project, the customer will be eager to consider any and all means of shortening the schedule.

FURTHER READING
For additional moral support in this situation, see "Spanish Theory Management" in *Peopleware* (DeMarco and Lister 1987).

If meeting the project's schedule is important enough to put pressure on you, it is important enough for the customer to increase the level of support for the project. If the company asks its developers to work harder, it must be willing to work harder, too. If you find yourself in a situation in which your customer is simply trying to get your team to work for free, there is probably almost nothing that you can do to improve it. Customers who practice this style of software development do not have your best interests in mind. Your most sensible options are to refuse to work on such projects or to change jobs.

So, Is All-Out Rapid Development Really What You Need?

It's a fact of life that customers—including end-users, marketers, managers, and others—will always clamor for new features and new releases. But customers are also aware of the disruption that a product upgrade can cause. Be aware that customers expect you to balance product, cost, and schedule for them. Of course, they will request that you provide a great product at low cost on a short schedule, but you usually get to pick only two out of these three desires. Releasing a low-quality product on a short schedule is usually the wrong combination. If you release a low-quality product on time, people will remember that it was low-quality—not that it was on time. If you release a late product that knocks their socks off, your customers will remember that you released a knockout product; in retrospect, the late delivery won't matter as much as it seems to now.

To determine whether customer requests justify an all-out rapid-development effort, try to determine whether the value line of your product looks more like the typical product or like products with strong schedule constraint shown in Figure 6-3. Find out whether an external date is driving the schedule or whether the date is really just "as soon as possible." Finally, find out whether top management will provide the level of support you'll need for a rapid-development effort. There's little point in going all out if you have to do it on your own.

If you're not sure that development speed occupies top priority, take your time and develop software you can be proud of. Develop a program that's worth waiting for; high-quality products are harder to compete with than are quickly delivered mediocre products.

CROSS-REFERENCE
For more on the development of Word for Windows, see "An Example of Overly Optimistic Scheduling" in Section 9.1.

The history of the microcomputer software industry is replete with examples of products that were delivered late but went on to achieve immense popularity. The development of Microsoft Word for Windows 1.0 was originally scheduled to take one year and took five (Iansiti 1994). Microsoft Windows 95 was delivered $1^1/_2$ years later than originally announced (Cusumano and Selby 1995) and became one of the fastest-selling products in software history. One financial product that I worked on was delivered 50 percent later than originally scheduled by its company but went on to become the most popular software product in that company's 25-year history. For each of these products, timely release (as originally defined) was not a key factor, even though everyone thought that the development schedule was critically important at the time.

6.3 Odds of Completing on Time

Many projects are perceived to be slow; however, not all projects are slow in the same way. Some development efforts really are slow, and others merely appear slow because of unreachable effort estimates.

One view of software-project estimation holds that every project has one exact time at which it should be completed. This view holds that if the project is run well, there is a 100-percent chance that it will be completed on a particular date. Figure 6-5 shows a graphical representation of that view.

Most developers' experience doesn't support this view. Many unknowns contribute to software schedules. Circumstances change. Developers learn more about the product they are building as they build it. Some practices work better than expected, others worse.

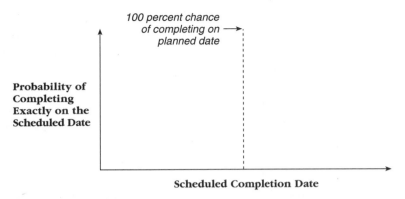

Figure 6-5. *One view of software scheduling. The project is thought to have a 100-percent chance of being completed on a specific date.*

Software projects contain too many variables to be able to set schedules with 100-percent accuracy. Far from having one particular date when a project would finish, for any given project there is a range of completion dates, of which some are more likely and some are less. The probability distribution of that range of dates looks like the curve shown in Figure 6-6.

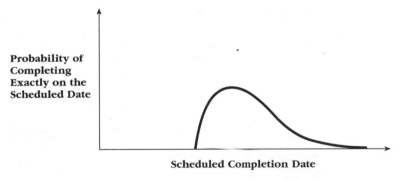

Figure 6-6. *The shape of a software schedule. Because of the unknowns that feed into a software project's schedule, some completion dates are more likely and some are less, but none are certain.*

CROSS-REFERENCE
For more on the shortest possible schedules, see "Shortest Possible Schedules" in Section 8.6.

The shape of this probability curve expresses several assumptions. One is that there is an absolute limit on how quickly you can complete any particular project. Completion in a shorter amount of time isn't just difficult; it's impossible. Another assumption is that the shape of the curve on the "early" side isn't the same as the shape on the "late" side. Even though there is a sharp limit to how quickly you can complete a project, there is no sharp limit to how slowly you can complete one. Since there are more ways to make a project late than there are to make it early, the slope of the curve on the late side is more gradual than it is on the early side.

Tom DeMarco proposed that projects should be scheduled so that the probability of coming in early would be the same as the probability of coming in late (DeMarco 1982). In other words, set the schedule for the project so that you have a 50/50 chance of completing on time, as shown in Figure 6-7.

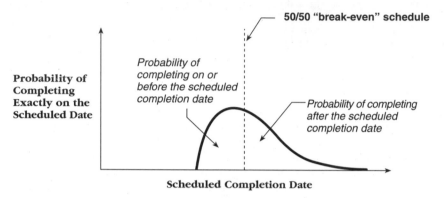

Figure 6-7. *Planning a break-even schedule. There is a limit to how quickly you can complete a project, but no hard limit to how long a project can take. This schedule provides a 50/50 chance of completing on time.*

DeMarco's break-even scheduling strategy is a useful starting point for gaining insight into the nature of slow development. You can start by dividing the probability graph into several zones, each representing a different development speed, as shown in Figure 6-8.

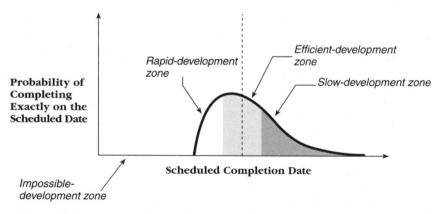

Figure 6-8. *The planning zones of a schedule curve. Many projects aim for the impossible-development zone (without knowing that it's impossible) and finish in the slow-development zone (without intending to).*

The area on the far left side of the graph is the "impossible-development zone." This zone represents a level of productivity that no project has ever achieved. Projects that are scheduled in this zone are guaranteed to overrun their planned schedules.

The area on the left side of the curve is the "rapid-development zone." A project that is completed in this zone is considered to be rapid because it had less than a 50-percent chance of being completed in the scheduled time. A development team that completes a project in this zone has beaten the odds.

The area in the middle of the curve is the "efficient-development zone." A project that is completed in this zone is considered to be efficient because it has neither beaten the odds nor been beaten by them. Most likely, the project has come in close to its estimated completion date. Effective software-development organizations consistently schedule and complete their projects in this zone, which represents a good combination of schedule and cost.

The area on the right side of the curve is the "slow-development zone." A project that is completed in this zone is considered to be slow because it actually had a better than 50-percent chance of coming in earlier. As far as the schedule is concerned, a project that has finished in this zone without intending to has blown it. Success at 50/50 scheduling depends both on accurate estimation and on getting an accurate estimate accepted, topics discussed in detail in Chapters 8 and 9.

6.4   Perception and Reality

Suppose that six months from now you plan to move to a new town 100 miles away and build a new house. You arrange with Honest Abe's Construction Company to construct the house for you. You agree to pay Abe $100,000, and Abe agrees to have the house ready in six months so that you can move into it when you move to town. You've already bought the site, and Abe agrees that it's suitable. So you shake hands, pay him half the money as a down payment, and wait for your house.

After a few weeks, you get curious about how work on the house is going, so one weekend you drive the 100 miles to the site to take a look at it. To your surprise, all you see at the site is an area where the dirt has been leveled. No foundation, no framing, no other work at all. You call Honest Abe and ask, "How's the work on my house going?" Abe says, "We're getting kind of a slow start because of another house that we've been finishing. I built some slack into my estimate for your house, though, so there's nothing to worry about."

Your job gets busy again, and by the time you have a chance to look at your house's progress again, three months have passed. You drive to the site again, and this time the foundation has been poured, but no other work is visible. You call the contractor, who says, "No problem. We're right on schedule." You're still nervous, but you decide to take Abe's word for it.

The fourth and fifth months go by. You call Abe a few times to check on progress, and each time he says it's going great. At the beginning of the sixth month, you decide to drive to look at the house one more time before it's finished. You're excited to see it. But when you get to the site, the only thing you see is the frame for the house. There's no roofing, siding, plumbing, wiring, heating, or cooling. You're nervous and tense, and you decide to check some of Honest Abe's references. You find that once in a while Abe has managed to complete a house when promised, but most of the time his houses are anywhere from 25 percent to 100 percent late. You're irate. "We're five months into a six-month schedule, and you hardly have anything done," you growl at him. "When am I going to get my house? I need to move into it a month from now." Abe says, "My crew is working as hard as possible. You'll get your house on time. Trust me."

Do you decide to trust Abe? Of course not! Not with his track record and the progress you've seen so far.

Yet in similar cycles in software development—with similar time frames and even larger amounts of money—we expect our customers to want less in the way of signs of progress than we would expect from someone building a house for us. We expect them to sign off on a set of requirements and then just sit tight for weeks or months or even years before we have anything tangible to show them. No wonder customers get nervous! No wonder customers think that software development takes a long time!

Even if you're completely on schedule, be aware that the perception of slow development can affect your project as much as the reality. Even though we do it all the time, it's unreasonable to expect customers to sit tight for months on end, and it's part of our job to provide them with steady signs of progress.

Unrealistic Customer Expectations

CROSS-REFERENCE
For details on problems associated with unrealistic schedules, see Section 9.1, "Overly Optimistic Scheduling."

Sometimes overcoming the perception of slow development requires more than providing steady signs of progress. Most of today's projects are scheduled in the rapid or impossible zones. Most projects lack the planning and resource commitments needed to meet their aggressive schedules. The project planners often do not even realize just how ambitious their schedules are, and, as Figure 6-9 suggests, they are usually completed in the slow zone.

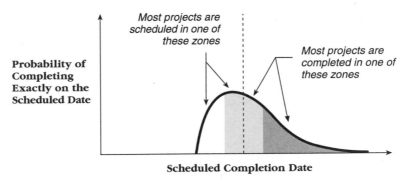

Probability of
Completing
Exactly on the
Scheduled Date

Most projects are
scheduled in one of
these zones

Most projects are
completed in one of
these zones

Scheduled Completion Date

Figure 6-9. *Typical planning in relation to the software-schedule curve. Because of unrealistic expectations, most projects will be perceived as slow even if they are completed in the efficient or rapid zones.*

The gap between the scheduled completion date and the actual completion date accounts for much of the perception that software projects are slow. If the average project is scheduled in the impossible zone but staffed and completed in the efficient zone, people will consider it to have failed even though its developers have completed it efficiently and might actually have completed it as quickly as possible given the resources provided.

Overcoming the Perception of Slow Development

In general terms, you can overcome the problem of slow development in either of two ways:

- *Address the reality of slow development.* Make the actual schedules shorter by moving from slow development to efficient development or by moving from efficient development to rapid development.

- *Address the perception of slow development.* Eliminate wishful thinking, and make planned schedules more realistic by lengthening them to close the gap between planned and actual completion dates. Use practices that highlight progress visibility. Sometimes customers don't want increased development speed as much as they just want you to keep them informed.

The development speed zone you're in currently will determine whether you should focus on slow development itself or on the perception of slow development. Most often, you'll need to address the problem on both levels.

6.5 Where the Time Goes

CROSS-REFERENCE
For details on figuring out where the time goes on your own projects, see Chapter 26, "Measurement."

One strategy for achieving rapid development is to determine the area in which most of the time is spent on a typical project and then try to reduce that time. You can shrink some areas more readily than others, and attempting to reduce some areas can inadvertently lengthen the schedule.

You can view time on a software project from many angles, and the different views produce different insights into where the time goes. The next subsection presents the classic (phase-by-phase) view, and the subsections after that present other views.

The Classic View

Most projects start out in an ill-defined, pre-requirements phase that can last for quite a long time. At some point, requirements gathering starts in earnest, and at some point after that, software development officially begins. The post-requirements activities tend to be the better defined part of the project. Table 6-1 provides a rough idea of where the time is spent on post-requirements activities on efficiently run small and large projects.

Table 6-1. Approximate Activity Breakdown by Size of Project

Activity	Small Project (2,500 lines of code)	Large Project (500,000 lines of code)
Architecture/design	10%	30%
Detailed design	20%	20%
Code/debug	25%	10%
Unit test	20%	5%
Integration	15%	20%
System test	10%	15%

Source: Adapted from *Code Complete* (McConnell 1993).

The most time-expensive activities of a small project are the construction activities of detailed design, code/debug, and unit test. If you were able to magically eliminate them, you could cut your project's effort by 65 percent. On a large project, construction activities take up less of the total effort. Magically eliminating them would reduce your project's effort by only about 35 percent.

HARD DATA

Most of us have learned through hard experience not to arbitrarily abbreviate the upstream activities of architecture and design. Cutting design time by 5 percent might seem as though it would reduce the development schedule by 5 percent, but what is more likely to happen is that any time saved by shortchanging design will be paid back with interest during the later stages of the project. (Actually, the amount you'll pay back will seem more like usury than interest.) Put another way, a design defect that takes an hour-and-a-half to fix at design time will take anywhere from two days to a month to fix if it isn't detected until system testing (Fagan 1976).

A more effective strategy than trying to abbreviate the earlier stages arbitrarily is to perform them as efficiently as possible or to pick practices that require less design. (An example would be using a code library for part of the system.) You're more likely to reduce total development time by spending more time in upstream activities, not less.

Soft Spots

HARD DATA

After surveying more than 4000 projects, Capers Jones reported that the software industry on the whole is probably about 35 percent efficient (Jones 1994). The other 65 percent of the time is spent on harmful or unproductive activities such as use of productivity tools that don't work, repair of carelessly developed modules, work lost because of lack of configuration control, and so on. Where might time be saved? The next few subsections describe some of those areas.

CROSS-REFERENCE
For more on the importance of avoiding rework, see Section 4.3, "Quality-Assurance Fundamentals."

Rework. Reworking defective requirements, design, and code typically consumes 40 to 50 percent of the total cost of software development (Jones 1986b; Boehm 1987a). Correcting defects early, when they're cheapest to correct and when such corrections preempt later rework, represents a powerful opportunity to shorten your projects.

CROSS-REFERENCE
For more on feature creep, see Section 14.2, "Mid-Project: Feature-Creep Control."

Feature creep. Feature creep can arise from requirements changes or developer gold-plating. The typical project experiences about a 25-percent change in requirements throughout its development, which adds more than 25-percent effort to the project (Boehm 1981, Jones 1994). Failing to limit changes to those that are absolutely essential is a classic development-speed mistake, and eliminating feature creep goes a long way toward eliminating schedule overruns.

CROSS-REFERENCE
For more on requirements analysis, see Section 14.1, "Early Project: Feature-Set Reduction."

Requirements specification. An activity that isn't shown in Table 6-1 is requirements specification. Whereas the activities listed in Table 6-1 are concerned with specifying the solution to a problem, requirements specification is concerned with specifying the problem itself. It is more open-ended than other development activities, and the amount of time you spend gathering requirements doesn't bear any particular relationship to the total time you'll spend building the program. You could spend 12 months amassing requirements for a system that will take 36 months to build. Or you could spend the same 12 months mediating among several groups to define a system that will ultimately take only 6 months to build. Typically, requirements specification takes between 10 percent and 30 percent of the elapsed time on a project (Boehm 1981).

Because requirements gathering is such an open-ended activity, it's possible to burn huge amounts of time unnecessarily. A moderate sense of urgency during requirements gathering can help to prevent a full-scale sense of panic at the end of a project.

Rapid-development practices that have been developed to combat wasted time during requirements specification include Joint Application Development (JAD), evolutionary prototyping, staged releases, and various risk management approaches. These practices are described elsewhere in this book.

CLASSIC MISTAKE

The "fuzzy front end." Another kind of activity that isn't described in Table 6-1 is the "fuzzy front end." The total time needed to develop a software product extends from the point at which the product is just a glimmer in someone's eye to the point at which the working software is put into the customer's hands. At some time after the software is a glimmer in someone's eye, a "go" decision is made, and the software project officially commences. The time between the initial glimmer and the "go" decision can be a long time indeed. That "fuzzy front end" can consume much of the time available for getting a product to market. A typical pattern is described in Case Study 6-1.

Case Study 6-1. Wandering in the Fuzzy Front End

Bill is a manager at Giga Safe Insurance Company. Here are the notes he took about the approval process for Giga-Quote 1.0, an insurance quote program:

October 1. We want to develop a new quote program for our field agents. We want the program to upload the day's quotes to the head office each night. It will take about 12 months to complete its development, so we can't get it done in time for this January's rate increase, but we should be able to get it done for the rate increase after that (15 months from now). We should aim to complete it by November 1 (13 months from now) so that we have time

(continued)

Case Study 6-1. Wandering in the Fuzzy Front End, *continued*

to train the field agents before the new rates go into effect. I'll propose the project at the executive committee meeting at the end of the month.

January 2. The Giga-Quote proposal got bumped off the executive committee agenda two months in a row. I finally brought it up at the end of December and got the approval to draw up a business-case analysis.

February 1. Business-case analysis is complete; it just needs to be reviewed.

March 1. Two key sales managers are on vacation. The business-case analysis can't be approved until they've reviewed it.

April 15. All reviews are complete, and the project is a "go." The executive committee still wants the project completed by November 1, though, so the team had better start coding now.

Because no formal management controls are in place—no schedule, no budget, no goals, and no objectives—progress during this period can be hard to track. Moreover, managers tend to give this phase a low priority because the financial impact is distant. You can lose time during the front end in several ways:

- No one has been assigned responsibility for the product's development.
- No sense of urgency exists for making a go/no-go decision about developing the product.
- No mechanism exists to keep the product from slipping into dormancy.
- No mechanism exists to revive the product once it has slipped into dormancy.
- Key aspects of the product's viability—technical feasibility and market appeal—can't be explored until the product receives budget approval.
- The product must wait for an annual product-approval cycle or budgeting cycle before it can receive budget approval.
- The team that develops the product isn't built from the team that worked for the product's approval. Time and momentum are lost assembling the development team, familiarizing it with the product, and handing off the product to it.

FURTHER READING
For more on the fuzzy front end, see *Developing Products in Half the Time* (Smith and Reinertsen 1991).

The effort expended in the front end of a project is usually low, but the cost resulting from delayed time-to-market can be high. The only way to recapture a month wasted on the front end is to shorten the product-development cycle by a month on the back end. Shortening the full-scale development effort by a month costs far more than shortening the front end by the same amount. The front end presents one of the cheapest and most effective rapid-development opportunities available.

6.6 Development-Speed Trade-Offs

> With rare exceptions, initial resource estimates and schedules are unacceptable. This is not because the programmers are unresponsive, but because the users generally want more than they can afford. If the job doesn't fit the available schedule and resources, it must either be pared down or the time and resources increased.
>
> *Watts Humphrey*

One of the philosophies undergirding this book is that it is better to make trade-off decisions with your eyes open than closed. If development speed is truly your top priority, then go ahead and increase the cost of the project and compromise the product's feature set in order to deliver it on time. But understand the implications of the decisions you make. Don't close your eyes and hope that somehow you'll be able to optimize your project for schedule, cost, and features all at the same time. You won't. Instead, you'll end up optimizing it for none of them; you'll waste time and money and deliver a product with less functionality than you otherwise could have.

Schedule, Cost, and Product Trade-Offs

A trade-off triangle with schedule, cost, and quality at its corners is a general management fundamental. In software, however, having a "quality" corner on a trade-off triangle doesn't make much sense. A focus on some kinds of quality reduces cost and schedule, and on other kinds increases them. In the software arena, a better way to think of trade-offs is among schedule, cost, and *product*. The product corner includes quality and all other product-related attributes including features, complexity, usability, modifiability, maintainability, defect rate, and so on. Figure 6-10 illustrates the software trade-off triangle.

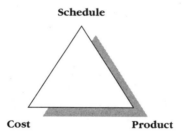

Schedule

Cost   **Product**

Figure 6-10. *Software trade-off triangle. You have to keep schedule, cost, and product in balance for the project to succeed.*

To keep the triangle balanced, you have to balance schedule, cost, and product. If you want to load up the product corner of the triangle, you also have to load up cost or schedule or both. The same goes for the other combinations. If you want to change one of the corners of the triangle, you have to change at least one of the others to keep it in balance.

To help me think about which option to manipulate, during planning discussions I like to visualize a large cardboard triangle with the corners labeled "schedule," "cost," and "product." The customers hold the corner or corners that they want to control. Our job as software developers is to let customers show us which corners they are holding and then to tell them what has to be done to balance the triangle. If a customer is holding the "product" and "cost" corners, we tell them what the "schedule" corner has to be. If they are holding only the "product" corner, we can give them a variety of cost-and-schedule combinations. But we developers absolutely must have at least one corner to hold on to. If your customer won't give you a corner of the triangle, you usually can't do the project.

CLASSIC MISTAKE

CROSS-REFERENCE
For more on negotiating in difficult environments, see Section 9.2, "Beating Schedule Pressure."

Jim McCarthy reports that in informal polling he has found that about 30 to 40 percent of all development projects suffer from simultaneously dictated features, resources, and schedules (McCarthy 1995a). If schedule, cost, and product aren't initially in balance—and they rarely are—that suggests that 30 to 40 percent of all development projects start out with no ability to balance their project characteristics for success. When a customer hands you a product definition, a fixed cost, and a fixed schedule, they are usually trying to put a 10-pound product into a 5-pound sack. You can try to force the 10-pounder into the sack, stretch the sack, and tear the sack, but in the end all you'll do is wear yourself out—because it just won't fit. And you'll still have to decide whether you want to get a bigger sack or put less into the sack you have.

Quality Trade-Offs

CROSS-REFERENCE
For details on the relationship between defect rate and development time, see Section 4.3, "Quality-Assurance Fundamentals."

Software products have two kinds of quality, which affect the schedule in different ways. One kind of quality is a low defect rate. To a point, low defects and short development times go together, so there is no way to trade off that kind of quality for schedule. The road to the shortest possible schedule lies in getting the product right the first time so that you don't waste time reworking design and code.

CROSS-REFERENCE
For details on how to use this kind of quality to reduce development time, see Chapter 14, "Feature-Set Control."

The other kind of quality includes all the other characteristics that you think of when you think of a high-quality software product—usability, efficiency, robustness, and so on. Attention to this kind of quality lengthens the development schedule, so there is an opportunity for trading off this kind of quality against the schedule.

Per-Person–Efficiency Trade-Off

Is there a conflict between trying to achieve the greatest per-person productivity and the greatest schedule efficiency? Yes, there is. The easiest way to maximize per-person productivity is to keep the team size small. One of the easiest ways to shorten a software schedule is to increase team size, which increases total productivity but usually makes each person less efficient. Rapid development isn't always efficient.

6.7 Typical Schedule-Improvement Pattern

Organizations that try to improve their development speed by moving toward efficient development follow a predictable pattern. If you take 100 typical projects, you'd find that their chances of coming in on time would look like Figure 6-11.

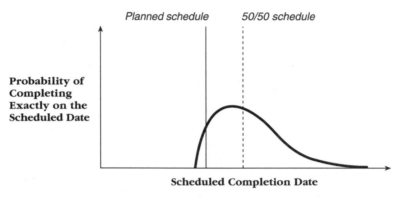

Figure 6-11. *Typical-development schedule curve. Typical projects make schedule plans that they have almost no chance of meeting.*

Among typical projects, the spread of project performance is wide, and many of the projects have severe overruns. Look at how much of the curve in Figure 6-11 is to the right of the planned-schedule line on typical projects. Few typical projects come anywhere close to meeting their cost or schedule goals.

FURTHER READING
For a similar discussion, see "Capability Maturity Model for Software, Version 1.1" (Paulk et al. 1993).

As Figure 6-12 shows, among efficient-development projects, the schedule spread is narrower, with most projects coming in close to their cost and schedule targets. About half the projects finish earlier than the target date, and about half finish later. The planned schedules are longer than they are in typical development, but the actual schedules are shorter. This is partly a result of learning how to set targets more realistically and partly a result of learning how to develop software faster. The move from wishful thinking to meaningful project planning is a big part of what it takes to move from typical development to efficient development.

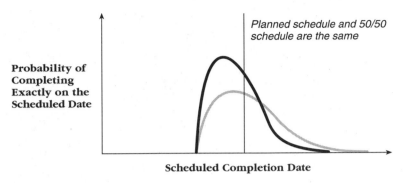

Figure 6-12. *Efficient-development schedule curve. Planned schedules in efficient projects are longer than planned schedules in typical projects, but actual schedules are shorter.*

Once you've achieved efficient development, the improvement pattern depends on whether you want to improve raw development speed or schedule predictability or both. Ideally, you could employ practices that would give you the tall, skinny curve shown in Figure 6-13.

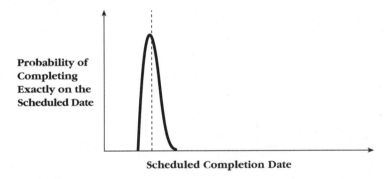

Figure 6-13. *Ideal rapid-development schedule curve. If every single thing goes as planned, the result is great speed and predictability.*

Unfortunately for all of us, the ideal curve in Figure 6-13 is as elusive in software development as it is in fad dieting. As shown in Figure 6-14, that means that most rapid-development practices are tilted either toward increasing development speed or reducing schedule risk, but not both.

129

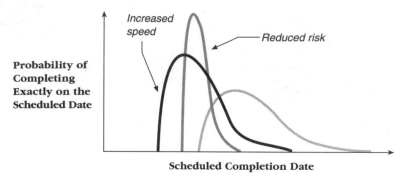

Figure 6-14. *Scheduling options. Rapid development can focus on either increasing development speed or reducing schedule-related risks.*

When you choose rapid-development practices, you need to decide whether you would rather improve the chance of delivering a product earlier or reduce the risk that the product will slip past a certain date. The rest of the book describes such practices.

6.8   Onward to Rapid Development

The remaining chapters in this part of the book describe approaches that contribute to rapid development. Here are the practices:

- Lifecycle Planning
- Estimation
- Scheduling
- Customer-Oriented Development
- Motivation
- Teamwork
- Team Structure
- Feature-Set Control
- Productivity Tools
- Project Recovery

Some of these topics could be considered as part of what I have described as "development fundamentals" or "efficient development." Because these approaches are critical to achieving maximum development speed, though, they are discussed in this part of the book.

Further Reading

DeMarco, Tom. *Controlling Software Projects.* New York: Yourdon Press, 1982. This book contains much of the inspiration for this chapter's discussion of the shape of software schedules. DeMarco paints a humorous and sometimes painfully vivid picture of current estimating practices—which as far as I can tell haven't changed since he published his book in 1982. He lays out one approach for improving estimation and scheduling.

Martin, James. *Rapid Application Development.* New York: Macmillan Publishing Company, 1991. This book presents a different perspective on the core issues of rapid development for IS applications.

Smith, P.G., and D.G. Reinertsen. *Developing Products in Half the Time.* New York: Van Nostrand Reinhold, 1991. Although not about software development specifically, this book contains many insights that relate to developing software products more rapidly. Chapter 3 contains a full discussion of the "fuzzy front end."

7

Lifecycle Planning

Contents

Related Topics

EVERY SOFTWARE-DEVELOPMENT EFFORT goes through a "lifecycle," which consists of all the activities between the time that version 1.0 of a system begins life as a gleam in someone's eye and the time that version 6.74b finally takes its last breath on the last customer's machine. A lifecycle model is a prescriptive model of what should happen between first glimmer and last breath.

For our purposes, the main function of a lifecycle model is to establish the order in which a project specifies, prototypes, designs, implements, reviews, tests, and performs its other activities. It establishes the criteria that you use to determine whether to proceed from one task to the next. This chapter focuses on a limited part of the full lifecycle, *the period between the first glimmer and initial release*. You can direct this focus either to new product development or to maintenance updates of existing software.

The most familiar lifecycle model is the well-known waterfall lifecycle model, which has some equally well-known weaknesses. Other lifecycle models are available, and in many cases they are better choices for rapid development than the waterfall model is. (The waterfall model is described in the next section, "Pure Waterfall.")

By defining the master plan for the project, the lifecycle model you choose has as much influence over your project's success as any other planning decision you make. The appropriate lifecycle model can streamline your project and help ensure that each step moves you closer to your goal. Depending on the lifecycle model you choose, you can improve development speed, improve quality, improve project tracking and control, minimize overhead, minimize risk exposure, or improve client relations. The wrong lifecycle model can be a constant source of slow work, repeated work, unnecessary work, and frustration. Not choosing a lifecycle model can produce the same effects.

Many lifecycle models are available. In the next several sections, I'll describe the models; and in the final section, I'll describe how to pick the one that will work best for your project.

Case Study 7-1. Ineffective Lifecycle Model Selection

The field agents at Giga-Safe were clamoring for an update to Giga-Quote 1.0, both to correct defects and to fix some annoying user-interface glitches. Bill had been reinstated as the project manager for Giga-Quote 1.1 after being removed at the end of Giga-Quote 1.0, and he brought in Randy for some advice. Randy was a high-priced consultant he had met at a sports bar.

"Here's what you should do," Randy said. "You had a lot of schedule problems last time, so this time you need to organize your project for all-out development speed. Prototyping is the fastest approach, so have your team use that." Bill thought that sounded good, so when he met with the team later that day, he told them to use prototyping.

Mike was the technical lead on the project, and he was surprised. "Bill, I don't follow your reasoning," he said. "We've got 6 weeks to fix a bunch of bugs and make some minor changes to the UI. What do you want a prototype for?"

"We need a prototype to speed up the project," Bill said testily. "Prototyping is the newest, fastest approach, and that's what I want you to use. Is there some kind of problem with that?"

(continued)

Touchy subject, Mike thought. "OK," he said. "We'll develop a prototype, if that's what you want."

Mike and another developer, Sue, went to work on the prototype. Since it was almost identical to their current system, it took only a few days to mock up the whole system.

At the beginning of week 2, they showed the prototype to the field-agents' manager, A.J. "Hell, I can't tell my agents this is all they're getting!" A.J. exclaimed. "It hardly does any more than the program does now! My agents are wailing about how they need something *better*. I've got some ideas for some new reports. Here, I'll show you." Mike and Sue listened patiently, and after the meeting Mike got together with Bill.

"We showed A.J. the prototype. He wants to add some new reports, and he won't take no for an answer. But we've got our hands full with the work we're already supposed to be doing."

"I don't see the problem," Bill said. "He's the field agents' manager. If he says they need some new reports, they need some new reports. You guys will just have to find a way to get them done in time."

"I'll try," Mike said. "But I have to tell you that there is only about a 1-percent chance that we'll finish on time if we add these reports."

"Well, you've got to do them," Bill said. "Maybe now that you're using prototyping, the work will go faster than you expect."

Two days later, A.J. stopped by Mike's cubicle. "I've been looking at that prototype, and I think we need to redesign some of the input screens too. I showed some of my agents your prototype yesterday at our monthly regional meeting. They said they'd call you with some more ideas. I gave them your phone number—I hope you don't mind. Keep up the good work!"

"Thanks," Mike said and slid down into his chair. Later, Mike asked Bill if he would try to talk A.J. out of the changes, but Bill said, "No."

The next day, Mike got phone calls from two agents who had been at the regional meeting. They both wanted more changes to the system. For the next couple of weeks, he got calls every day, and the list of changes piled up.

At the 4-week mark of their 6-week project, Mike and Sue estimated that they had received 6 months' worth of changes that they were supposed to have done in 2 weeks. Mike met with Bill again. "I'm disappointed in you," Bill said. "I've promised A.J. and those field agents that you would make the changes they requested. You're not giving the prototyping approach a chance. Just wait until it kicks in."

(continued)

Case Study 7-1. Ineffective Lifecycle Model Selection, *continued*

It already has kicked in, Mike thought. And I'm the one getting kicked. But Bill was resolute.

At the 8-week mark, Bill started to complain that Mike and Sue weren't working hard enough. At the 10-week mark, Bill began dropping by their cubicles twice a day to check their progress. By the time they hit the 12-week mark, the agents were complaining, and Bill said, "We've got to get something out. Just release what you have now." Since neither the new reports nor the new input screens were completed, Mike and Sue simply stubbed out the code under development and released a version that consisted mainly of bug fixes and corrections to annoying UI glitches—roughly what they had planned to develop and release in the first place, but it took 12 weeks instead of 6.

7.1 Pure Waterfall

The granddaddy of all lifecycle models is the waterfall model. Although it has many problems, it serves as the basis for other, more effective lifecycle models, so it's presented first in this chapter. In the waterfall model, a project progresses through an orderly sequence of steps from the initial software concept through system testing. The project holds a review at the end of each phase to determine whether it is ready to advance to the next phase—for example, from requirements analysis to architectural design. If the review determines that the project isn't ready to move to the next phase, it stays in the current phase until it is ready.

The waterfall model is document driven, which means that the main work products that are carried from phase to phase are documents. In the pure waterfall model, the phases are also discontinuous—they do not overlap. Figure 7-1 shows how the pure waterfall lifecycle model progresses.

The pure waterfall model performs well for product cycles in which you have a stable product definition and when you're working with well-understood technical methodologies. In such cases, the waterfall model helps you to find errors in the early, low-cost stages of a project. It provides the requirements stability that developers crave. If you're building a well-defined maintenance release of an existing product or porting an existing product to a new platform, a waterfall lifecycle might be the right choice for rapid development.

The pure waterfall model helps to minimize planning overhead because you can do all the planning up front. It doesn't provide tangible results in the form of software until the end of the lifecycle, but, to someone who is familiar with it, the documentation it generates provides meaningful indications of progress throughout the lifecycle.

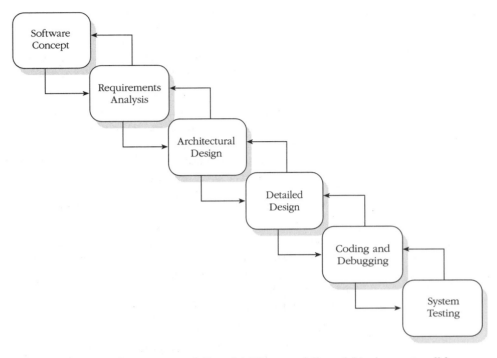

Figure 7-1. *The pure waterfall model. The waterfall model is the most well-known lifecycle model and provides good development speed in some circumstances. Other models, however, often provide greater development speed.*

The waterfall model works well for projects that are well understood but complex, because you can benefit from tackling complexity in an orderly way. It works well when quality requirements dominate cost and schedule requirements. Elimination of midstream changes eliminates a huge and common source of potential errors.

The waterfall model works especially well if you have a technically weak staff or an inexperienced staff because it provides the project with a structure that helps to minimize wasted effort.

The disadvantages of the pure waterfall model arise from the difficulty of fully specifying requirements at the beginning of the project, before any design work has been done and before any code has been written.

CROSS-REFERENCE
For details on problems with traditional specification methods, see "Problems with Traditional Specifications" in Section 14.1.

Developers complain about users who don't know what they want, but suppose the roles were reversed. Imagine trying to specify your car in detail to an automotive engineer. You tell the engineer that you want an engine, body, windows, steering wheel, accelerator pedal, brake pedal, emergency brake, seats, and so on. But can you remember to include everything that an automotive engineer will need to know to build your car?

Suppose you forget to specify that you need back-up lights that turn on when the car goes into reverse. The engineer goes away for 6 months and returns with a car with no back-up lights. You say, "Oh boy, I forgot to specify that the car needs back-up lights that turn on automatically when I shift into reverse."

The engineer goes ballistic. "Do you know what it's going to cost to take the car apart to connect wiring from the transmission to the rear of the car? We have to redesign the rear panel on the car, put in wiring for the brake lights, add another sensor to the transmission—this change will take weeks, if not months! Why didn't you tell me this in the first place?"

You grimace; it seemed like such a simple request...

Understandable mistake, right? A car is a complicated thing for an amateur to specify. A lot of software products are complicated too, and the people who are given the task of specifying software are often not computer experts. They can forget things that seem simple to them until they see the working product. If you're using a waterfall model, forgetting something can be a costly mistake. You don't find out until you get down to system testing that one of the requirements was missing or wrong.

Thus, the first major problem with the waterfall model is that it isn't flexible. You have to fully specify the requirements at the beginning of the project, which may be months or years before you have any working software. This flies in the face of modern business needs, in which the prize often goes to the developers who can implement the most functionality in the latest stage of the project. As Microsoft's Roger Sherman points out, the goal is often not to achieve what you said you would at the beginning of the project, but to achieve the maximum possible within the time and resources available (Sherman 1995).

Some people have criticized the waterfall model for not allowing you to back up to correct your mistakes. That's not quite right. As Figure 7-1 suggests, backing up is allowed, but it's difficult. A different view of the waterfall model that might put the matter into better perspective is the salmon lifecycle model, shown in Figure 7-2.

You're allowed to swim upstream, but the effort might kill you! At the end of architectural design, you participated in several major events that declared you were done with that phase. You held a design review, and you signed the official copy of the architecture document. If you discover a flaw in the architecture during coding and debugging, it's awkward to swim upstream and retrofit the architecture.

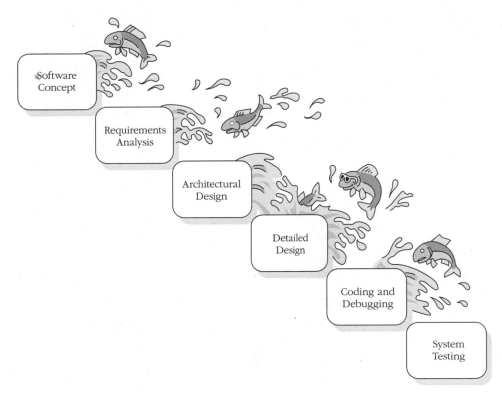

Figure 7-2. *Another depiction of the waterfall model—the salmon lifecycle model. It isn't impossible to back up using the waterfall model, just difficult.*

The waterfall lifecycle model has several other weaknesses. Some tools, methods, and activities span waterfall phases; those activities are difficult to accommodate in the waterfall model's disjoint phases. For a rapid-development project, the waterfall model can prescribe an excessive amount of documentation. If you're trying to retain flexibility, updating the specification can become a full-time job. The waterfall model generates few visible signs of progress until the very end. That can create the perception of slow development—even if it isn't true. Customers like to have tangible assurances that their projects will be delivered on time.

In summary, the venerable pure waterfall model's weaknesses often make it poorly suited for a rapid-development project. Even in the cases in which the pure waterfall model's strengths outweigh its weaknesses, modified waterfall models can work better.

7.2 Code-and-Fix

CROSS-REFERENCE
Code-and-fix is commonly combined with commitment-based development approaches. For details, see Section 2.5, "An Alternative Rapid-Development Strategy."

The code-and-fix model is a model that is seldom useful, but it is nonetheless common, so I'd like to discuss it. If you haven't explicitly chosen another lifecycle model, you're probably using code-and-fix by default. If you haven't done much project planning, you're undoubtedly using code-and-fix. Combined with a short schedule, code-and-fix gives rise to the code-like-hell approach described earlier.

When you use the code-and-fix model, you start with a general idea of what you want to build. You might have a formal specification, or you might not. You then use whatever combination of informal design, code, debug, and test methodologies suits you until you have a product that's ready to release. Figure 7-3 illustrates this process.

System Specification (maybe) → Code-and-Fix → Release (maybe)

Figure 7-3. *The code-and-fix model. Code-and-fix is an informal model that's in common use because it's simple, not because it works well.*

The code-and-fix model has two advantages. First, it has no overhead: you don't spend any time on planning, documentation, quality assurance, standards enforcement, or any activities other than pure coding. Since you jump right into coding, you can show signs of progress immediately. Second, it requires little expertise: anyone who has ever written a computer program is familiar with the code-and-fix model. Anyone can use it.

For tiny projects that you intend to throw away shortly after they're built, this model can be useful—for small proof-of-concept programs, for short-lived demos, or throwaway prototypes.

CLASSIC MISTAKE

For any kind of project other than a tiny project, this model is dangerous. It might have no overhead, but it also provides no means of assessing progress; you just code until you're done. It provides no means of assessing quality or identifying risks. If you discover three-quarters of the way through coding that your whole design approach is fundamentally flawed, you have no choice but to throw out your work and start over. Other models would set you up to detect such a fundamental mistake earlier, when it would have been less costly to fix.

In the end, this lifecycle model has no place on a rapid-development project, except for the small supporting roles indicated.

7.3 Spiral

At the other end of the sophistication scale from the code-and-fix model is the spiral model. The spiral model is a risk-oriented lifecycle model that breaks a software project up into miniprojects. Each miniproject addresses one or more major risks until all the major risks have been addressed. The concept of "risk" is broadly defined in this context, and it can refer to poorly understood requirements, poorly understood architecture, potential performance problems, problems in the underlying technology, and so on. After the major risks have all been addressed, the spiral model terminates as a waterfall lifecycle model would. Figure 7-4 on the next page illustrates the spiral model, which some people refer to affectionately as "the cinnamon roll."

Figure 7-4 is a complicated diagram, and it is worth studying. The basic idea behind the diagram is that you start on a small scale in the middle of the spine, explore the risks, make a plan to handle the risks, and then commit to an approach for the next iteration. Each iteration moves your project to a larger scale. You roll up one layer of the cinnamon roll, check to be sure that it's what you wanted, and then you begin work on the next layer.

Each iteration involves the six steps shown in bold on the outer edges of the spiral:

1. Determine objectives, alternatives, and constraints

2. Identify and resolve risks

3. Evaluate alternatives

4. Develop the deliverables for that iteration, and verify that they are correct

5. Plan the next iteration

6. Commit to an approach for the next iteration (if you decide to have one)

In the spiral model, the early iterations are the cheapest. You spend less developing the concept of operation than you do developing the requirements, and less developing the requirements than you do developing the design, implementing the product, and testing it.

Don't take the diagram more literally than it's meant to be taken. It isn't important that you have exactly four loops around the spiral, and it isn't important that you perform the six steps exactly as indicated, although that's usually a good order to use. You can tailor each iteration of the spiral to suit the needs of your project.

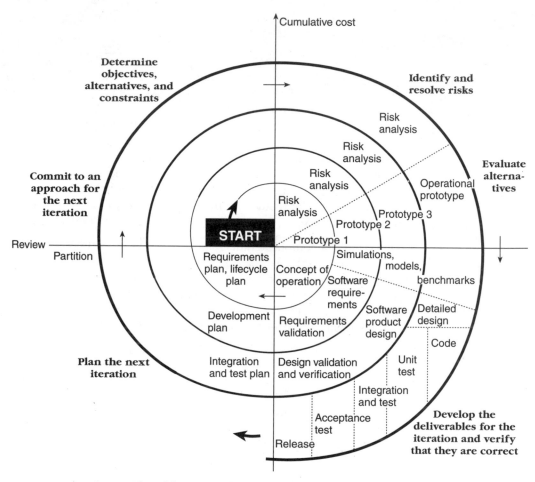

Source: Adapted from "A Spiral Model of Software Development and Enhancement" (Boehm 1988).

Figure 7-4. *The spiral model. In the spiral model, you start small and expand the scope of the project in increments. You expand the scope only after you've reduced the risks for the next increment to an acceptable level.*

CROSS-REFERENCE
For more on risk management, see Chapter 5, "Risk Management."

You can combine the model with other lifecycle models in a couple different ways. You can begin your project with a series of risk-reduction iterations; after you've reduced risks to an acceptable level, you can conclude the development effort with a waterfall lifecycle or other non-risk-based lifecycle. You can incorporate other lifecycle models as iterations within the spiral model. For example, if one of your risks is that you're not sure that your performance targets are achievable, you might include a prototyping iteration to investigate whether you can meet the targets.

One of the most important advantages of the spiral model is that as costs increase, risks decrease. The more time and money you spend, the less risk you're taking, which is exactly what you want on a rapid-development project.

The spiral model provides at least as much management control as the traditional waterfall model. You have the checkpoints at the end of each iteration. Because the model is risk oriented, it provides you with early indications of any insurmountable risks. If the project can't be done for technical or other reasons, you'll find out early—and it won't have cost you much.

The only disadvantage of the spiral model is that it's complicated. It requires conscientious, attentive, and knowledgeable management. It can be difficult to define objective, verifiable milestones that indicate whether you're ready to add the next layer to the cinnamon roll. In some cases, the product development is straightforward enough and project risks are modest enough that you don't need the flexibility and risk management provided by the spiral model.

7.4 Modified Waterfalls

The activities identified in the pure waterfall model are intrinsic to software development. You can't avoid them. You have to come up with a software concept somehow, and you have to get requirements from somewhere. You don't have to use the waterfall lifecycle model to gather requirements, but you do have to use something. Likewise, you can't avoid having an architecture, design, or code.

Most of the weaknesses in the pure waterfall model arise not from problems with these activities but from the treatment of these activities as disjoint, sequential phases. You can, therefore, correct the major weaknesses in the pure waterfall model with relatively minor modifications. You can modify it so that the phases overlap. You can reduce the emphasis on documentation. You can allow for more regression.

Sashimi (Waterfall with Overlapping Phases)

Peter DeGrace describes one of the modifications to the waterfall model as the "sashimi model." The name comes from a Japanese hardware development model (from Fuji-Xerox) and refers to the Japanese style of presenting sliced raw fish, with the slices overlapping each other. (The fact that this

143

model has to do with fish does not mean that it's related to the salmon lifecycle model.) Figure 7-5 shows my version of what the sashimi model looks like for software.

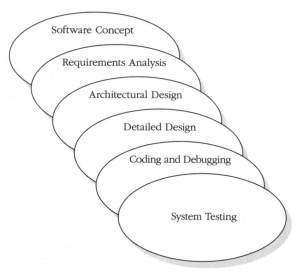

Source: Adapted from *Wicked Problems, Righteous Solutions* (DeGrace and Stahl 1990).

Figure 7-5. *The sashimi model. You can overcome some of the weaknesses of the waterfall model by overlapping its stages, but the approach creates new problems.*

The traditional waterfall model allows for minimal overlapping between phases at the end-of-phase review. This model suggests a stronger degree of overlap—for example, suggesting that you might be well into architectural design and perhaps partway into detailed design before you consider requirements analysis to be complete. I think this is a reasonable approach for many projects, which tend to gain important insights into what they're doing as they move through their development cycles and which function poorly with strictly sequential development plans.

In the pure waterfall model, the ideal documentation is documentation that one team can hand to a completely separate team between any two phases. The question is, "Why?" If you can provide personnel continuity between software concept, requirements analysis, architectural design, detailed design, and coding and debugging, you don't need as much documentation. You can follow a modified waterfall model and substantially reduce the documentation needs.

The sashimi model is not without problems. Because there is overlap among phases, milestones are more ambiguous, and it's harder to track progress accurately. Performing activities in parallel can lead to miscommunication, mistaken assumptions, and inefficiency. If you're working on a small, well-defined project, something close to the pure waterfall model can be the most efficient model available.

Waterfall with Subprojects

Another problem with the pure waterfall model from a rapid-development point of view is that you're supposed to be completely done with architectural design before you begin detailed design, and you're supposed to be completely done with detailed design before you begin coding and debugging. Systems do have some areas that contain design surprises, but they have other areas that we've implemented many times before and that contain no surprises. Why delay the implementation of the areas that are easy to design just because we're waiting for the design of a difficult area? If the architecture has broken the system into logically independent subsystems, you can spin off separate projects, each of which can proceed at its own pace. Figure 7-6 shows a bird's-eye view of how that might look.

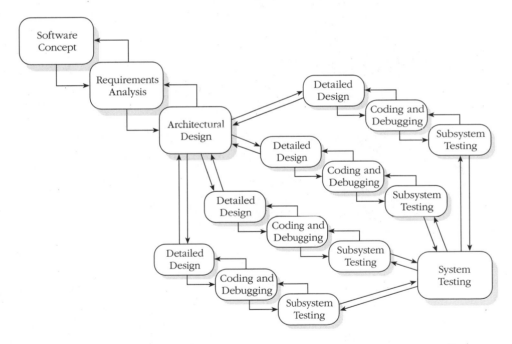

Figure 7-6. *The waterfall model with subprojects. Careful planning can allow you to perform some of the waterfall's tasks in parallel.*

The main risk with this approach is unforeseen interdependencies. You can partly account for that by eliminating dependencies at architecture time or waiting until after detailed-design time to break the project into subprojects.

145

Waterfall with Risk Reduction

Another of the waterfall model's weaknesses is that it requires you to fully define requirements before you begin architectural design, which seems reasonable except that it also requires you to fully understand the requirements before you begin architectural design. Modifying the waterfall—again, only slightly—you can put a risk-reduction spiral at the top of the waterfall to address the requirements risk. You can develop a user-interface prototype, use system storyboarding, conduct user interviews, videotape users interacting with an older system, or use any other requirements-gathering practices that you think are appropriate.

Figure 7-7 shows the waterfall model with risk reduction. Requirements analysis and architectural design are shown in gray to indicate that they might be addressed during the risk-reduction phase rather than during the waterfall phase.

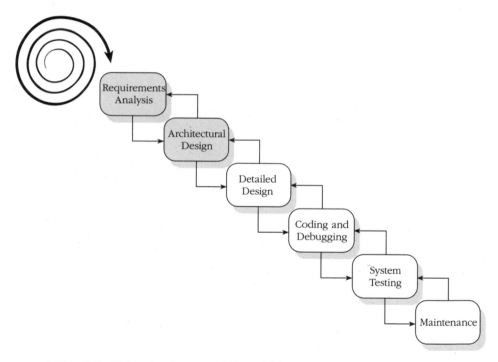

Figure 7-7. *Risk-reduction waterfall model. To overcome problems associated with the waterfall model's rigidity, you can precede a waterfall with a risk-reduction spiral for requirements analysis or architectural design.*

The risk-reduction preamble to the waterfall lifecycle isn't limited to requirements. You could use it to reduce architectural risk or any other risk to the project. If the product depends on developing a high-risk nucleus to the system, you might use a risk-reduction cycle to fully develop the high-risk nucleus before you commit to a full-scale project.

7.5 Evolutionary Prototyping

Evolutionary prototyping is a lifecycle model in which you develop the system concept as you move through the project. Usually you begin by developing the most visible aspects of the system. You demonstrate that part of the system to the customer and then continue to develop the prototype based on the feedback you receive. At some point, you and the customer agree that the prototype is "good enough." At that point, you complete any remaining work on the system and release the prototype as the final product. Figure 7-8 depicts this process graphically.

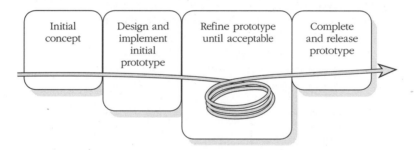

Figure 7-8. *Evolutionary-prototyping model. With evolutionary prototyping, you start by designing and implementing the most prominent parts of the program in a prototype and then adding to and refining the prototype until you're done. The prototype becomes the software that you eventually release.*

CROSS-REFERENCE
For details on evolutionary prototyping, see Chapter 21, "Evolutionary Prototyping."

Evolutionary prototyping is especially useful when requirements are changing rapidly, when your customer is reluctant to commit to a set of requirements, or when neither you nor your customer understands the application area well. It is also useful when the developers are unsure of the optimal architecture or algorithms to use. It produces steady, visible signs of progress, which can be especially useful when there is a strong demand for development speed.

The main drawback of this kind of prototyping is that it's impossible to know at the outset of the project how long it will take to create an acceptable product. You don't even know how many iterations you'll have to go through. This drawback is mitigated somewhat by the fact that customers can see steady signs of progress and they therefore tend to be less nervous about

147

eventually getting a product than with some other approaches. It's also possible to use evolutionary prototyping within a we'll-just-keep-prototyping-until-we-run-out-of-time-or-money-and-then-we'll-declare-ourselves-to-be-done framework.

Another drawback is that this approach can easily become an excuse to do code-and-fix development. Real evolutionary prototyping includes real requirements analysis, real design, and real maintainable code—just in much smaller increments than you'd find with traditional approaches.

7.6 Staged Delivery

The staged-delivery model is another lifecycle model in which you show software to the customer in successively refined stages. Unlike the evolutionary-prototyping model, when you use staged delivery, you know exactly what you're going to build when you set out to build it. What makes the staged-delivery model distinctive is that you don't deliver the software at the end of the project in one fell swoop. You deliver it in successive stages throughout the project. (This model is also known as "incremental implementation.") Figure 7-9 shows how the model works.

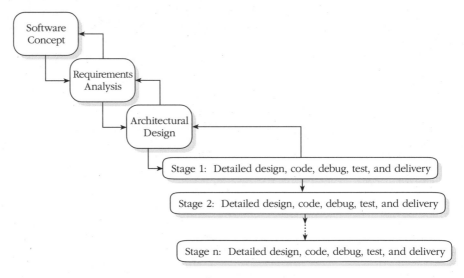

Figure 7-9. *Staged-delivery model. Staged delivery avoids the waterfall model's problem of no part of the system being done until all of it's done. Once you've finished design, you can implement and deliver the system in stages.*

CROSS-REFERENCE
For details on staged
delivery, see Chapter 36,
"Staged Delivery."
As Figure 7-9 suggests, with staged delivery you go through the waterfall model steps of defining the software concept, analyzing requirements, and creating an architectural design for the whole program you intend to build. You then proceed to do detailed design, coding, debugging, and testing within each stage.

The primary advantage of staged delivery is that it allows you to put useful functionality into the hands of your customers earlier than if you delivered 100 percent of the project at the end of the project. If you plan your stages carefully, you may be able to deliver the most important functionality the earliest, and your customers can start using the software at that point.

Staged delivery also provides tangible signs of progress earlier in the project than less incremental approaches do. Such signs of progress can be a valuable ally in keeping schedule pressure to a manageable level.

The main disadvantage of staged delivery is that it won't work without careful planning at both the management and technical levels. At a management level, be sure that the stages you plan are meaningful to the customer and that you distribute work among project personnel in such a way that they can complete their work in time for the stage deadline. At a technical level, be sure that you have accounted for all technical dependencies between different components of the product. A common mistake is to defer development of a component until stage 4 only to find that a component planned for stage 2 can't work without it.

7.7 Design-to-Schedule

The design-to-schedule lifecycle model is similar to the staged-release lifecycle model in that you plan to develop the product in successive stages. The difference is that you don't necessarily know at the outset that you'll ever make it to the last release. You might have five stages planned—but only make it to the third stage because you have an immovable deadline. Figure 7-10 on the next page illustrates this lifecycle model.

This lifecycle model can be a viable strategy for ensuring that you have a product to release by a particular date. If you absolutely must have functioning software in time for a trade show, or by year's end, or by some other immovable date, this strategy guarantees that you will have something. This strategy is particularly useful for parts of the product that you don't want on the critical path. For example, The Microsoft Windows operating system includes several "applets," including WordPad, Paint, and Hearts. Microsoft might use design-to-schedule for those applets to keep them from delaying Windows overall.

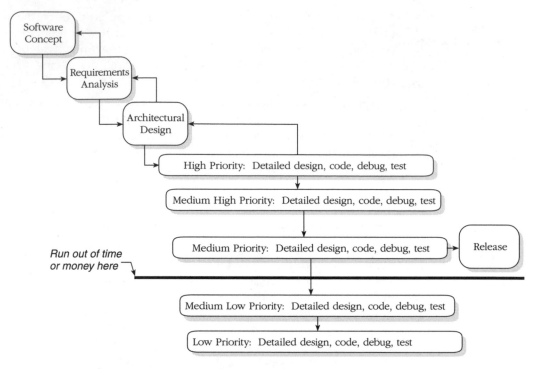

Figure 7-10. *Design-to-schedule model. Design-to-schedule is similar to the staged-release model and is useful when your system has a drop-dead delivery date.*

As Figure 7-10 suggests, one of the critical elements of this lifecycle model is that you prioritize the features and plan your stages so that the early stages contain the highest-priority features. You leave the lower-priority features for later. If the ship date arrives before you've completed all the stages, you don't want to have to leave out critical features because you've spent time implementing less critical ones.

The primary disadvantage of this approach is that if you don't get through all of the stages, you will have wasted time specifying, architecting, and designing features that you don't ship. If you hadn't wasted time on a lot of incomplete features that you didn't ship, you would have had time to squeeze in one or two more complete features.

The decision about whether to use the design-to-schedule model comes down mostly to a question of how much confidence you have in your scheduling ability. If you're highly confident that you can hit your schedule targets, this is an inefficient approach. If you're less confident, this approach just might save your bacon.

7.8   Evolutionary Delivery

Evolutionary delivery is a lifecycle model that straddles the ground between evolutionary prototyping and staged delivery. You develop a version of your product, show it to your customer, and refine the product based on customer feedback. How much evolutionary delivery looks like evolutionary prototyping really depends on the extent to which you plan to accommodate customer requests. If you plan to accommodate most requests, evolutionary delivery will look a lot like evolutionary prototyping. If you plan to accommodate few change requests, evolutionary delivery will look a lot like staged delivery. Figure 7-11 illustrates how the process works.

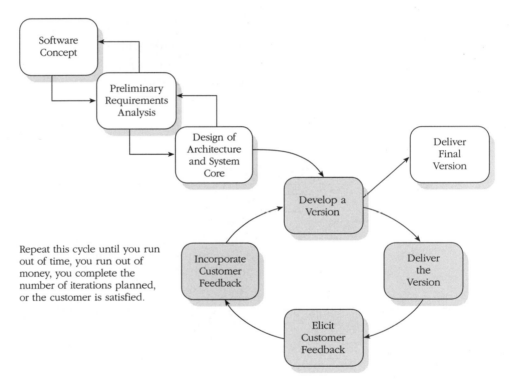

Figure 7-11.   *The evolutionary-delivery model. This model draws from the control you get with staged delivery and the flexibility you get with evolutionary prototyping. You can tailor it to provide as much control or flexibility as you need.*

CROSS-REFERENCE
For details on evolutionary delivery, see Chapter 20, "Evolutionary Delivery."

The main differences between evolutionary prototyping and evolutionary delivery are more differences in emphasis than in fundamental approach. In evolutionary prototyping, your initial emphasis is on the visible aspects of the system; you go back later and plug up holes in the system's foundation.

In evolutionary delivery, your initial emphasis is on the core of the system, which consists of lower level system functions that are unlikely to be changed by customer feedback.

Incremental Development Practices

The phrase "incremental development practices" refers to development practices that allow a program to be developed and delivered in stages. Incremental practices reduce risk by breaking the project into a series of small subprojects. Completing small subprojects tends to be easier than completing a single monolithic project. Incremental development practices increase progress visibility by providing finished, operational pieces of a system long before you could make the complete system operational. These practices provide a greater ability to make midcourse changes in direction because the system is brought to a shippable state several times during its development—you can use any of the shippable versions as a jumping-off point rather than needing to wait until the very end.

Lifecycle models that support incremental development include the spiral, evolutionary-prototyping, staged-delivery, and evolutionary-delivery models (discussed earlier in this chapter).

7.9   Design-to-Tools

The design-to-tools lifecycle model is a radical approach that historically has been used only within exceptionally time-sensitive environments. As tools have become more flexible and powerful—complete applications frameworks, visual programming environments, full-featured database programming environments—the number of projects that can consider using design-to-tools has increased.

CROSS-REFERENCE
For more on productivity tools, see Chapter 15, "Productivity Tools," and Chapter 31, "Rapid-Development Languages (RDLs)."

The idea behind the design-to-tools model is that you put a capability into your product only if it's directly supported by existing software tools. If it isn't supported, you leave it out. By "tools," I mean code and class libraries, code generators, rapid-development languages, and other software tools that dramatically reduce implementation time.

As Figure 7-12 suggests, the result of using this model is inevitably that you won't be able to implement all the functionality you ideally would like to include. But if you choose your tools carefully, you can implement most of the functionality you would like. When time is a constraint, you might actually be able to implement more total functionality than you would have been able to implement with another approach—but it will be the functionality that the tools make easiest to implement, not the functionality you ideally would like.

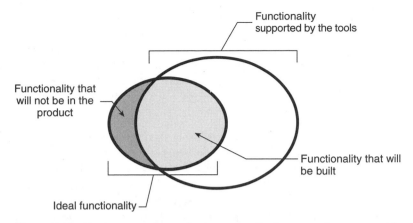

Figure 7-12. *Design-to-tools product concept. Design-to-tools can provide exceptional development speed, but it typically provides less control over your product's functionality than other lifecycle models would provide.*

This model can be combined with the other flexible lifecycle models. You might conduct an initial spiral to identify the capabilities of existing software tools, to identify core requirements, and to determine if the design-to-tools approach is workable. You can use a design-to-tools approach to implement a throwaway prototype, prototyping only the capabilities that can be implemented easily with tools. Then implement the real software using one of the other lifecycle models. You can also combine this model with staged delivery, evolutionary delivery, and design-to-schedule.

The design-to-tools model has a few main disadvantages. You lose a lot of control over your product. You might not be able to implement all the features that you want, and you might not be able to implement other features exactly the way you want. You become more dependent on commercial software producers—on both their product strategies and their financial stabilities. If you're writing small, mostly disposable programs, that might not be much of a problem; but if you're writing programs that you intend to support for a few years, each vendor whose products you use potentially becomes a weak link in the product chain.

7.10 Commercial Off-the-Shelf Software

One alternative that is sometimes overlooked in the excitement surrounding a new system is the option to buy software off the shelf. Off-the-shelf software will rarely satisfy all your needs, but consider the following points.

CROSS-REFERENCE
For details on problems
associated with relying
on outside vendors for
technical products, see
Chapter 28, "Outsourcing."

Off-the-shelf software is available immediately. In the intervening time between when you can buy off-the-shelf software and when you could release software of your own creation, your users will be provided with at least some valuable capabilities. They can learn to work around the products' limitations by the time you could have provided them with custom software. As time goes by, the commercial software might be revised to suit your needs even more closely.

Custom software probably won't turn out to match your mental vision of the ideal software. Comparisons between custom-built software and off-the-shelf software tend to compare the actual off-the-shelf software to the idealized custom-built software. However, when you actually build your own software, you have to make design, cost, and schedule concessions, and the actual custom-built product will fall short of the ideal you envisioned. If you were to deliver only 75 percent of the ideal product, how would that compare to the off-the-shelf software? (This argument applies to the design-to-tools model, too.)

7.11 Choosing the Most Rapid Lifecycle for Your Project

Different projects have different needs, even if they all need to be developed as quickly as possible. This chapter has described 10 software lifecycle models, which, along with all their variations and combinations, provide you with a full range of choices. Which one is fastest?

There is no such thing as a "rapid-development lifecycle model" because the most effective model depends on the context in which it's used. (See Figure 7-13.) Certain lifecycle models are sometimes touted as being more rapid than others, but each one will be fastest in some situations, slowest in others. A lifecycle model that often works well can work poorly if misapplied (as prototyping was in Case Study 7-1).

To choose the most effective lifecycle model for your project, examine your project and answer several questions:

- How well do my customer and I understand the requirements at the beginning of the project? Is our understanding likely to change significantly as we move through the project?

- How well do I understand the system architecture? Am I likely to need to make major architectural changes midway through the project?

- How much reliability do I need?

- How much do I need to plan ahead and design ahead during this project for future versions?

(continued on page 156)

Dinner Menu

Welcome to le Café de Lifecycle Rapide. Bon Appétit!

Entrees

Spiral
Handmade rotini finished with a risk-reduction sauce.
$15.95

Evolutionary Delivery
Mouth-watering mélange of staged delivery and evolutionary prototyping.
$15.95

Staged Delivery
A five-course feast. Ask your server for details.
$14.95

Design-to-Schedule
Methodology medley, ideal for quick executive lunches.
$11.95

Pure Waterfall
A classic, still made from the original recipe.
$14.95

Salads

Design-to-Tools
Roast canard generously stuffed with julienned multi-color beans.
Market Price

Commercial Off-the-Shelf Software
Chef's alchemic fusion of technology du jour. Selection varies daily.
$4.95

Code-and-Fix
Bottomless bowl of spaghetti lightly sprinkled with smoked design
and served with reckless abandon.
$5.95

Figure 7-13. *Choosing a lifecycle model. No one lifecycle model is best for all projects. The best lifecycle model for any particular project depends on that project's needs.*

- How much risk does this project entail?
- Am I constrained to a predefined schedule?
- Do I need to be able to make midcourse corrections?
- Do I need to provide my customers with visible progress throughout the project?
- Do I need to provide management with visible progress throughout the project?
- How much sophistication do I need to use this lifecycle model successfully?

CROSS-REFERENCE
For more on why a linear, waterfall-like approach is most efficient, see "Wisdom of Stopping Changes Altogether" in Section 14.2.

After you have answered these questions, Table 7-1 should help you decide which lifecycle model to use. In general, the more closely you can stick to a linear, waterfall-like approach—and do it effectively—the more rapid your development will be. Much of what I say throughout this book is based on this premise. But if you have reasons to think that a linear approach won't work, it's safer to choose an approach that's more flexible.

Table 7-1. Lifecycle Model Strengths and Weaknesses

Lifecycle Model Capability	Pure Waterfall	Code-and-Fix	Spiral	Modified Waterfalls	Evolutionary Prototyping
Works with poorly understood requirements	Poor	Poor	Excellent	Fair to excellent	Excellent
Works with poorly understood architecture	Poor	Poor	Excellent	Fair to excellent	Poor to fair
Produces highly reliable system	Excellent	Poor	Excellent	Excellent	Fair
Produces system with large growth envelope	Excellent	Poor to fair	Excellent	Excellent	Excellent
Manages risks	Poor	Poor	Excellent	Fair	Fair
Can be constrained to a predefined schedule	Fair	Poor	Fair	Fair	Poor
Has low overhead	Poor	Excellent	Fair	Excellent	Fair
Allows for midcourse corrections	Poor	Poor to excellent	Fair	Fair	Excellent
Provides customer with progress visibility	Poor	Fair	Excellent	Fair	Excellent
Provides management with progress visibility	Fair	Poor	Excellent	Fair to excellent	Fair
Requires little manager or developer sophistication	Fair	Excellent	Poor	Poor to fair	Poor

Each rating is either "Poor," "Fair," or "Excellent." Finer distinctions than that wouldn't be meaningful at this level. The ratings in the table are based on the model's best potential. The actual effectiveness of any lifecycle model will depend on how you implement it. It is usually possible to do worse than the table indicates. On the other hand, if you know the model is weak in a particular area, you can address that weakness early in your planning and compensate for it—perhaps by creating a hybrid of one or more of the models described. Of course, many of the table's criteria will also be strongly influenced by development considerations other than your choice of lifecycle models.

Here are detailed descriptions of the lifecycle-model criteria described in Table 7-1:

Works with poorly understood requirements refers to how well the lifecycle model works when either you or your customer understand the system's requirements poorly or when your customer is prone to change requirements. It indicates how well-suited the model is to exploratory software development.

Lifecycle Model Capability	Staged Delivery	Evolutionary Delivery	Design-to-Schedule	Design-to-Tools	Commercial Off-the-Shelf Software
Works with poorly understood requirements	Poor	Fair to excellent	Poor to fair	Fair	Excellent
Works with poorly understood architecture	Poor	Poor	Poor	Poor to excellent	Poor to excellent
Produces highly reliable system	Excellent	Fair to excellent	Fair	Poor to excellent	Poor to excellent
Produces system with large growth envelope	Excellent	Excellent	Fair to excellent	Poor	N/A
Manages risks	Fair	Fair	Fair to excellent	Poor to fair	N/A
Can be constrained to a predefined schedule	Fair	Fair	Excellent	Excellent	Excellent
Has low overhead	Fair	Fair	Fair	Fair to excellent	Excellent
Allows for midcourse corrections	Poor	Fair to excellent	Poor to fair	Excellent	Poor
Provides customer with progress visibility	Fair	Excellent	Fair	Excellent	N/A
Provides management with progress visibility	Excellent	Excellent	Excellent	Excellent	N/A
Requires little manager or developer sophistication	Fair	Fair	Poor	Fair	Fair

Works with poorly understood architecture refers to how well the lifecycle model works when you're developing in a new application area or when you're developing in a familiar applications area but are developing unfamiliar capabilities.

Produces highly reliable system refers to how many defects a system developed with the lifecycle model is likely to have when put into operation.

Produces system with large growth envelope refers to how easily you're likely to be able to modify the system in size and diversity over its lifetime. This includes modifying the system in ways that were not anticipated by the original designers.

Manages risks refers to the model's support for identifying and controlling risks to the schedule, risks to the product, and other risks.

Can be constrained to a predefined schedule refers to how well the lifecycle model supports delivery of software by an immovable drop-dead date.

Has low overhead refers to the amount of management and technical overhead required to use the model effectively. Overhead includes planning, status tracking, document production, package acquisition, and other activities that aren't directly involved in producing software itself.

Allows for midcourse corrections refers to the ability to change significant aspects of the product midway through the development schedule. This does not include changing the product's basic mission but does include significantly extending it.

Provides customer with progress visibility refers to the extent to which the model automatically generates signs of progress that the customer can use to track the project's status.

Provides management with progress visibility refers to the extent to which the model automatically generates signs of progress that management can use to track the project's status.

Requires little manager or developer sophistication refers to the level of education and training that you need to use the model successfully. That includes the level of sophistication you need to track progress using the model, to avoid risks inherent in the model, to avoid wasting time using the model, and to realize the benefits that led you to use the model in the first place.

Case Study 7-2. Effective Lifecycle Model Selection

Eddie had volunteered to oversee Square-Tech's development of a new product code named "Cube-It," a scientific graphics package. Rex, the CEO, felt that Square-Calc had given them a foot in the door they could use to become a market leader in scientific graphics.

Eddie met with George and Jill, both developers, to plan the project. "This is a new area for us, so I want to minimize the company's risk on this project. Rex told me that he wanted the preliminary product spec implemented within a year. I don't know whether that's possible, so I want you to use a spiral lifecycle model. For the first iteration of the spiral, we need to find out whether this preliminary spec is pure fantasy or whether we can make it a reality."

George and Jill worked for two weeks and then met with Eddie to evaluate the alternatives they had identified. "Here's what we found out. If the objective is to build the market-leading scientific-graphics package, there are two basic alternatives: beat the competition in features or beat them in ease of use. Right now, the easier niche to fill seems to be ease of use.

"We analyzed the risks for each alternative. If we go the full-feature route, we're looking at a minimum of about 200 staff-months to develop a market-leading product. We have the constraints of a maximum of 1 year to ship a product and a maximum team size of 8 people. We can't meet those constraints with the full-featured product. If we go the usability route, we're looking at more like 75 staff months. That fits with our constraints, and there will be more room in the market for us."

"That's good work," Eddie said. "I think Rex will like that." Eddie met with Rex later that day, and then he got back together with George and Jill the following morning.

"Rex pointed out that we need to develop some in-house usability experts. He thought that developing a product that emphasizes usability was a good strategic move, so he gave us the thumbs-up.

"Now we need to plan the next iteration of the spiral. Our goal for this iteration is to refine the product spec in ways that minimize our development time and maximize usability."

George and Jill spent 4 weeks on the iteration, and then they met with Eddie to review their findings. "We've created a prioritized list of preliminary requirements," George reported. "The list is sorted by usability and then by estimated

(continued)

Case Study 7-2. Effective Lifecycle Model Selection, *continued*

implementation time. We've made both best-case and worst-case effort estimates for each feature. You can see that there's a lot of variation, and a lot of that variation just has to do with how we define the specifics of each feature. In other words, we have a lot of control over how much time this product takes to implement.

"Having maximum usability as our clear, primary objective really makes some decisions easy for us. Some of the most time-consuming features to implement would also be the least usable. I recommend that we just eliminate some of them because it will be a win for both the schedule and the product."

"That's interesting," Eddie responded. "What high-level alternatives have you come up with?"

"We recommend either of two possibilities," Jill said. "We've got the 'safe' version, which puts a strong emphasis on usability but uses proven technology. And we've got the 'risky' version, which pushes the usability state of the art. Either one should be a lot more usable than anything else on the market. The risky version will make it harder for the competition to catch up with us, but it will also nominally take about 60 staff-months compared with the safe version's 40 staff-months. That's not all that much of a difference, but the worst case for the risky version is 120 staff-months compared with the safe version's 55."

"Wow!" Eddie said. "That's good information. Is it possible to implement the safe version but design ahead so that we can push the state of the art in version 2?"

"I'm glad you asked that," Jill said. "We estimated that the safe version with design-ahead for version 2 would nominally take 45 staff-months, with a worst-case of 60."

"That makes it pretty clear, doesn't it?" Eddie said. "We've got $10\frac{1}{2}$ months left, so let's do the safe version with design-ahead for version 2. While you all were focusing on the technical schedule risk, I've been focusing on the personnel schedule risk, and I've got three developers lined up. We'll add them to the team now and start the next iteration.

"George, you mentioned that a lot of the variation in schedule has to do with how each feature is ultimately defined, right? For the next spiral iteration, we need to focus on minimizing our design and implementation risk, and that means defining as many of those features to take as little implementation time as possible while staying consistent with our usability goal. I also want to have the new developers review your estimates to reduce the risk of any estimation error." George and Jill agreed.

The next iteration, which focused on design, took 3 months, bringing the project to the $4\frac{1}{2}$-month mark. Their reviews had convinced them that their

(continued)

Case Study 7-2. Effective Lifecycle Model Selection, *continued*

design was solid—including the design-ahead for version 2. The design work had allowed them to refine their estimates, and they now estimated that the remaining implementation would take 30 staff-months, with a worst case of 40. Eddie thought that was exceptional because it meant that the worst case had them delivering the software only 2 weeks late.

At the beginning of the coding iteration, the developers identified low code quality and poor status visibility as their primary risks. To minimize those risks, they established code reviews to detect and correct coding errors, and they used miniature milestones to provide excellent status visibility.

Their estimates hadn't been perfect, and the final iteration took 2 weeks longer than nominal. They delivered the first release candidate to system testing at 11 months instead of at $10\frac{1}{2}$. But the product's quality was excellent, and it took only two release candidates to declare a winner. Cube-It 1.0 was released on time.

Further Reading

DeGrace, Peter, and Leslie Hulet Stahl. *Wicked Problems, Righteous Solutions.* Englewood Cliffs, N.J.: Yourdon Press, 1990. The subtitle of this book is "A Catalog of Modern Software Engineering Paradigms," and it is by far the most complete description of software lifecycle models available. The book was produced through an unusual collaboration in which Peter DeGrace provided the useful technical content and Leslie Hulet Stahl provided the exceptionally readable and entertaining writing style.

Boehm, Barry W., ed. *Software Risk Management.* Washington, DC: IEEE Computer Society Press, 1989. This tutorial is interesting for the introduction to Section 4, "Implementing Risk Management." Boehm describes how to use the spiral model to decide which software lifecycle model to use. The volume also includes Boehm's papers, "A Spiral Model of Software Development and Enhancement" and "Applying Process Programming to the Spiral Model," which introduce the spiral lifecycle model and describe an extension to it (Boehm 1988; Boehm and Belz 1988).

Jones, Capers. *Assessment and Control of Software Risks.* Englewood Cliffs, N.J.: Yourdon Press, 1994. Chapter 57, "Partial Life-Cycle Definitions" describes the hazards of not breaking down your lifecycle description into enough detail. It provides a summary of the 25 activities that Jones says make up most of the work on a successful software project.

161

8

Estimation

Contents

Related Topics

HARD DATA

SOME ESTIMATES ARE CREATED CAREFULLY, and others are created by seat-of-the-pants guesses. Most projects overshoot their estimated schedules by anywhere from 25 to 100 percent, but a few organizations have achieved schedule-prediction accuracies to within 10 percent, and 5 percent is not unheard of (Jones 1994).

An accurate schedule estimate is part of the foundation of maximum development speed. Without an accurate schedule estimate, there is no foundation for effective planning and no support for rapid development. (See Case Study 8-1.)

This chapter provides an introduction to software project estimation. It describes how to come up with a useful estimate—how to crunch the numbers and create something reasonably accurate. Coming up with a perfect estimate doesn't do any good if you can't get the estimate accepted, so the next chapter describes how to handle the interpersonal elements involved in scheduling software projects.

Case Study 8-1. Seat-of-the-Pants Project Estimation

Carl had been put in charge of version 1 of Giga-Safe's inventory control system (ICS). He had a general idea of the capabilities desired when he attended the first meeting of the oversight committee for the project. Bill was the head of the oversight committee. "Carl, how long is ICS 1.0 going to take?" he asked.

"I think it will take about 9 months, but that's just a rough estimate at this point," Carl said.

"That's not going to work," Bill said. "I was hoping you'd say 3 or 4 months. We absolutely need to bring that system in within 6 months. Can you do it in 6?"

"I'm not sure," Carl said honestly. "I'd have to look at the project more carefully, but I can try to find a way to get it done in 6."

"Treat 6 months as a goal then," Bill said. "That's what it's got to be, anyway." The rest of the committee agreed.

By week 5, additional work on the product concept had convinced Carl that the project would take closer to his original 9-month guess than to 6 months, but he thought that with some luck he still might be able to complete it in 6. He didn't want to be branded a troublemaker, so he decided to sit tight.

Carl's team made steady progress, but requirements analysis took longer than they had hoped. They were now almost 4 months into what was supposed to be a 6-month project. "There's no way we can do the rest of the work we have to do in 2 months," he told Bill. He told Bill he needed a 2-month schedule slip and rescheduled the project to take 8 months.

A few weeks later, Carl realized that design wasn't proceeding as quickly as he had hoped either. "Implement the parts you can do easily," he told the team. "We'll worry about the rest of the parts when we get to them."

Carl met with the oversight committee. "We're now 7 months into our 8-month project. Detailed design is almost complete, and we're making good progress. But we can't complete the project in 8 months." Carl announced his second schedule slip, this time to 10 months. Bill grumbled and asked Carl to look for ways to bring the schedule back to around 8 months.

At the 9-month mark, the team had completed detailed design, but coding still hadn't begun on some modules. It was clear that Carl couldn't make the 10-month schedule either. He announced the third schedule slip number—to 12 months. Bill's face turned red when Carl announced the slip, and the pressure from him became more intense. Carl began to feel that his job was on the line.

Coding proceeded fairly well, but a few areas needed redesign and reimplementation. The team hadn't coordinated design details in those areas well,

(continued)

Case Study 8-1. Seat-of-the-Pants Project Estimation, *continued*

and some of their implementations conflicted. At the 11-month oversight-committee meeting, Carl announced the fourth schedule slip—to 13 months. Bill became livid. "Do you have any idea what you're doing?" he yelled. "You obviously don't have any idea! You obviously don't have any idea when the project is going to be done! I'll tell you when it's going to be done! It's going to be done by the 13-month mark, or you're going to be out of a job! I'm tired of being jerked around by you software guys! You and your team are going to work 60 hours a week until you deliver!" Carl felt his blood pressure rise, especially since Bill had backed him into an unrealistic schedule in the first place. But he knew that with four schedule slips under his belt, he had no credibility left. He felt that he had to knuckle under to the mandatory overtime or he would lose his job.

Carl told his team about the meeting. They worked hard and managed to deliver the software in just over 13 months. Additional implementation uncovered additional design flaws, but with everyone working 60 hours a week, they delivered the product through sweat and sheer willpower.

8.1 The Software-Estimation Story

Software estimation is difficult, and what some people try to do with software estimation isn't even theoretically possible. Upper management, lower management, customers, and some developers don't seem to understand why estimation is so hard. People who don't understand software estimation's inherent difficulties can play an unwitting role in making estimation even harder than it already is.

People remember stories better than they remember isolated facts, and there is a story to be told about why software estimation is hard. I think that we as developers need to make telling that story a priority. We need to be sure that customers and managers at all levels of our organizations have heard and understood it.

The basic software-estimation story is that software development is a process of gradual refinement. You begin with a fuzzy picture of what you want to build and then spend the rest of the project trying to bring that picture into clearer focus. Because the picture of the software you're trying to build is fuzzy, the estimate of the time and effort needed to build it is fuzzy, too. The estimate can come into focus only along with the software itself, which means that software-project estimation is also a process of gradual refinement.

The next several subsections describe the story in more detail.

Software and Construction

Suppose you go to your friend Stan, who's an architect, and say that you want to build a house. You start by asking Stan whether he can build a three-bedroom home for under $100,000. He'll say yes, but he'll also say that the specific cost will vary depending on the detailed characteristics you want. (See Figure 8-1.)

If you're willing to accept whatever Stan designs, it will be possible for him to deliver on his estimate. But if you have specific ideas about what kind of house you want—if you later insist on a three-car garage, gourmet kitchen, sunroom, sauna, swimming pool, den, two fireplaces, gold-plated fixtures, floor-to-ceiling Italian marble, and a building site with the best view in the state—your home could cost several times $100,000, even though the architect told you it was possible to build a three-bedroom home for under $100,000.

"A whole year to build
a house here?
No problem."

"Good. Let's get
started. I'm in
a hurry."

Figure 8-1. *It is difficult to know whether you can build the product that the customer wants in the desired time frame until you have a detailed understanding of what the customer wants.*

Software Development as a Process of Refinement

It is the mark of an instructed mind to rest satisfied with the degree of precision which the nature of a subject admits, and not to seek exactness when only an approximation of the truth is possible...

Aristotle

How much does a new house cost? It depends on the house. How much does a new billing system cost? It depends on the billing system. Some organizations want cost estimates to within ± 10 percent before they'll fund work on requirements definition. Although that degree of precision would be nice to have that early in the project, it isn't even theoretically possible. That early, you'll do well to estimate within a factor of 2.

Until each feature is understood in detail, you can't estimate the cost of a program precisely. Software development is a process of making increasingly detailed decisions. You refine the product concept into a statement of requirements, the requirements into a preliminary design, the preliminary design into a detailed design, and the detailed design into working code. At each of these stages, you make decisions that affect the project's ultimate cost and schedule. Because you can't know how each of these decisions will be made until you actually make them, uncertainty about the nature of the product contributes to uncertainty in the estimate.

Here are some examples of the kinds of questions that contribute to estimation uncertainty:

- Will the customer want Feature X?
- Will the customer want the cheap or expensive version of Feature X? There is typically at least a factor of 10 difference in the implementation difficulty of different versions of the same feature.
- If you implement the cheap version of Feature X, will the customer later want the expensive version after all?
- How will Feature X be designed? There is typically at least a factor of 10 difference in the design complexity of different designs for the same feature.
- What will be the quality level of Feature X? Depending on the care taken during implementation, there can be a factor of 10 difference in the number of defects contained in the original implementation.
- How long will it take to debug and correct mistakes made in the implementation of Feature X? Individual performance among different programmers with the same level of experience has been found to vary by at least a factor of 10 in debugging and correcting the same problems.
- How long will it take to integrate Feature X with all the other features?

CROSS-REFERENCE
For a detailed example of the
kinds of uncertainty that can
affect design and
implementation time, see
"Unclear or Impossible
Goals" in Section 14.2.

As you can see, the uncertainty about even a single feature can introduce a lot of uncertainty into an early-in-the-project estimate. Multiplied across an entire project, literally thousands of specification, design, and implementation decisions have to be made before the ultimate cost of the project can be determined. As you do make a greater percentage of those decisions, however, you can narrow the estimation range.

Amount of Refinement Possible

Researchers have found that project estimates fall within predictable precisions at various stages of a project. The estimate-convergence graph in Figure 8-2 shows how estimates become more precise as a project progresses.

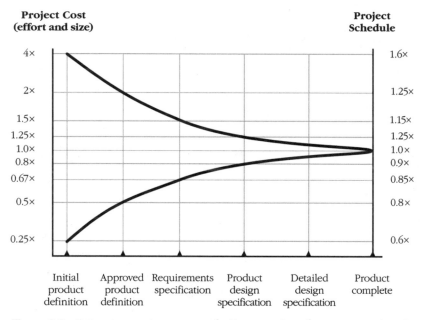

Figure 8-2. *Estimate-convergence graph. For any given feature set, estimation precision can improve only as the software itself becomes more refined. Source: Adapted from "Cost Models for Future Life Cycle Processes: COCOMO 2.0" (Boehm et al. 1995).*

Figure 8-2 captures the reason that software estimation is hard. At the time when developers are typically asked to provide a rough estimate, there can be a factor-of-16 difference between high and low effort estimates. Even after requirements have been completed, you can only know the amount of effort needed to within about 50 percent, and by that time most organizations want their estimates to the dollar. The estimation ranges implied in Figure 8-2 are summarized numerically in Table 8-1.

Table 8-1. Estimate Multipliers by Project Phase

Phase	Effort and Size		Schedule	
	Optimistic	Pessimistic	Optimistic	Pessimistic
Initial product concept	0.25	4.0	0.60	1.60
Approved product concept	0.50	2.0	0.80	1.25
Requirements specification	0.67	1.5	0.85	1.15
Product design specification	0.80	1.25	0.90	1.10
Detailed design specification	0.90	1.10	0.95	1.05

Source: Adapted from "Cost Models for Future Software Life Cycle Processes: COCOMO 2.0" (Boehm et al. 1995).

As the data in Table 8-1 suggests, your estimates throughout a project should start general and become more refined as the project progresses.

These ranges are broad, but even so, there are some extreme cases that they won't catch. No out-of-the-box estimation ranges can account for the case where your customer insists on the equivalent of floor-to-ceiling Italian marble.

To use the factors in the table, simply multiply your "most likely" single-point estimate by the optimistic factor to get the optimistic estimate and by the pessimistic factor to get the pessimistic estimate. You can then present your estimate as a range rather than as a point estimate. If your "most likely" estimate is 50 man-months and you've completed the requirements specification, you would multiply by 0.67 and 1.5 and estimate a range of 34 to 75 man-months. Sometimes your customers will insist on a "most likely" estimate, and you'll feel that you have to give it to them. But if that doesn't happen, you don't need to publish the single-point estimate except in your own notes.

CROSS-REFERENCE
For more on the relationship between schedule and effort estimates, see Section 8.5, "Schedule Estimation."

For reasons explained later in the chapter, the optimistic and pessimistic factors for schedule estimates are different than the factors for effort and size. They assume that you estimate the schedule by first creating an effort estimate and then computing the schedule from that. (The procedure for doing this is explained later in the chapter.) If you have estimated the schedule by simply eyeballing it, you'll be better off using the ranges listed under "Effort and Size" than the ranges listed under "Schedule."

Estimation vs. Control

Most software customers initially want more than they can afford. As Figure 8-3 suggests, that means that they have to bend either their ideas about the product or their ideas about the resources they are willing to commit. Sometimes the customer will want to bend both the resources and the feature set to meet each other halfway.

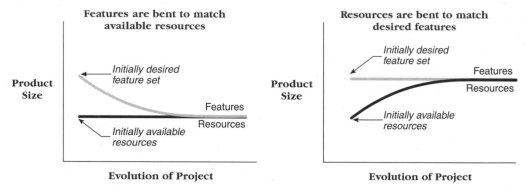

Figure 8-3. *Most software projects start with a mismatch between desired feature set and available resources. The feature set or the resources (or both) must be bent to meet the other.*

How can the feature set be bent to meet the available resources? In the case of building a new house, you might tell your friend Stan, "I might not know exactly what I want, but I do know that I don't need a sauna or a swimming pool, and I don't need the best view in the state. I don't have expensive tastes. I just want a normal house. Considering that, can you build me a house for $100,000?"

Stan will say, "I can definitely build you a house for $100,000, but you'll have to give me a lot of control over how the house is built. I'll have to use plans that the builder is already familiar with. I'll have to use standard doors, windows, appliances, and fixtures. I'll be able to give you only a small number of choices of countertops, rugs, and linoleum. You might not end up with the house you want."

"Fine," you say, because $100,000 is your limit.

Software builders face a choice between estimation accuracy and project control. If you can be flexible about the product characteristics, you can have some control over cost and schedule and can "build to budget." But each time you have to choose between putting a feature in or leaving it out, you'll have to leave it out. Each time you face a choice between implementing the better feature or the one that costs less, you'll have to choose the one that costs less. And you'll have to follow that pattern consistently. If you implement the better feature sometimes and the one that costs less other times, you're not building to budget. You're doing normal software development. If you can't accept the discipline and the trade-offs involved in a build-to-budget approach, you simply have to accept a lot of imprecision in early-in-the-project estimates.

Cooperation

CROSS-REFERENCE
For more on cooperating with the customer, see Section 9.2, "Beating Schedule Pressure"; Chapter 10, "Customer-Oriented Development"; and Chapter 37, "Theory-W Management."

So far, the estimation story has focused on all the reasons that you can't provide the precise estimates that people want. These reasons are good reasons; however, the people who want those precise estimates also have good reasons for wanting them, and I think that means we have an extra responsibility to offer as much estimate-related information as we can.

Help your customers by telling them about the parts of the project that you are able to estimate. If you can estimate the end of your current phase, tell them that. If you know when you'll have a better estimate, tell them that. Don't leave them feeling completely adrift. Tell them where the next landmark is.

Help your customers understand your strategy for the whole project by mapping out the whole set of estimates you intend to provide. Tell them that you'll update your estimates at the end of the product-definition, requirements-specification, product-design, and detailed-design stages. Offer to try to build to budget, if that will help, but be sure that your customers understand all the trade-offs that that approach involves.

If your customers still ask for more precise estimates than you can provide, tell them that you can't give them what they're asking for because you don't know yet yourself. But make it clear that you want to cooperate. Tell them, "As soon as I know, you'll know."

Convergence Between Estimates and Reality

Customers have a role to play in cooperating, too. If customers want the shortest possible schedule, they should not pressure you to lower your estimates or to provide them with misleadingly precise estimates.

As Figure 8-4 on the next page shows, the shortest actual schedule results from the most accurate, planned schedule (Symons 1991). If the estimate is too low, planning inefficiencies will drive up the actual cost of the project. If the estimate is too high, Parkinson's law (that work expands to fill available time) will drive up the actual cost of the project.

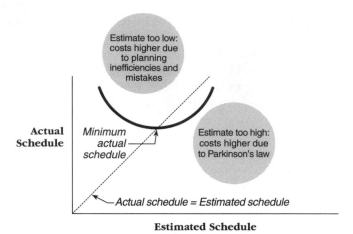

Figure 8-4. *Relationship between estimated effort and actual effort. An estimate that is either too low or too high will result in a longer-than-optimal actual schedule.*

The trick is to try to estimate neither high nor low, but right on the money. The goal of estimation is to seek a convergence between your estimates and reality. By definition, estimates and reality converge upon the software's release. The sooner the two track together, the better the business and product decisions you and your customers can make; the tighter all of you can plan your project and its interdependencies; the better the relationship between developers, managers, customers, marketers, and end-users will be; and the more rapid a development schedule you can attain.

The Estimation Story in a Nutshell

To tell the estimation story, you need to explain these four points:

- Constructing software is like constructing a house: you can't tell exactly how much it is going to cost until you know exactly what "it" is.

- As with building a house, you can either build your dream house—expense be hanged—or you can build to a budget. If you want to build to a budget, you have to be very flexible about the product characteristics.

- Whether you build to a budget or not, software development is a process of gradual refinement, so some imprecision is unavoidable. Unlike building a home, in software the only way to refine the product concept and thereby the estimate is to actually build the software.

- Estimates can be refined over the course of a project. Promise your customer that you will provide more refined estimates at each stage.

Case Study 8-2 at the end of the chapter provides an illustration of how the estimation story can be used on a live project.

Accuracy and Precision

"Accuracy" and "precision" are related but not identical concepts, and the difference between the two is important to software estimation. Accuracy refers to how close to the mark a measurement is: 3 is a more accurate representation of pi than 4 is. (To seven decimal places, pi equals 3.1415927.) Precision refers to how many significant digits a measurement has: 3.14 is a more precise representation of pi than 3 is.

A measurement can be precise without being accurate, and it can be accurate without being precise. 3 is an accurate representation of pi, but it is not precise. 3.3232 is a precise representation of pi, but it is not accurate. Airline schedules are usually precise to the minute, but they are not very accurate. Measuring people's heights in whole feet might be accurate, but it would not be precise.

In software estimation, false precision is the enemy of accuracy. An effort estimate of 40 to 70 man-months might be both the most accurate and the most precise estimate you can make. If you simplify it to 55 man-months, that's like representing pi as 3.3232 instead of 3. It looks more precise, but it's really less accurate.

Shortest-possible software schedules are achieved by creating the most accurate estimates possible, not the most precise. If you want to achieve maximum development speed, avoid false precision.

8.2 Estimation-Process Overview

Now that we've thoroughly explored the reasons that estimation is difficult, how do you actually make an estimate? The process of creating an accurate development schedule consists of three steps:

1. *Estimate the size of the product (number of lines of code or function points).* Some projects jump right into estimating the schedule itself, but effective estimation requires estimating the size of the software to be built first. This step is by far the most difficult intellectually, which might be part of the reason that people so often skip it.

2. *Estimate the effort (man-months).* If you have an accurate size estimate and historical data on your organization's performance on similar projects, computing the effort estimate is easy.

3. *Estimate the schedule (calendar months).* Once you've estimated the size and effort, for reasons explained later in the chapter, estimating the schedule turns out to be nearly trivial. But getting a realistic schedule estimate accepted can be the most difficult part of the project. I devote the entire next chapter to that topic.

Wrapped around these three steps is a more general step, a meta-step:

4. Provide estimates in ranges and periodically refine the ranges to provide increasing precision as the project progresses.

The following sections describe each of these steps in detail.

What Do People Usually Mean by "Estimate"?

"[The common definition of estimate is] *An estimate is the most optimistic prediction that has a non-zero probability of coming true.*'

"Accepting this definition leads irrevocably toward a method called what's-the-earliest-date-by-which-you-can't-prove-you-won't-be-finished estimating."

—*Tom DeMarco*

8.3 Size Estimation

You can estimate the size of a project in any of several ways:

- Use an algorithmic approach, such as function points, that estimates program size from program features. (I'll summarize this practice shortly.)

- Use size-estimation software that estimates program size from your description of program features (screens, dialogs, files, database tables, and so on).

- If you have already worked on a similar project and know its size, estimate each major piece of the new system as a percentage of the size of a similar piece of the old system. Estimate the total size of the new system by adding up the estimated sizes of each of the pieces.

CROSS-REFERENCE
For more on measuring projects, see Chapter 26, "Measurement."

Most software programs and some of the algorithmic approaches require that you calibrate the estimation practice to your environment before you use it. Accurate measurement of historical projects is a key to long-term success in using any kind of estimation. (See the sidebar on the next page.)

Function-Point Estimation

CROSS-REFERENCE
Rules for counting function points get much more detailed than what's presented here. For details, refer to the "Further Reading" section at the end of this chapter.

A function point is a synthetic measure of program size that is often used in a project's early stages (Albrecht 1979). Function points are easier to determine from a requirements specification than lines of code are, and they provide a more accurate measure of program size. Many different methods exist for counting function points; the one I describe here is closest to the "1984 IBM Method," which is the basis of IBM's and the International Function Point User Group's (IFPUG's) current practice (Jones 1991).

Program Size

As it's used in this chapter, "size" refers in a very general way to the total scope of a program. It includes the breadth and depth of the feature set as well as the program's difficulty and complexity.

Early in the project, the most accurate way to think of size is often in terms of function points. Sometimes it's useful to think of size in comparative terms—for example, "Umpty-Fratz version 2 will have about 30 percent more functionality than Umpty-Fratz version 1" or "Umpty-Fratz version 2 should be about three-quarters as big as Foo-Bar version 4."

As you work your way through a project from requirements analysis to implementation and test, your notion of size changes, typically shifting from number of function points at requirements time to number of classes or modules at design time to number of lines of code at implementation and test time.

The number of function points in a program is based on the number and complexity of each of the following items:

- *Inputs*—Screens, forms, dialog boxes, controls, or messages through which an end-user or other program adds, deletes, or changes a program's data. This includes any input that has a unique format or unique processing logic.

- *Outputs*—Screens, reports, graphs, or messages that the program generates for use by an end-user or other program. This includes any output that has a different format or requires a different processing logic than other output types.

- *Inquiries*—Input/output combinations in which an input results in an immediate, simple output. The term originated in the database world and refers to a direct search for specific data, usually using a single key. In modern GUI applications, the line between inquiries and outputs is blurry; generally, however, queries retrieve data directly from a database and provide only rudimentary formatting, whereas outputs can process, combine, or summarize complex data and can be highly formatted.

- *Logical internal files*—Major logical groups of end-user data or control information that are completely controlled by the program. A logical file might consist of a single flat file or a single table in a relational database.

- *External interface files*—Files controlled by other programs with which the program being counted interacts. This includes each major logical group of data or control information that enters or leaves the program.

The terminology in the function-point approach is fairly database oriented. The basic approach works well for all kinds of software, but you will have to fine-tune it for your own environment if you're not building database-intensive systems.

As Table 8-2 suggests, to compute the number of function points in a program, you take the number of low-complexity inputs in the program and multiply by 3, the number of low-complexity outputs and multiply by 4, and so on. The sum of those numbers gives you the "unadjusted function-point total."

Table 8-2. Function-Point Multipliers

Program Characteristic	Function Points		
	Low Complexity	Medium Complexity	High Complexity
Number of inputs	× 3	× 4	× 6
Number of outputs	× 4	× 5	× 7
Inquiries	× 3	× 4	× 6
Logical internal files	× 7	× 10	× 15
External interface files	× 5	× 7	× 10

Source: Adapted from *Applied Software Measurement* (Jones 1991).

You then compute an "influence multiplier" based on the influence that 14 factors have on the program, factors that include data communications, on-line data entry, processing complexity, and ease of installation. The influence multiplier ranges from 0.65 to 1.35.

When you multiply the unadjusted total by the influence multiplier, you get a total function-point count. Table 8-3 provides an example of how you would come up with that. The specific number of inputs, outputs, inquiries, logical internal files, and external interface files shown in the table are arbitrary. They and the influence multiplier were chosen solely for purposes of illustration.

The program illustrated in Table 8-3 works out to a size of 350 function points. If you had come up with that number, you could compare it to the sizes of previous projects and their schedules, and you could estimate a schedule from that. You could also use Jones's First-Order Estimation Practice, described later in this chapter.

Table 8-3. Example of Computing the Number of Function Points

Program Characteristic	Function Points		
	Low Complexity	Medium Complexity	High Complexity
Number of inputs	6 × 3 = 18	2 × 4 = 8	3 × 6 = 18
Number of outputs	7 × 4 = 28	7 × 5 = 35	0 × 7 = 0
Inquiries	0 × 3 = 0	2 × 4 = 8	4 × 6 = 24
Logical internal files	5 × 7 = 35	2 × 10 = 20	3 × 15 = 45
External interface files	9 × 5 = 45	0 × 7 = 0	2 × 10 = 20
Unadjusted function-point total			304
Influence multiplier			1.15
Adjusted function-point total			350

Estimation Tips

Here are some general guidelines for making size estimates.

CLASSIC MISTAKE

Avoid off-the-cuff estimates. Developers are sometimes trapped by off-the-cuff estimates. Your boss asks, "How long would it take to implement print preview on the Giga-Tron?" You say, "I don't know. I think it might take about a week. I'll check into it." You go off to your desk, look at the design and code for the program you were asked about, notice a few things you'd forgotten when you talked to your manager, add up the changes, and decide that it would take about five weeks. You hurry over to your manager's office to update your first estimate, but the manager is in a meeting. Later that day, you catch up with your manager, and before you can open your mouth, your manager says, "Since it seemed like a small project, I went ahead and asked for approval for the print-preview function at the budget meeting this afternoon. The rest of the budget committee was excited about the new feature and can't wait to see it next week. Can you start working on it today?"

What just happened here? Was it bad management? Bad development? Poor communication? It was probably a bit of all three, and I've found that the safest policy is simply not to give an off-the-cuff estimate. You never know how far it will travel, and it's futile to try to put conditions on it; people have enough trouble trying to remember the estimate itself, and it seems as if they never remember the conditions you put on it.

Allow time for the estimate, and plan it. Rushed estimates are inaccurate estimates. If you're estimating a large project, treat estimation as a miniproject, and take the time to plan the estimation activity itself so that you can do it well. Maybe it's just my Scots blood showing, but I am astounded at how often companies will spend a million dollars on a system based on a back-of-the-envelope estimate. If it were my money, I would want to spend enough on the estimate to know whether the system was really going to cost one million dollars or two.

CLASSIC MISTAKE

Use data from previous projects. By far the most common practice used for estimation is comparison with similar, past projects based solely on *personal memory* (Lederer and Prasad 1992). This practice is associated with cost and schedule overruns. Guessing and intuition are also common and are also associated with cost and schedule overruns. The use of documented data from similar past projects, however, is negatively correlated with cost and schedule overruns.

Use developer-based estimates. Estimates prepared by people other than the developers who will do the work are less accurate than estimates prepared by the developers who will do the work (Lederer and Prasad 1992). When estimator-developers do the estimate and the work, meeting their own estimates reflects positively on both their estimating and work abilities. Separate estimators are more likely to underestimate than estimator-developers (Lederer and Prasad 1992).

Estimate by walk-through. Have each team member estimate pieces of the project individually, and then have a walk-through meeting to compare estimates. Discuss differences in the estimates enough to understand the sources of the differences. Work until you reach consensus on the high and low ends of estimation ranges.

Estimate by categories. Simplify by classifying areas as easy, medium, and hard. Assign a fixed size to each category, and then add up the sizes.

Estimate at a low level of detail. Base the estimate on a detailed examination of project activities. In general, the more detailed your examination is, the more accurate your estimate will be. The Law of Large Numbers says that the error of sums will be greater than the sum of errors. In other words, a 10-percent error on one big piece is 10 percent high or 10 percent low. The 10-percent errors on 50 small pieces will be both high and low and will tend to cancel each other out. Summing task durations is negatively correlated with cost and schedule overruns (Lederer and Prasad 1992).

CLASSIC MISTAKE

Don't omit common tasks. People don't often omit tasks on purpose, but when they've been ordered to develop a product in the shortest possible time, they don't go out of their way to look for extra tasks. Here is a list of commonly omitted tasks: cutover, data conversion, installation, customization, management of the beta-test program, demonstrating the program to customers or users, attendance at change-control meetings, maintenance work on existing systems during the project, tech support of existing systems during the project, defect corrections, administration related to defect tracking, coordination with QA, support for user documentation, review of technical documents, integration, vacations, holidays, sick days, company and department meetings, and training.

Use software estimation tools. Software estimation tools can produce estimates for a wide variety of project sizes, project types, team sizes, staffing mixes, and other project variables. On large projects, software-estimation tools provide more accurate scheduling and lower incidence of cost overruns than do manual estimation methods (Jones 1994b).

Use several different estimation techniques, and compare the results. Try several different estimation techniques. Study the results from the different techniques. The most sophisticated commercial software producers tend to use at least three estimating tools and to look for convergence or spread among their schedule estimates. Convergence among the estimates tells them they've probably got a good estimate. Spread tells them there are probably factors they've overlooked and need to understand better.

Using only the information provided in this chapter, you can estimate a schedule based on assessing two different things:

- Lines of code and the schedules from Tables 8-8 through 8-10
- Function points and Jones's "first-order" measurement practice (described later in this chapter)

Change estimation practices as the project progresses. In the early stages of a project, an algorithmic or table-lookup estimate will be most accurate. During those stages, use estimation software or Tables 8-8 through 8-10 in this chapter. By about mid-design time, estimating each of the tasks individually and then adding them up will become the most accurate project estimate available and will remain so for the rest of the project (Symons 1991).

Estimate Presentation Styles

There's no point in being exact about something if you don't even know what you're talking about.

John von Neumann

The way you present an estimate initially can have a huge impact on what happens when the estimate needs changing later. Software estimation usually involves a great deal of risk and uncertainty, and a good estimate captures that risk and uncertainty.

179

Here are some techniques for presenting schedule estimates.

Plus-or-minus qualifiers. Use plus-or-minus style estimates to indicate both the amount and the direction of uncertainty in the estimate. Even when you have been forced into promising the software in an unrealistic time frame, you can let those around you know how risky the schedule is by presenting your estimates in plus-or-minus style. An estimate of 6 months, $+\frac{1}{2}$ month, $-\frac{1}{2}$ month says that the estimate is quite precise and that there's a good chance of meeting the estimate. An estimate of 6 months, +3 months, −2 months says that the estimate isn't very precise and that there's less chance of meeting the estimate. An estimate of 6 months, +6 months, −0 months says that the estimate is quite optimistic—probably unrealistic.

Ranges. One of the problems with plus-or-minus style estimates is that sometimes only the nominal part of the estimate is disseminated throughout the organization. The plus-or-minus factors are stripped off, which results in a significant loss of information. If that's the case, one alternative is to use ranges of estimates rather than plus-or-minus style estimates. For example, if your estimate is 6 months +3 months/−1 month, you could present the estimate as being 5–9 months instead.

Risk quantification. An extension of plus-or-minus estimation is to explain what the pluses and minuses represent in the estimate. Rather than simply saying "6 months, +3 months, −2 months," you can add information by putting the estimate into the form shown in Table 8-4.

Table 8-4. Example of a Risk-Quantification Estimate

Estimate: 6 months, +3 months, −2 months

+1 month for late delivery of graphics-formatting subsystem	−1 month for less delay in hiring new developers than expected
+1 month for new development tools not working as well as planned	−1 month from new development tools working better than planned
+0.5 month from staff sickness	
+0.5 month from underestimating size	

CROSS-REFERENCE
For more on addressing software-project risks, see Chapter 5, "Risk Management."

When you document the sources of uncertainty in your estimates, you provide your customers with information they can use to reduce the risks to the project and you lay the groundwork for explaining schedule changes if any of the risks materialize.

When you present estimates in this form, be prepared to answer questions about how you plan to address the risks and take advantage of the potential schedule reductions.

Cases. A variant of risk-quantified estimating is case-based estimating. Present your estimates for best case, worst case, planned case, and current case. The relationships between various of these different estimates will be interesting. If, for example, the planned case and the best case are the same, and the current case and the worst case are the same, your project is in trouble! Table 8-5 shows a sample estimate for a project that's not in quite that much trouble.

Table 8-5. Example of a Case-Based Estimate

Case	Estimate
Best case	April 1
Planned case	May 15
Current case	May 30
Worst case	July 15

Barry Boehm points out that, in practice, "planned case" or "most likely" estimates tend to cluster toward the "best case" end of the range, and actual results tend to cluster toward the "worst case" end of the range (Boehm 1981). Keep that in mind when creating and revising your set of cases.

Be prepared to explain to your customer what would have to occur for you to achieve the "best case" or fall into the "worst case." Customers will want to know about both possibilities.

Coarse dates and time periods. If your estimates are rough, use obviously coarse numbers such as 3Q97 or 10 man-years rather than misleadingly precise numbers such as July 19, 1997, or 520 man-weeks. In addition to expressing the message that the dates are approximate, the advantage of coarse numbers is that you don't risk losing information when they're simplified. An estimate of "6 months, +3 months, −1 month" can be simplified to "6 months." An estimate such as "3Q97" is immune to such simplification.

Confidence factors. One of the questions that people ask about a schedule is, "What chance do we have of making this date?" If you use the confidence-factor approach, you can answer that question by providing estimates that look like the one in Table 8-6 on the next page.

Table 8-6. Example of a Confidence-Factor Estimate

Delivery Date	Probability of Delivering On or Before the Scheduled Date
April 1	5%
May 1	50%
June 1	95%

CROSS-REFERENCE
For details on scheduling projects so that you have a 50-percent chance of completing them on time, see Section 6.3, "Odds of Completing on Time."

You can approximate these confidence intervals by using your "most likely" point estimate and the multipliers from Table 8-1 for the appropriate phase of your project. If you follow the advice in this book, you will have created the "most likely" estimate so that you can use it with 50-percent confidence. Multiplying your "most likely" estimate by Table 8-1's "optimistic" factor will provide you with the estimate you can use with 5-percent confidence. Multiplying by the "pessimistic" factor will provide the estimate you can use with 95-percent confidence.

8.4   Effort Estimation

Once you have the *size* estimate in hand, you can move to the second estimation step—deriving the *effort* estimate. Although the estimate is not strictly necessary for estimating a software schedule, you'll need an effort estimate in order to know how many people to put on your project; and having an effort estimate makes it easy to derive the schedule estimate.

Deriving the effort estimate is a straightforward process. Here are some of the ways you can convert a size estimate into an effort estimate:

- Use estimation software to create an effort estimate directly from the size estimate.

- Use the schedule tables in Tables 8-8 through 8-10 to convert a size estimate in lines of code to an effort estimate.

- Use your organization's historical data to determine how much effort previous projects of the estimated size have taken. Unless you have compelling reasons to think that the new project will be different from previous projects of a similar size, assume that it will take a proportional amount of effort. Once again, the most useful information you can have at this stage is historical data (not personal memory) from projects within your own organization.

- Use an algorithmic approach such as Barry Boehm's COCOMO model (Boehm 1981) or Putnam and Myers's lifecycle model (Putnam and Myers 1992) to convert a lines-of-code estimate into an effort estimate.

You can also apply many of the size-estimation tips described in the previous section to effort estimation.

8.5 Schedule Estimation

The third step in estimating a software project is to compute the schedule estimate. A rule of thumb is that you can compute the schedule from the effort estimate by using Equation 8-1.

Equation 8-1. Software Schedule Equation

$$\text{schedule in months} = 3.0 * \text{man-months}^{1/3}$$

If you've estimated that it will take 65 man-months to build the project, Equation 8-1 says that the optimal schedule is 12 months ($3.0 * 65^{1/3}$). That in turn implies an optimal team size of 65 man-months divided by the 12-month schedules—5 or 6 team members.

Unlike on many other topics in software project estimation, people have published remarkably similar findings on this topic (Boehm 1981). Opinions vary about whether the "3.0" in the equation should be 3.0 or 4.0 or 2.5 and about what exactly happens when you try to develop faster than the equation indicates—but if you don't have more accurate data from your own organization, Equation 8-1 is a good place to start.

This equation is the reason that the estimation ranges in Table 8-1 are broader for efforts than they are for schedules. Bigger projects take longer, but they also have bigger teams; and the inefficiencies associated with larger team sizes mean that effort increases disproportionately faster than schedule. The schedule ranges shown in Table 8-1 assume that you will add or remove team members as you learn more about the scope of the project. If you hold the team size constant, the schedule ranges will be just as large as the effort ranges.

Here are some alternative methods of computing the software schedule from the effort estimate:

- Use estimation software to compute the schedule from your size and effort estimates.
- Use historical data from your organization.
- Use the schedule tables—Tables 8-8 through 8-10—to look up a schedule estimate based on a size estimate.

- Use the schedule estimation step from one of the algorithmic approaches (for example, COCOMO) to provide an estimate that is more fine-tuned than what you'll get from Equation 8-1.

One of the common problems with schedule estimates is that they are usually done so crudely that people pad them to give themselves a margin of error. Sometimes people put in enough padding, and sometimes they don't.

CROSS-REFERENCE
Adding buffers for specific risks is a useful and sensible exception to the "no padding" rule. For details, see "Total Project Overrun and Buffers" in Section 5.3.

Equation 8-1 and the periodic-refinement approach allow you to quit using padding. Padding is a bad idea because it gives customers the wrong idea about why schedules are imprecise. Padding says, "I don't think our estimates are very good." An estimation range with periodic refinements says, "The estimates are good, but it's not possible for an estimate to be precise at this stage in the project. It will become more precise as we go along."

Use of software-estimation tools, algorithmic approaches, and the lookup tables in this book combined with the use of range estimates eliminates the need for padding and helps you to tell the estimation story clearly.

Commitment-Based Scheduling

CROSS-REFERENCE
For more on commitment-based scheduling, see Section 2.5, "An Alternative Rapid-Development Strategy," and Chapter 34, "Signing Up."

A few organizations proceed directly from requirements to scheduling without creating intermediate effort estimates. They typically do so within a commitment-based culture in which each developer is asked to make a schedule *commitment* rather than a schedule *estimate*. This practice pushes the responsibility for creating both the size estimate and the effort estimate onto the shoulders of the individual developers. It has the advantage of increasing developers' buy-in to schedules, tends to result in high morale for the period immediately following the commitment, and tends to elicit a lot of voluntary overtime from the developers.

HARD DATA

This practice also has several weaknesses. As far as estimation is concerned, surveys of estimated versus actual schedules have shown that developers' estimates tend to have an optimism factor of 20 to 30 percent (van Genuchten 1991). Within a commitment-based culture, that optimism is encouraged and it isn't subjected to any sanity checks. The overall effect is that it tends to produce large estimation errors.

CLASSIC MISTAKE

Commitment has a place in rapid development, but commitment-based planning as it is commonly practiced does not help to achieve short schedules. It is essential that the commitments be realistic and achievable so that your team can pile one success on top of another rather than get pounded down by one failure after another. The only good kind of schedule—commitment-based or otherwise—is an accurate one.

Jones's First-Order Estimation Practice

CROSS-REFERENCE
For details on function points, see "Function-Point Estimation" in Section 8.3.

If you have a function-point count, you can compute a rough schedule directly from that, using a practice that Capers Jones has described as "first-order estimation." To use it, you simply take the function-point total and raise it to the appropriate power selected from Table 8-7. The exponents in the table are derived from Jones's analysis of his database of several thousand projects.

Table 8-7. Exponents for Computing Schedules from Function Points

Kind of Software	Best in Class	Average	Worst in Class
Systems	0.43	0.45	0.48
Business	0.41	0.43	0.46
Shrink-wrap	0.39	0.42	0.45

Source: Adapted from "Determining Software Schedules" (Jones 1995c).

If you estimated your project's total number of function points to be 350 and you're working in an average shrink-wrap software organization, you would raise 350 to the 0.42 power ($350^{0.42}$), for a rough schedule of 12 calendar months. If you were working in a best-in-class shrink-wrap organization, you would raise 350 to the 0.39 power, for a schedule of 10 months.

This practice isn't a substitute for more careful schedule estimation, but it does provide a simple means of getting a rough schedule estimate that's better than guessing. It can also provide a quick reality check. If you want to develop a 350-function-point shrink-wrap product in 8 months, you should think again. The best-in-class schedule would be 10 months, and most organizations aren't best in class. Jones's first-order estimation practice allows you to know early on if you need to adjust your feature set, schedule expectations, or both.

8.6 Ballpark Schedule Estimates

The most unsuccessful three years in the education of cost estimators appears to be fifth-grade arithmetic.

Norman R. Augustine

One of the toughest obstacles to meaningful software scheduling is that usable, concrete information about software scheduling is hard to come by. The information that is available is usually found in one of two forms: it's either embedded in software-estimation programs, which at this time tend to be expensive ($1,000 to $10,000 or more), or it's in books with dozens of equations and multipliers, and it can take days to learn enough just to make a ballpark estimate.

What many people are looking for is a ballpark estimate of how long a program of a particular size will take, and that's what Tables 8-8 through 8-10 provide. The accuracy of the data in these tables won't be any match for the accuracy of data from projects within your own organization. But if your organization has not been keeping careful records about its past projects, this data should be more accurate than gut instinct.

Background

Tables 8-8 through 8-10 describe three kinds of projects:

CROSS-REFERENCE
For definitions of these kinds of software, see the sidebar, "Kinds of Projects," on page 22.

- Systems software
- Business software
- Shrink-wrap software

Systems software as it's defined here does not include firmware, real-time embedded software, avionics, process control, and the like. Productivity for those kinds of systems would be much lower.

If your project doesn't fit neatly into any of these categories, you can approximate an estimate for it by combining numbers from two or three of the columns. For example, if your project is a vertical-market product that seems as though it might be 60-percent business product and 40-percent shrink-wrap, you could add 60 percent of the business schedule to 40 percent of the shrink-wrap schedule to calculate the schedule for your product.

Schedules

The schedules are listed in terms of calendar months. They include all the design, construction, and testing time needed to complete a project. They do not include time for requirements specification. Schedules are given to one or two significant digits; greater precision than that would not be meaningful.

Efforts

The efforts are given in developer-team man-months (including management and quality assurance) to two or three significant digits. (They are given to three significant digits only when needed to more accurately represent the relationships between adjacent entries.)

CROSS-REFERENCE
For more on shortening and lengthening schedules, see "There is a shortest possible schedule, and you can't beat it," later in this section.

You can compute the average team size by dividing the effort months by the schedule months. The schedules do not attempt to represent the full range of possible combinations of schedules and team sizes. If you don't mind delivering the software a little later than the schedules in the tables, you can reduce overall project cost by lengthening the schedule and reducing the team size. A smaller team has less management and communication overhead, so it can work more productively (DeMarco 1982).

Lengthening the schedule beyond the nominal and keeping the team size the same doesn't produce similar savings. In that case, Parkinson's Law kicks in and work expands to fill the available time.

System sizes

The system sizes listed in Tables 8-8 through 8-10 are in lines of code, which are nonblank, noncomment source statements. In C and Pascal, a rough approximation would be the number of semicolons in the file. In Basic, it would be the number of nonblank, noncomment lines of source text. A statement that is formatted in such a way that it takes up more than one physical line still counts as only one "line of code" for purposes of these tables.

Small projects

The tables don't contain schedules for projects smaller than 10,000 lines of code. Projects in that range are usually completed by one person, and effort and schedule estimates for such projects are highly dependent on the capabilities of the individual performing the work. Many people work on smaller projects, and I would have liked to provide information that would be useful to them, but in the end I concluded that any numbers I provided would be meaningless. The individual assigned to do the work is best qualified to estimate such a project. You can still use the estimation practices described in the rest of this chapter to improve estimates for those projects.

Lines of code

Project sizes in these tables are given in lines of code. Line-of-code measurements have come under attack in recent years, and some people suggest using "function points" instead.

Line-of-code metrics do have some significant problems, but they are more commonly understood than function points, and, for any particular language, there is a high correlation between function points and lines of code (Albrecht and Gaffney 1983; Kemerer 1987).

Function points wouldn't be useful in tables like these because they don't translate well into effort if you don't know the specific language being used, and I don't know what language you're using. Fifty function points in macro assembler will take three or four times as long to implement as fifty function points in C++, but 1000 lines of code will take about the same amount of time in either language. Lines of code are thus as good a measure of program size as any other (for purposes of the schedule and effort estimates in these tables, anyway).

Accuracy of the estimates

Some people might also criticize these tables as being so oversimplified that they can't possibly produce useful estimates. It's true that these tables are simple. That's their purpose. It's also true that historical data from your own industry, organization, or group will allow you to make more accurate estimates than the estimates in these tables. But as simple as they are, Tables 8-8 through 8-10 provide estimates that for their intended purpose are about as accurate as some more complicated estimation models.

Chris Kemerer compared the effort predictions of five estimation models with a sample of 15 projects, and he found that the most accurate estimation model produced effort estimates that were, on average, within only about 100 percent of the actual efforts (Kemerer 1987). When subjected to Kemerer's test, the estimates from these tables produced a smaller average error than the most accurate estimation model he tested.

Considering this, the estimates in Tables 8-6 through 8-8 do serve their intended purpose of providing ballpark estimates that are more accurate than gut instinct. To anyone who claims to have more accurate estimation data, I say, that's great! Put your data into an easily usable form and make it publicly available.

Shortest Possible Schedules

CROSS-REFERENCE
For a hint on how to allocate time to different development activities, see Section 6.5, "Where the Time Goes."

This section contains Table 8-8, "Shortest Possible Schedules." When you're faced with a large project, a year or two can seem like an infinite amount of time. It might seem as though you should be able to complete any project in a year. But that's just not the case.

Use the schedules in Table 8-8 as sanity checks to help you be sure that your schedules are at least in the ballpark. If you think that you shouldn't have any trouble developing a 75,000 line shrink-wrap application in 9 months with 10 developers, think again! The shortest schedule for such an application is 10 months with 14 developers. Every schedule-reducing practice has already been included in that shortest possible schedule. It's almost certain that any particular project will take longer than 10 months. Achievable, optimistic schedules can still cause lots of problems, but you'll have a greater chance of success if you make sure that your initial estimate is at least somewhere in the possible range!

You might look at these schedules and think, "Shortest possible schedule? There's no way I could develop a 75,000 line shrink-wrap application in 10 months." If you think that, I'm sure that you're right. These schedules are the shortest schedules that can be achieved by the ideal software development organization. They will be out of reach for the majority of organizations. As you can see in Figure 8-5, even an organization that has a chance of achieving the shortest possible schedule still runs a large risk of coming in late.

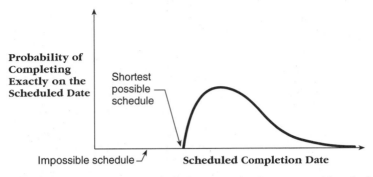

Figure 8-5. *An impossible schedule. Using the shortest possible schedule entails a high risk of late completion. Schedules shorter than that are simply impossible. Be sure that your planned schedule is at least as long as the shortest possible schedule.*

Assumptions

Because the schedules in Table 8-8 are the shortest possible schedules, they contain a hat full of extremely optimistic assumptions.

Staffing. Table 8-8's schedules assume that your team has drawn its talent from the top 10 percent of the talent pool. That means that the analysts who specified the requirements were in the top 10 percent and the developers are in the top 10 percent. Everyone has several years of experience working with the programming language you're using and with the programming environment you're developing in. The developers have a detailed knowledge of the applications area. Everyone is motivated, everyone shares the same vision of the product, everyone gets along with each other, everyone works as hard as possible, and there is no turnover.

CROSS-REFERENCE
For more on staffing patterns, see the "Further Reading" section at the end of this chapter.

Management. These schedules assume that the project has ideal project management, and that the developers' time isn't diverted into activities unrelated to technical development work. The project is staffed using a rectangular staffing pattern—that is, the entire staff starts working on Day 1 of the project and continues until the project is released.

Tool support. Advanced software tools are available, and the developers have unlimited access to computer resources. The office environment is ideal, and the entire project team is located within the same immediate area. All necessary communications tools such as individual phones, voicemail, fax, workgroup networks, and email with embedded documents are integrated into the work environment. Supplemental communications technologies such as video conferencing are available when needed.

Methodology. The most time-efficient development methods and development tools are also used. Requirements are completely known at the time design work starts, and they don't change.

Compression. These schedules have been compressed as much as possible below the nominal schedules for this set of assumptions. They can't be compressed any further.

Table 8-8. Shortest Possible Schedules

System Size (lines of code)	Systems Products		Business Products		Shrink-Wrap Products	
	Schedule (months)	Effort (man-months)	Schedule (months)	Effort (man-months)	Schedule (months)	Effort (man-months)
10,000	6	25	3.5	5	4.2	8
15,000	7	40	4.1	8	4.9	13
20,000	8	57	4.6	11	5.6	19
25,000	9	74	5.1	15	6	24
30,000	9	110	5.5	22	7	37
35,000	10	130	5.8	26	7	44
40,000	11	170	6	34	7	57
45,000	11	195	6	39	8	66
50,000	11	230	7	46	8	79
60,000	12	285	7	57	9	98
70,000	13	350	8	71	9	120
80,000	14	410	8	83	10	140
90,000	14	480	9	96	10	170
100,000	15	540	9	110	11	190
120,000	16	680	10	140	11	240
140,000	17	820	10	160	12	280
160,000	18	960	10	190	13	335
180,000	19	1,100	11	220	13	390
200,000	20	1,250	11	250	14	440
250,000	22	1,650	13	330	15	580
300,000	24	2,100	14	420	16	725
400,000	27	2,900	15	590	19	1,000
500,000	30	3,900	17	780	20	1,400

Sources: Derived from data in *Software Engineering Economics* (Boehm 1981), "An Empirical Validation of Software Cost Estimation Models" (Kemerer 1987), *Applied Software Measurement* (Jones 1991), *Measures for Excellence* (Putnam and Myers 1992), and *Assessment and Control of Software Risks* (Jones 1994).

Two facts of life

When it comes to scheduling, there are a few facts of life that we might prefer to be otherwise but which we can't change. Knowing what they are is perhaps some consolation. Here are two very important ones.

There is a shortest possible schedule, and you can't beat it. At some point, adding more software developers slows a project down instead of making it faster. Think about it: if one person can write a 1000-line program in a week, can five people write the same program in one day? Can 40 people write it in one hour?

It's easy to recognize the effect of communication and integration overhead in this simple example. It might be harder to recognize the effect on a larger project with a longer schedule, but the limiting factors are the same.

As Figure 8-6 illustrates, for a project of a particular size there's a point beyond which the development schedule simply can't be shortened. Not by working harder. Not by working smarter. Not by finding creative solutions. Not by making the team larger. It simply can't be done.

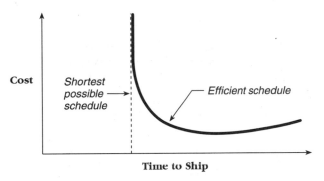

Figure 8-6. *Relationship between cost and schedule on a software project. The cost of achieving the efficient schedule is much less than the cost of achieving the shortest possible schedule.*

It is difficult to imagine any project that will possess all the characteristics assumed in these schedules, so it is hard to imagine that any project could actually achieve any of the shortest possible schedules. If your project doesn't match up to the assumptions underlying these schedules, it shouldn't be scheduled in the shortest-possible-schedule range. No project should ever be planned with a schedule shorter than the schedules in Table 8-8.

Costs increase rapidly when you shorten the schedule below nominal. Once your tools and methods are in place, you can reduce your schedule simply by increasing the number of developers or the amount of overtime. That's called "schedule compression." As Figure 8-6 illustrates, however, the other fact of life is that it becomes prohibitively expensive to shorten development time much below nominal. That's because you incur more communications and management overhead, and you have to use relatively inefficient staffing patterns.

Researchers have put forth many different methods for estimating the cost of schedule compression. A rule of thumb that is accurate enough for most purposes was put forth by Charles Symons (Symons 1991). You first estimate the initial effort and initial schedule. Then you combine those estimates with your desired schedule to compute the schedule compression factor using Equation 8-2.

Equation 8-2. Schedule Compression Factor

schedule compression factor = desired schedule ÷ initial schedule

If the initial schedule for your project is 12 months and you want to complete it in 10, the compression factor would be 0.83 (10 ÷ 12). Supposing that your initial effort estimate was 78 man-months, you then plug the 0.83 into the compressed schedule effort equation, Equation 8-3.

Equation 8-3. Compressed Schedule Effort

compressed schedule effort = initial effort ÷ schedule compression factor

That yields a compressed schedule effort of 94 man-months (78 ÷ 0.83), which means that the 17-percent reduction in the schedule requires a 21-percent increase in effort.

HARD DATA

Most researchers have concluded that it isn't possible to achieve a schedule compression factor lower than about 0.75 or 0.80 (Boehm 1981; Putnam and Myers 1992; Jones 1994). What this means is that there is a limit to how much you can reduce a schedule by adding people and requiring more overtime, and that limit is 25 percent at best. If your compression factor is lower than 0.75, you'll need to reduce the size of your product or lengthen your schedule instead of relying solely on schedule compression.

Incidentally, these schedule compression factors also work backwards. If you're willing to lengthen your schedule slightly, you can reduce the cost of your project by reducing the team size disproportionately. You can use Equations 8-2 and 8-3 to compute the effect of uncompressing a project's schedule.

Efficient Schedules

CROSS-REFERENCE
For details on what is meant by "efficient development," see "Efficient Development" in Section 2.3.

This section contains Table 8-9, "Efficient Schedules." Given that the shortest possible schedules are out of reach for nearly all organizations, scheduling according to the efficient schedules or the nominal schedules provided in the next section is the more realistic alternative.

Assumptions

The efficient schedules assume that you do most things right, but they stop short of making the ideal-case assumptions that underlie the shortest possible schedules.

CROSS-REFERENCE
For more information
on manpower buildup
patterns, see the "Further
Reading" references at the
end of the chapter.

These schedules assume that your team has drawn its talent from the top 25 percent of the talent pool, and that applies to both analysts and developers. Everyone has worked with the programming language and environment for a few years. Turnover is less than 6 percent per year. The team might not gel, but there is a shared consensus about the mission of the project and there are no significant conflicts. The project is staffed using an efficient staffing pattern, one that's known as a Rayleigh-style manpower-buildup pattern.

Aside from these assumptions, Table 8-9's schedules use the same assumptions as those for the shortest possible schedules: efficient use of programming tools, use of modern programming practices, active risk management, excellent physical environment, integrated use of communication tools, use of rapid-development practices, and so on.

These schedules have not been compressed below the nominal schedules for this set of assumptions. You can compress them up to 25 percent using the practice described in conjunction with Equations 8-2 and 8-3.

What if you're not sure whether to use the efficient schedules provided in Table 8-9 or the nominal schedules provided in Table 8-10? If you're working according to most of the efficient development practices described in Chapters 1 through 5, use these efficient schedules. If your project is shaky on the fundamentals, use the nominal schedules in Table 8-9.

Relationship between shortest possible and efficient schedules

One interesting aspect of the schedules in Table 8-9 is that the projects described require less effort overall than the projects in the shortest-possible-schedule table (Table 8-8)—in spite of the fact that the shortest possible schedules use more optimistic assumptions. That's a result of the fact that the shortest possible schedules are compressed as much as possible, and that compression carries a price.

Compressing the efficient schedules by the maximum amount (shortening them by 25 percent) will produce schedules that are of similar duration to the shortest possible schedules but that are more costly because of the less optimistic assumptions.

For most projects, these efficient schedules will represent "best case" schedules. The shortest possible schedules will simply be unachievable. These schedules will be achievable if nearly everything goes right.

Table 8-9. Efficient Schedules

System Size (lines of code)	Systems Products		Business Products		Shrink-Wrap Products	
	Schedule (months)	Effort (man-months)	Schedule (months)	Effort (man-months)	Schedule (months)	Effort (man-months)
10,000	8	24	4.9	5	5.9	8
15,000	10	38	5.8	8	7	12
20,000	11	54	7	11	8	18
25,000	12	70	7	14	9	23
30,000	13	97	8	20	9	32
35,000	14	120	8	24	10	39
40,000	15	140	9	30	10	49
45,000	16	170	9	34	11	57
50,000	16	190	10	40	11	67
60,000	18	240	10	49	12	83
70,000	19	290	11	61	13	100
80,000	20	345	12	71	14	120
90,000	21	400	12	82	15	140
100,000	22	450	13	93	15	160
120,000	23	560	14	115	16	195
140,000	25	670	15	140	17	235
160,000	26	709	15	160	18	280
180,000	28	910	16	190	19	320
200,000	29	1,300	17	210	20	360
250,000	32	1,300	19	280	22	470
300,000	34	1,650	20	345	24	590
400,000	38	2,350	22	490	27	830
500,000	42	3,100	25	640	29	1,100

Sources: Derived from data in *Software Engineering Economics* (Boehm 1981), "An Empirical Validation of Software Cost Estimation Models" (Kemerer 1987), *Applied Software Measurement* (Jones 1991), *Measures for Excellence* (Putnam and Myers 1992), and *Assessment and Control of Software Risks* (Jones 1994).

Nominal Schedules

This section contains Table 8-10, "Nominal Schedules." The nominal schedules are intended for use on average projects. Given that by definition most projects are average, most projects should use these nominal schedules rather than the efficient schedules or shortest possible schedules.

Assumptions

Nominal schedules use less optimistic assumptions than the other schedules do. They assume that your team has drawn its talent from the top 50 percent of the talent pool. The average team member has some familiarity with the programming language and the environment, but not necessarily extensive familiarity. The team has, on average, had some experience in the applications area—again, not necessarily extensive experience. These teams might not gel and might experience some conflicts. They can experience turnover of from 10 to 12 percent per year.

Programming tools and modern programming practices are used to some extent, but not as much as they would be on an efficient-development project. Some of the rapid-development practices in this book might be used, but they aren't used to their best advantage. Risks may be managed less actively than is ideal. Communications tools of individual phones, voicemail, fax, workgroup networks, and email are readily available, but they might not be integrated into the normal workflow. The office environment is somewhat less than ideal, but adequate: developers might be in cubicles rather than in private offices, but they aren't in open bays or programming bullpens.

As with the efficient-development schedules, these schedules have not been compressed below the nominal schedules, so you can compress them by up to 25 percent.

These schedules are not as speedy as the efficient-development schedules, but they are hardly worst-case schedules. They assume that you're doing a lot of things right, and achieving any of these nominal schedules will be a 50/50 bet for the average project.

Why develop efficiently?

These schedules not only take longer than the corresponding efficient schedules, they are far more expensive. The efficient development of a 250,000 line-of-code shrink-wrap application would consume about 470 man-months over 22 months. The same project developed in the nominal way would consume 800 man-months over a 26-month period.

Compressing the nominal schedules can produce schedules that are of similar duration to the efficient schedules but that are far more costly because of less efficient development practices. Compressing the nominal schedule for the 250,000-lines-of-code shrink-wrap application to finish in the same 22 months as efficient development would cost 950 man-months, twice as much as efficient development. Organizations reap significant benefits by using efficient development practices.

Table 8-10. Nominal Schedules

System Size (lines of code)	Systems Products		Business Products		Shrink-Wrap Products	
	Schedule (months)	Effort (man-months)	Schedule (months)	Effort (man-months)	Schedule (months)	Effort (man-months)
10,000	10	48	6	9	7	15
15,000	12	76	7	15	8	24
20,000	14	110	8	21	9	34
25,000	15	140	9	27	10	44
30,000	16	185	9	37	11	59
35,000	17	220	10	44	12	71
40,000	18	270	10	54	13	88
45,000	19	310	11	61	13	100
50,000	20	360	11	71	14	115
60,000	21	440	12	88	15	145
70,000	23	540	13	105	16	175
80,000	24	630	14	125	17	210
90,000	25	730	15	140	17	240
100,000	26	820	15	160	18	270
120,000	28	1,000	16	200	20	335
140,000	30	1,200	17	240	21	400
160,000	32	1,400	18	280	22	470
180,000	34	1,600	19	330	23	540
200,000	35	1,900	20	370	24	610
250,000	38	2,400	22	480	26	800
300,000	41	3,000	24	600	29	1,000
400,000	47	4,200	27	840	32	1,400
500,000	51	5,500	29	1,100	35	1,800

Sources: Derived from data in *Software Engineering Economics* (Boehm 1981), "An Empirical Validation of Software Cost Estimation Models" (Kemerer 1987), *Applied Software Measurement* (Jones 1991), *Measures for Excellence* (Putnam and Myers 1992), and *Assessment and Control of Software Risks* (Jones 1994).

What to Do First with the Ballpark Schedules

The first thing that most people will do when they see these schedules is to pull out notes from a recent project and compare how they did with the numbers in these tables. Was their project as fast as possible? Efficient? Nominal?

That's actually the best thing to do because it's the best way to learn about your projects. If the numbers in the tables estimate higher or lower than your last project, you'll know how to calibrate them before you use them to estimate your next project.

8.7 Estimate Refinement

One question that managers and customers ask is, "If I give you another week to work on your estimate, can you refine it so that it contains less uncertainty?" That's a reasonable request, but unfortunately it's not possible to act on it the way you'd like to. Research by Luiz Laranjeira suggests that the accuracy of the software estimate depends on the level of refinement of the software's definition (Laranjeira 1990). The more refined the definition, the more accurate the estimate. This makes sense intuitively because the more the system is nailed down, the less uncertainty feeds into the estimate.

The implication of Laranjeira's research is that the work you have to do to refine the software definition is the work of the software project itself: requirements specification, product design, and detailed design. It is simply not possible to know a schedule with ±10 percent precision at the requirements-specification stage. You can control it to come out on the low side, but if you just let the project flow wherever it wants to go, you'll get no better than +50 percent, −33 percent precision.

It is possible to refine a project estimate as the project progresses, and you should do that. The typical process that people follow is to allow themselves to be forced into making a single-point estimate early on and then be held accountable for it. For example, suppose a team lead provides the set of estimates listed in Table 8-11 over the course of a project.

Table 8-11. Example of a Single-Point–Estimation History

Point in Project	Estimate (man-months)
Initial product concept	100
Approved product concept	100
Requirements specification	135
Product design specification	145
Detailed design specification	160
Final	170

CLASSIC MISTAKE

When a team lead uses this single-point approach, the customer will consider the project to have slipped over budget and behind schedule the first time the estimate increases—when it increases from 100 to 135 man-months. After that, the project will be considered to be slipping into ever more trouble. That's absurd because not enough was known about the project when the 100-man-month estimate was made to create a meaningful estimate. The final tally of 170 man-months might actually represent excellent efficiency.

Contrast that scenario with one in which the team lead provides estimates in ranges that become narrower as the project progresses, such as those shown in Table 8-12.

Table 8-12. Example of a Range-Estimation History

Point in Project	Estimate (man-months)
Initial product concept	25–400
Approved product concept	50–200
Requirements specification	90–200
Product design specification	120–180
Detailed design specification	145–180
Final	170

These estimates contain a tremendous amount of imprecision, and all but the most sophisticated customers will try to get you to narrow the ranges. But it isn't possible to provide more precision than that shown in Table 8-12—it's only possible to lie about it or not to know any better. The imprecision isn't a sign of a bad estimate; it's part of the nature of software development. Failure to acknowledge imprecision is a sign of a bad estimate.

In the case illustrated in Table 8-12, as the team lead refines each estimate, management or the customer will consider the project to be staying within their expectations. Rather than losing the customer's confidence by taking one schedule slip after another, the team lead builds confidence by refusing to provide more precision than is reasonable and by consistently meeting the customer's expectations.

The number of times you revise an estimate can affect whether it is accepted. If you explain the estimation story ahead of time and promise to provide increasingly refined estimates at regular milestones such as those contained in Table 8-12, that will make for an orderly, respectable process.

Recalibration

Suppose that you have a 6-month schedule. You planned to meet your first milestone in 4 weeks, but it actually takes you 5 weeks. When you miss a scheduled date, there is a question about how to recalibrate the schedule. Should you:

1. Assume you can make up the lost week later in the schedule?

2. Add the week to the total schedule?

3. Multiply the whole schedule by the magnitude of the slip, in this case by 25 percent?

CLASSIC MISTAKE

The most common approach is #1. The reasoning typically goes like this: "Requirements took a little longer than we expected, but now they're solid, so we're bound to save time later. We'll make up the shortfall during coding and testing."

HARD DATA

A 1991 survey of more than 300 projects found that projects hardly ever make up lost time—they tend to get further behind (van Genuchten 1991). That eliminates option #1.

Estimation errors tend to be inaccurate for systemic reasons that pervade the whole schedule, such as pressure from management to use optimistic assumptions. It's unlikely that the whole schedule is accurate except for the part that you've had real experience with. So that eliminates option #2.

CROSS-REFERENCE
For more on recalibration, see "Regularly assess progress and recalibrate or replan" in Section 27.1.

With rare exception, the correct response to a missed milestone is option #3. That option makes the most sense analytically. It also matches my experience the best. If you aren't ready to extend the schedule by that amount, and people often aren't, then you can delay your decision and get more data by monitoring how you do in meeting the second milestone. But if you're still off by 25 percent in meeting the second milestone, it will be harder for you to take corrective action, and the corrective action you do take will have less time to work than it would if you had taken corrective action at the first available opportunity.

Changing the estimate after missing or beating a milestone isn't the only option, of course. You can change the "product" corner of the schedule/ product/cost triangle, or you can change the "cost" corner. You can change the spec to save time. You can spend more money. The only thing you can't do is to keep the schedule, the spec, and the cost the same and expect the project to improve.

The problems associated with schedule slips are mainly confidence problems. If you sign up to perform to a best-case estimate, a slip means that you have failed or are on the brink of failing. You're not meeting your planned schedule, and there's no basis for knowing what your completion date really is.

But if you've described ahead of time how your estimate will mature as the project matures and given your estimates as ranges, there will be fewer slips. As long as you're in the range, you're doing fine. A "slip" becomes something that's completely out of the estimation range, and that becomes a rare occurrence.

Case Study 8-2. Careful Project Estimation

Across town from Giga-Safe, Square-Tech was working on Cube-It 2.0, which, coincidentally, would turn out to be exactly the same size as the ICS 1.0 project described in Case Study 8-1. The team lead, George, met with Kim, the project manager; Carlos, a representative from marketing; and Rex, the CEO to whom both Kim and Carlos reported.

"Cube-It 1.0 has been a big hit, and we need to get an upgrade out fast, before the competition catches up," Carlos said. "We need a major upgrade in 6 months."

"Based on the preliminary product definition I've seen, that's not very likely," George said. "At this point, I would estimate the schedule at 2 to 5 quarters with a 'most likely' schedule of 3 quarters."

"Three *quarters*? Are you kidding me? I need something more specific than that," Carlos said.

"We haven't refined the product concept enough for me to provide a more precise estimate," George said. "With all the uncertainty in the product definition, it's not even theoretically possible. I've got to know what I'm going to build before I can say how long it will take. If we can trim a lot of features as we define the feature set, sure, we can bring it in in less time. But from what I've heard, this needs to be a full-featured version."

Rex spoke up. "You're right. We went for the pure-and-simple product with version 1.0, which gave us a terrific foot in the door. But we've got some significant functionality gaps that we need to close in version 2."

"Then I have to stick to my estimate of 2 to 5 quarters," George said.

"That's not good enough. You need to give us a more specific estimate," Kim said. "You said that you might be able to do it in 2 quarters. Let's just set a target of 6 months."

"I'm sorry, but I can't support that," George said. "We would just be fooling ourselves. Six months is the bare minimum to implement the absolute smallest feature set. My 'most likely' estimate is 3 quarters. That's 9 months, not 6.

"Believe me, I wish I could tell you what you want to hear," George continued. "It's not easy to sit here with a group of people who are all senior to me and tell you that I can't give you what you want. But if I did give you a more precise estimate, it would be worthless, and then the next time you wouldn't believe me at all. I'd rather tell you the truth now."

(continued)

Case Study 8-2. Careful Project Estimation, *continued*

George went over to the whiteboard and drew the estimate-convergence graph. "What I can promise is to refine the estimate steadily as we go along. I'll provide a schedule estimate that's accurate to within plus or minus 15 percent once we're finished with requirements and plus or minus 10 percent once we're finished with the detailed user-interface design. Once we're done with detailed design, I'll provide an estimate that's accurate to within 5 percent."

"I can support that," Rex said. "Let's get going on those requirements so that we figure out how soon we can release a product."

By week 5, George had completed the product concept, and he refined his estimate to 3 to 5 quarters with a "most likely" schedule of 5 quarters. He met again with Carlos, Kim, and Rex. Carlos and Kim pressed for a specific delivery date, but George politely refused. "There is still a huge amount of ambiguity in the product concept," he explained. "We've nailed it down a lot since last time, but there are still literally hundreds of details that need to be nailed down, and those can add up to a lot of time."

"The range goes from 3 to 5 quarters now instead of from 2 to 5," Kim pointed out. "Are you saying there's no chance of delivering the next version in 6 months?"

"That is what I'm saying," George said. "Based on the number of features that marketing has identified as make-or-break features, there's no way we can complete this project in less than 3 quarters."

"Why has the 'most likely' estimate increased from 3 quarters to 5?" Rex asked.

"Marketing wanted many more features in the product than I had originally assumed," George said. "But there's still plenty of time to redefine the feature set so that we can complete the project in less time."

"You should do that," Rex said. "We need features, but there's no way we can wait 5 quarters until the next release. Work with Carlos to define a feature set that you can deliver in a maximum of 4 quarters, ideally less."

By Week 17 George and his team had completed the requirements specification. They defined a product with a smaller feature set, and George refined his estimate to say that the project would take 9 to 12 months with a "most likely" estimate of 10 months.

"Ten *months!* That's great!" Rex said. "I was beginning to think that you would stay stuck on 'quarters' the whole project. Thanks to both you and Carlos for bringing the scope into line. When will you be able to provide a more specific estimate?"

"I'll have one at the end of product design, to within plus or minus 10 percent. That'll be in about 2 months," George said.

At 24 weeks, the Cube-It team completed the product design. George refined his estimate to say that the project would take 43 to 52 weeks, with a "most

(continued)

Case Study 8-2. Careful Project Estimation, *continued*

likely" completion time of 48 weeks. "It's safe to make plans based on the 52-week maximum schedule. It won't take any longer than that," he told Kim, Carlos, and Rex. They accepted the 52-week estimate without questions.

At 7 months, the Cube-It team completed detailed design, and George again refined the estimate. He reported that the project looked like it would take 47 to 51 weeks with a schedule of 49 weeks being most likely.

The Cube-It team delivered the product at the end of Week 50. Rex congratulated George on a job well done.

George took a few weeks off, and 55 weeks after Cube-It 2.0 began, he started a new project. He estimated the new project would take 2 to 4 quarters. "That doesn't give us much to go on. You've got to be more specific than that," a newly hired upper manager complained.

"No he doesn't," Kim explained as she drew the estimate-convergence graph on the whiteboard. "There's uncertainty in the schedule because there are uncertainties in the software product itself. George will refine the estimate in plenty of time to coordinate the other plans that depend on it."

Epilogue

The projects in the two case studies in this chapter were of identical sizes. The project in the first case study took 56 weeks instead of 50 because of its poor initial estimate. The poor estimate caused poor planning decisions and hasty, error-prone designs.

The projects in the two case studies made the same number of schedule adjustments. In the Giga-Safe case study, management thought the project was out of control as soon as Carl made his first schedule adjustment. They saw the adjustment as a schedule slip. The more schedule adjustments he made, the more out of control the project seemed. In the Square-Tech case study, management thought the project was under control the whole time, and each time George made a schedule adjustment, the project seemed even more under control.

By the ends of their projects, Carl's project was considered to be a failure, and he had lost nearly all credibility; and George's project was considered to be a success, and he had laid the groundwork for less confrontational project planning the next time around.

Further Reading

General Estimation

Boehm, Barry W. *Software Engineering Economics*. Englewood Cliffs, N.J.: Prentice Hall, 1981. This monumental book contains a thorough discussion of software estimation and scheduling, which is presented in terms of Boehm's COCOMO cost-estimation model. Because the book contains so many equations, graphs, and tables, it can look overwhelming, but most of the data Boehm presents is provided for reference purposes, and the part of the book that you actually need to read and understand isn't as long or complicated as it first appears.

Papers on an updated version of COCOMO have begun to trickle out. One is "Cost Models for Future Software Life Cycle Processes: COCOMO 2.0" (Boehm et al. 1995). Be on the lookout for an update to the material in Boehm's book sometime soon.

DeMarco, Tom. *Controlling Software Projects*. New York: Yourdon Press, 1982. Part III of DeMarco's book (Chapters 15 through 18) describes several software estimation models or "cost models." In the schedule tables in this chapter, I describe the assumptions that went into the schedules, but I don't describe why the assumptions affect the schedules the way they do. DeMarco explains why various factors affect software projects' costs and schedules. In complexity, his explanations are about halfway between the explanations in Boehm's book and the ones in this chapter.

Putnam, Lawrence H., and Ware Myers. *Measures for Excellence: Reliable Software On Time, Within Budget*. Englewood Cliffs, N.J.: Yourdon Press, 1992. Somewhat less daunting than Boehm's book, Putnam and Myers's book also presents a full-fledged software-project estimation methodology. The book is mathematically oriented, so it can be slow going. But I think it's worth the price just for Chapter 14, "A Very Simple Software Estimating System," which explains how to calibrate a simple cost-estimation model to your organization and how to use it to estimate medium to large projects. It discusses the phenomenon of lengthening a schedule slightly to reduce a project's cost, and it describes manpower-buildup patterns, including the Rayleigh curve.

Jones, Capers. *Assessment and Control of Software Risks*. Englewood Cliffs, N.J.: Yourdon Press, 1994. Although not specifically about estimation, this book contains discussions that relate to the topic. Of particular interest is a useful outline of the components of a typical estimate in Chapter 43, "Lack of Reusable Estimates (Templates)."

Gilb, Tom. *Principles of Software Engineering Management*. Wokingham, England: Addison-Wesley, 1988. Gilb provides practical advice for estimating software schedules. He puts a different emphasis on estimation than other authors, focusing on the importance of controlling the project to achieve your objectives rather than making passive predictions about it.

Function-Point Analysis

These three books contain complete discussions of function-point analysis.

Dreger, Brian. *Function Point Analysis*, Englewood Cliffs, N.J.: Prentice Hall, 1989.

Jones, Capers. *Applied Software Measurement: Assuring Productivity and Quality*. New York: McGraw-Hill, 1991.

Symons, Charles. *Software Sizing and Estimating: Mk II FPA (Function Point Analysis)*. Chichester, England: John Wiley & Sons, 1991.

9

Scheduling

Contents

Related Topics

MY TEAM SPENT SEVERAL DAYS WORKING ON a detailed project estimate. (Yes, this is my experience—not a case study.) We divided the project into several dozen features, and each person estimated each feature individually. We spent two long days discussing the estimates feature by feature so that we fully understood the variability in each one. We considered several approaches to combining the individual-feature estimates, and we finally came up with a most-likely schedule estimate of 15 months and a range of 12 to 18 months.

CROSS-REFERENCE For details on first-order estimation practice, see "Jones's First-Order Estimation Practice" in Section 8.5.

To sanity-check our work, we estimated the new project's size as a percentage of a similar, previous project's size and calculated the new schedule from the old one. That estimate came out to 15 months. Then we pumped our numbers into a commercial estimating tool, and the tool estimated 16 months. Jones's first-order estimation practice spit out a 16-month estimate, too.

On the way into the oversight committee meeting the next week, my boss asked, "What did your estimate come out to be?"

"15 months, plus or minus 3 months," I said.

"That's too long," he said. "I told you I wanted a short estimate. I'm going to tell the committee 9 months; that way, if we need some more time we can slide a little bit and still deliver in 12."

I protested. "Where did you get 9 months? We've already pared down the product in every way we can. That 15-month estimate is about as solid as estimates get. Nine months doesn't even make sense."

"To this committee, it does," my boss said sternly. By that time, other people on the committee were beginning to arrive, so I sat through the meeting and watched my boss sign me up for a schedule that I knew was impossible.

In the ideal world, you would create an estimate using practices such as those described in the previous chapter, and then you would be allowed to work to that schedule. In the real world, your boss, customer, marketing rep, or boss's boss can overrule your best estimate with a few waves of their magic wands and sign you up for an impossible deadline. But whether they know it or not, it's not in their best interest to underestimate your project.

What does scheduling have to do with rapid development? It has to do with creating an environment that isn't characterized by hasty, error-prone decision making and that is conducive to effective planning, thoughtful design, and time-saving quality assurance.

Creating an accurate, analytical estimate does not guarantee that the estimate will be accepted or that the project will actually be scheduled in a way that supports efficient development. Between current estimation practices and current scheduling practices, I am convinced that scheduling practices are the more serious problem.

The previous chapter described how to create an accurate estimate. This chapter discusses how to get that estimate accepted.

Where Do Schedules Come From?

"Most IS people I know—managers or not—don't control their own schedules. Schedules are handed down, like stone tablets (or, some would say, like bat guano) from on high—where 'on high' could mean the marketing department or top management.

"As a ranking curmudgeon in the field, I talk to a lot of people out there. Everyone I talk to—without exception—says that this schedule problem is the biggest plague of the field. Not fast-changing technology. Not new management philosophies. Working to impossible schedules is the biggest problem in IS."

—*Robert L. Glass*

9.1 Overly Optimistic Scheduling

First Law of Bad Management: "When something isn't working, do more of it."
Gerald Weinberg

Although you might think of impossible schedules as a modern problem, overly optimistic software schedules are a shop-worn tradition in software development. In 1967, Gene Bylinsky reported that "all significant programming problems turn out to be emergencies" (Bylinsky 1967). In the 1970s, Fred Brooks pointed out that "more software projects have gone awry for lack of calendar time than all other causes combined" (Brooks 1975). A decade later, Scott Costello observed that "deadline pressure is the single greatest enemy of software engineering" (Costello 1984).

HARD DATA

The situation hasn't changed in the 1990s. Capers Jones reports that excessive schedule pressure is the most common of all serious software engineering problems. "Excessive or irrational schedules are probably the single most destructive influence in all of software" (Jones 1991, 1994). Working under extreme deadline pressure has become a tradition. Fifty percent of projects set their schedules before requirements are set, and they don't set them with time to spare. It isn't uncommon for customers to insist on costs and schedules that are so far below U.S. norms that completion on time and within budget is technically impossible (Jones 1994).

This section examines the common practice of overly optimistic scheduling.

An Example of Overly Optimistic Scheduling

The development of Microsoft Word for Windows 1.0 provides an object lesson in the effects of optimistic scheduling practices. Word for Windows, aka "WinWord," spent 5 years in development, consumed 660 man-months of developer effort, and produced a system of 249,000 lines of code (Iansiti 1994). The final 5-year schedule was approximately five times as long as originally planned. Table 9-1 on the next page summarizes WinWord's scheduling history.

CROSS-REFERENCE
See Table 8-8 for the full set of shortest possible schedules.

WinWord had an extremely aggressive schedule. The shortest possible schedule for a project of its size is about 460 days. The *longest* estimate for WinWord 1.0's schedule was 395 days, which is 65 days shorter than the shortest possible schedule.

Development of WinWord 1.0 contained classic examples of the things that go wrong when a software project is scheduled too aggressively:

- WinWord was beset by unachievable goals. Bill Gates's directive to the team was to "develop the best word processor ever" and to do it as fast as possible, preferably within 12 months. Either of those goals individually would have been challenging. The combination was impossible.

Table 9-1. Scheduling History of Word for Windows 1.0

Report Date	Estimated Ship Date	Estimated Days to Ship	Actual Days to Ship	Relative Error
Sep-84	Sep-85	365	1887*	81%
Jun-85	Jul-86	395	1614	76%
Jan-86	Nov-86	304	1400	78%
Jun-86	May-87	334	1245	73%
Jan-87	Dec-87	334	1035	68%
Jun-87	Feb-88	245	884	72%
Jan-88	Jun-88	152	670	77%
Jun-88	Oct-88	122	518	76%
Aug-88	Jan-89	153	457	67%
Oct-88	Feb-89	123	396	69%
Jan-89	May-89	120	304	61%
Jun-89	Sep-89	92	153	40%
Jul-89	Oct-89	92	123	25%
Aug-89	Nov-89	92	92	0%
Nov-89	Nov-89	0	0	0%

*This value is approximate.

Source: Adapted from "Microsoft Corporation: Office Business Unit" (Iansiti 1994).

- Aggressive scheduling prevented accurate planning. As Table 9-1 shows, only one estimate was longer than a year, although at the times the estimates were made, ten estimates actually had more than a year to go. A 60- to 80-percent wishful-thinking factor remained a constant part of the schedule for the first 4 years of the project.

- The project experienced extremely high turnover. It had four development leads in 5 years, including two who quit the project because of the schedule pressure and one who quit for medical reasons.

- Because of schedule pressure, developers shortchanged their feature implementations, declaring them to be "done" even though they had low quality and were incomplete. The result was that WinWord spent 12 months in "stabilization," a period that had been expected to take only about 3 months.

Did WinWord's aggressive schedule help it to be delivered faster? No. Five years for a 250,000 line-of-code product isn't rapid development. In spite of its aggressive schedule, WinWord wasn't released in the time frame of even the nominal schedule for a project of its size. (The nominal schedule would have been 26 months.)

Should WinWord have been scheduled as a rapid-development project? Probably not. Innovation was more important than schedule speed on the WinWord project, and it should have been scheduled accordingly. If WinWord's project planners had planned WinWord as an "efficient" development project, they would have scheduled it to take about 22 months. That schedule would have been almost twice as long as the longest schedule actually planned for the project, but it would have relieved the pressure that caused development-lead turnover and excessive stabilization time.

CROSS-REFERENCE
In addition to the discussion in this chapter, for more on the value of accurate schedules, see "Convergence Between Estimates and Reality" in Section 8.1.

It's painful to schedule a project for 22 months when you want to finish it in 12, but wishful thinking is no substitute for careful planning, and "wishin' don't make it so." The schedule that will produce the most rapid delivery is the most accurate one, and projects that practice wishful scheduling pay a schedule penalty of weeks or months for doing so. The WinWord 1.0 team paid its penalty in years.

Root Causes of Overly Optimistic Schedules

CROSS-REFERENCE
One kind of overly optimistic schedule is the kind that is handed to the developer with schedule, resources, and features already defined. For details, see Section 6.6, "Development-Speed Tradeoffs."

The root causes of overly optimistic schedules are deep and manifold. Here are some of the causes:

- There is an external, immovable deadline such as the date of a computer trade show, change in tax laws, or Christmas shopping season.

- Managers or customers refuse to accept a range of estimates and make plans based on a single-point "best case" estimate.

- Managers and developers deliberately underestimate the project because they want a challenge or like working under pressure.

- The project is deliberately underestimated by management or sales in order to submit a winning bid.

- Developers underestimate an interesting project in order to get funding to work on it.

- The project manager believes that developers will work harder if the schedule is ambitious and therefore creates the schedule accordingly.

- Top management, marketing, or an external customer want a particular deadline, and the project manager can't talk them out of it.

- The project begins with a realistic schedule, but new features are piled on to the project, and before long the project is running under an overly optimistic schedule.

- The project is simply estimated poorly.

With this many sources of optimistic schedules, it's amazing that any realistic schedules are created at all.

Effects of Overly Optimistic Schedules

If you want to complete your project in the shortest possible time, it seems as though it would make sense to set a short schedule. It seems rational to think that even if you don't quite meet the short schedule, you might deliver the project earlier than you would have otherwise. You can exhort a person digging a ditch to shovel faster. Can't you exhort software developers to design and code faster?

As intuitively appealing as this simplistic argument is, it doesn't work in software. (And it probably doesn't work in ditch-digging either.) Why doesn't it work? Here are the reasons.

CROSS-REFERENCE
For more on 50/50 scheduling, see Section 6.3, "Odds of Completing On Time."

HARD DATA

Schedule accuracy. The first reason that optimistic scheduling doesn't work is that using an overly optimistic schedule reduces schedule accuracy. If you schedule in the middle of the schedule curve, you'll have a 50/50 chance of making your deadline. But it's difficult to schedule for a 50/50 chance of on-time completion. Programmers tend to underestimate their projects by 20 to 30 percent (van Genuchten 1991). As Figure 9-1 shows, if you use the developers' estimates as a baseline, you'll already be estimating on the left side of the curve—that is, with a less than 50-percent chance of completing your project on time.

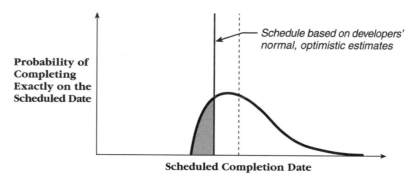

Figure 9-1. *Typical developer schedule. Developers typically estimate 20 to 30 percent lower than their actual effort. Merely using their normal estimates puts the chance of completing on time below 50 percent.*

Merely using the developer's "most likely" estimates gives you less accuracy than you would like. If you go beyond that to an optimistic estimate (as shown in Figure 9-2), you'll have little or no chance of delivering your product on time.

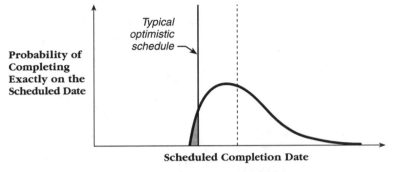

Figure 9-2. *Typical optimistic schedule. People sometimes think that setting a shorter schedule will increase the chance of early delivery, but all it really does is reduce accuracy and increase the chance of being late.*

Quality of project planning. An overly optimistic schedule undermines effective planning by feeding bad assumptions into phase planning, staffing-level planning, staff selection, staff-buildup planning, module-development planning, integration planning, test planning, and documentation planning. It would be convenient if plans would work when they are based on faulty assumptions; then we could use the same plans on every project! Unfortunately that doesn't happen, and faulty assumptions result in ineffective project plans. (See Figure 9-3 on the next page.)

Overly optimistic schedules don't result in plans that are off by just a little bit. The average small-project estimate is off by more than 100 percent (Standish Group 1994). The average large project is a year late (Jones 1994). With errors of this magnitude, the average project is doing planning that's virtually useless.

Adherence to plan. Even when planning is done effectively in the first place, a characteristic of all but the most sophisticated software organizations is that they throw out their plans and run free-form when they get into schedule trouble (Humphrey 1989). Setting an optimistic, unachievable schedule increases the risk that a project will run without a plan.

211

"I know everyone else thinks we should plan for 6 weeks to get over the pass, but I'm sure we can do it in 3 weeks—before it snows. Besides, we've got enough food for 4 weeks, and that will give us a whole week to spare!"

Figure 9-3. *Scheduling matters.*

Underscoping the project. An overly optimistic schedule can cause you to spend too little time on the upstream activities of requirements analysis and design. On a well-run project, you'll typically spend about one-third of your time on design. On a 12-month project, you would spend 4 months on design. If you estimated a 12-month project to take 6 months and planned design time accordingly, you would plan for only 2 months of design work, half of what you should plan for. It's already difficult enough to know whether you've done a good job on requirements and design—to know whether you're really done—and a short schedule encourages you not to think about it very hard. The usual effect of a short schedule is that the project rushes through requirements and design, either not completing the work or doing it sloppily. Those activities are inadvertently shortchanged.

Whatever you put into the project upstream, you get to fish out of the project downstream. Downstream from the shortchanged requirements and design, you'll fish out extra testing, defect correction, redesign, and rework—at anywhere from 10 to 100 times what it would have cost if it had been done properly in the first place (Fagan 1976, Boehm and Papaccio 1988).

CLASSIC MISTAKE

Officials from Loral admitted that their problems on the FAA's Advanced Automation System—which in 1994 was more than 5 years late and a *billion* dollars over budget—resulted from shortchanging their standard development processes in trying to meet the customer's unrealistic schedule demands. Time-to-market is greatly affected by the compromises a project inevitably makes when it sets an unachievable schedule (Curtis 1994).

Project focus. In addition to its effects on technical work, an overly optimistic schedule can divert managers away from activities that move the project forward. After the project fails to meet its initial delivery date, the project manager's efforts are diverted into "schedule politics" and into explaining how long the project will really take and why the new schedule is more reliable than the original one. Each time a project misses a deadline, it typically goes through a rescheduling exercise, and that saps developers' time too.

CROSS-REFERENCE
For more on customer relations, see Chapter 10, "Customer-Oriented Development."

Customer relations. Benjamin Franklin said that he would rather be a pessimist than an optimist; as a pessimist he would be pleasantly surprised more often. On the customer-relations side, when a project starts to look as though it won't meet its optimistic delivery date, customers, managers, and end-users are unpleasantly surprised. They naturally assume that the project is in trouble or out of control, even if it really is running smoothly. Once again, the project manager's attention is diverted from managing the project to managing the relationship with the customer, and the developer's attention is diverted from doing real work that moves the project forward to generating signs of progress to reassure the customer.

Over the long haul, optimistic scheduling erodes the relationship with the customer because customers lose faith in overly optimistic managers and developers.

CLASSIC MISTAKE

Premature convergence. Any sculptor will tell you that you don't start polishing a stone carving until you've roughed in the shape you want. Any home builder will tell you that there's no point in putting up wallboard and wallpaper until the electricity, plumbing, and heating and cooling systems are in place. Any software developer will tell you that there is no point in creating a shippable version of a software product until the product is feature-complete and stable. And yet that's exactly what's done when you work under an overly optimistic schedule.

If you're working on a project that's supposed to take about a year, 8 to 12 weeks before you're scheduled to ship the product you'll launch a major effort to prepare the product for release. You'll perform time-consuming activities that you ordinarily do not do until just before the product ships:

- Turning off debugging aids in the code
- Performance-tuning the product

- Removing or turning off partially implemented features that can't be completed in time to ship the product
- Implementing quick-and-dirty versions of features that absolutely must be completed in time to ship the product
- Fixing low-priority defects
- Polishing help files and user documents by checking spelling, coordinating page numbers between different source files, inserting exact cross-references and online help jumps, creating indexes, taking final screen shots, and so on
- Performing end-to-end system tests of the entire product and formally entering defects into the defect-reporting system

I think of these activities as forcing the product to *converge*. When a project tries to force convergence too early, it will fail to converge, and then it has to do all of those time-consuming activities again later.

Doing activities twice when they could be done once is inefficient. But there are other time-wasting aspects of premature convergence, too. If software is released to testing before it is ready, testers will find many more defects than they would find if it were not released until it was ready. When testers find more defects, they enter the defects into a formal bug-tracking system, which adds overhead that takes both testing and development time. Debugging aids have to be turned back on. Removed features have to be put back in. Quick-and-dirty "ship mode" changes that aren't reliable or maintainable come back to haunt the developers. To repeat, premature convergence is a waste of time.

Perhaps worse for the project is the effect that premature convergence has on developer morale. If you're running a foot race, when the gun goes off for the last lap, you'll give it your all. You want to arrive at the finish line with nothing left. With premature convergence, the gun goes off, you give it your all, and just before you reach the finish line someone moves it. That wasn't the last lap after all, but you're left with nothing more to give. In the long run, pacing is important, and premature convergence burns out developers too early.

Poorly managed projects often discover their schedule problems for the first time when their developers aren't able to force convergence. Better managed projects detect schedule problems much earlier. Symptoms of premature convergence include:

- Developers can't seem to fix defects without tearing the system apart; small changes take longer than they should.

- Developers have long lists of "trivial" changes, which they know they need to make but which they haven't made yet.
- Testers find defects faster than developers can correct them.
- Defect fixes generate as many new defects as they correct.
- Tech writers have trouble completing user documentation because the software is changing too fast to be able to document it accurately.
- Project estimates are adjusted many times by similar amounts; the estimated release date stays 3 weeks away for 6 months.

After you can't force convergence the first time, you'll need to back up, continue working, and try again to converge later. Optimistic schedules lead to premature and multiple attempts to converge, both of which lengthen schedules.

Excessive Schedule Pressure

CLASSIC MISTAKE

Customers' and managers' first response when they discover they aren't meeting their optimistic schedule is to heap more schedule pressure onto the developers and to insist on more overtime. Excessive schedule pressure occurs in about 75 percent of all large projects and in close to 100 percent of all very large projects (Jones 1994). Nearly 60 percent of developers report that the level of stress they feel is increasing (Glass 1994c).

Schedule pressure has become so ingrained in the software-development landscape that many developers have accepted it as an unalterable fact of life. Some developers are no longer even aware that the extreme schedule pressure they experience could be otherwise. That is unfortunate. Overly optimistic scheduling hurts the real development schedule in many ways, but excessive schedule pressure hurts it the most, so I want to explore this particular problem in detail.

HARD DATA

CROSS-REFERENCE
For more on error-prone modules, see "Error-prone modules" in Section 4.3.

Quality. About 40 percent of all software errors have been found to be caused by stress; those errors could have been avoided by scheduling appropriately and by placing no stress on the developers (Glass 1994c). When schedule pressure is extreme, about four times as many defects are reported in the released product as are reported for a product developed under less extreme pressure (Jones 1994). Excessive schedule pressure has also been found to be the most significant causative factor in the creation of extremely costly error-prone modules (Jones 1991).

With extreme schedule pressure, developers also increase the subtle pressure they put on themselves to focus on their own work rather than on quality-assurance activities. Developers might still hold code reviews, for example, but when they are faced with a choice between spending an extra hour reviewing someone else's code or working on their own routines, the developers usually will choose to spend the extra hour on their own code. They'll promise themselves to do better on the code review next time. Thus, quality starts its downward slide.

CROSS-REFERENCE
For more on the relationship
etween defect-level and schedule,
see Section 4.3, "Quality-
Assurance Fundamentals."

Projects that aim from the beginning at having the lowest number of defects usually also have the shortest schedules. Projects that apply excessive schedule pressure and shortchange quality are rudely awakened when they discover that what they have really shortchanged is the schedule.

CROSS-REFERENCE
For details on the occurrence
of gambling on rapid-
development projects, see
Section 5.6, "Risk, High Risk,
and Gambling."

Gambling. Since an overly optimistic schedule is impossible to achieve through normal, efficient development practices, project managers and developers are provided with an incentive to gamble rather than to take calculated risks. "I doubt that the Gig-O-Matic CASE tool will really improve my productivity by a factor of 100, but I have absolutely no chance of meeting my schedule without it, so what do I have to lose?"

On a rapid-development project, you should be doing everything possible to reduce risk. Software projects require you to take calculated risks but not close-your-eyes-and-hope-that-it-works risks. Schedule pressure contributes to poor risk management and mistakes that slow development.

CROSS-REFERENCE
For more on schedule
pressure and motivation,
see Chapter 11, "Motivation,"
and Section 43.1, "Using
Voluntary Overtime."

Motivation. Software developers like to work. A little bit of schedule pressure resulting from a slightly optimistic but achievable schedule can be motivating. But at some point the optimistic schedule crosses the threshold of believability, and at that point motivation drops—fast.

An overly optimistic schedule sets up developers to put in Herculean efforts only to be treated as failures for not achieving an impossible schedule—even when they have achieved a schedule that is nothing short of remarkable. The developers know this, and unless they are very young or very naive, they will not work hard—they will not commit, they will not "sign up"—to achieve a schedule that is out of reach. Anyone who tries to motivate by forcing commitment to an unachievable schedule will achieve exactly the opposite of what is desired.

Creativity. Many aspects of software development—including product specification, design, and construction—require creative thought. Creativity requires hard thinking and persistence when the sought-after solution doesn't immediately spring to mind. The drive to think hard and persist requires internal motivation. Excessive external motivation (aka stress) reduces internal motivation and in turn reduces creativity (Glass 1994a).

Aside from reducing the incentive to be creative, a pressure-cooker environment is simply the wrong kind of environment for creative thought. The cogitation required for a breakthrough solution requires a relaxed, contemplative state of mind.

HARD DATA

Given the same set of requirements, developers will create solutions that vary by as much as a factor of 10 in the amounts of code they require (Sackman, Erikson, and Grant 1968; Weinberg and Schulman 1974; Boehm, Gray, and Seewaldt 1984; De Marco and Lister 1989). If you're on a rapid-development schedule, you can't afford to create a pressure-cooker environment in which people are too rushed to find the solution that is one-tenth as expensive to implement as the others.

Burnout. If you use too much overtime in one project, your developers will more than make up for it on the next project. Programmers will putter around for months after putting in a big push on a major project—cleaning up their file systems, slowly commenting their source code, fixing low-priority bugs that they find interesting but which were not important enough to fix for the release (and may not be important enough to fix now), playing ping-pong, organizing their email, fine-tuning design documents, reading industry publications, and so on. If your schedule pushes developers too hard (perhaps by trying to force a premature convergence), you can experience that burnout on your current project rather than the next one.

Turnover. Overly optimistic schedules and the accompanying schedule pressure tend to cause extraordinarily high voluntary turnover, and the people who leave the project tend to be the most capable people with the highest performance appraisals (Jones 1991). Finding and training their replacements lengthens the schedule.

Long-term rapid development. Excessive overtime eliminates the free time that developers would otherwise spend on professional development. Developers who don't continue to grow don't learn about new practices, and that hurts your organization's long-term rapid-development capacity.

Relationship between developers and managers. Schedule pressure widens the gap between developers and managers. It feeds the existing tendency developers have to believe that management doesn't respect them, management doesn't care about them, and management doesn't know enough about software development to know when they're asking for something that's impossible. (See Figure 9-4.) Poor relationships lead to low morale, miscommunication, and other productivity sinkholes.

"If the book says that the shortest possible schedule is 6 months, you'll just have to work extra hard to finish in 4 months!"

Figure 9-4. *Unreasonable schedule pressure can cause developers to lose respect for their managers.*

The Bottom Line

Some people seem to think that software projects should be scheduled optimistically because software development should be more an adventure than a dreary engineering exercise. These people say that schedule pressure adds excitement.

How much sense does that make? If you were going on a *real* adventure, say a trip to the south pole by dogsled, would you let someone talk you into planning for it to take only 30 days when your best estimate was that it would take 60? Would you carry only 30 days' worth of food? Only 30 days' worth of fuel? Would you plan for your sled dogs to be worn out at the end of 30 days rather than 60? Doing any of those things would be self-destructive, and underscoping and underplanning a software project is similarly self-destructive, albeit usually without any life-threatening consequences.

In *Quality Software Management*, Gerald Weinberg suggests thinking about software projects as systems (Weinberg 1992). Each system takes in inputs and produces outputs. The system diagram for a project that's been accurately scheduled might look like the picture in Figure 9-5.

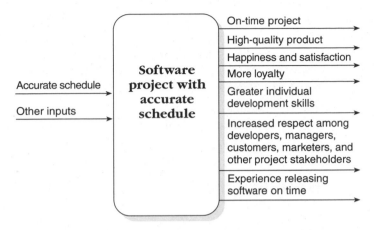

Figure 9-5. *System diagram for a project with an accurate schedule. Most people will be happy with the outputs from an accurately-scheduled project.*

The system diagram for a project that's been scheduled overly optimistically will, unfortunately, look more like the picture in Figure 9-6.

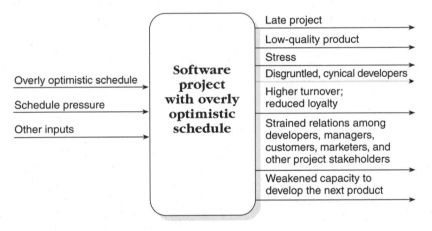

Figure 9-6. *System diagram for a project with an overly optimistic schedule. Most people won't like the outputs from a project with an overly optimistic schedule.*

When you compare the two systems, you can see that one is markedly healthier than the other.

In the end, I am opposed to the practice of overly optimistic scheduling because it undermines effective planning, eats into developers' personal lives, erodes relationships with customers, contributes to high turnover, contributes to low quality, and hurts the industry by stunting professional growth and creating the perception that software developers can't deliver what they promise.

But I am most opposed to overly optimistic scheduling because it doesn't work. It doesn't result in shorter actual schedules; it results in longer ones. That's what happened with WinWord 1.0. That's what happened with the FAA's Advanced Automation System. That's what happened with every other project I know of that has tried to work to an impossible schedule.

The shortest actual schedule results from the most accurate planned schedule. A project that has schedule problems needs to look no further for the source of its problems than an unachievable initial schedule.

9.2   Beating Schedule Pressure

Schedule pressure appears to be endemic to software development, and it has produced damaging, short-term thinking on two levels. At a local level, it has encouraged shortcut-taking on specific projects, which damages those specific projects. At a more global level, it has encouraged a fire-fighting mentality about schedule pressure itself. People view schedule pressure as a problem unique to their current project, even though they've felt schedule pressure on every project they've ever worked on and even though it has been one of the defining characteristics of the software industry for at least 30 years.

Ironically, we can't solve the problem of rapid development until we solve the problem of schedule pressure. As Figure 9-7 shows, schedule pressure creates a vicious circle of more stress, more mistakes, more schedule slips, and ever more schedule pressure.

Figure 9-7. *Vicious circle of schedule-pressure and schedule-slips. Anyone who wants to solve the problem of rapid development must first solve the problem of excessive schedule pressure.*

We as an industry need to learn how to beat schedule pressure. There cannot be a long-term solution to the schedule-pressure problem until we take time out to learn how to do our jobs better.

Three factors converge to make up the bulk of the problems associated with setting software schedules:

- *Wishful thinking*—Customers, managers, and end-users naturally and rationally want to get as much as they can for their money, and they want to get it as soon as possible. Most software project schedules are ambitious. Think about that. Most aren't average; most are ambitious. The previous section should provide all the reasons anyone needs to abandon their wishful thinking about software schedules.

- *Little awareness of the software estimation story or the real effects of overly optimistic scheduling*—Software can't be reliably estimated in its early stages. It's logically impossible. Yet we let people force us into unrealistic estimates. The estimation story described in Section 8.1 should help with this problem.

- *Poor negotiating skills*—Philip Metzger observed 15 years ago that developers were fairly good at estimating but were poor at defending their estimates (Metzger 1981). I haven't seen any evidence that developers have gotten any better at defending their estimates in recent years.

Developers tend to be bad negotiators for a few reasons.

CROSS-REFERENCE
For more on the profile of the average developer, see Section 11.1, "Typical Developer Motivations."

First, developers are, as a rule, introverts. About three-quarters of developers are introverts whereas only one-third of the general population would be described as such. Most developers get along with other people just fine, but challenging social interactions are not their strong suit.

Second, software schedules are typically set in negotiations between development and management or development and marketing. Gerald Weinberg points out that marketers tend to be 10 years older and negotiate for a living—that is, they tend to be seasoned, professional negotiators (Weinberg 1994). The deck is stacked against developers during schedule negotiations.

Third, developers tend to be temperamentally opposed to negotiating tricks. Such tricks offend their sense of technical accuracy and fairness. Developers won't offer lopsidedly high initial estimates even when they know that customers, marketers, or managers will start with lopsidedly low initial bargaining positions.

I have become convinced that developers need to become better negotiators, and I'll spend the rest of this chapter describing how to negotiate schedules effectively.

> ### Why Schedule Negotiations Are Difficult
>
> "False scheduling to match the patron's desired date is much more common in our discipline than elsewhere in engineering. It is very difficult to make a vigorous, plausible, and job-risking defense of an estimate that is derived by no quantitative method, supported by little data, and certified chiefly by the hunches of the managers."
>
> —*Fred Brooks*

Principled Negotiation

A good place to start improving your negotiating skills is the principled negotiation method described in *Getting to Yes* (Fisher and Ury 1981). This method has several characteristics that I find appealing. It doesn't rely on negotiating tricks, but it explains how to respond to tricks when others use them. It's based on the idea of creating win-win alternatives. You don't try to beat the person you're negotiating with; you try to cooperate so that both of you can win. It's an open strategy. You don't have to fear that the person you're negotiating with has read the same negotiating book and knows the same tricks. The method works best when all the parties involved know about it and use it.

CROSS-REFERENCE
For a related win-win strategy, see Chapter 37, "Theory-W Management."

The principled-negotiation strategy consists of four parts that deal with people, interests, options, and criteria:

- Separate the people from the problem
- Focus on interests, not positions
- Invent options for mutual gain
- Insist on using objective criteria

Each of these is described in the following sections.

Separate the People from the Problem

All negotiations involve people first, interests and positions second. When the negotiators' personalities are at odds—as, for example, developers' and marketers' personalities often are—negotiations can get hung up on personality differences.

CROSS-REFERENCE
People's expectations can affect negotiations. For more on expectations, see Section 10.3, "Managing Customer Expectations."

Begin by understanding the other side's position. I've had cases in which a non-technical manager had good business reasons for wanting a specific deadline. In one case, a manager felt pressure from the marketing organization and his boss to produce what was probably a 15-month project in 6 months. He told me that he had to have the software in 6 months. I told him that the best I could do was 15 months. He said, "I'm not giving you a choice. Our customers are expecting the software in 6 months." I said, "I'm sorry. I wish I could. But 15 months is the best I can do." He just froze and stared at me for 2 or 3 minutes.

Why did he freeze? Was he using silence as a negotiating maneuver? Maybe. But I think it was because he felt trapped and powerless. He had promised his boss a 6-month development schedule, and now the person who was supposed to head the project was telling him he couldn't keep his promise.

Understand that managers can be trapped by their organization's outdated policies. Some organizations fund software projects in ways that are essentially incompatible with the way software is developed. They don't allow managers to ask for funding just to develop the product concept and come up with a good cost estimate. To get enough funding to do a decent estimate, managers have to get funding for the whole project. By the time they get a decent estimate, it can be embarrassing or even career-threatening to go back and ask for the right amount of funding. People at the highest levels of such organizations need to hear the software-estimation story so that they can institute sensible funding practices.

Most middle managers aren't stupid or irrational when they insist on a deadline that you know is impossible. They simply don't know enough about the technical work to know that it's impossible, or they know all too well how much pressure they feel from their own bosses, customers, or people higher up in the organization.

CROSS-REFERENCE
For more on the software estimation story, see Section 8.1, "The Software-Estimation Story."

What can you do? Work to improve the relationship with your manager or customer. Be cooperative. Work to set realistic expectations. Be sure that everyone understands the software-estimation story. Be an advisor on schedule matters, and avoid slipping into the role of adversary. Suggest ways to change the project that will reduce the schedule, but hold firm to not just writing down a different date.

It's also useful to try to take emotions out of the negotiating equation. Sometimes the easiest way to do that is to let the other people blow off steam. Don't react emotionally to their emotions. Invite them to express themselves fully. Say something like, "I can see that those are all serious concerns, and I want to be sure I understand your position. What else can you tell me about your situation?" When they are done, acknowledge their emotions and reiterate your commitment to find a win-win solution. The other parts of principled negotiation will help you to follow through on that commitment.

Focus on Interests, Not Positions

Suppose you're selling your car in order to buy a new boat, and you've figured that you need to get $5000 for your car in order to buy the boat you want. A prospective buyer approaches you and offers $4500. You say, "There's no way I can part with this car for less than $5000." The buyer says, "$4500 is my final offer."

When you negotiate in this way, you focus on positions rather than interests. Positions are bargaining statements that are so narrow that in order for one person to win, the other person has to lose.

Now suppose that the car buyer says, "I really can't go over $4500, but I happen to know that you're in the market for a new boat, and I happen to be the regional distributor for a big boat company. I can get the boat you want for $1000 less than you can get it from any dealer. Now what do you think about my offer?" Well, now the offer sounds pretty good because it will leave you with $500 more than you would have gotten if the buyer had just agreed to your price.

Underlying interests are broader than bargaining positions, and focusing on them opens up a world of negotiating possibilities. Your boss might start out by saying, "I need Giga-Blat 4.0 in 6 months," and you might know immediately that you can't deliver it in less than 9 months. Your boss's interest might be keeping a promise made to the sales organization, and your interest might be working less than 60 hours a week for the next 6 months. Between the two of you, you might be able to create a product that would satisfy the sales organization and would be deliverable within 6 months. If you focus on interests, you're more likely to find a win-win solution than if you dig into bargaining positions.

One of the major problems with schedule negotiations is that they tend to become one-dimensional, focusing only on the schedule. Don't get dug into a position. Make it clear that you're willing to consider a full-range of alternatives—just not pie-in-the-sky options. If other people have dug themselves into demanding a specific schedule, here are some points you can use to dislodge them:

Appeal to true development speed. Point out that the worst fault of overly optimistic schedules is that they undermine actual development speed. Explain the negative effects of overly optimistic scheduling that were described in Section 9.1. True rapid development requires that you be firmly connected to reality, including to a realistic schedule.

Appeal to increasing the chance of success. Point out that you have estimated the most likely completion date and that you already have only a 50/50 chance of meeting that. Shortening the schedule will further reduce your chances of completing on time.

Invoke your organization's track record. Point to your organization's history of underestimating projects, coming in late, and all the problems that lateness has caused. Appeal to the other person's good sense not to do the same thing again.

Invent Options for Mutual Gain

CROSS-REFERENCE
For more on the value of cooperation, see "Cooperation" in Section 8.1.

Rather than thinking of negotiating as a zero-sum game in which one person wins at the other's expense, think of it as an exercise in creative problem-solving; the truly clever negotiator will find a way for both parties to win.

Your most powerful negotiating ally in schedule negotiations is your ability to generate options that the other person has no way of knowing about. You hold the key to a vault of technical knowledge, and that puts the responsibility for generating creative solutions more on your shoulders than on the nontechnical person you're negotiating with. It's your role to explain the full range of possibilities and trade-offs.

CROSS-REFERENCE
For details on the schedule, cost, and product triangle, see "Schedule, Cost, and Product Trade-offs" in Section 6.6.

I find it useful to think about how many degrees of freedom there are in planning a software project. The basic degrees of freedom are defined by the schedule, cost, and product triangle. You have to keep the three corners in balance for the project to succeed. But there are infinite variations on that triangle, and the person you're negotiating with might find some of those variations to be a lot more appealing than others. Here are some of the degrees of freedom you might suggest related to the product itself:

- Move some of the desired functionality into version 2. Few people need all of what they asked for exactly when they asked for it.
- Deliver the product in stages—for example, versions 0.7, 0.8, 0.9, and 1.0—with the most important functionality coming first.
- Cut features altogether. Features that are time-consuming to implement and often negotiable include the level of integration with other systems, level of compatibility with previous systems, and performance.
- Polish some features less—implement them to some degree, but make them less fancy.
- Relax the detailed requirements for each feature. Define your mission as getting as close as possible to the requirements through the use of prebuilt commercial components.

Here are some degrees of freedom related to project resources:

- Add more developers, if it's early in the schedule.
- Add higher-output developers (for example, subject-area experts).
- Add more testers.
- Add more administrative support.

- Increase the degree of developer support. Get quieter, more private offices, faster computers, on-site technicians for network and machine support, approval to use higher priced developer-support services, and so on.

- Eliminate company red tape. Set your project up as a skunkworks project.

- Increase the level of end-user involvement. Devote a full-time end-user to the project who is authorized to make binding decisions about the product's feature set.

- Increase the level of executive involvement. If you've been trying to introduce JAD sessions to your organization but haven't been able to get the executive sponsorship you need, this is a good time to ask for it.

Here are some degrees of freedom you can suggest related to the project's schedule:

- Set a schedule *goal* but not an ultimate deadline for the whole project until you've completed the detailed design, product design, or at least the requirements specification.

- If it's early in the project, agree to look for ways to reduce the development time as you refine the product concept, specification, and design.

- Agree to use estimation ranges or coarse estimates and to refine them as the project progresses.

You can propose a few additional degrees of freedom in certain circumstances. They can make a difference in development time, but they also tend to be political hot potatoes. Don't bring them up unless you know the person on the other side of the table is already sympathetic to your cause.

- Provide exceptional developer support so that developers can focus more easily on the project—shopping service, catered meals, laundry, housecleaning, lawn care, and so on.

- Provide increased developer motivation—paid overtime, guarantee of comp time, profit sharing, all-expenses-paid trips to Hawaii, and so on.

Whatever you do, don't agree to a lopsided schedule-cost-product triangle. Remember that once you've settled on a feature set, the size of the triangle is practically a law of physics—the three corners have to be in balance.

Throughout the negotiations, focus on what you can do and avoid getting stuck on what you can't. If you're given an impossible combination of feature set, resources, and schedule, say, "I can deliver the whole feature set with my current team 4 weeks later than you want it. Or I could add a person to the team and deliver the whole feature set when you want it. Or I can cut features X, Y, and Z and deliver the rest with my current team by the time you want it."

The key is to take attention away from a shouting match like this one: *I can't do it.* "Yes you can." *No I can't.* "Can!" *Can't!* Lay out a set of options, and focus your discussion on what you can do.

One warning: In the cooperative, brainstorming atmosphere that arises from this kind of free-wheeling discussion, it's easy to agree to a solution that seems like a good idea at the time but by the next morning seems like a bad deal. Don't make any hard commitments to new options until you've had enough time to analyze them quietly by yourself.

Insist on Using Objective Criteria

The ultimate act of disempowerment is to take away the responsibility for the schedule from those who must live by it.
Jim McCarthy

One of the oddest aspects of our business is that when careful estimation produces estimates that are notably longer than desired, the customer or manager will often simply disregard the estimate (Jones 1994). They'll do that even when the estimate comes from an estimation tool or an outside estimation expert—and even when the organization has a history of overrunning its estimates. Questioning an estimate is a valid and useful practice. Throwing it out the window and replacing it with wishful thinking is not.

A key to breaking deadlocks with principled negotiations is the use of objective criteria. The alternative is to break negotiation deadlocks based on whoever has the most willpower. I've seen schedules for million-dollar projects decided on the basis of which person could stare the longest without blinking. Most organizations will be better off using a more principled approach.

In principled negotiation, when you reach a deadlock, you search for objective criteria you can use to break the deadlock. You reason with the other people about which criteria are most appropriate, and you keep an open mind about criteria they suggest. Most important, you don't yield to pressure, only to principle.

Here are some guidelines for keeping schedule negotiations focused on principles and not just desires.

Don't negotiate the estimate itself. You can negotiate the inputs to the estimate—the degrees of freedom described in the previous section—but not the estimate itself. As Figure 9-8 suggests, treat the estimate as something that's determined from those inputs almost by a law of nature. Be extremely open to changing the inputs and be ready to offer alternatives, but match your flexibility in those areas with a firm stance on the estimate itself.

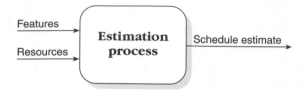

Figure 9-8. *Treating an estimate as something determined by a law of nature. You can negotiate the inputs, but you can't change the output without changing the inputs.*

Suppose you're negotiating with an in-house customer. You could say something like this: "This is my best estimate. I can write a different date on a piece of paper, but that won't be a valid estimate. I can write a bigger number in my checkbook, too, but that doesn't mean that I'll have any more money. I've already given the team only about a 50-percent chance of delivering the software on time. Planning for a shorter schedule won't shorten the amount of time it will take them to create the product you want. It will just increase the risk of being late."

Point out that by refusing to accept an impossible deadline you're really looking out for your customer's best interests. Point to your organization's history of schedule overruns, and tell the in-house customer that you're unwilling to set either of you up for failure. It's easy to make this argument once you've demonstrated your willingness to look for win-win solutions.

FURTHER READING
For an illustration of using a software-estimating tool as an impartial expert, see Section 2.3.2 of "Theory-W Software Project Management: Principles and Examples" (Boehm and Ross 1989).

Insist that the estimate be prepared by a qualified party. Sometimes negotiations produce the absurd situation in which customers who have no idea how to build a software system nevertheless claim to know how long it will take to build it. Insist that the estimate be prepared by someone with appropriate qualifications. That will often be you.

Some organizations have had good success creating an independent estimation group. Those groups are effective because they do not have a vested interest either in delivering the product in the shortest possible time or in avoiding hard work. If negotiations become deadlocked on the topic of the estimate, propose submitting the estimate to a third party and pledge to accept their results. Ask your negotiation foe to pledge to do the same.

A variation on this theme is to bring in a consultant or noted authority to review your schedule. (An unfamiliar expert sometimes has more credibility than a familiar one.) Some organizations have also had success using software-estimation tools. They've found that once developers calibrate the estimation tool for a specific project, the tool allows them to easily and objectively explore the effects of different options in an unbiased way.

Insist on a rational estimation procedure. Chapter 8, "Estimation," explains the basis for creating software project estimates. Insist that the procedure that is used to create the estimate comply with the following guidelines:

- *Nails down features before it nails down the estimate.* You can't know how much a new house costs until you know quite a lot about the house. You can't tell how much a new software system will cost until you know quite a lot about the system.

- *Doesn't provide unrealistic precision.* Provide your estimates in ranges that become increasingly refined as the project progresses.

- *Reestimates after changes.* The estimate should be the last step in the process. It's irrational to create an estimate, pile on more features, and keep the estimate the same.

Don't bow to the pressure to commit to impossible deadlines. That short-term fix damages your long-term credibility. No one really benefits from pretending that you can meet an impossible schedule, even though sometimes people think they do. Improve your credibility by pushing for solutions that respond to the real business needs of your bosses and customers.

> **In reality, you don't need permission to do your job well.**
> *Larry Constantine*

Weather the storm. Although people have different tolerances for withstanding pressure, if your customers, managers, or marketers want you to change your estimate without also changing the feature set or resources, I think the best approach is to politely and firmly stand by your estimate. Batten down the hatches and endure the thunderstorm of an unwelcome estimate early in the project rather than the hurricane of schedule slips and cost overruns later on.

Case Study 9-1. A Successful Schedule Negotiation

Tina's team had put a lot of work into their estimate for the Giga-Bill 1.0 project, which they had estimated would probably take 12 months. Her boss, Bill, wasn't happy with the estimate the team came up with. He said it needed to be shorter. Tina found herself sitting across from Bill at the oversight committee meeting.

"The team has estimated it can deliver the product in 6 months," Bill said.

"Err—ahem." Tina cleared her throat. "What Bill means is that we estimated an ideal-world, best case of 6 months, but in order to achieve that best case, every single thing on the project has to go perfectly. And you know software projects—nothing ever goes perfectly. Our most likely estimate is 12 months, with a realistic range of 10 to 15 months." Tina was sweating and wished she had a handkerchief to wipe her forehead.

(continued)

Case Study 9-1. A Successful Schedule Negotiation, *continued*

Catherine from accounting spoke up. "We really were hoping for something shorter. Can't you shorten your estimate?"

"I wish I could," Tina said. "But my team has been over this ground carefully. If I shortened my estimate, it wouldn't be worth the paper it's printed on. Giving you a shorter estimate wouldn't make the project take less time; it would just guarantee that it would be late. There is still a lot of flexibility in this product concept, and as we refine our product concept we can refine it with the schedule in mind." She moved into a discussion of the estimate-convergence curve and felt some relief at being on familiar ground.

"This process of refinement isn't entirely neutral," Tina concluded. "We can continue to work with the product concept and resources to shorten the schedule. There are lots of things we can do." She explained a few of the degrees of freedom.

Committee members asked several questions about specific options Tina had proposed, and they seemed satisfied with her answers.

"I'm going to need to think this over," Catherine said. "Twelve months is a long time, but you've given us a lot of interesting possibilities." Tina invited her to call with questions or to discuss more options.

After the meeting, Bill was still steaming. "Don't mess with me again," he growled at Tina. "Where do you get off changing my estimate in front of the committee?"

"Your 'estimate'?" Tina replied. "You didn't have an estimate. You had a schedule target, and that target happened to be impossible. My team isn't just throwing darts at a board. They did a lot of work to come up with an unusually solid estimate, and 12 months is the best number we have for this project. This organization, including you, has a history of overrunning its schedule and budget targets, and I couldn't let you set yourself up for failure. I was careful not to make you look bad. The committee took the news pretty well, I thought."

"They did take it better than I expected," Bill admitted. "I'll let it slide this time. That was a gutsy move, but don't ever pull a stunt like that again."

"OK," Tina agreed, wondering whether she would ever need to pull a stunt like that again. Her stomach had done flip flops when she corrected Bill during the meeting, but she knew if she didn't do it then, she'd just have to do it 9 months later when it became obvious that they weren't going to meet their schedule. If she waited until later, the next 9 months would be a miserable exercise in code-like-hell development. Bad planning and poor quality would push out their real deadline, and they probably wouldn't even deliver in 12 months. On the whole, she thought she'd made the right call.

Further Reading

DeMarco, Tom. *Why Does Software Cost So Much?* New York: Dorset House, 1995. The title essay contains an insightful investigation into the topic of software costs. DeMarco is as eloquent as ever, and he places himself squarely on the side of sensible, effective, developer-oriented development practices.

DeMarco, Tom, and Timothy Lister. *Peopleware: Productive Projects and Teams.* New York: Dorset House, 1987. Several sections of this book contain energetic attacks against unrealistically ambitious software schedules, and the whole book provides moral support for anyone who's feeling too much pressure.

Maguire, Steve. *Debugging the Development Process.* Redmond, Wash.: Microsoft Press, 1994. Chapter 5, "Scheduling Madness," discusses how to make a schedule aggressive but not damagingly aggressive, and Chapter 8, "That Sinking Feeling," explores the problems associated with excessive overtime.

Gilb, Tom. *Principles of Software Engineering Management.* Wokingham, England: Addison-Wesley, 1988. Gilb provides practical advice for working with bosses and customers to align expectations with reality. The book includes a nice chapter on "Deadline pressure: how to beat it."

Costello, Scott H. "Software engineering under deadline pressure." *ACM Sigsoft Software Engineering Notes,* 9:5 October 1984, pp. 15–19. This is an insightful peek into the many effects that schedule pressure has on good software-engineering practices. Costello has a keen sense of the pressures that developers feel and how they respond to them, and he advances a three-pronged solution that managers can use to counteract the damaging effects of deadline pressure.

Fisher, Roger, and William Ury. *Getting to Yes.* New York: Penguin Books, 1981. Although it's not about software, this is one of the most valuable 154-page books you're likely to read. The book arose from work conducted by the Harvard Negotiation Project. Unlike some negotiation books that consist mainly of tricks for beating the other side, this book focuses on win-win negotiating and lays out the method of "principled negotiation." It describes how to counter negotiating tricks without stooping to the use of tricks yourself.

Iansiti, Marco. "Microsoft Corporation: Office Business Unit." Harvard Business School Case Study 9-691-033, revised May 31, 1994, Boston: Harvard Business School, 1994. This is a fascinating study of the development of Word for Windows 1.0.

10

Customer-Oriented Development

Contents

Related Topics

A GROUP OF SOFTWARE DEVELOPERS and their customers went to a software trade show by train. Each of the customers bought a train ticket, but the developers bought only one ticket among them. The customers thought the software developers must be pretty foolish.

One of the developers said, "Here comes the conductor," and all the developers piled into the bathroom. The conductor came aboard, said, "Tickets please," and took a ticket from each customer. He then went to the bathroom, knocked on the door, and said, "Ticket please." The developers pushed the ticket under the door. The conductor took it, and the developers came out of the bathroom a few minutes later. Now the customers were the ones who felt foolish.

On the way back from the trade show, the group of customers thought they would be smarter this time, so they bought one ticket for their whole group. But this time the developers didn't buy even one ticket, and some of the customers snickered at them. After awhile, the developer lookout said, "Conductor coming!" All the developers piled into a bathroom. All the customers piled into another bathroom. Then, before the conductor came on board, one of the developers left the bathroom, knocked on the door to the customers' bathroom, and said, "Ticket please."

The moral: Not every solution invented by software developers is good for their customers (and sooner or later the customers will figure that out).

Customer orientation seems as though it might be too intangible to have much of an effect on development speed. Intangible or not, the companies that have made customer relations a top priority have made many of their development problems disappear, including the problem of slow development.

CLASSIC MISTAKE

The need to pay attention to your customers becomes obvious when you realize that, in the end, your customers' perception of whether your development is slow or fast is all that matters. If customers don't like your product, they won't pay for it, and if they don't pay for it, nothing else you do matters. Even if you build the wrong product quickly, you've still built the wrong product. Managers, marketers, and senior executives care about development speed because they think that customers care about it. If you can satisfy your customers, you can satisfy your manager, your company's brass, and everyone else.

Who "the customer" is varies considerably from project to project. On some projects, the customer is the person who plunks down $200 for a shrink-wrap software package. On other projects, it's a real flesh-and-blood client who directly pays your project's development costs. On still other projects, it's another group within your organization. Regardless of who pays for the software, it's also beneficial to think of your end-users as customers. Depending on your situation, you might read "customer" as "client," "marketing group," "end-user," or "boss." In all cases, the principles of increasing development speed by improving customer relations are about the same.

This chapter identifies practices that can help to maintain good relationships and puts the practices into context. Specific customer-oriented practices are described in the "Best Practice" part of the book.

Case Study 10-1. The Requirements Club

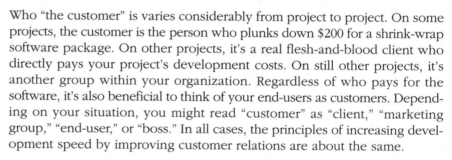

Carl had returned from a requirements-analysis workshop and was eager to put his new knowledge to work. The workshop had convinced him that formalizing a stable set of requirements was important. Downstream requirements changes could cost anywhere from 50 to 200 times as much as it would cost to get the requirements right in the first place, so he wanted to do a good job.

Carl's first project after the workshop was a major upgrade to his company's in-house billing system, Giga-Bill 2.0. He set up extensive interviews with the system's users in the accounting department, and his team compiled an exhaustive list of requirements. Carl had Catherine, the accounting-department representative, review the requirements spec, agree to it, and sign it before his team began design. With detailed requirements in hand, the team estimated

(continued)

the project would take about 5 months. Accounting thought that was acceptable; it meant the system would be completed by November 1, in plenty of time for year-end processing.

The team completed architecture the first month and all of the design by the end of the second month. About that time, Catherine called Carl.

"We're wondering how hard it would be to add a few new reports," she said. Carl explained that they had based their design on the requirements and reminded her that she had signed the requirements document. "I know," she said. "But a lot of people are asking for these reports, and we'd really like to get them into this version." Carl had been through this before, and he knew that adding a lot of late requirements would ruin his schedule. Allowing Catherine to add requirements now would set a bad precedent for the rest of the project. He said he was sorry, but the team had already started coding and it was too late to make the changes. He agreed to add the reports in the version after this one. A few weeks later, Catherine tried to add data to some of the existing reports, but Carl stood his ground.

By the end of the fourth month, the team had met all their deadlines and fully expected to deliver the product on time. Three weeks before the delivery date, Catherine met with Carl again, and this time she asked for only two new reports. She was irritated that Carl had been so unresponsive to her earlier requests. "We didn't absolutely need those other reports, but we have to have these for our year-end processing. I'm sorry they weren't included in the spec, but they are based on new requirements from the IRS, and we have to have them."

"We can't add them now," Carl said pointedly. "We're virtually done coding, and all that's left now is system testing. In order to add those reports, we'd have to code the reports themselves, add two new input screens to support them, and change our database schema. My team based its plans on the requirements spec. What was the point of creating a requirements spec if we weren't going to stick to it? Adding those reports now would cost probably 5 or 10 times as much as they would've if you'd asked for them when we were doing requirements. If we start making changes now, we couldn't even guarantee that you'd have any part of the new system by year-end. We've got to stick to the requirements for the project to succeed. You agreed to these requirements, remember? You signed off on them, remember?" Catherine pointed out that she didn't have any control over what the IRS asked for, but Carl refused to make the changes so late.

Catherine went to Claire, Carl's manager, and complained that Carl was using the requirements as a club. "I'm the customer, aren't I?" she said. "Why won't he listen to me? I don't care if it takes another two months. We've got to have those reports."

(continued)

Case Study 10-1. The Requirements Club, *continued*

Claire told Carl to add the two new reports. "What are they supposed to do, Carl? Say 'no' to the IRS? Come on." Carl complained bitterly that Catherine had agreed to the requirements and it would wreck the deadline his team almost had within its grasp, but he finally agreed. Two of the people on his team canceled their end-of-project vacations, and they completed the changes by December 31.

Users were lukewarm about the new system and said that it was confusing and inflexible. But it did generate the new reports they needed, so they kept their complaints to a minimum. Catherine asked Claire to keep Carl away from her projects in the future. Claire moved Carl to a new area and didn't assign him to another technical-lead role.

10.1   Customers' Importance to Rapid Development

HARD DATA

In a survey of over 8,000 projects, the Standish Group found that the number one reason that projects succeed is user involvement (Standish Group 1994). Some experts in rapid development have stated that easy access to end-users is one of three critical success factors in rapid-development projects (Millington and Stapleton 1995). Depending on your situation, you could just as easily read that as "customer involvement."

In the Standish Group Survey, the top three reasons that projects were completed late, over budget, and with less functionality than desired were a lack of user input, incomplete requirements specifications, and changing requirements and specifications. You can handle all of these problems through the use of customer-oriented practices. Similarly, you can address four of the top six reasons that projects were canceled with customer-oriented practices.

> There are only two things of importance. One is the customer, and the other is the product. If you take care of customers, they come back. If you take care of product, it doesn't come back.
>
> *Stanley Marcus (of Neiman Marcus)*

Here are the two main reasons that you should pay attention to customer relations on a rapid-development project:

- Good relations with customers improve actual development speed. If you have a cooperative rather than antagonistic relationship and good communications with your customer, you eliminate a significant source of inefficiency and major development errors.

- Good relations with customers improve perceived development speed. Much of customers' concern about development speed arises from a fear that you might not complete the project at all. If you structure your project to provide high visibility for your progress, you increase customers' confidence in you, and raw development speed becomes a lesser concern. Their attention will shift to functionality, quality, and other matters, and development speed will take its place as just one of many priorities.

The following sections describe in detail how focusing on customers improves both real and perceived development speed.

Improved Efficiency

Customer involvement can be on the critical path of a custom-software project. Customers often don't understand what they need to do to support rapid development. They don't allocate time for reviews, management, monitoring progress, or considering what they are asking for. Customers sometimes don't realize that a week's delay in reviewing a key document can translate into a week's delay in delivering the product. A common problem is that customers provide several points of contact, and you can never be sure who you need to talk to get a decision on a particular issue. By focusing on customer relations early in the project, you can select customer-oriented development approaches that eliminate these inefficiencies.

Less Rework

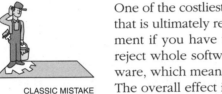

CLASSIC MISTAKE

One of the costliest mistakes in software development is to develop software that is ultimately rejected by the customer. You can't achieve rapid development if you have to develop the software twice. Customers don't usually reject whole software systems outright; rather, they reject parts of the software, which means that you have to redesign and reimplement those parts. The overall effect is that you deliver the system late. Avoiding such rework is a key to mastering rapid development.

Reduced Risk

Here are some ways that customers can pose risks to the schedule:

CROSS-REFERENCE
For a different list of customer-related risks, see the "Customer" entry in Table 5-3, "Potential schedule risks."

- Customers don't understand what they want.
- Customers won't commit to a set of written requirements.
- Customers insist on new requirements after the cost and schedule have been fixed.
- Communication with customers is slow.
- Customers will not participate in reviews or are incapable of doing so.
- Customers are technically unsophisticated.
- Customers won't let people do their jobs.
- Customers don't understand the software-development process.
- A new customer is an unknown entity, and specific risks are unknown.

Establishing good relationships with your customers allows you to do a better job of identifying risks and monitoring them throughout the project.

Lack of Friction

Occasionally, I found myself thinking, 'If it weren't for the customers, this job could be fun.'

Naomi Karten

HARD DATA

When you don't get along with your customers, you spend more time managing customer relationships. That takes time, and it can be distracting. While you're thinking about the software architecture, in the back of your mind you're also thinking about how to tell your customers that the software will be 3 weeks late. Those distractions make you less efficient, and they're demotivating. It's hard to put in extra hours for customers you don't like.

The problem of friction with customers is endemic to the industry. For outsourced software projects (projects with real clients), the severity of friction between clients and software contractors is great enough that on average both parties consider canceling the project (Jones 1994). About 40 percent of all outsourced projects experience this level of friction, and about 65 percent of all fixed-price contracts experience it.

Friction can arise either from the developer's side or from the customer's side. From the customer's side, sources of friction for developers include demanding impossible delivery dates, demanding new requirements and refusing to pay for them, omitting clear acceptance criteria from the contract, insisting that every last trivial bug be fixed in the first release, and inadequately monitoring the contract's progress.

From the developer's side, sources of friction for customers can include promising impossible delivery dates, bidding artificially low, bidding on projects for which the developers lack necessary skills, developing products with low quality, missing delivery dates, and providing inadequate status reports.

Making partners of customers means they become more likely to understand technical constraints. You start to get rid of the "I need it all now" phenomenon, and customers begin cooperating to find realistic, mutually satisfying technical solutions.

10.2 Customer-Oriented Practices

Customer-oriented practices come in several categories. Here are the categories for rapid-development purposes:

- *Planning*—Customer-oriented practices help you build customer satisfaction into your project.

- *Requirements analysis*—Customer-oriented practices help you to understand the real requirements and avoid rework.

- *Design*—Customer-oriented practices help you build in the flexibility needed to respond quickly to customer-generated change requests.

- *Construction*—Customer-oriented practices help to keep the customer confident about your progress.

Each of these are discussed further in the following sections. In addition, Section 10.3 discusses *managing customer expectations.*

Planning

Here are some planning practices you can use to build customer satisfaction into your project:

CROSS-REFERENCE
For details on these practices, see Chapter 7, "Lifecycle Planning"; Chapter 20, "Evolutionary Delivery"; Chapter 21, "Evolutionary Prototyping"; Chapter 36, "Staged Delivery"; and Chapter 37, "Theory-W Management."

- *Select an appropriate lifecycle model.* Provide your customer with steady, tangible signs of progress. Possibilities include the spiral model, evolutionary delivery, evolutionary prototyping, and staged delivery.
- *Identify the real customer.* Sometimes the person you need to keep happy is not the person you have the most contact with. If you're building software for another group within your organization, you might spend most of your time with a contact-person from that group, but the person you might really need to keep happy is your boss. If you're working with an external customer, the customer's representative might not be the decision maker who decides whether to continue the project or cancel it. Be sure to identify the real decision maker, and keep that person happy too.
- *Establish an efficient method for interacting with the customer.* If at all possible, insist that the customer provide a single point of contact. That person will occasionally need to get input from other people or do some consensus-building on the customer side, but there is no such thing as a rapid-development project in which you have to get the approval of six customer representatives for every decision.
- *Create a win-win project.* Use Theory-W project management to identify the "win" conditions for all of the parties involved. Create a plan to achieve the win conditions, and then monitor the project for risks that would keep any party from becoming a winner.
- *Manage risks.* Pay special attention to customer-related risks in your risk-management planning and risk monitoring.

Requirements Analysis

CLASSIC MISTAKE

Whenever you gather requirements, the challenge is to gather the real requirements. Sometimes the real requirements are in conflict with the requirements you gather; more often they are simply missing. Sometimes discovering the real requirements calls for digging beyond the surface requirements. This was the problem in Case Study 10-1: Carl did requirements analysis by the

239

book, but he initially did not uncover the requirements for two key reports. Requirements are often stated vaguely, which creates the possibility of confusion. Customers tend to interpret requirements broadly, and developers tend to interpret them narrowly—another source of friction is born.

Customer-oriented requirements-gathering practices help you to discover more of the real requirements and to maximize your understanding of all the requirements. Obviously, the more time you spend working on the real requirements, the less time you'll spend working on extraneous requirements, and the faster you'll be able to deliver the software that your customer wants.

Figure 10-1 shows the difference between the requirements you gather with customer-oriented practices and without.

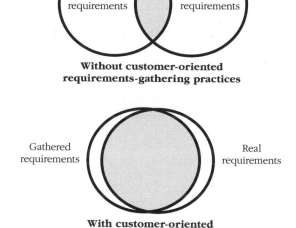

**Without customer-oriented
requirements-gathering practices**

**With customer-oriented
requirements-gathering practices**

Figure 10-1. *The difference between typical and customer-oriented requirements-gathering practices. Customer-oriented practices increase the proportion of real requirements you can gather.*

HARD DATA

One empirical study found that productivity was about 50 percent higher than average when customers had a "high" level of participation in specifying the requirements (Vosburgh et al. 1984). As Figure 10-2 shows, productivity was about 10 percent higher than average with a "medium" level of participation, and about 20 percent below average with a "low" level of participation.

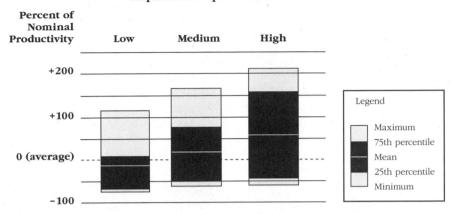

Figure 10-2. *Findings for "Client Participation in Requirements Specification" factor (Vosburgh et al. 1984). Active customer participation can produce dramatic improvements in productivity, but it is not by itself a guarantee of success.*

CROSS-REFERENCE
For details on this point, see Section 3.2, "Effect of Mistakes on a Development Schedule."

HARD DATA

Figure 10-2 sounds a familiar refrain. Both the top end and the average are significantly better with greater customer participation, but the low end is virtually unchanged. Customer involvement can help development speed tremendously, but it isn't sufficient by itself to improve productivity.

As important as it is to involve your customers in specifying requirements, avoid letting the customers write the requirements spec entirely. The same study that found that productivity increased with high customer participation also found that productivity was lower when customers wrote the spec. In fact, over half the specs written by customers had to be rewritten (Vosburgh et al. 1984).

Here are some practices you can use to involve your customers in requirements gathering:

- Use requirements-eliciting practices that help customers figure out what they want—user interface prototyping, evolutionary prototyping, and Joint Application Development (JAD) sessions, for example.
- Conduct focus groups that help you figure out what the customer wants.
- Videotape customers using the software.
- Conduct customer-satisfaction surveys to obtain a quantitative measurement of your relationship to your customers.

FURTHER READING
For tips on using videotaping to improve software usability, see *Constantine on Peopleware* (Constantine 1995a).

Which specific customer-oriented requirements practices you should use depends on what a "customer" is to your organization. If your customer is another group within your organization, you might use JAD sessions and evolutionary prototyping. If your customer is someone who buys shrink-wrapped software, you might use focus groups and customer-satisfaction surveys.

Jim McCarthy tells a story that vividly illustrates the value of finding out what customers really want (McCarthy 1995a). McCarthy was working on the development of Visual C++ version 1.0. At that time, Microsoft was getting clobbered by Borland in the C/C++ market. McCarthy's group finally conducted a survey and ran some focus groups, and they learned that the biggest challenge developers faced was not the challenge of using the more exotic features of C++ but of switching to C++ at all. So they defined the primary goal of Visual C++ 1.0 to be to make it possible for developers to use C++ without climbing an incredibly steep learning curve. Meanwhile, Borland continued its focus on expert C++ developers and added support for templates and exceptions and other hard-core C++ language features.

In support of their objective of making C++ easier to use, the Visual C++ group came up with the idea of an Applications Wizard, which is a utility that builds the shell of a C++ application automatically. The result? Visual C++ gained dozens of points of market share almost immediately upon its release.

Design

CROSS-REFERENCE
For more on good design practices, see "Design" in Section 4.2 and Chapter 19, "Designing for Change."

You might have done a perfect job of gathering requirements—but you probably didn't. Here is the most productive thing you can do during design to maintain a customer orientation:

- Employ design practices that allow your customers to change their minds occasionally.

This boils down to identifying the changes you think are likely and then using as much information hiding and encapsulation as you can. Lack of design flexibility was apparently one of the weaknesses of the project described in Case Study 10-1, beginning on page 234. That development team created a design that couldn't accommodate two new reports without causing major trauma to the system.

Construction

If you've laid the groundwork during planning, requirements analysis, and design, by the time you get to full-scale construction your customers will be so invested in the development process that you won't have to worry about them.

Here are some customer-oriented practices that work especially well during construction:

CROSS-REFERENCE
For details on these practices, see "Tracking" in Section 4.1 and Chapter 27, "Miniature Milestones."

- Employ implementation practices that create readable, modifiable code, which will improve your ability to respond to customer change requests.

- Use progress-monitoring practices such as mini milestones so that you can inform the customer about your progress.

- Select a lifecycle model that provides the customer with steady, tangible signs of progress. This becomes especially important at implementation time because, without it, the project starts to seem as though it's dragged on for eons without really moving forward.

An interesting aspect of choosing an incremental lifecycle model is that it allows you to deliver working software to your customers frequently. The mere act of handing a working product to your customer every week or month provides more effective communication about your progress than a traditional status report. Customers like progress more than promises, and they especially like progress that they can hold in their hands or see on their computer screens.

10.3 Managing Customer Expectations

HARD DATA

Many problems in software development, especially in the area of development speed, arise from unstated, unrealistic expectations. One survey even found that 10 percent of all projects are canceled because of unrealistic expectations (Standish Group 1994). It is in your interest to try to set expectations explicitly so that you can bring to light any unrealistic assumptions your customers might have about the schedule or deliverables.

CROSS-REFERENCE
For details on the problems associated with overly optimistic schedules, see Section 9.1, "Overly Optimistic Scheduling."

One kind of unrealistic expectation can arise from the schedule. Many projects have their schedules set by their customers before the requirements and resources are fully known. As I've mentioned elsewhere in this book, agreeing to unrealistic schedules creates unrealistic expectations in the minds of your customers. Working with your customers to establish realistic expectations about their schedules is a key to success.

FURTHER READING
For more on managing customer expectations, see *Managing Expectations* (Karten 1994).

Making the effort to understand your customer's expectations can save a lot of friction and extra work. In 1992 I had a customer who wanted two changes made during beta testing of the Windows product I was working on. They presented both of these as "must have" changes. The first change was to add

243

a button to a toolbar so that the user could click and insert a new output page rather than going through some menus to do the same thing. The second change was to add a "blank output" page that would allow users to drag and drop pages from their word processor, spreadsheet, charting program, or other application into this product, preferably using hot links so that when they updated the pages in the other application the changes would automatically flow into our application.

The first change was no problem. It would take about one-half day to implement and a little time to write new test scripts, but that was about it. The second change was a different story. It would have required full OLE support, which in 1992 was supposed to take about one full-time developer the entire duration of the project.

After asking a few questions, it turned out that between the two features, the customer thought that the new toolbar button was the more crucial item. Once they understood that it would take from 6 to 9 staff months to implement the blank output page, they said "No way! It's not that important. Forget about it." Since dragging and dropping was easy for them to do, they had assumed that it would be easy for us to implement—believing it to be a 1-day or 2-day change.

You've probably had experiences in which your customers misunderstand something so basic that it didn't even occur to you that it was possible to misunderstand it. Customers sometimes think that if you're done with a prototype, you must be almost done with the product itself. They wonder where the "any" key is. They put diskettes into disk drives upside down and backwards. They think that if they can see color output on their screen they should be able to get color output on their laser printer. They move their mouse to the edge of the table and don't know what to do. They think you should know all of their requirements without having to explain them to you. (These are, by the way, all real examples.)

Yet despite how it sometimes seems, customers aren't stupid; rather, it's that they just don't understand what goes into software development. That's fair, because sometimes developers don't understand their customers' business environment, and customers think we're stupid for that.

Part of our jobs as software developers is to educate our customers so that they understand software development better, which makes it possible for us to live up to their expectations. (See Figure 10-3.) When customers become educated—when they have experience with software in general, with

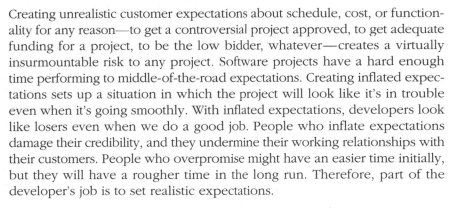

Figure 10-3. *Developers' and customers' views of the same phenomenon can be quite different.*

automation in their job areas, and as participants in software projects—productivity of the entire project improves (Jones 1991).

Sometimes customer expectations make it impossible to succeed. I know of one in-house software organization that delivered three projects to an internal customer within a 3-month period. One project finished early. The customer accused the developers of sandbagging their estimates. One finished on time.

The customer accused the developers of estimating conservatively and stretching out their work to match the estimate. One finished late, and the customer accused the developers of not being committed to the project.

CLASSIC MISTAKE

Creating unrealistic customer expectations about schedule, cost, or functionality for any reason—to get a controversial project approved, to get adequate funding for a project, to be the low bidder, whatever—creates a virtually insurmountable risk to any project. Software projects have a hard enough time performing to middle-of-the-road expectations. Creating inflated expectations sets up a situation in which the project will look like it's in trouble even when it's going smoothly. With inflated expectations, developers look like losers even when we do a good job. People who inflate expectations damage their credibility, and they undermine their working relationships with their customers. People who overpromise might have an easier time initially, but they will have a rougher time in the long run. Therefore, part of the developer's job is to set realistic expectations.

Case Study 10-2. The Requirements Club Revisited

Mike led the development effort on version 3 of Giga-Safe's billing system. At the beginning of the project, he met with Catherine to map out the project. "We're going to try to be more responsive to requests for changes this time," he told her. "That doesn't mean that we can include the kitchen sink, but we want to make sure not to leave you out in the cold." Catherine said that she appreciated that.

Mike led his team through a traditional requirements-gathering exercise that looked similar to the one that Chip had led the team through on Giga-Bill 2. When they were done, Mike's team mocked up the new reports and put together a live prototype of the input screens. They showed them to Catherine. "I never noticed it before," she said, "but we really ought to combine these two reports into one."

"No problem," Mike said. "What else?" Catherine said she'd like some other users in the accounting department to look at the screens and reports, so they set up an appointment for the next day.

By the time they were done the next day, they had changed every report in at least one minor respect. They had added two new reports and eliminated two entirely. They had also rearranged several input screens so that the users wouldn't have to enter as much redundant data. They went through the same routine with several more users over the next few days, and by the end they thought they had a clear picture of what the users wanted.

"We're going to make flexibility a design goal," Mike told Catherine. "If you try to limit additional change requests, we'll try to accommodate you on the really important ones."

Version 3 had been conceived as a smaller upgrade than version 2, and the team estimated that it would take 3 months instead of the 7 months the previous version had taken. As the deadline approached, the team waited for the inevitable requests for new input screens and reports. Low-priority requests trickled in and were marked "version 4", but release day arrived without a single high-priority request, and the system was released on time. Users were enthusiastic about version 3 and said it was what they'd hoped for last time.

After they released the product, one of the team members pointed out that they'd wasted time building flexibility into their design and code. "That's OK," Mike said. "We'll use it when we build the next version."

Further Reading

Karten, Naomi. *Managing Expectations*. New York: Dorset House, 1994. Karten's book deals with the problem of customers who, as she says, want more, better, faster, sooner, now. She discusses communications fundamentals, such as use of technical jargon, different communications styles, and careful listening. The book contains many enjoyable examples, some software-related and some not. The book emphasizes customer-service expectations, and, unfortunately, contains little discussion of managing schedule expectations specifically.

Whitaker, Ken. *Managing Software Maniacs*. New York: John Wiley & Sons, 1994. Chapter 1 of Whitaker's book discusses the importance of putting customers at the top of your priority list.

Peters, Tomas J., and Robert H. Waterman, Jr. *In Search of Excellence*. New York: Warner Books, 1982. This classic management book contains analysis and case studies about the value of keeping the customer satisfied.

11

Motivation

Contents

Related Topics

HARD DATA

OF THE FOUR AREAS OF RAPID-DEVELOPMENT leverage—people, process, product, and technology—"people" has the greatest potential to shorten software schedules across a variety of projects. Most people who work in the software industry have personally observed the enormous differences in output between average developers, mediocre developers, and genius developers. Researchers have identified performance differences on the order of 10 to 1 or more between different developers with the same levels of experience (Sackman, Erikson, and Grant 1968; Curtis 1981; Mills 1983; DeMarco and Lister 1985; Curtis et al. 1986; Card 1987; Valett and McGarry 1989).

Motivation is undoubtedly the single greatest influence on how well people perform. Most productivity studies have found that motivation has a stronger influence on productivity than any other factor (Boehm 1981).

Considering the critical role that motivation plays in development speed, you would expect a full-fledged motivation program to occupy a position of central importance on every rapid-development project. But that's not the case. Motivation is a "soft" factor: it's difficult to quantify, and it often takes a back seat to other factors that might be less important but that are easier

[Handwritten margin notes: "Assumption A motivated team does not necessarily stay motivated", "Motivated team on target", "Added pressure assumed handle"]

to measure. Every organization knows that motivation is important, but only a few organizations do anything about it. Many common management practices are penny-wise and pound-foolish, trading huge losses in morale for minor methodology improvements or dubious budget savings. Some motivational attempts backfire and actually hurt motivation.

Although motivation is a soft factor, the knowledge of how to motivate software developers is not a total mystery. This chapter describes how to tap into motivation to improve development speed.

Case Study 11-1. A Disheartening Lunch with the Boss

Tina had been working for about 1 year on a 2-year project. She was the lead on a commercial PC product for the first time, and she was really enjoying using C++ on an industrial-strength application. Although no one had asked them to, Tina and her team had already put in a lot of overtime; they were excited about the product concept and seemed to enjoy working long days together. The whole team had pitched in to remove every ounce of fat from their development process so that they could work efficiently. She was proud that they had hit all their milestones so far and was sure that they would hit the rest of them, too.

Her boss, Bill, asked her to lunch after they met their first coding milestone, and Tina thought, "Fabulous. He wants to congratulate me on the great job I've been doing."

Lunch started pleasantly, and Bill did congratulate her for doing a great job. "You know, the oversight committee is really excited about the progress you've been making on this project. But there are a few things we need to talk about. First, since your team seems like it's meeting its deadlines easily, we'd like to move the completion date up 3 months. With your track record, we think you'll be able to make that date without any trouble."

"But that's impossible—" Tina started to object, but her boss cut her off.

"Just wait until I finish my other points. Second, your last status report mentioned that your team will be taking an advanced C++ training course 4 hours a week for the next 10 weeks. In view of our schedule goals, we'd like you to cancel that course. You've got a strong team, and we are confident that you already know everything you need to about C++. Third, I know you're a mentor in the company's mentoring program and some of your team members are, too. Since the developers you're mentoring aren't working on your project, we'd like you to suspend your participation in that program until you ship the product. Finally, I know you have put a lot of work into making a really elegant design for the product. A couple of people on the oversight committee reviewed it and said it looks great. But we'd like you to refocus your design and cut the fluff so that you can implement it faster. I know you've tried hard to make the design flexible, so that won't be any trouble, will it?"

(continued)

Case Study 11-1. A Disheartening Lunch with the Boss, *continued*

Tina objected to her boss's "suggestions," but Bill prevailed. Afterwards, she wondered how she would report this to her team. She finally decided to report it exactly the way it had happened. Her team listened without saying anything. When she was done, one of the senior developers said, "They haven't learned anything, have they?"

When Tina went home for the day at 5:00, she noticed that everyone else had already left.

11.1 Typical Developer Motivations

Different people are motivated by different factors, and developers are not always motivated by the same factors as their managers or by the same factors as the general public. Table 11-1 on the next page shows a ranked ordering of motivational factors for developers, managers, and the general population.

The data in Table 11-1 deals specifically with "programmer analysts" rather than "developers." It is a statistical summary, so any single developer might actually match the manager column or the general-population column better than the programmer analyst column.

The data in Table 11-1 is also pretty old. Some of the factors such as the importance of job security are bound to change as economic conditions change. Different companies are hiring programmers now than were hiring in 1981. Maybe only the first few entries in each column are significant. But in the main, I think the data in Table 11-1 captures some important insights about the differences between developers, their managers, and the population at large:

- *Compared to the general population*, developers are much more motivated by possibility for growth, personal life, opportunity for technical supervision, and interpersonal relations with their peers. Developers are much less motivated by status, interpersonal relationships with subordinates, responsibility, and recognition.
- *Compared to their managers*, developers are somewhat more motivated by possibility for growth, personal life, and technical-supervision opportunity. Developers are much less motivated by responsibility, recognition, and interpersonal relationships with subordinates.

The comparisons between developers and managers are particularly interesting, and they help to explain some of the miscommunications that occur

Table 11-1. Comparison of Motivators for Programmer Analysts vs. Managers and the General Population

Programmer Analysts	Managers of Programmers	General Population
1. Achievement	1. Responsibility	1. Achievement
2. Possibility for growth	2. Achievement	2. Recognition
3. Work itself	3. Work itself	3. Work itself
4. Personal life	4. Recognition	4. Responsibility
5. Technical-supervision opportunity	5. Possibility for growth	5. Advancement
6. Advancement	6. Interpersonal relations, subordinate	6. Salary
7. Interpersonal relations, peers	7. Interpersonal relations, peers	7. Possibility for growth
8. Recognition	8. Advancement	8. Interpersonal relations, subordinate
9. Salary	9. Salary	9. Status
10. Responsibility	10. Interpersonal relations, superior	10. Interpersonal relations, superior
11. Interpersonal relations, superior	11. Company policies and administration	11. Interpersonal relations, peers
12. Job security	12. Job security	12. Technical-supervision opportunity
13. Interpersonal relations, subordinate	13. Technical-supervision opportunity	13. Company policies and administration
14. Company policies and administration	14. Status	14. Working conditions
15. Working conditions	15. Personal life	15. Personal life
16. Status	16. Working conditions	16. Job security

Sources: Adapted from *Software Engineering Economics* (Boehm 1981) and "Who Is the DP Professional?" (Fitz-enz 1978).

between developers and managers. *If you're a manager and you try to motivate your developers the same way that you would like to be motivated, you're likely to fail.* Developers care little about the responsibility or recognition that would motivate you. If you want to motivate developers, emphasize technical challenges, autonomy, the chance to learn and use new skills, and career planning—and respect their personal lives.

If you're a developer, be aware that your manager might have your interests at heart more than you think. The phony-sounding "attaboy" or hokey award might be your manager's sincere attempt to motivate you in the way that your manager likes to be motivated.

Another source of insight into developer motivations comes from surveys conducted to determine the personality types of developers using the Myers-Briggs Type Indicator (MBTI) test. The MBTI measures people's preferences along four dimensions and comes up with a four-letter categorization. The categories are:

- Extroversion (E) or introversion (I)
- Sensing (S) or intuitive (N)
- Thinking (T) or feeling (F)
- Judging (J) or perceiving (P)

There are 16 four-letter combinations, which means that there are 16 personality types.

HARD DATA

Not too surprisingly, two extensive surveys have found that computer professionals are much more "introverted" than the general population. "Introverts" in the context of MBTI doesn't mean quite the same thing it does in the non-MBTI world. In this case, it simply means that the person is more interested in the inner world of ideas than the external world of people and things. Somewhere between one-half to two-thirds of the computing population is introverted, compared with one-quarter to one-third of the general population (Lyons 1985; Thomsett 1990). This tendency toward an inner orientation seems consistent with the data in Table 11-1 that shows that developers in general are more interested in the possibility for growth than the other groups are and less interested in status and recognition.

The same surveys found that 80 percent of computer professionals have a preference for thinking (T) over feeling (F) compared to 50 percent of the general population. Ts have a preference for making decisions based on a logical and impersonal basis rather than on subjective personal values. This planned, logical bent is reinforced by computer professionals' preference for judging (J) over perceiving (P)—two-thirds of computer professionals are Js compared to about one-half of the general population. Js tend to live in a planned, orderly way, whereas Ps tend to be more flexible and adaptable.

CROSS-REFERENCE
For more on the importance of scheduling realistically, see Section 9.1, "Overly Optimistic Scheduling."

The implication of this preference is clear: If you want to appeal to a developer, you'd better use logical arguments. For example, a lot of what's been written about motivation suggests that one key to exceptional productivity is to set seemingly impossible goals. That's fine for Fs, who might find such goals inspiring. But Ts will reject such goals out of hand for being "illogical." This is one reason that it is a rare group of developers who will respond positively to an impossible schedule goal. The boss in Case Study 11-1 who moved the deadline up 3 months failed to take the probable reaction of T personality types into account.

Motivation, Morale, and Job Satisfaction

The terms motivation, morale, and job satisfaction are used more or less interchangeably in casual discussions, but they are not identical.

Motivation refers to the forces that cause you to engage in work-related behavior and that determine the form, direction, intensity, and duration of your efforts.

Morale refers to your current desire to work at your job. There is a loose association between motivation and morale, but morale can be high when motivation is low—you might want to continue working on a project because the project is easy, your teammates are fun, and you like goofing off. Conversely, motivation can be high when morale is low—you might want to do an outstanding job on a project you despise so that the company will feel sorry when you quit.

Job satisfaction refers to your perception that your job allows you to fulfill your important job-related values. Job satisfaction is similar to morale, but it involves a longer view. Your morale might be low because a well-liked boss got a promotion and won't be your boss anymore, but your overall job satisfaction might be high because you think that your organization is making good promotion decisions. Once again, there is a loose association between job satisfaction and motivation, but you can have high job satisfaction when your motivation is low, and you can be highly motivated when your job satisfaction is low.

From a rapid-development point of view, motivation matters most on single projects, and job satisfaction matters most for an organization's long-term rapid-development capability.

Remind yourself that different forms of motivation work with different people. Generalities about motivation can provide broad-brushed insights, but you'll be most successful if you try to identify the most effective motivation for each individual. Try to put yourself inside each team member's head and understand how he or she thinks. Better yet, ask people what they think. Figure out what will make the project a success for each person.

11.2   Using the Top Five Motivation Factors

A kick in the pants is a particularly bad form of motivation. As Frederick Herzberg points out, a kick in the pants doesn't produce motivation; it just produces movement (Herzberg 1987). To tap into the "10" of that 10-to-1 difference in individual performance, you have to go beyond movement and tap into developers' internal motivations.

254

Excite your developers. Create an environment in which they can satisfy their internal drives. When people are excited, they will put in long hours and enjoy it. You can generate a sense of excitement by focusing on the five factors that most influence developer motivation: achievement, possibility for growth, work itself, personal life, and technical-supervision opportunity. The following sections take up these five factors in detail.

Achievement

Software developers like to work. The best way to motivate developers is to provide an environment that makes it easy for them to focus on what they like doing most, which is developing software.

Ownership

CROSS-REFERENCE
For details on problems associated with ownership, see Section 34.2, "Managing the Risks of Signing Up." For details on the hazards of too much voluntary overtime, see Chapter 43, "Voluntary Overtime."

Ownership—"buy-in"—is one key to achievement motivation. People will work harder to achieve their own goals than to achieve someone else's. Microsoft's Chris Peters points out that if you let developers create their own schedules, they take ownership of their schedules, and you get their buy-in. You don't have to worry about long schedules because the schedules that developers generate are always ambitious (Cusumano and Selby 1995). You might have to worry about some of the problems associated with overly optimistic schedules or developers voluntarily working too much overtime, but those aren't motivation problems.

Goal setting

Goal setting is another key to achievement motivation. Explicitly setting development-speed objectives is a simple, obvious step in achieving accelerated software development, and it's easy to overlook. You might wonder, if you set a development-time objective, do developers actually work to achieve it? The answer is yes, if they know how that objective fits in with other objectives and if the set of objectives taken as a whole is reasonable. Developers can't respond to objectives that change daily or that are collectively impossible to meet.

Gerald Weinberg and Edward Schulman conducted a fascinating experiment to investigate the effect of objectives on developer performance (Weinberg and Schulman 1974). They gave five teams of developers the assignment of working on five versions of the same program. They gave the same five objectives to each of the five teams; however, they told each team to maximize a different objective. They told one team to minimize memory required, another to produce the clearest possible output, another to make the most readable program, another to use the minimum number of statements, and the last group to complete the program in the least amount of time. The results are shown in Table 11-2 on the next page.

Table 11-2. Team Performance Ranked Against Objectives That Teams Were Told to Optimize

Objective that Team was Told to Optimize	Team Ranking on Each Objective				
	Memory Use	Output Readability	Program Readability	Minimum Statements	Minimum Programming Time
Memory use	**1**	4	4	2	5
Output readability	5	**1**	1	5	3
Program readability	3	2	**2**	3	4
Minimum statements	2	5	3	**1**	3
Minimum programming time	4	3	5	4	**1**

Source: "Goals and Performance in Computer Programming" (Weinberg and Schulman 1974).

HARD DATA

The results of this study were remarkable. Four of the five teams finished first in the objective they were told to optimize; one team finished second in its objective. They also gave each team a secondary objective, and, on those, three of the teams finished second in their secondary objective, one team finished first, and one team finished last. None of the teams did consistently well in all objectives.

The implication of this study is that developers do what you ask them to do. They have high achievement motivation: they will work to the objectives you specify, but you have to tell them what those objectives are. If you want your team to develop a program in the minimum time, tell them! You can also tell them you want to minimize risk or maximize progress visibility. Depending on your situation, any of those goals could be the most important contributor to "rapid development."

Successful projects use goal setting to their advantage. Boeing captured its design goals and objectives for the 747 in a book titled *Design Objectives and Criteria*. If you think that goal setting isn't critical to the success of a project, consider that Boeing turned down an offer of $100 million from the Soviet government for a copy of that book (Larson and LaFasto 1989).

CROSS-REFERENCE
Goals should be clear, but they don't necessarily have to be simple to work. For a different angle on goal setting, see "Shared, Elevating Vision or Goal" in Section 12.3.

Be aware that it is possible to go too far in goal setting. If you give a team several objectives at once, it's often not possible for them to do well on all of them. None of the teams in the Weinberg and Schulman study did well on all criteria. A study at ITT found that productivity dropped sharply when multiple goals were present (Vosburgh et al. 1984).

HARD DATA

Setting too many goals at once is a common problem. A review of 32 management teams found that, in response to the question, "What does the leader do that keeps the team from functioning more effectively?" the most common response was that the leader diluted the team's efforts with too many priorities (Larson and LaFasto 1989). The researchers identified this as a major leadership blind spot because most team leaders gave themselves high ratings in the area of setting priorities. For best results, select one objective and make it clear that it is the most important one.

Possibility for Growth

One of the most exciting aspects of being a software developer is working in a field that is constantly changing. You have to learn something every day just to stay current, and half of what you need to know to do your job today will be out of date 3 years from now. Considering the nature of the industry developers have chosen to work in, it isn't surprising that they are motivated by possibilities for growth.

An organization can tap into that motivation by providing developers with opportunities to grow on their projects. This requires aligning the growth goals of the organization with the growth goals of the individual. Barry Boehm (1981) puts it this way:

> The principle of career progression indicates that it is in an organization's best interest to help people determine how they wish to grow professionally, and to provide them with career development opportunities in those directions. This may seem like a somewhat obvious principle, but in practice there are many software organizations which follow strongly opposing principles.

The boss in Case Study 11-1 undercut the team's possibility for growth by canceling the advanced C++ classes, thereby undercutting the team's motivation at the same time.

An organization can show interest in its developers' professional growth in any of these ways:

- By providing tuition reimbursement for professional-development classes
- By giving time off to attend classes or to study
- By providing reimbursement for purchase of professional books
- By assigning developers to projects that will expand their skill sets
- By assigning a mentor to each new developer (which shows both the mentor and the new developer that the organization is dedicated to professional growth)

- By avoiding excessive schedule pressure (which tells developers that the real, top priority is getting the next product out the door regardless of the personal cost)

HARD DATA

How much should you spend? There really is no upper limit. In *Thriving on Chaos*, Tom Peters reports that Nissan budgeted $30,000 per person in start-up training costs when they opened their plant in Smyrna, Tennessee (Peters 1987). Companies that are in the top 10 percent of their industries in quality and productivity typically provide 2 weeks of training per year for software developers and 3 weeks for software managers (Jones 1994).

A focus on personal growth can have both short-term and long-term impacts on your organization's productivity. In the short term, it will increase your team's motivation, causing them to work harder. In the long term, your organization will improve its ability to attract and keep people from the top of the talent pool. As John Naisbitt and Patricia Aburdene say in *Reinventing the Corporation*, "The best and brightest people will gravitate toward those corporations that foster personal growth" (Naisbitt and Aburdene 1985). In other words, support for professional development is vital to the health of any corporation—and especially so in the software field.

Work Itself

Richard Hackman and Greg Oldham argue that, generally, people's internal motivation comes from three sources: They must experience meaning in their work; they must experience responsibility for the outcome of their work; and they must know the actual results of their work activities (Hackman and Oldham 1980).

Hackman and Oldham identified five dimensions of the work itself that contribute to these sources of motivation. The first three of these job characteristics contribute to how meaningful people find their work to be:

- *Skill variety* is the degree to which your work requires you to exercise a variety of skills so that you can avoid boredom and fatigue. People find meaning in jobs that offer variety, even in work that is not very significant or important in any absolute sense.

- *Task identity* is the degree to which your job requires you to complete a whole, identifiable piece of work. People care more about their work when they have a whole job to do and when they feel that their contribution matters.

- *Task significance* is the degree to which your work affects other people and contributes to social welfare. People need to feel that the final product has value. As Hackman and Oldham point out, people who tighten nuts on airplanes will feel that their work is more important and meaningful than people who tighten nuts on decorative mirrors. Likewise, developers who are allowed to meet customers and understand the big picture within which they do their work are likely to feel more motivated by their work than developers who are kept in the dark (Zawacki 1993).

The fourth job characteristic contributes to a person's feeling of responsibility for the outcome of the work:

- *Autonomy* is the degree to which you have control over the means and methods you use to perform your work—the sense of being your own boss, and the amount of elbow room you have. The more autonomy people have, the greater sense of personal responsibility they tend to feel for the outcome of their work.

The fifth and final job characteristic contributes to how much people know about the actual results of their work activities:

- *Job feedback* is the degree to which carrying out the job itself provides you with direct and clear information about how effective you are. (This is different from receiving feedback from a supervisor or co-worker.) Software development provides great job feedback because the work itself—the program—provides the feedback: you can see immediately whether the program works when you run it.

HARD DATA

One key to motivation is to control these five dimensions to create meaningful work and then match up that work with people who have a high desire to achieve. Robert Zawacki reported that his 15 years of research indicate that about 60 percent of a developer's motivation comes from the matchup between the job and the developer (Zawacki 1993).

CROSS-REFERENCE
For a practice that pushes this kind of motivation to the extreme, see Chapter 34, "Signing Up."

The importance of the work itself is one reason that quality is usually more motivating to software developers than schedule. Creating something on the leading edge is a rush to a technically oriented person. It provides a level of motivation that's hard to create outside of a project team that's pushing the state of the art in some way or other.

Opportunity to focus on the work itself

Another motivational aspect of the work itself is the degree to which the environment allows a developer to focus on the work itself compared to how much it requires the developer to focus on related concerns.

CLASSIC MISTAKE

In most of the organizations I have been associated with, I have spent a significant portion of my time each day on trivial administrative tasks that broke the day into a series of distractions that didn't contribute to the project I was working on. In one organization, to get a pad of paper I had to walk from the fifth floor to the second floor, pick up the pad of paper in the supply room, and sign for it with my name and project account number. If I couldn't remember my project account number, I had to call someone back on the fifth floor to get it (and interrupt them) or I had to walk back up to my desk, look up the account number, and then walk back down to the second floor and start over.

In another organization, to make more than 10 photocopies I had to walk several buildings away, leave the copies overnight, and pick them up the next morning. When I have had problems with my computer, the most common organizational response has been to have me try to fix it myself. If that fails, the organization will bring in a professional computer technician a day or two later. In the meantime, the typical response is something along the lines of, "You don't absolutely *need* a computer to do your work, do you?"

Procuring anything unusual—bookcases, whiteboards, corkboards, an extra monitor for debugging, and so on—has taken anywhere from weeks to months. For a software developer who wants nothing more than to develop software, it can be incredibly frustrating (and demotivating) to have to spend time filling out a form just to get a notepad.

Aside from not eliminating administrative hassles, some traditional corporations inadvertently divert attention from the work itself by placing an emphasis on nonwork aspects of their environments. Enforcing a dress code suggests that the work itself, while important, is not of utmost importance. Enforcing strict work hours suggests the same thing. In some organizations, such policies are beneficial to the organization's image, but every organization should be sure to understand the message those non-work-itself policies convey to developers. Ask whether the image is important enough to justify the loss in motivation and productivity.

Personal Life

Achievement, possibility for growth, and work itself are in the top five motivators for both developers and managers (although they prioritize the factors differently). Those factors present a significant opportunity for developers and managers to understand what makes the other tick. But personal life is fourth for developers, fifteenth for managers. Thus, the motivational impact of a developer's personal life is likely to be the hardest motivational factor for a manager to understand. A close second is probably responsibility, which is ranked first for managers and tenth for developers.

One upshot of this disparity is that managers sometimes reward their best developers by assigning them to their highest-profile, highest-pressure projects. To the manager, the extra responsibility would be a treat, and the diminished personal life wouldn't matter much. To a developer, the extra responsibility is more trick than treat, and the diminished personal life is a keen loss. The developer interprets the manager's "reward" as punishment.

Fortunately, a manager doesn't have to understand in detail why developers' personal lives are important to them. A company can't do much to use personal lives as motivators except to schedule projects realistically so that developers have time for personal lives, to respect vacations and holidays, and to be sensitive to occasional requests for time off during the workday.

Technical-Supervision Opportunity

Managers are less motivated by opportunity for technical supervision than are developers. The easiest way to understand this is to recognize the connection between technical-supervision opportunity and achievement. For a developer, a technical-supervision opportunity represents an achievement. An opportunity to supervise technical work implies that the developer has achieved a level of technical expertise sufficient to direct others. For a manager, a technical-supervision opportunity would probably represent a step backwards; the manager is already supervising others and is quite happy not to be supervising technical details. So it's really not surprising that developers are more motivated by technical-supervision opportunity than managers are.

Technical-supervision opportunities are not limited to assigning one person to be the technical lead on a project. You can use this motivator more broadly:

- Assign each person on a project to be the technical lead for a particular product area—user-interface design, database operations, printing, graphics, report formatting, analytics, networking, interfacing with other applications, installation, data conversion, and so on.

- Assign each person to be the technical lead for a particular process area—technical reviews, reuse, integration, tool evaluation, performance evaluation, system testing, and so on.

- Assign all but the most junior developers to be mentors. You can assign second-level mentors to work with the first-level mentors. The second-level mentors can help with the mentoring activity itself, or they might provide more technically-experienced advice to the first-level mentors.

11.3   Using Other Motivation Factors

In addition to the top five motivators, there are a few other factors that you can use to motivate your team.

Rewards and Incentives

In *Inside RAD*, Kerr and Hunter chronicle the day-to-day activities of a rapid-development project (Kerr and Hunter 1994). At the end of their client company's first successful RAD project, top management met with the development team to figure out how to repeat the project's success. The team made many recommendations, most of which were accepted. Among other things, the team recommended establishing an awards program and listed a variety of possible rewards—recognition dinners with company executives, cash bonuses, vacation-time bonuses, gifts of appreciation (theater tickets or dinners for two), and award ceremonies. Kerr and Hunter reported that the awards-program proposal was clearly management's least-favorite recommendation, and at the time *Inside RAD* was published, nothing had been done to implement that recommendation.

CLASSIC MISTAKE

When you take a step back from Kerr and Hunter's story, you see something incredible. Kerr and Hunter describe a project that was successful enough to write a book about, but the company that received the benefit of this exceptional project balked at rewarding its developers. When the development team actually asked to be rewarded, the company responded by pocket-vetoing any reward. How many more successful rapid-development projects do you think that company will get from that team?

Developers grow tired of working for unappreciative companies, and rewards are therefore important to long-term motivation. But monetary rewards have to be handled carefully. Developers are good at math, and they can figure out when a reward is not commensurate with the sacrifice they've made. In "Improving Software Productivity," Barry Boehm reported that poor reward systems are systems in which an organization gives its top performers 6-percent raises and its mediocre performers 5-percent raises. Eventually the top performers get frustrated and leave (Boehm 1987a).

Do rewards motivate people? Absolutely. They motivate people to get rewards.

Alfie Kohn

It's also important to present any reward purely as a gesture of appreciation rather than an incentive. At least two-dozen studies over the last 30 years have shown conclusively that people who expect to receive a reward for doing their jobs successfully don't perform as well as those who expect no reward at all (Kohn 1993). The work itself is the greatest motivator, and the more a manager stresses an external reward, the less interested the developer becomes in the work itself, and the more potential motivation is lost.

Here are some possible gestures of appreciation that are often appropriate:

- Sincere praise directed at a specific accomplishment
- Team T-shirts, polo shirts, rugby shirts, watches, pins, mugs, posters, and so on

- Humorous or serious awards in the form of plaques, certificates, trophies, and the like
- Special events to celebrate significant accomplishments; depending on your team's preferences, an event might be a dinner at a favorite restaurant, a show, a trip, a ski day, or a dinner at the boss's house (or, for maximum effect, the boss's boss's house)
- Exceptions to company policies for the team, such as casual-dress Friday, a Ping-Pong table in your team's section of the building, free soda pop in the team refrigerator, and so on
- Special courses (outside the local area)
- Sponsorship at conferences that the organization would not ordinarily sponsor
- Grade-level promotions
- Special bonuses

In *In Search of Excellence,* Peters and Waterman (1982) report that the companies that manage to stay in the top halves of their industries over 20-year periods make extensive use of nonmonetary incentives. They put it this way:

> We were struck by the wealth of nonmonetary incentives used by the excellent companies. Nothing is more powerful than positive reinforcement. Everybody uses it. But top performers, almost alone, use it extensively. The volume of contrived opportunities for showering pins, buttons, badges, and medals on people is staggering at McDonald's, Tupperware, IBM, or many of the other top performers. They actively seek out and pursue endless excuses to give out rewards.

As with any show of appreciation, it's the thought that counts. Be sure that your rewards say "appreciation" rather than "incentive" or "manipulation."

Pilot Projects

In one of the most famous experiments in motivation and productivity, Elton Mayo and his associates ran a series of tests on worker productivity from 1927 to 1932 at the Hawthorne Works of the Western Electric Company in Chicago. Their aim was to determine the effect of lighting on productivity. First they tried turning the lights up, and productivity went up. Then they tried turning the lights down, and productivity went up again. They tried holding the lights constant, and productivity went up yet again (Boehm 1981).

After many more experiments, Mayo drew a conclusion that had nothing to do with lighting levels. He concluded that the simple act of conducting the experiments had increased productivity.

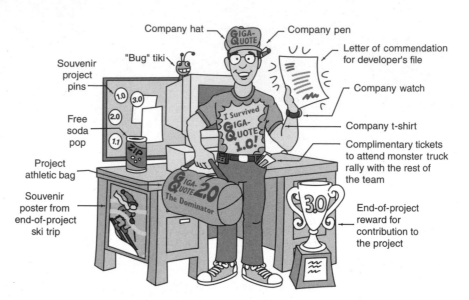

Figure 11-1. *The well-appreciated software developer.*

The "Hawthorne effect" (as it has come to be known) has been confounding productivity experiments and software metrics programs for decades. If you are a scientist, you would like to eliminate the Hawthorne effect because it interferes with your ability to determine whether the introduction of a new technology really improves productivity or whether the improvement is merely an example of the Hawthorne effect. But if you're a technical lead or manager, the Hawthorne effect is pure gold. If you're in the business of producing software, it doesn't matter whether the improvement in productivity comes from the new technology or the Hawthorne effect. If your experimental results are skewed, they'll be skewed on the high side, which is what you were after anyway.

FURTHER READING
For another view of the Hawthorne effect, see "What Happened at Hawthorne" (Parsons 1974).

The implication for software projects is clear. Run every software project as an experiment, as a pilot project. Try out some new methodology or new technology on each new project, and be sure that your team knows that the project is a pilot project. If you gather conclusive data on the effectiveness of the new methodology or new technology, great! You can use that data as a basis for spreading the methodology or technology to other projects in your organization. If the data you gather is inconclusive, you still get the benefit of the Hawthorne effect. As with rewards, remember that there is a fine line between motivation and manipulation. Don't manipulate.

Performance Reviews

Proper execution of a performance review significantly increases motivation, and improper execution of a performance review significantly decreases motivation. Andrew Grove, president of Intel, says that a performance review "is the *single most important form of task-relevant feedback* we as supervisors can provide" (Grove 1982). He goes on to say that, "The review will influence a subordinate's performance—positively or negatively—for a long time, which makes the appraisal one of the manager's highest-leverage activities."

W. Edwards Deming once stated the point a little differently when he said that most American reviews are conducted poorly, and it takes the average manager half a year to recuperate from his or her performance review (Peters 1988). He said that the American propensity for negative performance appraisals is our number-one management problem.

If your organization conducts performance reviews once or twice a year, take advantage of this high-leverage activity. Be sure that the reviews you're involved with increase rather than reduce motivation.

11.4 Morale Killers

Just as important as the factors that motivate are the factors that demotivate. In the 1960s, Fred Herzberg conducted research that identified two kinds of motivators (Herzberg 1987). He differentiated between motivating factors ("satisfiers"), which stimulate performance when they are present, and hygiene factors ("dissatisfiers"), which degrade performance when they are absent. This section identifies hygiene factors and other morale killers.

Hygiene Factors

Hygiene factors are the basic conditions a worker needs to work effectively. At best, hygiene factors create no dissatisfaction. At worst, their absence creates dissatisfaction. Adequate lighting is a hygiene factor because if adequate lighting is not present, the worker's ability to work effectively is impaired, and that hurts motivation. But adding extra lighting beyond a certain point does nothing to improve motivation. Good developers tend to gravitate toward organizations that provide work environments in which they can be productive—environments that meet their hygiene needs.

Here is a list of hygiene factors for software developers:

- Appropriate lighting, heating, and air-conditioning
- Adequate desk and shelf space
- Enough quiet to allow concentration (including the ability to turn off the telephone)
- Enough privacy to prevent unwanted interruptions
- Access to office equipment (such as a photocopy machine and a fax machine)
- Readily available office supplies
- Unrestricted access to a computer
- Up-to-date computing equipment
- Immediate or near-immediate repair of broken computer equipment
- Up-to-date communications support (including email, individual telephones, voice mail, and ready access to well-equipped conference rooms)
- Applicable software tools (word processor, design tools, programmer's editor, compiler, code libraries, debugging aids, and so on)
- Applicable hardware (for example, a color printer if you are working on a graphics application and expect most of your customers to print in color)
- Applicable reference manuals and trade publications
- Auxiliary reference books and on-line reference aids
- At least minimal training in new computer software, tools, and methodologies (additional training can be a growth motivator)
- Legal copies of all software used
- Freedom to set work hours—both generally (choosing to work 8–5, 11–8, or some other hours) and specifically (taking the afternoon off to attend a child's school play)

Other Morale Killers

Aside from not meeting a hygiene factor adequately, management can damage morale in other ways.

CLASSIC MISTAKE

Management manipulation. Developers are sensitive to being manipulated by management. Developers tend to deal with issues head-on, and they want management to deal with developers in a straightforward manner.

A few managers try to manipulate developers by setting phony deadlines, and most developers can smell a phony deadline 100 yards away. Management says, "We really, really have to have this project done by the end of the year." The developers say, "That sounds ambitious. If we really, really have to have it done by the end of the year, what features can we cut if we get into trouble?" Management says, "We need to keep all the features intact. We can't cut any of them." Development says, "Yeah, but what if we start to run out of time and we don't have any other choice but to cut features to make the schedule? What features should we cut then?" Management hems and haws and says, "We don't have a choice. You need to deliver all the features, and you need to deliver them by year-end."

Any particular manager might have good reasons to ask for such a deadline without giving a full explanation. Lower-level managers might not understand the reasons for deadlines they've been handed from someone higher up. The company might need to time a product's release in preparation for a public stock offering, and management might be legally restricted from explaining all the details. But answers like the ones described above appear to be evasive and manipulative—and developers respond poorly to that.

Barring extenuating circumstances, any manager who asks developers to commit to extra work on a project owes them a straight explanation. In Case Study 11-1, why did the boss move the deadline up 3 months? He didn't say. It seemed like he was moving it up just for the sake of moving it up. Managers who find themselves forced not to provide details about why a deadline is important should bear in mind that developers will probably find their explanations to be demotivating.

CROSS-REFERENCE
For a full discussion of the effects of excessive schedule pressure, see Section 9.1, "Overly Optimistic Scheduling."

Excessive schedule pressure. If the deadline is real, it still might not be realistic. One of the quickest ways to drop motivation to zero is to present developers with an impossible deadline. Few people will work hard to meet a deadline they know is impossible, especially if they are MBTI type Ts (those who respond to logic more than to emotion).

CLASSIC MISTAKE

Lack of appreciation for development's efforts. Ken Whitaker described a meeting his software-development team had with his organization's marketing branch. Here's what the marketing representative said at their meeting: "Marketing never gets off the hook! Why don't you give development half of the action items we get? Let's get products out dramatically faster—we all know that development 'sandbags' its schedules...."

Whitaker comments that "[The developers] knew how to deliver software products to market and had established an outstanding track record in doing just that—delivering. There was *no* sandbagging. Development made incredible efforts to deliver on marketing's expected and (sometimes) unrealistic delivery schedule. In fact, we all thought we were part of a great team" (Whitaker 1994).

I think this is a common dynamic—people don't *see* how much work developers are doing, so they don't think they're doing much and therefore must

don't need extra?

be sandbagging. In reality, developers are extremely self-motivated, work long and hard hours, and find being accused of "loafing" to be very demotivating. If you want your developers to do more than merely show up at the office, never, ever tell them they're not working hard when they are.

Inappropriate involvement of technically inept management. Developers can be motivated by technically inept managers as long as those managers recognize that they are technically inept and confine their control of the project to nontechnical decisions. If they try to meddle in technical decisions that they don't understand, they will become the butt of the development team's jokes, and most people can't be motivated by someone they don't respect. The nontechnical manager in Case Study 11-1 made a serious mistake when he ordered the development team to "cut the fluff" from its design.

Not involving developers in decisions that affect them. Not involving developers in decisions that affect them creates the impression that the manager either doesn't care about the development team or that management doesn't respect them enough to want their contributions. Here are some classic cases in which management must involve developers if it wants to keep their motivation high:

CLASSIC MISTAKE

- Committing to new schedules
- Committing to new features or feature modifications
- Hiring new team members
- Volunteering developers for short-term assignments outside the project
- Designing the product
- Making technical trade-off decisions (for example, whether to improve the performance of Feature A at Feature B's expense or vice versa)
- Changing office space
- Changing computer hardware
- Changing software tools
- Committing to deliver work products that might or might not already be planned by the team (for example, a prototype for use by the customer or a prerelease version of the product)
- Committing to new development procedures (for example, a new form of change control or a new kind of requirements specification)

If you are a manager, you might find it necessary to make the commitment or the change described in each of the above cases. As a manager, you have a right to do that. You also have a right to drive the motivation of your team to zero. If you want to drive motivation to less than zero, try soliciting the team's input to whitewash a decision after you've already made it. That combination of failure to involve developers and manipulation is especially demotivating. If you want to keep motivation high, involve the development team in the decision before you make the commitment or agree to the change.

Productivity barriers. If the environment is set up in a way that thwarts developers' best efforts to be productive, you can be quite sure that their motivation will suffer. Try to remove productivity roadblocks so that your team can focus on the work rather than on overcoming distractions.

CLASSIC MISTAKE

Low quality. Developers derive some of their self-esteem from the products they develop. If they develop a high-quality product, they feel good. If they develop a low-quality product, they don't feel as good. For a developer to be motivated by pride of ownership, there has to be ownership of the work, and there has to be pride in the work. A few developers can take pride in their response to the challenge of developing a low-quality product in the shortest possible time. But most developers are motivated more by quality than by sheer output.

If you as the manager insist that your developers shortchange quality in order to meet a tight schedule, you remove both halves of the pride-of-ownership motivator. You remove the pride, because the developers will not be proud of a low-quality product, and you remove the ownership, because you (rather than they) are making the decision to shortchange quality. With a low-quality product, some developers will feel terrible even if they meet their deadlines and receive bonuses.

If you feel that your developers won't be able to build a high-quality product in the time available, let the developers come to that conclusion themselves. They might choose to design a less-demanding product, or they might choose to develop a lower-quality product in the desired time frame. Regardless of what they decide, it won't do you any good to try to force them to develop a low-quality product. That's kick-in-the-pants motivation, and it doesn't work.

Heavy-handed motivation campaigns. With posters, slogans, pep talks, and other rah-rah! motivational practices, it's easier to insult developers' intelligence than it is to motivate them. With software developers, a light touch works best.

Case Study 11-2. A Highly Motivational Environment

Whatever else its critics might say about Microsoft, everyone agrees that it has succeeded in motivating its developers to an extraordinary degree. Stories of 10-, 12-, 14-, even 18-hour days are common, as are stories of people who live in their offices for weeks at a time (Maguire 1995). I have seen fold-out couches, cots, and sleeping bags in offices at Microsoft. I know of one developer who had a Murphy bed custom-made to fit his office. Dave Moore, Microsoft's director of development, described a typical day at Microsoft like this: "Wake up, go to work, do some work. 'Oh, I'm hungry.' Go down and eat some breakfast. Do some work. 'Oh, I'm hungry.' Eat some lunch. Work until you drop. Drive home. Sleep" (Cusumano and Selby 1995).

In its local area, Microsoft is known as "The Velvet Sweatshop," which suggests that, if anything, Microsoft might be doing too good a job of motivating its employees.

How does Microsoft achieve such a high level of motivation? It's simple. Microsoft explicitly focuses on morale. Each group at Microsoft has a morale budget that can be used for anything the group wants to use it for. Some groups buy movie-theater-style popcorn poppers. Some groups go skiing or go bowling or have a cookout. Some groups make T-shirts. Some groups rent a whole movie theater for a private screening of their favorite movie.

While Microsoft was still involved with OS/2, the OS/2 development group requested that the company install a washer and dryer in their building so that they wouldn't have to go home to do their laundry. Although the group never got its washer and dryer, the message was clear: this team wanted to work. The group didn't ask for promotions, more money, bigger offices, or fancy carpets; rather, it asked for management to remove every conceivable roadblock so that it could concentrate on shipping a product.

When I first began consulting at Microsoft, I was pleasantly surprised to find how much time each day I could actually spend working. Every floor in every building has a supply room stocked with common and not-so-common office supplies. You just take what you need, and you don't even need to sign anything. Most other things are only an email message away. If you need office equipment—bookcases, whiteboards, and so on—you just send email, put a note on the wall where you want the office furniture, and within 24 hours someone will have installed the furniture in your office. If you have a computer problem, you call the company's help desk, and within an hour or two a knowledgeable computer technician will have fixed your problem. They loan you a computer if necessary, and they will even swap your hard disk into the loaner to minimize downtime.

Microsoft also makes extensive use of nonmonetary rewards. I spent a year at Microsoft working on Windows 3.1. During that time, I received three team T-shirts, a team rugby shirt, a team beach towel, and a team mouse pad. I also

(continued)

Case Study 11-2. A Highly Motivational Environment, *continued*

took part in a team train ride and a nice dinner on the local "Dinner Train" and another dinner at a nice restaurant. If I had been an employee, I would also have received a few more shirts, a Microsoft watch, a plaque for participating in the project, and a big Lucite "Ship-It" award for shipping the project. The total value of this stuff is probably only two or three hundred dollars, but as Tom Peters and Robert Waterman say, companies with excellent motivation don't miss any opportunity to shower their employees with nonmonetary rewards.

Microsoft doesn't ignore developers' personal lives, either. For example, during the time I was there, the developer who had the office next to mine had his 10-year-old daughter come by every day after school. She did her homework quietly in his office while he worked. No one at the company even raised an eyebrow.

Self-motivation and motivation of other employees are part of the Microsoft corporate culture. Microsoft doesn't have an explicit practice of signing up for a project, but it is not uncommon for an employee who expresses doubt about meeting a deadline to be asked whether he or she is "signed up." Microsoft avoids the problem of phony-sounding management motivational speeches because, as often as not, the question doesn't come from a manager; instead, it comes from the person who will have to do the work if the person in question doesn't.

In addition to providing explicit support for morale, Microsoft gladly trades other factors to keep morale high, sometimes trading them in ways that would make other companies shudder (Zachary 1994). I've seen them trade methodological purity, programming discipline, control over the product specification, control over the schedule, management visibility—almost anything to benefit morale. Whatever you might think of the other effects, the motivational efficacy of this approach speaks for itself.

Further Reading

These three books are specifically about motivating software developers:

DeMarco, Tom, and Timothy Lister. *Peopleware: Productive Projects and Teams.* New York: Dorset House, 1987. DeMarco and Lister present many guidelines both for what to do and what not to do in motivating software teams.

Weinberg, Gerald M. *Becoming a Technical Leader.* New York: Dorset House, 1982. Part 3 of this book is about obstacles to motivation and learning how to motivate others.

271

Weinberg, Gerald M. *The Psychology of Computer Programming.* New York: Van Nostrand Reinhold, 1971. Chapter 10 of this classic book deals with motivation specifically, and the rest of the book provides insight into the programming mind-set, which will be useful to anyone who wants to understand what makes developers tick.

These two books provide insight into how Microsoft motivates its developers:

Cusumano, Michael, and Richard Selby. *Microsoft Secrets: How the World's Most Powerful Software Company Creates Technology, Shapes Markets, and Manages People.* New York: Free Press, 1995.

Zachary, Pascal. *Showstopper! The Breakneck Race to Create Windows NT and the Next Generation at Microsoft.* New York: Free Press, 1994.

These three books and articles are about motivation in general:

Herzberg, Frederick. "One More Time: How Do You Motivate Employees?" *Harvard Business Review*, September–October 1987, 109–120. This enlightening article discusses motivating employees through focusing on job enrichment and "growth motivators" rather than on hygiene motivators. The original article was published in 1968 and was republished in 1987 with some new comments by the author. By the time it was republished, the article had sold more than a million reprints, making it the most popular article in the history of the *Harvard Business Review*. I rarely laugh out loud while reading professional publications, but I did while reading this one. It is probably one of the most humorous articles ever published by the *Harvard Business Review*.

Peters, Tomas J., and Robert H. Waterman, Jr. *In Search of Excellence.* New York: Warner Books, 1982. This book is not about software, but snippets about how to motivate technical and nontechnical workers are threaded throughout the book.

Hackman, J. Richard, and Greg R. Oldham. *Work Redesign.* Reading, Mass.: Addison-Wesley, 1980. This book explores work-itself related motivations and proposes a framework for redesigning work to improve motivation, productivity, and quality. It contains valuable information, and the authors have earnestly attempted to make the book easy to read, but it's a heavy-duty psychology book. As someone without a psychology background, I found it to be slow going.

12

Teamwork

Contents

Related Topics

THE MOVIE *WITNESS* CAPTURES THE MARVEL of an Amish barn raising. Shortly after dawn, several dozen farmers and their families arrive at the site of a newlywed Amish couple's farm to put up a barn. The farmers raise the supporting members of the frame in the early morning, and by noon they complete the framing from the ground up to the rafters. After lunch, the farmers nail on the sides and the roofing. They work quietly, happily, and hard. And they do their work without the aid of electricity or power tools.

There are jobs for everyone from the youngest girls and boys to the oldest men and women. The kids carry water, tools, and supplies to the adults. The oldest men and women direct others' activities. Two men who might be viewed as rivals put aside their differences and cooperate toward their common goal. Several dozen people contribute their skills in ways that best support the common cause. The result of all this is an incredible feat: By the time the sun goes down, a team of farmers (and their families) has built an entire barn in a single day.

Several things are notably absent from this remarkable scene. The Amish use traditional tools and traditional building methods to erect the barn. No one delays the project to argue the merits of adopting more modern approaches. No one gripes because they can't use power tools. None of the farmers takes time out to talk to his stockbroker on his cellular phone. No one embroils the project in a debate about whether the newlywed couple really needs a new barn, or whether they should open a bed and breakfast instead. No one leaves the Amish community at the end of the day because the pressure of the project has been too intense.

The farmers are united by a clear vision of the barn they will build and by the seemingly impossible challenge of building it in about 15 hours. When they're done, they feel a strong sense of accomplishment—both individually and collectively—and they feel even stronger ties to their neighbors than they felt before.

If ever there was a model of a perfect team, this is it.

Case Study 12-1. You Call This a Team?

The Giga-Quote 2.0 project team had five team members: Joe, Carl, Angela, Tomas, and Tina. The project was organized with Tomas as the chief programmer on a chief-programmer team. In seeming contradiction to the chief-programmer-team structure, Tina served as the informal project manager and Angela as the QA manager. Decisions were made primarily by consensus and enforced by peer pressure. None of the other group members seemed to recognize Tomas's authority as chief programmer.

Early in the project, the group experienced problems with group dynamics. The group had several strong-willed individuals with differing opinions, and four of the group members described their group as having "all chiefs and no Indians." Tomas, the nominal chief programmer, denied that there were any personality problems. The group spent considerable energy in heated discussions about technical issues and project direction. These discussions often failed to reach a resolution. For example, the group decided to skip risk analysis, not because they had technical reasons to skip it but because they thought it would be too controversial.

The group (except for Tomas) recognized from the beginning that they had a group-dynamics problem, but they actually seemed to enjoy conflict. They felt that strong disagreements had resulted in spirited participation by all group members and thorough examinations of major technical issues.

In fact, the poor group dynamics had serious damaging effects. The group originally planned to develop Giga-Quote 2.0 under a classical waterfall lifecycle model, but they did not follow their plan. Different group members described their current lifecycle model as anything from an "overlapping waterfall" model to "chaos."

(continued)

Case Study 12-1. You Call This a Team? *continued*

> The group also did not follow recommended development practices. For example, the group had planned to use code inspections and reviews, but these were voluntary and they quit using them after they caused too many arguments. The group also could not agree on acceptance criteria for the end of the architecture, design, and unit-construction phases. After a few contentious initial attempts at design, they decided to proceed with coding and work out the details as they went along.
>
> When the Giga-Quote group reached integration, they experienced a big bang. They had allowed for 1 week to integrate 9 months of work. Group members had been confident about integration because they had defined the interfaces at the "data structure level." But they had defined only the syntax; their poor group dynamics had prevented them from defining interface semantics.
>
> As the deadline approached, personality conflicts came to a head. Carl folded his arms and protested, "I've said all along that this design approach would never work. That's why we're having all of these integration problems. We should have used my design." Angela, Joe, and Tina decided that they'd had enough and left for other positions within the company. That left Tomas and Carl as the only surviving team members. Tomas disliked Carl so much that he committed to work virtually nonstop until he completed the project if management would remove Carl. He finally completed the project 7 months after its original delivery date.

12.1 Software Uses of Teamwork

It takes more than just a group of people who happen to work together to constitute a team. In their book *The Wisdom of Teams*, Katzenbach and Smith (1993) define a team as "a small number of people with complementary skills who are committed to a common purpose, performance goals, and approach for which they hold themselves mutually accountable."

Teamwork can come into play on software projects on any number of specific tasks:

- Developing and reviewing the project's requirements
- Developing the project's architecture and the design guidelines that will be used by the whole project
- Defining aspects of the technical environment that will be used on the project (including the programming languages, compilers, source-code libraries, code generators, editors, and version-control tools)
- Developing coding standards that will be used by the whole project
- Coordinating work on related pieces of a project (including defining interfaces between subsystems, modules, and classes)

- Designing difficult parts of the system
- Reviewing individual developers' designs and code
- Debugging difficult parts of the system
- Testing of requirements, design, and code
- Auditing a project's progress
- Maintaining software once it has been built (including responding to maintenance requests and making emergency fixes)

Although any of these tasks could be done by a single person, they can all benefit from the involvement of two or more brains, which requires interaction among project members. If the brains are working in cooperation, the whole can sometimes be greater than the sum of its parts. If the brains are on a collision path, it can be less. A "team" exists whenever two heads together are better than two heads individually.

> ## Groups and Teams
>
> Not all groups are teams. Some projects can be done well enough by a group of cooperative people who don't form into a team. Some projects don't call for the level of commitment that teamwork entails.

12.2 Teamwork's Importance to Rapid Development

CROSS-REFERENCE
For general reasons that a peopleware focus is key to success on a rapid-development project, see "People" in Section 2.2.

Small projects can get away with not addressing teamwork issues, but they will benefit from addressing them. Large projects are group efforts, and characteristics of the groups play an important role in those projects' success.

Variations in Team Productivity

HARD DATA

Researchers have found differences in individual productivity on the order of 10 to 1. Researchers have also identified dramatic differences in the productivity levels of entire teams. After analyzing 69 projects at TRW and other companies, Barry Boehm concluded that the best teams were at least 4 times as productive as the worst (Boehm 1981). DeMarco and Lister identified productivity differences of 5.6 to 1 in a study of 166 professional programmers from 18 organizations (DeMarco and Lister 1985). An earlier study of programming teams observed a 2.6 to 1 variation in the times required for teams to complete the same project (Weinberg and Schulman 1974).

This difference holds even among groups of developers with similar levels of experience. In one study of seven identical projects, the developers were all professional programmers with several years of experience who were enrolled in a computer-science graduate program. The products still ranged in effort by a factor of 3.4 to 1 (Boehm, Gray, and Seewaldt 1984). Similarly, Valett and McGarry reported 2-to-1 and 3-to-1 differences in productivity between different projects at NASA's Software Engineering Laboratory (Valett and McGarry 1989).

CROSS-REFERENCE
For details on individual differences in productivity, see "People" in Section 2.2.

When you cut across this set of studies, the bottom line is that among groups with different backgrounds and different levels of experience, there is about a 5-to-1 difference in productivity. Among groups with similar backgrounds and similar levels of experience, there is about a 2.5-to-1 difference in productivity.

Cohesiveness and Performance

If your experience has been like mine, you'll agree that members of cohesive groups work hard, enjoy their work, and spend a great percentage of their time focused on the project goals. As Case Study 12-1 illustrates, participants in projects with poor team dynamics are frequently unfocused and demoralized, and they spend a great deal of their time working at cross purposes.

HARD DATA

In a study published in 1993, B. Lakhanpal reported on how group cohesiveness, individual capabilities, and experience were related to overall project performance on 31 software projects (Lakhanpal 1993). The projects ranged in duration from 6 to 14 months and in size from 4 to 8 developers. Lakhanpal found that group cohesiveness contributed more to productivity than project members' individual capabilities or experience did. (Individual capabilities were a close second.)

Lakhanpal points out that managers commonly assign project members based on level of experience and individual capabilities. The study of 31 projects suggests that managers who are concerned about rapid development would be better off to assign developers based on their abilities to contribute to a cohesive team first and only then based on their individual capabilities.

Case Study 12-2. A High-Performance Team

One illustration of a productive team is the group of Amish farmers at the beginning of the chapter. That might not have much to do with software teams, but, then again, it might.

The most productive team I ever worked on shared many characteristics with the Amish barn raisers. After I graduated from college, I worked for a startup company in the actuarial consulting business. The owner was cheap, so he

(continued)

Case Study 12-2. A High-Performance Team, *continued*

hired fresh-out-of-college graduates to minimize his labor costs rather than pay more for experienced developers. Our group members soon found we had a lot in common since our jobs at this company were the first professional, adult jobs any of us had had.

Because it was a startup company, we broke a lot of new ground for the company, and we worked to a lot of challenging deadlines. We set up friendly rivalries, such as buying each other donuts for finding bugs in our code. Because we were recent college graduates, we had more responsibility than we had ever had before.

We had all been hired with the same job title, so it wasn't too long before we started referring to ourselves as "Analysts Incorporated." Like a lot of other teams, we had a set of in-jokes and rituals that people outside of the team had a hard time understanding. We spent our programming time in a programming bull pen, and since we thought our boss pushed us way too hard, we sometimes put up a sign that read "Closed Door Analyst Meeting," closed the door, and sang spirituals while we programmed.

One day I took a new hire to get a joint assignment from our supervisor. The supervisor was an honorary member of Analysts Incorporated, and he and I made jokes and traded barbs about previous projects while we went over the new project. After a few minutes, the supervisor needed to attend a meeting, so he excused himself and said he would check back after the meeting to see how our work was going. After he had left, the new hire said, "It doesn't seem like we got much accomplished. All you two did was make jokes and insult each other, and we don't really know what we're supposed to do, do we? When are we going to get our assignment?" As I explained the assignment we had just received point-by-point to the new hire, I realized how far our group had gone toward establishing its own mode of communication and unique identity.

12.3 Creating a High-Performance Team

Productive teams are sometimes characterized as teams that have jelled or as teams that are highly cohesive. What characteristics does a high-performance, jelled, cohesive team have? The team has:

- A shared, elevating vision or goal
- A sense of team identity
- A results-driven structure
- Competent team members
- A commitment to the team

- Mutual trust
- Interdependence among team members
- Effective communication
- A sense of autonomy
- A sense of empowerment
- Small team size
- A high level of enjoyment

In 1989, Larson and LaFasto published a study that found unusual consistency among the attributes of highly effective teams. This was true for teams as diverse as the McDonald's Chicken McNugget team, the space-shuttle Challenger investigation team, cardiac-surgery teams, mountain-climbing teams, the 1966 Notre Dame championship football team, and White House cabinets (Larson and LaFasto 1989). The following sections explain how each of the attributes apply to software teams.

Shared, Elevating Vision or Goal

HARD DATA

Before the project gets really rolling, a team needs to "buy in" to a common vision or common goals. The Amish farmers shared a common vision of the barn they were going to raise, why they were raising it, how they would raise it, and how long it would take. Without such a shared vision, high-performance teamwork cannot take place. Larson and LaFasto's study of 75 teams found that in every case in which an effectively functioning team was identified, the team had a clear understanding of its objective.

Sharing a vision is useful to rapid development on several levels. Having agreement on the project vision helps to streamline decision making on the smaller issues. Small issues stay small because the big vision keeps them in perspective, and everyone agrees on the big vision. The team is able to make decisions and then execute them without squabbling and without revisiting issues that have already been decided. A common vision builds trust among the team members because they know that they are all working toward the same objective. It also helps to keep the team focused and avoid time-wasting side trips. An effective team builds a level of trust and cooperation that allows them to outperform a collection of individuals with similar skills.

Occasionally a highly cohesive team will lock onto a shared vision that is at odds with the organization's objectives. In this case, the team might get a lot of work done, but not the kind of work the organization needs. To be productive, a cohesive group needs to have a focus compatible with the organization they are a part of.

Challenging Work

The shared vision can be of something important—such as putting a man on the moon by 1970—or it can be of something relatively trivial—getting the latest update of the billing system out 3 weeks faster than last time. The vision can be virtually arbitrary, but as long as the whole team shares it, it will serve the same purpose of helping to bring the team together.

To have a motivating effect, the vision also needs to be elevating. The team needs to be presented with a challenge, a mission. The Amish farmers responded to the seemingly impossible challenge of building an entire barn in one day. High-performance teams don't form around ho-hum goals. "We'd like to create the third-best database product and deliver it in an average amount of time with below average quality." Ho hum. Yawn. No team is going to rally around that. (See Figure 12-1.)

But the response to challenge is an emotional reaction, and it is influenced as much by the way the work is assigned or described as by the work itself. Here's a restatement of the ho-hum goal: "We're going to create a database product that will take us from zero market share to 25-percent market share in 18 months. Marketing and production need absolutely reliable schedule estimates to pull this off, so we're going to make it our goal to set internal milestones and a final ship date that we can meet with 100-percent assurance." A team just might form around the vision of 100-percent scheduling accuracy.

"Aren't you a team? Why aren't you getting more done? Work Harder."

Figure 12-1. *The way you present the project will determine whether your team sees its job as a mission or a hardship.*

A real team needs a mission, and how you frame the project has a lot to do with whether the team sees a mission.

Sense of Team Identity

As team members work together toward their common vision, they begin to feel a sense of team identity. Teams name themselves. "The Black Team." "Analysts Incorporated." "The Camobap Boys." "Seance." Some teams have a team motto. Others, like IBM's famous Black Team, adopt a team dress code. Their senses of humor begin to gravitate toward one another's, finding humor in things that other people don't understand. They look for common characteristics that differentiate them from the rank and file. IBM's Black Team continued even after all the original team members had gone. That's a strong sense of identity. Smart companies reinforce the team's sense of identity by providing team T-shirts, notepads, mugs, and other paraphernalia that validate the team as a legitimate entity.

Team members allow their sense of team identity to overshadow their identities as individuals. They derive satisfaction from the team's accomplishments. They see the common goal as more important than their personal agendas. They have the opportunity to achieve something with the team that they couldn't achieve individually. For example, from 1957 to 1969, the Boston Celtics won the NBA championship 11 times without ever having a player among the top three scorers in the league. The team came first. Team members talk more about what "we" did than what "I" did, and they seem to take more pride in what "we" did than in what "I" did.

Along with the feeling of identity, high-performance teams often develop a sense of eliteness. Team members get to be team members by going through some kind of trial by fire—a rigorous interview and audition process, successfully completing an especially challenging first assignment, or being recruited on the basis of exceptional past performance.

One project I know of used up all the money in its morale budget and later made team shirts available for $30 apiece to new team members. That is a good example of how *not* to create team spirit. (The message the team hears from the company is that the team ranks so low in the company that it has to buy its own team shirts.) The same project was identified as responsible for one of the company's "low-revenue products." Characterizing a team that way is a mistake because that isn't the sort of identity that most teams will rally around.

Results-Driven Structure

CROSS-REFERENCE
For more on team structures,
see Chapter 13, "Team
Structure."

You can structure teams for optimal output, or you can structure them in such a way that it is almost impossible for them to produce anything at all.

For rapid development, you need to structure the team with maximum development speed in mind. You don't put John in charge just because he's the owner's cousin, and you don't use a chief-programmer team structure on a three-person project when the three people have roughly equal skills.

Here are four essential characteristics of a results-driven team structure:

- Roles must be clear, and everyone must be accountable for their work at all times. Accountability is critical to effective decision making and to rapid execution after the decisions have been made.

- The team must have an effective communication system that supports the free flow of information among team members. Communication must flow freely both from and to the team's management.

- The team must have some means of monitoring individual performance and providing feedback. The team should know whom to reward, who needs individual development, and who can assume more responsibilities in the future.

- Decisions must be made based on facts rather than on subjective opinions whenever possible. The team needs to be sure that the facts are interpreted without biases that undercut the functioning of the team.

There are practically an infinite number of team structures that can satisfy these essential characteristics. It is amazing that so many team structures do not.

Competent Team Members

Just as team structures are chosen for the wrong reasons, team members are often chosen for the wrong reasons: for example, they are often chosen because they have an interest in the project, because they are cheap, or most often simply because they are available. They are not chosen with rapid development in mind. Case Study 12-3 describes the way in which team members are typically selected.

Case Study 12-3. Typical Team-Member Selection

Bill had a new application to build, and he needed to put a team together fast. The project was supposed to take about 6 months and was going to involve a lot of custom graphics, and the team would have to work closely with the

(continued)

Case Study 12-3. Typical Team-Member Selection, *continued*

customer. It should take about four developers. Ideally, Bill thought, he'd like to get Juan, who had worked on GUI custom graphics on that platform before, and Sue, who was a database guru and great with customers. But they were both busy on other projects for the next 2 or 3 weeks.

At the manager's meeting Bill found out that Tomas, Jennifer, Carl, and Angela would be available at the end of the week. "They'll do OK," he said. "That will let us get started right away."

He planned the project this way: "Tomas can work on the graphics. He hasn't worked on this platform before, but he's done some graphics work. Jennifer would be good for the database side. She said she was tired of working on databases, but she agreed to work on them again if we really needed her to. Carl's done some work on this platform before, so he could lend Tomas a hand with the graphics. And Angela is an expert in the programming language. Carl, Angela, and Tomas have had a few problems working together before, but I think they've put their differences behind them. None of them are particularly strong in working with customers, but I can fill in that gap myself."

Case Study 12-3 describes a team that's selected based on who's available at exactly the right time without much concern for the long-term performance consequences. It's almost certain that the team would do better on its 6-month project if it waited the 3 weeks until Juan and Sue were available.

For rapid development, team members need to be chosen based on who has the competencies that are currently needed. Three kinds of competencies are important:

- Specific technical skills—application area, platform, methodologies, and programming language
- A strong desire to contribute
- Specific collaboration skills required to work effectively with others

Mix of Roles

On an effective team, the team members have a mix of skills and they play several different roles. It obviously doesn't make sense to have a team of seven people who are all experts in assembly language if your project is in C++. Likewise, it doesn't make sense to have seven people who are all experts in C++ if no one of them knows the applications area. Less obviously, you need team members who have a blend of technical, business, management, and interpersonal skills. In rapid development, you need interpersonal leaders as much as technical leaders.

FURTHER READING
These labels are not
Belbin's but are taken from
Constantine on Peopleware
(Constantine 1995a).

Dr. Meredith Belbin identified the following leadership roles:

- *Driver*—Controls team direction at a detailed, tactical level. Defines things, steers and shapes group discussions and activities.

- *Coordinator*—Controls team direction at the highest, strategic level. Moves the problem-solving forward by recognizing strengths and weaknesses and making the best use of human and other resources.

- *Originator*—Provides leadership in ideas, innovating and inventing ideas and strategies, especially on major issues.

- *Monitor*—Analyzes problems from a practical point of view and evaluates ideas and suggestions so that the team can make balanced decisions.

- *Implementer*—Converts concepts and plans into work procedures and carries out group plans efficiently and as agreed.

- *Supporter*—Builds on team members' strengths and underpins their shortcomings. Provides emotional leadership and fosters team spirit. Improves communications among team members.

- *Investigator*—Explores and reports on ideas, developments, and resources outside the group. Creates external contacts that may be useful to the group.

- *Finisher*—Ensures that all necessary work is completed in all details. Seeks work that needs greater than average attention to detail, and maintains the group's focus and sense of urgency.

Even on a rapid-development project, it's best not to staff a project with nothing but high-performance individuals. You also need people who will look out for the organization's larger interests, people who will keep the high-performance individuals from clashing, people who will provide technical vision, and people who will do all the detail work necessary to carry out the vision.

One symptom of a team that isn't working is that people are rigid about the roles they will and won't play. One person will do database programming only and won't work on report formatting. Or another person will program only in C++ and won't have anything to do with Visual Basic.

On a well-oiled team, different people will be willing to play different roles at different times, depending on what the team needs. A person who normally concentrates on user-interface work might switch to database work if there are two other user-interface experts on the team. Or a person who usually plays a technical-lead role may volunteer to play a participant role if there are too many leaders on a particular project.

Commitment to the Team

CROSS-REFERENCE
For more on commitment to a project, see Chapter 34, "Signing Up."

The characteristics of vision, challenge, and team identity coalesce in the area of commitment. On an effective team, team members commit to the team. They make personal sacrifices for the team that they would not make for the larger organization. In some instances, they may make sacrifices to the team to spite the larger organization, to prove that they know something that the larger organization doesn't. In any case, the minimum requirement for team success is that the team members contribute their time and energy—their effort—and that calls for commitment.

When team members commit, there must be something for them to commit to. You can't commit to unstated goals. You can't commit at any deep level to "doing whatever management wants." Vision, challenge, and team identity provide the things to which team members commit.

Getting project members to commit to a project is not as hard as it might sound. IBM found that many developers were eager for the opportunity to do something extraordinary in their work. They found that simply by asking and giving people the option to accept or decline, they got project members to make extraordinary commitments (Scherr 1989).

Mutual Trust

Larson and LaFasto found that trust consisted of four components:

- Honesty
- Openness
- Consistency
- Respect

If any one of these elements is breached, even once, trust is broken.

Trust is less a cause than an effect of an effective team. You can't force the members of a team to trust each other. You can't set a goal of "Trust your teammates." But once project members commit to a common vision and start to identify with the team, they learn to be accountable and to hold each other accountable. When team members see that other team members truly have the team's interests at heart—and realize that they have a track record of being honest, open, consistent, and respectful with each other—trust will arise from that.

Interdependence Among Members

Team members rely on each other's individual strengths, and they all do what's best for the team. Everybody feels that they have a chance to contribute and that their contributions matter. Everybody participates in decisions. In short, the team members become interdependent. Members of healthy teams sometimes look for ways they can become dependent on other team members. "I could do this myself, but Joe is especially good at debugging assembly language code. I'll wait until he comes back from lunch and then ask him for help."

On the most effective one-project teams that I've been on, the beginning of the project is characterized by an unusual measure of tentativeness. Team members might feel that they have specific strengths to offer the team, but they are not pushy about asserting their rights to occupy specific roles. Through a series of tacit negotiations, team members gradually take on roles that are not just best for them individually but that are best for the team as a whole. In this way, everyone gravitates toward productive positions, and no one feels left out.

Effective Communication

CROSS-REFERENCE
For more on the role of communication in teamwork, see "Effective communication" in Section 13.1.

Members of cohesive teams stay in touch with each other constantly. They are careful to see that everyone understands when they speak, and their communication is aided by the fact that they share a common vision and sense of identity. Amish barn raisers communicate efficiently during a barn raising because they live in a tight-knit community and nearly all of them have been through barn raisings before. They are able to communicate precise meanings with a few words or gestures because they have already established a baseline of mutual understanding.

Team members express what they are truly feeling, even when it's uncomfortable. Sometimes team members have to present bad news. "My part of the project is going to take 2 weeks longer than I originally estimated." In an environment characterized by interdependence and trust, project members can broach uncomfortable subjects when they first notice them, when there's still time to take effective corrective action. The alternative is covering up mistakes until they become too serious to overlook, which is deadly to a rapid-development effort.

Sense of Autonomy

Effective teams have a sense that they are free to do whatever is necessary to make the project succeed. One reason that skunkworks projects work as well as they do is that they give team members a chance to do what's right without worrying about doing what appears to be right. They can work without interference. The team might make a few mistakes—but the motivational benefit will more than offset the mistakes.

This sense of autonomy is related to the level of trust they feel from their manager. It is imperative that the manager trust the team. That means not micromanaging the team, second-guessing it, or overriding it on tough decisions. Any manager will support a team when the team is clearly right—but that's not trust. When a manager supports the team when it looks like it might be wrong—*that's trust.*

Sense of Empowerment

An effective team needs to feel empowered to take whatever actions are needed to succeed. The organization doesn't merely allow them to do what they think is right, it supports them in doing it. An empowered team knows that it can, as they say at Apple Computer, *push back* against the organization when it feels the organization is asking for something unreasonable or is headed in the wrong direction.

One common way that teams are denied empowerment is in the purchase of minor items they need to be effective. I worked on an aerospace project in which it took 6 months to get the approval to buy two scientific hand-held calculators. This was on a project whose mission was to analyze scientific data!

As Robert Townsend says, "Don't underestimate the morale value of letting your people 'waste' some money" (Townsend 1970). The most extreme example I know of was an episode during the development of Windows 95. To ensure that Windows 95 worked well with every program, the project manager and the rest of the team headed over to the local software store and loaded up a pickup truck with one of every kind of program available. The total tab was about $15,000, but the project manager said that the benefit to morale was unbelievable. (The benefit to morale at the software store wasn't bad, either.)

Small Team Size

Some experts say that you must have fewer than 8 to 10 people for a team to jell (Emery and Emery 1975, Bayer and Highsmith 1994). If you can keep the group to that size, do so. If your project requires you to have more than 10 project members, try to break the project into multiple teams, each of which has 10 or fewer members.

The 10-person limitation applies mainly to single-project teams. If you can keep a team together across several projects, you can expand the size of the team as long as the team shares a deep-rooted culture. The Amish farmers formed a cohesive team of several dozen people, but they had been together for generations.

On the other end of the scale, it is possible for a group to be too small to form a team. Emery and Emery point out that with less than four members, a group has a hard time forming a group identity, and the group will be dominated by interpersonal relationships rather than a sense of group responsibility (Emery and Emery 1975).

High Level of Enjoyment

CROSS-REFERENCE
For more on what motivates developers, see Section 11.1, "Typical Developer Motivations."

Not every enjoyable team is productive, but most productive teams are enjoyable. There are several reasons for this. First, developers like to be productive. If their team supports their desire to be productive, they enjoy that. Second, people naturally spend more time doing things that they enjoy than doing things that they don't enjoy, and if they spend more time at it, they'll get more done. Third, part of what makes a team jell is adopting a group sense of humor. DeMarco and Lister describe a jelled group in which all the members thought that chickens and lips were funny (DeMarco and Lister 1987). Chickens with lips were especially funny. The group actually rejected a well-qualified candidate because they didn't think he would find chickens with lips amusing. I don't happen to think that chickens with lips are funny, but I know what DeMarco and Lister are talking about. One group I was a part of thought that cream soda was hilarious and another thought that grape Lifesavers were a riot. There's nothing intrinsically comical about cream soda or grape Lifesavers, but those jokes were part of what gave those teams their identities. I haven't personally seen a cohesive team that didn't have a keen sense of humor. That might just be a quirk of my specific experience, but I don't think so.

How to Manage a High-Performance Team

CROSS-REFERENCE
For the difference between managers and team leaders, see Section 13.3, "Managers and Technical Leads."

FURTHER READING
For excellent discussions of each of these points, see *Quality Software Management, Volume 3: Congruent Action* (Weinberg 1994).

A cohesive team creates an "us" and the manager is in the sticky position of being not completely "us" and not completely "them." Some managers find that kind of team unity threatening. Other managers find it exhilarating. By taking on a great deal of autonomy and responsibility, a high-performance team can relieve a manager of many of the usual management duties.

Here are some keys to success in managing a cohesive team:

- Establish a vision. The vision is all-important, and it is up to the manager and team leader to put it into play.

- Create change. The manager recognizes that there is a difference between the way things should be and the way they are now. Realize that the vision requires change, and make the change happen.

- Manage the team as a team. Make the team responsible for its actions rather than making individuals on the team responsible for their individual actions. Team members often set higher standards for themselves than their leaders do (Larson and LaFasto 1989).

- Delegate tasks to the team in a way that is challenging, clear, and supportive. Unleash the energy and talents of the team members.
- Leave details of how to do the task to the team, possibly including the assignment of individual work responsibilities.
- When a team isn't functioning well, think about the MOI model, which states that most team problems arise from Motivation, Organization, or Information. Try to remove roadblocks related to these three factors.

12.4 Why Teams Fail

FURTHER READING
For an excellent discussion of team failure, see Chapter 20, "Teamicide," in *Peopleware* (DeMarco and Lister 1987).

The cohesiveness of a group depends on the total field of forces that act on that group. As with other aspects of rapid development, you have to do a lot of things right to succeed, but you only have to do one thing wrong to fail. Teams don't need to have all the characteristics described in the previous section, but they do need to have most of them.

Teams can fail for any of the reasons listed in Section 11.4, "Morale Killers." Those morale killers can keep a team from jelling just as easily as they can undercut individual morale.

Here are some other reasons that teams fail.

Lack of common vision. Teams rarely form without a common vision. Organizations sometimes prevent teams from forming by undercutting their visions. A team might form around the vision of producing "the best word processor in the world." That vision takes a beating if the organization later decides that the word processor doesn't have to be world class, but it does have to be completed within the next 3 months. When the vision takes a beating, the team takes a beating too.

Lack of identity. Teams can fail because they don't establish a team identity. The team members might be willing, but no one plays the role of Supporter, and without anyone to look after the team, the team doesn't form. This risk is particularly strong on rapid-development projects because of pressure not to "waste time" on "nonproductive" activities such as developing a team logo or shared sense of humor. Each team needs to have someone who will take responsibility for maintaining the health of the team.

Teams can also lack identity because one or more members would rather work alone than be part of a team. Some people aren't joiners, and some people think the whole idea of teams is silly. Sometimes a group is composed of 9-to-5ers who don't want to make the commitment to their jobs that team membership entails. There are lots of appropriate places for people who work like this, but their presence can be deadly to team formation.

Lack of recognition. Sometimes project members have been part of a project team that gave its heart and soul—only to find that its efforts weren't appreciated. One young woman I know worked practically nonstop for 3 months to meet a deadline. When her product shipped, the manager thanked her in a fatherly way and gave her a stuffed animal. She thought the gesture was patronizing, and she was livid. I wouldn't blame her for not signing up for another all-out team project. If an organization wants to create a high-performance team more than once, it should be sure to recognize the extraordinary efforts of the first team appropriately. If group members' previous experience has conditioned them to ask, "What's in it for me?" you'll have an uphill battle in getting a high-performance team to form.

Productivity roadblocks. Sometimes teams fail because they feel that they can't be productive. People can't survive if the environment doesn't contain enough oxygen, and teams can't survive if they're prevented from getting their work done. Some experts say that the primary function of a software-project manager is to remove barriers to productivity so that the naturally self-motivated developers can be productive (DeMarco and Lister 1987).

Ineffective communication. Teams won't form if they can't communicate regularly. Common barriers to communication include lack of voicemail, lack of email, insufficient number of conference rooms, and separation of the team members into geographically dispersed sites. Bill Gates has pointed out that doing all of Microsoft's new-product development on one site is a major advantage because whenever interdependencies exist, you can talk about them face to face (Cusumano and Selby 1995).

Lack of trust. Lack of trust can kill a team's morale as quickly as any other factor. One reason that teams usually don't form within bureaucratic organizations is that the organizations (to varying extents) are based on lack of trust. You've probably heard something similar to this: "We caught someone buying an extra pack of 3-by-5 cards in August of 1952, so now all purchases have to go through central purchasing." The lack of trust for employees is often institutionalized.

Managers who pay more attention to how their teams go about administrative details than to the results they achieve are demonstrating a lack of trust. Managers who micromanage their team's activities, who don't allow them to meet with their customers, or who give them phony deadlines are giving a clear signal that they don't trust them.

Instead of micromanaging a project team, set up a high-level project charter. Let the team run within that charter. Set it up so that management can't overrule the team unless they've gone against their charter.

Problem personnel. The software field is littered with stories of developers who are uncooperative in legendary proportions. I worked with one belligerent developer who said things like, "OK, Mr. Smarty Pants Programmer, if you're so great, how come I just found a bug in your code?" Some programmers browbeat their co-workers into using their design approaches. Their nonconfrontational co-workers would rather acquiesce to their design demands than prolong their interactions with them. I know of one developer who was so difficult to work with that the human resources department had to be brought in to resolve module-design disputes.

If you tolerate even one developer whom the other developers think is a problem, you'll hurt the morale of the good developers. You are implying that not only do you expect your team members to give their all; you expect them to do it when their co-workers are working against them.

In a review of 32 management teams, Larson and LaFasto found that the most consistent and intense complaint from team members was that their team leaders were unwilling to confront and resolve problems associated with poor performance by individual team members (Larson and LaFasto 1989). They report that, "[m]ore than any other single aspect of team leadership, members are disturbed by leaders who are unwilling to deal directly and effectively with self-serving or noncontributing team members." They go on to say that this is a significant management blind spot because managers nearly always think their teams are running more smoothly than their team members do.

Problem personnel are easy to identify if you know what to look for:

- They cover up their ignorance rather than trying to learn from their teammates. "I don't know how to explain my design; I just know that it works" or "My code is too complicated to test." (These are both actual quotes.)

- They have an excessive desire for privacy. "I don't need anyone to review my code."

- They are territorial. "No one else can fix the bugs in my code. I'm too busy to fix them now, but I'll get to them next week."

- They grumble about team decisions and continue to revisit old discussions after the team has moved on. "I still think we ought to go back and change the design we were talking about last month. The one we picked isn't going to work."

- Other team members all make wisecracks or complain about the same person. Software developers often won't complain directly, so you have to ask if there's a problem when you hear many wisecracks.

- They don't pitch in on team activities. On one project I worked on, 2 days before our first major deadline a developer asked for the next day off. The reason? He wanted to spend the day at a men's-clothing sale in a nearby city—a clear sign that he hadn't integrated with the team.

Coaching the problem person on how to work as part of a team sometimes works, but it's usually better to leave the coaching to the team than to try to do it as the team leader or manager. You might have to coach the team on how to coach the problem team member.

If coaching doesn't produce results quickly, don't be afraid to fire a person who doesn't have the best interests of the team at heart. Here are three solid reasons:

- It's rare to see a major problem caused by lack of skill. It's nearly always attitude, and attitudes are hard to change.

- The longer you keep a disruptive person around, the more legitimacy that person will gain through casual contacts with other groups and managers, a growing base of code that person has to maintain, and so on.

- Some managers say that they have never regretted firing anyone. They've only regretted not doing it sooner.

You might worry about losing ground if you replace a team member, but on a project of almost any size, you'll more than make up for the lost ground by eliminating a person who's working against the rest of the team. Cut your losses, and improve the rest of your team's morale.

12.5 Long-Term Teambuilding

The team of Amish farmers is a good model of the perfect, jelled team. But that team didn't form overnight. Those farmers had been together for years, and their families had been together for years before that. You can't expect performance as dramatic as raising a barn in a single day from a temporary team. That kind of productivity comes only from permanent teams.

Here are some reasons to keep teams together permanently.

Higher productivity. With a permanent-team strategy, you keep a group together if it jells into a team, and you disband it if it doesn't. Rather than breaking up every team and rolling the dice on every new project to see whether new teams jell or not, you roll the dice only after you've lost. You stockpile your winnings by keeping the productive teams together. The net effect is an "averaging up" of the level of performance in your organization.

Lower startup costs. The startup costs for building a team are unavoidable, so why not try to reuse the team and avoid additional startup costs? By keeping the effective teams together, you preserve some of the vision, team identity, communication, trust, and reservoir of good will built up from completing an enjoyable project together. You're also likely to preserve specific technical practices and knowledge of specific tools within a group.

Lower risk of personnel problems. Personnel issues arising from people who work poorly together cost your projects time and money. You can avoid these problems altogether by keeping teams together when they jell.

HARD DATA

Less turnover. The current annual turnover rate is about 35 percent among computer people (Thomsett 1990). DeMarco and Lister estimate that 20 percent of the average company's total labor expense is turnover cost (DeMarco and Lister 1987). An internal Australian Bureau of Statistics estimate placed the average time lost by a project team member's resignation at 6 weeks (Thomsett 1990). Studies by M. Cherlin and by the Butler Cox Foundation estimate the cost of replacing an experienced computer person at anywhere from $20,000 to $100,000 (Thomsett 1990).

HARD DATA

Costs are not limited simply to the loss of the employee. Productivity suffers generally. A study of 41 projects at Dupont found that projects with low turnover had 65 percent higher productivity than projects with high turnover (Martin 1991).

Not surprisingly, people who have formed into cohesive teams are less likely to leave a company than people who have not (Lakhanpal 1993). Why should they leave? They have found an environment they enjoy and can feel productive in.

The idleness question. Organizations are sometimes leery of keeping teams together because they might have to pay a team to sit idle until a project comes along that's appropriate for them to work on. That's a valid objection, but I think that in most organizations it isn't ultimately a strong objection.

Organizations that look exclusively at the cost of idle time overlook the costs of rebuilding teams for each new project. The cost of building a new team includes the cost of assembling the team and of training the team to work together.

Organizations tend to overlook how much they lose by breaking up a high-performance team. They take a chance that individuals who could be working as part of a high-performance team will instead become part of an average team or a poor one.

Some organizations worry that if they keep teams together, they won't be able to get any teams to work on certain projects. But others have found that if you give people the chance to work with other people they like, they'll work on just about any project (DeMarco and Lister 1987).

Finally, I have yet to see a software organization that has long idle periods. To the contrary, every project that I've ever worked on has started late because personnel weren't available to staff it until their previous projects were completed.

HARD DATA

Peopleware issues tend to lose out in the bean-counter calculations because in the past they have lacked the quantitative support that staff-days-spent-idle has. But the situation has changed. Australian software consultant Rob Thomsett has shown that there is a tremendous return on investment from teambuilding—for example, it is an order of magnitude better than for CASE tools (Constantine 1995a). We now know that among groups of people with equivalent skills, the most productive teams are 2 to 3 times as productive as the least productive teams. They're 1½ to 2 times as productive as the average teams. If you have a team that you know is on the top end of that range, you would be smart to allow them to sit idle for up to one-third or even one-half of their work lives just to avoid the risk of breaking them up and substituting a merely average team in their place.

12.6 Summary of Teamwork Guidelines

Larson and LaFasto distilled the results of their research into a set of practical guidelines for team leaders and team members. If your team wants to adopt a set of rules, the guidelines in Table 12-1 on the facing page are a good place to start.

Case Study 12-4. A Second High-Performance Team

Frank O'Grady captured the intense efficiency that a jelled team can have:

"I would sit in on design meetings, amazed at what I was seeing. When they were on a roll, it was as if they were all in some kind of high-energy trance during which they could see in their mind's eye how the program would unfold through time. They spoke in rapid-fire shorthand, often accompanied by vivid hand gestures when they wanted to emphasize a point. After 15 minutes or so, a consensus was reached as to what had to be done. Everyone knew which programs had to be changed and recompiled. The meeting adjourned." (O'Grady 1990)

Table 12-1. Practical Guidelines for Team Members and Leaders

Team Leader	Team Members
As a team leader, I will:	As a team member, I will:
1. Avoid compromising the team's objective with political issues.	1. Demonstrate a realistic understanding of my role and accountabilities.
2. Exhibit personal commitment to the team's goal.	2. Demonstrate objective and fact-based judgments.
3. Not dilute the team's efforts with too many priorities.	3. Collaborate effectively with other team members.
4. Be fair and impartial toward all team members.	4. Make the team goal a higher priority than any personal objective.
5. Be willing to confront and resolve issues associated with inadequate performance by team members.	5. Demonstrate a willingness to devote whatever effort is necessary to achieve team success.
6. Be open to new ideas and information from team members.	6. Be willing to share information, perceptions, and feedback appropriately.
	7. Provide help to other team members when needed and appropriate.
	8. Demonstrate high standards of excellence.
	9. Stand behind and support team decisions.
	10. Demonstrate courage of conviction by directly confronting important issues.
	11. Demonstrate leadership in ways that contribute to the team's success.
	12. Respond constructively to feedback from others.

Source: Adapted from *TeamWork* (Larson and LaFasto 1989).

Further Reading

Here are three books and articles about teambuilding in software:

DeMarco, Tom, and Timothy Lister. *Peopleware: Productive Projects and Teams*. New York: Dorset House, 1987. Part IV of this book focuses on growing productive software teams. It's entertaining reading, and it provides memorable stories about teams that worked and teams that didn't.

Weinberg, Gerald M. *Quality Software Management, Volume 3: Congruent Action*. New York: Dorset House, 1994. Part IV of this book is on managing software teams. Weinberg's treatment of the topic is a little more systematic, a little more thorough, and just as entertaining as *Peopleware*'s. Parts I through III of his book lay the foundation for managing yourself and people who work in teams.

Constantine, Larry L. *Constantine on Peopleware*. Englewood Cliffs, N.J.: Yourdon Press, 1995. Constantine brings his expertise in software development and family counseling to bear on topics related to effective software teams.

Here are some sources of information on teambuilding in general:

Larson, Carl E., and Frank M. J. LaFasto. *Teamwork: What Must Go Right; What Can Go Wrong*. Newbury Park, Calif: Sage, 1989. This remarkable book describes what makes effective teams work. The authors conducted a 3-year study of 75 effective teams and distilled the results into eight principles, each of which is described in its own chapter. At 140 pages, this book is short, practical, easy to read, and informative.

Katzenbach, Jon, and Douglas Smith. *The Wisdom of Teams*. Boston: Harvard Business School Press, 1993. This is a full-scale treatment of teams in general rather than just software teams. It's a good alternative to Larson and LaFasto's book.

Dyer, William G. *Teambuilding*. Reading, Mass: Addison-Wesley, 1987. This book describes more of the nuts and bolts of teambuilding than Larson and LaFasto's book does. Whereas Larson and LaFasto's intended audience seems to be the leader of the team, this book's intended audience seems to be the leader of a teambuilding workshop. It makes a nice complement to either Larson and LaFasto's book or Katzenbach and Smith's.

Witness. Paramount Pictures. Produced by Edward S. Feldman and directed by Peter Weir, 1985. The Amish barn-raising scene is about 70 minutes into this love-story/thriller, which received Oscars for best original screenplay and best editing and was nominated for best picture, best direction, best actor, best cinematography, best art direction, and best original score.

13

Team Structure

Contents

Related Topics

HARD DATA

EVEN WHEN YOU HAVE SKILLED, MOTIVATED, hard-working people, the wrong team structure can undercut their efforts instead of catapulting them to success. A poor team structure can increase development time, reduce quality, damage morale, increase turnover, and ultimately lead to project cancellation. Currently, about one-third of all team projects are organized in ineffective ways (Jones 1994).

This chapter describes the primary considerations in organizing a rapid-development team and lays out several models of team structure. It concludes with a discussion of one of the most nettlesome team-structure issues: the relationship between project managers and technical leads.

Case Study 13-1. Mismatch Between Project Objectives and Team Structure

After several failed projects, Bill was determined to bring the Giga-Bill 4.0 project in on time and within budget, so he brought in Randy, a high-priced consultant, to help him set up the project.

Randy talked to Bill about his project for a while and then recommended that he set up the project as a skunkworks team. "Software people are creative, and they need lots of flexibility. You should set them up with an off-site office and give them lots of autonomy so they can create. If you do that, they'll work day and night, and they can't help but complete the project on time."

(continued)

Case Study 13-1. Mismatch Between Project Objectives and Team Stucture, *continued*

Bill was uncomfortable with the idea of setting up an off-site office, but the project was important, and he decided to take Randy's advice. He put the developer he considered to be his best lead, Carl, in charge of the project.

"Carl, we need to get this project finished as fast as possible. The end-users are clamoring for an upgrade to solve all of the problems with Giga-Bill 4.0. We've got to hit a home run with this project. We've got to make the users happy. The users are so eager to get a new product that they have already drafted a set of requirements. I've looked at the requirements, and it looks to me like their requirements tell us exactly what we need to build. We need to get this next version out in as close to 6 months as we can."

Bill continued. "Randy recommended that I not interfere with your day-to-day activities, so you're in charge. I'll give you whatever flexibility you want. You do whatever it takes to get this project done now!"

Carl was excited about the idea of working off-site, and he knew he would enjoy working with the other people on the team. He met with Juan and Jennifer later that day. "I've got good news and better news," he told them. "The good news is that Bill has gotten the word that the users are fed up with Giga-Bill 4.0, and we need to hit a home run with this project. He's willing to give us all the flexibility we need to hit the ball out of the park. The better news is that we're going to be set up with an off-site office and no interference from Bill or anyone else. Good-bye dress code!"

Juan and Jennifer were as excited about the project as Carl, and when they started the project officially two weeks later, their morale was sky-high. Carl went to work early the first day thinking that he would get some work done before the others arrived, and Juan and Jennifer were already there. They stayed late every day the first week, and had no trouble staying focused on the project. It felt great to have a chance to develop a truly great product.

At the end of the first week, Carl had a status meeting with Bill. "We've had some great ideas that are going to make a truly great product. We've come up with some ways to meet the users' requirements that will knock their socks off." Bill thought it was great to see Carl so charged about the project, and he decided not to risk squashing his blossoming morale by asking him about the schedule.

Carl continued to report status semimonthly, and Bill continued to be impressed with the team's extraordinary morale. Carl reported that the team was working at least 9 or 10 hours a day and most Saturdays without being asked. After the first meeting, Bill always asked whether the project was on schedule and Carl always reported that they were making great progress. Bill wanted more details, but Randy had emphasized that pushing too hard could hurt morale. So he didn't push.

At the 5½-month mark, Bill couldn't wait any more and asked, "How are you doing on the schedule?"

(continued)

Case Study 13-1. Mismatch Between Project Objectives and Team Stucture, *continued*

"We're doing great," Carl answered. "We've been working night and day, and this program is really coming together."

"OK, but are you going to be able to deliver the software in 2 weeks?" Bill asked.

"Two weeks? No, we can't deliver in 2 weeks. This is a complicated program, and it will probably be more like 8 weeks," Carl said. "But it is really going to blow you away."

"Wait a minute!" Bill said. "I thought you told me that you were on schedule. The users are expecting to get this software in 2 weeks!"

"You said we needed to hit a home run. That's what we're doing. We needed more than exactly 6 months to do that. It should take about 7 1/2 months. Don't worry. The users are going to love this software."

"Holy cow!" Bill said. "This is a disaster! You guys need to get that software done now! I've had users breathing down my neck for 6 months while I waited for you to get this done. They told us exactly what a home run would be 6 months ago. All you needed to do was follow their instructions. I spent a lot of personal chits to get approval to put the project off-site so that you could get it done fast. They're going to pin my ears back."

"Gee, I'm sorry Bill. I didn't realize that the schedule was the main thing here. I thought hitting a home run was. I'll talk with everyone on the team and see what we can do."

Carl went back to the team and told them about the change in direction. By that time, they had already done all of the design and a lot of the implementation for the home-run project, so they decided that the fastest way to finish would be to continue as planned. They had only 8 weeks to go. Changing course now would introduce all kinds of unpredictable side effects that would probably just prolong the schedule.

They continued to work as hard as possible, but their estimates had not been very good. At the 8-month mark, Bill decided that he had let this team goof off enough, and moved them back on-site. The team's morale plummeted, and they quit working voluntary nights and weekends. Bill responded by ordering them to work 10-hour days and mandatory Saturdays until they were done. The team remained enthusiastic about their product, but they had lost their enthusiasm for the project. They finally finished after 9 1/2 months. The users loved the new software, but they said they wished they could have gotten it 4 months earlier.

13.1 Team-Structure Considerations

The first consideration in organizing a team is to determine the team's broad objective. Here are the broad objectives according to Larson and LaFasto (1989):

- Problem resolution
- Creativity
- Tactical execution

Once you've established the broad objective, you choose a team structure that matches it. Larson and LaFasto define three general team structures for effective, high-performance teams. The structure that's most appropriate depends on the team's objective.

The users in Case Study 13-1 had described exactly what they wanted, and the team really just needed to create and execute a plan for implementing it. Bill got some bad advice from Randy, who should have identified the primary goal of the team as tactical execution. The users were more interested in getting a timely upgrade than they were in creative solutions. The effect of the bad advice was predictable: organized for creativity, the team came up with a highly creative solution but didn't execute their plan efficiently. They weren't organized for that.

Kinds of Teams

Once you've identified the team's broadest objective—problem resolution, creativity, or tactical execution—then you set up a team structure that emphasizes the characteristic that is most important for that kind of team. For a problem-resolution team, you emphasize trust. For a creativity team, autonomy. And for a tactical-execution team, clarity.

Problem-resolution team. The problem-resolution team focuses on solving a complex, poorly defined problem. A group of epidemiologists working for the Centers for Disease Control who are trying to diagnose the cause of a cholera outbreak would be a problem-resolution team. A group of maintenance programmers trying to diagnose a new showstopper defect is too. The people on a problem-resolution team need to be trustworthy, intelligent, and pragmatic. Problem-resolution teams are chiefly occupied with one or more specific issues, and their team structure should support that focus.

Creativity team. The creativity team's charter is to explore possibilities and alternatives. A group of McDonald's food scientists trying to invent a new kind of McFood would be a creativity team. A group of programmers who are breaking new ground in a multimedia application would be another kind of creativity team. The creativity team's members need to be self-motivated, independent, creative, and persistent. The team's structure needs to support the team members' individual and collective autonomy.

Tactical-execution team. The tactical-execution team focuses on carrying out a well-defined plan. A team of commandos conducting a raid, a surgical team, and a baseball team would all be tactical-execution teams. So would a software team working on a well-defined product upgrade in which the purpose of the upgrade is not to break new ground but to put well-understood functionality into users' hands as quickly as possible. This kind of team is characterized by having highly focused tasks and clearly defined roles. Success criteria tend to be black-and-white, so it is often easy to tell whether the team succeeds or fails. Tactical-execution team members need to have a sense of urgency about their mission, be more interested in action than esoteric intellectualizing, and be loyal to the team.

Table 13-1 summarizes the different team objectives and the team structures that support those objectives.

Table 13-1. Team Objectives and Team Structures

	Broad Objective		
	Problem Resolution	Creativity	Tactical Execution
Dominant feature	Trust	Autonomy	Clarity
Typical software example	Corrective maintenance on live systems	New product development	Product-upgrade development
Process emphasis	Focus on issues	Explore possibilities and alternatives	Highly focused tasks with clear roles, often marked by clear success or failure
Appropriate lifecycle models	Code-and-fix, spiral	Evolutionary prototyping, evolutionary delivery, spiral, design-to-schedule, design-to-tools	Waterfall, modified waterfalls, staged delivery, spiral, design-to-schedule, design-to-tools
Team selection criteria	Intelligent, street smart, people sensitive, high integrity	Cerebral, independent thinkers, self-starters, tenacious	Loyal, committed, action-oriented, sense of urgency, responsive
Appropriate software-team models	Business team, search-and-rescue team, SWAT team	Business team, chief-programmer team, skunkworks team, feature team, theater team	Business team, chief-programmer team, feature team, SWAT team, professional athletic team

Source: Adapted from *TeamWork* (Larson and LaFasto 1989).

Additional Team-Design Features

Beyond the three basic kinds of teams, there are four team-structure features that seem to characterize all kinds of effectively functioning teams:

Clear roles and accountabilities. On a high-performance team, every person counts, and everyone knows what they are supposed to do. As Larson and LaFasto say, "EVERYONE IS ACCOUNTABLE ALL THE TIME on successful teams" *[authors' emphasis]* (Larson and LaFasto 1989).

Monitoring of individual performance and providing feedback. The flip side of accountability is that team members need some way of knowing whether they are living up to the team's expectations. The team needs to have mechanisms in place to let team members know in what ways their performance is acceptable and in what ways it needs improvement.

Effective communication. Effective communication depends on several project characteristics.

Information must be easily accessible. Meting out information on a "need to know" basis is bad for morale on a rapid-development project. Put all relevant information including documents, spreadsheets, and project-planning materials into version control and make them available on-line.

Information must originate from credible sources. The team's confidence in its decision making—the extent to which it's willing to make decisions actively or boldly—depends on how confident it is in the information on which it bases its decisions.

There must be opportunities for team members to raise issues not on the formal agenda. The word "formal" is key. Team members need informal opportunities to raise issues in an environment where titles, positions, office sizes, and power ties are not part of the equation. This is part of the underlying reason for the success of informal management approaches such as Management By Walking Around.

The communication system must provide for documenting issues raised and decisions made. Keeping accurate records prevents the team from retracing its steps through old decisions.

Fact-based decision making. Subjective judgments can undercut team morale. High-performance team members need to understand the bases for all decisions that affect them. If they find that decisions are made for arbitrary, subjective, or self-serving reasons, their performance will suffer.

Which Kind of Team Is Best for Rapid Development?

CROSS-REFERENCE
For more on the need to tailor the development approach to the project, see Section 2.4, "Which Dimension Matters the Most?" and Section 6.1, "Does One Size Fit All?"

A key to organizing a team for rapid development is understanding that there is no single team structure that achieves the maximum development speed on every project.

Suppose you're working on a brand new word-processing product and your goal is to create the best word processor in the world. You don't know at the beginning of the project exactly what the world's best word processor looks like. Part of your job will be to discover the characteristics that make up an exceptional product. For the most rapid development within that context, you should choose a team structure that supports creativity.

Now suppose that you're working on version 2 of that same word-processing product. You learned on version 1 what it would take to create a world-class product, and you don't view version 2 as exploratory. You have a detailed list of features that need to be implemented, and your goal is to implement them as fast as possible so that you stay ahead of the competition. For the most rapid development within that context, you should choose a team structure that supports tactical execution.

There's no such thing as a single best "rapid-development team structure" because the most effective structure depends on the context. (See Figure 13-1.)

"We're the right team to
win this game."

"No, we're the right team
to win this game."

Figure 13-1. *No single team structure is best for all projects.*

13.2   Team Models

CROSS-REFERENCE
For more on the roles that people play in effective teams, see "Mix of Roles" in Section 12.3.

Team leads, project managers, writers, and researchers have come up with many team models over the years, and this section catalogs a few of them. Some of the models affect only how the team operates on the inside and thus could be implemented by the technical lead or the team itself. Others affect how the team looks to management and would ordinarily require management approval.

The models in this section don't make up an orthogonal set. You will find overlaps and contradictions among the models, and you could combine elements from several different models to make up your own model. This section is intended more to generate ideas about different ways to structure a team than to be a systematic presentation of all possible team structures.

Business Team

The most common team structure is probably the peer group headed by a technical lead. Aside from the technical lead, the team members all have equal status, and they are differentiated by area of expertise: database, graphics, user interface, and various programming languages. The technical lead is an active technical contributor and is thought of as the first among equals. The lead is usually chosen on the basis of technical expertise rather than management proficiency.

Most commonly, the lead is responsible for making final decisions on tough technical issues. Sometimes the lead is a regular team member who merely has the extra duty of being the team's link to management. In other cases, the lead occupies a first-level management position. The specific amount of management responsibility the technical lead has varies from one organization to another, and I'll discuss that topic more later in the chapter.

From the outside, the business-team structure looks like a typical hierarchical structure. It streamlines communication with management by identifying one person as principally responsible for technical work on the project. It allows each team member to work in his or her area of expertise, and it allows the team itself to sort out who should work on what. It works well with small groups and with long-standing groups that can sort out their relationships over time.

It is adaptable enough that it can work on all kinds of projects—problem resolution, creativity, and tactical execution. But its generality is also its weakness, and in many cases a different structure can work better.

Chief-Programmer Team

The idea of the chief-programmer team was originally developed at IBM during the late 1960s and early 1970s (Baker 1972, Baker and Mills 1973). It was popularized by Fred Brooks in the *Mythical Man-Month* (Brooks 1975, 1995), in which Brooks referred to it as a surgical team. The two terms are interchangeable.

CROSS-REFERENCE
For more on variations
individual performance, see
"People" in Section 2.2.

The chief-programmer team takes advantage of the phenomenon that some developers are 10 times as productive as others. Ordinary team structures put mediocre programmers and superstars on equal footing. You take advantage of the high productivity of the superstars, but you're also penalized by the lower productivity of other team members. In the surgical-team concept, a programming superstar is identified as the surgeon, or chief programmer. That person then drafts the entire specification, completes all of the design, writes the vast majority of the production code, and is ultimately responsible for virtually all of the decisions on a project.

With the surgeon handling the bulk of the design and code, other team members are free to specialize. They are arrayed about the surgeon in support roles, and the chief-programmer team takes advantage of the fact that specialists tend to outperform generalists (Jones 1991).

A "backup programmer" serves as the chief programmer's alter ego. The backup programmer supports the surgeon as critic, research assistant, technical contact for outside groups, and backup surgeon.

The "administrator" handles administrative matters such as money, people, space, and machines. Although the surgeon has ultimate say about these matters, the administrator frees the surgeon from having to deal with them on a daily basis.

The "toolsmith" is responsible for creating custom tools requested by the surgeon. In today's terminology, the toolsmith would be in charge of creat ing command scripts and make files, of crafting macros for use in the programming editor, and of running the daily build.

The team is rounded out by a "language lawyer" who supports the surgeon by answering esoteric questions about the programming language the surgeon is using.

Several of the support roles suggested in the original chief-programmer proposal are now regularly performed by nonprogrammers—by documentation specialists, test specialists, and program managers. Other tasks such as word processing and version control have been simplified so much by modern software tools that they no longer need to be performed by support personnel.

When it was first used more than 20 years ago, the chief-programmer team achieved a level of productivity unheard of in its time (Baker and Mills 1973). In the years since, many organizations have attempted to implement chief-programmer teams, and most have not been able to repeat the initial stunning success. It turns out that true superstars capable of serving as chief programmers are rare. When individuals with such exceptional capabilities are found, they want to work on state-of-the-art projects, which is not what most organizations have to offer.

In spite of 20 years worth of changes and the rarity of superstar programmers, I think this structure can still be appropriate when used opportunistically. You can't start out by saying, "I need to get this project done fast, and I want to use a chief-programmer team structure." But what if you do happen to have a superstar who's willing to work exceptionally hard, who has few other interests, and who is willing to put in 16 hours a day? In that case, I think the chief-programmer team can be the answer.

The chief-programmer team is appropriate for creative projects, in which having one mind at the top will help to protect the system's conceptual integrity. It's also well suited to tactical-execution projects, in which the chief programmer can serve as near dictator in plotting out the most expeditious means of reaching project completion.

Skunkworks Team

The skunkworks team is an integral part of the lore of the engineering world. A skunkworks project takes a group of talented, creative product developers, puts them in a facility where they will be freed of the organization's normal bureaucratic restrictions, and turns them loose to develop and innovate.

Skunkworks teams are typically treated as black-boxes by their management. The management doesn't want to know the details of how they do their job; they just want to know that they're doing it. The team is thus free to organize itself as it sees fit. A natural leader might emerge over time, or the team might designate a leader from the outset.

Skunkworks projects have the advantage of creating a feeling of intense ownership and extraordinary buy-in from the developers involved. The motivational effect can be astounding. They have the disadvantage of not providing much visibility into the team's progress. Some of this is probably an inevitable effect of the unpredictability involved in any highly creative work. Some of it is an explicit trade-off—trading a loss in visibility for an increase in motivation.

Skunkworks teams are most appropriate for exploratory projects on which creativity is all-important. Skunkworks teams are rarely the most rapid structure when you need to solve a narrowly defined problem or when you need to execute a well-understood plan.

Feature Team

In the feature-team approach, development, quality assurance, documentation, program management, and marketing personnel are arranged in traditional hierarchical reporting structures. Marketing people report to marketing managers, developers report to development managers, and so on.

Layered on top of this traditional organization are teams that draw one or more members from each of these groups and that are given responsibility for a chunk of the product's functionality (McCarthy 1995a). You might have a feature team assigned to printing, or reporting, or graphing. The feature team then becomes ultimately responsible for decisions about that part of the product.

Feature teams have the advantages of empowerment, accountability, and balance. The team can sensibly be empowered because it contains representatives from development, quality assurance, documentation, program management, and marketing—in short, from each of the concerned parties. The team will consider all necessary viewpoints in its decisions, and thus there will hardly ever be a basis for overriding its decisions.

For the same reason, the team becomes accountable. They have access to all the people they need to make good decisions. If they don't make good decisions, they have no one to blame but themselves. The team is balanced. You wouldn't want development, marketing, or quality assurance alone to have ultimate say over a product's specification, but you can get balanced decisions from a group that includes representatives from each of those categories.

Feature teams are appropriate for problem-resolution projects because they have the empowerment and accountability needed to resolve issues expediently. They are also good for creativity projects because the interdisciplinary team composition can stimulate ideas. The additional overhead incurred with feature teams will be wasted on tactical-execution projects—if all the tasks are clearly defined, feature teams have little to contribute.

Search-and-Rescue Team

In the search-and-rescue team model, the software team acts like a group of emergency medical technicians who go looking for missing mountain climbers. The search-and-rescue team focuses on solving a specific problem. It combines specialized emergency medical training with mountaineering or other wilderness survival skills. It needs intimate knowledge of the terrain it will search, it needs to be ready to go at a moment's notice, and it needs excellent knowledge of first-aid practices so that it can stabilize and possibly improve the victims' conditions until they can be transported to appropriate medical facilities.

The software equivalent is to combine specialized knowledge of specific hardware and software tools with equally specialized knowledge of a particular business environment. For example, you might have software that tracks an overnight delivery service's packages. If that software breaks down, it will need to be fixed immediately, not by noon tomorrow. The team charged with maintaining that software could be conceived as a search-and-rescue team. Such a team needs intimate knowledge of the terrain it will be searching (the package-tracking software), an ability to respond to problems immediately, and an excellent knowledge of how to stabilize the system in the short-term—addressing the immediate problem of lost packages.

The search-and-rescue team model is most appropriate for teams that need to focus on problem resolution. It is too bottom-line oriented to support much creativity and too short-term oriented to support tactical execution.

SWAT Team

The SWAT team model is based on military or police SWAT teams, in which "SWAT" stands for "special weapons and tactics." On that kind of team, each member is highly trained in some specialty such as sharpshooting, explosives, or high-speed driving. The team trains extensively so that when the crisis hits, they can work together as one seamless unit.

In software, "SWAT" stands for "skilled with advanced tools." It originated as part of James Martin's RAD methodology (Martin 1991). The idea behind a SWAT team is to take a group of people who are highly skilled with a particular tool or practice and turn them loose on a problem that is well suited to being solved by that tool or practice. A SWAT team might specialize in any of the following areas:

- A particular DBMS package, such as Microsoft Access, FoxPro, Oracle, Paradox, or Sybase
- A particular programming environment, such as Delphi, PowerBuilder, or Visual Basic
- A particular development practice, such as JAD sessions or user-interface prototyping
- A particular project phase, such as project estimation, planning, performance optimization, or recovery

SWAT teams are usually permanent teams. They might not perform SWAT duties full-time, but they are accustomed to working together and have well-defined roles. If they are trained in Access, for example, they understand each other's strengths and weaknesses and know how to work together to create an Access application in record time.

SWAT teams are especially appropriate on tactical-execution projects. Their job is not to be creative but to implement a solution within the limits of a tool or a practice that they know well. SWAT teams can also work well on problem-resolution projects. Team members trust each other, and their focus on a particular project phase allows them to treat completion of that phase as a single problem that they can quickly overcome.

Professional Athletic Team

The professional-athletic-team model emphasizes several characteristics that are common to shrink-wrap software production and probably to other kinds of software development, too. For simplicity's sake, I'll use a baseball team in the examples, but almost any kind of professional athletic team could serve as a model.

Some software project teams are similar to professional baseball teams in that the players—software developers—are selected at least as carefully as the management is and are probably more critical to the project's success. The athletes are the stars of the baseball team, and the developers are the stars of the software team.

Before the program manager can be worth anything to the team, he or she must be thoroughly disabused of the notion that he or she has any direct control.

Jim McCarthy

HARD DATA

An athletic team manager handles the back-office decisions, which are strategically important, but the manager is not the one who swings the bat, scores the runs, or throws out the runners. The fans don't come to watch the manager; they come to watch the players.

Similarly, the software manager is important, but not because of any development capabilities. The manager's role is to clear roadblocks and enable developers to work efficiently. Developers might be able to develop a product without the manager, but the manager couldn't develop a product without the developers.

Athletic teams also have highly specialized roles. The pitcher doesn't say, "I'm sick of pitching. I want to play third base today." Likewise with software teams. The project manager can hire a database specialist, a user-interface specialist, and a software-metrics specialist, but no one should expect the database specialist to do graphics any more than they should expect the pitcher to play third base. Of course, in baseball there are only 9 positions, while in software more than 100 specialties have been identified (Jones 1994). Specialties in software can include system architecture, reusability, package evaluation, specific hardware, specific software environments (such as Macintosh, X-Window, and Microsoft Windows), specific programming languages, performance, LAN, CASE, customer support, maintenance test, customer liaison, and many more.

In professional baseball, as in software, the manager is often a former star player. There is no sense in which the manager is better than or hierarchically above the superstar players. He might have the authority to hire and fire some of the weaker players, but if he has a personality conflict with the team's biggest star, he is as likely to get the ax as the player is.

This specific model applies best to tactical-execution projects, which emphasize the highly specialized roles that individual players play. You can apply the model's general idea that management plays a supporting role to development to all kinds of projects.

Theater Team

FURTHER READING
For a similar idea, see Chapter 13, "The Choir and the Team," in *Why Does Software Cost So Much?* (DeMarco 1995).

The theater team is characterized by strong direction and a lot of negotiation about project roles. The central role on the project is occupied by the director, who maintains the vision of the product and assigns people responsibility for individual areas. Individual contributors can shape their roles, their parts of the project, as their own artistic instincts move them. But they can't take their ideas so far that they clash with the director's vision. If their ideas conflict with the director's, the director's vision has to prevail for the sake of the project.

In the theater model, you are not just assigned to a project. You audition, and then you accept a role. A lot of negotiation goes on before you accept the role:

- "I need to play the lead this time; I can't play something else."
- "I want to play the villain."
- "I'll play anything but the villain."
- "I'm committed to work on another play, so I don't have much time; I'll just do lights this time."
- "I'll work on this project if I can be the technical lead for graphics."
- "I'm tired of doing databases; I want to do user-interface code this time."
- "I want to coach a baseball team this summer. I'll work hard, but I can only put in 40 hours a week."

In the theater model, you don't sign up to play the lead role and then get moved to villain (or database).

The software manager occupies the role of producer. The producer is responsible for obtaining funding, coordinating schedules, and being sure that everyone is in the right place at the right time. The producer generally does not play an active role in the artistic aspects of the project.

The theater model's strength is that it provides a way to integrate strong individual contributions within a strong central vision on creativity projects. As Fred Brooks argues, conceptual integrity is the most important consideration in system design, and if a system is to have it, one person must control the concepts (Brooks 1975). It also helps to explain why even with a strong cast and strong direction, some projects still turn out mediocre or fail. Some software projects might be out of control, but anyone who's seen a terrible movie that cost $50 million can see that sometimes projects just don't work out.

The theater model is particularly appropriate for software teams that are dominated by strong personalities. Everyone knows that actors and actresses are temperamental, and some software developers have reputations as prima donnas too. If a project role is important enough, and if a particular developer is the only one who can play it, the director might decide that he or she is willing to put up with the prima donna for the sake of the project. But if the rest of the cast is strong, the director might pass up a prima donna in order to have a smoother project.

The theater model is an appropriate model for modern multimedia projects. Whereas software projects used to have to integrate the contributions of multiple software developers, now they have to integrate the contributions of graphic designers, writers, video producers, audio producers, editors, illustrators, content coordinators—and multiple software developers.

Large Teams

Large teams pose special problems of communication and coordination. If you're the only person on a project, you can work any way you want to because you don't have to communicate or coordinate with anyone. As the number of people on a project increases, however, the number of communication paths and the amount of coordination needed increases, too. It doesn't increase additively, as the number of people increases. It increases multiplicatively, proportional to the *square* of the number of people. Figure 13-2 on the next page shows how.

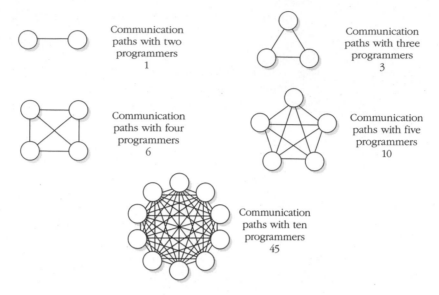

Figure 13-2. *Communication paths on projects of various sizes.*

A two-person project has only one path of communication. A five-person project has 10 paths. A ten-person project has 45 paths, assuming that every person talks to every other person. The two percent of projects that have 50 or more programmers have at least 1200 potential paths. The more communication paths you have, the more time you spend communicating and the more opportunities there are for communication mistakes.

A project with 1200 communication paths has far too many paths to operate effectively, and, in practice, 50-person projects aren't organized so that every person communicates with every other person. Large projects call for organizational practices that formalize and streamline communication. Formalizing communication is an important element of success on large projects, but it's out of scope in a chapter on team structure. Streamlining communication, on the other hand, can be greatly affected by team structure.

FURTHER READING
For more on the effect that project size has on a software project, see Chapter 21 of *Code Complete* (McConnell 1993).

All the ways to streamline communication rely on creating some kind of hierarchy, that is, creating small groups, which function as teams, and then appointing representatives from those groups to interact with each other and with management. You can create these small groups in several ways:

- Form a set of business teams, and within each team appoint a team liaison to communicate with other groups.

- Form a set of chief-programmer teams, and make the backup programmer responsible for communicating with other groups.

- Form feature teams, and make the program-management representative on each feature team responsible for communicating with other groups.

Regardless of how the small teams are organized, I think it is critical that there be a single person who is ultimately responsible for the product's conceptual integrity. That person can be cast as the architect, surgeon, director, or even sometimes the program manager, but there must be a person whose job it is to be sure that all the teams' good local solutions add up to a good global solution.

13.3 Managers and Technical Leads

On a lot of team projects, there are two or three regular developers and one developer who has some management responsibilities. This person is usually called a "lead" or "technical lead." The person is usually assigned to this role on the basis of technical rather than management expertise. Straddling the fence between development and management is a tricky business for this person and one that can destroy the project if not handled well—either because the lead relates poorly to the team or to upper managers.

Managers and technical leads don't always work closely together. A lot of problems—overlapping responsibilities, motivation, customer relations, low quality, poor alignment on project goals, and so on—can be improved when they communicate effectively about the issues they're dealing with.

One of the biggest obstacles to effective performance of the technical-lead role is the lack of a clear division of responsibilities between the technical lead and the manager. There is often a muddling of responsibilities. For example, the manager may know little about how the team functions day to day but may still be responsible for conducting the team members' performance reviews.

In its purest form, the technical lead is responsible for the technical work and is responsible for a single team. The manager is responsible for the nontechnical direction of the team and is responsible for two or more projects. From the team's point of view, the manager's role is to unburden the technical lead by handling certain nontechnical tasks. From the organization's point of view, the manager's role is to control the team so that it conforms to the goals of the organization. Some of the team models, particularly the professional athletic team and the theater team, are better than others at helping to keep the distinctions between the two roles in mind.

Since the specifics of the technical-lead/manager relationship vary so much, it's useful for the technical lead and manager to discuss their roles at the beginning of the project. That helps to avoid responsibility clashes in which both people think they're responsible for the same thing and responsibility vacuums in which both people think the other person is responsible.

John Boddie published an interesting diagram that described his view of the relationship between the project manager and the technical lead (shown in Figure 13-3), and I think the diagram brings some key issues to light (Boddie 1987). You can use the diagram as a focal point to discuss and clarify the technical lead's and manager's responsibilities.

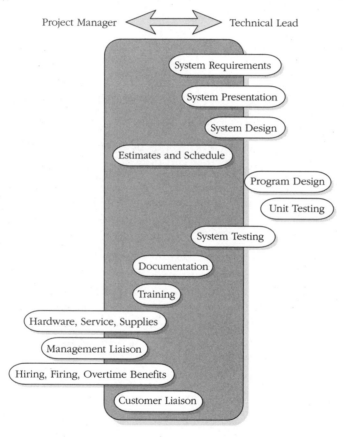

Figure 13-3. *Project manager's and technical lead's responsibilities. Since specific roles can vary from project to project, a discussion that uses this illustration as a focal point can help to clarify the division of responsibilities on a particular project. Source: Adapted from* Crunch Mode *(Boddie 1987).*

**Case Study 13-2. Good Match Between
Project Objectives and Team Structure**

Across the company from Bill's Giga-Bill 4.0 project, Claire had been tapped to oversee an update to the inventory control system (ICS). Like every other project in the company, this one needed to be completed as soon as possible—in about two months. Unfortunately, none of the original team members for ICS 1.0 were available to work on version 1.1, so Claire brought in Charles, a software engineering consultant, and asked him how she should set up the team.

"Well," Charles said, "it sounds to me like this is a straightforward product update. You have a good idea of what the users are asking for, right? This is version 1.1, which is an incremental release, so it doesn't seem like there's any great call for product innovation. But the update does require more work than just a few bug fixes. I'd say that the best kind of team structure for this project is a tactical-execution team. You could set it up as a chief-programmer team, a SWAT team, or a professional athletic team. I don't think it makes sense to set up full-fledged feature teams on this project because there just isn't that much work to do. It seems like that would be too much overhead. Who are you going to put on the project?"

"I'd like to have Kip lead the project," Claire said. "He is a competent all-around programmer. He's careful and good at working with end-users, but I don't think he is strong enough to be a chief programmer. I also plan to use Sue, who is good at debugging and making fixes, and Tomas, our in-house reporting expert. The biggest work items are working through a list of low-priority bug fixes that we didn't have time to fix in version 1.0. We also need to add some new reports. There are some minor user-interface enhancements, but they aren't as significant as the reporting changes."

"Based on what you've told me, I think you should use an athletic-team model," Charles said. "Each person has an existing area of expertise. Why don't you make Tomas the reporting specialist. Since there isn't as much work in the UI area, make Sue the bugmeister and the user-interface specialist, too. Make Kip the team captain; he's careful, so he can be the primary reviewer of Sue's and Tomas's code. He can also be the main link to both you and the customers." Claire agreed, and set up a meeting with Kip, Sue, and Tomas.

The developers liked the idea of specializing in specific areas and were happy with the roles Claire suggested. Claire emphasized that the project needed to be completed as fast as possible, so they dove in.

They had a clear picture of what they needed to do, and they spent their first few days reviewing the old project. Then they began designing the reporting and user-interface enhancements. Tomas proposed a safe but clumsy design for the reports. Sue and Kip pointed out some design alternatives that would

(continued)

**Case Study 13-2. Good Match Between
Project Objectives and Team Structure,** *continued*

cut the reporting work by about half. Tomas accepted their suggestions gladly since he didn't want to be the person everyone was waiting for at the end of the project. He began coding. Kip read through Tomas's code about once a week, and Tomas was grateful that Kip, rather than the users, was catching his bugs.

Sue plunged into the long list of bug fixes, and Kip reviewed her fixes one-by-one. Sue was good, but at first about a quarter of her fixes seemed to produce unintended side effects. Kip's reviews caught almost all of those. Sue gained momentum as she worked, and by the 4-week mark she had been over so many different parts of the system that she seemed to be carrying the whole system around in her head. By that time she was making bug fixes at a brisk pace and with hardly any errors.

Tomas and Sue began to rely on each other for advice. Sue helped Tomas think through the systemwide ramifications of his detailed designs, and Tomas helped Sue spelunk through old reporting code.

Kip made regular status reports in person to Claire and the end-users. The end-users appreciated being able to talk to a live person and ask questions about how the project was going.

When they got deeper into the details of the project, the developers found that their assigned roles didn't completely cover all of the work that needed to be done. There were some database updates that involved considerably more work than "bug fixes" normally would. Kip volunteered to take on that work, and Sue and Tomas agreed.

As the 2-month mark approached, the team was performing in high gear. They voluntarily worked the last two weekends just to make sure they would have time for any unexpected problems, and they finally delivered ICS 1.1 2 days ahead of schedule.

Further Reading

Here are three sources of general information on team structure:

Larson, Carl E., and Frank M. J. LaFasto. *Teamwork: What Must Go Right; What Can Go Wrong.* Newbury Park, Calif.: Sage, 1989. Chapter 3 of this book describes the relationship between project objectives and effective team structures.

Communications of the ACM, October 1993. This issue is devoted to the topic of project organization and management and contains several articles on team structure.

Constantine, Larry L. *Constantine on Peopleware*. Englewood Cliffs, N.J.: Yourdon Press, 1995. Part 3 of this book describes team structures. Constantine uses Larson and LaFasto's theory as a jumping off point for defining four of his own kinds of teams.

Here are some sources of information on specific team structures:

Brooks, Frederick P., Jr. *The Mythical Man-Month, Anniversary Edition*. Reading, Mass.: Addison-Wesley, 1995. Chapter 3 of this book describes the chief-programmer team.

Thomsett, Rob. "When the Rubber Hits the Road: A Guide to Implementing Self-Managing Teams," *American Programmer*, December 1994, 37–45. This article contains a description of self-managed teams and some practical tips on overcoming initial problems with them.

McCarthy, Jim. *Dynamics of Software Development*. Redmond, Wash.: Microsoft Press, 1995. Rule #7 in this book is "Use Feature Teams." McCarthy explains the ins and outs of feature teams at Microsoft.

Heckel, Paul. *The Elements of Friendly Software Design*. New York: Warner Books, 1984. Chapter 11 of this book explores the relationship between animated film making and software development. It goes in a different direction than the theater model described in this chapter, but it's in the same spirit.

Martin, James. *Rapid Application Development*. New York: MacMillan Publishing Company, 1991. Chapter 10 of this book describes the use of SWAT teams within RAD projects.

Peters, Tomas J., and Robert H. Waterman, Jr. *In Search of Excellence*. New York: Warner Books, 1982. This book contains discussions of several skunkworks projects.

DeMarco, Tom. *Why Does Software Cost So Much?* New York: Dorset House, 1995. Chapter 13, "The Choir and the Team," proposes that the best way to think about a software-development group is as a choir in which the success of the choir depends at least as much on cooperation as on individual performance.

14

Feature-Set Control

Contents

Related Topics

SOFTWARE DEVELOPERS AND MANAGERS SAY that they understand the need for feature-set control, but industry reports indicate otherwise. Developers, managers, marketers, and end-users continue to stuff so many features into already bloated products that one of the elders of the software industry has publicly pleaded for leaner software products (Wirth 1995).

HARD DATA

The most serious feature-set control problem is the problem of creeping requirements, requirements that are added late in a product's development. Projects that fail to control creeping requirements are highly susceptible to excessive schedule pressure (Jones 1994). Several studies have found that creeping requirements are the most common or one of the most common sources of cost and schedule overruns (Vosburgh et al. 1984, Lederer and Prasad 1992, Jones 1991, 1994, Standish Group 1994). They are also a major factor in project cancelations: changes resulting from creeping requirements can destabilize a product to such a degree that it can't be finished at all (Jones 1994).

Everyone says they understand the need to control creeping requirements, but people who should know better don't seem to take the need seriously. It is rare to read an account of a "software project disaster" that doesn't mention a deep and wide creeping-requirements problem. Wayt Gibbs reported that the Denver airport lost $1.1 million a day for months while waiting for late baggage-handling software, but what really happened was that the airport planners had saddled the software contractor with $20 million worth of late changes (Gibbs 1994). It's easy to surmise that the real cost of those changes was more than $20 million.

Reports of late software projects are often accompanied by commentary to the effect of, "Why can't these software guys figure out how to deliver software on time?" The FAA's multi-billion dollar air-traffic-control workstation software has been plagued by late changes, and Gibbs's story stated that an FAA report "bemoaned" that "every line of code developed needs to be rewritten" (Gibbs 1994). But there is no call for moaning. Creeping requirements are the reason that the software has needed to be rewritten, and that reason is in plain view.

A *Wall Street Journal* report (Carroll 1990) on the development of On Location told the following story:

> The software was late and far over budget; in fact, it almost didn't make it out the door. And it bore little resemblance to their original plans.... Most software-development planning stinks.

I find this report amazing. In the same breath the author comments both that the software *bore little resemblance to their original plans* and that the software was late and far over budget. The author treats these problems as unrelated and concludes that the *planning* is what stinks. Incredible! Neither the author of the article nor the development team described in the article seemed to have any awareness that there might be a connection between the feature changes and the software's lateness.

These twin phenomena of late-breaking changes and late software are cause and effect. To succeed at rapid development, we need to understand that relationship, take it to heart, and address it at the most fundamental levels of our project planning. Feature-set control makes up the product part of the people-process-product-technology foursome—the four dimensions of development speed. Feature-set control is where all your product-related leverage comes into play.

There are three general kinds of feature-set control:

- Early-project control of defining a feature set that is consistent with your project's schedule and budget objectives
- Mid-project control of controlling creeping requirements

- Late-project control of trimming features to meet a schedule or cost goal.

Successful projects learn to use all three kinds of feature-set control to their advantage. Boeing's 777 project, which includes a massive software component but which also includes major nonsoftware components, was delivered on time. One of the reasons for the project's success was that the chief engineer was keenly aware of the need to control late-breaking software changes (Wiener 1993). He hung this sign over his desk:

If Boeing can control changes and deliver an entire jet aircraft on time, I think it's possible for the software industry to control changes and deliver its software on time. The rest of this chapter explains how.

14.1 Early Project: Feature-Set Reduction

Feature-set control in the early part of a project consists primarily of not putting unnecessary features into the product in the first place. In *Inside RAD*, Kerr and Hunter say that the first commandment of rapid development is to "narrow your scope" (Kerr and Hunter 1994). There are three basic ways to do this:

- Minimal specification
- Requirements scrubbing
- Versioned development

Each of these is described in the following sections.

Minimal Specification

When you specify requirements for a project, there is usually a question about how much detail to provide in the specification. Conventional wisdom holds that more detail is better. The attempt to create a detailed requirements specification catches more of the requirements than a less detailed one would, which avoids the time and cost problems associated with adding requirements late in the project. It provides a thorough basis for planning and tracking the project. And it provides developers with a secure foundation upon which to base their design and code.

Problems with traditional specifications

From a development-speed point of view, detailed specifications also have some disadvantages.

Wasted specification effort. You can spend time specifying in enormous detail the characteristics of the system that the users don't even care about. Analysts sometimes force users to make decisions about button sizes and placement in dialog boxes, ordering of tab fields, and other aspects of a system that both the users and the developers would be just as happy to leave to the developers' discretion.

Obsolescence. Changes mid-way through a project can quickly render a requirements document obsolete. Changes that can be made relatively simply to the design and code in its early stages require time-consuming retrofits to the requirements document. Maintaining the requirements document becomes a moral or bureaucratic task rather than one that contributes to progress. It's possible to spend time specifying in enormous detail a feature set that you'd like to be able to change later in response to changing market conditions or customer demands.

Lack of efficacy. The net effect of specifying a system in enormous detail is often insufficient to guarantee the success of the system. The system can satisfy the letter of the specification and still not be satisfactory.

Overly constrained design. Overspecifying the software can force design and implementation approaches that waste time. For example, the requirements document might require that the dialog boxes use 3-D group boxes like the one shown in Figure 14-1.

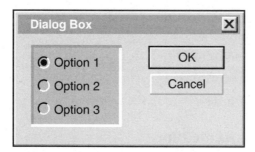

Figure 14-1. *A dialog box with the ideal group box.*

At implementation time, it might turn out that another kind of 3-D group box that looks like the one in Figure 14-2 is commercially available and easier to implement.

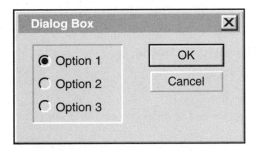

Figure 14-2. *A dialog box with the quick-to-implement group box. Relaxing requirements by a small amount can make a large difference in implementation time if the change allows for better tool support.*

The only differences between the two group boxes shown in Figures 14-1 and 14-2 are the widths of their outlines and the shading of the boxes' interiors, which gives the first one a deeper look.

If it makes sense to leave details like this to the developer's discretion, you should do so. One of these group-box styles can be implemented virtually for free. The other might require a developer to delve into the details of writing a custom control. What's really hazardous here, from a schedule point of view, is that developers *like* to delve into such details, and you might not even know that you've passed a decision point at which your team decided to spend an extra week or two so that you could have 3-D style #1 instead of 3-D style #2.

Users might genuinely have an opinion at requirements time that the group box in the first example looks better than the group box in the second. But that preference is probably based on an assumption that their costs are equal. Few users would choose 3-D style #1 over 3-D style #2 if they knew it would take an extra week to develop.

In summary, some of the drive to create a traditional spec is based on practical necessity, some on a desire to avoid high downstream costs, and some on a not-always-rational desire to control every aspect of the project from the beginning. A traditional specification approach can make it seem as though the goal of software development is to build the software exactly as planned. But the goal is not to build exactly what you said you would at the beginning. It is to build the best possible software within the available time. If project conditions are right, a minimal specification can help.

Creating a minimal specification

A minimal specification consists of what it sounds like it should consist of: the minimal amount of information needed to meaningfully specify the product. It could consist of any of the following elements:

CROSS-REFERENCE
For more on the importance of aligning the development team on a shared vision, see "Shared, Elevating Vision or Goal" in Section 12.3.

- *A short paper spec*—This is a text description of the software you want to build, which should be 10 pages or less.

- *Point-of-departure spec*—This is a one-shot approximation spec, which is not intended to be maintained after it is initially written. Its primary purpose is to align the development group, customers, and end-users on a common vision of the product. Once that alignment is achieved, the spec has served its purpose and does not need to be maintained.

- *User manual as spec*—Instead of writing a traditional specification, write a user manual, and require the software to conform to the manual. Since you have to write the user manual at some point anyway, you might as well write it first and eliminate the redundancy you would otherwise incur by writing both a user manual and a specification. A variation on this idea is to write an on-line help system for use as the spec.

- *User-interface prototypes*—A user-interface prototype can either serve as a de facto spec or it can supplement a written spec. If created carefully, a picture can be worth a thousand words and can take a lot less time to generate.

- *Paper storyboards*—Sometimes low-tech works best. If you work with customers or end-users who can visualize software without having to see it on a computer screen, sometimes it's quicker and easier to draw reports, screens, and other UI elements on flip charts and to design the product that way.

- *Vision statement*—Create a vision statement that describes both what to put in and what to leave out of the product. Describing what to leave out is difficult, but that's the essential function of this kind of vision statement. The natural tendency is to try to make a product be all things to all people, and a good vision statement draws the line by stating what a product is *not*. As Microsoft's Chris Peters says, "The hard part is figuring out what not to do. We cut two-thirds of the features we want to do in every release off the list" (Cusumano and Selby 1995).

- *Product theme*—Create a theme for the product. Themes are related to visions, and they are good mechanisms for controlling featureitis. In Excel 3.0, the theme was to make the release as "sexy" as possible. Features such as three-dimensional worksheets were ruled out because they weren't sexy. Slick graphics were ruled in because they were.

You can create one of these minimal specifications in any of several ways. You can use a traditional one-on-one interview approach, keeping the amount of detail to a minimum. You can hold standard Joint Application Development (JAD) sessions and capture the outcome of the JAD session in a minimal-spec format. Or you can split the difference between one-on-one interviews and full-up JAD sessions by holding on-site meetings to define the software product. Live prototypes and paper storyboards can be valuable discussion aids in such a setting.

CROSS-REFERENCE
For more on the importance of setting realistic expectations, see Section 10.3, "Managing Customer Expectations."

Success in using minimal specification requires considerable flexibility in requirements. Projects like the Boeing 777 that need more rigidity are not good candidates for using a minimal specification. As part of the minimal-specification effort, you might want to present an "Article of Understanding" or something similar to your customers just to make sure they know what to expect. It could read something like this:

> We have all tried to capture every important requirement in the requirements specification, but there will inevitably be gaps, which the software developers will need to interpret on their own. On a typical project, there are hundreds of such gaps, which makes it impractical for developers and customers to confer about each one. The vast majority of those gaps are typically resolved by the developers without the customer even becoming aware that an ambiguity ever existed.

> In some cases, the customer will have a strong feeling about how an ambiguity has been resolved and will want to have it resolved differently. This happens to a greater or lesser degree on virtually every software project. To the extent that such ambiguities are clarified by the customer later in the project to mean something different than what the developer assumed, there will probably be negative impacts to cost or schedule or both. The developers will try to design the software to minimize these negative impacts, but we all know from long experience that this unpleasant feature of software development is unavoidable. We will all try to remember when that happens that it is unavoidable.

> As developers, we will try to be responsive to the customers' needs and create a solution that satisfies the customers' desires with minimum disruption to cost and schedule. As customers, we will try to remember that developers have done the best job they could in interpreting the gaps in what we have told them.

An article of understanding like this can help to reduce late-project haggling. Instead of the traditional bickering about whether a proposed change is a bug or a feature, you can simply ask, "Is the change in the project's best interest?"

Benefits of minimal specifications

When the minimal-specification approach is used effectively, it can produce several schedule-related benefits.

Improved morale and motivation. The greatest productivity benefit arising from the minimal-spec approach is its contribution to developer morale.

With minimal specification, you in effect have the developers do much of the specification themselves. When they specify the product, it becomes *their* product, and they will do whatever is needed to make their product a success.

Opportunistic efficiency. With a minimal spec, developers are more free to design and implement the software in the most expeditious way possible. When every detail is spelled out in advance, they are more constrained.

Less wasted effort. Developers often expend effort trying to get users or customers to specify things they don't really care about. A minimal spec avoids that wasted effort and in general avoids the bureaucratic problems associated with traditional specification efforts.

Shorter requirements phase. A minimal spec takes less time to create than a traditional spec; you can save time during the requirements definition itself.

Risks of minimal specifications

The minimal-spec approach is also subject to several risks.

CLASSIC MISTAKE

Omission of key requirements. When you create a minimal spec, you leave out everything that you're sure the customer doesn't care about, but you risk leaving out things that the customer does care about. The minimal spec is a gamble. You bet that the time you would waste specifying unnecessary details in a traditional, detailed spec would outweigh the time you will waste by overlooking requirements and making more expensive changes later with a minimal spec. If you lose the bet, you deliver the software later than you would have if you had used traditional methods.

CROSS-REFERENCE
For more on the problem of setting too many goals at once, see "Goal Setting" in Section 11.2 and the discussion of "Unclear or Impossible Goals" in Section 14.2, later in this chapter.

Unclear or impossible goals. Crystal-clear goals are essential to the success of a minimal-spec approach. The approach works because it allows developers to use ambiguities in the spec to their advantage. Goals tell them in which direction to resolve those ambiguities. Do they resolve them toward maximum usability, maximum "Wow!" factor, or minimum development time? If minimum development time is clearly the top priority, developers will resolve ambiguities to favor development speed.

If the development-speed goal is not the clear top priority, developers might favor development speed or they might favor something else. The effect will not be the shortest possible development schedule. If you have a complex set of goals, you'll be better off to create a traditional specification and spell out what you want in detail.

CROSS-REFERENCE
For more on gold-plating, see Chapter 5, "Risk Management," and Chapter 39, "Timebox Development."

Gold-plating. Minimal specifications increase the risk of developer gold-plating; it is a natural consequence of the ownership that they feel from being able to specify much of the product themselves. They want their product to be as good as possible, and their internal notions of product quality can take precedence over the project's development-speed goals. At other times, gold-plating comes from developers who want to explore a technically challenging new area such as artificial intelligence or instant response time. A rapid-development project is the wrong forum in which to explore challenging new areas.

CLASSIC MISTAKE

The extra work from gold-plating can be deceptive. Most developers are conscientious enough not to implement an extra feature that will take a huge amount of time. The extra time needed might seem small—a couple hours here to fix an additional bug, a couple hours there to tweak the code to be compatible with other changes. But that's the real hazard of gold-plating. It eats up time in ways that you don't realize until you look back and see how it all adds up.

Even at Microsoft, where schedule pressure is intense, almost every post-mortem in every group gives rise to the complaint that major schedule problems arose when team members couldn't resist adding new features (Cusumano and Selby 1995).

You can address this risk on two levels—as the technical lead or as the manager. If you're the technical lead, you hold the reins on externally visible aspects of the product. Create a detailed user-interface prototype, and allow developers complete flexibility on their designs as long as they produce something really close to the prototype. But don't allow developers to add major functionality beyond what's expressed in the prototype. As the technical lead, you can probably make that point to the developers yourself.

If you're the manager, you're better off addressing the risk indirectly. The second way to address gold-plating is to hold regular design reviews that focus on minimal and time-effective designs. If the team as a whole has bought into the goal of minimum delivery time, it will apply pressure to any developer who is self-indulgently gold-plating a feature rather than supporting the group's objective.

Lack of support for parallel activities. One of the strengths of a traditional specification is that it provides superb support for parallel work. If the spec is done well, technical writers can create user documentation directly from the spec, and they can start writing as soon as the spec is complete. Testers can begin creating test cases at the same time.

For minimal specification to work, you have to set a milestone early in the project at which time visible changes to the product stop. At that point, user documentation and testing can begin in earnest. You need to set that point, often called "visual freeze," early enough that documentation and testing don't become critical-path activities. From that point forward, allow only the most critical changes.

Increased developer attachment to specific features. The increased ownership that developers feel with a minimal-spec approach can be a double-edged sword. You get extra motivation, but you can also encounter more resistance when you want to change one of the developer's features. Keep in mind that when product changes are suggested, they are no longer implicitly critical of only the product; they are implicitly critical of the developer's work.

CROSS-REFERENCE
For details on incremental delivery strategies, see Chapter 7, "Lifecycle Planning."

Use of minimal specification for the wrong reason. Don't use a minimal specification to reduce time on the requirements-specification activity itself. If you use this practice as a lazy substitute for doing a good job of requirements specification, you'll end up with a lot of rework—designing and implementing features twice, the second time at a point in the project when it's expensive to change your mind. But if you use this practice to avoid doing work that would be wasted, you follow through with clear goals, and you give developers latitude in how they implement their features, then you can develop more efficiently.

CLASSIC MISTAKE

If you use this approach, both you and your customers have to be prepared to accept a version of the product that doesn't match your vision of what the product should look like. Sometimes people start out saying they want to use this approach—and then, when the product departs from their mental image, they try to bring it into line. Worse, some customers will try to use the looseness of this specification approach to their advantage, shoehorning in extra features late in the project and interpreting every feature in the most elaborate way possible. If you allow much of that, you'll waste time by making late, costly changes; you would have done better specifying your intent up front and then designing and implementing the product efficiently the first time.

Know yourself and your customers well enough to know whether you'll accept the results of giving developers this much discretion. If you're uncomfortable with ceding such control, you'll be better off using a traditional specification approach or an incremental-delivery strategy.

Keys to success in using minimal specifications

There are several keys to success in using minimal specifications.

Use a minimum specification only when requirements are flexible. The success of this approach depends on the flexibility of the requirements. If you think the requirements are really less flexible than they appear, take steps to be sure that they are flexible before you commit to use a minimal specification. Flexible initial requirements have been identified by some people as a key to success with any rapid-development approach (Millington and Stapleton 1995).

Keep the spec to a minimum. With any of these approaches, you'll need to make it clear that one of the objectives is to specify only the minimum detail necessary. For items that users might or might not care about, the default option should be to leave further specification to the developers. When in doubt, leave it out!

Capture the important requirements. Although you should try not to capture requirements that the users don't care about, you must be careful to capture all of the requirements that they do care about. Doing a good minimal spec requires a special sensitivity to what users really care about.

CROSS-REFERENCE
For more on flexible development approaches, see Chapter 7, "Lifecycle Planning," and Chapter 19, "Designing for Change."

Use flexible development approaches. Use development approaches that allow mistakes to be corrected. With a minimal-spec approach, more mistakes will occur than with a traditional-spec approach. The use of flexible development approaches is a means of hedging your bet that you can save more time than you waste.

Involve key users. Find people who understand the business need or organizational need for the software, and involve them in product specification and development. This helps to avoid the problem of omitted requirements.

Focus on graphically oriented documentation. Graphics in the form of diagrams, sample outputs, and live prototypes tend to be easier to create than written specifications and more meaningful to users. For the graphically oriented parts of your system, focus your documentation efforts on creating graphically oriented materials.

Requirements Scrubbing

Entirely removing ("scrubbing") a feature from a product is one of the most powerful ways to shorten a software schedule because you remove every ounce of effort associated with that feature: specification, design, testing, documentation—everything. The earlier in the project you remove a feature, the more time you save. Requirements scrubbing is less risky than minimal specification. Because it reduces the size and complexity of the product, it also reduces the overall risk level of the project. (See Figure 14-3 on the next page.)

The idea behind requirements scrubbing is simple: After you create a product specification, go over the specification with a fine-tooth comb and with the following aims:

- Eliminate all requirements that are not absolutely necessary.
- Simplify all requirements that are more complicated than necessary.
- Substitute cheaper options for all requirements that have cheaper options.

As with minimal specification, the ultimate success of this practice depends on follow-through. If you begin with 100 requirements and the requirements-scrubbing activity pares that number down to 70, you might well be able to complete the project with 70 percent of the original effort. But if you pare the list down to 70 only to reinstate the deleted requirements later, the project will likely cost more than it would have if you had retained the entire 100 requirements the whole time.

Figure 14-3. *Smaller projects take less time to build.*

Versioned Development

CROSS-REFERENCE
For more on versioned development, see "Define Families of Programs" in Section 19.1; Chapter 20, "Evolutionary Delivery"; and Chapter 36, "Staged Delivery."

An alternative to eliminating requirements altogether is eliminating them from the current version. You can plan out a set of requirements for a robust, complete, ideal project but then implement the project in pieces. Put in any hooks you'll need to support the later pieces, but don't implement the pieces themselves. The development practices of evolutionary delivery and staged delivery can help in this area.

The inevitable effect of using these practices is that by the time you finish version 1 and begin work on version 2, you scrap some of the features you had originally planned to have in the version 2 and add others. When that happens, you become especially glad that you didn't put the scrapped features into version 1.

14.2 Mid-Project: Feature-Creep Control

If you do a good job of specifying a lean product, you might think you have your feature set under control. Most projects aren't that lucky. For many years, the holy grail of requirements management has been to collect a set of requirements—scrubbed, minimally specified, or otherwise—encase them in permafrost, and then build a complete product design, implementation, documentation, and quality assurance atop them. Unfortunately for developers and their ulcers, projects that have successfully frozen their requirements have proven to be almost as hard to find as the Holy Grail itself. A typical project experiences about a 25-percent change in requirements during development (Boehm 1981, Jones 1994).

Sources of Change

Mid-project changes arise from many sources. End-users want changes because they need additional functionality or different functionality or because they gain a better understanding of the system as it's being built.

Marketers want changes because they see the market as feature-driven. Software reviews contain long lists of features and check marks. If new products with new features come out during a product's development, marketers naturally want their products to stack up well against the competition, and they want the new features added to their product.

Developers want changes because they have a great emotional and intellectual investment in all of the system's details. If they're building the second version of a system, they want to correct the first version's deficiencies, whether such changes are required or not. Each developer has an area of special interest. It doesn't matter whether a user interface that's 100 percent compliant with user-interface standards is required, or whether lightning-fast response time, perfectly commented code, or a fully normalized database are specified: developers will do whatever work is needed to satisfy their special interests.

CROSS-REFERENCE
For tips on resisting pressure, including pressure to add requirements, see Section 9.2, "Beating Schedule Pressure."

All these groups—end-users, marketers, and developers—will try to put their favorite features into the requirements spec even if they didn't make it during the formal requirements-specification activity. Users sometimes try to end-run the requirements process and coax specific developers into implementing their favorite features. Marketers build a marketing case and insist later that their favorite features be added. Developers implement unrequired features on their own time or when the boss is looking the other way.

HARD DATA

All in all, projects tend to experience about a 1-percent change in requirements per month. On average, the longer your project takes, the more your product will change before it's complete (Jones 1994). A few factors can make that figure considerably worse.

Killer-app syndrome

Shrink-wrap products are particularly susceptible to "killer-app syndrome." The development group at Company A sets developing "the best application in its class" as its design goal. The group designs an application that meets that criteria and then begins to implement it. A few weeks before the software is scheduled to ship, Company B's application enters the market. Their application has some features that Company A never thought of and others that are superior to Company A's. The development group at Company A decides to slide its schedule a few months so that it can redesign its application and truly clobber Company B. It works until a few weeks before its revised ship date, and then Company C releases its software, which is again superior in some areas. The cycle begins again.

Unclear or impossible goals

It's difficult to resist setting ambitious goals for a project: "We want to develop a world-class product in the shortest possible time at the lowest possible cost." Because it isn't possible to meet that entire set of goals or because the goals are unclear, the most likely result is meeting *none* of the goals. If developers can't meet the project's goals, they will meet their own goals instead, and you will lose much of your influence over the project's outcome.

To illustrate the way in which clear goals can have a significant effect on a development schedule, consider the design and construction of a charting program. There is a tiny part of the charting program that deals with "polymarkers"—squares, circles, triangles, and stars that designate specific points on a graph. Figure 14-4 shows an example. Suppose that the specification is silent on the question of whether to provide the user with the ability to control the polymarkers' sizes. In such a case, the developer who implements the polymarkers can provide such control in any of many ways:

1. Do not provide any control at all.

2. Set up the source code to be modified in one place for the whole set of polymarkers (that is, sizes of all polymarkers are set by a single named constant or preprocessor macro).

3. Set up the source code to be modified in one place, on a polymarker-by-polymarker basis, for a fixed number of polymarkers (that is, size of each polymarker—square, triangle, and so on—is set by its own named constant or preprocessor macro).

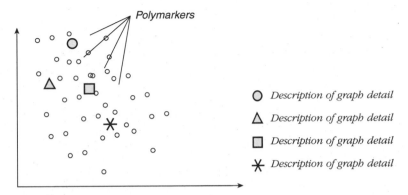

Polymarkers

◯ *Description of graph detail*

△ *Description of graph detail*

▢ *Description of graph detail*

✳ *Description of graph detail*

Figure 14-4. *Examples of polymarkers. There can be at least a 10-to-1 difference in size and implementation time of even seemingly trivial features.*

4. Set up the source code to be modified in one place, on a polymarker-by-polymarker basis, for a dynamic number of polymarkers (for example, you might later want to add cross-hairs, diamonds, and bull's-eyes to the original set of polymarkers).

5. Allow for modification of an external file that the program reads at startup, one setting for the whole set of polymarkers (for example, an .ini file or other external file).

6. Allow for modification of an external file that the program reads at startup, different settings for each polymarker, for a fixed number of polymarkers.

7. Allow for modification of an external file that the program reads at startup, different settings for each polymarker, for a dynamic number of polymarkers.

8. Allow for interactive, end-user modification of a single polymarker-size specification.

9. Allow for interactive, end-user modification of polymarker-size specifications, with one setting per polymarker, for a fixed number of polymarkers.

10. Allow for interactive, end-user modification of polymarker-size specifications, with one setting per polymarker, for a dynamic number of polymarkers.

These options represent huge differences in design and implementation times. At the low end, a fixed number of polymarkers have their sizes hard-coded into the program. This requires only that polymarkers be represented in an array of fixed size. The amount of work required to implement that beyond the base work required to implement polymarkers would be negligible, probably on the order of a few minutes.

At the high end, a variable maximum number of polymarkers have their sizes set at runtime, interactively, by the user. That calls for dynamically allocated data, a flexible dialog box, persistent storage of the polymarker sizes set by the user, extra source-code files put under version control, extra test cases, and documentation of all the above in paper documents and online help. The amount of work required to implement this would probably be measured in weeks.

The amazing thing about this example is that it represents weeks of potential difference in schedule arising from a *single, trivial* characteristic of a charting program—the size of the polymarkers. We haven't even gotten to the possibility that polymarkers might also be allowed to have different outline colors, outline thicknesses, fill colors, orderings, and so on. Even worse, this seemingly trivial issue is likely to interact with other seemingly trivial issues in combination, meaning that you multiply their difficulties together rather than merely add them.

The point of this is that the devil really is in the details, and implementation time can vary tremendously based on how developers interpret seemingly trivial details. *No specification can hope to cover every one of these trivial details.*

HARD DATA

Without any guidelines to the contrary, developers will pursue flexible approaches that tend more toward option #10 than #1. Most conscientious developers will intentionally try to design some flexibility into their code, and as the example illustrates, the amount of flexibility that a good developer will put into code can vary tremendously. As my friend and colleague Hank Meuret says, the programmer ideal is to be able to change one compiler switch and compile a program as a spreadsheet instead of a word processor. When you multiply the tendency to choose flexibility rather than development speed across dozens of developers and hundreds of detailed decisions on a project, it's easy to see why some programs are vastly larger than expected and take vastly longer than expected to complete. Some studies have found up to 10-to-1 differences in the sizes of programs written to the same specification (DeMarco and Lister 1989).

CROSS-REFERENCE
For more on goal setting, see "Goal Setting" in Section 11.2.

If you were to proceed through implementation with the assumption that whenever you encountered an ambiguity in the specification you would tend toward the #1 end of the set of options rather than toward the #10 end, you could easily implement your whole program an order of magnitude faster than someone who took the opposite approach. If you want to leverage your product's feature set to achieve maximum development speed, you must make it clear that you want your team to tend toward #1. You must make it clear that development speed is the top design-and-implementation goal, and you must not confuse that goal by piling many other goals on top of it.

Effects of Change

HARD DATA

People are far too casual about the effects that late changes in a project have. They underestimate the ripple effects that changes have on the project's design, code, testing, documentation, customer support, training, configuration management, personnel assignments, management and staff communications, planning and tracking, and ultimately on the schedule, budget, and product quality (Boehm 1989). When all these factors are considered, changes typically cost anywhere from 50 to 200 times less if you make them at requirements time than if you wait until construction or maintenance (Boehm and Papaccio 1988).

As I said at the beginning of the chapter, several studies have found that feature creep is the most common source of cost and schedule overruns. A study at ITT produced some interesting results in this area (Vosburgh et al. 1984). It found that projects that experienced enough change to need their specifications to be rewritten were significantly less productive than projects that didn't need to rewrite their specs. Figure 14-5 illustrates the difference.

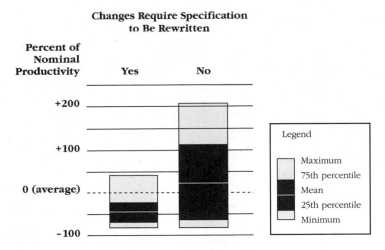

Figure 14-5. *Findings for "Changes Require Specification to Be Rewritten" factor (Vosburgh et al. 1984). Controlling changes can produce dramatic improvements in productivity, but that control does not by itself guarantee success.*

CROSS-REFERENCE
For details on this point, see
Section 3.2, "Effect of
Mistakes on a Development
Schedule."

As you can see in Figure 14-5, both the average and maximum productivities were higher when changes were controlled, and this study suggests that it is hardly ever possible to achieve high productivity unless you control changes. At the bottom ends of the ranges, some projects had the same low productivity regardless of whether they did a good job of controlling changes. As with other effective development practices, controlling changes is not by itself sufficient to guarantee high productivity. Even when you do a good job of controlling changes, there are other ways to torpedo a project.

Wisdom of Stopping Changes Altogether

Requirements that don't change are great. If you can develop software to an unchanging set of requirements, you can plan with almost 100-percent accuracy. You can design and code without wasting time to make late changes inefficiently. You can use any of the unstable-requirements practices and any of the stable-requirements practices too. The whole universe of speed-oriented development practices is open to you. Such projects are a joy to work on and a joy to manage. You can reach project completion faster and more economically than you can in any other circumstances.

That's nice work if you can get it. When you do need some flexibility, however, pretending that no changes are allowable or desirable is just a way to lose control of the change process. Here are some circumstances in which it is unwise to try to stop changes altogether.

When your customers don't know what they want. Refusing to allow changes assumes that your customers know what they want at requirements time. It assumes that you can truly know requirements at the outset, before design and coding begin. On most projects, that's not possible. Part of the software developer's job is to help customers figure out what they want, and customers often can't figure out what they want until they have working software in their hands. You can use the various incremental development practices to respond to this need.

When you want to be responsive to your customer. Even when you think your customers know what they want, you might want to keep the software flexible to keep your options open. If you follow a frozen-requirements plan, you might deliver the product on time, but you might seem unresponsive, and that can be just as bad as late delivery. If you're a contract software developer, you might need to stay flexible to stay competitive. If you're an in-house developer, your company's well-being might depend on your providing that flexibility.

In-house development organizations are especially susceptible to being unresponsive to their users. They quit looking at their users as true customers because they have an exclusive engagement. Friction results over time, and then the developers use the requirements specification as a weapon to force their users to behave. No one likes working in the face of a steady stream of arbitrary changes, but there are more constructive ways to respond than beating the users on the head with a requirements document. Developers who do that are finding with increasing frequency that their engagements aren't as exclusive as they had once thought (Yourdon 1992).

When the market is changing rapidly. In the 1960s and earlier, when business needs changed more slowly than they do today, it might have been wise to plan a product in detail two years before you released it. Today, the most successful products are often those that had the most change implemented the latest in the development cycle. Rather than automatically trying to eliminate requirements changes, the software developer's job today is to strike a balance between chaos and rigidity—rejecting low-priority changes and accepting changes that represent prudent responses to changing market conditions.

When you want to give latitude to the developers. One big change associated with the PC revolution has been that project sponsors are more willing to leave large parts of the specification to the developers' discretion (for the reasons described in the "Minimal Specification" section early in this chapter). If you want to leave part of the product concept to the developers, you can't freeze the product concept as soon as requirements specification is complete; you have to leave at least part of it open for the developers to interpret.

Stable or not stable?

How stable your requirements are has a huge impact on how you go about software development, and particularly on what you need to do to develop rapidly. If your requirements are stable, you develop one way. If they are unstable, you develop another way. From a rapid-development point of view, one of the worst mistakes you can make is to think your requirements are stable when they aren't.

If your project doesn't have stable requirements, it isn't sufficient any more to throw up your hands and shout "Yikes! We don't have stable requirements!"—and proceed the same as you would have if you did have stable requirements. You can take certain steps to compensate for unstable requirements, and you must take those steps if you want to develop rapidly.

Methods of Change Control

Because stopping changes altogether is rarely in a project's best interest, the question for most projects turns to how to manage change most effectively. Any change-management plan should aim for several goals:

- Allow changes that help to produce the best possible product in the time available. Disallow all other changes.

- Allow all parties that would be affected by a proposed change to assess the schedule, resource, and product impacts of the change.

- Notify parties on the periphery of the project of each proposed change, its assessed impact, and whether it was accepted or rejected.

- Provide an audit trail of decisions related to the product content.

The change process should be structured to perform these jobs as efficiently as possible. Here are some options for accomplishing that objective.

Customer-oriented requirements practices

CROSS-REFERENCE
For more on customer-oriented requirements practices, see Chapter 10, "Customer-Oriented Development." For details on throwaway prototypes, see Chapter 38, "Throwaway Prototyping."

One change-control strategy is to try to minimize the number of changes needed. Customer-oriented requirements-gathering practices do a better job of eliciting the real requirements than traditional practices. For example, one study found that the combination of JAD and prototyping can drop creeping requirements to below 5 percent (Jones 1994). Prototyping helps to minimize changes because it strikes at what is often the root of the problem— the fact that customers don't know what they want until they see it. Throwaway prototypes are generally the most effective in this regard and provide the most resistance to requirements creep (Jones 1994).

Change analysis

In most cases, it's not the developer's or technical lead's job to say "No" to changes. But you can use the change-analysis process to screen out superfluous changes. Rather than saying "No" to each change, you provide cost and schedule impacts. Explain that you have to adjust the schedule for the time spent analyzing new feature requests. That explanation will screen out most of the frivolous change requests.

You can also screen out changes by making it harder to submit a change request. You can insist on a complete written specification of the change, a business-case analysis, a sample of the inputs and outputs that will be affected, and so on.

John Boddie tells the story of being called to the main office for an emergency schedule meeting on a rush project. When he and his team arrived, his boss asked "Is everything on schedule for delivery on the 18th?" Boddie said it was. Then the boss asked, "So we'll have the product on the 18th?"

Boddie said, "No, you'll have to wait until the 19th because this meeting has taken a day from our schedule" (Boddie 1987).

In the last few weeks of a project, you might say that the minimum schedule slide for any feature change is an entire day or more. You could even say that the minimum slide for *considering* a feature change is an entire day or more. This is appropriate since late-project changes tend to impact all aspects of the project, often in ways that are hard to predict without careful analysis.

You would probably want to make it a little easier to get defect-related change requests accepted. But even minor defects can have far-reaching consequences, so, depending on the kind of program and the stage of the project, you might not.

Version 2

One great help in saying "No" to changing the current product is being able to say "Yes" to putting those changes into some future product. Create a list of future enhancements. People should understand that features won't necessarily make it into version 2 just because they didn't make it into version 1, but you don't need to emphasize that point. What you do need to emphasize is that you're listening to people's concerns and plan to address them at the appropriate time. On a rapid-development project, the appropriate time is often "Next project."

A useful adjunct to the version-2 strategy is to create a "multi-release technology plan," which maps out a multi-year strategy for your product. That helps people to relax and see that the feature they want will be more appropriate for some later release (McCarthy 1995a).

Short release cycles

One of the keys to users and customers agreeing to the version-2 approach is that they have some assurance that there will in fact be a version 2. If they fear that the current version will be the last version ever built, they'll try harder to put all their pet features into it. Short release cycles help to build the user's confidence that their favorite feature will eventually make it into the product. The incremental development approaches of evolutionary delivery, evolutionary prototyping, and staged delivery can help.

Change board

Formal change-control boards have proven effective against creeping requirements for large projects (Jones 1994). They can also be effective for small projects.

Structure. The change board typically consists of representatives from each party that has a stake in the product's development. Concerned parties typically include development, QA, user documentation, customer support, marketing, and management. Each party should own the area it has control over. Development should own the development schedule, and user documentation should own the user-documentation schedule. In some organizations, marketing owns the product spec; in other organizations, development or management does.

Change analysis. The change board's function is to analyze each proposed change. The change should be analyzed from each corner of the classic trade-off triangle: How will the change affect the product's schedule, cost, and features? It should also be analyzed from the point of view of each organization affected: How will it affect development, documentation, customer support, quality assurance, and marketing? If the feature request is not worth the time it takes to analyze it, then it isn't worth the time it will take to implement it, and the change board should reject the proposed change out of hand. You can also apply the preceding section's change-analysis suggestions to change boards.

Triage. In addition to analyzing each change, the change board has to accept or reject each one. Some organizations refer to this part of the change board's job as "triage," a term from emergency medicine that refers to the activity of sorting injured people into groups so that the people who will most benefit from medical treatment receive it first.

"Triage" has some connotations that are particularly appropriate to the operation of a software change board. Triage connotes that you are allocating a scarce resource and that there is not enough of the resource to go around. That's true in software. There will never be enough time or money to add every feature that everyone wants. Triage also connotes that some people will not receive aid even though they desperately need it. In software, some changes that seem as though they are desperately needed will not make it into the next release of the software. Some features will not be implemented, and some low-priority defects will not be corrected. Finally, triage also connotes that you are doing something life-critical. And when you're prioritizing change requests on a rapid-development project, you are definitely performing a job that is critical to the life of your project.

Bundling. The change board can also group small changes so that developers can handle them in bundles. A series of uncoordinated small changes can be maddeningly distracting to developers in the late stages of a project. Each one requires the overhead of a code review, documentation update, testing, checking files in and out of version control, and so on. Developers appreciate being able to handle small changes in groups rather than one at a time.

The bureaucracy issue. Change boards have been stigmatized as being overly bureaucratic. Part of the bad rap comes from ineffective change boards. Some change boards interpret their charter narrowly as saying "No" rather than as being responsible to produce the best possible product in the time available. But the fact that some change boards have been poorly conducted does not mean that the idea is flawed.

The other part of the bad rap comes from the fact that the change board's job is unpopular! If the team has done a respectable job of specifying the product, a properly functioning change board will say "No" to more feature requests than it says "Yes" to. To the people who have been told "No," that will make it seem overly bureaucratic. It might well be that the organization that complains the most about a change board is the organization that most needs to be protected from uncontrolled changes.

An effective change board guarantees that you will understand the consequences of each change before you make it. As with many other aspects of speed-oriented development practices, a change board is valuable because it helps you to make decisions with your eyes fully open to the development-speed consequences.

14.3   Late Project: Feature Cuts

Feature-set control continues to be important through the end of a project. Even if you were successful at specifying a minimum feature set up front and controlling changes through the middle of the project, for a variety of all-too-familiar reasons you can still find yourself behind schedule at the end of the project.

By the time you reach that point, one of the most potent schedule-reduction options is the elimination of low-priority features. This practice is effective because it eliminates effort associated with further implementation, testing, and documentation. This practice is in common use at Microsoft, where it has been found to be an effective means of reining in late software projects (Cusumano and Selby 1995, McCarthy 1995b).

The drawback of this practice is that by the time you reach the end of the project, you've probably already done the design work and part of the implementation and testing for the features that you cut. You might even have to do some small amount of work to remove the feature—strip out unused code or disable it, remove test cases that exercise the feature, remove documentation that refers to the feature, and so on. If you plan to release another version of the product, this is only a small problem because you'll eventually use the work that you strip out or disable for the current version.

For maximum efficiency, start with a scrubbed requirements document, design and implement the features you know will be in the product, and then add lower-priority features if you have time. Don't waste time working on features that will be cut later.

CROSS-REFERENCE
For more on development styles that support late-in-the-project changes, see Chapter 7, "Lifecycle Planning."

If you don't think you can live up to that ideal, then plan ahead for the eventuality of cutting features late in the project. Use a lifecycle model such as evolutionary prototyping, evolutionary delivery, design-to-schedule, or design-to-tools that supports late-project feature changes.

Case Study 14-1. Managing Change Effectively

Six weeks before Square-Calc 4.0 was scheduled to ship, Kim walked into Eddie's office. "Eddie, we've got a problem. Our competitors have just released a new version, and it has several new features that our product doesn't have. We need to add some new features before we ship this product."

Eddie nodded. "OK. Make a list of the new features, and we'll discuss them at the change-board meeting this afternoon." Kim agreed and went back to her office to prepare the list.

At the change-board meeting, Kim proposed a dozen new features that their competitor's new product had and their new product did not. She felt strongest about the fact that their competitors had greatly simplified their menus, moving many items to context-sensitive pop-up menus. She argued that this seemed like a major user-interface enhancement, and their product would look out of date if it came out without similar menus.

After Kim finished describing the new features, Eddie took over. "First of all, it will probably push our schedule out about a day just to estimate this many changes. Does the group think that these changes are important enough to justify the estimation time?" The group agreed that they were that important. "OK, then," Eddie said. "I'll distribute these new features as change requests to all of the affected groups. I don't want to interrupt their workflow any more than necessary at this critical stage in the project, so I'll give them a few days to respond. Let's plan to decide on these changes at our regular change-board meeting next week." The group agreed, and the meeting broke up.

At the next meeting, the estimates were ready. "According to these preliminary estimates, it would push our schedule out 3 to 4 months to implement all of these changes," Eddie reported. "Development considers them to be relatively minor changes and estimates that they could implement all of them in about 4 weeks, but testing and documentation would be more strongly affected. The pop-up menu change is the most costly in terms of calendar time because it significantly changes the program's user interface. Testing says that that change alone would require rewriting about a third of their test cases, which would take about 6 weeks. Documentation has a long lead-time for printing, and they are scheduled to go to press at the end of this week. They would have to change 80 percent of their document pages and help screens, reshoot virtually all of their screen shots, and then redo their final proofing cycle. That would push their schedule out 3 to 4 months, depending on how

(continued)

Case Study 14-1. Managing Change Effectively, *continued*

quickly they can hire a contract writer. The usability group is lukewarm about whether we should even make this change, so I don't think it's worth doing."

"I still think it's important," Kim said. "But I don't think we should slip the schedule 3 months for it." The group quickly agreed to postpone the pop-up menu change. They added it to a list of features to be considered for the next version.

From among the rest of the change requests, the change board identified three that were estimated to have a total impact on development, testing, and documentation of 1 week. Carlos from marketing wanted those new features and said that a 1-week slip was an acceptable price to pay. The board accepted those changes. Five more changes were identified as features they would like to add if they had time, but the board concluded that they weren't important enough to move the release date. They added those changes to the list of features to be considered for the next version and rejected the remaining requests.

After the meeting, the affected groups were notified of the change board's decision. Since each group's input had been considered in the decision, they all adjusted their schedules accordingly and took the changes in stride.

Further Reading

Carroll, Paul B. "Creating New Software Was Agonizing Task for Mitch Kapor Firm," *The Wall Street Journal*, May 11, 1990, A1, A5. This is a fascinating case study of the development of On Location 1.0 and illustrates what a blind spot feature creep can be.

Gibbs, W. Wayt. "Software's Chronic Crisis," *Scientific American*, September 1994, 86–95. This article describes some recent software projects that have been plagued by changing requirements, including the Denver airport's baggage-handling software and the FAA's air-traffic-control workstation software.

Jones, Capers. *Assessment and Control of Software Risks*. Englewood Cliffs, N.J.: Yourdon Press, 1994. Chapter 9, "Creeping User Requirements," contains a detailed discussion of the root causes, associated problems, cost impact, and methods of prevention and control of feature creep.

McConnell, Steve. *Code Complete*. Redmond, Wash.: Microsoft Press, 1993. Sections 3.1 through 3.3 describe how costs increase when you accept requirements changes late in a project. They also contain an extended argument for trying to get accurate requirements as early in a project as possible.

Bugsy. TriStar Pictures. Produced by Mark Johnson, Barry Levinson, and Warren Beatty, and directed by Barry Levinson, 1991. This movie begins as a story about a gangster moving to California to take over the Hollywood rackets, but it quickly turns into a tale of Bugsy Siegel's obsession with building the first casino in Las Vegas. Bugsy's casino ultimately costs six times its original estimate, largely due to what we would think of as feature creep. As a software developer who's been on the builder's side of that problem, it's hard not to feel a sense of justice when Bugsy is finally gunned down for changing his mind too often and spending too much of the mob's money.

15

Productivity Tools

Contents

Related Topics

SOFTWARE MANAGERS AND DEVELOPERS ARE DRAWN TO productivity tools like ants to a picnic, children to mud puddles, and late-night TV lawyers to auto accidents. Sometimes they're drawn to productivity tools the way that drunken sailors are drawn to the sirens' call.

Productivity tools make up the technology dimension of the people-process-product-technology foursome—and as such, they have a significant role to play in rapid development. Adopting a new tool can be one of the quickest ways to improve productivity. But it can also be one of the riskiest.

The most productive organizations have found ways to minimize the risks and maximize the productivity gains. Their strategy depends on recognizing three critical realities:

- Productivity tools seldom produce the schedule savings their vendors promise.
- Learning any new tool or practice initially lowers productivity.
- Productivity tools that have been discredited sometimes produce significant schedule savings anyway, just not as significant as originally promised.

The rest of this chapter explores these realities in detail.

What Is a "Productivity Tool"?

I mean something fairly specific when I refer to "productivity tools" in this chapter. When I talk about a productivity tool, I am not referring to a specific brand of compiler that is incrementally better than another brand, or to compilers, linkers, source-code editors, or to other code-level tools in general. In this chapter, I'm talking about tools that have the potential to significantly change the way you work: 4GLs (fourth-generation languages), visual-programming languages, code generators, code or class libraries—tools that offer dramatic reductions in workload and equally dramatic improvements in development schedules.

Case Study 15-1. Ineffective Tool Use

"I don't know how I let myself get talked into another impossible deadline," Mike complained to the team. "We're supposed to write a whole new billing system in 3 months, and it probably will take at least 5 months. I think we're screwed."

"Maybe not," Angela said. "I just got a brochure for version 1 of the Blaze-O-Matic visual-programming language. The brochure says that we can easily double or triple our development speed. It uses object-oriented programming. I've wanted to try it anyway. What do you think about trying that?"

"Double or triple, huh," Mike said. "I don't know if I believe that. Still, I don't know what other choice we've got. Even if it doesn't cut our schedule by a half or two-thirds, it might shave off a month or two. I think object-oriented programming would help our project, too. All right. Let's do it!"

The project started immediately, and the group was amazed at how quickly they were able to construct the basic user interface in Blaze-O-Matic. Its database support was good, and that part of the program went quickly, too. Other parts of the tool were harder to learn, but at the 2-month mark, they had about half of their product done. Since they'd been climbing a learning curve on the first half of the project, they felt optimistic about finishing the last half of the product by the 3-month deadline.

Then they found a chink in their armor. "Hey, Mike, I just discovered that the help screens aren't as easy to hook up as we thought. I thought I could set up the hooks for all the screens in an afternoon, but Blaze-O-Matic doesn't support context-sensitive help. It's going to take longer." Angela looked disappointed. Mike told her that integrated help was one of the critical features of the new billing system, so she should spend as long as needed.

(continued)

As Month 3 wore on, team members discovered more and more Blaze-O-Matic limitations: Blaze-O-Matic had advertised that it could automatically import records from ASCII files into the database. They'd counted on that feature to convert old billing records to the new database format. But Blaze-O-Matic wouldn't handle the kinds of records their files used, so they had to code all the access routines by hand. The reporting module was flaky and wouldn't support the exact report format they wanted, so they spent a lot of time coding workarounds for that, and report-formatting bugs kept popping up after they thought they were done.

The team still had about 25 percent of the product to implement when they reached their 3-month deadline, and they agreed that they had at least 2 weeks to go, even working full tilt. "I'll go deliver the bad news," Mike said. When he returned, Angela had news of her own to report.

"You know those help screens? It turns out that Blaze-O-Matic doesn't support context-sensitive help hooks *and* it doesn't provide any way to launch help from inside an application. I figured out how to launch help as a generic application, but then I found out that Blaze-O-Matic does something weird with the task ID of the program you launch from it, and if any other application has already opened help, Blaze-O-Matic closes their help but doesn't open ours! I've been on the phone to tech support all day, and they said they would send us a patch for the problem. But they're working on a new release, and it will probably be 3 weeks before they can send us the patch."

"Damn!" Mike said. "I just told the boss that we would have the whole thing wrapped up in 2 weeks. Can they speed it up at all?"

"No can do," Angela said. She'd already checked that possibility on the phone. "I think we're stuck."

The team had plenty to do while they waited for the patch. It arrived 4 weeks later instead of 3, but the last 25 percent of the product took 6 weeks instead of the 2 weeks they'd hoped for. They finally delivered the product at the $4\frac{1}{2}$-month mark.

After releasing the product, the team conducted a postmortem and recommended that the company not use Blaze-O-Matic again. They concluded that it had allowed them to speed up their development some, but it had also required too many design compromises. They hadn't been able to implement the program they had wanted to.

A year later, Angela talked to a friend from a different part of the company and discovered that her project had had a similar experience with Blaze-O-Matic. That project had started a month after Angela's team completed their postmortem.

15.1   Role of Productivity Tools in Rapid Development

Computers are good at automatic, repetitive tasks. Most of the things that software-development technology has automated so far have been the repetitive tasks—conversion of assembler code into machine language, conversion of high-level language code into assembler, creating database descriptions from English-like descriptions, handling the same kinds of window-processing calls again and again, and so on. But there are many aspects of software development that are not repetitive and that are therefore not well suited to being automated by hardware and software tools.

In 1987, Frederick P. Brooks, Jr. published the article "No Silver Bullets—Essence and Accidents of Software Engineering," and that article has become one of the most influential and famous articles in the field of software engineering (Brooks 1987). Brooks argues that the difficult part of software development arises from the fact that a computer program's essence is a set of interlocking concepts—data sets, relationships among data sets, algorithms, and functions. These concepts are highly precise and rich with detail. The hard part of software development, Brooks says, is specifying, designing, and testing these concepts themselves.

A different Brooks, Ruven Brooks, published a study that suggested it would take on the order of tens of thousands or even hundreds of thousands of rules to capture the knowledge of an expert developer (Brooks 1977). Capturing the end-product of thinking through all these rules in a programming language is the easy part of software development. Thinking them through in the first place is what's difficult.

The fact that software programs are highly precise and rich with detail is not going to change. Software programs are becoming more precise, more detailed, and more complex, not less. Someone has to think through the conceptual essence of any new computer program or any change to any old computer program. That person must understand each detail of the program's functionality and must understand how each of the details relate to each other. Such understanding is difficult, error-prone, and time-consuming. The time required to achieve that understanding is one of the main contributors to the time required to complete a software-development project.

Fred Brooks maintains that to achieve a dramatic reduction in development time, a new technology would have to simplify the essence of software development; it would have to make it much easier to formulate the set of interlocking concepts that make up a computer program. As a rule of thumb, the more a technology strikes at the essence of what makes software development difficult, the more effort it is likely to save.

CROSS-REFERENCE
For more on rapid-development languages, see Chapter 31, "Rapid-Development Languages (RDLs)."

A high-level language compiler saves a lot of effort because it moves the whole set of concepts that you have to be concerned with to a higher level. That's what the move to higher-level programming languages has accomplished over the years. The switch from low-level languages like assembler to higher-level languages like C and Pascal freed you from having to think about what the underlying machine was doing when it ran your program. The move to visual-programming languages such as Delphi, PowerBuilder, and Visual Basic provides a similar kind of simplification, allowing you to forget about many of the tasks a windowing environment performs when it runs a graphically oriented program.

Tools that do not strike at the conceptual essence—the hard part of programming—don't help as much. A programming editor helps only a little because it allows you to type in code faster; it's handy, but it doesn't strike at the essence of what makes software development difficult. The same is true for source-code control tools, debuggers, execution profilers, automated testing tools, and so on; those tools provide only incremental productivity gains for the same reason.

Tools such as CASE tools and code libraries or class libraries are somewhere between high-level languages and coding tools in their ability to improve productivity—they strike at the root of the problem, but most of them don't strike very hard.

Fred Brooks pointed out that our industry has been involved in a long search for a magic silver bullet to slay the low-productivity werewolf. Alexander the Great wept because there were no more worlds to conquer. In 1987, Brooks asserted that, although it had been done before, no single technology or practice looked as though it would be capable of producing a 10-fold improvement in productivity in the next 10 years. Rearranging the math a little, Brooks was arguing that no single tool or practice could produce a sustained productivity improvement of 25 percent per year for 10 years. Eight years later, in 1995, he reaffirmed that position, and I think he's right. We have to be satisfied with individual practices and technologies that generate productivity improvements of less than 25 percent per year, or we have to look for combinations of practices and technologies to have any chance at greater improvements.

Areas of Special Applicability

CROSS-REFERENCE
For details on the portion of a project taken up by construction, see Section 6.5, "Where the Time Goes."

Productivity tools tend to focus on software construction. How effective they are in supporting rapid development depends on how much of your project consists of software construction. How large is your project? How complicated is your project? How much of the lifecycle is occupied by software construction? Some kinds of projects are better supported than others.

349

DBMS-oriented applications. Database applications are well supported by productivity tools on nearly all platforms. Productivity tools exist to generate database schemas, generate queries, format reports, create data-entry screens, and so on. If you need to develop 100 data-entry screens for use with a database, I can't imagine coding that sort of thing by hand anymore because many good database tools (such as Visual FoxPro, Access, PowerBuilder, CA Visual Objects, FileMaker, Focus, and a raft of CASE tools) take the repetitiveness out of that process.

Custom applications. Rapid-development languages work well for small applications in which the design envelope is well understood. If your customer will be happy with standard data-entry forms, standard graphics, standard reports—in short, with an application that looks like a lot of other applications—then you should be able to develop it in a 4GL or visual-programming language. In many if not most custom-software projects, the customer is willing to accept a few limitations in look and feel in exchange for dramatically faster development time.

Throwaway prototyping. Rapid-development languages are extremely well-suited to the development of throwaway user-interface prototypes. You'd almost have to be crazy to develop a throwaway prototype in C/C++ or plain Pascal these days. You might develop the nucleus of an evolutionary prototype in those languages so that you could extend it later on, but it's hard to imagine why you'd use anything other than a visual-programming language to develop rapid iterations of a user-interface design that you planned to throw away later.

In general, the smaller and simpler the application, the more valuable productivity tools will be. On small projects, most of the project is consumed by code construction, which is the part that is usually helped the most by such tools. On larger projects, a smaller proportion of the project is devoted to coding, so the potential contribution of code-focused, rapid-development tools will be smaller.

Productivity Tool Limitations

"Three steps forward and two steps back" is a fact of life with productivity tools. Productivity tools giveth, and productivity tools taketh away.

On one project, my team used a user-interface class library for the Microsoft Windows environment. Using the class library generally made our lives much easier. But then we got to the part of the project where we were supposed to copy graphics from our application to the clipboard in "metafile format." The class library advertised support for metafiles, and its technical documentation said that it supported metafiles. But when we actually tried to use metafiles, they didn't work. Our full-screen metafiles came out about 1/8 of an inch square.

After many calls to the class-library company and to Microsoft, we eventually determined that both Microsoft Windows and the class library contained errors in handling metafiles. We then spent several days designing and coding a workaround to the problem. By the time we got to the metafile work, we were so thoroughly committed to our design that we really didn't have any alternative but to code the time-consuming workaround the way that we did.

On balance, we still saved a lot of time by using the class library. But in the metafile area, if we had known at the outset that metafiles were poorly supported, we would have designed our program differently, and we wouldn't have wasted as much time.

I haven't seen any systematic study of the issue, but my best estimate is that if you plan to use a productivity tool, you should add about 25 percent on top of the total time you expect to spend working with the tool for use in working around the tool's limitations. There are always things that are harder to do because you're using a tool, and sometimes there are defects in the tool itself.

Ultimate Role of Productivity Tools on Rapid-Development Projects

HARD DATA

When you weigh the advantages and disadvantages of productivity tool use, the argument for emphasizing productivity tool use on rapid-development projects is far from clear-cut. In a review of 10 software projects that several organizations had selected as their best projects, Bill Hetzel concluded that, "Best projects do not necessarily have state-of-the-art methodologies or extensive automation and tooling. They do rely on basic principles such as strong team work, project communication, and project controls. Good organization and management appears to be far more of a critical success factor than technology" (Hetzel 1993). Other studies have also concluded that productivity tools are only a secondary contributor to an organization's overall level of productivity (Zelkowitz, et al. 1984, Zawacki 1993).

Charles Symons reinforces the point when he reports that there are so many other influences on a software schedule that there isn't any clear-cut data to support the contention that projects that use fourth-generation languages are delivered any faster than projects that use third-generation languages (Symons 1991). This is not to say that specific bits of functionality on those projects aren't developed faster—just that any significant variations in schedule are more likely to result from differences in planning, management, requirements specification, and a host of other factors than they are from the technology used to construct the system.

HARD DATA

In a 17-year study involving more than 100 experiments with live projects and 50 technologies, NASA's Software Engineering Laboratory concluded that improvements are characterized by continual, sustained, and methodical change. We should not wait for or depend on technological breakthroughs (Glass 1993).

Leading-edge productivity tools can play an important role in shortening development schedules, but it's good to keep their role in perspective. By themselves, they are neither necessary nor sufficient for achieving rapid development.

15.2   Productivity-Tool Strategy

Somewhat counter to common practice, tool use is best treated as a long-term, strategic issue rather than a short-term, tactical fix. Tool usage is not a short-term solution because it takes time and money to acquire and deploy tools effectively. If you don't spend time and money on it, then you stand to waste time and money using tools that you ultimately find to be ineffective. Brand new tools (not just new to you, but new) introduce unpredictability into both quality and schedule. It's no accident that the state-of-the-art is called "the bleeding edge."

Tool usage is also unlikely to provide any major competitive advantage. Tools tend to be advertised heavily, which means that any tool you know about, your competitors know about too. The advantage you get from switching to a new tool is the time between when you start using it to proper advantage and the time when your competitors start using it. Switching to a new tool is easier than a lot of the other means of improving development speed, and that means everyone else is as highly motivated to switch to new tools as you are. Long-term, strategic advantages come from improvements in people, process, and product. Being up to date in productivity tools is part of the ante for staying in the game, but it won't give you a winning hand.

If you deploy new tools in a haphazard way, the benefit that you receive from them will wax and wane. There isn't much advantage in jumping onto a cool-tool bandwagon three months ahead of the competition if you jump onto a crappy-tool bandwagon three months ahead of them, too. But, as Figure 15-1 shows, if you can find a way to implement only the good tools, and if you can consistently do it sooner than the competition, that would provide a continual strategic competitive advantage.

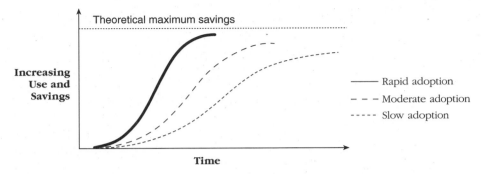

Figure 15-1. *An effective deployment strategy can maximize gains through systematic rapid adoption of new tools. But it must also avoid productivity losses caused by deploying ineffective tools.*

A strategy for acquiring and deploying new tools effectively should include the following elements:

- Early identification of promising new tools
- Timely and accurate evaluation of new tools
- Rapid deployment of new tools that are found to be effective
- Nondeployment of new tools that are found to be ineffective
- Continuing reliance on older, proven tools

If you implement a program containing these elements within your organization, you will achieve a strategic competitive advantage. You will adopt the good new tools more quickly. You will avoid the lost productivity associated with adopting the wrong tools. And over time you will build on your successes by continuing to use older, proven tools. The following sections describe how to implement this kind of program, and Case Study 15-2 at the end of this chapter illustrates one such program.

15.3 Productivity-Tool Acquisition

HARD DATA

Organizations that have random or casual methods of acquiring software tools waste about 50 percent of all the money they spend on tools. Worse, poor tool investments are associated with long schedules. Organizations that use formal acquisition strategies can drop their wastage to about 10 percent and avoid the associated schedule problems (Jones 1994).

FURTHER READING
For more on problems associated with tool acquisition, see *Assessment and Control of Software Risks* (Jones 1994).

Here are some common problems with acquisition tools:

- The software tool market is prone to gimmickry and exaggerated claims.
- Bad-tool acquisition precludes acquisition of more beneficial tools.
- Thirty percent of acquired tools do not meet enough user needs to be effective.
- Ten percent are never used after acquisition.
- Twenty-five percent are used less than they could be because of lack of training.
- Fifteen percent are seriously incompatible with existing tools and trigger some form of modification to fit the new tool into the intended environment.

The ultimate cost of a tool is only slightly related to its purchase price. Learning expense and efficiency gains or losses are much more important in determining the lifetime cost of a tool than is the purchase price.

Acquisition Plan

An organization that waits until it needs a tool to begin researching has waited too long. Tool evaluation and dissemination should be an ongoing activity.

Tools group

An effective, ongoing approach is to identify a person or group to be responsible for disseminating information about software tools. Depending on the size of the organization, that person or group can be assigned tools responsibilities either full- or part-time and should be responsible for the following activities:

Intelligence gathering. The tools group should stay abreast of developments in the tools market and literature related to tools—news reports, marketing materials, comparative reviews, anecdotal reports from tool users, online discussion threads, and so on.

Evaluation. The group should evaluate new tools as they become available. It should maintain a "recommended list" of tools for general use. It should track how well each tool works on large projects, small projects, short projects, long projects, and so on. Depending on the size of the organization, it might recommend tools to be used on pilot projects on a trial basis, monitoring those pilot projects to identify winners and losers.

The tools group should continue to evaluate new releases of tools that have earlier been found lacking. With less-formal evaluations, people sometimes develop mental blocks about tools they have had bad experiences with. They will shun version 5 of a tool because version 2 had more problems than their tool of choice—ignoring that versions 3, 4, and 5 of their tool have also had problems of their own.

Coordination. Different groups within an organization can all try new tools, but without coordination they might all try the same new tool. There might be six promising new tools and six groups to try them, but without coordination maybe only three of the six tools will be tried. Some of those groups might have been just as happy to try one of the three untried tools as the one they did try. The tools group should coordinate tool experimentation so that groups don't all learn the same lessons the hard way and so that the organization learns as much as it can as efficiently as it can.

Dissemination. The tools group should get the word out to people who need tool information. The group should maintain reports on different groups' experiences with each tool and make those reports available to other groups who are considering using a particular tool. If the organization is large enough, it could desktop publish an informal monthly or bimonthly tools newsletter that reports on the results of tool use on pilot projects and solicits groups to become pilots for tools under evaluation. It could facilitate informal communications among different tool users, perhaps by hosting monthly brown-bag lunch presentations on new tools or by moderating bulletin-board discussions.

Risks of setting up a tools group

There are several risks in setting up a centralized tools group, the worst being overcontrol. It's important that the tools group collect and disseminate information about effective tools; however, if the group is to support rapid development, it can't be allowed to calcify into a bureaucratic standards organization that insists that all groups use only the tools it has "approved."

The tools group should be set up as a service organization rather than as a standards organization. The tools group's job is to help those working on real projects to do their jobs better. The people working on the front lines of projects know best what they need. The tools people can make recommendations, provide advice, and lend support, but their judgments about which tools to use should not prevail over the judgments of the people who actually have to live with the tools.

The tools group needs to be staffed by people whose recommendations will be heard. If the group is prioritized low and staffed with cast-off developers, the group's recommendations may be ignored, possibly for good reason.

Selection Criteria

CROSS-REFERENCE
The considerations in selecting tools overlap with considerations in selecting outsourcing vendors. For those criteria, see Chapter 28, "Outsourcing."

This section contains criteria to use in your tool acquisitions. You can use these criteria within the context of a standing tools group or for the evaluation of a specific tool for a specific project.

Estimated gain. Foremost on the list for a rapid-development project is to estimate the efficiency gain you expect to realize from the use of a particular tool. This is often difficult to measure, and for reasons spelled out in detail throughout this chapter, should be estimated conservatively.

A good rule of thumb is to assume that any vendor claim of more than 25-percent improvement in productivity per year from a single tool is either specious or false (Jones 1994). You can decide what to do with a vendor who makes such a claim; some people avoid dealing with them entirely.

Vendor stability. You stake your future on the future of the vendor who provides the tools. How long has the vendor company been in business? How stable are they? How committed are they to the specific tool of interest? Is the tool in the vendor's main line of business, or is it a sideline? Is the tool likely to be supported by another company if the current vendor goes out of business?

If you have concerns about the vendor's stability and you're still interested in the tool, you should consider what you will do if the vendor goes out of business. Do you need the tool for more than one project or version? Can you maintain the tool yourself? Will the vendor provide source code? If so, what is the quality level of that source code?

Quality. Depending on the kind of tool you're looking at, it could be that the quality of the vendor's tool will determine the quality of your program. If the vendor tool is buggy, your program will be buggy. If the vendor tool is slow, your program will be slow. Check under the hood before you jump on the vendor's bandwagon.

Maturity. A tool's maturity is often a good indication of both quality and vendor commitment. Some organizations refuse to buy version 1 of any tool from a new vendor—no matter how good it is reported to be—because there is too much risk of unknown quality and, regardless of the vendor's good intentions, unknown ability to stay in business. Some organizations follow the "version 3 rule."

CLASSIC MISTAKE

Version 1 is often tantamount to prototyping code. The product focus is often unclear, and you can't be sure of the direction in which the vendor will take future versions of the tool. You might buy version 1 of a class library because of the vendor's all-out emphasis on performance, only to find that by version 3 the vendor has shifted its focus to portability (with terrible performance consequences).

The product direction in version 2 is usually more certain, but sometimes version 2 is just a bug-fix release or displays the second-system effect: the developers cram in all the features they wanted to include the first time, and product quality suffers. Product direction can still be unclear.

Version 3 is frequently the first really stable, usable version of a tool. By the time version 3 rolls around, the product focus is usually clear and the vendor has demonstrated that it has the stamina needed to continue development of its product.

Training time. Consider whether anyone who will use the tool has direct experience with the tool. Has anyone on your team attended a training class? How available are freelance programmers who know how to use the tool? How much productivity will you lose to the learning curve?

CROSS-REFERENCE
For more on design to tools, see Section 7.9, "Design to Tools."

Applicability. Is the tool really applicable to your job, or will you have to force-fit it? Can you accept the trade-offs that a design-to-tools strategy will entail? It's fine to use a design-to-tools strategy. Just be sure to do it with your eyes open.

Compatibility. Does the new tool work well with the tools you're already using? Does it restrict future tool choices?

Growth envelope. In addition to the direction in which you *know* you want your product to go, will the tool support the directions in which you *might* want your product to go?

CLASSIC MISTAKE

It's the nature of a software project to expand beyond its original scope. I participated in one project in which the team had to choose between low-end, in-house database management software and a high-end commercial DBMS. The engineer who favored the commercial database manager pointed out that under heavy data loads the commercial DBMS was likely to be several times faster. The engineer who favored the in-house DBMS insisted that there was no processing-speed requirement, and so the performance consideration was irrelevant. By selecting the in-house DBMS instead of its more powerful competitor, the company didn't have to pay a licensing fee, so that's what they selected.

CROSS-REFERENCE
For more on growth envelopes, see "Define Families of Programs" in Section 19.1.

In the end, the company might not have paid a licensing fee to use the in-house DBMS, but it did pay, and it paid, and it paid some more. Although the in-house DBMS had operated reasonably fast with small test databases, under full data loads it inched along. Some common operations took more than 24 hours. In the face of performance this abysmal—surprise! surprise!—a performance requirement was added. By that time, thousands of lines of code had been written to use the in-house database software, and the company wound up having to rewrite its DBMS software.

Avoid selecting a tool that's only minimally sufficient for the job.

Customizing selection criteria. In defining a set of criteria to use in tool selection, be sure that you buy tools according to your own criteria rather than someone else's. It's fine to read comparative reviews to see what issues are involved in using a particular class of tool, because you often discover important issues that you hadn't thought about. But once you've seen what the issues are, decide for yourself what matters. Don't add criteria to your list solely because magazine reviewers have them on their lists. It's unlikely that even half the things mentioned in a typical magazine review will be of concern to any one of your individual projects.

Commitment

Once you've made the tool selection, commit to it. Don't keep looking over your shoulder and wondering if some other tool would have been better. Let the other tools go! As Larry O'Brien says, "When the project hits its first big bump, it's natural to worry that you're wasting effort. But every project and every tool has a first, big bump" (O'Brien 1995). You don't have to enjoy the bumps, but realize that you'll encounter at least a few no matter how good a job of tool-selection you've done. Switching tools mid-project just guarantees you'll have at least one more big bump.

15.4 Productivity-Tool Use

Once you've developed an effective tool-acquisition strategy, a few issues still remain in the area of tool use. How you match tools to projects can have a major impact on your rapid-development capability.

When to Deploy

On a software project, there is a trade-off between the learning curve you climb in becoming familiar with a new tool and the productivity you gain once you become familiar. The first time you use a new tool, it often takes more time than if you hadn't used the tool at all. You incur overhead for training, experimentation, learning about the tool's weak spots (as in my Windows metafile project), and arguing among team members about how to use the tool to maximum advantage.

As Figure 15-2 suggests, if you expect your project to take as long as Project B, you can expect to recoup your learning-curve investment. But if you expect your project to finish sooner, as Project A does, you would be better off not adopting that tool, at least from the point of view of that project.

At an organizational level, the considerations are a little different. If you always have short projects like Project A and learning curves for new tools

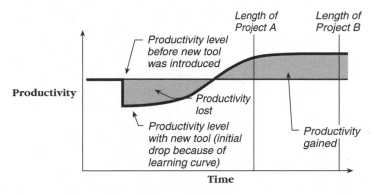

Figure 15-2. *Learning curve's effect on productivity. Introducing a new tool on a short project, such as Project A, doesn't allow you to recoup the productivity you lose to the learning curve.*

like the one shown in Figure 15-2, you'll never be able to justify introducing a new tool on a single project. But to maintain the long-term development capability of your organization, to continue raising your productivity level, you sometimes have to adopt a new tool on a project even though it's a suboptimal solution for that particular project.

You can draw two conclusions from this for rapid development. First, long-term, you need to keep introducing new and more effective tools to improve productivity. You can't make those decisions purely on the basis of what's best for individual projects. Second, short-term, a rapid-development project is usually not the right project on which to introduce a new tool. The time you're in a hurry is the worst time to take a new shortcut. Choose a less time-sensitive project, and soak up the learning curve on that project.

Importance of Training

CLASSIC MISTAKE

The more powerful a tool is, the more difficult it can be to use effectively. Without adequate training, tools that could provide significant productivity benefits often sit on shelves unused. Wayne Beardsley puts it this way:

> Think of our software company as a construction company. Our task is to dig a ditch from the street to a farmhouse five miles away. We've purchased the latest backhoe systems for the work crew. On a typical day, the crew members drive the backhoe from the street to the end of the ditch, hop off, and use the shovels that came with the backhoe to dig another few feet. At the end of the day, they hop back onto the backhoe and drive it back to the street. Maybe we should explain that the backhoe wasn't purchased for commuting. (Beardsley 1995)

This analogy fits altogether too closely to many software projects.

How Much Schedule Reduction to Expect

No practice is implemented in a vacuum, and the environment in which the practice is used plays a large role in determining whether it succeeds (Basili and McGarry 1995). Vendor productivity claims are usually claims for the maximum potential of a practice in an ideal environment; you'll have to try it to determine how well it works in your environment.

To estimate how much schedule reduction to expect from a productivity tool, think in terms of the entire lifecycle you plan to use, and then determine how much effort you expect to save during each part of the lifecycle.

CROSS-REFERENCE
For details on the waterfall lifecycle model, see Section 7.1, "Pure Waterfall."

Suppose you plan to use a fourth-generation language (4GL) such as Focus, Visual Basic, or Delphi for 50 percent of your system within a classical, waterfall lifecycle. Suppose further that you expect the project to consist of about 32,000 lines of code if it were implemented completely in a third-generation language (3GL) such as C, Basic, or Pascal. Table 15-1 shows approximately how that kind of project would break down by activity.

HARD DATA

Switching to a 4GL is one of the more powerful ways to employ productivity tools in your behalf. Estimates vary, but in moving from a 3GL to a 4GL, you can typically expect to reduce your coding effort by 75 percent or so (Jones 1995). You can expect to reduce your design effort by about the same amount (Klepper and Bock 1995).

That 75-percent savings in design and coding unfortunately doesn't translate into a 75-percent savings in schedule. In the example, only 50 percent of the program is implemented in a 4GL, so the 75-percent savings applies only to that 50 percent. Moreover, the savings does not apply to the activities of architecture, unit test, or system test, and it applies only partially to integration. When all is said and done, you come out with about a 20-percent reduction in effort as a result of using a 4GL for 50 percent of your program.

CROSS-REFERENCE
For details on the relationship between effort and schedule, see Section 8.5, "Schedule Estimation."

Unfortunately, we're still not quite done whittling down the savings. A woman might be able to have twins in 9 months, but that doesn't mean she could have had one baby in $4\frac{1}{2}$ months. Effort savings don't translate straight across the board to schedule savings. That 20-percent savings in effort translates to only an 8-percent savings in schedule.

Now here's the really bad news. This example didn't even include the time needed for requirements specification or learning curve. If you included that, the savings as a percentage of the end-to-end project time would be even smaller. Ugh!

CROSS-REFERENCE
The effort estimates in this table are derived from data in Table 8-10, "Nominal Schedules." The schedule estimates are calculated using Equation 8-1 described in Section 8.5.

Table 15-1. Example of Savings Realized by Switching from a 3GL to a 4GL for 50 Percent of a 32,000 LOC Project

Activity	Nominal Effort (man-months)	Expected Savings by Activity	Final Effort (man-months)	Explanation
Architecture (high-level design)	6	0%	6	Same amount of architecture required. Any savings would be offset by the need to architect the combination of 3GL and 4GL languages.
Detailed design	8	38%	5	75% reduction for the 50% of the program coded in a 4GL.
Code/debug	8	38%	5	75% reduction for the 50% of the program coded in a 4GL.
Unit test	6	0%	6	Same unit tests required for same functionality.
Integration	6	30%	4	75% reduction for the part coded in 4GL, but extra integration required to mix 3GL and 4GL partially offsets the savings.
System test	6	0%	6	Same system tests required for same functionality.
Total Effort (man-months)	40	20%	32	
Schedule Savings				
Expected schedule (calendar months)	10.3	8%	9.5	

Here's a somewhat more encouraging example. This time, suppose that you're working on the same application as the last example, but that you can implement it completely in a 4GL. Table 15-2 on the next page illustrates the savings you can expect in this case.

CROSS-REFERENCE
The effort estimates in this table are derived from data in Table 8-10, "Nominal Schedules." The schedule estimates are calculated using Equation 8-1 described in Section 8.5.

Table 15-2. Example of Savings Realized by Switching from a 3GL to a 4GL for 100 Percent of a 32,000 LOC Project

Activity	Nominal Effort (man-months)	Expected Savings by Activity	Final Effort (man-months)	Explanation
Architecture (high-level design)	6	80%	1	Program is so much smaller that little architecture is needed.
Detailed design	8	75%	2	75% reduction due to switch from 3GL to 4GL.
Code/debug	8	75%	2	75% reduction due to switch from 3GL to 4GL.
Unit test	6	0%	6	Same unit tests required for same functionality.
Integration	6	75%	1	75% reduction due to switch from 3GL to 4GL.
System test	6	0%	6	Same system tests required for same functionality.
Total Effort (man-months)	40	55%	18	
Schedule Savings				
Expected schedule (calendar months)	10.3	23%	7.9	

Here, the payoff in effort is terrific—55-percent savings overall. But the payoff in schedule is still a relatively modest 23 percent, and that assumes that there's no learning-curve effect associated with switching to the 4GL. The switch from a 3GL to a 4GL is one of the most powerful productivity improvements you can make, but even when you can implement a program entirely in a 4GL, you cut the schedule by only about 25 percent.

HARD DATA

You might disagree with the specific percentage savings I've estimated in these tables, but don't let that obscure the messages of these examples: it is extremely difficult for any productivity tool to deliver as much as a 25-percent reduction in schedule, and you can simply dismiss more ambitious claims. Most tools' real savings will be more in line with the first example, delivering schedule savings of 10 percent or less. A few leading-edge companies have sustained productivity improvements of 15 to 25 percent per year for several years by using combinations of tools, and that seems to be the upper limit (Jones 1994).

Tools and Methodologies

This section has focused on productivity tools, but the problems associated with deploying tools, training people to use them, and estimating savings from their use apply just as much to the use of new methodologies. The next section applies to both tools and methodologies, too.

15.5 Silver-Bullet Syndrome

Once upon a time, there was a poor widow who lived with her son, Jack. One day when they had no money for food, Jack's mother sent him to market to sell their cow.

On the way to the market, Jack encountered an old man who offered him five brightly colored beans and a plastic square for the cow. Jack was a good boy and at first he refused, but the man said that the bright beans and the plastic square were magic and were really worth 10 cows. Jack gave him the cow. The man put the beans and the plastic square into a cardboard box and said to call it a "CASE tool."

Jack ran home to find his mother. "I gave the cow to a man I met," Jack said, "and he gave me this. It's a 'CASE tool.' It's magic." He opened the cardboard box and showed his mother the magic beans and the plastic square.

"Beans!" his mother cried. "Oh, Jack, there is no such thing as magic. You stupid boy! We're ruined!" She took the CASE tool and threw it out the window. She sent Jack to bed without any supper.

What happened after Jack traded the cow for a CASE tool? Did the CASE tool grow into a magic beanstalk? Or did Jack just lose his mother's cow?

The biggest risk associated with software tool use is undoubtedly silver-bullet syndrome—the naïve belief that a single tool or technology will by itself dramatically reduce development time. (See Figure 15-3 on the next page.) Switching to a new programming language, trying out a CASE tool, moving to object-oriented programming, adopting Total Quality Management—these have become classic exercises in wishful thinking. The desire to believe in silver bullets on rapid-development projects is especially strong.

*"This CASE tool is magic. It's easily
worth 10 of your cows."*

Figure 15-3. *When dealing with tool vendors, software developers must learn to separate true claims from fairy tales.*

Most of us are software developers because we think there is something inherently exciting about computer software. When we see a new software tool, we can't help but find it mesmerizing. Who cares if it's practical! It's got 3-D scroll bars! And customizable menus! Look! It even emulates Brief and vi and EMACS! New tools are seductive to software developers, and I believe that silver-bullet syndrome is an occupational hazard. We wouldn't be in this business if we weren't prone to believe that software tools could solve our problems.

I hope that Abraham Lincoln was right when he said that you couldn't fool all of the people all of the time, but sometimes our industry seems determined to prove otherwise. Software developers are bombarded with extravagant productivity claims—"Reduce your development time by a factor of 10!" (Or 100!! Or 1000!!!) Capers Jones estimates that there have been false productivity claims in about 75 percent of the marketing materials published by CASE, language, methodology, and software tool vendors in recent years. CASE tool vendors are the worst, followed by information engineering, RAD, 4GLs, and object-oriented methods (Jones 1994). On average, the tools for which silver-bullet claims have been made produce no visible improvement or only marginal improvement. Some people have indeed been fooled.

HARD DATA

Even when software developers succeed in overcoming their natural gullibility and reject silver-bullet claims, their managers goad them on. After reviewing more than 4000 projects, Jones concluded that at least 70 percent of all US software managers naïvely believe that a single factor can produce large productivity and quality gains. What's worse, he noted that organizations that succumb to the silver-bullet syndrome tend never to improve at all; indeed, they often go backwards (Jones 1994). He notes that the silver-bullet syndrome is especially common among lagging-edge organizations.

CLASSIC MISTAKE

Unfortunately the effects of this naïveté are far from benign. Silver-bullet syndrome poses a risk to software schedules in the same way that Laetrile poses a risk to cancer patients: pursuit of false cures diverts attention from other cures or sets of cures that would be more effective. Exaggerated productivity claims have encouraged the adoption of ineffective tools and slowed down and reduced the adoption of other tools that would have been more effective. Because we buy magic beans instead of real ones, we go to bed hungry. The naïve belief that a single tool can dramatically reduce development time leads us to try new tools one at a time rather than to take a more systematic approach. We adopt beneficial tools in serial rather than in parallel. We plan for short-term improvements and neglect long-term planning altogether. In the end, silver-bullet syndrome is a causative factor for canceled projects and cost overruns as well as for excessive development times. The only bright side to this sorry tale is that there's little chance of a giant shouting "Fee Fi Fo Fum" and eating us on toast for breakfast.

Identifying Silver Bullets

You can dismiss any claim of an ability to improve productivity by more than 25 percent per year out of hand as a silver-bullet claim. As time goes by, for each tool that's presented as a silver bullet, people gain real experience with the silver bullet, and eventually the industry learns that it is not a silver bullet after all. The unfortunate side effect is that we sometimes throw out the baby with the bath water, completely discounting a valuable practice just because it didn't live up to early, inflated claims.

Here are some current silver bullets that don't live up to the claims made for them.

4GLs. 4GLs (fourth-generation languages) can be powerful aids to software productivity, but they provide incremental gains, not revolutionary ones. Realistic gains are on a par with those described in Table 15-2 on page 362. As Fred Brooks points out, the last really large gain was obtained when we moved from assembler to 3GLs (third-generation languages) and were able to stop worrying about the hardware details of specific machines (Brooks 1987). Any additional gains from language improvements are bound to be more modest.

CASE tools. The ability of CASE tools to contribute to software development in a major way has been perennially overrated. CASE can be genuinely beneficial in some environments, particularly in database-intensive ones. But in other organizations, CASE tools essentially amount to high-end tools for creating design diagrams. Al Davis put it best:

> CASE tools help a software engineer in the same way a word processor helps an author. A word processor does not make a poor novelist a good one, but it will make every author more efficient and their material more grammatical. A CASE tool does not make a poor engineer a good one, but it will make every engineer more efficient and their products prettier.

Practitioners have started to draw the same conclusion. A survey by Tesch, Klein, and Sobol found that practitioners were generally convinced that CASE tools did not improve design quality (Tesch, Klein, and Sobol 1995).

The bottom line is that CASE can help, and in some situations it can help a lot. But it isn't a silver bullet.

RAD. RAD is an IS-oriented set of practices that are somewhat adaptable to individual circumstances. RAD was defined with some precision when it was introduced in *Rapid Application Development* (Martin 1991) and refers to a combination of JAD sessions, prototyping, SWAT teams, timeboxed deliverables, and CASE tools, all tied together with a fairly well-defined methodology. Because it is a collection of practices rather than a single practice, it can sometimes provide silver-bullet-like gains within its specific areas of applicability. But RAD doesn't apply to any kind of unique software—custom, shrink-wrap, or systems software, for example—which tends to be the most problematic kind. Outside of its origins in database-centered IS systems, RAD has become more of a rallying cry for faster development than a meaningful methodology.

Automatic programming. This is a popular silver bullet that seems to resurface every few years. In a paper titled "Automatic Programming: Myths and Prospects," Charles Rich and Richard Waters argue that automatic programming is most commonly a "cocktail-party myth" (Rich and Waters 1988). According to the cocktail-party myth, end-users will simply tell the computer what kind of program they want, and the computer will generate it for them. The only communication necessary to create a computer program will be the users providing the computer with a precise statement of requirements.

The problem with even this cocktail-party myth is that end users have enough trouble completely and precisely specifying requirements to human software analysts. There is no reason to think that they would be better at specifying them to a computer. Certainly we'll see differences between what is input to the computer today and in the future and in what is called a "program."

But the highest level programming language we can hope for, I think, is one that operates exactly at the level of the person's business or profession—tools as useful as spreadsheets, but tailored to different needs.

Rich and Waters conclude that, "The automatic programming systems of the future will be more like vacuum cleaners than like self-cleaning ovens. With a self-cleaning oven, all you have to do is decide that you want the oven cleaned and push a button. With vacuum cleaners, your productivity is greatly enhanced, but you still have a lot of work to do."

HARD DATA

Object-oriented programming. Object-oriented technologies haven't panned out the way that people had hoped they would. One survey found that object-oriented projects had dropped from a 92-percent success rate in 1991 to a 66-percent success rate two years later. The explanation for the change was that object-oriented projects in 1991 were staffed with "champions" who might have been biased about their results or more highly skilled than average. More recent projects have been staffed with typical developers who are more critical about the strengths and weaknesses of object-oriented practices (Glass 1994b).

CROSS-REFERENCE
For other comments on object-oriented programming, see Chapter 19, "Designing for Change."

Object-oriented programming is delivering major benefits in the area of reusability, but the promised benefits in the areas of naturalness and ease of use have been disproved (Scholtz, et al. 1994). Object-oriented programming integrates many of the best ideas of the last 35 years of software development, but learning to use it well is difficult. It places more of a burden on the developer rather than less, and it should be viewed as an expert's technology. When viewed that way, it is a valuable addition to the developer's toolbox.

Any of the practices in this book, taken individually. None of the individual practices described in this book should be taken to be silver-bullet solutions individually. Collectively, over time, they can make dramatic differences in your ability to deliver software quickly.

Biting the Bullet

In the fairy-tale version of *Jack and the Beanstalk*, the magic beans grow into a giant beanstalk, and Jack has a great adventure. But in the software version, when Jack's mother throws the beans out the window, that's the end of the story. The beans don't contain any magic, and Jack has just wasted his mother's cow.

Software people buy magic beans whenever they believe claims that their best judgment tells them are impossible. Vendors continue to promise that they have beans that will produce huge beanstalks and allow the purchasers to scale to impossible heights of productivity. Developers and managers continue to spend millions of dollars based on those claims. The $64 question for our industry is, "How many times are we going to buy the same magic beans?"

It's human nature to look for an easy way out, and it's entirely rational to look for the cheapest, fastest, easiest solution. But it's hard to believe that trained professionals would continue to act against their best judgment for 30 years, which is what we as an industry have done.

Software development is a tough, time-consuming business. For 30 years we've been told that the magic that will enable us to slay giant schedules and budgets is just around the corner. For 30 years it hasn't come. I say, enough is enough. There is no magic. There is no point in waiting for it. The more we wait, the more we deprive ourselves of valuable, incrementally better solutions to many of our problems. There aren't any *easy* solutions, but there are *easier* solutions, which can provide modest improvements individually and dramatic improvements collectively.

This whole book, in a sense, is an entreaty to stop buying magic beans and looking for silver bullets. We as an industry need to grit our teeth, bite the bullet, and do the hard work necessary to achieve real productivity gains.

Case Study 15-2. Effective Tool Use

To her surprise, Angela suddenly found herself in charge of the new tools group in her company. She had complained that no one had read her postmortem on Blaze-O-Matic version 1. Another group in the company had had a similar experience with Blaze-O-Matic after her group did, which meant that the company had made the same costly mistake twice. A few weeks after she complained, someone had asked her if she would head the new group.

Months went by, and one day Mike dropped in to ask if she'd heard anything about Gung-HO-OO, a new user-interface library that was supposed to be better than Blaze-O-Matic.

"Sure," she said. "There's one group in the company that's already completed a project with it, and another group that's using it now and is almost finished with their project. I've got a copy of the first group's postmortem right here, which you can have. A guy named Kip is the contact person for the project that's using Gung-HO-OO now. Here's his email address."

Mike thanked her, and went off to read the postmortem. It sounded from the report like Gung-HO-OO was a stable package, but that it had a weak statistics library. The group that wrote the postmortem hadn't cared about that, but they'd flagged it as a potential problem for other groups. That was a problem for Mike's project, which needed to do some number crunching. He got in touch with Kip and found that his group was also doing some statistics work. They had spent about a month trying tools from different vendors

(continued)

Case Study 15-2. Effective Tool Use, *continued*

and had identified another package called Tally-HO-OO, which worked well with Gung-HO-OO. Mike recommended to his group that they use the combination of Gung-HO-OO and Tally-HO-OO, and they agreed.

Mike's group proceeded to develop their program with the two packages, and they encountered few problems, finishing in record time.

At Angela's suggestion, they had also decided to use a new graphics library that no one else in the company had used yet. She had conducted a preliminary analysis, but she cautioned them to beware of weaknesses that could only be detected through use on a real project.

At the end of the project, Mike's group concluded that the graphics library was only so-so. The library supported about half of the graphs that they needed to draw, but they had to hand-code the other half. They felt that if they had known all along how much they would be hand-coding, they could have created a better design for the graphs they had hand-coded and built the other graphs without much more work. They commented to that effect in the project postmortem and sent a copy to Angela. She filed it for future projects' reference.

Further Reading

Brooks, Frederick P., Jr. *The Mythical Man-Month, Anniversary Edition.* Reading, Mass.: Addison-Wesley, 1995. This book contains the essays, "No Silver Bullet—Essence and Accident in Software Engineering" and "No Silver Bullet Refired." The first title is Brooks' famous essay reprinted from the April 1987 issue of *Computer* magazine. Brooks argues that there will not be, and more important, that there *cannot* be, any single new practice capable of producing an order-of-magnitude reduction in the effort required to build a software system within the 10 year period that started in 1986. "No Silver Bullet Refired" is a reexamination 9 years later of the claims made in the earlier essay.

Glass, Robert L. "What Are the Realities of Software Productivity/Quality Improvements," *Software Practitioner*, November 1995, 1, 4–9. This article surveys the evaluative research that's been done on many of the silver-bullet practices and concludes that in nearly all cases there is little research to support either productivity or quality claims.

Jones, Capers. *Assessment and Control of Software Risks.* Englewood Cliffs, N.J.: Yourdon Press, 1994. This book contains a detailed discussion of the risks associated with tool acquisition ("poor technology investments"), silver-bullet syndrome, and related topics such as short-range improvement planning.

Jones, Capers. "Why Is Technology Transfer So Hard?" *IEEE Computer*, June 1995, 86–87. This is a thoughtful inquiry into why it takes as long as it does to deploy new tools and practices in an organization.

O'Brien, Larry. "The Ten Commandments of Tool Selection," *Software Development*, November 1995, 38–43. This is a pithy summary of guidelines for selecting tools successfully.

16

Project Recovery

Contents

16.1 General Recovery Options

16.2 Recovery Plan

Related Topics

Rapid-development strategy: Chapter 2

Some projects discover their need for rapid development long after they are underway, usually at some point after the project has been determined to be late. The project might have missed an early deadline. It might have missed its final delivery date. No matter. The project is in trouble and needs to be rescued.

In this chapter, when I refer to a project that's in trouble, I'm not talking about a project that's slipped off its schedule a bit. I'm talking about a project that's crying for help and about to go under for the third time. Such projects have the following characteristics:

- No one has any idea when the project will finish, and most people have given up trying to guess.

- The product is laden with defects.

- Team members are working excessive numbers of hours—60 hours per week or more of involuntary or peer-pressure-induced overtime.

- Management has lost its ability to control progress or even to ascertain the project's status with any accuracy.

- The customer has lost confidence that the development group will ever deliver the promised software.

- The team is defensive about its progress. They feel threatened if anyone outside the team suggests that the project might be in trouble.

- Relations between developers, marketers, managers, quality assurance, and customers are strained.

- The project is on the verge of being canceled; customers and managers are actively considering that option.

- The morale of the development team has hit rock bottom. The fun has gone out of the project, and the team members are grim.

To save a project that's in this much trouble, minor adjustments won't work. You need to take strong corrective action. This chapter describes a strong rescue plan.

Case Study 16-1. An Unsuccessful Project Recovery

Carl's inventory-control system project, ICS 2.0, was racing toward the finish line. His team had been working on the system for a little more than 4 months, and now the deadline was just 3 weeks away. He called the team meeting to order. "According to the schedule, everybody should be checking in the final versions of their code this week. How's that going?"

"Pretty good, but not good enough," Joe responded honestly. "I've run into a few problems, and I'm working as hard as I can, but I don't see any way I can finish in less than 5 weeks."

"That goes double for me," Jennifer said. "I'm making good progress, but this never should have been scheduled as a 5-month project. It's more like a 7-month project. I've got 5 or 6 weeks of work left."

Carl instinctively reached for his Rolaids. "All right. I'm going to think about how to break this news to my boss. Give me the rest of the day to come up with a recovery plan, and I'll let you know the plan."

The next day, Carl laid out his plan. He had talked his boss, Bill, into slipping their schedule 3 weeks. He was going to borrow Kip from another group to help Jennifer and Joe. And he had a line on a top-notch contractor named Keiko to pick up the rest of the slack.

"Are you serious?" Jennifer asked, incredulously. "Haven't you heard of the mythical man-month syndrome? Adding developers at this point will make our project *later*. It'll take a lot of time to get two new people up to speed. It'll take a lot of *my* time."

"I've thought of that, and I want to avoid that problem too," Carl said. "I think we can divide up our project so that you hardly notice the two new developers. I'll train them myself."

"They might be able to help a little," Joe chimed in. "But I honestly need 5 weeks, and I don't see any way to divide up my work so that I can give any of it to anyone else."

"Are you signed up for this project or not?" Carl said. "The project isn't in that much trouble. Just do your best, and let's see what happens. OK?" Jennifer

(continued)

Case Study 16-1. An Unsuccessful Project Recovery, *continued*

and Joe didn't see any point in arguing about it, so they said OK and went back to work.

They worked almost nonstop for the next 3 weeks, but at the end of that time they were barely any closer to the finish line. "How are we doing?" Carl asked.

"About the same," Jennifer reported. "I've still got at least 4 or 5 weeks worth of work left."

"Same here," Joe reported.

"What have you guys been doing?" Carl fumed. "Jennifer, you said you had 5 or 6 weeks of work left, and that was 3 weeks ago. How can you still have 4 or 5 weeks left?"

"Some things took longer than I expected," she said. "Plus, no offense to Kip and Keiko, but getting them up to speed is taking a lot of time. They didn't understand how we handle our source-code files, and Keiko overwrote some of our master source files. Re-creating them took Joe and me several days."

"How could he overwrite your files?" Carl asked. "Aren't you using automated source-code control and making periodic backups?"

Jennifer's patience was wearing thin. She was tired and had poured everything she had into the project. "Listen, we've been going all-out for more than 2 months. We're doing our best. No one's had time to set up automated version control, and we've just had a couple of minor setbacks. Look, I said I'll be done in 4 or 5 weeks, and that's when I'll be done." The meeting broke up, and Carl optimistically told Bill that the team would be done in 4 weeks.

Four weeks later, the team reported making good progress, but they still thought it would be another 3 weeks or so until they were done. A few weeks after that, Jennifer and Joe discovered some design flaws that they couldn't code around, and they had to redesign a major chunk of the system. Each bug fix seemed to give rise to two more defect reports, and the group's estimated completion times started getting further away instead of closer. Carl admitted that he didn't really know when the project would be finished.

Two months later, after three more 3-week schedule slips, Bill canceled the project. He notified the users that they would have to continue using ICS 1.0 or find an off-the-shelf substitute.

16.1 General Recovery Options

Only three fundamental approaches are available to someone rescuing a project:

- Cut the size of the software so that you can build it within the time and effort planned.

- Increase the process productivity by focusing on short-term improvements.

- Face the fact that the software will not be ready on time, slip the schedule, and proceed with damage control, possibly including canceling the project.

Combine these three approaches and a fourth approach emerges:

- Drop a few features, increase productivity as much as you can, and slip the schedule as needed.

This last approach is the option that this chapter describes.

Philosophy

When you're in project-recovery mode, it's easy to focus on the wrong issue: how to finish *quickly,* how to *catch up?* This is rarely the real problem. For projects that are in this much trouble, the primary problem is usually how to finish *at all.*

There are lots of directions to go with a recovery plan; the plan in this chapter focuses on regaining project control. "Control" can have a negative connotation, especially to independent-minded developers, but I don't think it's possible to rescue a project without concentrating on it. In my experience, as well as the experiences captured in Software Engineering Institute audits and other published and anecdotal reports, the most common reason that projects get into trouble in the first place is that they have not been adequately controlled. A desire for all-out development speed leads projects to take unwise shortcuts, and they inadvertently sacrifice real development speed in the bargain. In the end, there is so little control that neither developers nor managers even know how far off track their projects are.

It's difficult to take back control that you've given away, so the moment that you and your team are forced to confront the reality that recovery is needed represents a singular leadership opportunity. It gives you a chance to redefine your project in fundamental ways, which you can't do if your project is in only a little trouble.

This is a time for decisive action. If you're going to make changes, make big changes and make them all at once. Lots of small corrections are demoralizing to the development team and make it look to your management like you don't know what you're doing. It's easier to recapture control all at once than it is to try to take back a little now and a little more later.

"I'm really glad we found this island. Our situation seemed out of control for a while."

Figure 16-1. *A weak attempt to regain control of a project can lead to a false sense of security.*

16.2 Recovery Plan

A set of guidelines exists that can work to rescue floundering projects; the guidelines operate along the lines of people, process, and product. You can combine the practices in this book in endless ways to create an endless number of recovery plans. This section contains one such plan.

The plan in this chapter is designed to rescue projects that are in deep trouble. Those are the projects that need the most help, so I have described a thorough approach. If your project is not in that much trouble, you can use a less thorough approach. Adapt this project-recovery plan to the specific needs of your project.

CROSS-REFERENCE
For more on the most effective means of introducing new technology, see "When to Deploy" in Section 15.4.

One plan that virtually never works is cutting corners. Far from being a time to cut corners, project recovery is a time to return to basics. The plan described here is consistent with the four pillars of rapid development: avoiding classic mistakes, applying fundamental development practices, managing risks, and looking for ways to apply speed-oriented practices.

First Steps

Before you launch a recovery plan, find out what kind of plan you need.

CROSS-REFERENCE
For details on identifying development priorities, see "Invent Options for Mutual Gain" in Section 9.2.

Assess your situation. Determine how critical the deadline really is and what precisely is needed to meet it. You might find out that there isn't really any hard deadline, and you don't need to worry about project recovery at all. Or you might find that your customers are much more willing to negotiate the feature set to avoid a late project than they were at the beginning.

CROSS-REFERENCE
For details, see Chapter 10, "Customer-Oriented Development," and Chapter 37, "Theory-W Management."

Apply Theory-W analysis. What do you and your team need to succeed? What do your customers need? What do you need to do to salvage the customer relationship? Don't focus on the past. Focus on the present. If you can't find a way to make winners out of everyone by their own standards, scuttle the project.

Prepare yourself to fix the project. If your project is in recovery mode and not merely a little behind, your project is broken. Realize that your project is broken. Realize that you can't fix it by doing the same things you've been doing. Mentally prepare yourself to make significant changes. Prepare both your team and your management for the reality that significant changes will be needed if they want to rescue the project. If people aren't willing to make significant changes, you've already lost the battle. Consider canceling the project.

Ask your team what needs to be done. Ask everyone on your team to contribute at least five practical ideas about how to rescue the project. Evaluate the ideas, then implement as many of them as you can.

Be realistic. If you're in project-recovery mode, you're probably wearing a string of broken schedule promises around your neck. They drag you down as much as the albatross around the neck of the Ancient Mariner dragged him down. If you're in recovery mode, your team desperately needs a strong dose of clear-headed, realistic project leadership. When you start your project recovery, admit that you don't know how long it will take to finish. Explain your plan for getting the project back on track, and then give a date by which you can commit to a new deadline. Don't commit to a new deadline until you have good reasons to think you can meet it.

People

People are the most important point of leverage in rapid development, and you need to put that room of your rapid-development house in order before you proceed to the areas of process and product.

CROSS-REFERENCE
For details on motivation, see
Chapter 11, "Motivation."

FURTHER READING
For more on the team
dynamics of sacrificing
sacred cows, see rule #48 in
Software Project Dynamics
(McCarthy 1995).

CROSS-REFERENCE
For details on factors that
hurt morale, see Section
11.4, "Morale Killers."

CROSS-REFERENCE
For details, see "Problem
personnel" in Section 12.4.

Do whatever is needed to restore the group's morale. During project recovery, morale plays a critical role in your team's productivity. Upper managers will want to know how to motivate your group more. This is a false question during project recovery. If your group has been working hard, the question is not how to motivate them to the utmost, but how to restore their morale so that they will be motivated at all.

One of the best ways to restore morale is to take a symbolic action that shows you're behind the developers, and one of the best ways to do that is to sacrifice one of your organization's sacred cows. That shows the developers that the company is behind them and illustrates the importance of the project. Your actions say, "We are committed to releasing this product, and we will do whatever it takes to make that happen." Sacred cows vary among different organizations, but as long as you're breaking precedent, the developers will get the message. Let them come to work later than the rest of the organization. Let them go home early. Suspend the dress code. Move them off-site. Buy them the new large-screen monitors they've wanted. Bring in catered meals. In short, make them feel important. To your project, they are.

One of the most sacred of sacred cows to a project that's behind schedule is the disallowance of time off. If you've been in 3-weeks-until-product-release mode for several months, not only will time off be appreciated by the developers, it will be necessary to keep your team healthy and productive. A whole weekend off can seem like a lifetime to a developer who has been working with no end in sight.

Be sure that you're providing for the team's hygiene factors. Remove excessive schedule pressure, poor working conditions, management manipulation, and other morale killers.

Clean up major personnel problems. The most common complaint about team leaders is that they don't address problems caused by troublesome team members. If you think you have a problem person, face up to that fact and eliminate the problem. Replace uncooperative team members even if they're key contributors. They cost more in team morale than they contribute technically. You're regrouping anyway, so this is a good time to cut your losses.

Clean up major leadership problems. The leader who has brought the project to the brink of disaster might not have enough credibility left to make the changes needed to lead the project to success. In some cases, the ineffective leader is the technical lead; in other cases, it's the project manager. If you're in a position to do so, consider shaking up the project leadership. Replacing the leader is one option, but if you're the technical lead, you probably can't fire an ineffective manager. If you're the manager, firing a technical lead isn't always the best course of action anyway. Fortunately, several options that are more subtle and often more effective than "you're fired!" are available.

- Change the manager's boss. Sometimes a manager needs different leadership.

- Move the manager into a participatory role. Sometimes a technically-oriented manager can make a technical contribution that will help the project succeed more than his or her leadership contribution can.

- Provide the manager with an assistant. Depending on what's needed, the assistant either can focus on technical details, freeing up the manager to concentrate on big-picture issues, or can handle administrative issues, freeing up the manager to focus on technical matters. In the extreme case, sometimes, the "assistant" can take over nearly all of the manager's responsibilities, leaving the manager in place to handle administrative duties and reports to upper management.

These points focus on management changes, but they apply just as well to changes in the project's technical leadership.

CLASSIC MISTAKE

Add people carefully, if at all. Remember Brooks's law that adding people to a late project is like pouring gasoline on a fire (Brooks 1975). Don't add people to a late project willy-nilly.

But remember the whole law. If you can partition your project's work in such a way that an additional person can contribute without interacting with the other people on the project, it's OK to add a person. Think about whether it makes sense to add someone who will spend 8 hours doing what an existing developer could do in 1 hour. If your project is that desperate, go ahead and add someone. But stick to the plan. Some people can't abide watching another person spend 8 hours on a 1-hour job regardless of their original intentions. Know what kind of person you are. If you think you might err, err on the side of not adding anyone.

Focus people's time. When you're in project-recovery mode, you need to make the best possible use of the people who are already familiar with the project. Consider taking the money you would have spent adding people and use it instead to focus the efforts of your existing people. You'll come out ahead.

You can focus existing people in a variety of ways. Give them private offices. Move them off-site. Be sure that they are not distracted by other projects within your organization, so relieve them of tech-support duty, maintenance of other systems, proposal work, and all of the other responsibilities that eat into a developer's time. The point is not to hold their noses to the grindstone, but to relieve them of all nonessential tasks.

If you must hire additional people, consider not hiring developers. Hire administrative people who can take care of clerical work and help your developers minimize personal downtime (for example, laundry, shopping, bill paying, yard work, and so on).

CROSS-REFERENCE
Allowing different levels of commitment is different at the beginning of a project. For details, see Chapter 34, "Signing Up."

Allow team members to be different. Some people will rise to the challenge of project recovery and become heroes. Others will be too burned out and will refuse to give their all. That's fine. Some people want to be heroes, and other people don't. In the late stages of a project, you have room for quiet, steady contributors who don't rise to heroic heights but who know their way around the product. What you don't have room for are loud naysayers who chide their heroic teammates for being heroic. Morale during project recovery is fragile, and you can't tolerate people who bring the rest of the team down.

CROSS-REFERENCE
For more on seeing that developers pace themselves, see Section 43.1, "Using Voluntary Overtime."

See that developers pace themselves. Runners run at different speeds depending on the distance to the finish line. Runners run faster toward a nearby finish line than they do toward a finish line that's miles away. The best runners learn to pace themselves.

Allow your team to break the vicious circle of schedule pressure leading to stress leading to more defects leading to more work leading back to more schedule pressure. Ease the schedule pressure, give the developers time to focus on quality, and the schedule will follow.

Process

Although you'll find your greatest leverage in the area of people, you must also clean up your process if you want to rescue a project that's in trouble.

CROSS-REFERENCE
For a list of many more classic mistakes, see Section 3.3, "Classic Mistakes Enumerated."

Identify and fix classic mistakes. Survey your project to see whether you're falling victim to any of the classic mistakes. Here are the most important questions to ask:

- Is the product definition still changing?
- Is your project suffering from an inadequate design?
- Are there too few management controls in place to accurately track the project's status?
- Have you shortchanged quality in the rush to meet your deadline?
- Do you have a realistic deadline? (If you've slipped your schedule two or more times already, you probably don't.)
- Have people been working so hard that you risk losing them at the end of the project or earlier? (If you've already lost people, they're working too hard.)
- Have you lost time by using new, unproved technology?

- Is a problem developer dragging the rest of the group down?
- Is team morale high enough to finish the project?
- Do you have accountability leaks? People or groups who might mean well but who have not been accountable for the results of their work?

Fix the parts of your development processes that are obviously broken. When a project is in trouble, everyone usually knows that a few parts of the process are broken. This is where back-to-basics really comes into play— the broken parts are often broken because the project has consciously or unconsciously been ignoring the software fundamentals.

If the team is tripping over itself because you haven't set up version control, set up version control. If you're losing track of the defects being reported, set up a defect tracking system. If end-users or the customer have been adding changes uncontrollably, set up a change-control board. If the team hasn't been able to concentrate because of a steady stream of interruptions, move them off-site, have the facilities group physically wall-off their area, or put up your own floor-to-ceiling boundary with empty computer boxes. If people haven't been getting the timely decisions they need, set up a war room: meet at 5:00 p.m. every day and promise that anybody who needs a decision will get one.

CROSS-REFERENCE
For details, see Chapter 27, "Miniature Milestones."

Create detailed miniature milestones. In rescuing a drowning project, it is absolutely essential that you set up a tracking mechanism that allows you to monitor progress accurately. This is your key to controlling the rest of the project. If the project is in trouble, you have all the justification you need to set up miniature milestones.

Miniature milestones allow you to know on a day-by-day basis whether your project is on schedule. The milestones should be miniature, binary, and exhaustive. They're *miniature* because each of them can be completed in one or two days, no longer. They're *binary* because either they're done or they're not—they're not "90 percent done." They're *exhaustive* because when you check off the last milestone, you're done with the project. If you have tasks that aren't on the milestone schedule, add them to the schedule. No work is done "off schedule."

Setting and meeting even trivial milestones provides a boost to morale. It shows that you can make progress and that there's a possibility of regaining control.

One of the biggest problems with setting up mini milestones at the beginning of a project is that you don't know enough to identify all the work in detail. In project-recovery mode, the situation is different. At that late stage in the project, developers have learned enough about the product to be able to say in detail what needs to be done. Thus mini milestones are particularly appropriate for use in project recovery.

Set up a schedule linked to milestone completion. Plan completion dates for each mini milestone. Don't plan on massive overtime: that hasn't worked so far, and it won't work going forward. If you plan massive overtime into your schedule, developers can't catch up by working more overtime when they get behind. Set the schedule so that if developers get behind on their miniature milestones, they can catch up by working overtime the same day. That allows them to stay on schedule on a day-by-day basis. If you stay on schedule day by day, you stay on schedule week by week and month by month, and that's the only way it's possible to stay on schedule for a whole project.

Track schedule progress meticulously. If you don't track progress after you set up the mini milestones, the schedule-creation process will have been just an exercise in wasting time. Check with developers daily to assess their progress against the mini milestones. Be sure that when a milestone is marked "done" it is truly, 100 percent done. Ask the developer, "If I take the source code for this module that's 'done' and lock it in a vault for the rest of the project, can we ship it? Do you still have some tweaking or polishing to do, or is it 100 percent done?" If the developer says, "It's 99 percent done," then it's *not* done, and the milestone has not been met.

Do not allow developers to get off track on their mini-milestone schedules. The easiest way to get off track is to miss one milestone and then to stop keeping track. A 1-day slip turns into a 2-day slip, which turns into 3 days, and then into a week or more. Soon there is no correspondence between the developer's work and the milestone schedule. Once a schedule has been calibrated, do not take schedule slips lightly. If a single developer falls behind on a single milestone, expect him or her to work overtime that day to catch up. (If a developer meets a single milestone early, it's OK to allow him or her to go home early that day.) Daily milestones must be met consistently or the schedule must be recalibrated so that they can be met consistently.

Record the reasons for missed milestones. Having a record of the reasons that each milestone was missed can help to detect the underlying causes. A record might point to an individual developer's need for training or highlight organizational dynamics that make it hard for any developers to make good on their estimates. It can help to distinguish between estimate-related problems and other schedule-related problems.

Recalibrate after a short time—one or two weeks. If a developer consistently misses milestones and falls more than ½ day behind, it's time to recalibrate that developer's schedule. Recalibrate by increasing the current schedule by the percentage of the slip so far. If the developer has needed 7 days to do 4 days' work, multiply the rest of the work by $7/4$. Don't play games by thinking that you'll make up the lost time later. If you're in project-recovery mode, that game has already been lost.

Never trade a bad
date for an equally
bad date. That's a
bad deal. You're just
hemorrhaging
credibility if you
do that.

Jim McCarthy

Don't commit to a new schedule until you can create a meaningful one. Do not give a new schedule to upper management until after you have created a mini-milestone schedule, worked to it for at least a week or two, recalibrated, and worked a week or two more to check your recalibration. Giving a new schedule to management any other way is tantamount to replacing one bad schedule with a different but equally bad schedule. If you follow these steps first, you will have a more solid basis for your future schedule commitments.

Manage risks painstakingly. Focus on risk management using the guidelines spelled out in Chapter 5, "Risk Management." Create a top-10 risks list, and hold daily risk-monitoring meetings. You can expand the 5:00 p.m. war-room meetings to review risks and address new issues that have arisen as well as to provide timely decisions.

Product

It's often not possible to recover a project until you rein in the product's feature set.

CROSS-REFERENCE
For details on change control,
see Section 14.2, "Mid-Project:
Feature-Creep Control."

Stabilize the requirements. If requirements have been changing throughout the project, you don't need to look any further for the source of your problems. You must stabilize requirements before you can bring your project to a successful conclusion. A system with significantly changing requirements cannot be developed quickly and often cannot be developed at all.

It is not uncommon to need to do a nearly complete requirements specification at this stage. Some products change so much during their development that, by the time the crisis hits, no one knows for sure what features the product is supposed to contain. Developers and testers are working on features that might or might not need to be in the product.

Some projects will resist the work involved with formalizing a statement of requirements this late in the project, but keep in mind that *the other approach is the one that's causing all the problems.* You have to do something different, and you have to know what your feature set is before you can finish the product, before you can even be sure that the development team is working on the product you want.

If the project has been running for some time, formalizing requirements will be a painful step because it will involve eliminating some people's pet features. That's too bad, but it should have been done early on, and it has to be done before you can complete the project. If you can't get the parties involved to commit to a set of requirements when the project is hanging on by its fingernails in recovery mode, then you might as well give up. You're fighting a battle you can't win.

After you do get a set of requirements, set the bar for accepting changes very high. Require a full day even to consider a change. Require more than a day as the minimum time needed to implement a change. (This is for feature changes, not defect corrections.)

CROSS-REFERENCE
For more on trimming requirements, see "Requirements Scrubbing" in Section 14.1.

Trim the feature set. Recovery mode presents an opportunity to reduce the requirements to the minimal acceptable set. Cut low-priority features ruthlessly. You don't need to fix everything, and you don't need to implement every feature. Prioritize. Remember, the real problem at this stage is not developing the product in the shortest possible time or creating the best possible product: it's completing the product at all. Worry about low-priority features on the next version.

People should be ready and willing to define a minimal feature set at this point. If they aren't willing to sacrifice pet features when the project is in recovery mode, they probably won't ever be willing to.

Assess your political position. If people aren't willing to freeze requirements or fall back to minimal requirements, this is a good time to take a step back and look at what's really happening on your project. Think about why the other parties are still not focused on the product. What are they focused on? What is more important to them than the product? Are they focused on a power struggle? Are they focused on making you or your boss look bad? As ugly as organizational politics can be, they do exist, and an unwillingness to make crucial compromises when there's no other choice is a telltale sign. If you're caught in the middle of a political skirmish rather than a product development, the project-recovery plan in this chapter won't be of much help, and you should choose your actions accordingly.

CROSS-REFERENCE
For details, see "Error-prone modules" in Section 4.3.

Take out the garbage. Find out if there are any parts of the product that everyone knows are extremely low quality. When you've found a lot of defects in a particular piece of code, it's tempting to think that you've found the last one. But buggy modules tend to produce an amazing, continuing stream of defects. Error-prone modules are responsible for a disproportionate amount of the work on a project, and it is better to throw them out and start over than to continue working with them.

Throw them out. Go through a design cycle. Review the design. Implement the design. Review the implementation. This will seem like work that you can't afford when you're in recovery mode, but what will really kill you in recovery mode is getting nickeled-and-dimed to death by an uncontrollable number of defects. Systematic redesign and implementation reduces your risk.

Reduce the number of defects, and keep them reduced. Projects that are in schedule trouble often start to focus on schedule and expedient shortcuts to the exclusion of quality. Those compromises invariably return to haunt the developers before the product is released. If you've been in 3-weeks-to-ship mode for awhile, you've almost certainly been making quality compromises and shortcuts during that time that will make your project take longer rather than shorter.

Start using an "open-defects" graph, and update it daily. Figure 16-2 is an example.

CROSS-REFERENCE
For details on why this graph will reduce defects, see Chapter 26, "Measurement."

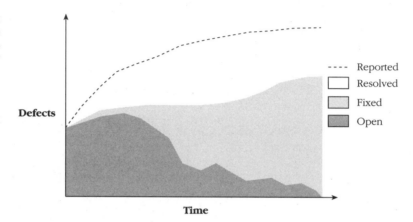

Figure 16-2. *Example of an "open defects" graph. Publishing this graph emphasizes that reducing defects is a high priority and helps to gain control on projects with quality problems.*

The goal of the open-defects graph is to emphasize how many open defects there are and to highlight the priority of reducing them. Bring the number of open defects down to a manageable level, and keep it there. Start using design and code reviews to maintain a consistent level of low defects. Development time is wasted working and reworking low-quality software. Focusing on quality is one way to reduce development time, and doing so is essential to project recovery.

CROSS-REFERENCE
For details, see Chapter 18, "Daily Build and Smoke Test."

Get to a known good state, and build on that. Plot out the shortest possible course from wherever your product is now to a state at which you can build and test some subset of it. When you get the product to that point, use daily builds to keep the product in a buildable, testable state every day. Add code to the build, and make sure that the code you add doesn't break the build. Make maintaining the build a top priority. Some projects have developers wear beepers and require them to fix the build day or night if they are responsible for breaking it.

Timing

Surprisingly, the best time to launch a project-recovery plan might not be the first moment you notice your project is in trouble. You need to be sure that your management and the development team are ready to hear the message and ready to take the steps needed to truly recover the project. This is something that you need to do right the first time.

You have to walk a line between two considerations. If you launch your recovery plan too early, people won't yet believe that there's a need for it. It is not in your best interest to cry "Wolf!" before other people can see that the wolf is there. If you launch it too late, it will likely follow on the heels of a series of small corrections or mini-recovery attempts that didn't completely work, and you will have undermined your credibility in leading a more effective, larger-scale recovery effort. You will have cried "Wolf!" too many times.

I don't recommend letting your project run into the weeds merely so that you can do a better job of rescuing it. However, if your project has already run into the weeds, I do recommend that you time the presentation of your recovery plan so that everyone else on the project will be receptive enough for it to succeed.

Case Study 16-2. A Successful Project Recovery

End-user reaction to canceling the new inventory-tracking system had been fierce, and a few weeks after Bill canceled the project, he reconsidered. He concluded that they should finish it after all. By that time, Keiko, the contractor, had moved on to a different project. Kip had been reassigned to a short-term project but could be brought back to the team. Jennifer and Joe were just returning from vacation, and Bill thought they might be ready to try again. He called Carl, who had been team lead on the canceled project, into his office. Carl saw a stranger in his boss's office.

"Carl, I've decided to resuscitate ICS 2.0, and I'm going to give you another chance. Meet Charles. He's a project-recovery expert, and I've hired him to help you bring this sucker in. He's already told me that you can't come up with a new schedule right away. He said it might take a few weeks before we know exactly how long it will take to fix the project. I really got my butt kicked for canceling this thing, so now we've got to finish it no matter what. Let me know as soon as you have a new schedule."

Carl was glad to get another chance at rescuing the project. He had thought of some things he could do better, and he knew that Jennifer and Joe had been depressed about the project being canceled. He and Charles left Bill's office together.

(continued)

Case Study 16-2. A Successful Project Recovery, *continued*

Charles started talking. "From what I've heard, I think the main task here is just to finish the project. I'd like to identify each group's win conditions, and then manage the rest of the project so that those are met. Based on the end-users I've talked to, getting a replacement for the old system by the end of the year would be a win as long as it fixes a few long-standing problems. I've got a list of the major problems, and I got the end-users to agree that the rest could wait. Of course they'd like the next release sooner, but they really just want a guarantee that they'll get it eventually.

"Bill's win condition is the same. He wants to follow through with the user group. What do you need to make this a win for you?"

Carl thought a minute. "I need to show that I can rescue this project and meet everybody else's win conditions. I've had a rest, and I can work as hard as I need to." Later that day, Carl talked to Jennifer, Joe, and Kip. Their win conditions were that they wanted to finish the job they'd started, and they wanted to lead normal lives outside work while they were doing that.

"I can't sacrifice the rest of my life to this project anymore," Jennifer said. "Even after 3 weeks of vacation I'm too burned out to do that. It would be nice to finish this project, but I'd rather work on a different project and never finish this one than get that burned out again." Kip said he was willing to work hard, but Joe said he felt the same as Jennifer.

Charles asked the team what they thought needed to be done to save the project, and Jennifer and Joe were in complete agreement. "We were in such a hurry last time that we took all kinds of low-quality shortcuts. We need to go back and clean up some of the product. We shouldn't add any new people this time, either." Carl agreed. He didn't want to make the same mistake twice.

Charles stepped in. "What I'd like you all to do is create a detailed list of every task that needs to be done to release the product, and I really mean everything. Rewriting bad modules, fixing the build script, setting up automated version control, documenting old code, duplicating diskettes, talking to end-users on the phone, everything. And I want you to estimate how long each task will take. If you have any tasks that take more than 2 days, I want you to break them up into smaller tasks that take less time. Then we're going to sit down and plan out the rest of the project.

"I want you to know that your estimates aren't commitments. They're just estimates, and nobody outside of this room will know about them until we're confident that they're right. I know I'm asking for a lot of detail, and it will take time to do all those estimates. I wouldn't be surprised if it takes you at least a day to come up with them. But this project is broken, and this is what we need to do to get it back on track."

The developers spent the next 2 days coming up with incredibly detailed task lists. Joe was surprised at some of his estimates. He took tasks that he had

(continued)

Case Study 16-2. A Successful Project Recovery, *continued*

originally estimated would take 3 days, broke them down into more detail, and found that the sum of the parts for a few of them was more like 5 or 6 days. Charles said he wasn't surprised. The whole group put together a schedule based on the detailed task lists, and Charles told Bill that they would have a revised completion date in about 15 days.

Carl and Charles checked the team's progress every day for the next week. Kip completed his tasks consistently on time. Jennifer found that one day she finished all of her work by mid afternoon, and one day she had to work until 9:00 in the evening. She was getting the work done, but by the end of the week she had logged almost 50 hours. She told Carl that that was too much. Joe had had trouble completing his tasks on time, and by the end of the week he had completed only half of what he had planned.

The team met to look over their progress. Charles insisted that they recalibrate Joe's schedule by multiplying all of his estimates by 2.0. Even though Jennifer was meeting her deadlines, he reminded them that Jennifer's win condition included leading a normal life outside of work, and they recalibrated her schedule by multiplying her estimates by 1.25. The recalibration made everyone's schedules come out uneven, so they reshuffled the work so that everybody on the team had about the same amount of work.

Carl was surprised at the result. If their estimates were right, they would finish the project in 10 weeks, which wasn't nearly as bad as he had feared. "Should I give Bill the good news?" he asked Charles.

"No, we'll work another week to the recalibrated schedule, and if we're hitting the mini milestones consistently, then we'll tell Bill. But we will let Bill know that we'll have a revised schedule for him a week from Monday."

The next week went surprisingly smoothly. Carl continued to check with each developer every day to be sure that each milestone task was getting done, and each one was. Jennifer stayed late one night, but she told Carl that was mainly because she had goofed off part of the day, not because she had too much work to do. By the end of the week, everybody was on schedule. More important, everybody was happy. Jennifer had originally thought she would be annoyed by the mini milestones' micro management, but it actually felt good to be able to check off a task every day and to tell someone that she was making progress. Morale had improved.

Carl and Charles told Bill that they would be done in 9 weeks. Bill said that was good news and had been worth the wait. For the remainder of the project, Charles and Carl continued to check progress daily. Each person put in a few late nights to keep to their mini-milestone schedules, but by the end of the 9 weeks they were really and truly finished. They delivered the software to their end-users and notified Bill. Everyone considered the project a win.

Further Reading

McCarthy, Jim. *Dynamics of Software Development*. Redmond, Wash.: Microsoft Press, 1995. This is an entertaining set of lessons that McCarthy learned from his experiences working on Microsoft's Visual C++ and other products. McCarthy describes an enthusiastic but essentially grim vision of software development at Microsoft. He presents Microsoft projects as spending nearly all their time doing what this chapter has called "project recovery." If you recognize that that is what McCarthy is writing about and read his book on that level, he has some valuable things to say.

Zachary, Pascal. *Showstopper! The Breakneck Race to Create Windows NT and the Next Generation at Microsoft*. New York: Free Press, 1994. This is a description of the development of Microsoft Windows NT 3.0. According to the author's description, the NT project spent more time in recovery mode than in normal development. Like McCarthy's book, if you read this book as a project-recovery fable, you can gather some valuable lessons. Once you've read the book, you'll be glad that you didn't learn these particular lessons firsthand!

Boddie, John. *Crunch Mode*. New York: Yourdon Press, 1987. This book is not specifically about project recovery, but it is about how to develop software under tight schedules. You can apply a lot of Boddie's approach to a project in recovery mode.

Weinberg, Gerald M. *Quality Software Management, Volume 1: Systems Thinking*. New York: Dorset House, 1992. Pressure is a constant companion during project recovery. Chapters 16 and 17 of this book discuss what Weinberg calls "pressure patterns." He describes what happens to developers and leaders under stress as well as what to do about it.

Thomsett, Rob. "Project Pathology: A Study of Project Failures," *American Programmer*, July 1995, 8–16. Thomsett provides an insightful review of the factors that get projects into trouble in the first place and of early warning signs that they're in trouble.

BEST
PRACTICES

Introduction to Best Practices

This part of the book contains 27 "best practices":

The sample best-practice summary table shown in Figure III-1 is an example of the summary tables that describe each practice's defining characteristics. By reading each of the summaries in Chapters 17–43, you should be able to determine which practices are appropriate for your project or organization.

100

Sample Best-Practice Summary Table

Each best practice has a summary table that describes the practice's defining characteristics. By reading each of the summaries in Chapters 17–43 you should be able to determine which practices are appropriate for your project or organization.

Efficacy

Potential reduction from nominal schedule:	None (≈0%), Fair (0–10%), Good (10–20%), Very Good (20–30%), Excellent (30%+)
Improvement in progress visibility:	None (≈0%), Fair (0–25%), Good (25–50%), Very Good (50–75%), Excellent (75%+)
Effect on schedule risk:	Decreased Risk, No Effect, Increased Risk
Chance of first-time success:	Poor (≈0–20%), Fair (20–40%), Good (40–60%), Very Good (60–80%), Excellent (80–100%)
Chance of long-term success:	Poor (≈0–20%), Fair (20–40%), Good (40–60%), Very Good (60–80%), Excellent (80–100%)

Major Risks

- This section summarizes the major risks that this practice poses *to the rest of the project*. It does not include risks to the success of the practice itself.

Major Interactions and Trade-Offs

- This section summarizes the practice's major interactions with other practices and trade-offs involved in using the practice.

Figure III-1. *A sample best-practice summary table, with explanations of its features.*

The chapters in this part of the book describe best practices in rapid development. These practices represent the state of the art in development speed. Some of them are new. Others have been in use for 20 years or more. Some of them might seem like common sense. (If only common sense were commonly practiced!) Others might not seem like best practices until you read the chapter.

These practices are not intended to be used all at once. Some of them are mutually exclusive. But you will probably find a few that you can use on your current development projects without radically altering your software development approach. Other practices might be so appealing that you'll want to radically alter your development approach to be able to use them.

Organization of Best-Practice Chapters

All the best-practice chapters are similarly organized. Each begins with a table that looks like the example at the beginning of this chapter. The table presents a summary of each practice's efficacy, risks, and interactions and trade-offs. Each summary comment is explained in more detail in the body of the chapter.

The first three entries under "Efficacy" in Figure III-1 describe the three kinds of schedule improvements that are discussed in Section 1.2, "Attaining Rapid Development":

- Potential reduction from nominal schedule
- Improvement in progress visibility
- Effect on schedule risk

The following paragraphs explain these three entries and the rest of the entries in the best-practice summary section.

"Potential reduction from nominal schedule." This entry provides an estimate of the effect that use of the practice will have on a project's schedule. The potential reductions all assume that the practice is executed expertly. Projects that use a practice for the first time will usually make mistakes that will cut into the practice's efficacy.

I've provided this rating on a verbal scale—None, Fair, Good, Very Good, and Excellent—rather than a numeric scale. The sample best-practice table in Figure III-1 shows the approximate correspondence between this verbal scale and percentage reductions. In some cases, the basis for the percentage reduction has been estimated by a third party and is described in the "Bottom Line" section later in the chapter; in others, it is my best estimate of the practice's effectiveness.

You can translate from the verbal scale back to the percentage ranges, but the verbal scale is the best description of the potential reduction. The state of software development does not generally allow someone to make precise statements such as "Prototyping cuts schedules by 24.37 percent." One study might find that prototyping reduced development time by 25 percent; another might find that it reduced it by 45 percent. A third might find no savings at all. The verbal scale reflects the imprecision of the underlying data.

CROSS-REFERENCE
For more on the waterfall
lifecycle model, see
Section 7.1,
"Pure Waterfall."

"Improvement in progress visibility." This rating is also provided on a verbal scale rather than a numeric one. It is difficult to pin down something as amorphous as "improvement in progress visibility," and I have created the best approximation I can think of by defining the improvement as the percent of the project that a practice makes more visible than a traditional waterfall lifecycle model would. The ratings in this category arise from my best estimate. Once again, there is an approximate correspondence between the verbal ratings and the underlying quantifications, but the verbal ratings better convey the inexactness of the data.

"Effect on schedule risk." Some practices, such as evolutionary prototyping, generally decrease development time compared with traditional methods, but they make it more difficult to predict specifically when the project will be finished. A traditional development effort might take an average of 3 months and vary by plus or minus 2 weeks. An evolutionary-prototyping approach to the same project might take an average of 2 months and vary by plus 6 weeks/minus 2 weeks. Such practices are considered to increase schedule risk. This rating—Decreased Risk, No Effect, or Increased Risk—indicates whether a practice improves the ability to meet a specific deadline or doesn't affect it or worsens it.

I have included some practices as best practices specifically because they have a strong positive effect on schedule risk. They might have little or no effect on average schedule lengths, but they will dampen wild schedule fluctuations and help to bring out-of-control schedules under control.

"Chance of first-time success." Some of the practices are more difficult to learn to use than others. You can expect to be immediately successful with some practices; for others you'll probably have to settle for delayed gratification. A few practices (such as Reuse) require a substantial investment in infrastructure before they begin to pay off. Those have virtually no chance of "first-time" success and are rated as low as "Poor" in this category even though they have terrific long-term potential.

CROSS-REFERENCE
For more on CASE tools, see
"CASE tools" in Section 15.5.

"Chance of long-term success." Even when you factor out the learning-curve effect, some practices are simply successful more often than others. This rating describes the chance that a practice will be successful if you stick with it long enough to become proficient at using it. Theoretically, the rating scale in this category goes from Poor to Excellent, but because these chapters describe *best* practices, there aren't actually any practices rated lower than Good. Some practices, such as CASE tools, were specifically not included in this book as best practices because the chance of long-term success has proved to be only Fair or Poor.

A comparison between the rating in this category and the "chance of first-time success" category will give you an indication of the steepness of the learning curve associated with the practice. Some practices, such as the Top-10 Risks List, have the same rating for both first-time and long-term success. Those practices are exceptionally easy to learn to use. Others, such as Designing for Change, have a difference of more than one rating level; such practices are relatively difficult to learn to use.

"Major risks." The word "risk" can be used in a variety of senses including risks to the successful use of the practice itself. Those risks are described in the body of the chapter (in the "Using *Best Practice*" section) but are not described in this table. This entry summarizes the major risks that the use of the practice poses to the rest of the project.

"Major Interactions and Trade-Offs." This entry describes how the practice interacts with other rapid-development and efficient-development practices and what trade-offs are involved in using the practice. Some speed-oriented practices involve virtually no trade-offs, but others require that you spend more money, sacrifice flexibility, or accept more risk in order to shorten the schedule.

Other Sections

In addition to the summary table, the best-practice chapters have roughly the same organization, including the following sections:

- Using *Best Practice*
- Managing the Risks of *Best Practice*
- Side Effects of *Best Practice*
- *Best Practice*'s Interactions with Other Practices
- The Bottom Line on *Best Practice*
- Keys to Success in Using *Best Practice*
- Further Reading

Summary of Best-Practice Candidates

CROSS-REFERENCE
For more on the three kinds of schedule-related practices, see Section 1.2, "Attaining Rapid Development."

Each practice described in a best-practice chapter has been chosen for one of the following reasons:

- Reduction of development schedules
- Reduction of perceived development schedules by making progress more visible
- Reduction of schedule volatility, thus reducing the chance of a runaway project

Some of the best practices are described in Part I of this book, and those best practices are merely summarized in this part of the book.

You might ask, "Why did you ignore Object-Structured FooBar Charts, which happen to be my favorite practice?" That's a fair question and one that I struggled with throughout the creation of this book. A candidate for best-practice status could have been excluded for any of several reasons.

Fundamental development practices. Many best-practice candidates fell into the category of fundamental development practices. One of the challenges in writing this book has been to keep it from turning into a general software-engineering handbook. In order to keep the book to a manageable size, I introduce those practices in Chapter 2, "Software Development Fundamentals" and provide references to other sources of information. A lot of information is available from other sources on the fundamental practices.

In a few cases, you might rightly consider a practice to be a fundamental one, but if it has a profound impact on development speed, I included it as a best-practice chapter anyway.

Best philosophy, but not best practice. Some best-practice candidates seemed to be more like theories or philosophies than practices. The distinction between theory, practice, and philosophy in software development is not clear, and so an approach that I call a "philosophy" you might call a "practice" and vice versa. Regardless of what it's called, if I considered it to be "best," I discussed it in the book somewhere. But if I considered it to be a philosophy, it's in the first or second part of the book. (See Table III-1 for a list of where each best philosophy is discussed.)

Best practice, maybe, but not for development speed. Some best-practice candidates might very well be best practices for their effect on quality or usability, but they could not pass the tests of improving actual development schedules, perceived schedules, or schedule volatility. Those practices were not included in this book.

Insufficient evidence for a practice's efficacy. A few promising practices were not supported by enough evidence to deem them to be best practices. If the development community has not yet had enough experience with a practice to publish a handful of experiments or experience reports about it, I didn't include it. Some of the practices that fell into this category will no doubt someday prove that they have large speed benefits, and I'll include those in a future edition of this book.

In a few instances in which published support by itself was not sufficient to justify treating a practice as a best practice, I had personal experience with the practice that convinced me that it was indeed a best practice. I included those in spite of the lack of published support from other sources.

Questionable evidence for a practice's efficacy. A few best-practice candidates seemed promising, but the only published information I could find was from vendors or other parties who had vested interests in promoting the practices, so I excluded them.

Not a best practice. A few best-practice candidates are highly regarded (even zealously regarded) in some quarters, but that does not make them best practices. In some cases, experience reports indicated that a well-regarded practice typically failed to live up to expectations. In some, a practice is a good practice, but not a best practice. And in some, the practice works fabulously when it works, but it fails too often to be considered a best practice.

In one case (RAD), the candidate practice consisted of a combination of many of the other practices described in this book. That might very well be an effective combination in some circumstances. But because this book advocates selecting rapid-development practices that meet the needs of your specific project, that specific pre-fab combination of practices was not itself considered to be a best practice.

I know that most readers will still wonder about how I categorized specific practices, Object-Structured FooBar Charts or whatever. (I would.) To satisfy that curiosity, Table III-1 summarizes the best-practice candidates and indicates where they are discussed in this book or why they were left out.

The table can also serve as a comprehensive reference to speed-oriented practices for someone planning a rapid-development project.

Table III-1. Summary of Best-Practice Candidates

Best-Practice Candidate	Where Referenced or Reason Not Included
4GLs	Best practice. See Rapid-Development Languages (RDLs).
Analysis, requirements	Fundamental.
Architecture	Fundamental.
Buy vs. build planning	Fundamental.
CASE tools	Insufficient evidence for practice's efficacy. See "CASE tools" in Section 15.5.
Change board	Best practice discussed within another chapter. See "Change Board" in Section 14.2 and summary in Chapter 17.
Cleanroom development	Best practice, maybe, but not for development speed.
Code, readable, high-quality	Fundamental.
Construction practices, effective	Fundamental.

(continued)

Table III-1. Summary of Best-Practice Candidates, *continued*

Best-Practice Candidate	Where Referenced or Reason Not Included
Customer orientation	Best philosophy. See Chapter 10, "Customer-Oriented Development."
Daily build and smoke test	Best practice. See Chapter 18, "Daily Build and Smoke Test."
Design storyboarding	Insufficient information available to consider it to be a best practice.
Design, object-oriented, structured, etc.	Fundamental.
Design-to-schedule lifecycle model	Not a best practice. See Section 7.7, "Design to Schedule."
Design-to-tools lifecycle model	Not a best practice. See Section 7.9, "Design to Tools."
Designing for change	Best practice. See Chapter 19, "Designing for Change."
Education, management	Best practice, maybe, but not for development speed.
Education, technical staff	Best practice, maybe, but not for development speed.
Error-prone modules	Fundamental.
Estimating tools, automated	Fundamental.
Estimation and scheduling, accurate	Best philosophy. See Chapter 8, "Estimation," and Chapter 9, "Scheduling."
Evolutionary-delivery lifecycle model	Best practice. See Chapter 20, "Evolutionary Delivery."
Evolutionary-prototyping lifecycle model	Best practice. See Chapter 21, "Evolutionary Prototyping."
Feature-set control	Best philosophy. See Chapter 14, "Feature-Set Control."
Goal setting	Best practice discussed within another chapter. See "Goal Setting" in Section 11.2 and summary in Chapter 22.
Hiring top talent	Fundamental. See "People" in Section 2.2.
Information engineering	Insufficient evidence for practice's efficacy.
Inspections	Fundamental. Best practice discussed within another chapter. See "Inspections" in Section 4.3 and summary in Chapter 23.
Integration strategies	Fundamental.
Joint Application Development (JAD)	Best practice. See Chapter 24, "Joint Application Development (JAD)."
Joint Requirements Planning (JRP)	Not a best practice. See "JAD Planning" in Section 24.1.

(continued)

Table III-1. Summary of Best-Practice Candidates, *continued*

Best-Practice Candidate	Where Referenced or Reason Not Included
Leadership	Fundamental.
Lifecycle model selection	Best practice discussed within another chapter. See Chapter 7, "Lifecycle Planning," and summary in Chapter 25.
Measurement	Best practice. See Chapter 26, "Measurement."
Meetings, efficient	Fundamental.
Milestones, major	Not a best practice. See "Major Milestones" sidebar on page 484.
Milestones, miniature	Best practice. See Chapter 27, "Miniature Milestones."
Minimal specification	Not a best practice. See "Minimal Specification" in Section 14.1.
Motivation	Best philosophy. See Chapter 11, "Motivation."
Object technology	Fundamental. See Section 4.2, "Technical Fundamentals."
Outsourcing	Best practice. See Chapter 28, "Outsourcing."
Overtime, excessive	Not a best practice. See Section 43.1, "Using Voluntary Overtime."
Overtime, voluntary	Best practice. See Chapter 43, "Voluntary Overtime."
Parallel development	Fundamental.
Planning tools, automated	Fundamental.
Planning, effective	Fundamental.
Principled negotiation	Best practice discussed within another chapter. See Section 9.2, "Beating Schedule Pressure," and summary in Chapter 29.
Process improvement	Best philosophy. See "Process" in Section 2.2 and Chapter 26, "Measurement."
Productivity environments	Best practice. See Chapter 30, "Productivity Environments."
Productivity tools	Best philosophy. See Chapter 15, "Productivity Tools."
Quality assurance	Fundamental.
Rapid Application Development (RAD)	Combination of best practices—not a best practice itself.
Rapid-development languages (RDLs)	Best practice. See Chapter 31, "Rapid-Development Languages (RDLs)."
Requirements analysis	Fundamental.

(continued)

Table III-1. Summary of Best-Practice Candidates, *continued*

Best-Practice Candidate	Where Referenced or Reason Not Included
Requirements scrubbing	Best practice discussed within another chapter. See "Requirements Scrubbing" in Section 14.1 and summary in Chapter 32.
Reuse	Best practice. See Chapter 33, "Reuse."
Reviews, walk-throughs, and code reading	Fundamental.
Risk management	Best philosophy. See Chapter 5, "Risk Management."
Scheduling tools, automated	Fundamental.
SEI CMM Levels	Best philosophy. See "Process" in Section 2.2 and "Further Reading" in Chapter 2.
Signing up	Best practice. See Chapter 34, "Signing Up."
Software configuration management (SCM)	Fundamental.
Software engineering process group (SEPG)	Best practice. Considerations involved are very similar to those in setting up a tools group. See "Tools Group" in Section 15.3 and summary in Chapter 40.
Source code control	Fundamental.
Spiral lifecycle model	Best practice discussed within another chapter. See Section 7.3, "Spiral," and summary in Chapter 35.
Staff specialization	Best practice. See Chapter 13, "Team Structure."
Staffing levels (how much and when to add)	Fundamental.
Staged-delivery lifecycle model	Best practice. See Chapter 36, "Staged Delivery."
Structured programming	Fundamental.
Team structure	Best philosophy. See Chapter 13, "Team Structure."
Teamwork	Best philosophy. See Chapter 12, "Teamwork."
Testing	Fundamental.
Theory-W management	Best practice. See Chapter 37, "Theory-W Management."
Throwaway prototyping	Best practice. See Chapter 38, "Throwaway Prototyping."
Timebox development	Best practice. See Chapter 39, "Timebox Development."

(continued)

Table III-1. Summary of Best-Practice Candidates, *continued*

Best-Practice Candidate	Where Referenced or Reason Not Included
Tools group	Best practice discussed within another chapter. See "Tools Group" in Section 15.3 and summary in Chapter 40.
Top-10 risks list	Best practice discussed within another chapter. See "Top-10 Risks List" in Section 5.5 and summary in Chapter 41.
Tracking	Fundamental.
User-interface prototyping	Best practice. See Chapter 42, "User-Interface Prototyping."
Win-win negotiating	See Chapter 29, "Principled Negotiation."

Summary of Best-Practice Evaluations

Table III-2 provides a side-by-side comparison of the best practices discussed in Chapters 17–43.

Table III-2. Summary of Best-Practice Evaluations

Best-Practice Name	Potential Reduction From Nominal Schedule	Improvement in Progress Visibility	Effect on Schedule Risk	Chance of First-Time Success	Chance of Long-Term Success
Change Board	Fair	Fair	Decreased	Very Good	Excellent
Daily Build and Smoke Test	Good	Good	Decreased	Very Good	Excellent
Designing for Change	Fair	None	Decreased	Good	Excellent
Evolutionary Delivery	Good	Excellent	Decreased	Very Good	Excellent
Evolutionary Prototyping	Excellent	Excellent	Increased	Very Good	Excellent
Goal Setting (goal of shortest schedule)	Very Good	None	Increased	Good	Very Good
Goal Setting (goal of least risk)	None	Good	Decreased	Good	Very Good
Goal Setting (goal of maximum visibility)	None	Excellent	Decreased	Good	Very Good

(continued)

Table III-2. Summary of Best-Practice Evaluations, *continued*

Best-Practice Name	Potential Reduction From Nominal Schedule	Improvement in Progress Visibility	Effect on Schedule Risk	Chance of First-Time Success	Chance of Long-Term Success
Inspections	Very Good	Fair	Decreased	Good	Excellent
Joint Application Development (JAD)	Good	Fair	Decreased	Good	Excellent
Lifecycle Model Selection	Fair	Fair	Decreased	Very Good	Excellent
Measurement	Very Good	Good	Decreased	Good	Excellent
Miniature Milestones	Fair	Very Good	Decreased	Good	Excellent
Outsourcing	Excellent	None	Increased	Good	Very Good
Principled Negotiation	None	Very Good	Decreased	Very Good	Excellent
Productivity Environments	Good	None	No Effect	Good	Very Good
Rapid-Development Languages (RDLs)	Good	None	Increased	Good	Very Good
Requirements Scrubbing	Very Good	None	Decreased	Very Good	Excellent
Reuse	Excellent	None	Decreased	Poor	Very Good
Signing Up	Very Good	None	Increased	Fair	Good
Spiral Lifecycle Model	Fair	Very Good	Decreased	Good	Excellent
Staged Delivery	None	Good	Decreased	Very Good	Excellent
Theory-W Management	None	Very Good	Decreased	Excellent	Excellent
Throwaway Prototyping	Fair	None	Decreased	Excellent	Excellent
Timebox Development	Excellent	None	Decreased	Good	Excellent
Tools Group	Good	None	Decreased	Good	Very Good
Top-10 Risks List	None	Very Good	Decreased	Excellent	Excellent
User-Interface Prototyping	Good	Fair	Decreased	Excellent	Excellent
Voluntary Overtime	Good	None	Increased	Fair	Very Good

17

Change Board

A Change Board is an approach to controlling changes to a software product. It works by bringing together representatives from each concerned party—for example, development, QA, user documentation, customer support, marketing, and management—and giving them ultimate authority for accepting or rejecting proposed changes. It produces its rapid-development benefit by raising the visibility of feature creep and reducing the number of uncontrolled changes to the product. Change Boards can be used in virtually any kind of environment—business, shrink-wrap, or systems.

SUMMARY

Efficacy

Potential reduction from nominal schedule:	Fair
Improvement in progress visibility:	Fair
Effect on schedule risk:	Decreased Risk
Chance of first-time success:	Very Good
Chance of long-term success:	Excellent

Major Risks

- Approving too few or too many changes

Major Interactions and Trade-Offs

- Can be combined freely with other practices

For more on change boards, see "Change Board" in Section 14.2.

18

Daily Build and Smoke Test

The Daily Build and Smoke Test is a process in which a software product is completely built every day and then put through a series of tests to verify its basic operations. This process is a construction-stage process, and it can be initiated even when projects are already underway. The process produces its savings by reducing the likelihood of several common, time-consuming risks—unsuccessful integration, low quality, and poor progress visibility. The process provides critical control for projects in recovery mode. Its success depends on developers taking the process seriously and on well-designed smoke tests. The Daily Build and Smoke Test can be used effectively on projects of virtually any size and complexity.

**S
U
M
M
A
R
Y**

Efficacy

Potential reduction from nominal schedule:	Good
Improvement in progress visibility:	Good
Effect on schedule risk:	Decreased Risk
Chance of first-time success:	Very Good
Chance of long-term success:	Excellent

Major Risks

- Pressure to release interim versions of a program too frequently

Major Interactions and Trade-Offs

- Trades small increase in project overhead for large reduction in integration risk and improvement in progress visibility
- Especially effective when used in conjunction with Miniature Milestones
- Provides support needed for incremental-development lifecycle models

If you have a simple computer program that consists of only one file, building the program consists of compiling and linking the file to create an executable program. On a typical team project that involves dozens, hundreds, or even thousands of files, the process of creating an executable product becomes more complicated and time-consuming. The product must be "built" in order for it to run.

In the daily-build-and-smoke-test process, the entire product is built every day. That means that every file is compiled, linked, and combined into an executable program every day. The product is then put through a "smoke test," a relatively simple test to see whether the product "smokes" when you turn it on.

This simple process produces significant time savings on several fronts.

FURTHER READING
For more on software integration, see Chapter 27, "System Integration," in *Code Complete* (McConnell 1993).

It minimizes integration risk. One of the greatest risks that a project faces is that when team members combine or "integrate" the code that they have been working on separately, their code does not work well together. Depending on how late in the project such an incompatibility is discovered, debugging might take longer than it would have if integration had occurred earlier—because program interfaces might have to be changed, or major parts of the system might have to be redesigned and reimplemented. In extreme cases, integration errors have caused projects to be canceled. The daily-build-and-smoke-test process keeps integration errors small and manageable, and it prevents runaway integration problems.

CROSS-REFERENCE
For details on the effect that low quality has on a development schedule, see Section 4.3, "Quality-Assurance Fundamentals."

It reduces the risk of low quality. Related to the risk of unsuccessful or problematic integration is the risk of low quality. By minimally smoke testing all the code in the product every day, quality problems are prevented from taking control of the project. You bring the system to a known, good state, and then you keep it there. It is simply not allowed to deteriorate to the point where time-consuming quality problems can occur.

CLASSIC MISTAKE

It supports easier defect diagnosis. When the product is built and tested every day, it's much easier to pinpoint why the product is broken on any given day. If the product worked on Day 17 and is broken on Day 18, something that happened between the builds on Days 17 and 18 broke the product. If you're building and testing the product only weekly or monthly, the problem could be anywhere between Day 17 and Day 24, or between Day 17 and Day 47.

It supports progress monitoring. When you build the system every day, the features that are present and not present are obvious. Both technical and nontechnical managers can simply exercise the product to get a sense of how close it is to completion.

It improves morale. As Fred Brooks points out, an incredible boost in morale results from seeing a product work. It almost doesn't matter what the product does; developers can be excited just to see it display a rectangle! With daily builds, a little bit more of the product works every day, and that keeps morale high.

It improves customer relations. If daily builds have a positive effect on developer morale, they also have a positive effect on customer morale. Customers like signs of progress, and daily builds provide signs of progress frequently.

18.1 Using the Daily Build and Smoke Test

The idea behind the daily-build-and-smoke-test process is simple: build the product and test it every day. The following sections describe some of the ins and outs of this simple idea.

Build daily. The most fundamental part of the daily build is to build the product every day. As Jim McCarthy says, treat the daily build as the heartbeat of the project (McCarthy 1995c). If the heart isn't beating, the project is dead.

A little less metaphorically, some describe the daily build as the synch pulse of a project (Cusumano and Selby 1995). Different developers' code can get a little bit out of synch between synch pulses, but with each synch pulse, all the code has to come back into alignment. When you insist on keeping the pulses close together, you prevent some developers from getting out of synch entirely.

Use an automated build tool (such as *make*) to reduce the repetitive work associated with building daily.

Check for broken builds. In order for the daily-build process to be effective, the software that's built has to work. If the software isn't usable, the build is considered to be broken, and fixing the build becomes top priority.

Each project sets its own standard for what constitutes "breaking the build." The standard needs to set a quality level that's strict enough to keep showstopper defects out of the daily build but lenient enough to disregard trivial defects (because undue attention to trivial defects can paralyze progress).

At a minimum, a good build should:

- Compile all files, libraries, and other components successfully
- Link all files, libraries, and other components successfully

- Not contain any showstopper bugs that prevent the program from being launched or that make it hazardous to operate
- Pass the smoke test

Some projects set stricter standards and include compiler and linker errors and warnings in their definitions of good builds. The litmus test in any case is whether the build is stable enough to be released to testing. If it's stable enough to test, it isn't broken.

Smoke test daily. The smoke test should exercise the entire system from end to end. It does not have to be an exhaustive test, but it should be capable of detecting major problems. By definition, if the build passes the smoke test, that means that it is stable enough to be tested and is a good build.

Without the smoke test, the daily build is meaningless. The smoke test indicates whether the build worked. If you treat the build itself as the heartbeat of the project, the smoke test is the stethoscope that allows you to determine whether the heart is beating. It is the first line of testing, the first line of defense against program deterioration. Without the smoke test, the daily build is just a way of verifying that you have a clean compile.

The smoke test must evolve as the system evolves. At first, the smoke test will probably be something simple, such as testing whether the system can say, "Hello World." As the system develops, the smoke test will become more thorough. The first test might take a matter of seconds to run. As the system grows, the smoke test can grow to thirty minutes, an hour, or more.

The build group should make maintaining the smoke test its top priority. The quality of their work on the smoke test should factor into their performance evaluations. The build group will be under pressure from the developers not to make the smoke test too "picky," so its members should be chosen from the ranks of quality assurance rather than from the ranks of developers. Regardless of everyone's best intentions, putting a developer in charge of the smoke test is too much like putting a fox in charge of the chicken coop. The group's members should report to the QA lead rather than to the development lead.

This is one of the areas in which designing your system for testing comes in handy. The smoke test should be automated, and sometimes it's easier to automate if you have built-in hooks for testing.

Establish a build group. On most projects, tending the daily build becomes a big enough task that it needs to be an explicit part of someone's job. On large projects, it can become a full-time job for more than one person. For example, on Windows NT 3.0, there were four full-time people in the build group (Zachary 1994). It also takes effort to keep the smoke test up to date as the product grows and evolves.

On smaller projects you might not need to devote a whole person to the daily build. In that case, put someone from quality assurance in charge of it.

Add code to the build only when it makes sense to do so... Although daily builds require that you build the system daily, they do not require that developers add every new line of code they write to the system every day. Individual developers usually don't write code fast enough to add meaningful increments to the system every day. They work on a chunk of code and then integrate it when they have a collection of code in a consistent state. Developers should maintain private versions of the source files they're working on. Once they have created a complete set of modifications, they make a private build of the system using their modifications, test it, and check it in.

...but don't wait too long to add code to the build. Although few developers will check in code every day, beware of developers who check in code infrequently. It's possible for a developer to become so embroiled in a set of revisions that every file in the system seems to be involved. That undermines the value of the daily build. The rest of the team will continue to realize the benefit of incremental integration but that particular developer will not. If a developer goes more than a few days without checking in a set of changes, consider that developer's work to be at risk.

FURTHER READING
For many details on developer-level testing practice, see *Writing Solid Code* (Maguire 1993).

Require developers to smoke test their code before adding it to the system. Developers need to test their own code before they add it to the build. A developer can do this by creating a private build of the system on a personal machine, which the developer then tests individually. Or the developer can release a private build to a "testing buddy," a tester who focuses on that developer's code. The goal in either case is to be sure that the new code passes the smoke test before it's allowed to influence other parts of the system.

Create a holding area for code that's to be added to the build. Part of the success of the daily-build process depends on knowing which builds are good and which are not. In testing their own code, developers need to be able to rely on a known good system.

Most groups solve this problem by creating a holding area for code that developers think is ready to be added to the build. New code goes into the holding area, the new build is built, and if the build is acceptable, the new code is migrated into the master sources.

On small- and medium-sized projects, a version-control system can serve this function. Developers check new code into the version-control system. Developers who want to use a known good build simply set a date flag in their version-control–options file that tells the system to retrieve files based on the date of the last-known good build.

On large projects or projects that use unsophisticated version-control software, the holding-area function has to be handled manually. The author of a set of new code sends email to the build group to tell them where to find the new files to be checked in. Or the group establishes a "check-in" area on a file server where developers put new versions of their source files. The build group then assumes responsibility for checking new code into version control after they have verified that the new code doesn't break the build.

Create a penalty for breaking the build. Most groups that use daily builds create a penalty for breaking the build. If the build is broken too often, it's hard for developers to take the job of not breaking the build seriously. Breaking the build should be the exception, not the rule. Make it clear from the beginning that keeping the build healthy is the project's top priority. Refuse to take a broken build casually. Insist that developers who have broken the build stop their other work until they've fixed the build.

A fun penalty can help to emphasize the priority of keeping the build healthy. Some groups give out suckers to developers who break the build. The sucker who broke the build has to tape a sucker to his office door until he fixes the build. Other projects make the person who broke the build responsible for running the build until someone else breaks it. On one project I worked on, the person who broke the build had to wear a hat made out of an umbrella until he fixed the build. Other groups have guilty developers wear goat horns or contribute $5 to a morale fund.

Some projects establish a penalty with more bite. Microsoft developers on high-profile projects such as NT, Windows 95, and Excel have taken to wearing beepers in the late stages of their projects. If they break the build, they are called in to fix the build regardless of the time of day or night. The success of this practice depends on the build group being able to determine precisely who broke the build. If they aren't careful, a developer who's mistakenly called to fix the build at 3:00 in the morning will quickly become an enemy of the daily-build process.

Release builds in the morning. Some groups have found that they prefer to build overnight, smoke test in the early morning, and release new builds in the morning rather than the afternoon. There are several advantages to smoke testing and releasing builds in the morning.

First, if you release a build in the morning, testers can test with a fresh build that day. If you generally release builds in the afternoon, testers feel compelled to launch their automated tests before they leave for the day. When the build is delayed, which it often is, the testers have to stay late to launch their tests. Because it's not their fault that they have to stay late, the build process becomes demoralizing.

When you complete the build in the morning, you have more reliable access to developers when there are problems with the build. During the day, developers are down the hall. During the evening, developers can be anywhere. Even when developers are given beepers, they're not always easy to locate.

It might be more macho to start smoke testing at the end of the day and call people in the middle of the night when you find problems, but it's harder on the team, it wastes time, and in the end you lose more than you gain.

CLASSIC MISTAKE

Build and smoke even under pressure. When schedule pressure becomes intense, the work required to maintain the daily build can seem like extravagant overhead. The opposite is true. Under pressure, developers lose some of their discipline. They feel pressure to take design and implementation shortcuts that they would not take under less stressful circumstances. They review and unit test their own code less carefully than usual. The code tends toward a state of entropy more quickly than it would during less stressful times.

Against this backdrop, the daily-build-and-smoke-test process enforces discipline and keeps pressure-cooker projects on track. The code still tends toward a state of entropy, but you bring that tendency to heel every day. If you build daily and the build is broken, identifying the developer responsible and insisting on an immediate code fix is a manageable task. Bringing the code back from its state of entropy is a relatively small undertaking.

If you wait two days—until twice as many defects are inserted into the code—then you have to deal both with twice as many defects and with multiplicative interaction effects of those defects. It will take more than twice as much effort to diagnose and correct them. The longer you wait between builds, the harder it is to bring the build back into line.

What Kinds of Projects Can Use the Daily-Build-and-Smoke-Test Process?

Virtually any kind of project can use daily builds—large projects, small projects, operating systems, shrink-wrap software, and business systems.

Fred Brooks reports that software builders in some organizations are surprised or even shocked by the daily-build process. They report that they build every week, but not every day (Brooks 1995). The problem with weekly builds is that you tend not to build every week. If the build is broken one week, you might go for several weeks before the next good build. When that happens, you lose virtually all the benefit of frequent builds.

Some developers protest that it is impractical to build every day because their projects are too large. But the project that was perhaps the most complex software-development effort in recent history used daily builds successfully. By the time it was first released, Microsoft NT consisted of 5.6 million lines of code spread across 40,000 source files. A complete build took as many as 19 hours on several machines, but the NT development team still managed to build every day (Zachary 1994). Far from being a nuisance, the NT team attributed much of their success on that huge project to their daily builds. Those of us who work on projects of less staggering proportions will have a hard time explaining why we don't use daily builds.

For technical leads, daily builds are particularly useful because you can implement them at a purely technical level. You don't have to have management authority to insist that your team build successfully every day.

CROSS-REFERENCE
For more on project recovery, see Chapter 16, "Project Recovery."

Daily builds are especially valuable in project-recovery mode. If you can't get to a good-build state, you have no hope of ever shipping the product, so you might as well work toward a good build as one of your first project-recovery objectives. Once you get to a known good state, you make incremental additions and stay in a known good state. It's a morale boost during project recovery to have a working product at all times, and it makes for clear progress indications.

18.2 Managing the Risks of the Daily Build and Smoke Test

The daily-build process has few drawbacks. Here is the main one.

CROSS-REFERENCE
The problems of premature releases are related to the problems of premature convergence discussed in "Premature convergence" in Section 9.1.

Tendency toward premature releases. When people outside the development group see that the product is being built every day, pressure mounts to create frequent releases for outside groups. Creating external releases can look easy to a product manager, and it is easier than when you're not using daily builds, but it still sucks up developers' time in subtle ways:

- Developers spend time preparing materials that are not needed for the final product but that are needed to support the release. These materials include documentation, interim versions of features still under development, stubbing out hazardous areas of the product, hiding debugging aids, and so on.

- Developers make quick fixes so that features will work for a particular release rather than waiting until they can make more careful changes. These quick fixes eventually break, and the developers then have to make the more careful changes that they should have made in the first place. The net effect is that the developers waste time fixing the same code twice.

- Developers spend more time responding to minor problems on an ad hoc basis early in the development cycle, problems that could be taken care of more efficiently as part of the developers' normal work cycle.

You wouldn't want to eliminate interim releases entirely. What you can do is to plan for a specific number of interim releases and then try not to increase that number.

18.3 Side Effects of the Daily Build and Smoke Test

Some developers who have used daily builds claim that it improves overall product quality (Zachary 1994). Other than that general claim, the daily build's effect is limited to its improvements in integration risk, quality risk, and progress visibility.

18.4 The Daily Build and Smoke Test's Interactions with Other Practices

Daily builds combine nicely with the use of miniature milestones (Chapter 27). As Chris Peters says, "Scheduling rule #1 is constant vigilance" (Peters 1995). If you have defined a complete set of mini milestones and you know that your daily build is not broken, then you will have exceptional visibility into your progress. You can check the build every single day to determine whether your project is meeting its mini milestones. If it is meeting its mini milestones, it will finish on time. If it is falling behind, you will detect that immediately, and you can adjust your plans accordingly. The only kind of scheduling error you can make is to leave tasks off the schedule.

CROSS-REFERENCE
For more on incremental development practices, see Chapter 7, "Lifecycle Planning."

Daily builds also provide support for incremental-development practices (Chapter 7). Those practices depend on being able to release interim versions of the software externally. The effort required to prepare a good build for release is relatively small compared to the effort needed to convert an average, infrequently built program into a good build.

18.5 The Bottom Line on the Daily Build and Smoke Test

CROSS-REFERENCE
For more on the importance of making progress visible, see Section 6.3, "Perception and Reality."

The daily-build-and-smoke-test process is at heart a risk-management practice. Because the risks it addresses are schedule risks, it has a powerful ability to make schedules more predictable and to eliminate some of the risks that can cause extreme delays—integration problems, low quality, and lack of progress visibility.

I don't know of any quantitative data on the schedule efficacy of the daily-build process, but the anecdotal reports on its value are impressive. Jim McCarthy has said that if Microsoft could evangelize only one idea from its development process, the daily-build-and-smoke-test process would be the one (McCarthy 1995c).

18.6 Keys to Success in Using the Daily Build and Smoke Test

Here are the keys to success in using daily builds:

- Build every day.
- Smoke test every day.
- Grow the smoke test with the product. Be sure that the test remains meaningful as the product evolves.
- Make a healthy build the project's top priority.
- Take steps to ensure that broken builds are the exception rather than the rule.
- Don't abandon the process under pressure.

Further Reading

Cusumano, Michael, and Richard Selby. *Microsoft Secrets: How the World's Most Powerful Software Company Creates Technology, Shapes Markets, and Manages People.* New York: Free Press, 1995. Chapter 5 describes Microsoft's daily-build process in detail, including a detailed listing of the steps that an individual developer goes through on applications products such as Microsoft Excel.

McCarthy, Jim. *Dynamics of Software Development.* Redmond, Wash.: Microsoft Press, 1995. McCarthy describes the daily-build process as a practice he has found to be useful in developing software at Microsoft. His viewpoint provides a complement to the one described in *Microsoft Secrets* and in this chapter.

McConnell, Steve. *Code Complete.* Redmond, Wash.: Microsoft Press, 1993. Chapter 27 of this book discusses integration approaches. It provides additional background on the reasons that incremental integration practices such as daily builds are effective.

19

Designing for Change

Designing for Change is a broad label that encompasses several change-oriented design practices. These practices need to be employed early in the software lifecycle to be effective. The success of Designing for Change depends on identifying likely changes, developing a change plan, and hiding design decisions so that changes do not ripple through a program. Some of the change-oriented design practices are more difficult than people think, but when they are done well they lay the groundwork for long-lived programs and for flexibility that can help to minimize the schedule impacts of late-breaking change requests.

Efficacy

Potential reduction from nominal schedule:	Fair
Improvement in progress visibility:	None
Effect on schedule risk:	Decreased Risk
Chance of first-time success:	Good
Chance of long-term success:	Excellent

Major Risks

- Overreliance on the use of programming languages to solve design problems rather than on change-oriented design practices

Major Interactions and Trade-Offs

- Provides necessary support for incremental-development practices
- Design methods involved work hand-in-hand with software reuse

Many developers recognize designing for change as a "good" software engineering practice, but few recognize it as a valuable contributor to rapid development.

Some of the most damaging influences on a development schedule are late, unexpected changes to a product—changes that occur after initial design is complete and after implementation is underway. Projects that deal poorly with such changes are often perceived as slow even if they were on schedule up to the point where the changes were introduced.

Current development practices place an increasing emphasis on responding to changes—changes in market conditions, changes in customer understanding of the problem, changes in underlying technology, and so on.

Against this backdrop, Designing for Change does not produce direct schedule savings. The care needed to design for change might actually lengthen the nominal development schedule. But the schedule equation is seldom so simple as to contain the nominal schedule as its only variable. You must factor in the likelihood of changes, including changes in future versions. Then you must weigh the small, known increase in effort needed to design for change against the large potential risk of not designing for change. On balance, it is possible to save time. If you use incremental-development practices such as Evolutionary Delivery and Evolutionary Prototyping, you build a likelihood of change into the development process, so your design had better account for it.

19.1   Using Designing for Change

"Designing for change" does not refer to any single design methodology, but to a panoply of design practices that contribute to flexible software designs. Here are some of the things you can do:

- Identify areas likely to change.
- Use information hiding.
- Develop a change plan.
- Define families of programs.
- Use object-oriented design.

The rest of this section lays out each of these practices. Some of the practices overlap, but I think that each of them has distinctive heuristic value.

Identify Areas Likely to Change

The first key to success in Designing for Change is to identify the potential changes. Begin design work by listing design decisions that are likely to change. Robert L. Glass has pointed out that one characteristic of great designers is that they are able to anticipate more kinds of possible change than average designers can (Glass 1994a). Here are some frequent sources of change:

- Hardware dependencies
- File formats
- Inputs and outputs
- Nonstandard language features
- Difficult design and implementation areas
- Global variables
- Implementations of specific data structures
- Implementations of abstract data types
- Business rules
- Sequences in which items will be processed
- Requirements that were barely excluded from the current version
- Requirements that were summarily excluded from the current version
- Features planned for the next version

Identifying changes needs to be done at design time or earlier. Identifying possible requirements changes should be a part of identifying requirements.

Use Information Hiding

CROSS-REFERENCE
For more on information hiding, see "Further Reading" at the end of the chapter.

Once you have created your list of potential changes, isolate the design decisions related to each of those changes inside its own module. By "module" I am not necessarily referring to a single routine. A module in this context could be a routine or a collection of routines and data. It could be a "module" in Modula-2, a "class" in C++, a "package" in Ada, a "unit" in Turbo, Pascal, or Delphi, and so on.

HARD DATA

The practice of hiding changeable design decisions inside their own modules is known as "information hiding," which is one of the few theoretical techniques that has indisputably proven its usefulness in practice (Boehm 1987a). In the time since David Parnas first introduced the technique, large programs that use information hiding have been found to be easier to modify—by a factor of four—than programs that don't (Korson and Vaishnavi 1986). Moreover, information hiding is part of the foundation of both structured design and object-oriented design. In structured design, the notion of black boxes comes from information hiding. In object-oriented design, information hiding gives rise to the notions of encapsulation and visibility.

In the 20th anniversary edition of *The Mythical Man-Month*, Fred Brooks concludes that his criticism of information hiding was one of the few shortcomings of the first edition of his book. "Parnas was right, and I was wrong about information hiding," he proclaims (Brooks 1995).

To use information hiding, begin design by listing design decisions that are likely to change (as described above) or especially difficult design decisions. Then design each module to hide the effects of changes to one of those design decisions. Design the interface to the module to be insensitive to changes inside the module. That way, if the change occurs, it will affect only one module. The goal should be to create black boxes—modules that have well-defined, narrow interfaces and that keep their implementation details to themselves.

CLASSIC MISTAKE

Suppose you have a program in which each object is supposed to have a unique ID stored in a member variable called *ID*. One design approach would be to use integers for the IDs and to store the highest ID assigned so far in a global variable called *MaxID*. Each place a new object is allocated, perhaps in each object's constructor, you could simply use the statement *ID = ++MaxID*. (This is a C-language statement that increments the value of *MaxID* by 1 and assigns the new value to *ID*.) That would guarantee a unique ID, and it would add the absolute minimum of code in each place an object is created. What could go wrong with that?

A lot of things could go wrong. What if you want to reserve ranges of IDs for special purposes? What if you want to be able to reuse the IDs of objects that have been destroyed? What if you want to add an assertion that fires when you allocate more IDs than the maximum number you've anticipated? If you allocated IDs by spreading *ID = ++MaxID* statements throughout your program, you would have to change the code associated with every one of those statements.

The way that new IDs are created is a design decision that you should hide. If you use the phrase *++MaxID* throughout your program, you expose the information that the way a new ID is created is simply by incrementing *MaxID*. If, instead, you put the statement *ID = NewID()* throughout your program, you hide the information about how new IDs are created.

Inside the *NewID()* function you might still have just one line of code, *return (++MaxID)* or its equivalent, but if you later decide to reserve certain ranges of IDs for special purposes, to reuse old IDs, or to add assertions, you could make those changes within the *NewID()* function itself—without touching dozens or hundreds of *ID = NewID()* statements. No matter how complicated the revisions inside *NewID()* might become, they wouldn't affect any other part of the program.

Now suppose that you further discover you need to change the type of the ID from an integer to a string. If you've spread variable declarations like *int ID* throughout your program, your use of the *NewID()* function won't help. You'll still have to go through your program and make dozens or hundreds of changes.

In this case, the design decision to hide is the ID's type. You could simply declare your IDs to be of *IDTYPE*—a user-defined type that resolves to *int*—rather than directly declaring them to be of type *int*. Once again, hiding a design decision makes a huge difference in the amount of code affected by a change.

Develop a Change Plan

For the areas that are likely to change, develop change plans. Change plans can prescribe the use of any of the following practices:

FURTHER READING
For details on all these
practices, see *Code
Complete* (McConnell 1993).

- Use abstract interfaces to modules rather than interfaces that expose the implementation details.

- Use named constants for data-structure sizes rather than hard-coded literals.

- Use late-binding strategies. Look up data-structure sizes in an external file or registry in the Windows environment. Allocate data structures dynamically based on those sizes.

- Use table-driven techniques in which the operation of the program changes based on the data in the table. Decide whether to store the data table inside the program (which will require recompilation to change) or outside the program in a data file, initialization file, Windows registry, or resource file.

- Use routines rather than duplicating lines of code—even if it's only one or two lines.

- Use simple routines that perform single, small functions. If you keep routines simple, they'll be easier to use in ways you didn't originally anticipate.

- Keep unrelated operations separate. Don't combine unrelated operations into a single routine just because they seem too simple to put into separate routines.

- Separate code for general functionality from code for specialized functionality. Distinguish between code for use throughout your organization, for use in a specific application, and for use in a specific version of an application.

These practices are all good software-engineering practices, which, among other things, help to support change.

419

Define Families of Programs

David Parnas pointed out as early as 1976 that the developer's job had changed from designing individual programs to designing families of programs (Parnas 1976, 1979). In the 20 years since he wrote that, the developer's job has shifted even more in that direction. Developers today use the same code base to produce programs for different languages, different platforms, and different customers. Figure 19-1 illustrates how this is done.

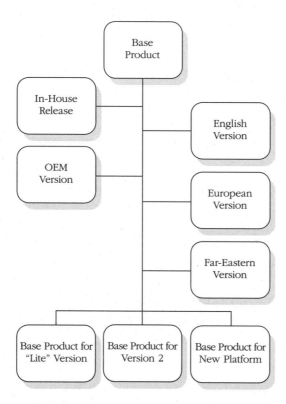

Figure 19-1. *Family of products. Since most products eventually turn into a family of products, most design efforts should concentrate on designing a family of programs instead of just one.*

In this environment, Parnas argues that a designer should try to anticipate the needs of the family of programs in developing the base product. The designer should anticipate lateral versions such as in-house releases, English, European, and Far-Eastern versions, and the designer should also anticipate follow-on versions. The designer should design the product so that the decisions that are least likely to change among versions are placed closest to the root of the tree. This holds true whether you're consciously designing a family of programs or just a single program that you'd like to prepare for change.

CROSS-REFERENCE
For more on defining minimal feature sets and on versioned-release practices, see Chapter 20, "Evolutionary Delivery"; Chapter 36, "Staged Delivery"; and "Versioned Development" in Section 14.1.

A good practice is first to identify a minimal subset of functionality that might be of use to the end-user and then to define minimal increments beyond that. The minimal subset usually won't be large enough to make up a program that anyone would want to use; it is useful for the purpose of preparing for change, but it usually isn't worth building for its own sake. The increments you define beyond that should also be so small as to seem trivial. The point of keeping them small is to avoid creating components that perform more than one function. The smaller and sharper you make the components, the more adaptable to change the system will be. Designing minimal components that add minimal incremental functionality also leads to systems in which you can easily trim features when needed.

Use Object-Oriented Design

CROSS-REFERENCE
For more comments on object-oriented programming, see "Identifying Silver Bullets" in Section 15.5.

One of the outgrowths of information hiding and modularity has been object-oriented design. In object-oriented design, you divide a system into objects. Sometimes the objects model real-world entities; sometimes they model computer-science structures or more abstract entities.

A study at NASA's Software Engineering Laboratory found that object-oriented development practices increased reusability, reconfigurability, and productivity, and they reduced development schedules (Scholtz, et al. 1994).

Use object-oriented design, but don't expect it to be a cure-all. The success of object-oriented design in a high-change environment depends on the same factors that information hiding does. You still need to identify the most likely sources of change, and you still need to hide those changes behind narrow interfaces that insulate the rest of the program from potential changes.

19.2 Managing the Risks of Designing for Change

CLASSIC MISTAKE

Using the best practice of Designing for Change poses no risks to the rest of the project. The main risk associated with Designing for Change is simply the risk of failing to use the practice to its full benefit.

Overreliance on languages and pictures rather than on design. The mere act of putting objects into classes does not create an object-oriented design, does not provide information hiding, and does not protect a program from changes. The mere act of drawing a module-hierarchy chart does not create a change-tolerant design. Good designs come from good design work, not from pictures of design.

CROSS-REFERENCE
For another broad view of
object-oriented technology,
see "Identifying Silver
Bullets" in Section 15.5.

Doing object-oriented design effectively is harder than people have made it out to be. As discussed in Section 15.5, it is an expert's technology. David Parnas writes that object-oriented (O-O) programming has caught on slowly for the following reason:

> [O-O] has been tied to a variety of complex languages. Instead of teaching people that O-O is a type of design, and giving them design principles, people have been taught that O-O is the use of a particular tool. We can write good or bad programs with any tool. Unless we teach people how to design, the languages matter very little. The result is that people do bad designs with these languages and get very little value from them. (Parnas in Brooks 1995)

To design for change, you must actually *design*. Focusing on areas that are likely to change, information hiding, and families of programs make up the strategic backbone of object-oriented design. If you don't follow those design steps, you might as well be working in Fortran, plain old C, or assembler.

19.3 Side Effects of Designing for Change

HARD DATA

Programs that are designed for change continue to yield benefits long after their initial construction. Capers Jones reports that programs that are well-structured and developed with high quality are nearly guaranteed to have long and useful service lives. Programs that are poorly structured and developed with low quality are nearly always taken out of service or become catastrophically expensive to maintain within 3 to 5 years (Jones 1994).

19.4 Designing for Change's Interactions with Other Practices

The flexibility provided by Designing for Change is an important part of the support needed for incremental-development practices such as Evolutionary Delivery (Chapter 20) and Evolutionary Prototyping (Chapter 21). The change-oriented design practices also provide moderate support for Reuse (Chapter 33).

19.5 The Bottom Line on Designing for Change

The bottom line is that Designing for Change is a risk-reduction practice. If the system is stable, it doesn't produce immediate schedule reductions, but it helps to prevent the massive schedule slips that can occur when unanticipated changes cause widespread ripple effects through the design and code.

19.6   Keys to Success in Using Designing for Change

Here are the keys to success in designing for change:

- Identify the most likely changes.
- Use information hiding to insulate the system from the effects of the most likely changes.
- Define families of programs rather than considering only one program at a time.
- Don't count on the mere use of an object-oriented programming language to do the design job automatically.

Further Reading

The three Parnas papers below are the seminal presentations of the ideas of information hiding and designing for change. They are still some of the best sources of information available on these ideas. They might be difficult to find in their original sources, but the 1972 and 1979 papers have been reproduced in *Tutorial on Software Design Techniques* (Freeman and Wasserman 1983), and the 1972 paper has also been reproduced in *Writings of the Revolution* (Yourdon 1982).

Parnas, David L. "On the Criteria to Be Used in Decomposing Systems into Modules," *Communications of the ACM,* v. 5, no. 12, December 1972, 1053–58 (also in Yourdon 1979, Freeman and Wasserman 1983).

Parnas, David L. "Designing Software for Ease of Extension and Contraction," *IEEE Transactions on Software Engineering,* v. SE-5, March 1979, 128–138 (also in Freeman and Wasserman 1983).

Parnas, David Lorge, Paul C. Clements, and David M. Weiss. "The Modular Structure of Complex Systems," *IEEE Transactions on Software Engineering,* March 1985, 259–266.

McConnell, Steve. *Code Complete.* Redmond, Wash.: Microsoft Press, 1993. Section 6.1 of this book discusses information hiding, and Section 12.3 discusses the related topic of abstract data types. Chapter 30, "Software Evolution," describes how to prepare for software changes at the implementation level.

20

Evolutionary Delivery

Evolutionary Delivery is a lifecycle model that strikes a balance between Staged Delivery's control and Evolutionary Prototyping's flexibility. It provides its rapid-development benefit by delivering selected portions of the software earlier than would otherwise be possible, but it does not necessarily deliver the final software product any faster. It provides some ability to change product direction mid-course in response to customer requests. Evolutionary Delivery has been used successfully on in-house business software and shrink-wrap software. Used thoughtfully, it can lead to improved product quality, reduced code size, and more even distribution of development and testing resources. As with other lifecycle models, Evolutionary Delivery is a whole-project practice: if you want to use it, you need to start planning to use it early in the project.

Efficacy

Potential reduction from nominal schedule:	Good
Improvement in progress visibility:	Excellent
Effect on schedule risk:	Decreased Risk
Chance of first-time success:	Very Good
Chance of long-term success:	Excellent

Major Risks

- Feature creep
- Diminished project control
- Unrealistic schedule and budget expectations
- Inefficient use of development time by developers

Major Interactions and Trade-Offs

- Draws from both Staged Delivery and Evolutionary Prototyping
- Success depends on use of designing for change

Some people go to the grocery store carrying a complete list of the groceries they'll need for the week: "2 pounds of bananas, 3 pounds of apples, 1 bunch of carrots," and so on. Other people go to the store with no list at all and buy whatever looks best when they get there: "These melons smell good. I'll get a couple of those. These snow peas look fresh. I'll put them together with some onions and water chestnuts and make a stir-fry. Oh, and these porterhouse steaks look terrific. I haven't had a steak in a long time. I'll get a couple of those for tomorrow." Most people are somewhere in between. They take a list to the store, but they improvise to greater and lesser degrees when they get there.

In the world of software lifecycle models, Staged Delivery is a lot like going to the store with a complete list. Evolutionary Prototyping is like going to the store with no list at all. Evolutionary Delivery is like starting with a list but improvising some as you go along.

The Staged Delivery lifecycle model provides highly visible signs of progress to the customer and a high degree of control to management, but not much flexibility. Evolutionary Prototyping is nearly the opposite: like Staged Delivery, it provides highly visible signs of progress to the customer—but unlike Staged Delivery, it provides a high degree of flexibility in responding to customer feedback and little control to management. Sometimes you want to combine the control of Staged Delivery with the flexibility of Evolutionary Prototyping. Evolutionary Delivery straddles the ground between those two lifecycle models and draws its advantages and disadvantages from whichever it leans toward the most.

CROSS-REFERENCE
For details on these kinds of support for rapid development, see the introductions to Chapter 21, "Evolutionary Prototyping," and Chapter 36, "Staged Delivery."

Evolutionary Delivery supports rapid development in several ways:

- It reduces the risk of delivering a product that the customer doesn't want, avoiding time-consuming rework.

- For custom software, it makes progress visible by delivering software early and often.

- For shrink-wrap software, it supports more frequent product releases.

- It reduces estimation error by allowing for recalibration and reestimation after each evolutionary delivery.

- It reduces the risk of integration problems by integrating early and often—whenever a delivery occurs.

- It improves morale because the project is seen as a success from the first time the product says, "Hello World" until the final version is ultimately delivered.

As with other aspects of Evolutionary Delivery, the extent to which it supports rapid development in each of these ways depends on whether it leans more toward Staged Delivery or Evolutionary Prototyping.

20.1   Using Evolutionary Delivery

To use Evolutionary Delivery, you need to have a fundamental idea of the kind of system you're building at the outset of the project. As Figure 20-1 suggests, in the evolutionary-delivery approach, you start with a preliminary idea of what your customer wants, and you create a system architecture and core based on that. That architecture and core serve as the basis for further development.

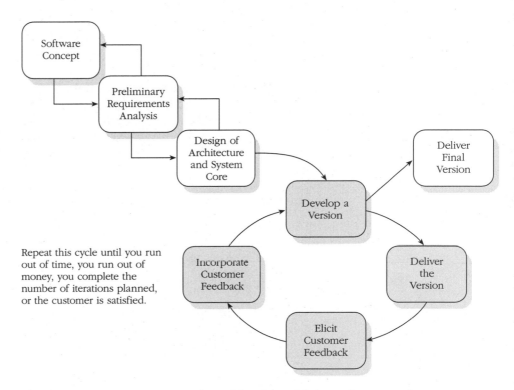

Figure 20-1. *The Evolutionary Delivery lifecycle model draws from Staged Delivery's control and Evolutionary Prototyping's flexibility. You can tailor it to provide as much control or flexibility as you need.*

The architecture should anticipate as many of the possible directions the system could go as it can. The core should consist of lower-level system functions that are unlikely to change as a result of customer feedback. It's fine to be uncertain about the details of what you will ultimately build on top of the core, but you should be confident in the core itself.

Properly identifying the system core is one key to success in using Evolutionary Delivery. Aside from that, the most critical choice you make in Evolutionary Delivery is whether to lean more toward Evolutionary Prototyping or Staged Delivery.

In Evolutionary Prototyping, you tend to iterate until you and the customer agree that you have produced an acceptable product. How many iterations will that take? You can't know for sure. Usually you can't afford for a project to be that open-ended.

In Staged Delivery, on the other hand, you plan during architectural design how many stages to have and exactly what you want to build during each stage. What if you change your mind? Well, pure Staged Delivery doesn't allow for that.

With Evolutionary Delivery, you can start from a base of Evolutionary Prototyping and slant the project toward Staged Delivery to provide more control. You can decide at the outset that you will deliver the product in four evolutionary deliveries. You invite the customer to provide feedback at each delivery, which you can then account for in the next delivery. But the process will not continue indefinitely: it will stop after four deliveries. Deciding on the number of iterations in advance and sticking to it is one of the critical factors to success in this kind of rapid development (Burlton 1992).

With Evolutionary Delivery, another option is to start from a base of Staged Delivery and slant the project toward Evolutionary Prototyping to provide more flexibility. You can decide at the outset what you will deliver in stages 1, 2, and 3, but you can be more tentative about stages 4 and 5, thus giving your project a direction but not an exact road map.

Whether you slant more toward Evolutionary Prototyping or Staged Delivery should depend on the extent to which you need to accommodate customer requests. If you need to accommodate most requests, set up Evolutionary Delivery to be more like prototyping. Some experts recommend delivering the software in increments as small as 1 to 5 percent (Gilb 1988). If you need to accommodate few change requests, plan it to be more like Staged Delivery, with just a handful of larger releases.

Release Order

CROSS-REFERENCE
For details on the value of mapping out possible changes to a system at design time, see "Define Families of Programs" in Section 19.1.

You use Evolutionary Delivery when you're not exactly sure what you want to build. But unlike Evolutionary Prototyping, you do have at least some idea, so you should map out a preliminary set of deliveries at the beginning of your project, while you're developing the system architecture and system core.

Your initial delivery schedule will probably contain some functionality that will definitely be in the final system, some that will probably be, and some that might not be. Still other functionality will be identified and added later.

Be sure that you structure your delivery schedule so that you develop the functionality you are most confident in first. You can show the system to your customers, elicit their feedback, and gain confidence that the remaining functionality is really what they want—before you begin working on it.

When to Use Evolutionary Delivery

CROSS-REFERENCE
For a related discussion of planning decisions that depend on how well-understood your system is, see Section 13.1, "Team-Structure Considerations."

If you understand your system so well that you don't expect many surprises, you will be better off using Staged Delivery than Evolutionary Delivery. You have more control over the project when you map out exactly what will be delivered at the end of each stage ahead of time. That style of development is most often appropriate for maintenance releases or product upgrades in which you already understand the product area thoroughly and don't expect to discover any revolutionary insights along the development path.

If your system is poorly understood and you expect a lot of surprises, including surprises that are likely to affect the system in fundamental ways, you will be better off using Evolutionary Prototyping than Evolutionary Delivery. Evolutionary Delivery requires that you know enough about the project at the outset to design an architecture and to implement core functionality. With Evolutionary Prototyping, you don't have to do those things at the beginning.

Evolutionary Delivery isn't limited to completely new systems. On an existing system, each new delivery can replace part of the old system and can also provide new capabilities. At some point, you'll have replaced so much of the old system that there's nothing left. The architecture of the new system needs to be designed carefully so that you can transition to it without being infected by the old system's restrictions. That might mean that you can't create certain portions of the new system right away; you might want to wait until the new system can support those portions without kludges.

20.2   Managing the Risks of Evolutionary Delivery

Here are the risks you should plan for if your version of Evolutionary Delivery leans more toward Evolutionary Prototyping:

CROSS-REFERENCE
For details on these risks, see Section 21.2, "Managing the Risks of Evolutionary Prototyping."

- Unrealistic schedule and budget expectations arising from rapid early progress
- Diminished project control

- Feature creep
- Poor user feedback
- Poor product performance
- Unrealistic performance expectations
- Poor design
- Poor maintainability
- Inefficient use of development time by developers

Here are the risks you should watch for if your project leans more toward Staged Delivery:

CROSS-REFERENCE
For details on these risks, see Section 36.2, "Managing the Risks of Staged Delivery."

- Feature creep
- Missed technical dependencies
- Insufficient developer focus, leading to inefficient use of development time

20.3 Side Effects of Evolutionary Delivery

Evolutionary Delivery improves your ability to make mid-course project corrections. At each incremental delivery, if the results weren't what you expected, you can improve the design, modify the cost/benefit analysis, or cancel the project early.

Delivering early and often helps to improve your estimation by giving you more chances to practice. That doesn't increase your development speed, but it does improve your ability to deliver what you promise, which can be just as important in a speed-sensitive environment. Tom Gilb calls this the "future-shock principle": data from past projects might be useful, but it can't be as useful to you as current data from your present project (Gilb 1988).

Another benefit is that you can pretend to ship your product every few weeks or months. In doing that, you shorten the amount of time it takes to learn all the lessons that you learn by completing a product cycle. End-to-end product development experience is great experience to have, and when you shorten the feedback loop, you're able to get that experience faster.

CROSS-REFERENCE
For details on these side effects, see Section 21.3, "Side Effects of Evolutionary Prototyping."

If your version of Evolutionary Delivery is tilted toward Evolutionary Prototyping, you might experience these side effects:

- Improved morale of users, customers, and developers because progress is visible

- Early feedback on whether the final system will be acceptable
- Decreased overall code length
- Defect reduction due to better requirements definition
- Smooth effort curves that reduce the deadline effect (which commonly arises when using traditional development approaches)

CROSS-REFERENCE
For details on these side effects, see Section 36.3, "Side Effects of Staged Delivery."

If your version of Evolutionary Delivery is tilted toward Staged Delivery, you might experience these side effects:

- More even distribution of development and testing resources
- Improved code quality
- More likely project completion
- Support for build-to-budget efforts

20.4 Evolutionary Delivery's Interactions with Other Practices

Success of Evolutionary Delivery depends on the effective use of Designing for Change (Chapter 19). Evolutionary Delivery invites changes, and your system needs to be set up to accommodate them.

20.5 The Bottom Line on Evolutionary Delivery

CROSS-REFERENCE
For more on the importance of making progress visible, see Section 6.3, "Perception and Reality."

The bottom line on Evolutionary Delivery is that, whether or not it reduces overall development time, it provides tangible signs of progress that can be just as important to rapid development as all-out development speed. It might appear that this incremental approach takes longer than a more traditional approach, but it almost never does because it keeps you and your customer from getting too far out of touch with your real progress.

HARD DATA

Evolutionary Prototyping has been reported to decrease development effort by from 45 to 80 percent (Gordon and Bieman 1995). Staged Delivery, on the other hand, does not generally reduce development time, but it makes progress more visible. The specific reduction in development time that you experience from Evolutionary Delivery will depend on the specific mix of Evolutionary Prototyping and Staged Delivery that you use.

20.6   Keys to Success in Using Evolutionary Delivery

Here are the keys to using Evolutionary Delivery successfully:

- Be sure that the product architecture supports as many of the system's possible directions as you can imagine.
- Define the system's core carefully.
- Decide whether to lean more toward Evolutionary Prototyping or Staged Delivery, based on the extent to which you need to accommodate customer change requests.
- Order the functionality in your initial set of releases from "most certain" to "least certain." Assume that the number of changes will increase in later releases.
- Explicitly manage user expectations having to do with schedule, budget, and performance.
- Consider whether pure Staged Delivery or pure Evolutionary Prototyping might be a better fit for your project.

Further Reading

Gilb, Tom. *Principles of Software Engineering Management.* Wokingham, England: Addison-Wesley, 1988. Chapters 7 and 15 contain thorough discussions of staged delivery and evolutionary delivery.

McConnell, Steve. *Code Complete.* Redmond, Wash.: Microsoft Press, 1993. Chapter 27 describes the evolutionary-delivery practice.

Cusumano, Michael, and Richard Selby. *Microsoft Secrets: How the World's Most Powerful Software Company Creates Technology, Shapes Markets, and Manages People.* New York: Free Press, 1995. Chapter 4 describes Microsoft's milestone process, which could be considered to be a cousin to evolutionary delivery. Cusumano and Selby are professors at MIT and UC Irvine, respectively, and they present the outsider's view of the process.

McCarthy, Jim. *Dynamics of Software Development.* Redmond, Wash.: Microsoft Press, 1995. McCarthy describes the insider's view of Microsoft's milestone process. From an evolutionary-delivery viewpoint, his book is particularly interesting because it focuses on Visual C++, a subscription shrink-wrap product that's shipped every four months.

21

Evolutionary Prototyping

Evolutionary Prototyping is a lifecycle model in which the system is developed in increments so that it can readily be modified in response to end-user and customer feedback. Most evolutionary-prototyping efforts begin by prototyping the user interface and then evolving the completed system from that, but prototyping can start with any high-risk area. Evolutionary Prototyping is not the same as Throwaway Prototyping, and making the right choice about whether to develop an evolutionary prototype or a throwaway prototype is one key to success. Other keys to success include using experienced developers, managing schedule and budget expectations, and managing the prototyping activity itself.

S
U
M
M
A
R
Y

Efficacy

Potential reduction from nominal schedule:	Excellent
Improvement in progress visibility:	Excellent
Effect on schedule risk:	Increased Risk
Chance of first-time success:	Very Good
Chance of long-term success:	Excellent

Major Risks

- Unrealistic schedule and budget expectations
- Inefficient use of prototyping time
- Unrealistic performance expectations
- Poor design
- Poor maintainability

(continued)

Major Interactions and Trade-Offs

- Trades a reduction in project control for increased end-user and customer feedback and for better progress visibility
- Can be combined with User-Interface Prototyping and Throwaway Prototyping
- Can serve as a basis for Evolutionary Delivery

Evolutionary Prototyping is a development approach in which you develop selected parts of a system first and then evolve the rest of the system from those parts. Unlike other kinds of prototyping, in Evolutionary Prototyping you don't discard the prototyping code; you evolve it into the code that you ultimately deliver. Figure 21-1 shows how this works.

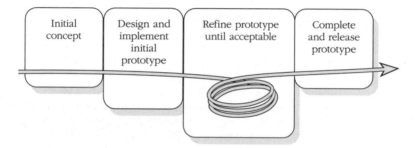

Figure 21-1. *Evolutionary Prototyping model. With Evolutionary Prototyping, you start by designing and implementing the most prominent parts of the program in a prototype. You then continue adding to and refining the prototype until you're done. The prototype eventually evolves into the software that you release.*

Evolutionary Prototyping supports rapid development by addressing risks early. You start development with the riskiest areas of your system. If you can overcome the obstacles, you can evolve the rest of the system from the prototype. If you can't, you can cancel the project without having spent any more money than necessary to discover that the obstacles were insurmountable.

Rapid Prototyping

Evolutionary Prototyping is one of a set of practices that are often described as "rapid prototyping." The term "rapid prototyping" is a loose description that generally refers to Evolutionary Prototyping but which often refers to any prototyping practices.

21.1   Using Evolutionary Prototyping

Evolutionary Prototyping is an exploratory activity that you use when you don't know at the outset exactly what you need to build. Because the areas of uncertainty in a development effort vary from one project to another, your first step is to identify the part of the system to use as a starting point. The two main options are to start with the most visible parts or the riskiest parts. The user interface is often both the most visible and the riskiest part, so it is often the obvious place to start.

After you've built the first part of the system, you demonstrate it and then continue to develop the prototype based on the feedback you receive. If your prototyping effort is customer-oriented, you'll continue to solicit feedback from the customer and to refine the user interface until everyone agrees that the prototype is good enough. Then you develop the rest of the system using the prototype's design and code as a foundation.

If your prototyping effort is technically oriented, you might develop some other part of the system first, such as the database. The feedback you'll look for in that case won't necessarily come from the customer. Your mission might be to benchmark database size or performance with a realistic number of end-users. But the general prototyping pattern is the same. You continue to look for feedback and to refine your prototype until everyone agrees that the prototype is good enough, and then you complete the system. The same principle applies to prototyping of user interfaces, complex calculations, interactive performance, real-time timing constraints, data sizing, and proof-of-concept aspects of leading-edge systems.

You can use Evolutionary Prototyping to greater or lesser degrees on most kinds of projects. It is probably best suited to business systems in which developers can have frequent, informal interactions with end-users. But it is also well suited to commercial, shrink-wrap, and systems projects as long as you can get end-users involved. The user interaction for these kinds of projects will generally need to be more structured and formal.

21.2   Managing the Risks of Evolutionary Prototyping

HARD DATA

In spite of a long list of risks to watch for, Evolutionary Prototyping is a relatively low-risk practice. Of published case studies, 33 of the 39 have reported success (Gordon and Bieman 1995). Here are some risks to keep in mind.

CROSS-REFERENCE
For related risks, see Section 38.2, "Managing the Risks of Throwaway Prototyping," and Section 42.2, "Managing the Risks of User-Interface Prototyping."

Unrealistic schedule and budget expectations. Evolutionary Prototyping may create unfulfillable expectations about the overall development schedule. When end-users, managers, or marketers see rapid progress on a prototype, they sometimes make unrealistic assumptions about how quickly you can develop the final product. In some instances, the sales staff passes along unrealistic schedule expectations to customers. Customers later become upset when they hear that the software will take longer than they expected.

It's easy to complete the most visible work quickly, but a great deal of the work in a programming project isn't obvious to the customer or end-user. Low-visibility work includes robust database access, maintenance of database integrity, security, networking, data conversion between successive product versions, design for high-volume usage, multi-user support, and multi-platform support. The better this work is done, the less noticeable it will be.

Another problem with the effort expectations created when prototyping starts with the user interface is that some of the functionality that looks easiest from the end-user's point of view is the most difficult to implement from the developer's point of view. Difficult areas that look easy include cut-and-paste within an application, cut-and-paste from other applications, printing, print preview, and WYSIWYG screen displays.

HARD DATA

Finally, prototypes are generally designed to handle only the nominal cases; they aren't expected to handle the exceptional cases. But as much as 90 percent of a normal program consists of exception handling (Shaw in Bentley 1982), which suggests that even if a prototype were completely functional for all nominal cases, it would still take up to 9 times as much effort to implement the exceptional cases as it took to implement the fully functioning, nominal-case prototype.

If management does not understand the difference between creating a limited prototype and a full-scale product, it will be at risk of seriously under-budgeting prototyping projects. Scott Gordon and James Bieman reported a case in which management bought a 2-year project as a 6-week project. Management believed that the prototyping would produce fully functional results in an amount of time that was out of touch with real-world needs by a factor of almost 20 (Gordon and Bieman 1995).

CROSS-REFERENCE
For more on expectation management, see Section 10.3, "Managing Customer Expectations."

You can manage this risk by explicitly managing the expectations of end-users, managers, developers, and marketers. Be sure they interact with the prototype in a controlled setting in which you can explain the prototype's limitations, and be sure that they understand the difference between creating a prototype and creating completely functional software.

Diminished project control. With Evolutionary Prototyping, it's impossible to know at the outset of the project how long it will take to create an acceptable product. You don't know how many iterations it will take or how long each iteration will last.

CROSS-REFERENCE
For details on realizing benefits of both Evolutionary Prototyping and Staged Delivery, see Chapter 20, "Evolutionary Delivery."

This risk is mitigated somewhat by the fact that customers can see steady signs of progress and tend to be less nervous about eventually getting a product than with traditional development approaches. It's also possible to use an evolutionary-delivery approach that's strongly tilted toward Evolutionary Prototyping, which provides some of the control of Staged Delivery and some of the flexibility of Evolutionary Prototyping.

CROSS-REFERENCE
For details on the risk of poor feedback, see "End-User Feedback and Involvement" in Section 42.1.

Poor end-user or customer feedback. Prototyping doesn't guarantee high-quality end-user or customer feedback. End-users and customers don't always know what they're looking at when they see a prototype. One common phenomenon is that they are so overwhelmed by the live software demonstration that they don't look past the glitz to understand what the prototype really represents. If they give you a rubber-stamp approval, you can be virtually certain that they don't fully understand what they're seeing. Be sure that end-users and customers study the prototype carefully enough to provide meaningful feedback.

Poor product performance. Several factors can contribute to poor product performance, including:

- Not considering performance in the product's design
- Keeping poorly structured, inefficient code that was developed quickly for the prototype instead of evolving it to production quality
- Keeping a prototype that was originally intended to be thrown away

You can take three steps to minimize the risk of poor performance:

- Consider performance early. Be sure to benchmark performance early, and be sure that the prototype's design supports an adequate level of performance.
- Don't develop quick-and-dirty code for the prototype. A prototype's code quality needs to be good enough to support extensive modifications, which means that it needs to be at least as good as the code of a traditionally developed system.
- Don't evolve a throwaway prototype into the final product.

Unrealistic performance expectations. The risk of unrealistic performance expectations is related to the risk of poor performance. This risk arises when the prototype has much better performance than the final product. Because a prototype doesn't have to do all of the work that a final product does, it can sometimes be very fast compared to the final product. When customers see the final product, it can appear to be unacceptably slow.

This risk also has an evil twin. If a prototyping language is used that has much worse performance than the target language, customers may equate weaknesses in the prototype's performance with weaknesses in the final product. More than one case study has reported project failure as a result of low expectations created by a prototype (Gordon and Bieman 1995).

You can address this risk by explicitly managing the expectations that customers develop from interacting with the prototype. If the prototype is very fast, add artificial delays to the prototype so that the prototype's performance approximates the performance of the final product. If the prototype is very slow, explain to customers that the performance of the prototype isn't indicative of the performance of the final product.

Poor design. Many prototyping projects have better designs than traditional projects, but several factors contribute to the risk of poor design.

- A prototype's design can deteriorate and its implementation can drift from its original design during successive stages (just as most software products tend to deteriorate during maintenance). The final product can inherit design patches from the prototype system.

- Sometimes customer or end-user feedback steers the product in an unexpected direction. If the design didn't anticipate the direction, it might be twisted to fit without doing a full redesign.

- The design that flows out of a user-interface–focused prototyping activity might focus on the user interface excessively; it might fail to account for other parts of the system that should also have strong influences on the system's design.

CROSS-REFERENCE
For more on pushing the envelope with rapid-development languages, see Section 28.3, "Managing Risks of RDLs."

- The use of a special-purpose prototyping language can result in a poor system design. Environments that are well suited to making rapid progress during the early stages of development are sometimes poorly suited to maintaining design integrity in the later stages of development.

You can mitigate design-quality risks by striking at the root of the problem. Limit the scope of the prototype to specific areas of the product, for example, to the user interface. Develop this limited part of the product using a prototyping language, and evolve it; then develop the rest of the product using a traditional programming language and nonprototyping approaches.

When creating the overall system design, make a conscious effort not to overemphasize the user interface or any other aspect of the system that has been prototyped. Minimize the impact that design in one area can have on the design as a whole.

Include a design phase with each iteration of the prototype to ensure that you evolve the design and not just the code. Use a design checklist at each stage to check the quality of the evolving product.

CLASSIC MISTAKE

Avoid using inexperienced developers on a prototyping project. Evolutionary Prototyping requires that developers make far-reaching design decisions much earlier in the development process than when other development approaches are used. Inexperienced developers are often poorly equipped to make good design decisions under such circumstances. Case studies of prototyping projects have reported projects that have failed because of the involvement of inexperienced developers. They have also reported projects that have succeeded only because of the involvement of experienced developers (Gordon and Bieman 1995).

Poor maintainability. Evolutionary Prototyping sometimes contributes to poor maintainability. The high degree of modularity needed for effective Evolutionary Prototyping is conducive to maintainable code. But when the prototype is developed extremely rapidly, it is also sometimes developed extremely sloppily—Evolutionary Prototyping can be used as a disguise for code-and-fix development. Moreover, if a special-purpose prototyping language is used, the language may be unfamiliar to maintenance programmers, which will make the program difficult to maintain. In the published literature on prototyping, more sources than not have observed worse maintainability with Evolutionary Prototyping than with traditional approaches (Gordon and Bieman 1995).

Minimize the maintainability risk by taking a few simple steps. Be sure that the design is adequate by using the guidelines listed in the discussion of the "Poor design" risk (in the preceding section). Use code-quality checklists at each stage to keep the prototype's code quality from slipping. Follow normal naming conventions for objects, methods, functions, data, database elements, libraries, and any other components that will be maintained as the prototype matures. Follow other coding conventions for good layout and commenting. Remind your team that they will have to use their own code throughout multiple product-release cycles—that will give them a strong incentive to make their code maintainable and to keep it that way.

CROSS-REFERENCE
For details on change management, see Chapter 14, "Feature-Set Control."

Feature creep. Customers and end-users typically have direct access to the prototype during an evolutionary-prototyping project, and that can sometimes lead to an increased desire for features. In addition to managing their interactions with the prototype, use normal change-management practices to control feature creep.

CLASSIC MISTAKE

Inefficient use of prototyping time. Prototyping is usually intended to shorten the development schedule. Paradoxically, projects often waste time during prototyping and don't save as much time as they could. Prototyping is an exploratory, iterative process, so it is tempting to treat it as a process that can't be managed carefully. Developers don't always know how far to develop a prototype, so they sometimes waste time fleshing out features that are summarily excluded from the product later. Developers sometimes give the prototype a robustness it doesn't need or waste time working on the prototype without moving it in any clear direction.

To spend prototyping time effectively, make project tracking and control a priority. Carefully schedule prototyping activities. Later in the project you might break the project into chunks of a few days or weeks, but during prototyping break it into hours or days. Be sure that you don't put a lot of work into prototyping and evolving any part of the system until you're certain it's going to remain part of the system.

Developers need to have a well-developed sense of how little they can do to investigate the risky areas a prototype is intended to explore. On one project I worked on, we needed to create a user-interface prototype to demonstrate our user-interface design to our sponsor. One of the other developers thought it would take a team of three developers 6 weeks to build the prototype. I thought I could do all the work myself in about 1 week, which turned out to be accurate. The difference in our estimates didn't arise because I was six times as fast as three developers; they arose because the other developer didn't have a good sense of all the things that could be left out of that kind of a prototype. Ergo, avoid using inexperienced developers on prototyping projects.

21.3   Side Effects of Evolutionary Prototyping

In addition to its rapid-development benefits, Evolutionary Prototyping produces many side effects, most of which are beneficial. Prototyping tends to lead to:

- Improved morale of end-users, customers, and developers because progress is visible
- Early feedback on whether the final system will be acceptable
- Decreased overall code length because of better designs and more reuse
- Lower defect rates because of better requirements definition
- Smoother effort curves, reducing the deadline effect (which is common when using traditional development approaches)

21.4 Evolutionary Prototyping's Interactions with Other Practices

HARD DATA

Evolutionary Prototyping is an effective remedy for feature creep when it is used with other practices. One study found that the combination of prototyping and JAD (Chapter 24) was capable of keeping creeping requirements below 5 percent. Average projects experience levels of about 25 percent (Jones 1994).

Evolutionary Prototyping is also an effective defect-removal practice when combined with other practices. A combination of reviews, inspections, and testing produce a defect-removal strategy with the highest defect-removal efficacy, lowest cost, and shortest schedule. Adding prototyping to the mix produces a defect-removal strategy with the highest cumulative defect-removal efficacy (Pfleeger 1994a).

If Evolutionary Prototyping provides less control than you need or you already know fundamentally what you want the system to do, you can use Evolutionary Delivery (Chapter 20) or Staged Delivery (Chapter 36) instead.

Relationship to Other Kinds of Prototyping

On small systems, Evolutionary Prototyping is preferable to Throwaway Prototyping because the overhead of creating a throwaway prototype makes it economically unfeasible. If you're considering developing a throwaway prototype on a small-to-medium–size project, be sure that you can recoup the overhead over the life of the project.

On large systems (systems with more than 100,000 lines of code), you can use either Throwaway Prototyping or Evolutionary Prototyping. Developers are sometimes leery of using Evolutionary Prototyping on large systems, but the published reports on the use of Evolutionary Prototyping on large systems have all reported success (Gordon and Bieman 1995).

21.5 The Bottom Line on Evolutionary Prototyping

HARD DATA

In case studies, Evolutionary Prototyping has decreased development effort dramatically, by from 45 to 80 percent (Gordon and Bieman 1995). To achieve this kind of reduction, you must manage development risks carefully, particularly the risks of poor design, poor maintenance, and feature creep. If you don't do that, overall effort can actually increase.

Prototyping yields its benefits quickly. Capers Jones estimates that Evolutionary Prototyping will return roughly two dollars for every dollar spent within the first year, and scaling up to roughly ten dollars for every dollar spent within four years (Jones 1994).

Prototyping also produces steady, visible signs of advancement, improving progress visibility and contributing to the impression that you're developing rapidly. That can be especially useful when the demand for development speed is strong.

The up-front cost of initiating an evolutionary-prototyping program is low—only the costs needed for developer training and prototyping tools.

21.6 Keys to Success in Using Evolutionary Prototyping

Here are the keys to successful Evolutionary Prototyping:

- Decide at the beginning of the project whether to evolve the prototype or throw it away. Be sure that managers and developers are both committed to whichever course of action is selected.

- Explicitly manage customer and end-user expectations having to do with schedule, budget, and performance.

- Limit end-user interaction with the prototype to controlled settings.

- Use experienced developers. Avoid using entry-level developers.

- Use design checklists at each stage to ensure the quality of the prototyped system.

- Use code-quality checklists at each stage to ensure the maintainability of the prototyped code.

- Consider performance early.

- Carefully manage the prototyping activity itself.

- Consider whether Evolutionary Prototyping will provide the most benefit or whether Evolutionary Delivery or Staged Delivery would be better.

Further Reading

Gordon, V. Scott, and James M. Bieman. "Rapid Prototyping: Lessons Learned," *IEEE Software*, January 1995, 85–95. This article summarizes the lessons learned from 22 published case studies of prototyping and several additional anonymous case studies.

Connell, John, and Linda Shafer. *Object-Oriented Rapid Prototyping*. Englewood Cliffs, N.J.: Yourdon Press, 1995. This book overviews the reasons that you would prototype and different prototyping styles. It then presents an intelligent, full discussion of evolutionary, object-oriented prototyping including the topics of design guidelines, tools, prototype refinement, and prototyping-compatible lifecycle models.

22

Goal Setting

S
U
M
M
A
R
Y

Goal Setting makes use of the fact that human motivation is the single, strongest contributor to productivity. In Goal Setting, a product manager or customer simply tells developers what is expected of them. Because Goal Setting contributes to motivation, developers will generally work hard to achieve a goal of "shortest schedule" (or least risky schedule or most visible progress or whatever the goal is). The primary obstacle to success is an unwillingness to define a small, clear set of goals and commit to them for an entire project.

Efficacy	**Goal of Shortest Schedule**	**Goal of Least Risk**	**Goal of Maximum Visibility**
Potential reduction from nominal schedule:	Very Good	None	None
Improvement in progress visibility:	None	Good	Excellent
Effect on schedule risk:	Increased Risk	Decreased Risk	Decreased Risk
Chance of first-time success:	Good	Good	Good
Chance of long-term success:	Very Good	Very Good	Very Good

Major Risks

- Significant loss of motivation if goals are changed

Major Interactions and Trade-Offs

- Provides key support for signing up, timebox development, voluntary overtime, and motivation in general

The summary ratings in this table depend on the specific goal. For more on goal setting, see "Goal Setting" in Section 11.2.

23

Inspections

Inspections are a kind of formal technical review in which participants in the review are well-trained in review practices and assigned specific roles to play. Participants inspect review materials before the review meeting, using checklists of common errors. The roles played during the review meeting help to stimulate discovery of additional errors. Inspections have been found to be much more effective at finding errors than execution testing—both in percentage of total defects found and in time spent per defect. They derive their rapid-development benefit by detecting errors early in the development process, which avoids costly, downstream rework. Inspections can be used on virtually any kind of project and on both new development and maintenance.

S
U
M
M
A
R
Y

Efficacy

Potential reduction from nominal schedule:	Very Good
Improvement in progress visibility:	Fair
Effect on schedule risk:	Decreased Risk
Chance of first-time success:	Good
Chance of long-term success:	Excellent

Major Risks

None

Major Interactions and Trade-Offs

- Can be combined with virtually any other rapid-development practice.

For more on inspections, see "Inspections" in Section 4.3 and "Further Reading on QA Fundamentals" at the end of Section 4.3.

24

Joint Application Development (JAD)

JAD is a requirements-definition and user-interface design methodology in which end-users, executives, and developers attend intense off-site meetings to work out a system's details. JAD focuses on the business problem rather than technical details. It is most applicable to the development of business systems, but it can be used successfully for shrink-wrap and systems software. It produces its savings by shortening the elapsed time required to gather a system's requirements and by gathering requirements better, thus reducing the number of costly, downstream requirements changes. Its success depends on effective leadership of the JAD sessions; on participation by key end-users, executives, and developers; and on achieving group synergy during JAD sessions.

S U M M A R Y

Efficacy

Potential reduction from nominal schedule:	Good
Improvement in progress visibility:	Fair
Effect on schedule risk:	Decreased Risk
Chance of first-time success:	Good
Chance of long-term success:	Excellent

Major Risks

- Unrealistic productivity expectations following the JAD sessions
- Premature, inaccurate estimates of remaining work following JAD sessions

Major Interactions and Trade-Offs

- Works best when combined with an incremental-development lifecycle model
- Can be combined with rapid-development languages and prototyping tools

JAD stands for "Joint Application Development." The "joint" refers to the fact that developers, end-users, and other concerned parties together design the product concept. It's a structured process for requirements gathering and negotiation. The focal point of the process is a series of workshops that are attended by executives, end-users, and developers.

JAD leverages group dynamics, extensive use of visual aids, WYSIWYG documentation, and an organized, rational process to gather requirements in a short time. JAD is one of the most powerful requirements-specification practices yet developed, and it produces its savings in several ways.

CROSS-REFERENCE
For more on reducing time at the front end of the product-development cycle, see Section 6.5, "Where the Time Goes."

It commits top executives to the software-planning process. JAD involves top executives from the beginning of a product's development. Early executive involvement shortens the product-approval cycle.

It shortens the requirements-specification phase. JAD reduces the amount of time needed to gather requirements, which shortens the overall development cycle. This is particularly useful because requirements specification can be an essentially unbounded activity that adds weeks or months to a project's front end.

It eliminates features of questionable value. By eliminating questionable features and making the product smaller, JAD reduces development time.

It helps to get requirements right the first time. Requirements analysts and end-users speak different languages, which means that the chances of them communicating effectively about software requirements are slim. JAD improves communication and eliminates costly rework resulting from mistaken requirements.

It helps to get the user interface right the first time. Some products require extensive rework because end-users reject the product's user interface. JAD-design sessions focus on user-interface design. Because end-users are involved in those sessions, the user interface that's developed is usually ultimately acceptable to end-users.

It reduces organizational infighting. Many projects are hobbled by conflicting objectives or hidden agendas. By bringing all the decision makers together to design the system, JAD brings these issues to light early in the project, when they can still be addressed effectively and before they've had time to do much damage.

24.1   Using JAD

JAD consists of two main phases, a JAD-planning phase and a JAD-design phase. Both of these phases deal with what is traditionally thought of as the system's requirements, but at different levels. In both phases, JAD focuses on the business-design problem rather than on purely technical details.

During the JAD-planning phase, the emphasis is on mapping out broad capabilities of the software system. The emphasis is more on business concerns than detailed technical concerns. The main outcomes of the JAD-planning phase are the system's goals, preliminary effort and schedule estimates, and a decision about whether to continue with further product development. JAD planning also sets up the JAD-design phase.

If the decision is made to go ahead with the product, the JAD-design phase comes next. JAD design elicits more detailed requirements, and its purpose is to create the user-level design of the software. In spite of being called "design," it does not focus on the functional design of the system, which is what you might think of when you think of "design." JAD design uses prototyping extensively, and the main outcomes of this phase are a detailed user-interface design, a database schema (if appropriate), and refined budget and schedule estimates. At the end of this phase, the project must again be approved before it can continue.

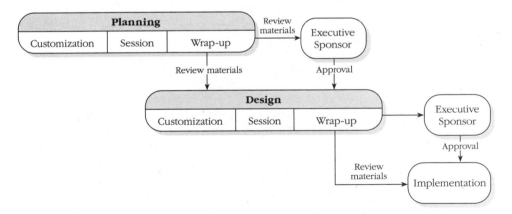

Figure 24-1. *Overview of the JAD process. JAD planning and JAD design are organized into similar sequences of activities. Source: Adapted from* Joint Application Design *(August 1991)*.

As Figure 24-1 suggests, both the planning phase and the design phase are broken into three parts:

1. *Customization*—The session leader and perhaps a few other people take the out-of-the-box JAD methodology and tailor it to the specific project. This typically requires from 1 to 10 days.

2. *Session*—The session, the time when all the parties are brought together, is the main focus of JAD. It typically lasts from 1 to 10 days, depending on the size of the system.

3. *Wrap-up*—Wrap-up is the documentation or packaging of the session activity. Handwritten notes and visual aids are converted into one or more formal documents. This takes from 3 to 15 days.

CROSS-REFERENCE
For more on incremental lifecycle models, see Chapter 7, "Lifecycle Planning."

Once the JAD-design phase is over, as much output as possible is carried electronically into the program-design and construction phases. JAD does not dictate any particular program-design or construction practices, but it is especially compatible with incremental lifecycle models and with the use of CASE tools.

Although JAD was originally developed for use in IS mainframe environments, it has been used successfully in client-server software development too (August 1991, Martin 1991, Sims 1995). The practice of bringing all the stakeholder parties together to thrash out a system's requirements is equally applicable to commercial products, vertical-market software, shrink-wrap software, and systems software. You can use the customization subphases of JAD planning and JAD design to adapt JAD to projects of virtually any size or kind.

JAD Planning

JAD planning focuses on requirements and planning. Its objectives are to identify high-level requirements, define and bound the system scope, plan the JAD-design activity, publish the JAD-plan document, and obtain approval for the JAD-design activity. The JAD-planning phase is also sometimes called Joint Requirements Planning, or JRP (Martin 1991). The following subsections describe the customization, session, and wrap-up subphases.

Customization

The purpose of the customization activity is to tailor the JAD-planning session to the needs of the specific project. The main activities during customization are:

1. Orient participants to the JAD process
2. Organize the JAD team

3. Tailor JAD tasks and outputs to the specific project

4. Prepare the materials for the JAD-planning session

The people who participate in planning are usually not the same people who participate in design. The participants in a planning session tend to be higher up in the organization. JAD design makes use of participants who will own the system or work with it when it's built. If these higher-level people and hands-on people are all the same, you can combine planning and design into one phase.

Session

The JAD session is what sets JAD apart from other requirements-gathering methods. Critical ingredients of the JAD session include leadership from a trained JAD leader, participation by the executive sponsor and other key decision-makers, use of a structured process, and an ability to work without normal day-to-day interruptions.

Timeline

CROSS-REFERENCE
For more on the factors that cause teams to jell, see Chapter 12, "Teamwork."

As I mentioned earlier, a JAD session can last anywhere from 1 to 10 days. JAD is a team activity, so typical teamwork guidelines apply. It usually takes 2 days for a JAD team to jell (Martin 1991). If the JAD session lasts 5 days, the team will do most of its work on days 3, 4, and 5.

Regardless of the duration of the JAD session, the participants must attend full-time. If some participants attend only part-time, you waste time briefing them and re-covering old ground. To achieve the group synergy of a JAD session, all group members need to be present.

Facilities

The JAD room is located off-site, ideally in a hotel or conference facility. JAD participants are normally key people in the organization, and key people usually have dozens of potential distractions. The facility should free participants from their normal distractions and allow them to focus exclusively on the JAD session. Allowing participants to respond to interruptions during a session suggests that the JAD session isn't important.

The JAD room for both planning and design should include visual-aid support, computer support, copy machine, notepads, pens, Polaroid camera to record whiteboard contents, name cards (if needed), and drinks and refreshments. This combination of facilities sends an important message to the JAD participants: "This job is important, and the organization is behind you."

Roles

A JAD session includes a number of people.

Session leader. The session leader is most instrumental in the success or failure of JAD, and the successful leader needs a rare combination of skills. The leader must have excellent communication and mediation skills. The leader must mediate political disputes, power struggles, and personality clashes. The leader needs to be impartial (arriving at the JAD session with no political baggage) and able to keep an open mind and control controversies. The leader should be sensitive to hidden agendas and able to redirect them constructively. The leader should bridge communication gaps. The leader must be comfortable speaking to and controlling a group of people that includes high-level executives. The leader should encourage quiet members of the group to participate and prevent strong personalities from dominating the sessions.

To achieve all this, the leader needs to have the respect of all the parties at the session, needs to prepare thoroughly, and needs adequate knowledge of the business area and development practices that will be used. Finally, the leader needs to be enthusiastic about JAD.

When JAD fails, it is almost always because of the JAD session leader (Martin 1991). Some organizations appoint different leaders for each project. The result is that each project uses an unskilled leader and realizes unsatisfactory results. An organization that intends to use JAD should train one or more JAD leaders and expect them to stay in that job for two years or more. It usually takes about four JAD sessions for a new JAD leader to become proficient.

Executive sponsor. This is the person who bears the financial responsibility for the system. This person is the focal point for the go/no-go decision that follows the planning session. Sometimes more than one executive sponsor will attend, especially during the planning sessions.

End-user representative. This is a key representative from the end-user community who should have the authority to make binding decisions about the program. Like the other participants, the end-user representative should be a good communicator. More than one end-user representative can participate, although the design session held later provides the main forum for end-user involvement.

Developer. This person's job is to assist end-users, to steer them away from specifying a "blue sky" system that is not implementable, and to learn the end-user's perspective. The developer answers questions about other systems, feasibility of proposed features, and costs. Developers should be careful to avoid saying "yes" or "no" to any user ideas. Their role is to provide information, not to make judgments. Developers must learn the system during the planning and design sessions so that they can hit the ground running after the JAD-design phase. More than one developer can (and often should) participate in the session.

Scribe. The scribe is someone from the software-development department whose primary responsibility is to record what happens during the session. The scribe is an active participant, asking for clarification and pointing out inconsistencies from day to day.

Specialists. These people are invited as needed to provide any special expertise required for the session. The specialist is an exception to the rule that all participants need to be present at all times. You can call in this person as-needed because the specialist is a resource to the JAD group rather than a full member of the group.

Common problems

JAD sessions are subject to several common problems:

- JAD sessions give an organization an opportunity to leverage the performance of its star performers. Great performers can work wonders during a JAD session, while mediocre performers can produce mediocre results. Sometimes an organization doesn't spare its stars to participate in JAD. Participation of all key people is essential. If you can't get key people to participate, don't do the JAD session at all. The chance of success is greatly reduced, and the key people who do attend the session won't appreciate having several days wasted if the session fails.

- Observers are a risk at JAD sessions because they typically are not able to confine themselves to observer roles. If you need to allow observers, treat them as participants, and make sure that they attend the same training sessions other participants do and are adequately prepared.

- Too many participants can keep the JAD team from jelling, which will impair the group's progress. The complete JAD group should have a total of 8 people or fewer (Martin 1991). Some experts have reported good success with as many as 15 participants (August 1991), but it is hard for the team to jell when it contains more than 8 people. If your organization is skilled at JAD, you might be able to approach the upper limit of 15 participants, but do so cautiously.

What happens during a session

A JAD-planning session typically goes through eight main activities:

- *Conducting the orientation*—Introduce the group to the purpose of the session, timetable, and agenda.

- *Defining the high-level requirements*—Map out the system, including identification of the business needs the system is intended to address; system objectives; anticipated benefits; list of possible system functions; rough prioritization of system functions; and strategic and future considerations.

- *Limiting the system scope*—Place limits on what the system can include. Your decisions about what the system will not include are as important to development speed as decisions about what the system will include.

- *Identifying and estimating the JAD-design phase or phases*—This is the first step in planning follow-on JAD activities.

- *Identifying the JAD-design participants*—Identify the people who will participate in the follow-on JAD-design phases.

- *Scheduling the JAD-design phases*—End-users, development, and the executive sponsor agree on a schedule for JAD design.

- *Documenting the issues and considerations*—Document the issues that were considered during the JAD-planning session so that you have a record of options that were considered and a record of the reasons that issues were resolved in the way they were.

- *Concluding the session*.

For each of these activities, you go through roughly the same process. The JAD session leader presents the task, such as defining high-level requirements. Participants then generate ideas. The ideas are displayed where everyone can see them on whiteboards or overhead projectors. It's essential during this period that all team members participate, and a good JAD leader will make sure that happens.

Once the ideas have been generated, you evaluate the ideas. This is the time when the different points of view of executive sponsors, end-users, development representatives, and specialists come into play. The JAD leader keeps the group focused on the main topic, cuts through political disputes, minimizes the effects of strong and weak personalities, and redirects side issues that can't be resolved during the JAD session. During evaluation, participants often generate ideas that resolve conflicting needs in creative ways.

Finally, the group commits to whatever has been decided during the evaluation phase—system objectives, rough prioritization of system functions, restrictions on the system's scope, participants in the JAD-design phase, and so on.

Wrap-Up

The wrap-up follows the JAD session and produces a JAD document, which should look as much as possible like what was generated during the session. Output from the planning session includes:

- List of system objectives, including strategic and future considerations

- Details of possible system functions, including the functions themselves, the business needs that each function addresses, benefits of each function, estimate of the return on investment of each function, and a rough prioritization of each function

- Limitations on the system's scope, including a list of functions that the system will not include
- List of interfaces to other systems
- List of issues that couldn't be resolved during the JAD session, including the name of the issue, the person responsible, and the promised resolution date
- Plan for what happens next, including identification of follow-on JAD-design phases, JAD-design participants, JAD-design schedules, and rough target dates for implementation

In some JAD approaches, one of the outputs of the JAD session is a presentation to the executive sponsor, which includes all the information needed to make a go/no-go decision. In other approaches, the executive sponsor attends the whole JAD-planning session, and no such presentation is needed.

JAD Design

JAD design focuses on requirements and user-interface design. Its objectives are to define detailed requirements, define scope, design screen and report layouts, develop the prototype, and gather the editing, data-validation, processing, and system-interface requirements. It should also produce a design for the database schema if one is needed. The outcome of a JAD-design session is a JAD-design document, which is used to obtain approval for implementation.

Customization

The main activities during design customization are the same as they were for planning. Preparation for the session includes arranging for a session room, equipment, and supplies; preparing visual aids and forms; readying software and personnel for the documentation and prototype efforts; and setting up the session room. The session leader should also prepare a list of possible specifications before the session. These specifications should be treated as "proposed."

If end-users are not familiar with JAD, you should train them before they attend the JAD session. This will familiarize them with the objectives of the session, the roles of the leader and scribe, what they are expected to contribute, and any special diagrammatic techniques that you plan to use.

Session

Critical ingredients of the JAD-design session are similar to those of the planning session: leadership from a trained JAD leader, participation by key decision-makers, use of a structured process, and freedom from interruptions. The design session is highly visual, using whiteboards, flip charts, overhead projectors, and large-screen monitors or projectors.

JAD-design sessions typically last longer than JAD-planning sessions, from a few days to 10 days or more, typically lasting about a week. The facilities needed are identical to those used for JAD planning.

The roles of session leader, development representative, scribe, and specialist are similar to what they were for planning. The development representatives are busier because they are required to participate in the sessions during the day and to build the prototype in the evenings. The executive sponsor is not required to be at the JAD session but may drop in from time-to-time to answer questions and offer support. Rather than use a single end-user representative, a group of key end-users should be present, end-users who can devote enough time to work with the details of the product from JAD design through program design, implementation, test, and release. The project manager might also be present but should not lead the session because the JAD leader must be absolutely impartial.

What happens during a session

A JAD-design session typically goes through ten main activities:

- *Conducting the orientation*—The session leader lays out the purpose of the session, timetable, and agenda.

- *Reviewing and refining the JAD-planning requirements and scope*— You can use the session plan that came out of the JAD-planning phase as a starting point, but you will probably want to refine the plan before you move into the rest of the JAD-design session.

- *Developing a workflow diagram*—Create a diagram that shows how work will be done with the new software system.

- *Developing a workflow description*—Describe in words how work will be done with the new software system.

- *Designing the screens and reports*—Design screen layouts and report formats. JAD-design sessions make extensive use of interactive prototypes, which are created by developers and end-users during and between meetings.

- *Specifying the processing requirements*—Specify data volumes, rates, audit requirements, security requirements, and so on.

- *Defining the interface requirements*—Specify the systems that the new system must interface to.

- *Identifying the system data groups and functions*—Map out the system's data, including major data structures, data-structure components, and data-structure relationships. If the system is database-oriented, create a normalized database schema.

- *Documenting the issues and considerations*—As with planning, you'll want to have a record of options that were considered and a record of the reasons that issues were resolved the way they were.

- *Concluding the session.*

The group dynamics of design meetings are essentially the same as they were in planning. For each of these tasks, the team steps through a process of presenting the task, generating ideas, evaluating ideas, and committing to a resolution.

JAD design saves time because group sessions are more efficient than one-on-one requirements-gathering sessions. Traditionally, analysts come away from end-user interviews with incomplete understandings of the desired requirements. Later they try to second-guess what the end-user said or wanted. During a JAD session, end-users talk with analysts and each other about what they want. The group focuses its combined knowledge of the business area, the business problem to be solved, technical limits and possibilities, strategic considerations, exceptional cases, and especially difficult areas.

CROSS-REFERENCE
For more on the beneficial effect that time pressure can have, see Chapter 39, "Timebox Development."

The time pressure of a JAD-design session helps the group to focus on the main task and reach consensus. Time pressure encourages the participants to work hard and cooperate.

Wrap-Up

JAD documentation takes the place of a traditional requirements specification, so carefully documenting the design session is important. Here are the wrap-up activities that follow a design session:

- Complete the JAD-design document, which again should look as much as possible like what was generated during the session.

- Complete the prototype based on the direction set during the session. In some cases it might be possible to complete the prototype during the design session itself.

- Have all participants review the design document and prototype.

- Present the results to the executive sponsor, including a summary of the design session, the JAD design, preliminary target implementation dates, and the project's current status.

It's important to move quickly from JAD design into functional design and implementation. If a project has to wait several months for approval after JAD design, the requirements can begin to get out of date, you can lose key participants, and you lose end-user support.

24.2   Managing the Risks of JAD

JAD is a sophisticated process that must be done well to work. Here are the main problems it can cause.

CROSS-REFERENCE
For more on the problems caused by unusually rapid progress early in a project, see "Unrealistic schedule and budget expectations" in Section 21.2.

Unrealistic expectations following the JAD session. The JAD session can generate so much excitement that development can't possibly meet the demand for the new system fast enough. Participants in the session see how quickly developers can create a prototype, and they don't always understand why it takes so much longer to create the real system. The positive momentum generated during the sessions can turn against developers if they don't deliver the real system fast enough.

CROSS-REFERENCE
For more on setting realistic expectations, see Section 10.3, "Managing Customer Expectations."

You can mitigate this risk in two ways. First, part of the JAD-design session should be spent setting realistic expectations about how long it will take for development to create the new system. The whole group should commit to a development schedule by the end of the design session.

Second, you should choose an incremental development approach to use with JAD. This allows for relatively quick signs of progress after the JAD-design session as well as garnering the other advantages of incremental development approaches.

CROSS-REFERENCE
For details on how to make and refine estimates, see Chapter 8, "Estimation."

Premature, inaccurate estimates of remaining work following JAD sessions. In standard JAD, a target date for completing implementation comes out of JAD planning, and the estimate is not revised as part of the JAD-design phase. That creates an estimate far too early in the development cycle and contributes to the risk of unrealistic expectations. You'll know much more about the system after JAD design than after JAD planning. JAD participants will probably want an estimate after the planning phase, so make a rough estimate after planning and a more refined estimate after design. I've modified the standard JAD-phase outputs in this chapter to use this two-estimate approach instead of the standard approach.

24.3   Side Effects of JAD

Aside from its impact on development speed, JAD has many side effects, all of them positive:

- It results in a higher-quality user interface from the end-user's point of view. Prototypes make the software's design tangible, and participants are better able to contribute to a hot prototype than a cold paper spec.
- It results in higher end-user satisfaction because of the end-users' participation in the software's design.

- It results in systems that have greater business value, for the same reason.

- It helps developers gain appreciation for the practical business needs and concerns of executives and end-users.

- It cuts across organizational barriers and reduces the effects of politics. When the mission is clear, the group dynamics during the JAD session will expose hidden agendas, conflicting needs, and politics that might otherwise cripple a project or result in an unsatisfactory product.

- It keeps developers from being trapped in the middle of political conflicts between different departments and end-users.

- It helps to educate end-users about software development through their participation in JAD sessions.

24.4 JAD's Interactions with Other Practices

CROSS-REFERENCE
For more on incremental development approaches, see Chapter 7, "Lifecycle Planning."

JAD should be combined with an incremental lifecycle model—such as Evolutionary Delivery, Evolutionary Prototyping, or Staged Delivery (Chapters 7, 20, 21, and 36)—that delivers part of the software relatively soon after the JAD-design session.

HARD DATA

JAD and prototyping (Chapters 21, 38, and 42) appear to be synergistic practices, and the combination can drop creeping requirements below 5 percent (Jones 1994).

If the technical environment supports it, do the prototyping and design work during the JAD-design session in such a way that you can transfer it to the implementation stage. This is easier to do in IS development than in many other kinds of development. JAD is an integral part of James Martin's RAD methodology, and some organizations integrate JAD into a RAD lifecycle supported by ICASE tools. If it makes sense to do that within your environment, plan for that integration during JAD-planning customization.

24.5 The Bottom Line on JAD

HARD DATA

JAD's effectiveness varies. In early use, companies such as American Airlines, Texas Instruments, and IBM reported that JAD cut the time to do requirements specification by 15 to 35 percent (Rush 1985). CNA Insurance Company reported that it cut requirements effort by almost 70 percent. More recently, Judy August reported that JAD cuts the elapsed time of requirements specification anywhere from 20 to 60 percent compared with traditional methods, and it cuts total effort by 20 to 60 percent at the same time (August 1991).

Requirements gathering takes between 10 percent and 30 percent of the elapsed time on a typical project, depending on the size and complexity of the project (Boehm 1981). If you assume that your project would consume closer to 30 percent than 10 percent of your time without JAD, you can expect JAD's requirements savings to translate into a total-development-time reduction of 5 to 15 percent. To be safe, plan to realize savings on the low end of that range during your initial use of JAD. As your experience with JAD increases, you'll be able to track its effectiveness specifically within your own organization and use your own experience to estimate future projects.

24.6   Keys to Success in Using JAD

Here are the keys to success in using JAD:

- Use an experienced JAD leader to conduct the JAD sessions.
- Be sure that an executive sponsor is committed to the JAD process.
- Have key participants attend the JAD sessions—full-time.
- Hold the workshops off-site, with no telephone and no interruptions. Have participants keep their evenings clear for the duration of the session.
- Prepare participants thoroughly; be sure they understand the JAD process and the specific objectives of the JAD session.
- Set realistic end-user expectations for the work to be done after JAD design.
- Follow up JAD design with an incremental lifecycle model.

To succeed in using JAD for the first time, try to use it on a project that would normally take 12 to 18 staff months of effort in an applications area that is well-understood and not controversial.

Further Reading

JAD is a complex, well-defined process, and a full description of how to do it takes much more than one chapter. If you don't have access to a trained facilitator, the first book below is a good place to start.

Wood, Jane, and Denise Silver. *Joint Application Development, 2d Ed.* New York: John Wiley & Sons, 1995. This book thoroughly explores the many variations of JAD and describes how to become a JAD facilitator. It's well-written and loaded with practical suggestions.

August, Judy. *Joint Application Design.* Englewood Cliffs, N.J.: Yourdon Press, 1991. This is a well-organized, easily readable discussion of JAD that focuses on the way JAD has been done at IBM. It maps out each of the JAD steps and contains much practical advice, such as which visual aids to prepare before the JAD session, how to conduct the JAD kickoff meeting, and much more.

Martin, James. *Rapid Application Development.* New York: Macmillan Publishing Company, 1991. Chapters 7 and 8 describe JAD, and the rest of the book describes a rapid-development context (RAD) that relies on JAD.

25

Lifecycle Model Selection

A software lifecycle is a model that describes all the activities that go into creating a software product. Product development styles vary tremendously among different kinds of projects, requiring different kinds of tasks and different task orderings. Choice of the wrong lifecycle model can result in missing tasks and inappropriate task ordering, which undercuts project planning and efficiency. Choice of an appropriate lifecycle model has the opposite effect—ensuring that all effort is used efficiently. Every project uses a lifecycle of one kind or another—explicitly or implicitly—and this practice ensures that the choice is made explicitly and to maximum advantage.

S
U
M
M
A
R
Y

Efficacy

Potential reduction from nominal schedule:	Fair
Improvement in progress visibility:	Fair
Effect on schedule risk:	Decreased Risk
Chance of first-time success:	Very Good
Chance of long-term success:	Excellent

Major Risks

- The practice of selecting a lifecycle does not in itself contain any risks. Specific lifecycle models may contain additional risks.

Major Interactions and Trade-Offs

None

The summary entries in the table describe only the effect of explicitly choosing a lifecycle model. In addition to those effects, the specific lifecycle model chosen will also have greater or lesser ability to reduce schedule, improve progress visibility, and affect risk level. For more on lifecycle model selection, see Chapter 7, "Lifecycle Planning."

26

Measurement

Measurement is a practice that has both short-term motivational benefits and long-term cost, quality, and schedule benefits. Measurement provides an antidote to the common problems of poor estimates, poor scheduling, and poor progress visibility. Companies that have active measurement programs tend to dominate their industries. Virtually any organization or project can benefit from applying Measurement at some level. For greatest effect, Measurement should have high-level management commitment and be enacted through a permanent measurement group. Measurement can also be implemented to a lesser degree on individual projects by the project team or individual team members.

Efficacy

Potential reduction from nominal schedule:	Very Good
Improvement in progress visibility:	Good
Effect on schedule risk:	Decreased Risk
Chance of first-time success:	Good
Chance of long-term success:	Excellent

Major Risks

- Overoptimization of single-factor measurements
- Misuse of measurements for employee evaluations
- Misleading information from lines-of-code measurements

Major Interactions and Trade-Offs

- Provides the foundation for improvements in estimation, scheduling, productivity-tool evaluation, and programming-practice evaluation

Software products and projects can be measured in dozens of ways: size in lines of code or function points; defects per thousand lines of code or function point; hours spent designing, coding, and debugging; developer satisfaction—these are just the tip of the iceberg.

Measurement programs support rapid development in several ways.

Measurement provides status visibility. The only thing worse than being late is not knowing that you're late. Measuring your progress can help you know exactly what your status is.

CROSS-REFERENCE
For more on the importance of objectives, see "Goal Setting" in Section 11.2.

Measurement focuses people's activities. As I've mentioned elsewhere, people respond to the objectives you set for them. When you measure a characteristic of your development process and feed it back to the people involved, you're implicitly telling them that they should work to improve their performance against that characteristic. If you measure the program's bug count and feed that back, they'll reduce the bug count. If you measure the percentage of modules marked as done, they'll increase the percentage of modules marked as done.

What gets measured gets optimized. If you measure development-speed related characteristics of the project, those will get optimized.

Measurement improves morale. Properly implemented, a measurement program can improve developer morale by bringing attention to chronic problems such as excessive schedule pressure, inadequate office space, and inadequate computing resources.

CROSS-REFERENCE
For more on setting expectations, see Section 10.3, "Managing Customer Expectations."

Measurement can help to set realistic expectations. You'll be in a much stronger position to make and defend schedule estimates if you have measurements to support you. When your customer asks you to work to an impossible deadline, you can say something like this: "I will work hard to deliver the system by the time you want it, but historically, based on the figures I have just described to you, it will take longer than your imposed deadline. We might set a new record on this project, but I recommend that you modify your plans in light of our history" (Rifkin and Cox 1991).

Measurement lays the groundwork for long-term process improvement. The most significant benefit of Measurement can't be realized in the short-term on a single project, but it will pay off over two or three years. By measuring your projects on a consistent basis, you lay a groundwork for comparing projects and analyzing which practices work and which don't. A measurement program helps you avoid wasting time on practices that aren't paying off. It helps you identify silver-bullet technologies that aren't living up to their claims. It helps you to accumulate a base of experience that will support more accurate project estimation and more meaningful planning. Measurement is the cornerstone of any long-term process-improvement program.

26.1   Using Measurement

There are several keys to using Measurement effectively.

Goals, Questions, Metrics

Some organizations waste both time and money by measuring more things than they need to. A good way to avoid that problem is to be sure that you're collecting data for a reason. The Goals, Questions, Metrics practice can help (Basili and Weiss 1984):

- *Set goals.* Determine how you want to improve your projects and products. Your goal, for example, might be to reduce the number of defects put into the software in the first place so that you don't spend so much time debugging and correcting the software downstream.

- *Ask questions.* Determine what questions you need to ask in order to meet your goals. A question might be, "What kinds of defects are costing us the most to fix?"

- *Establish metrics.* Set up metrics (measurements) that will answer your questions. You might start collecting data on defect types, creation times, detection times, cost to detect, and cost to correct.

A review of data collection at NASA's Software Engineering Laboratory concluded that the most important lesson learned in 15 years was that you need to define measurement goals before you measure (Valett and McGarry 1989).

Measurement Group

Some organizations set up a separate measurement group, and that is usually a good idea because effective measurement requires a specialized set of skills. The group can consist of typical developers, but the ideal measurement group would have knowledge of the following areas (Jones 1991):

- Statistics and multivariate analysis
- Literature of software engineering
- Literature of software project management
- Software planning and estimating methods
- Software planning and estimating tools
- Design of data-collection forms
- Survey design
- Quality-control methods, including reviews
- Walk-throughs, inspections, and all standard forms of testing

- Pros and cons of specific software metrics
- Accounting principles

This is the skill-set that experienced measurement groups at AT&T, DuPont, Hewlett-Packard, IBM, and ITT have.

You don't necessarily need to have an organization-level, full-time measurement group to measure aspects of specific projects. A team leader or an individual team member can introduce specific measures at the project level to take advantage of Measurement's short-term motivational benefits.

What to Measure

Each organization needs to decide what to measure based on its own priorities—its own goals and questions. But, at a minimum, most organizations will want to keep historical data on project sizes, schedules, resource requirements, and quality characteristics. Table 26-1 lists some of the data elements that different organizations collect.

Table 26-1. Examples of Kinds of Measurement Data

Cost and resource data

Effort by activity, phase, and type of personnel (see also Table 26-2)

Computer resources

Calendar time

Change and defect data

Defects by classification (severity, subsystem, time of insertion, source of error, resolution)

Problem-report status

Defect detection method (review, inspection, test, etc.)

Effort to detect and correct each defect

Process data

Process definition (design method, programming language, review method, etc.)

Process conformance (is code reviewed when it's supposed to be, etc.)

Estimated time to complete

Milestone progress

Code growth over time

Code changes over time

Requirements changes over time

Product data

Development dates

Total effort

(continued)

Table 26-1. Examples of Kinds of Measurement Data, *continued*

Product data, *continued*

Kind of project (business, shrink-wrap, systems, etc.)

Functions or objects included in project

Size in lines of code and function points

Size of documents produced

Programming language

Once you've started collecting even a few data elements, you can gain insight from the raw data, and you can also combine data elements to gain other insights. Here are some examples of combined data elements you can create:

- Number of open defects vs. total defects reported (to help predict project release dates)
- Number of defects found by inspection vs. by execution testing (to help plan quality-assurance activities)
- History of estimated vs. actual days remaining in a project, as a percentage (to help track and improve estimation accuracy)
- Average lines of code per staff month, broken down by programming language (to help estimate and plan programming activity)
- Average function points per staff month, broken down by programming language (to help estimate and plan programming activity)
- Percentage of total defects removed before product release (to help assess product quality)
- Average time to fix a defect, by severity, by subsystem, and by time of defect insertion (to help plan defect-correction activity)
- Average hours per page of documentation (to help plan documentation activity on a project)

Most projects don't collect the raw data that would allow them to create this information, but as you can see, this information requires the collection of only a few measurements.

Granularity

CLASSIC MISTAKE

One of the problems with the data that most organizations collect is that it's collected at too large a granularity to be useful. For example, an organization might accumulate data on the total number of hours spent on project FooBar but not distinguish between how much time was spent on specification, prototyping, architecture, design, implementation, and so on. Such large-grain data might be useful to accountants, but it's not useful to someone who wants to analyze planning and estimation data or data that will be used to improve the software-development process.

Table 26-2 lists a set of categories and activities for time accounting that will provide as much granularity as most projects need to start with.

FURTHER READING
For a different list of activities that you can use as a basis for time accounting, see Table 1.1 in *Applied Software Measurement* (Jones 1991).

Table 26-2. Example of Time-Accounting Activities

Category	Activity
Management	Plan
	Manage customer or end-user relations
	Manage developers
	Manage quality assurance
	Manage change
Administration	Downtime
	Development lab setup
Process development	Create development process
	Review or inspect development process
	Rework/fix development process
	Educate customer or team members about development process
Requirements specification	Create specification
	Review or inspect specification
	Rework/fix specification
	Report defects detected during specification
Prototyping	Create prototype
	Review or inspect prototype
	Rework/fix prototype
	Report defects detected during prototyping
Architecture	Create architecture
	Review or inspect architecture
	Rework/fix architecture
	Report defects detected during architecture
Design	Create design
	Review or inspect design
	Rework/fix design
	Report defects detected during design
Implementation	Create implementation
	Review or inspect implementation
	Rework/fix implementation
	Report defects detected during implementation
Component acquisition	Investigate or acquire components, either commercial or in-house
	Manage component acquisition

(continued)

Table 26-2. Example of Time-Accounting Activities, *continued*

Category	Activity
Component acquisition, continued	Test acquired components
	Maintain acquired components
	Report defects in acquired components
Integration	Create and maintain build
	Test build
	Distribute build
System testing	Plan system testing
	Create manual for system testing
	Create automated system test
	Run manual system test
	Run automated system test
	Report defects detected during system test
Product release	Prepare and support intermediate release
	Prepare and support alpha release
	Prepare and support beta release
	Prepare and support final release
Metrics	Collect measurement data
	Analyze measurement data

Using the Data You Collect

Collecting the data doesn't do much good if you don't use it. The following sections explain what to do with the data you collect.

CROSS-REFERENCE
For details on how average projects spend their time, see Section 6.5, "Where the Time Goes."

Pareto analysis

If you're concerned about development speed, one of the most powerful things you can do with the data you collect is to perform a Pareto analysis—look for the 20 percent of activities that consume 80 percent of the time. Optimizing a software project for speed is similar to optimizing a software program for speed. Measure where you spend your time, and then look for ways to make the most time-consuming areas more efficient.

Analysis vs. measurement

CLASSIC MISTAKE

On the opposite end of the scale from organizations that collect data that's too coarse are organizations that are so excited about software measurement that they collect data about everything. Collecting too much data is actually not much better than collecting too little. It's easy to bury yourself in data that's so unreliable you can't know what any of it means. To be meaning-

473

ful, metrics need to be defined and standardized so that you can compare them across projects.

HARD DATA

NASA's Software Engineering Laboratory (SEL) has had an active measurement program for almost 20 years. One of the lessons SEL has learned is to spend more effort on analysis and less on data collection. In the early years of the program, SEL spent about twice as much on data collection as on analysis. Since then, data collection effort has dropped by half, and SEL now spends about three times as much on analysis and packaging as on collection (NASA 1994).

After the data is analyzed, SEL has found that packaging the lessons learned is key to making the data collection and analysis useful. You might package data and analysis in any of the following forms:

- Equations, such as the amount of effort or computing resources typically needed to develop a program of a particular size
- Pie charts, such as distributions of errors by severity
- Graphs defining ranges of normal, such as growth in lines of code checked into version control over time
- Tables, such as expected time-to-ship for various numbers of open defects
- Defined processes, such as code-inspection or code-reading process
- Rules of thumb, such as, "Code-reading finds more interface defects than execution testing"
- Software tools that embody any or all of the above

If you're just beginning a measurement program, use a simple set of measurements, such as number of defects, effort, dollars, and lines of code. (The time-accounting data described in Table 26-2 would make up a single "effort" measurement.) Standardize the measurements across your projects, and then refine them and add to them as you gain experience (Pietrasanta 1990, Rifkin and Cox 1991).

HARD DATA

Organizations that are just starting to collect software data tend on average to collect about a dozen different measurements. Even organizations that have a great deal of experience with measurement programs still tend to collect only about two-dozen measurements (Brodman and Johnson 1995).

Feedback

HARD DATA

Once you set up a measurement program, it's important to update developers and managers on the results of the measurements. Providing feedback to developers can be an organizational blind spot; organizations tend to feed the data back to managers but overlook developers. In one survey, 37 percent of managers thought that feedback was given on measurement data, but only 11 percent of developers thought so (Hall and Fenton 1994).

Developers tend to be leery of how measurement data will be used. Both managers and developers think that managers manipulate measurement data at least one-third of the time (Hall and Fenton 1994). When developers can't see what's being done with the data, they lose confidence in the measurement program. A poorly implemented metrics program can actually damage developer morale.

HARD DATA

When an organization does provide feedback on measurement data, developers are enthusiastic about the measurement program. With feedback, they say that the measurement program is "quite useful" or "very useful" about 90 percent of the time. When an organization doesn't provide feedback, they say the measurement program is "quite useful" or "very useful" only about 60 percent of the time (Hall and Fenton 1994).

Another way to increase developer enthusiasm is to ask developers to participate in the design of the data-collection forms. If you do, the data you collect will be better, and your invitation will improve the likelihood of their buy-in (Basili and McGarry 1995).

Baseline report

One specialized kind of feedback that measurement organizations provide is an annual software-baseline report. The baseline report is similar to an annual financial report, but it describes the state of the organization's software-development capability. It includes summaries of the projects conducted that year; strengths and weaknesses in the areas of people, process, product, and technology; staffing levels; schedules; productivity levels; and quality levels. It describes non-software personnel's perceptions of the software-development organization and the development organization's perceptions of itself. It also includes a description of the organization's existing software inventory.

The baseline is built on the basis of historical data, surveys, roundtable discussions, and interviews. It isn't evaluative; it doesn't tell you whether your software-development capability is good or bad. It's purely descriptive. As such, it provides a critical foundation for comparing your status year-to-year and for future improvements.

Limitations

Where is the wisdom we have lost in knowledge? Where is the knowledge we have lost in information?

T. S. Eliot

Measurement is useful, but it is not a panacea. Keep these limitations in mind.

Overreliance on statistics. One of the mistakes that NASA's Software Engineering Laboratory (SEL) made initially was that it assumed it would gain the most insight through statistical analysis of the data it collected. As SEL's measurement program matured, SEL discovered that it did get some insight from statistics but that it got more from talking about the statistics with the people involved (Basili and McGarry 1995).

HARD DATA

Data accuracy. The fact that you measure something doesn't mean the measurement is accurate. Measurements of the software process can contain a lot of error. Sources of errors include unpaid and unrecorded overtime, charging time to the wrong project, unrecorded user effort, unrecorded management effort, unrecorded specialist effort on projects, unreported defects, unrecorded effort spent prior to activating the project-tracking system, and inclusion of non-project tasks. Capers Jones reports that most corporate tracking systems tend to omit 30 to 70 percent of the real effort on a software project (Jones 1991). Keep these sources of error in mind as you design your measurement program.

26.2 Managing the Risks of Measurement

In general, Measurement is an effective risk-reduction practice. The more you measure, the fewer places there are for risks to hide. Measurement, however, has risks of its own. Here are a few specific problems to watch for.

Overoptimization of single-factor measurements. What you measure gets optimized, and that means you need to be careful when you define what to measure. If you measure only lines of code produced, some developers will alter their coding style to be more verbose. Some will completely forget about code quality and focus only on quantity. If you measure only defects, you might find that development speed drops through the floor.

It's risky to try to use too many measurements when you're setting up a new measurement program, but it's also risky not to measure enough of the project's key characteristics. Be sure to set up enough different measurements that the team doesn't overoptimize for just one.

CLASSIC MISTAKE

Measurements misused for employee evaluations. Measurement can be a loaded subject. Many people have had bad experiences with measurement in SAT scores, school grades, work performance evaluations, and so on. A tempting mistake to make with a software-measurement program is to use it to evaluate specific people. A successful measurement program depends on the buy-in of the people whose work is being measured, and it's important that a measurement program track projects, not specific people.

Perry, Staudenmayer, and Votta set up a software research project that illustrated exemplary use of measurement data. They entered all data under an ID code known only to them. They gave each person being measured a "bill of rights," including the right to temporarily discontinue being measured at any time, to withdraw from the measurement program entirely, to examine the measurement data, and to ask the measurement group not to record something. They reported that not one of their research subjects exercised these rights, but it made their subjects more comfortable knowing they were there (Perry, Staudenmayer, and Votta 1994).

FURTHER READING
For an excellent discussion
of problems with lines-of-
code measurements, see
Programming Productivity
(Jones 1986a).

Misleading information from lines-of-code measurements. Most measurement programs will measure code size in lines of code, and there are some anomalies with that measurement. Here are some of them:

- Productivity measurements based on lines of code can make high-level languages look less productive than they are. High-level languages implement more functionality per line of code than low-level languages. A developer might write fewer lines of code per month in a high-level language and still accomplish far more than would be possible with more lines of code in a low-level language.

- Quality measurements based on lines of code can make high-level languages look as if they promote lower quality than they do. Suppose you have two equivalent applications with the same number of defects, one written in a high-level language and one in a low-level language. To the end-user, the applications will appear to have exactly the same quality levels. But the one written in the low-level language will have fewer defects per line of code simply because the lower-level language requires more code to implement the same functionality. The fact that one application has fewer defects per line of code creates a misleading impression about the applications' quality levels.

To avoid such problems, beware of anomalies in comparing metrics across different programming languages. Smarter, quicker ways of doing things may result in less code. Also consider using function points for some measurements. They provide a universal language that is better suited for some kinds of productivity and quality measurements.

26.3 Side Effects of Measurement

The main side effect of a measurement program is that what you measure gets optimized. Depending on what you measure, you might end up optimizing defect rates, usability, execution efficiency, schedule, or some other factor.

26.4 Measurement's Interactions with Other Practices

A measurement program provides the foundation for improvement in areas including estimation (Chapter 8), scheduling (Chapter 9), and productivity-tool evaluation (Chapter 15). Although it is possible to design a measurement program so that it undercuts a rapid-development project, there is no reason that a well-designed measurement program should interact negatively with any other practice.

26.5 The Bottom Line on Measurement

HARD DATA

Measurement programs naturally have some of the best data available to support their efficacy. Metrics guru Capers Jones reports that organizations that have established full software-measurement programs have often improved quality by about 40 percent per year and productivity by about 15 percent per year for 4 to 5 years consecutively (Jones 1991, 1994). He points out that only a handful of U.S. organizations currently have accurate measures of software defect rates and defect removal and that those organizations tend to dominate their industries (Jones 1991). The cost for this level of improvement is typically from 4 to 5 percent of the total software budget.

26.6 Keys to Success in Using Measurement

Here are the keys to success in using Measurement:

- Set up a measurement group. Put it in charge of identifying useful measurements and helping projects to measure themselves.
- Track time-accounting data at a fine level of granularity.
- Start with a small set of measurements. Select what you want to measure by using the Goals, Questions, Metrics approach.
- Don't just collect the data. Analyze it and provide feedback about it to the people whose work it describes.

Further Reading

Software Measurement Guidebook. Document number SEL-94-002. Greenbelt, Md.: Goddard Space Flight Center, NASA, 1994. This is an excellent introductory book that describes the basics of how and why to establish a measurement program. Among other highlights, it includes a chapter of experience-based guidelines, lots of sample data from NASA projects, and an extensive set of sample data-collection forms. You can obtain a single copy for free by writing to Software Engineering Branch, Code 552, Goddard Space Flight Center, Greenbelt, Maryland 20771.

Grady, Robert B., and Deborah L. Caswell. *Software Metrics: Establishing a Company-Wide Program.* Englewood Cliffs, N.J.: Prentice Hall, 1987. Grady and Caswell describe their experiences in establishing a software-metrics program at Hewlett-Packard and how to establish one in your organization.

Grady, Robert B. *Practical Software Metrics for Project Management and Process Improvement.* Englewood Cliffs, N.J.: PTR Prentice Hall, 1992. This book is the follow-on to Grady and Caswell's earlier book and extends the discussion of lessons learned at Hewlett-Packard. It contains a particularly nice presentation of a set of software business-management graphs, each of which is annotated with the goals and questions that the graph was developed in response to.

Jones, Capers. *Applied Software Measurement: Assuring Productivity and Quality.* New York: McGraw-Hill, 1991. This book contains Jones's recommendations for setting up an organization-wide measurement program. It is a good source of information on functional metrics (the alternative to lines-of-code metrics). It describes problems of measuring software, various approaches to measurement, and the mechanics of building a measurement baseline. It also contains excellent general discussions of the factors that contribute to quality and productivity.

Conte, S. D., H. E. Dunsmore, and V. Y. Shen. *Software Engineering Metrics and Models.* Menlo Park, Calif.: Benjamin/Cummings, 1986. This book catalogs software-measurement knowledge, including commonly used measurements, experimental techniques, and criteria for evaluating experimental results. It is a useful, complementary reference to either of Grady's books or to Jones's book.

IEEE Software, July 1994. This issue focuses on measurement-based process improvement. The issue contains articles that discuss the various process-rating scales and industrial experience reports in measurement-based process improvement.

27

Miniature Milestones

The Miniature Milestones practice is a fine-grain approach to project tracking and control that provides exceptional visibility into a project's status. It produces its rapid-development benefit by virtually eliminating the risk of uncontrolled, undetected schedule slippage. It can be used on business, shrink-wrap, and systems software projects, and it can be used throughout the development cycle. Keys to success include overcoming resistance of the people whose work will be managed with the practice and staying true to the practice's "miniature" nature.

S U M M A R Y

Efficacy

Potential reduction from nominal schedule: Fair

Improvement in progress visibility: Very Good

Effect on schedule risk: Decreased Risk

Chance of first-time success: Good

Chance of long-term success: Excellent

Major Risks

None

Major Interactions and Trade-Offs

- Especially well-suited to project recovery
- Especially effective when combined with the Daily Build and Smoke Test practice
- Works well with Evolutionary Prototyping, User-Interface Prototyping, Requirements Specification, and other hard-to-manage project activities
- Trades increase in project-tracking effort for much greater status visibility and control

Imagine that you're a pioneer heading from the east coast to the west. Your journey is much too long to be completed in a single day, so you define a set of points that will mark the significant milestones on your journey. It's a 2500 mile journey, so you mark five milestones, each about 500 miles apart.

Major milestones 500 miles apart are great for setting long-term direction, but they are lousy for figuring out where to go each day—especially when you're traveling only, say, 25 miles per day. For that, you need finer-grain control. If you know that your big milestone is 500 miles away, north-by-northwest, you can take a compass reading, find a closer landmark that's roughly north-by-northwest, and then strike out toward that. Once you reach that closer landmark, you take another compass reading, find another landmark, and strike out again.

The close landmarks that you pick—the tree, rock formation, river, or hilltop—serve as your miniature milestones. Reaching the miniature milestones provides you with a steady sense of accomplishment. Since you pick only milestones that are between you and your next big milestone, reaching the miniature milestone also gives you confidence that you will eventually reach your larger objective.

Miniature Milestones' support for rapid development boils down to four factors: improved status visibility, fine-grain control, improved motivation, and reduced schedule risk.

Improved status visibility. One of the most common problems on software-development projects is that neither developers, project leaders, managers, nor customers are able to assess the project's status accurately. Say nothing about whether they can predict when the project will be done, they don't even know how much they've already completed!

CLASSIC MISTAKE

Jim McCarthy cautions against letting a developer "go dark" (McCarthy 1995a). You believe that everything's going along OK. Why? Because every day you ask your developers, "How's it going?" They say, "Fine." And then one day you ask, "How's it going?" And they say, "Um, we're going to be about 6 months late." Wow! They slipped 6 months in 1 day! How did that happen? It happened because they were "working in the dark"—neither you nor they had enough light on their work to know that they had been slipping all along.

With Miniature Milestones, you define a set of targets that you have to meet on a near-daily basis. If you start missing milestones, your schedule isn't realistic. Since your milestones are fine-grained, you will find out early that you have a problem. That gives you an early opportunity to recalibrate your schedule, adjust your plan, and move on.

Fine-grain control. In *Roger's Version*, John Updike describes a diet plan in which a woman weighs herself every Monday morning. She is a small woman, and she wants to weigh less than 100 pounds. If on Monday morning she finds that she weighs more than 100 pounds, she eats only carrots and celery until she again weighs less than 100 pounds. She reasons that she can't gain more than 1 or 2 pounds in a week, and if she doesn't gain more than 1 or 2 pounds, she certainly won't gain 10 or 20. With her approach, her weight will always stay close to where she wants it to be.

The Miniature Milestone practice applies this same idea to software development, and it's based on the idea that if your project never gets behind schedule by more than a day or so, it is logically impossible for it to get behind schedule by a week or a month or more.

Milestones also help to keep people on track. Without short-term milestones, it is too easy to lose sight of the big picture. People spend time on detours that seem interesting or productive in some vague sense but that fail to move the project forward. With larger-grain tracking, developers get off schedule by a few days or a week, and they stop paying attention to it.

With Miniature Milestones, everyone has to meet their targets every day or two. If you meet most of your milestones just by working a full day—and meet the rest by working an extra full day—you will meet the overall, big milestones as well as the little ones. There's no opportunity for error to creep in.

CROSS-REFERENCE
For more on developer motivations, see Chapter 11, "Motivation."

Improved motivation. Achievement is the strongest motivator for software developers, and anything that supports achievement or makes progress more palpable will improve motivation. Miniature Milestones make progress exceptionally tangible.

CROSS-REFERENCE
For more on detailed estimation, see "Estimate at a low level of detail" in Section 8.3.

Reduced schedule risk. One of the best ways to reduce schedule risk is to break large, poorly defined tasks into smaller ones. When creating an estimate, developers and managers tend to concentrate on the tasks they understand best and to shrug off the tasks they understand least. The frequent result is that a 1-week "DBMS interface" job can turn out to take an unexpected 6 weeks because no one ever looked at the job carefully. Miniature Milestones address the risk by eliminating large schedule blobs entirely.

> ## Major Milestones
>
> Major milestones are the far-apart milestones that help you set general directions for your projects. Such milestones are typically months apart. On traditional, waterfall projects, the major milestones typically consist of product definition complete, requirements specification complete, architecture complete, detailed design complete, code complete, system testing complete, and product acceptance.
>
> On modern shrink-wrap projects, a typical set of major milestones might consist of project approval, visual freeze, feature complete, code complete, and release to manufacturing.
>
> Major milestones are useful for setting direction, but they are too far apart to provide good project control. The combination of major and miniature milestones can work well, with major milestones providing the project's strategic objectives and miniature milestones providing the tactical means to achieve each objective.

27.1   Using Miniature Milestones

You can apply the Miniature Milestones practice throughout the life of a project. You can apply it to early activities such as Requirements Specification and Evolutionary Prototyping; in fact, it is particularly useful in focusing those hard-to-direct activities.

For maximum benefit, the Miniature Milestones practice will be implemented at the project level by the technical lead or manager, whichever is appropriate. But individual contributors can implement it on a personal level even if their leaders don't.

The amount of detail required when implementing Miniature Milestones will give pause to whoever has responsibility for tracking those details, especially on large projects. But large projects are the projects that most commonly spin out of control, and it is on those projects that this kind of detailed tracking is especially needed.

CROSS-REFERENCE
For more on initiating new measures in response to a crisis, see "Timing" in Section 16.2.
Initiate Miniature Milestones early or in response to a crisis. Miniature Milestones provide a high degree of project control. Set them up early in the project or in response to an acknowledged crisis. If you set them up at other times, you run the risk of seeming Draconian. As with other aspects of project control, it's easier to overcontrol in the beginning and relax control as the project progresses than it is the other way around. As Barry Boehm and Rony Ross say, "Hard-soft works better than soft-hard" (Boehm and Ross 1989).

Have developers create their own mini milestones. Some developers will view Miniature Milestones as micro-management, and, actually, they'll be right. It *is* micro-management. More specifically, it's micro project-tracking. However, not all micro-management is bad. The micro-management that developers resist is micro-management of the details of how they do their jobs.

If you let people define their own miniature milestones, you allow them to control the details of their jobs. All you're asking is that they tell you what the details are, which improves buy-in and avoids seeming like micro-management. Some people don't understand the details of their jobs, and those people will feel threatened by this practice. If you handle their objections diplomatically, learning to work to a miniature-milestone schedule will serve as an educational experience for them.

Keep milestones miniature. Make mini milestones that are achievable in 1 or 2 days. There's nothing magical about this size limit, but it's important that anyone who misses a milestone can catch up quickly. If people have done generally good jobs of estimating their work, they should be able to catch up on any particular missed milestone by working overtime for 1 or 2 days.

CLASSIC MISTAKE

Another reason to keep milestones small is to reduce the number of places that unforeseen work can hide. Developers tend to view a week or weekend as an infinite amount of time—they can accomplish anything. They don't think about exactly what's involved in creating the "data conversion module," and that's why the job takes 2 weeks instead of the estimated one weekend. But most developers won't commit to tackling a problem in 1 or 2 days unless they understand what it involves.

To be sure you're basing your schedule on meaningful estimates, insist on further decomposing tasks that are above the "infinite amount of time" threshold for your environment.

Make milestones binary. Define milestones so that they are either done or not. The only two statuses are "done" and "not done." Percentages are not used. As soon as people are allowed to report that they are "90 percent done," the milestones lose their ability to contribute to a clear view of project progress.

CROSS-REFERENCE
For another example of this, see "Track schedule progress meticulously" in Section 16.2.

Some people can't resist the temptation to fudge their status reporting with Miniature Milestones. "Are you done?" you ask. "Sure!" they say. "Are you 100 percent done?" you ask. "Well, uh, I'm 99 percent done!" they say. "What do you mean, '99 percent done'?" you ask. And they say, "Uh, I mean that I still need to compile and test and debug the module, but I've got it written!"

Be fanatic about interpreting milestones strictly.

CLASSIC MISTAKE

Make the set of milestones exhaustive. Be sure that your list of milestones includes every task needed to release your product. The most common source of software estimation errors is omitting necessary tasks (van Genuchten 1991). Do not allow developers to keep a list of "off schedule" work in their heads; little "cleanup" tasks can add up fast. Such work can accumulate to a mass capable of sinking a project. Insist that every task be on the milestone list. When you mark the last milestone as complete, your project should be done, and you should be able to fold up the tents and go home. (Actually, folding up the tents should be on the milestone list too!)

CROSS-REFERENCE
For more on the way that visibility improves as a project progresses, see Section 8.1, "The Software-Estimation Story."

Use Miniature Milestones for short-term (but not long-term) planning. The Miniature Milestones practice is appropriate for tracking short-term progress toward a larger goal. Mini milestones are the trees, rock formations, rivers, and hilltops that you travel to next. Don't overdrive your headlights. It is usually not practical or even possible to create a detailed milestone list for an entire project at the beginning of the project. You simply don't know enough before design is complete, for example, to be able to create mini milestones for construction.

Keep the pioneer metaphor in mind. Periodically you want to find a vantage point that allows you to survey the surrounding terrain. That's what larger milestones are for. In defining mini milestones, you are planning out the route toward the next major landmark. You only map out a detailed route for the part of the terrain that you can see from your current vantage point.

Regularly assess progress and recalibrate or replan. One of the main advantages of using the Miniature Milestones practice is that it allows you to make frequent comparisons between your estimates and your actual progress. You can recalibrate your estimates based on your actual progress, and you can improve your estimating skills in short order.

CROSS-REFERENCE
For more on recalibrating estimates, see "Recalibration" in Section 8.7.

If you find that you are missing milestones frequently, stop trying to catch up. You will get further behind. You have only two choices: (1) You can recalibrate your schedule, multiplying the rest of your schedule by the size of the schedule slip so far; (2) You can take corrective action to get back on schedule, which might consist of trimming the product's feature set, clearing away distractions so the developers can focus better, reassigning parts of the project to developers who seem to be meeting their milestones easily, and so on.

CROSS-REFERENCE
For more on the hazards of too much schedule pressure, see Section 9.1, "Overly Optimistic Scheduling."

If a developer has kept to a schedule only by working extraordinary amounts of overtime, recalibrate that developer's schedule. That developer does not have any schedule cushion, and any task that's been underestimated more severely than the rest will blow the schedule out of the water. You also need to give that developer enough time to quit making rushed, stupid decisions that ultimately make the project take longer. Recalibrate the schedule so that it can be met by working normal, 8-hour days.

If after recalibration you find that some milestones have grown to more than 1 or 2 days in size, have the developer break those milestones into smaller milestones and reestimate them.

When you recalibrate several developers' schedules, you'll probably find that some developers' schedules become longer than others. If those differences are large, shift some of their work around so that it comes out more evenly.

Miniature Milestones vs. Task Lists

You might wonder what the difference is between Miniature Milestones and generic task lists. The two practices are similar in that they keep track of the work to be done at a fine grain. The differences are primarily differences in emphasis. The Miniature Milestones practice insists that tasks be reported as either 100 percent done or not done; generic tasks have no such restriction. Miniature Milestones defines a task as taking only 1 or 2 days; generic tasks can be any length. Miniature Milestones require that you recalibrate if you get off track; generic tasks include no such notion. In short, using Miniature Milestones requires more discipline than using generic task lists.

27.2   Managing Risks of Miniature Milestones

There is a risk of failing to use the Miniature Milestones practice effectively. The use of mini milestones does not pose any risks to the project itself.

27.3   Side Effects of Miniature Milestones

Using the Miniature Milestones practice requires detailed, active management. Setting up mini milestones demands time and effort both from developers and their leaders. It requires an ongoing commitment to status reporting and tracking. The Miniature Milestones practice takes more management effort than other, less detailed approaches; however, those other approaches tend not to work. Saying that the use of mini milestones takes more time than other practices may be equivalent to saying that effective management takes more time than ineffective management.

A second side effect of Miniature Milestones is that it prevents a project leader from losing touch with the project. A leader who uses mini milestones is in regular contact with every person on the project every time a milestone is supposed to be done, which should be approximately every day. Lots of incidental communication takes place, and that helps with risk management, motivation, personnel issues, and most other management activities.

27.4 Miniature Milestones' Interactions with Other Practices

The Miniature Milestones practice is particularly useful during project recovery (Chapter 16) because it provides excellent progress visibility. Because mini milestones support almost daily comparisons of estimated and actual progress, they also support a relatively quick assessment of how much longer a project will really take.

A project that's in recovery mode is often especially capable of mapping out the rest of the project in mini milestones. Most projects don't realize that they're in trouble until mid- or late-construction. By that time, developers usually know in detail what work remains to be done. Because people realize that they're facing a crisis, they are ready for strong corrective action and are receptive to the control implied by the Miniature Milestones practice.

The Miniature Milestones practice is well-suited for use with the Daily Build and Smoke Test practice (Chapter 18), which improves your ability to verify that each mini milestone is being met.

Mini milestones are also useful as a means of adding control to amorphous development practices that can otherwise be hard to control: Evolutionary Prototyping (Chapter 21), User-Interface Prototyping (Chapter 42), and so on.

You can use mini milestones as an estimation-calibration practice (Section 8.7) even if you don't use it for project control. Plan out the first few weeks of your project using mini milestones and see how you perform against your estimates. If you meet your estimates, maybe you'll want to quit using mini milestones. If you find that your estimates are off by significant amounts, that tells you that you should reestimate and try again.

27.5 The Bottom Line on Miniature Milestones

In Chapter 14, "Feature-Set Control," I described the development of On Location, a project that got into serious schedule trouble. The same article that described how the project got into trouble also described what it finally took to ship it:

> They gathered the team together and produced an excruciatingly detailed accounting of all the work still to be done. They decided they could finish in a bit more than a month, but only by stopping work on the second project and devoting three more programmers to On Location.... Office tensions heated up again, but the process stayed remarkably close to the new schedule. The product—the 30th version circulated internally—finally went to manufacturing. (Carroll 1990)

A project that was in deep trouble—enough trouble that it was reported in *The Wall Street Journal*—finally got things under control by using "an excruciatingly detailed accounting of all the work still to be done"—mini milestones. They should have been using mini milestones all along.

CROSS-REFERENCE
For more on the importance of making progress visible, see Section 6.3, "Perception and Reality."

The value of Miniature Milestones lies primarily in the increased visibility and project control that it affords. Its schedule benefit arises mostly from reducing the risk of a large accumulation of individually small schedule slips. If you think you're 3 months from completion and you can't create a mini-milestone schedule for the rest of the project, then you probably don't know in detail what needs to be done to finish the project, and you're probably really at least 6–9 months from completion.

The Miniature Milestones practice produces a secondary schedule benefit by focusing developer's activities. Since all work is on schedule, there is less opportunity to explore interesting but ultimately unproductive development detours. The effect can be a small reduction in development time.

27.6 Keys to Success in Using Miniature Milestones

Here are the keys to success in using Miniature Milestones:

- Initiate its use at an appropriate time, either early in the project or in response to a crisis.
- Keep the milestones small, a day or two in duration.
- Be sure that your list of milestones is exhaustive.
- Foster accurate milestone-progress reporting.
- Regularly assess progress, and recalibrate or replan if you start to slip off the milestone schedule.

Further Reading

Gilb, Tom. *Principles of Software Engineering Management.* Wokingham, England: Addison-Wesley, 1988. Gilb doesn't use the term "miniature milestones," but much of the approach he describes is similar. His book contains a particularly good discussion of recalibrating in response to the experience you gain from meeting miniature milestones.

28

Outsourcing

Outsourcing is the practice of paying an outside organization to develop a program instead of developing it in-house. Outsourcing companies can have more expertise in an applications area, more developers available to work at a given time, and a larger library of reusable code to draw from. The combination can result in a dramatic reduction in the time needed to deploy a new product. In some instances, Outsourcing can save development cost, too.

Efficacy

Potential reduction from nominal schedule:	Excellent
Improvement in progress visibility:	None
Effect on schedule risk:	Increased Risk
Chance of first-time success:	Good
Chance of long-term success:	Very Good

Major Risks

- Transfer of expertise outside the organization
- Loss of control over future development
- Compromise of confidential information
- Loss of progress visibility and control

Major Interactions and Trade-Offs

- Trades loss of control and reduced in-house development capacity for improved development speed or reduced cost or both

Outsourcing can be faster than in-house development for the same reason that buying a loaf of bread at the store is faster than baking it yourself. There are people whose primary business is to bake bread, and there are people whose primary job is to develop outsourced software. Here are some of the reasons that Outsourcing can save time.

CROSS-REFERENCE
For details on reuse, see Chapter 33, "Reuse."

Reuse. As with bread manufacturers, commercial outsourcing companies can achieve economies of scale within an industry that an individual organization cannot. If you develop a single inventory-control program, you might not be able to justify tripling the cost in order to develop a library of reusable inventory-control components. For one program, that might just cost more without providing any benefit. But an outsourcing vendor that develops dozens of inventory-control systems cannot afford not to develop such reusable components. Its one-time development costs might triple, but reusable components will allow it to develop each additional inventory-control program for a small fraction of the one-time development cost.

Even without reusable components, Outsourcing supports rapid development in several ways.

Staffing flexibility. The outsourcing vendor might be able to devote more developers to the project than you could provide for the same project. Or it might have developers who are motivated to work more overtime than your staff is.

Experience. If the applications area is new to you or involves the use of unfamiliar technology, the vendor might have more experience in the area than you do.

CROSS-REFERENCE
For more on the importance of good requirements specification, see "Requirements Management" in Section 4.2.

Better requirements specification. Depending on the details of your contract with the vendor, you might be required to create a more careful requirements specification than you would otherwise. A high-quality requirements analysis can save time whether the project is outsourced or not, but the incentive to pay attention to requirements quality is stronger when you outsource.

CROSS-REFERENCE
For more on feature creep, see Section 14.2, "Mid-Project: Feature-Creep Control."

Reduced feature creep. The costs of feature creep can be hidden or confused when you develop in-house, but vendors are highly sensitive to the cost of changes. As with high-quality requirements specification, reduced feature creep can save time whether you outsource or develop in-house, but the incentive is stronger with Outsourcing.

If you're a technical lead, you probably won't initiate outsourcing, but you should know what it involves. Upper management can call on you to evaluate whether your organization should outsource a project or to participate in vendor evaluations. One of the most interesting things about outsourcing is that it puts you on the customer side of software development; that can give you insight into what your customers experience.

28.1   Using Outsourcing

CLASSIC MISTAKE

Organizations sometimes turn to outsourcing because they are frustrated by the difficulties of managing in-house software development. They assume that if someone else builds the software for them, their job will be much easier. But the reality is almost the opposite. You have less visibility into the project's progress when it is being conducted across town or across the globe, and compensating for that lack of visibility requires astute and attentive management. As a rule, Outsourcing requires even more skillful management than in-house development.

CROSS-REFERENCE
For more on risk management, see Chapter 5, "Risk Management."

Develop a management plan including risk management.   Develop plans for managing outsourced development just as you would for an in-house project. Your plans should include descriptions of how you intend to select a vendor, negotiate the contract, develop requirements, handle requirements changes, track the vendor's progress, monitor quality, and validate that the delivered software meets requirements. You might develop these plans in cooperation with the vendor you choose.

Plan to spend time on risk management. Overseeing a project done by another organization can involve risks that you haven't experienced in your organization. (More on this later.)

Learn about contract management.   There is a well-defined body of knowledge having to do with managing outsourced work. A good place to start learning about this topic is by reading *Software Acquisition Management* (Marciniak and Reifer 1990), which is described in the "Further Reading" section at the end of this chapter.

Make communication with the vendor a priority.   Plan to stay in regular communication with the outsourcing vendor even when it doesn't seem like there's anything to communicate about. Some software projects use "management by walking around"; when you outsource, you should plan to "manage by phoning around."

Remote outsourcing companies will sometimes provide a dedicated data link for exchanging email, computer files, and so on. In one case, the existence of a dedicated 64-kilobit satellite link was considered key to the project's success. The clients reported that the computer link made up 25 percent of the total project cost and that its advantages far outweighed its cost (Dedene and De Vreese 1995).

Count on using some of your own technical resources.   Organizations sometimes want to outsource because they don't have the technical skills needed to develop a product. Outsourcing definitely reduces demands on the technical staff, but it doesn't eliminate them. Plan to spend more time on the product specification than you normally would. The specification will normally become part of the outsourcing contract, and you'll get only what you ask for. If you forget to ask for something in the spec, few vendors will provide it out of goodwill. Also plan to allocate technical resources to provide support for vendor questions and to test the quality and acceptability of the delivered product.

Be leery of unstable requirements. Except in rare cases, you won't be able to define your requirements precisely enough for vendors to bid accurately on your project before the vendor does some initial work. If you insist on fixed-price bids on the basis of a vague requirements statement, you'll get high bids from the competent vendors. The only low bids you'll get will be from vendors who don't understand software development well enough to know the risks involved with incompletely specified software.

The first part of your project—whether conducted in-house or by a vendor—should be devoted to defining and stabilizing requirements so that you could, in principle, do the remainder of the project on a fixed-price basis without excessive estimate padding.

Some vendors specialize in prototyping, JAD sessions, and other fast requirements practices. They can help you to shorten the schedule even when you don't have a clear set of requirements. Other vendors just do design and implementation. If you use them, you'll have to nail down your requirements before they'll be able to help you save time.

Retain enough control to pull the work back in-house if needed. With all the things that can go wrong with outsourced work, be sure to have a Plan B.

Especially consider outsourcing legacy-systems reengineering. A legacy-system reengineering project is an especially good candidate for Outsourcing. Users have spent years getting the system the way they want it, and they don't usually want to change anything; the requirements tend to be stable. The maintenance staff on legacy systems is usually already overwhelmed and will therefore appreciate the relief they get from having someone else reengineer the system.

System testing on reengineering projects can constitute a major part of the development effort because other work gets substantial assistance from code-translation tools. Consider Outsourcing a major part of the testing as well.

Be sure to develop a plan for handling changes to the reengineered software after it has been brought back in-house. Will the reengineered code be maintainable by your in-house developers? Who will handle defect corrections and enhancements?

Avoid double standards for outsourced work. Organizations sometimes hold outsourcing vendors to different standards than in-house developers. If you're considering the Outsourcing practice, consider what effect holding in-house developers to the vendor's standards would have on quality and schedule.

Kinds of Arrangements

The basic kinds of contracts are time-and-materials; fixed-price; and no-cure, no-pay. The kind of contract determines many characteristics of the relationship you'll have with the vendor.

Time-and-materials contracts provide the most flexibility, and you don't have to know much technically. You can simply say, "I want a foobar," and the vendor will keep working on the foobar until it gets it right or you run out of money. You can change your mind about what you meant by "foobar," as long as you keep the money flowing. The downside is that time-and-materials contracts often overrun their estimates. Moreover, vendors usually require a substantial down payment before they begin work—as much as 50 percent—so by the time they start to overrun their estimates, you'll feel that you don't have the option of pulling out of the contract.

Fixed-price contracts are an alternative to time-and-materials contracts. With fixed-price, you get a guarantee that the vendor will not overrun its estimate, or at least that it will soak up the cost if it does. But that guarantee can add as much as 50 percent to the cost of an equivalent time-and-materials project. Fixed-price contracts also require you to specify in detail what you mean when you say, "I want a foobar." Requirements changes will require you to negotiate for more time and money; if you thought negotiating with your in-house developers for feature changes was tough, wait until you do it with a third party. Fixed-price contracts typically require a substantial down payment, so pulling out of them can be costly, too.

A few vendors now offer a third kind of contract—no-cure, no-pay. This kind of contract tends to be cheaper than either time-and-materials or fixed-price. You typically pay only 20 percent down, and you don't make any additional payment until the vendor reaches a significant milestone. You define the milestone in such a way that when the vendor reaches it, you can be confident that the project will ultimately succeed. The only drawback of no-cure, no-pay is that the vendor is likely to insist that you stay actively involved throughout the project. That's not really much of a disadvantage since successful execution of the other kinds of arrangements requires the same thing.

There are many variations on these basic kinds of contracts, including cost-plus contracts—basically fixed-price contracts with an incentive added for on-time delivery. You'll usually want to negotiate the details of a specific outsourcing contract.

Offshore Outsourcing

HARD DATA

One of the outsourcing options that's become increasingly popular is offshore outsourcing. Offshore companies offer lower labor costs than you might find locally—on the order of 35 percent lower (Dedene and De Vreese 1995)—and some offer quality that is at least as good as companies in the United States. There are several issues to keep in mind.

Communication. Communication is a key to success with any outsourcing project, and it becomes a more prominent concern when you're outsourcing to a distant country. Services that we take for granted, such as a reliable phone system, can become major obstacles.

Be sure that language differences will not be a problem. If you're working with people who speak the same language you do, you're likely to have fewer problems than if you're working with people who speak a different language.

Some companies have advertised that they have foreign engineering talent backed by U.S. management. The idea is that you talk to people who speak your language and they talk to the people who speak the other language. That approach can work fine, or it can backfire when at the end of the project you receive 100,000 lines of code documented in Russian or Japanese, and you speak only English.

Time differences. Time differences can work for or against you. If you need to have daily, real-time interactions, a significant time difference can result in few or no overlapping business hours—so either you or the vendor will end up working strange hours.

If you can conduct most of your communication via email, a large time difference can be more a help than a hindrance. The vendor can answer your email questions while you sleep and vice versa. If you're sharing a computer, the offshore vendor might be able to use your computer during its normal business hours, which will be your off-peak hours. Between your site and the vendor's, you can work around the clock with none of the stress typically associated with such a schedule.

Travel. Plan on some travel time and expense. You can't resolve all issues via email or over the phone, and face-to-face meetings help to prevent time-wasting communication problems. At a minimum, plan to hold face-to-face meetings at the beginning of the project, at the end of the project, and every couple of months throughout the project.

Characteristics of the vendor's country. Working with a foreign vendor can expose you to risks that you don't have to consider in working with U.S. vendors. For example, you need to understand the vendor's local copyright, patent, and intellectual-property laws. Also, you need to consider the vendor country's political and economic climate and other factors that could interfere with your project.

Vendor Evaluation

CROSS-REFERENCE
Vendor evaluation has some things in common with tool evaluation. For details on that, see Section 15.3, "Productivity-Tool Acquisition."

One of the tasks you'll face in outsourcing a software project is evaluating a vendor. If your confidence in the vendor's abilities is ill-founded, you will almost certainly realize less benefit than you had hoped for. One revealing exercise is to use a commercial estimation tool to compare your in-house developers' likely performance against that of a potential vendor. If the tool estimates that the vendor's schedule won't be significantly better than your in-house schedule, you'll be better off to keep the project in-house.

Table 28-1 lists considerations to keep in mind when evaluating vendors.

Table 28-1. Vendor-Evaluation Questionnaire

Management Considerations

- ❑ What is the ability of the vendor to meet its schedule and budget commitments? What is its track record in meeting its commitments?
- ❑ What are the satisfaction levels of the vendor's current customers, including long-term customers? Does the vendor have any long-term customers?
- ❑ What are the vendor's project-management capabilities? Does it have expertise in all aspects of software-project management, including size estimation, cost estimation, project planning, project tracking, and project control?
- ❑ Can you trust the confidentiality of the vendor? Does the vendor also serve your competitors?
- ❑ Who will provide product support? you or the vendor? Do you want the vendor to provide support to your customers?
- ❑ Is any litigation pending against the vendor?

Technical Considerations

- ❑ What is the vendor's ability to rise to the technical challenges of the project?
- ❑ Has the vendor's software-development capability been evaluated by your technical staff or a third party? Were both technical work products and development processes included in the evaluation?
- ❑ What is the vendor's level of expertise in the application area?
- ❑ What is the vendor's level of expertise in the implementation environment?
- ❑ Is the quality of the vendor's other software acceptable? Does the vendor have quantitative data to support its quality claims?
- ❑ Is the quality of the vendor's work sufficient to support future enhancements?

(continued)

Table 28-1. Vendor-Evaluation Questionnaire, *continued*

General Considerations

❑ Is the vendor financially stable? What would happen to your project if the vendor encountered a severe financial downturn?

❑ Has the vendor developed software in an outsourcing capacity before? Is building outsourced software its primary business? What is the level of the vendor's commitment to outsourcing?

Contract Considerations

At some point in your dealings with an outsourcing vendor, you'll want to create a contract that describes the outsourcing agreement. Nominally, the contract will spell out the kind of software the vendor will provide and when it will provide it. It will also spell out how much money you'll pay the vendor and when you'll pay it. It might include penalties on both sides for nonperformance.

Beyond those basics, Table 28-2 lists a number of other issues to consider before you sign anything.

Table 28-2. Contract Considerations

❑ What work products (aside from the software itself) will be produced as part of the contract—architecture description, design description, source code, inline documentation, external documentation, test plan, test cases, test results, quality metrics, user documentation, maintenance plan?

❑ Does the contract contain provisions for periodic review and assessment of the vendor's progress?

❑ Have you included a detailed statement of requirements as part of the contract?

❑ Does the contract provide for changes in requirements?

❑ Who retains ownership of or has rights to original code written for the project?

❑ Who retains ownership of or has rights to code the vendor provides from its code library?

❑ Who retains ownership of or has rights to code you provide from your code library?

❑ Will the vendor provide documentation for code that it provides from its code library?

❑ Who is responsible for maintaining the code, including code originally provided by your organization?

❑ If the vendor is responsible for correcting defects, does the contract specify critical repair scenarios and reaction times?

❑ Does the vendor have the right to sell the software developed for you to other customers?

(continued)

Table 28-2. Contract Considerations, *continued*

❑ If you provide source code to the vendor for inclusion in your product, is the vendor restricted from reusing that source code in other products or selling that source code to other customers?

❑ Who has rights to the source code if the vendor becomes insolvent? Can you place the source code in escrow so that you get it if that happens?

❑ Will you need to provide proprietary tools for the vendor's use? Are your rights to those tools protected?

❑ If the vendor uses tools to build the product, will those tools be delivered to you at the end of the project? Who owns them if they are delivered to you?

❑ Are developers from your organization who interact with the vendor required to sign nondisclosure agreements? What are the implications of the vendor doing that? Will it restrict your organization's ability to develop its own products in the future?

❑ Is the vendor prevented from hiring developers from your organization?

❑ Is your organization prevented from hiring developers from the vendors? Even if the vendor becomes insolvent?

❑ Does the vendor require that a licensing message containing its name be shown on the splash screen, About box, and help screens and/or appear in printed documentation?

❑ What are the criteria for accepting the final product? Who is responsible for determining acceptability? What mechanisms protect both parties from disagreements regarding the delivered product's acceptability?

❑ If the software is licensed, how are licensing fees handled? Will the vendor be allowed to increase licensing fees for future versions of the product? If yes, by how much?

28.2   Managing the Risks of Outsourcing

Outsourcing can be a useful practice, but it has some well-known risks as well as organization-wide consequences.

Loss of visibility. The most significant risk associated with Outsourcing is probably the loss of visibility needed to ascertain the project's progress. It isn't uncommon for projects to report that they are on time right up to the day they are supposed to deliver, and then to take a schedule slip of several months. Be sure that your contract with the vendor provides for timely and meaningful progress assessments.

Transfer of expertise outside your organization. One major risk of Outsourcing is that it transfers expertise about the product area outside your organization. As a result, two things happen: your ability to develop that kind of software diminishes, and the vendor's knowledge of your data and algorithms increases. Whether that transfer is sensible depends on how you answer this question: "Should this software product be considered to be part of our core business?" If it is, Outsourcing might be expedient in the short term, but it will reduce your competitive position in the long term.

Here are some guidelines for determining whether to consider a product to be part of your core business:

- How important is it for your organization to maintain a technical capability to develop software in this area?
- Does this software currently give your organization a significant competitive advantage?
- If your organization decides to drop out of developing software in this area now, what is the chance that it will want to drop back in later?
- What will be the cost of dropping back in later?
- Does your software contain trade secrets or other proprietary data?
- Do you sell products based upon proprietary characteristics of this software?
- Is your organization's software development more effective than your competitors'? enough so to be considered a competitive advantage?
- How does your time to market for software products compare with that of your competitors?
- Is your software quality level better than your competitors'?

If you answer "yes" to most of these questions, Outsourcing is not in your long-term best interest. If you answer "no" to most of these questions, your project is a good candidate for Outsourcing.

Loss of morale. If the project you outsource is a project that in-house developers have wanted to work on, transferring that project outside the organization can adversely affect developers' performance on other projects. Moreover, Outsourcing can give developers the impression that their own jobs are at risk, which can cast an unproductive pall over your entire development organization.

Loss of control over future programs. By transferring development of a program to an outside organization, you might lose the ability to extend the program in the future. Your technical staff is unlikely to be familiar with vendor-developed code. The vendor might make design or implementation choices that limit future flexibility. Depending on the details of your contract, you might lose the right to modify the program you paid for. Or you might not have rights to the design or source code. Be sure that your contract provides the flexibility you need.

Compromise of confidential information. Be sure that you identify proprietary data and algorithms and that your contract ensures that this intellectual property stays carefully protected.

28.3 Side Effects of Outsourcing

Outsourcing has two beneficial side effects.

Welcome relief. Outsourcing a project can give your staff a break. If your staff has been working on one rush project after another, they might welcome the opportunity to get out of the kitchen and let someone else feel the heat for a while. Outsourcing can provide a welcome change in routine, and your developers can benefit from exposure to another software-development organization.

Reduced manpower fluctuations. Outsourcing eliminates the need to staff up for a rush project.

28.4 Outsourcing's Interactions with Other Practices

On the customer side, effective outsourcing is an exercise in effective project management (Section 4.1) and risk management (Chapter 5), and you need to be especially conscientious about those activities. Other than that, the Outsourcing practice does not interact with other rapid-development practices.

28.5 The Bottom Line on Outsourcing

HARD DATA

Not much quantitative data exists on the success or failure of outsourcing arrangements, but anecdotal reports have been favorable. For example, Capers Jones reports that outsourcing averages about twice the productivity of in-house development in New England banking applications (Jones 1991).

28.6 Keys to Success in Using Outsourcing

Here are the keys to success in using Outsourcing:

- Select the Outsourcing vendor carefully.
- Craft the contract with the vendor carefully.
- Plan to manage the outsourced project at least as carefully as you would an in-house project.
- Make communication with the vendor a priority, both electronically and in person.

- Do at least as good a job of specifying requirements as you would do for an in-house project (unless requirements specification is one of the vendor's strengths).

- Be sure that Outsourcing of the rapid-development project is in your organization's long-term best interest.

Further Reading

Marciniak, John J., and Donald J. Reifer. *Software Acquisition Management*. New York: John Wiley & Sons, 1990. Marciniak and Reifer fully explore the considerations on both the buying and selling sides of outsourced software relationships. The book has a strong engineering bent, and it discusses how to put work out for bid, write contracts, and manage outsourced projects from start to completion.

Humphrey, W. S., and W. L. Sweet. *A Method for Assessing the Software Engineering Capability of Contractors*. SEI Technical Report CMU/SEI-87-TR-23, Pittsburgh: Software Engineering Institute, 1987. This report contains more than 100 detailed questions that you can use to assess a vendor's software-development capability. The questions are divided into categories of organizational structure; resources, personnel, and training; technology management; documented standards and procedures; process metrics; data management and analysis; process control; and tools and technology. Vendor evaluation has been a major emphasis of work at the Software Engineering Institute, and this report also describes an overarching framework that you can use to evaluate the vendor's general development capabilities.

Humphrey, Watts S. *Managing the Software Process*. Reading, Mass.: Addison-Wesley, 1989. Chapter 19 is devoted to contracting for software. It contains insightful guidelines for establishing a relationship with a vendor, developing a set of requirements, tracking progress, monitoring quality, and managing vendors at different competency levels.

Dedene, Guido, and Jean-Pierre De Vreese. "Realities of Off-Shore Reengineering," *IEEE Software*, January 1995, 35–45. This is an interesting case study in outsourcing two software projects overseas.

29

Principled Negotiation

Principled Negotiation is a negotiating strategy that relies on improving communications and the creation of win-win options rather than on negotiating tricks. It can be used during requirements analysis, schedule creation, feature-change discussions, and at other times throughout a project. It produces its rapid-development benefit by clarifying expectations and identifying exactly what is needed to set the project up for success. Effective use of Principled Negotiation depends on separating people from the problem; focusing on interests, not positions; inventing options for mutual gain; and insisting on the use of objective criteria. It can be used on any kind of project.

S
U
M
M
A
R
Y

Efficacy

Potential reduction from nominal schedule:	None
Improvement in progress visibility:	Very Good
Effect on schedule risk:	Decreased Risk
Chance of first-time success:	Very Good
Chance of long-term success:	Excellent

Major Risks

None

Major Interactions and Trade-Offs

None

For more on principled negotiation, see Section 9.2, "Beating Schedule Pressure."

30

Productivity Environments

Software development is a highly intellectual activity that requires long periods of uninterrupted concentration. Productivity Environments provide developers with the freedom from noise and interruptions they need in order to work effectively. The use of Productivity Environments can benefit any kind of project—business, shrink-wrap, or systems. In addition to productivity improvements, some organizations have experienced improvements in developer morale and retention rates after establishing Productivity Environments.

Efficacy

Potential reduction from nominal schedule:	Good
Improvement in progress visibility:	None
Effect on schedule risk:	No Effect
Chance of first-time success:	Good
Chance of long-term success:	Very Good

Major Risks

- Lost productivity from status-oriented office improvements
- Transition downtime
- Political repercussions of preferential treatment for software professionals

Major Interactions and Trade-Offs

- Trades small increase in cost for large increase in productivity

If you were in the oil business, before you could make a single dollar you would need to locate a source of oil, drill a hole in the ground, pump the oil out of the ground, refine the oil, pump it into ships or trucks or barrels, and sell it. Part of the profitability of your business would be determined by how efficiently you could pump the oil out of the ground. If your pumping technique left 50 percent of the oil underground, you would be leaving 50 percent of your potential revenues underground, too.

You can't pump software out of a hole in the ground. Our nation's software reserves are located predominately inside the brains of our nation's software developers, and extracting that software from those brains requires every bit as much finesse as extracting oil from an oil well.

CLASSIC MISTAKE

Paradoxically, the majority of developers today work under conditions that almost seem designed to prevent the extraction of working software from their brains. More than 70 percent of all software organizations have crowded office conditions, and the average time between interruptions under those conditions is only about 11 minutes (Jones 1994).

Unlike most management tasks, which are interrupt based and which survive and thrive on frequent interruptions, software development tasks require long periods of uninterrupted concentration. Because managers generally do not need long uninterrupted periods to do their work, developers' requests for peace and quiet can seem like requests for preferential treatment. But developers are usually highly self-motivated, and what they're really asking for is to be provided with conditions that will allow them to work efficiently.

Flow time. During the analysis and design stages, software development is an ephemeral, conceptual activity. Like any conceptual activity, the quality of the work is dependent on the worker's ability to sustain a "flow state"— a relaxed state of total immersion in a problem that facilitates understanding of it and the generation of solutions for it (DeMarco and Lister 1987). Converting brain waves to computer software is a delicate process, and developers work best during the hours they spend in this state of effortless concentration. Developers require 15 minutes or more to enter a state of flow, which can then last many hours, until fatigue or interruption terminates it. If developers are interrupted every 11 minutes, they will likely never enter a flow state and will therefore be unlikely to ever reach their highest levels of productivity.

CROSS-REFERENCE
For more on hygiene needs, see "Hygiene Factors" in Section 11.4.

Hygiene needs. In addition to the enhanced ability to enter a flow state, the Productivity Environments practice addresses a major motivational factor for software developers. Office space appropriate for development work is a "hygiene" motivational factor: that is, adequate office space does not increase motivation or productivity, but below a certain threshold inadequate office space can seriously erode motivation and productivity.

For developers, the need for productivity environments is obvious and basic. Productivity environments are in the same motivational category as adequate lighting, reliable power, and accessible bathroom facilities. An organization that doesn't provide an environment in which developers can work effectively is not providing the basics that developers need to be productive, and developers tend to view such organizations as irrationally working against their own interests. Good developers tend to gravitate toward organizations that provide work environments in which they can be productive. Developers who stay in less productive environments tend to lose their motivation and morale, and productivity suffers. (See Figure 30-1.)

Figure 30-1. *DILBERT reprinted by permission of United Feature Syndicate, Inc.*

Developers, team leads, and lower-level managers don't usually have the latitude to move a team to more productive offices. But if your project is under schedule pressure and your management is serious about productivity improvements, you might try negotiating for quieter, more private office space in return for promises of higher productivity.

30.1   Using Productivity Environments

Productivity environments have the following characteristics:

- At least 80 square feet of floor space per developer.

- At least 15 square feet of desk space capable of holding books, files, notes, source-code listings, and computer equipment simultaneously. The desk supports should be designed so that they do not obstruct leg movements. The workspace should be configurable to the preferences of the individual developer (for example, either a right-hand or left-hand return).

- Some means of stopping phone interruptions. A "ringer off" switch combined with voicemail or the ability to forward calls to an administrative assistant are the most common solutions. Engraining use of email rather than phone calls throughout an organization is also an effective step toward preventing phone interruptions.

- Some means of stopping in-person interruptions. A private office with a door is the most common solution. The corporate culture should allow and encourage developers to close their doors; some companies with "open door" policies discourage the practice (apparently unaware that this harms developer productivity).

- Some means of shutting out unwanted noise. Business and social conversations should not carry into the developer's workspace and the PA system should not intrude to announce anything less serious than a building fire. Again, a private office with a door is the most common solution.

- At least 15 linear feet of bookshelf space.

CROSS-REFERENCE
For more on other published reports about productivity environments, see "The Bottom Line on Productivity Environments," later in the chapter.

In addition to these factors, which are supported by published reports, my experience leads me to believe that several additional factors are important:

- Offices with external windows. The view does not have to be spectacular, and the window can even look through another external window, but it should provide a sense of the world outside the office building, and it should allow the developer to refocus periodically on something more than 24 inches away. In one office, I looked through five windows to an outside view, but that was enough to rest my eyes and to provide a break from the computer equipment. High-tech work requires a "high-touch" environment for morale (Naisbitt 1982).

- At least 12 square feet of whiteboard space.

- At least 12 square feet of bulletin board space.

- Convenient access to other project team members. The team should have offices that are together; even being on different floors can put too much "distance" between the team members.
- Convenient access to a high-speed printer.
- Convenient access to a photocopy machine with an automatic document feeder.
- Convenient access to conference rooms. Private offices go a long way toward addressing the need for conference rooms, but conference rooms are still needed whenever a group of three or more people meets.
- Convenient access to common office supplies—pens, pencils, refill leads, highlighters, paper clips, rubber bands, staples, tape, notepads, spiral notebooks, 3-ring binders, blank diskettes, diskette labels, blank backup tapes, Post-it notes of various sizes, standard business envelopes, large mailing envelopes, stamps, file folders, file folder labels, hanging files, pushpins, paper towels, whiteboard markers, whiteboard cleaner, and screen cleaner.

Figure 30-2 shows some of the productivity office designs that were developed for IBM's highly regarded Santa Teresa office facility.

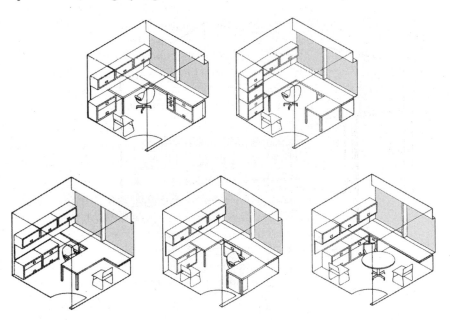

Figure 30-2. *Designs for productivity offices at IBM's Santa Teresa Laboratory. Developers reported that their productivity increased about 11 percent when they moved into these offices. Copyright 1978 International Business Machines Corporation. Reprinted with permission from* IBM Systems Journal, *vol. 17, No. 1.*

30.2 Managing the Risks of Productivity Environments

Providing productivity environments is not a particularly risky activity, but the few risks involved are worth noting.

Lost productivity from status-oriented office improvements. One hazard of stepping up to providing Productivity Environments is that management might treat the improvement in the office environment as a status upgrade instead of a productivity upgrade. In some organizations, private offices are status symbols, and management sometimes interprets developers' lobbying for private offices as lobbying for improved status. As a result, organizations sometimes spend money on cosmetic improvements that don't improve productivity—and that sometimes damage it. Management might upgrade the developers' cubicles from standard cloth walls to walls with smoked-glass inserts. They might assign developers to larger cubicles that hold small conference tables. They might replace the standard cubicle furniture with tasteful antique wood furniture.

Though well intentioned, each of these measures is more likely to damage productivity than to improve it. Smoked-glass inserts reduce the already limited amount of privacy available to a developer who works in a cubicle. Conference tables increase the chance of holding impromptu meetings in a cubicle, which increases the number of distractions to the developers in adjacent cubicles. Antique wood furniture reduces leg movement and therefore reduces the usable work area inside the cubicle. I haven't met a developer yet who wouldn't prefer working at two large, fold-up, banquet tables instead of a small, finely crafted antique desk.

If true productivity offices cannot be provided, more effective productivity measures would include increasing the height of the cubicle walls from 5 feet to 7 feet and adding doors to them. Be sure that your office improvements stay focused on productivity.

Transition downtime. Changing office space nearly always involves a host of administrative headaches that have an adverse effect on productivity. I've seen problems in the transfer of file boxes and other materials from the old site to the new one and problems with new phone systems, new voicemail systems, computer network installations, power supply reliability, delivery of office furniture and equipment, and a variety of other areas.

In addition to administrative headaches, there is the inevitable downtime associated with a move or a remodel. Developers lose time packing and unpacking. People succumb to the temptation to reorganize their files and bookshelves at moving time. If the move is to a new building, people spend time exploring their new environment. And there is sometimes a loss of morale on the part of developers who do not get the new office locations they had hoped for.

CROSS-REFERENCE
Sometimes you can boost the productivity of a project in recovery mode by moving to better office space. For comments on the general idea, see "Do whatever is needed to restore the group's morale" in Section 16.2.

All things considered, you should assume a minimum of one lost person-week per developer for any group move. Moving to productivity offices will produce positive benefits in the long run, but the final stage of a project under pressure is usually a poor time to make such a move. Such a move should generally be made between projects or in the early stages of a new project.

Political repercussions of preferential treatment for software professionals. In an organization that doesn't generally provide private offices to its staff, non-software staff members can interpret the provision of private offices to software developers as preferential treatment. You can mitigate this risk by explaining the special needs of software developers to other staff members who feel slighted or by locating software developers in a separate area where the differences in office accommodations won't be as noticeable.

30.3 Side Effects of Productivity Environments

Developers appreciate improvements in their working conditions. Organizations that adopt Productivity Environments have found that they have a positive influence on developer satisfaction and retention rates (Boehm 1981).

30.4 Productivity Environments' Interactions with Other Practices

You can use Productivity Environments in conjunction with any other productivity practice. Its effect is independent of the effects of other practices.

30.5 The Bottom Line on Productivity Environments

Tom DeMarco and Timothy Lister sponsored a programming competition in which 166 developers competed on the basis of both quality and speed (DeMarco and Lister 1985). The competitors provided information on the characteristics of their physical work environments, and it turned out that the developers who performed in the top 25 percent had bigger, quieter, and more private offices and had fewer interruptions from people and phone calls than the rest of the group. Table 30-1 contains a summary of the differences in office environments between the best and worst performers.

Table 30-1. Differences in Office Environments Between Best and Worst Performers in a Programming Competition

Environmental Factor	Top 25%	Bottom 25%
Dedicated floor space	78 square feet	46 square feet
Acceptably quiet workspace	57% yes	29% yes
Acceptably private workspace	62% yes	19% yes
Silenceable phone	52% yes	10% yes
Calls can be diverted to voicemail or receptionist	76% yes	19% yes
Frequent needless interruptions	38% yes	76% yes
Workspace makes developers feel appreciated	57% yes	29% yes

Source: Adapted from *Developer Performance and the Effects of the Workplace* (DeMarco and Lister 1985).

DeMarco and Lister thought that this correlation between office environment and productivity might be the result of a hidden factor, namely that better developers might naturally have better offices because they had been promoted. But when they further examined their data, they found that that wasn't the case: developers from the same organizations had similar facilities, and their performance still varied.

HARD DATA

The data shows a strong correlation between productivity and quality of the workplace. Developers in the top 25 percent had productivity 2.6 times better than developers in the bottom 25 percent. This suggests that moving from a bottom 25-percent environment to a top 25-percent environment is likely to result in a better than 100-percent improvement in productivity.

In the 1970s, IBM studied developer needs, created architectural guidelines, and designed their Santa Teresa facility with developers in mind. Developers participated throughout the design process. The result is that the physical facilities at Santa Teresa are rated the highest in the company each year in annual opinion surveys. IBM reports that the facility improved productivity by about 11 percent—and IBM didn't start out in the bottom 25 percent (Jones 1994).

Office space in my area costs anywhere from $1.00 to $2.00 per square foot per month. Developer time, including salary and benefits, costs anywhere from $4,000 to $10,000 per month. The average cost to go from the bottom 25 percent to the top 25 percent (46 to 78 square feet and least-expensive to most-expensive office space) would be about $110 a month per developer. The average productivity improvement is calculated by multiplying productivity by a factor of 2.6, which would work out to about $11,000 a month.

A decision to skimp on office space seems to me to be "office-space-wise and developer-time-foolish"—by a factor of about 100.

All in all, an organization that currently has an average environment can probably expect to improve its development productivity by 20 percent or more by providing its developers with productivity environments. The gain for organizations that currently have above average or below average facilities will vary accordingly.

30.6 Keys to Success in Using Productivity Environments

Here are the keys to using the Productivity Environments practice successfully:

- Avoid status-oriented office improvements. Focus on the office characteristics that count, such as privacy, freedom from noise, adequate work surfaces, and an ability to shut out interruptions.
- Plan the change in office space for a noncritical time in the project. Changing office space between projects is best.
- Develop a plan to manage the political repercussions of providing developers with private offices.

Further Reading

DeMarco, Tom, and Timothy Lister. *Peopleware: Productive Projects and Teams.* New York: Dorset House, 1987. This book deals with human factors in the programming equation, including the need for flow time and the productivity effects of office environments.

McCue, Gerald M. "IBM's Santa Teresa Laboratory—Architectural Design for Program Development," *IBM Systems Journal*, vol. 17, no. 1, 1978, 4–25. McCue describes the process that IBM used to create its Santa Teresa office complex.

31

Rapid-Development Languages (RDLs)

"Rapid-development language" is a general term that refers to any programming language that offers speedier implementation than do traditional third-generation languages such as C/C++, Pascal, or Fortran. Rapid-Development Languages (RDLs) produce their savings by reducing the amount of construction needed to build a product. Although the savings are realized during construction, the ability to shorten the construction cycle has projectwide implications: shorter construction cycles make incremental lifecycles such as Evolutionary Prototyping practical. Because RDLs often lack first-rate performance, constrain flexibility, and are limited to specific kinds of problems, they are usually better suited to the development of in-house business software and limited-distribution custom software than to shrink-wrap or systems software.

S U M M A R Y

Efficacy

Potential reduction from nominal schedule:	Good
Improvement in progress visibility:	None
Effect on schedule risk:	Increased Risk
Chance of first-time success:	Good
Chance of long-term success:	Very Good

Major Risks

- Silver-bullet syndrome and overestimated savings
- Failure to scale up to large projects
- Encouragement of sloppy programming practices

(continued)

Major Interactions and Trade-Offs

- Trades some design and implementation flexibility for reduced implementation time
- Improved construction speed supports Evolutionary Prototyping and related incremental approaches

A weekend warrior using a nail gun, belt sander, and paint sprayer can slap together a doghouse a whole lot faster than someone using only a hammer, sanding block, and paint brush. The power-tool user is also more likely to make a trip to the hospital for emergency medical attention. And if quality is a concern, the power tools will be replaced or supplemented by old-fashioned hand tools anyway. The rewards, risks, and trade-offs of power-tool use in software are much the same.

By "rapid-development language," I am referring to a broad class of development environments that offer more rapid implementation than do third-generation languages such as Basic, C/C++, Cobol, Pascal, and Fortran. Here are the kinds of development environments I'm talking about:

- Fourth-generation languages (4GLs) such as Focus and Ramis
- Database management systems such as Microsoft Access, Microsoft FoxPro, Oracle, Paradox, and Sybase
- Visual programming languages such as Borland Delphi, CA Visual Objects, Microsoft Visual Basic, Realizer, and Visual Age
- Domain-specific tools such as spreadsheets, statistical packages, equation editors, and other tools that solve problems that would otherwise have to be solved by creating a computer program

CROSS-REFERENCE
For more on productivity tools in general, see Chapter 15, "Productivity Tools."
In this chapter, I refer to these languages as "RDLs" for commonality with 3GLs (third-generation languages) and 4GLs (fourth-generation languages). In talking about RDLs, I am not specifically talking about class libraries or function libraries, even though you can apply many of the same considerations to use of those tools.

RDLs support rapid development by allowing developers to develop programs at a higher level of abstraction than they could with traditional languages. An operation that would take 100 lines of code in C might take only 25 lines of code in Visual Basic. An operation that would require opening a file, advancing a file pointer, writing a record, and closing a file in C might require only a single Store() statement in an RDL.

CROSS-REFERENCE
For more on function points,
see "Function-Point
Estimation" in Section 8.3.

Because different programming languages produce such different bangs for a given number of lines of code, much of the software industry is moving toward a measure called "function points" to estimate program sizes. A function point is a synthetic measure of program size that is based on a weighted sum of the number of inputs, outputs, inquiries, and files. Function points are useful because they allow you to think about program size in a language-independent way. A low-level language such as assembler will require many more lines of code to implement a function point than does a higher-level language such as C or Visual Basic. Function points provide a common currency for making comparisons between languages.

Researchers have been able to derive rough approximations of the average amount of work required to implement a function point in different languages. Table 31-1 shows how function points relate to lines of code for programs of various sizes. Lines of code are nonblank, noncomment source statements.

Table 31-1. Approximate Function-Points to Lines-of-Code Conversions

Size in Function Points	Size in Lines of Code					
	Fortran	Cobol	C	C++	Pascal	Visual Basic
1	110	90	125	50	90	30
100	11,000	9,000	12,500	5,000	9,000	3,000
500	55,000	45,000	62,500	25,000	45,000	15,000
1,000	110,000	90,000	125,000	50,000	90,000	30,000
5,000	550,000	450,000	625,000	250,000	450,000	150,000

Source: Derived from data in "Programming Languages Table" (Jones 1995a).

This data is approximate, and some of the numbers vary a lot, depending on coding style. For example, some people use C++ as a type-safe version of C, in which case the C++ figure would be much closer to the C figure than the table shows. But on average, the comparisons between different languages in the table tell an important story.

Suppose you had a word-processing program that was specified to be about 5,000 function points. According to the data in this table, it would take you roughly 625,000 lines of C code to implement the word processor, 250,000 lines of C++ code, or 150,000 lines of Visual Basic code. It would take you roughly 25 percent of the code to implement a program in Visual Basic that it would take to implement the same program in plain old C. That difference can translate to a significant savings in development time.

In general, working in a higher-level language produces savings during both coding and design. Developers tend to be able to write about the same number of lines of code per month regardless of the language they use (Boehm 1981, Putnam and Myers 1992). When they use a higher-level language, coding goes faster simply because they write fewer lines of code for a given amount of functionality. Design also goes faster because less code means there is less to design.

In the word-processor example, you could cut the number of lines of code required by 75 percent by using Visual Basic rather than C. That means that you could cut your design and implementation effort by the same 75 percent. You might have other considerations that would force you to use C in spite of Visual Basic's savings potential, but if development speed is an important consideration, you should at least know what you're missing.

Table 31-2 shows the approximate "language levels" for a wider variety of languages than Table 31-1. The "language level" is intended to be a more specific replacement for the level implied by the phrases "third-generation language" and "fourth-generation language." It is defined as the number of assembler statements that would be needed to replace one statement in the higher-level language. Thus, on average, it would take approximately 2.5 assembler statements to replace 1 C-language statement or 10 to replace 1 Visual Basic statement.

The numbers in Table 31-2 are subject to a lot of error, but they are the best numbers available at this time, and they are accurate enough to support this point: from a development-speed point of view, you should implement your projects in the highest-level language possible. If you can implement something in C rather than assembler, C++ rather than C, or Visual Basic rather than C++, you can develop faster.

The table contains several other interesting data points. One is that the 3GLs are all roughly comparable: C, Cobol, Fortran, and Pascal all require about 100 statements per function point. The 4GLs, DBMSs, and visual programming languages such as dBase IV, Focus, Oracle, Paradox, Sybase, and Visual Basic are roughly comparable to each other too, each requiring about 35 statements per function point. Tools such as spreadsheets—which are occasionally viewed as end-user programming tools—boost productivity through the roof, needing only 6 "statements" on average to implement a function point that would require 128 statements in C.

Table 31-2. Approximate Language Levels

Language	Level	Statements per Function Point
Assembler	**1**	**320**
Ada 83	4.5	70
AWK	15	25
C	2.5	125
C++	6.5	50
Cobol (ANSI 85)	3.5	90
dBase IV	9	35
Excel, Lotus 123, Quattro Pro, other spreadsheets	≈50	6
Focus	8	40
Fortran 77	3	110
GW Basic	3.25	100
Lisp	5	65
Macro assembler	1.5	215
Modula 2	4	80
Oracle	8	40
Paradox	9	35
Pascal	3.5	90
Perl	15	25
Quick Basic 3	5.5	60
SAS, SPSS, other statistics packages	10	30
Smalltalk 80; Smalltalk/V	15	20
Sybase	8	40
Visual Basic 3	10	30

Source: Adapted from data in "Programming Languages Table" (Jones 1995a).

31.1 Using RDLs

In general, select specific RDLs using the selection criteria listed in Section 15.3, "Productivity-Tool Acquisition," and deploy them using the guidelines described in Section 15.4, "Productivity-Tool Use." Beyond those general guidelines, the way you use specific RDLs will vary from one RDL to another, and the keys to success will vary as well.

31.2   Managing the Risks of RDLs

The power of an RDL can be seductive, and most of the risks associated with the use of RDLs arise from not recognizing the limits of that power.

CROSS-REFERENCE
For more on silver-bullet syndrome, see Section 15.5, "Silver-Bullet Syndrome."

Silver-bullet syndrome and overestimated savings. As with other productivity tools, RDLs are prone to gimmickry and exaggerated claims. Regardless of vendors' claims, it is unlikely that even the most powerful RDL will allow you to reduce your end-to-end development time by as much as 25 percent. Be leery of any product that claims otherwise, or at least don't bank on saving as much time as you're promised.

Even if you see through vendors' silver-bullet claims and have a realistic idea of the design- and code-time savings from an RDL, estimating the end-to-end time savings is tricky. See "How Much Schedule Reduction to Expect" in Section 15.4 for estimation guidelines.

Application to unsuitable projects. RDLs are not well-suited to some kinds of products. Performance of the code they generate is sometimes not adequate to support real-time or shrink-wrap software development, and RDLs sometimes lack the flexibility needed to implement customized user interfaces, graphics, output, or interfaces to other programs. Sometimes your requirements will call for functionality that the RDL should support, but you find out well into your project that the RDL doesn't support that functionality after all. RDLs work best when your requirements are somewhat flexible, allowing you to play to the RDL's strengths and to avoid its weaknesses.

Failure to scale up to large projects. RDLs frequently lack the software-engineering features needed to support large projects. The same features of the language that seem so convenient on small projects (such as not having to declare your variables before you use them) can create nightmares on large projects or team projects.

Here are some common weaknesses:

- Weak data typing
- Weak data-structuring abilities
- Poor support for modularity
- Weak or nonexistent debugging facilities
- Weak editing facilities
- Weak ability to call routines written in other languages or to make calls from routines written in other languages
- Lack of support for free-form source-code formatting (that is, some RDLs are like line-oriented languages such as Basic or Fortran instead of statement-oriented languages such as C/C++ or Pascal)

- Poor support for group work, including lack of source-code control tools

To minimize the risk of failure to scale up, before you put an RDL into use on a large project, conduct a feasibility study to be sure that the RDL's software-engineering weaknesses won't cost your project more than it will save over the development and maintenance cycle. Be conservative in estimating the savings you expect to realize. RDLs usually save time, but if the project is large enough to make the schedule an issue, it is large enough to be cautious about an RDL's limitations.

Encouragement of sloppy programming practices. With traditional programming languages, you tend to build infrastructure into your program to anticipate areas that aren't well-supported by the language itself. You develop highly modular code so that changes won't ripple through your program. You use coding standards to make code readable, and you avoid known worst practices such as using GOTOs and global variables.

CLASSIC MISTAKE

One of the ironic weaknesses of RDLs is that in pushing back a lot of complexity, they lull you into a false sense of security—they make you believe they will do everything for you automatically. You can get far into a project before you realize that you even need things like design and coding standards. By the time you realize that you do need them, you're so far into your project that it's hard to retrofit your code with them. When you hit the wall, you hit it hard. Your work slows to a crawl, and you might find yourself wishing that you were back in 3GL land.

This experience is so aggravating that some developers claim that you don't really save time overall by switching to a higher-level language. Sometimes that claim is right. The quality of some RDLs is poor, and sometimes RDLs fail to scale up well on large projects.

CROSS-REFERENCE
For problems associated with sloppy programming practices, see "Construction" in Section 4.2 and Section 4.3, "Quality-Assurance Fundamentals."

But other times the problem is not so much the result of the RDLs' weaknesses as it is of the tendency to use sloppy design and coding practices on RDL projects. In that case, the bad experience is more a result of the aggravation people feel when they run into an RDL's limitations and have to slow down. It's like what you experience when you've been driving at 65 mph for hours and then hit a 25-mph speed zone. You feel like you're barely moving. You feel like you could jump out of the car and jog faster. But of course you can't really jog faster than 25 mph, and you usually can't develop whole programs faster in C or assembler than you can in a good RDL.

To avoid the risk of sloppiness, use design and coding practices to compensate for the RDL's weaknesses. If you must err, err on the side of overdesigning your program and being too careful with your coding standards. This is a classic case in which an ounce of prevention is worth a pound of cure.

521

31.3   Side Effects of RDLs

Specific RDLs can have influences on quality, usability, functionality, and other product characteristics, and you should consider those factors when you evaluate specific RDL products.

31.4   RDLs' Interactions with Other Practices

Nearly all of the general guidelines for using productivity tools (Chapter 15) apply to RDLs.

RDLs provide schedule-reduction leverage because of their ability to reduce construction time. Because they reduce construction time so much, they also make new kinds of lifecycle models possible. If switching from a 3GL to an RDL cuts detailed design and coding effort by 75 percent (which is a good rule of thumb), that will significantly reduce the amount of time between iterations in an iterative lifecycle model. An iteration that takes 2 months in C might be cut to as little as 2 weeks in Visual Basic. The difference in those two time periods is the difference between customers or end-users seeing you as responsive and unresponsive. To derive maximum benefit from an RDL, employ it within an incremental, iterative lifecycle model (Chapter 7).

If you're working on shrink-wrap, real-time, or other software that is not well-suited to implementation in an RDL, you can still use RDLs for User-Interface Prototyping (Chapter 42) and Throwaway Prototyping (Chapter 38). One of the goals of prototyping is to use the minimum effort possible, and RDLs can contribute to that goal.

31.5   The Bottom Line on RDLs

HARD DATA

As suggested by Tables 31-1 and 31-2, the bottom line on RDLs is that the specific savings you can expect depends both on the specific language you're using now and on the specific RDL you switch to. It also depends on whether the kind of program you need to build is the kind the RDL is good at building. If you're currently using a 3GL, you can probably expect to cut construction effort by about 75 percent when you switch to an RDL. That amount will continue to improve as new and improved languages become available—but it probably won't improve as quickly as tool vendors will want you to believe!

If you can't switch completely to an RDL, you might still be able to implement some of your project in an RDL. The 75 percent rule of thumb applies: you can expect to cut your design and construction effort by about 75 percent for the part of the code you implement in the RDL (Klepper and Bock 1995).

FURTHER READING
For more on the effects of project size on project activities, see Chapter 21, "Project Size," in *Code Complete* (McConnell 1993).

As project size increases, the savings you realize from switching to an RDL decreases. RDLs yield their savings by shortening the construction part of a project. On small projects, construction activities can make up as much as 80 percent of the project's total effort. On larger projects, however, detailed design, coding, and debugging shrink to something like 25 percent of the total effort, and the savings from streamlining those activities will shrink accordingly (McConnell 1993).

31.6 Keys to Success in Using RDLs

Here are the keys to success in using RDLs:

- All other things being equal, for maximum development speed use the language with the highest language level in Table 31-2 (keeping in mind the limitations of that table's data).

- Select specific RDLs using the selection criteria listed in Section 15.3, "Productivity-Tool Acquisition."

- Put specific RDLs into use using the guidelines described in Section 15.4, "Productivity-Tool Use."

- Estimate the savings you expect to realize from RDL usage conservatively. Consider your project's size and the part of the lifecycle you expect to compress by using the RDL. On all but the smallest and simplest projects, schedule in time for working around the limitations of the RDL.

- Be careful about using RDLs on large projects. Bear in mind that as project size increases, the limitations of RDLs become more severe and the savings potential decreases.

- Err on the side of overdesign and overly careful coding standards when using an RDL.

- When you switch to an RDL, look for opportunities to use new lifecycle models that allow you to be increasingly responsive to your customers.

Further Reading

Jones, Capers. "Software Productivity Research Programming Languages Table," 7th Edition, March 1995, Burlington, Mass.: Software Productivity Research, 1995. This table provides language levels and statements per function point for several hundred languages. You can access the full table on the Internet at http://www.spr.com/library/langtbl.htm.

McConnell, Steve. *Code Complete*. Redmond, Wash.: Microsoft Press, 1993. Much of the book describes how to work around programming-language limitations, advice which applies to RDLs as well as any other language. Chapter 21 describes the effect that program size has on project activities and therefore on the potential that an RDL has to reduce overall development time.

32

Requirements Scrubbing

Requirements Scrubbing is a practice in which a product specification is carefully examined for unnecessary or overly complex requirements, which are then removed. Since product size is the largest contributor to a project's cost and duration, reducing the size of the product produces a commensurately less expensive project and shorter schedule. Requirements Scrubbing can be used on virtually any project.

Efficacy

Potential reduction from nominal schedule:	Very Good
Improvement in progress visibility:	None
Effect on schedule risk:	Decreased Risk
Chance of first-time success:	Very Good
Chance of long-term success:	Excellent

Major Risks

- Elimination of requirements that are later reinstated

Major Interactions and Trade-Offs

None

For more on requirements scrubbing, see "Requirements Scrubbing" in Section 14.1.

33

Reuse

Reuse is a long-term strategy in which an organization builds a library of frequently used components, allowing new programs to be assembled quickly from existing components. When backed by long-term management commitment, Reuse can produce greater schedule and effort savings than any other rapid-development practice. What's more, it can be used by virtually any kind of organization for any kind of software. Reuse can also be implemented opportunistically, as a short-term practice, by salvaging code for a new program from existing programs. The short-term approach can also produce significant schedule and effort savings, but the savings potential is far less dramatic than with Planned Reuse.

Efficacy

Potential reduction from nominal schedule:	Excellent
Improvement in progress visibility:	None
Effect on schedule risk:	Decreased Risk
Chance of first-time success:	Poor
Chance of long-term success:	Very Good

Major Risks

- Wasted effort if the components that are prepared for reuse are not selected carefully

Major Interactions and Trade-Offs

- Reuse needs to be coordinated with productivity-tool use.
- Planned Reuse must be built on a foundation of software-development fundamentals.

Reuse is sometimes thought to apply only to code, but it can involve reusing anything from a previous development effort—code, designs, data, documentation, test materials, specifications, and plans. For IS applications, planning for data reuse can be just as important as planning for code reuse. Although you might not think of it as reuse, reusing personnel from similar projects is one of the easiest and most potent kinds of reuse.

For purposes of this chapter, there are two basic categories of reuse:

- Planned Reuse
- Opportunistic Reuse

Planned Reuse is what experts are usually talking about when they refer to reuse, but Opportunistic Reuse can provide schedule reductions too. Opportunistic Reuse breaks down into two topics:

- Reuse of components from internal sources
- Reuse of components from external sources

Use of external components is not typically thought of as reuse; it's usually thought of as a buy-vs.-build decision. But the issues involved are similar, so I discuss some aspects of that topic in this chapter.

Reuse produces its schedule savings for the obvious reason that it's often quicker, easier, and more reliable to reuse something that's already been created than it is to create that thing anew. You can employ Reuse on projects of virtually any size, and it is as appropriate for in-house business systems as it is for mass-distribution shrink-wrap or systems software.

33.1 Using Reuse

The considerations involved in Opportunistic Reuse and Planned Reuse are quite different and are discussed in the next two sections.

Using Opportunistic Reuse

You can reuse opportunistically when you discover that an existing system has something in common with a system that you are about to build. You then save time by salvaging pieces of the existing system and using them in the new system.

Adapt or salvage?

If you want to reuse opportunistically, you have two options: adapt the old system to the new use, or design the new system from the ground up and salvage components from the old system. I have found that it works best to create a fresh design for the new system and then to salvage parts from existing systems. The reason that approach works better is that it requires you to understand only small pieces of the old program in isolation. Adapting an old program to a new use requires you to understand the whole program, which is a much harder job. Of course, if the people who wrote the old program are the same people who are working on the new one, or if the new one is extremely similar to the old one, you might be better off adapting the old program.

The salvaging approach is opportunistic because it takes some luck to be able to reuse designs and code from a previous system without planning ahead for it. You can succeed if the old system is well-designed and well-implemented. It helps if the old system made use of modularity and information hiding. You can also succeed if the staff overlaps between the old system and the new one. Without some overlap, trying to salvage parts of an old system can be more an exercise in cryptography than reuse.

Overestimated savings

CLASSIC MISTAKE

The biggest problem with Opportunistic Reuse is that it is easy to overestimate potential effort and schedule savings. Even if the old system is quite similar to the new one—say, 80 percent of the code could potentially be reused—you have to consider requirements analysis, design, construction, test, documentation, and other activities in your effort and schedule planning. Depending on the specific situation, you might be able to reuse all of the requirements analysis and design or none of them; if the old project was not created and packaged to be reused, you should count on reusing none of them. If the code is the only thing that you can reuse, that 80-percent overlap in code can shrink to a 20-percent reduction in effort and even less reduction in schedule, even though the systems are 80-percent similar.

Part of the work of reusing 80 percent of the code will be figuring out which 80 percent to reuse. That can be deceptively time-consuming and can quickly eat into the 20-percent savings.

Another common problem occurs when parts of the old system are used in ways that weren't anticipated in the old system's design and implementation—new defects surface in the old system's code. When that happens, if your staff isn't intimately familiar with the old system, they suddenly find themselves debugging and fixing unfamiliar code, and that will eat into that 20-percent savings too.

Experience with Opportunistic Reuse

HARD DATA

Some projects that have reused opportunistically have had good success. A project done for the French military produced a 37-percent improvement in productivity by salvaging code from a similar existing system (Henry and

529

Faller 1995). Project leaders credited the project's success to the use of modularity and information hiding in the first system, similar scopes of the old and new systems, and half of the same staff working on the old and new systems.

A study at NASA's Software Engineering Laboratory studied ten projects that pursued reuse aggressively (McGarry, Waligora, and McDermott 1989). The initial projects weren't able to take much of their code from previous projects because previous projects hadn't established a sufficient code base. In subsequent projects, however, the projects that used functional design were able to take about 35 percent of their code from previous projects. Projects that used object-based design were able to take more than 70 percent of their code from previous projects.

One of the advantages of this kind of reuse is that it doesn't necessarily require high-level management commitment. Capers Jones reports that individual developers often reuse their own code, which can make up 15 to 35 percent of any given program (Jones 1994). You might be able to encourage developers to reuse as much as possible at the technical-lead or individual-contributor level.

External reuse

HARD DATA

There isn't any *technical* reason to develop a component internally when you can buy a packaged component externally, but there might be a *business* reason, such as wanting to control a technology that's critical to your business. From a technical point of view, an external vendor can probably put more resources into a packaged component than you could and do it at less cost to you. Reusable code modules are typically offered at from 1 to 20 percent of what they would cost the customer to develop (Jones 1994).

CROSS-REFERENCE
For more on commercial code libraries, see Chapter 31, "Rapid-Development Languages (RDLs)," and Chapter 15, "Productivity Tools."

For a lot of people, the free market is moving quickly to address reuse. It's been the subject of industrial and academic research for years, and vendors have long provided commercial code libraries for specific application domains such as user interfaces, databases, mathematics, and so on. But commercial reuse finally began in earnest on the PC platform with Microsoft Visual Basic and VBXs (Visual Basic Controls). Recognizing their popularity, Microsoft strengthened support for reuse with OCXs (OLE Controls). Language providers such as Borland, Gupta, Microsoft, and PowerSoft have rushed to support both VBXs and OCXs in their language products.

The problems traditionally cited as obstacles to reuse are also being addressed by the free market. For example, companies do not need to create their own repositories of reusable components because VBX vendors do it for them. The vendors' success depends partly on how well they organize, catalogue, and publicize their reuse products so that customers can find the components they need and buy them.

When I see a
VB custom control,
I think, 'There's
1000 hours of my
life that I don't have
to spend in front
of a computer.'

Al Corwin

Some people have been puzzled by the success of VBXs, but I think the reason is apparent. VBXs provide for extremely good encapsulation and information hiding, which are the keys to successful reuse. The reuse promised for object-oriented programming languages such as C++ has been compromised by the design of the languages themselves. In C++, for example, the code's developers can develop a class interface that exposes the internal workings of the class. That sabotages information hiding and encapsulation. Or they can use function names that don't give the potential user any idea how to use the class. Because the language doesn't require developers to provide documentation, it can be difficult for someone else to understand a class well enough to reuse it.

In contrast, the developer of a VBX has no choice but to provide a property sheet, which essentially makes the VBX interface self-documenting. The property sheet completely hides the VBX's implementation, which enforces information hiding and encapsulation. VBXs have succeeded simply because they provide better support for encapsulation than many object-oriented languages do. Modularity and information hiding provide the support for reuse that people want. This finding is consistent with the reports of organizations that have set up their own planned-reuse programs, which I'll discuss later.

Using Planned Reuse

Planned Reuse, as the name implies, is a long-term strategy that won't help you on the first project you use it on. In spite of that, no other practice has the capacity to reduce development schedules as much in the long term.

To begin a reuse program, you should first survey your organization's existing software and identify components that occur frequently. You should then plan to make those components reusable over the long-term, either by purchasing them from a reliable vendor or by developing reusable versions yourself.

Management considerations

Reuse links projects that previously could be conducted in isolation, which broadens the scope of decisions about projects. It implies that different projects will have to standardize their software processes, languages, and tools. Effective reuse requires a long-term investment in training and a multi-project plan for building and maintaining reusable components. These are difficult challenges, and virtually every survey of reuse programs or report on a specific program says that management commitment rather than technical prowess is the key to success (Card and Comer 1994, Joos 1994, Jones 1994, Griss and Wosser 1995).

Here are some of the management tasks involved in conducting a reuse program:

- Designate a management champion—from top management—for the reuse program. There is no incentive at the first-line-manager level for developing reusable components on a single project, because it makes your project look bad, and there's no incentive for making the next project look good.

- Secure a long-term commitment to the program. It's important that reuse not be treated as a fad, since it can take 2 years or more for the development of reusable components to begin to pay off (Jones 1994).

- Make reuse an explicit and integral part of the development process. Reuse won't just happen on its own, and it won't happen as a by-product of otherwise good processes. To make its priority clear, make supporting reuse an employee-review level activity.

- Convert the organization's software-productivity measurement programs from measuring how much software is developed to measuring how much software is delivered. This will help to ensure that developers receive credit for using reusable components.

- Establish a separate reuse group to take charge of the care and feeding of reusable components. In a small organization, the "group" might consist of a single person or even just a part-time person.

- Provide training for the reuse group and for the group's potential clients.

- Heighten organizational awareness of the reuse initiative through an active public-relations campaign.

- Create and maintain a formal list of the people who are reusing components so that they can be notified in the event of problems with the components they're using.

- Work out a cost or charge-back system for using components from the reusable components library.

One of the most challenging aspects of setting up a reuse program is that it is difficult to make Reuse succeed without support from other key development practices such as quality assurance and configuration management. Some experts have argued that a reuse program should be implemented as part of a broader process-improvement program (Card and Comer 1994).

Technical considerations

CROSS-REFERENCE
Reuse groups have a lot in common with productivity-tools groups. For details on those, see "Tools Group" in Section 15.3.

The group charged with the care and feeding of reusable components will have a lot of work to do. Here are some of its tasks:

- Evaluate whether the organization's current software architectures support reuse, and develop architectures that support reuse if needed.

- Evaluate whether current coding standards support reuse, and recommend new standards if appropriate.

- Create programming-language and interface standards that support reuse. It's nearly impossible to reuse components if they are written in different languages, use completely different function-call interfaces, and use different coding conventions.

- Set up processes that support reuse. Recommend that each project start by surveying the components that it might reuse.

- Create a formal reusable components library, and provide some means of browsing the library to look for components that might be reused.

Beyond these general tasks, the group will need to do design, implementation, and quality-assurance work on the reusable components themselves.

Focus on domain-specific components. The reuse programs that are the most successful focus on building reusable components for specific application domains. If you're working on financial applications, focus on building reusable financial components. On insurance-quote programs, focus on building reusable insurance components. Try to focus on reuse at the "application domain" or "business component" level (Pfleeger 1994b).

HARD DATA

Create small, sharp components. You might be better off focusing your reuse work on the creation of small, sharp, specialized components rather than on large, bulky, general components. Developers who try to create reusable software by creating general components rarely anticipate future users' needs adequately. Future users will look at the large, bulky component, see that it doesn't meet all of their needs, and decide not to use the component at all. "Large and bulky" means "too hard to understand," and that means "too error-prone to use." Data from the NASA Software Engineering Lab suggests that if a component needs to be modified by more than 25 percent, it's as cost-effective to develop a new one-off component as it is to reuse an old one (NASA 1990).

FURTHER READING
This opinion is somewhat controversial. For a fuller discussion of the RISC vs. CISC debate as it applies to software reuse, see *Confessions of a Used Program Salesman* (Tracz 1995).

You're better off breaking the large component into several small, sharp components and focusing your reuse efforts on those. In structured-design language, *fully factor* any component that you intend to reuse. Don't present large components as single, monolithic entities. With smaller, sharper components, you give up the hope of solving the future user's problem in one fell swoop, but that hope is usually unrealistic anyway. With smaller components, you improve the chances of providing at least something of value.

HARD DATA

Focus on information hiding and encapsulation. Another key to success is focusing on information hiding and encapsulation—the core of "object-based" design (McGarry, Waligora, and McDermott 1989, Scholtz, et al. 1994, Henry and Faller 1995). Most of the existing, successful reuse projects have used traditional languages such as Ada, C, Cobol, and Fortran (Griss and Wosser 1995). One survey of 29 organizations found that programs developed in languages that are often thought to promote reuse (such as Ada and C++) actually showed no more reuse than those developed in traditional languages (Frakes and Fox 1995).

"Object-oriented" design adds the ideas of inheritance and polymorphism to object-based design, but the addition of those characteristics does not appear to make reuse any more achievable. A panel of researchers and practitioners at the International Conference on Software Engineering in 1994 agreed that object-oriented development by itself was neither necessary nor sufficient for reuse (Pfleeger 1994b). Information hiding and encapsulation are the real keys to success.

HARD DATA

Create good documentation. Reuse also requires good documentation. When you create a reusable component, you are not just creating a program; you are creating a product. For it to be used, its level of polish needs to be comparable to products that your organization buys commercially. For that reason, Fred Brooks estimates that developing a reusable component will cost approximately three times as much as developing the same component for stand-alone use (Brooks 1995). Others also estimate that creating components for reuse doubles or triples the cost (Jones 1994, Tracz 1995).

One kind of documentation that's especially valuable for reuse is a list of known limitations for each component. Software is often released with known defects because some bugs are of too low a priority to fix. But a defect that's low priority in one context can become high priority when the component is reused in another product. Don't make people discover defects on their own when you know about them already: document known limitations.

CROSS-REFERENCE
For more on the development-speed costs of low quality, see Section 4.3, "Quality-Assurance Fundamentals."

Make reusable components error-free. Successful reuse requires the creation of components that are virtually error-free. If a developer who tries to employ a reusable component finds that it contains defects, the reuse program will quickly lose its shine. A reuse program based on low-quality programs can actually increase the cost of developing software. Instead of paying the original developer to fully debug a component, you pay a developer who is unfamiliar with the component to debug it, probably less efficiently.

Focus on the quality of the reusable component library, not size. The sheer amount of code available to be reused does not appear to affect the level of reuse; small code libraries are used at least as heavily as large ones

(Pfleeger 1994b, Frakes and Fox 1995). Choosing from a large menu of reusable, existing components can be so difficult that Smalltalk developers refer to the phenomenon as "climbing the Smalltalk mountain." If you want to implement reuse, focus on quality, not quantity.

HARD DATA

Don't worry too much about whether developers will accept reuse. Finally, there is less to worry about on the client side of the reuse relationship than people sometimes think. Conventional wisdom holds that developers don't like to use code unless they developed it themselves. But a 1995 survey found that more than 70 percent of developers would actually rather reuse components than develop them from scratch (Frakes and Fox 1995).

33.2 Managing the Risks of Reuse

Reuse programs generally improve quality and productivity and lower cost. At the project level, reuse tends to reduce risk because less of the product needs to be hand-coded, and the quality of reused components is generally higher than that of one-off components. At the organization level, however, a family of risks clusters around the difficulty of predicting which components will need to be reused.

Wasted effort. Creation of reusable components costs two to three times as much as creation of a one-off component. Once the component is developed, you have to use it at least two or three times just to break even. Ted Biggerstaff calls this the "Rule of Three": before you receive any benefit from reusing a component, you have to reuse it three times (Tracz 1995). If you're not sure that you will reuse a component at least three times, it might still make sense to have prebuilt components available from a future-development-speed point of view, but that speed will come at a price.

Misdirected effort. If you establish a separate group to develop reusable components, there is a chance that the group will develop components that are never used. If the reuse group guesses wrong and one out of four of its components are never used, you would have to plan to use each component that you do reuse at least five times just to break even. Within a single organization that doesn't develop an awful lot of really similar systems, that can be a difficult break-even point to meet.

A practical strategy that reduces this risk might be to implement a "Rule of Two": implement every component as a one-off component the first time—and then, the second time it's needed, consider making it reusable. At that point, you know that you're going to be using it at least twice, so you are implicitly accepting less risk if you believe that some reuse now implies more reuse later. But be careful. Some experts warn that if you have not yet built

535

three real systems in a particular domain, you probably don't yet know enough about it to create reusable components successfully (Tracz 1995).

Shifting technology. A risk of Planned Reuse arises from the fact that it's a long-term strategy. Not only do you need to use a component several times to break even, you need to use it before the bottom drops out of the technology it's based on. As Chris Peters says, "You can spend so much time making something sharable, only to have it be obsolete two years later. In a world where things change so fast and so furiously, you tell me what part ought to be shared" (Peters in Cusumano and Selby 1995).

CROSS-REFERENCE
For more on estimating time savings, see "How Much Schedule Reduction to Expect" in Section 15.4.

Overestimated savings. Don't assume that reusing code will produce large time savings. If you reuse only code, you'll mostly save only coding time. If you reuse other project artifacts, you can save other time too.

HARD DATA

Keep in mind that it costs something to reuse a component because of the time needed to find that component and to learn how to use it. Plan to spend about one-fifth as much to reuse a line of code as to develop it from scratch (Tracz 1995).

33.3 Side Effects of Reuse

Opportunistic Reuse doesn't have any notable side effects, but Planned Reuse programs have one.

Improved performance. Reused components improve performance in two ways. They are often better-designed and more polished than one-off components, which means they are often faster (Pfleeger 1994b). They also allow systems to be assembled more quickly, which allows systems to be tested for performance bottlenecks sooner. But because they tend to be more general, reusable components can sometimes be slower than one-off components, so you'll need to assess the performance of any particular component you're interested in instead of assuming that it's faster or slower.

33.4 Reuse's Interactions with Other Practices

Reuse is related to the use of productivity tools (Chapter 15) and Rapid-Development Languages (Chapter 31). For example, you might be able to reuse a tool that quickly generates user-interface code in Pascal or reuse a library of database components written in C but not be able to do both at the same time. Reuse can either help or hinder the use of specific tools.

Because reusable components have to be more change tolerant than one-off components, reuse helps with Designing for Change (Chapter 19). Reuse can also factor heavily in a design-to-tools practice (Section 7.9). Finally, Planned Reuse is hard to implement successfully unless an organization has the software-development fundamentals down cold (Chapter 4).

33.5 The Bottom Line on Reuse

The bottom line on Opportunistic Reuse varies considerably, depending on how big the reuse opportunity is. Small amounts of Opportunistic Reuse will produce small savings. Large amounts of reuse could probably produce effort savings in the range of from 20 to 25 percent over the life of an entire project, assuming that large amounts of code and design can be reused and that there is some staff continuity between the new program and the one being salvaged.

HARD DATA

Planned Reuse is not a short-term practice, but the long-term payoff makes it an appealing strategy. In one study of software process improvement in 13 organizations, some organizations demonstrated much greater productivity gains than others (Herbsleb et al. 1994). One company improved its productivity by 58 percent per year for 4 years. Another cut its time-to-market by 23 percent per year for 6 years—that's a total reduction of 79 percent. The authors of the study attributed both of these extraordinary gains to reuse programs.

Because of the organizational and quality-assurance challenges, it can take a reuse program 2 years to develop any components that are truly reusable (Jones 1994). But productivity with significant reuse can exceed 35 function points per staff month compared to a national average of about 5 function points per staff month. Because use of reusable components completely eliminates design and construction and reduces the amount of quality assurance needed for those components, a successful reuse program is by far the most effective productivity practice available (Jones 1994).

33.6 Keys to Success in Using Reuse

The keys to success for Opportunistic Reuse are simple:

- Take advantage of personnel continuity between old and new programs.
- Don't overestimate your savings.

The keys to success for Planned Reuse are more demanding:

- Secure long-term, high-level management commitment to the reuse program.
- Make reuse an integral part of the development process.
- Establish a separate reuse group whose job it is to identify reusable component candidates, create standards that support reuse, and disseminate information about reusable components to potential users.
- Focus on small, sharp, domain-specific components.
- Focus design efforts on information hiding and encapsulation.
- Bring the quality of the reusable components up to the "products" level by documenting them well and assuring that they are virtually error-free.

Further Reading

Tracz, Will. *Confessions of a Used Program Salesman.* Reading, Mass.: Addison-Wesley, 1995. This book contains a series of columns that Tracz wrote for *IEEE Computer* and additional material, all of which is written from a practitioner's perspective. It covers management, technical, and a few philosophical issues. A few of the essays are pure entertainment. The writing is lighthearted, and readers who don't enjoy word games should be advised that Tracz' writing is exceptionally punishing.

Freeman, Peter, ed. *Tutorial: Software Reusability.* Washington, D.C.: IEEE Computer Society Press, 1987. This collection of seminal papers on reuse describes fundamental reuse concepts, techniques, and ongoing research circa 1987.

IEEE Software, September 1994. This issue focuses on planned reuse. It includes 10 articles on the topic, including a case study of reuse and several other articles that describe real-world experiences with reuse programs.

Udell, John. "Component Software," *Byte*, May 1994, 45–55. This article describes the rapid adoption of VBXs and surveys competing industrywide reusable-component strategies.

34

Signing Up

Motivation is probably the most significant influence on productivity. Signing Up is a practice that in some cases has led to extraordinary levels of motivation. It has produced remarkable successes on both hardware and software projects in a variety of industries. Its success depends on having a clear vision that team members can sign up to and on actively monitoring the project to ensure that the signed-up team develops the product in an acceptable direction.

Efficacy

Potential reduction from nominal schedule:	Very Good
Improvement in progress visibility:	None
Effect on schedule risk:	Increased Risk
Chance of first-time success:	Fair
Chance of long-term success:	Good

Major Risks

- Increased inefficiency
- Reduced status visibility and control
- Smaller available talent pool for the project
- Burnout

Major Interactions and Trade-Offs

- Trades possible decreases in visibility, control, and efficiency for a major increase in motivation

With the Signing Up practice, a manager or team leader asks potential team members to make an unconditional commitment to seeing that a project succeeds. The team is then allowed to complete the project in its own way. Signing Up derives its rapid-development benefit from its tremendous motivational ability. Developers who sign up make a voluntary, personal commitment to the project, and they often go to extraordinary lengths to make the project succeed. Teams that have signed up work at such a hectic pace that they are bound to make some mistakes, but the sheer amount of effort they put in can swamp the effects of those mistakes.

34.1 Using Signing Up

Kerr and Hunter point out that the Antarctic explorer Shackleton found his crew by advertising for men to perform hard work under dangerous conditions for low pay, *with the possibility of tremendous glory if successful* (Kerr and Hunter 1994). That, in a nutshell, is how you use signing up. You offer developers little reward except those intrinsic in the work itself: the chance to work on something important, to stretch their capabilities, to surmount a seemingly impossible goal, and to achieve something that no one in the organization has achieved before.

In *The Soul of a New Machine*, Tracy Kidder describes a signed-up team in which the main benefit of signing up is something called "pinball" (Kidder 1981). In pinball, the only benefit of winning the game is that you get to play again. If you sign up for a development project and succeed, you get to sign up again, on the next exciting project. That's the reward, and that's all the reward that many developers need.

Some people don't like playing pinball, and some people don't like signing up. To them, it seems like an exercise in illogic and masochism. To some, it seems like management manipulation. But to others, it represents a long-awaited opportunity. IBM found that it had no problem getting people to sign up. They found that people wanted to commit to producing extraordinary results at work; all that was missing was the opportunity (Scherr 1989).

CROSS-REFERENCE
For details on motivation and teamwork, see Chapter 11, "Motivation," and Chapter 12, "Teamwork." For details on creating visions, see "Goal Setting" in Section 11.2 and "Shared, Elevating Vision or Goal" in Section 12.3.

Frame a challenge and a vision. The keys to success with Signing Up are similar to the keys to success in motivation in general and in building high-performance teams. At the top of all the lists is providing a clear vision of what the project is supposed to accomplish. To get people to sign up, the vision needs to be of an extraordinary accomplishment. Merely completing a project is not good enough. Here are some examples of extraordinary visions:

- Be the first group of explorers to reach the south pole

- Be the first country to put an astronaut on the moon
- Design and build a totally new computer without the company's support
- Design the best computer operating system in the world
- Be the first team in the organization to develop a complete shrink-wrap software product in less than a year
- Create a DBMS package that places number one in its first *InfoWorld* comparative test and beats all its competitors by at least 0.5 points
- Decisively leapfrog the competition in the same software category

Give people a choice about signing up. The Signing Up practice doesn't work if people don't have a choice about whether they sign up. You have to accept the possibility that some of the people you'd like to have on your team won't make the extraordinary commitment that Signing Up requires. The fact that some qualified people don't make the team works partly in your favor. The team members who do sign up can see that some people don't have what it takes to be on it, and that helps to foster their sense of team identity.

If you've already put the team together, you can't use Signing Up unless you're prepared to kick people off the team who won't sign up midway through the project. Signing Up needs to be implemented at the beginning of the project or in response to a crisis. It's not a practice you can initiate midstream.

Once developers have made their choice, however, the commitment must be unequivocal. They must commit to make the project succeed no matter what.

Sign up at the team level. The Signing Up practice seems to work best on teams that are small enough to have a team identity. It's hard for someone to sign up with a large organization. Some companies have used this practice successfully on large projects by creating small teams within the large projects and having people sign up for those.

People need to identify with a group that's small enough so that they know their contribution matters. When people are signed up, each and every one of them will feel personally responsible for completing the product. When the product is done, each person will feel that he or she was the key person that the project could not have survived without. And each of those people will be right.

Because Signing Up is best done at the team level, it doesn't have to be initiated by management. It can be initiated by the team lead or even by a de facto leader—someone who happens to be exceptionally self-motivated and wants to pull the rest of the team along.

Follow through by empowering the team. Signing Up won't work unless you let the team run with the ball. Point the direction, but don't specify how to get to the end.

Don't use Signing Up on a project with shaky requirements. Your highly motivated team needs to be able to charge full-steam ahead, not full-steam right, then full-steam left, then full-steam backwards. The only exception to this rule is when the team itself is responsible for defining requirements. Then sometimes they can tolerate numerous changes in direction without losing motivation.

Signing Up in Different Environments

You can use Signing Up on virtually any kind of project—business, shrink-wrap, systems, and so on. Signing Up always requires an "extraordinary commitment," but the exact nature of that extraordinary commitment means different things in different environments.

In the world of RAD, James Kerr wrote about a dedicated RAD team that signed up, which meant that they were willing to sweep aside their normal mix of responsibilities and work a hard, focused 8 hours a day on one project (Kerr and Hunter 1994). Kerr reports that this team sometimes had to work at home in the evenings or for a few hours on the weekend. The high point of this project for Kerr was the night that the team of four people stayed late to implement a set of help screens. Kerr talks at length about what a grueling day it was. The team worked a full day, took a half-hour break for pizza and beer, and kept going almost until midnight. Kerr describes this as a "breakneck schedule."

In contrast, on the Microsoft Windows NT project, signing up meant fore-going *everything* to be able to work on the project: evenings, weekends, holidays, normal sleeping hours, you name it (Zachary 1994). When they weren't sleeping, they were working. Developers sacrificed hobbies, health, and families to work on the project. One team member answered email from the hospital while his wife was in labor. The NT development team wore beepers so that they could be called at 3:00 in the morning if their code had broken the build. People kept cots in their offices, and many would go several days without going home. Tracy Kidder describes a similar level of commitment in *The Soul of a New Machine* (Kidder 1981).

Some organizations, like Microsoft, don't mind if the signing-up commitment results in a lot of overtime. Other organizations, like IBM, have found that part of the commitment can be not to work any overtime (Scherr 1989). They've found that placing a set of severe, seemingly impossible constraints on a project forces the team to consider and implement radically productive solutions that they would normally not even consider.

The level of commitment will vary with the degree of the challenge. The Windows NT team was faced with the challenge of developing the best operating system in the world. Kerr's RAD team was faced with the relatively mundane challenge of developing a business system for in-house use. Not surprisingly, one team was willing to sacrifice much more than the other.

34.2   Managing the Risks of Signing Up

The Signing Up practice is a double-edged sword. It offers tremendous motivational potential, but it also offers as many hazards as any other practice described in this book.

> I think of that statistic that the best programmers are 25 times as productive as the worst programmers, and it seems that I am both of those guys.
>
> *Al Corwin*

Increased inefficiency. Teams that are signed up have a tendency to work hard rather than to work smart. Although it's theoretically possible to work hard *and* work smart, most people seem to be able to do one or the other, but not both. A focus on working hard almost guarantees that they'll make mistakes that they'll live to regret, mistakes that will take more project time rather than less. Some experts have even argued that people who work more than 40 hours per week don't get any more done than people who work about 40 hours (Metzger 1981, Mills in Metzger 1981, DeMarco and Lister 1987, Brady and DeMarco 1994, Maguire 1994).

If you're working on a project in which people are signed up, watch for an increase in the number of time-consuming mistakes and other signs that people are not working as smart as they should.

Decreased status visibility. People who sign up make a personal commitment to deliver a product in the shortest possible time. In some cases, that can-do mentality makes it hard to assess the real status of the project.

CLASSIC MISTAKE

CROSS-REFERENCE
All the problems discussed here are characteristic of this kind of scheduling. For details, see "Commitment-Based Scheduling" in Section 8.5.

Monday:	"Will you be done by Friday?" *"You bet!"*
Wednesday:	"Will you be done by Friday?" *"You bet!"*
Friday:	"Are you done?" *"Um, no, but I will be really soon. I'll be done by Monday."*
Monday:	"Are you done?" *"Um, no. I should be done in a few hours."*
Friday:	"Are you done?" *"I'm getting really close. I'll be done any time now."*
Monday:	"Are you done?" *"No. I ran into some setbacks, but I'm on top of them. I should be done by Friday."*

Multiply this phenomenon across an entire project and you have a project whose status is virtually impossible to determine. Some organizations are willing to trade this kind of loss of management visibility for higher morale, and some aren't. Be aware of the trade-off your project is making.

543

Loss of control. The signed-up team takes on a life of its own, and the life it takes on is sometimes not the life that the company wants it to have. The team (and the product) might be headed in a different direction than management wants them to go. Forcing the team to change direction can give the team the impression that they aren't as empowered as they thought they were, and that can be fatal to morale.

Addressing this risk requires that you make a judgment about the trade-off between morale and efficiency as well as between morale and control. Are you getting enough of a morale boost from having a signed-up team to justify letting them go their own direction?

Smaller available talent pool for the project. Enthusiasm can work wonders, but it has its limits too. Some older, more-experienced developers who have signed up before simply won't sign up for Windows NT-like projects. The result can be an averaging down of the experience level on a project in which Signing Up is used. Such projects can be characterized more by their exceptional energy levels than by their exceptional results.

Burnout. Even when developers work overtime voluntarily, long hours can take a heavy toll. The anecdotal reports of developers who sign up for projects and work lots of overtime also include lengthy lists of developers who leave their companies at the ends of their projects (Kidder 1981; Zachary 1994).

34.3 Side Effects of Signing Up

Signing Up does not have any consistent, predictable effect on a product's characteristics. Side effects arise from the fact that the development team will have more control over the character of the product than it might otherwise, and that can mean that the product's quality, usability, functionality, or other attributes turn out better, worse, or simply different than you expect.

34.4 Signing Up's Interactions with Other Practices

Signing Up has a close relationship with teamwork (Chapter 12). People sign up for a team, and it's hard to have a team in which half the people are signed up and half are not. Usually, if the Signing Up practice is going to work, everyone on the team needs to be signed up.

You can expect teams that are signed up to work some Voluntary Overtime (Chapter 43). In exchange, the team will expect the organization to support their efforts, at least in the form of providing them with a productive work environment (Chapter 30). The team might also resist more active, hands-on management practices such as Miniature Milestones (Chapter 27). You'll probably have to use commitment-based scheduling ("Commitment-Based Scheduling" in Section 8.5) and accept all of the trade-offs it involves.

34.5 The Bottom Line on Signing Up

The bottom line with Signing Up is that the degree of commitment you elicit will vary depending on the excitement that you're able to generate about the project. When you have an extraordinary project, you can see extraordinary commitment, extraordinary morale, and extraordinary productivity. On more mundane projects, you can expect less.

34.6 Keys to Success in Using Signing Up

Here are the keys to success in using Signing Up:

- Create a compelling vision for the project so that team members will have something that's worth signing up for.
- Make Signing Up voluntary.
- Empower the team so that it can succeed at the challenge it has been motivated to respond to.
- Be prepared to address or accept the inefficiencies that result from people working hard rather than smart.

Further Reading

Kidder, Tracy. *The Soul of a New Machine.* Boston: Atlantic Monthly/Little Brown, 1981. This book describes how computer hardware developers signed up to work on Data General's Eagle computer. It lays out the signing-up process in detail and illustrates the motivational benefit of the process—Eagle's developers worked practically 24 hours a day throughout the project. It is also an object lesson in the risks associated with signing up: much of the development team quit the company when the project was finished.

35

Spiral Lifecycle Model

The Spiral Lifecycle Model is a sophisticated lifecycle model that focuses on early identification and reduction of project risks. A spiral project starts on a small scale, explores risks, makes a plan to handle the risks, and then decides whether to take the next step of the project—to do the next iteration of the spiral. It derives its rapid-development benefit not from an increase in project speed, but from continuously reducing the project's risk level—which has an effect on the time required to deliver it. Success at using the Spiral Lifecycle Model depends on conscientious, attentive, and knowledgeable management. It can be used on most kinds of projects, and its risk-reduction focus is always beneficial.

Efficacy

Potential reduction from nominal schedule:	Fair
Improvement in progress visibility:	Very Good
Effect on schedule risk:	Decreased Risk
Chance of first-time success:	Good
Chance of long-term success:	Excellent

Major Risks

None

Major Interactions and Trade-Offs

- Trades increased project planning and tracking for greatly improved progress visibility and greatly reduced risk

For more on the spiral lifecycle model, see Section 7.3, "Spiral."

36

Staged Delivery

Staged Delivery is a lifecycle model in which software is developed in stages, usually with the most important capabilities being developed first. Staged Delivery doesn't reduce the time needed to build a software product, but it substantially reduces the risks involved in building one and also provides tangible signs of progress that are visible to the customer and useful to management in assessing project status. Keys to success include being sure that the product architecture is solid and defining delivery stages carefully. Staged Delivery can improve overall code quality, reduce the risk of project cancelation, and support build-to-budget efforts.

S U M M A R Y

Efficacy

Potential reduction from nominal schedule:	None
Improvement in progress visibility:	Good
Effect on schedule risk:	Decreased Risk
Chance of first-time success:	Very Good
Chance of long-term success:	Excellent

Major Risks

- Feature creep

Major Interactions and Trade-Offs

- Can plan each delivery stage using Miniature Milestones
- Success depends on defining a family of programs (part of Designing for Change)
- Less flexibility than Evolutionary Delivery or Evolutionary Prototyping; can serve as a basis for Evolutionary Delivery
- Trades increased planning effort for increased progress visibility

Staged Delivery is a lifecycle model in which you develop software in successive stages and either show it to the customer or actually deliver it at the end of each stage. Figure 36-1 provides a graphical depiction of this lifecycle model.

As Figure 36-1 suggests, with Staged Delivery you go through the waterfall model steps of defining the software concept, analyzing requirements, and creating an architectural design. You then proceed to do detailed design, coding, debugging, and testing within each stage, creating a releasable product at the end of each stage.

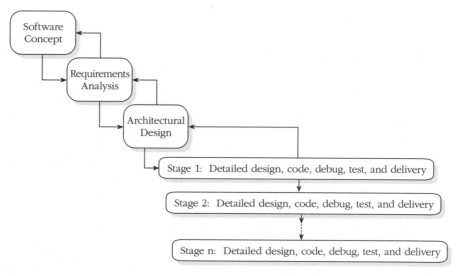

Figure 36-1. *The Staged Delivery lifecycle model. Staged Delivery allows you to deliver a product in stages after first developing requirements and architectural design in a traditional way.*

Staged Delivery supports improvements in the perceived schedule more than in the actual schedule.

More visible progress for custom-software development. With some software-development approaches, you complete large sections of the lifecycle almost in secret. Technical projects often provide status reports such as "90 percent complete." That's not enough for customers who have learned the hard way that if the first 90 percent of a project takes 90 percent of the time, the last 10 percent of the project can take another 90 percent of the time. It's easier to keep your customers happy when you're regularly showing them evidence of your progress.

For custom software, an approach that puts something in front of the customer on a regular basis increases the customer's confidence that you will eventually complete the project. Your progress is obvious. The customer's perception of your speed improves.

Shorter product-release cycles for shrink-wrap software development. With typical development approaches for shrink-wrap software, you define version 1 and then design, code, and test until you complete it. If development takes longer than planned, the product ships late and revenue from the product comes in late. If your company's finances are shaky and you're slow in finishing version 1, you might never get a chance to start version 2.

Using the Staged Delivery practice, you can define internal versions at a finer granularity than version 1 and version 2. You can define versions 2a through 2f and plan to have them ready at 1-month intervals. You might plan to have 2a ready at 7 seven months into a 1-year schedule, 2b ready at 8 months, 2c ready at 9 months, and so on. If you meet your 1-year schedule, you'll have 2f ready and you can ship the full product. If you don't complete 2f, you'll still have a working product in 2c, 2d, or 2e. Any of those versions is an improvement over version 1, and you can ship it instead of 2f. Once you ship it, you can define new increments for version 3 and continue.

This approach supports more frequent and predictable product releases. From your customer's point of view, you've released two versions, 1 and 2, and you released those two versions on time. From your point of view, you've developed several versions but released only the two that were ready at the time your company needed them.

This approach requires sophisticated coordination with marketing and user-documentation efforts, but if you're working in the highly competitive world of packaged software, it can be an effective way to reduce the risk of a product-development cycle.

Early warning of problems. When you plan to deliver releases early and often, you get early, frequent, indisputable progress reports. Either the release is done on time or it isn't. The work's quality is obvious from the release's quality. If the development team is in trouble, you discover that within the first one or two releases; you don't have to wait until the project is "99 percent complete" and 0 percent functional.

Less overhead. Staged Delivery also goes a long way toward eliminating the administrative time that developers spend creating progress reports and other traditional progress-tracking reports. The working product is a more accurate status report than any paper report could ever be.

Makes more options available. Even if you're uneasy about releasing version 2c to your customer when you planned to release version 2f, using Staged Delivery provides you with something you can release if business needs call for it. You might ultimately decide that it's not in your best interest to release version 2c and defer release to version 2d. But if you don't use Staged Delivery, you won't have the option.

CROSS-REFERENCE
For more on refining estimates based on experience, see "Recalibration" in Section 8.7.

Reduces estimation error. Staged Delivery sidesteps the problem of bad estimates by delivering early and often. Instead of making one large estimate for the whole project, you can make several smaller estimates for several smaller releases. With each release, you can learn from the mistakes in your estimates, recalibrate your approach, and improve the accuracy of future estimates.

CROSS-REFERENCE
For more on frequent integration, see Chapter 18, "Daily Build and Smoke Test."

Integration problems minimized. A common risk to software projects is difficulty in integrating components that were developed separately. The likelihood of serious integration problems is related to the time between successive integration attempts. If the time between attempts is long, the chance of problems is large. When you deliver software early and often, as you do with Staged Delivery, you must also perform integration early and often. That minimizes potential integration problems.

36.1 Using Staged Delivery

In Staged Delivery, you start with a clear idea of the product you will ultimately deliver. Staged Delivery is a late-in-the-project development practice. If you're following a traditional waterfall lifecycle model, you don't need to start planning for it until after you've completed requirements analysis and architectural design.

Once you've completed architectural design, to use Staged Delivery you plan a series of deliveries. As Figure 36-1 on page 550 suggests, within each stage you do a complete detailed design, construction, and test cycle, and at the end of each stage you deliver a working product. For example, if you were developing a word processing program, you might create the following delivery plan:

Table 36-1. Example of a Staged-Delivery Schedule for a Word Processor

Stage 1	Text editor is available, including editing, saving, and printing.
Stage 2	Character and basic paragraph formatting is available.
Stage 3	Advanced formatting is available, including WYSIWYG page layout and on-screen formatting tools.
Stage 4	Utilities are available, including spell checking, thesaurus, grammar checking, hyphenation, and mail merge.
Stage 5	Full integration with other products is complete.

The first delivery should be the germ of the product you will ultimately deliver. Subsequent releases add more capabilities in a carefully planned way. You deliver the final product in the last stage.

Planning for the first release is unique in that it needs to include some global architectural thinking, which raises questions such as: "Is the software architecture open enough to support modifications, including many that we haven't fully anticipated?" It's also a good idea to plot a general direction for the software at the beginning of the project—although, depending on whether you intend to use a pure Staged Delivery approach or an Evolutionary Delivery approach, that general direction might just be a best guess that you'll override later.

You don't have to deliver each release to a customer to use the Staged Delivery practice, and you can implement it on a technical-lead level. In the case of the word processor, you might not even release a version to your customer until delivery 3 or 4 or even 5. But you could use Staged Delivery as an aid to track progress, coordinate drops to quality assurance, or reduce the risk of integration problems.

For the approach to work well, each stage should include size, performance, and quality targets in addition to functionality targets. Too much hidden work accumulates as you go along if you don't deliver a truly releasable product at the end of each stage.

As a general goal, try to deliver the software's capabilities from most important to least important. Defining the deliveries in this way forces people to prioritize and helps to eliminate gold-plating. If you do a good job of this, by the time you've delivered 80 percent of the product your customer will be wondering what could possibly be left in that last 20 percent.

Technical Dependencies

In a single large release, the order of component delivery doesn't matter much. Multiple small releases of a product require more planning than a single large release does, and you have to be sure that you haven't overlooked any technical dependencies in your planning. If you plan to implement autosave in delivery 3, you'd better be sure that manual save isn't planned for delivery 4. Be sure that the development team reviews the delivery plan with an eye toward technical dependencies before you promise specific features at specific times to your customers.

Developer Focus

Staged Delivery requires that each developer meet the deadline for each stage. If one developer misses a deadline, the whole release can slide. Some developers are used to working solo, performing their assignments in whatever order they choose. Some developers might resent the restrictions that a Staged Delivery plan imposes. If you allow developers the amount of freedom they are used to, you'll miss your delivery dates and lose much of the value of staged deliveries.

With Staged Delivery, developers can't follow their noses as much as they're used to doing. You need to be sure that the developers have bought into the delivery plan and agreed to work to it. The best way to ensure developer buy-in is to involve developers intimately in the creation of the plan. If the delivery plan is *their* delivery plan—and if there was no heavy hand influencing their work—you won't have to worry about getting their buy-in.

Theme Releases

CROSS-REFERENCE
For details of another kind of theme, see "Shared, Elevating Vision or Goal" in Section 12.3.

A good way to define the stages is to use themes for each incremental release (Whitaker 1994). Defining releases can give rise to feature-by-feature negotiations that can take up a lot of time. The use of themes raises those negotiations to a higher level.

In the delivery schedule mapped out in Table 36-1 on page 552, the themes are text editing, basic formatting, advanced formatting, utilities, and integration. These themes make it easier to decide into which release to put a particular capability. Even if the feature straddles a gray area—you could classify automatic list numbering as either advanced formatting or a utility, for example—your job will be easier because you only have to decide which of the two themes is most appropriate. You don't have to consider every feature for every release.

When you use themes, you probably won't be able to deliver features in exact priority order. Instead, plan to prioritize the themes in order of importance, and then deliver the themes in priority order.

CROSS-REFERENCE
You can use the Miniature Milestones practice to track progress during each stage. For details, see Chapter 27, "Miniature Milestones."

The use of themes, shouldn't be taken as an invitation to abbreviate release planning. Map out exactly which features you plan to have in each release. If you don't, you won't know exactly what to expect at each delivery stage, and you'll lose much of the project-tracking benefit of this lifecycle model.

Kinds Of Projects

Staged Delivery works best for well-understood systems. If you're not sure what features your product should have, then the Staged Delivery practice isn't a good choice. You have to understand the product well enough to plan the stages by the time you're done with architectural design.

Staged Delivery works especially well when your customers are eager to begin using a relatively small portion of the product's functionality. You can provide a valuable service to your customers if you can provide the 20 percent of the product they most need in a fraction of the development time needed for the complete product.

Staged Delivery is also an appropriate practice for very large projects. Planning a series of four 9-month projects is considerably less risky than planning a single 3-year project. You would probably have stages within stages for a project of that size; even a 9-month project is too large to provide good progress visibility to your customer, and you should break it up into several incremental releases.

Staged Delivery works well only for systems in which you can develop useful subsets of the product independently. Most end-user products can be defined in such a way that you can make meaningful intermediate deliveries before you deliver the final product. But operating systems, some kinds of embedded systems, and some other kinds of products might not be usable without complete or nearly complete functionality; for those kinds of systems, Staged Delivery is not appropriate. So if you can't figure out how to break the delivery of your product up into stages, Staged Delivery is not the right approach for you.

36.2 Managing the Risks of Staged Delivery

The preceding discussion might give you the idea that Staged Delivery works almost every time, but keep this limitation in mind.

Feature creep. The main risk associated with Staged Delivery is the risk of feature creep. When customers begin to use the first release of your product, they are likely to want to change what has been planned for the other releases.

CROSS-REFERENCE
For a variation of Staged Delivery that works better when requirements aren't stable, see Chapter 20, "Evolutionary Delivery."

The best way to manage this risk is not to use Staged Delivery if you're uncertain what features need to be developed. Pure Staged Delivery does not provide much flexibility to respond to customer requests. Staged Delivery works best when you have a broad and deep consensus about what should be in the product.

If you decide to use Staged Delivery, you can still build time into your schedule to accommodate unknown features. You might define the last stage as the stage for making late-breaking changes. By allocating that time, you make it clear to your customers that you intend to be flexible, but you also make it clear that you expect to limit the number of unknown features that you implement. Of course, when you get to the last stage you can renegotiate the schedule if your customers want more features than you have time for. By then your customers will have working software in their hands, and they might well find that their initial schedule goal is no longer as important as it once seemed.

In addition to these practices specific to Staged Delivery, you can use any of the general means of managing feature creep. Those are described in Chapter 14, "Feature-Set Control."

36.3 Side Effects of Staged Delivery

In addition to its positive effect on project scheduling, Staged Delivery can benefit several other project characteristics.

More even distribution of development and testing resources. Projects using Staged Delivery consist of several minicycles of planning, requirements analysis, design, code, and test. Design isn't bunched up at the beginning, programming isn't bunched up in the middle, and testing isn't bunched up at the end. You can distribute analysis, programming, and testing resources more uniformly than you can with approaches that are closer to the pure waterfall model.

Improved code quality. In traditional approaches, you know that "someone" will have to read your code and maintain it. That provides an abstract motivation to write good code. With Staged Delivery, you know that *you* will need to read and modify the code many times. That provides a concrete motivation to write good code, which is a more compelling incentive (Basili and Turner 1975).

More likely project completion. A staged-delivery project won't be abandoned as easily as a waterfall-model project. If the project runs into funding trouble, it's less likely to be canceled if the system is 50 percent complete, 50 percent operational, and in the users' hands than if it's 90 percent complete, doesn't work at all, and has never been touched by anyone outside the development team.

Support for build-to-budget. The premise of Staged Delivery is that you deliver something useful as early as possible. The project will be partially complete even if your customers run out of money. At the end of each stage you and your customers can examine the budget and determine whether they can afford the next stage. Thus, even if the well runs dry, the product still might be largely usable. In many cases, the last 10 or 20 percent of the product consists of optional capabilities that aren't part of the product's core. Even if a few frills are missing, the customers will get most of the necessary capabilities. If funding runs out at the 90-percent mark, imagine how much happier your customers will be with a mostly functioning product than if you had used a pure waterfall lifecycle model—and "90 percent complete" meant "0 percent operational."

36.4 Staged Delivery's Interactions with Other Practices

Although there are a few similarities, Staged Delivery is not a form of prototyping. Prototyping is exploratory, and Staged Delivery is not. Its goal is to make progress visible or to put useful software into the customers' hands more quickly. Unlike prototyping, you know the end result when you begin the process.

If the Staged Delivery practice provides less flexibility than you need, you can probably use Evolutionary Delivery (Chapter 20) or Evolutionary Prototyping (Chapter 21) instead. If your customers get the stage 1 release and tell you that what you're planning to deliver for stage 2 won't suit them, you'd have to be pigheaded not to change course. If you know the general nature of the system you're building but still have doubts about significant aspects of it, don't use Staged Delivery.

Staged Delivery combines well with Miniature Milestones (Chapter 27). By the time you get to each stage, you should know enough about what you're building to map out the milestones in detail.

Success at developing a set of staged deliveries depends on designing a family of programs ("Define Families of Programs" in Section 19.1). The more you follow that design practice, the better able you'll be to avoid disaster if the requirements turn out to be less stable than you thought.

Why Is Staged Delivery So Rigid?

Staged Delivery doesn't always have to be as rigid as it's described in this chapter. Sometimes it's desirable to map out an entire product and deliver it in stages, as described here. Sometimes you'll want more flexibility—rigidly defining the early stages and allowing for more flexibility in later stages. Sometimes you'll want to evolve the product throughout its development, as you do with Evolutionary Prototyping (Chapter 21).

This chapter describes the most rigid version of Staged Delivery in order to provide a clear contrast between it (at one end of the scale) and Evolutionary Prototyping (at the other). For your own use, you can adapt Staged Delivery (or Evolutionary Delivery or Evolutionary Prototyping) to the specific needs of your project and call it anything you like.

36.5 The Bottom Line on Staged Delivery

CROSS-REFERENCE
For more on the importance
of making progress visible,
see Section 6.3,
"Perception and Reality."

The bottom line with the Staged Delivery practice is that, although it doesn't reduce the overall development time needed to build a software product, it reduces the risk involved in building a product and it provides tangible signs of progress that can be as important to rapid development as all-out development time is.

36.6 Keys to Success in Using Staged Delivery

Here are the keys to using Staged Delivery successfully:

- Be sure that the product architecture supports as many of the possible future directions of the software as you can imagine.

- Define the first delivery stage so that you can deliver it as early as possible.

- Define the delivery stages in terms of themes, and be sure to involve developers intimately in defining the themes and the specific capabilities that make up each theme.

- Deliver the theme releases in order of importance.

- Consider whether pure Staged Delivery will provide the most benefit, or whether Evolutionary Delivery or Evolutionary Prototyping would provide more benefit. Carefully consider how you plan to handle customer change requests.

Further Reading

Gilb, Tom. *Principles of Software Engineering Management.* Wokingham, England: Addison-Wesley, 1988. Chapters 7 and 15 contain a thorough discussion of both staged and evolutionary delivery. (Gilb doesn't distinguish between the two.) Gilb was one of the first people to emphasize the value of incremental development approaches such as these. He has first-hand experience using the practice on large projects, and much of the management approach described in the rest of his book assumes that it's used.

37

Theory-W Management

A software project involves many stakeholders with competing interests, including bosses, developers, end-users, customers, and maintainers. Theory-W provides a project-management framework for reconciling competing interests. It is based on making an explicit effort to understand what the different stakeholders need in order to "win," negotiating conflicts among the stakeholders' win conditions, and then structuring the project so that everyone realizes their win conditions. Theory-W produces its schedule savings through improved efficiency of working relationships, improved progress visibility, and reduced risk.

Efficacy

Potential reduction from nominal schedule:	None
Improvement in progress visibility:	Very Good
Effect on schedule risk:	Decreased Risk
Chance of first-time success:	Excellent
Chance of long-term success:	Excellent

Major Risks

None

Major Interactions and Trade-Offs

- Designed to be combined with the Spiral Lifecycle Model
- Particularly effective during schedule negotiations
- Relies on the use of the Principled Negotiation practice

One practical management approach that supports rapid development is called "Theory-W Management" (Boehm and Ross 1989). Theory-W takes its name from its most important principle: *Make everyone a Winner.*

Most software projects begin with a group of project stakeholders who have competing objectives. Table 37-1 shows the stakeholders and their typical objectives.

Table 37-1. Project Stakeholders and Their Objectives

Customers	Bosses	Developers	End-Users	Maintainers
Quick schedule	No overruns	Interesting design work	Lots of features	No defects
Low budget	No surprises	Exploration of new technical areas	User-friendly software	Good documentation
	Successful project		Fast software	Easy modifiabiltiy
		No grunt work	Robust software	
		Home life		

Source: Adapted from "Theory-W Software Project Management: Principles and Examples" (Boehm and Ross 1989).

As you can see from the table, many of the objectives conflict. The end-users' goal of "lots of features" might easily be in conflict with the customers' goals of "quick schedule" and "low budget." The developers' goal of "interesting design work" could be in conflict with the customers' goals of "quick schedule," and their goal of "no grunt work" might be in conflict with the maintainers' goal of "good documentation."

Most project teams don't do a good job of reconciling these objectives. The result is that a project can seem sometimes like a turtle on Valium to the customer at the same time it seems like a rapid-development death march to the developers.

Theory-W software-project management argues that making winners of all the stakeholders in a software process is both a necessary and a sufficient condition for running a successful software project. Projects that set up win-lose or lose-lose scenarios will be unsuccessful.

Theory-W Management supports rapid development by putting all the stakeholders on the same side of the negotiating table. Conflicts between these groups are at the root of most software-project management problems and affect your ability to set goals, define delivery dates, prioritize assignments, and adapt to changes.

Specifically, Theory-W Management supports rapid development in the following ways.

CROSS-REFERENCE
For more on the importance
of clear objectives, see "Goal
Setting" in Section 11.2.

Clearer project objectives. Because a Theory-W project begins by identifying each of the stakeholders' "win" conditions, the project's objectives are clear from the start. The negotiation that takes place at the beginning of the project reinforces and documents the project's objectives. Setting clear objectives is probably the most important key to motivating developers, and motivating developers is probably the most important key to rapid development.

Better customer relations. Many projects are set up to provide a win for the customer and a loss for the developers, or vice versa. It's hard to maintain good relations when one of the parties is losing. Theory-W projects by their very nature improve relations between developers and customers because everyone stands to gain.

Several development-speed savings arise from improved customer relations:

CROSS-REFERENCE
For details on using
customer relations to
improve development speed,
see Chapter 10, "Customer-
Oriented Development."

- Efficiency improves as a result of better communication and better customer understanding of the customer role in the project.

- The amount of rework drops because you do a better job of analyzing requirements. Negotiations over feature details take less time because everyone is aligned on the main goals they want to achieve.

- Early goal-setting produces realistic schedule expectations, which improves the perceived development speed and eliminates problems associated with overly optimistic schedules.

Reduced customer-related risk. Many risks arise from the customer side of a development relationship, including feature creep, slow communication, and micro-management. Establishing a Theory-W relationship with your customer helps to minimize or eliminate such risks. It helps you to manage the remaining risks because you can keep a close eye on customer-related risks and get early warnings about them.

37.1 Using Theory-W Management

When you use the Theory-W Management practice, you have everyone sit down at the beginning of the project and identify their win conditions. Then everyone negotiates to create a projectwide set of win conditions that you can reasonably achieve. Project management for the rest of the project consists of monitoring the project to ensure that each stakeholder continues to win. If one of the stakeholders starts to slide into a lose condition, you adjust the project accordingly.

Make Everyone a Winner

CROSS-REFERENCE
For more on negotiating and the four steps of *Getting to Yes*, see Section 9.2, "Beating Schedule Pressure."

The best work in developing win-win situations has been done in the field of negotiating. Here is the outline of a general process you can use to set up a win-win situation from "getting to yes" (Fisher and Ury 1981):

1. Separate people from the problem.

2. Focus on interests rather than positions.

3. Invent options for mutual gain.

4. Insist on using objective criteria.

Table 37-2 provides a summary of how these win-win steps apply to Theory-W Management.

Table 37-2. Steps in Theory-W Project Management

1. Establish a set of win-win preconditions before you start the project.
   - Understand how people want to win.
   - Establish reasonable expectations on the parts of all stakeholders.
   - Match people's tasks to their win conditions.
   - Provide an environment that supports the project's goals.

2. Structure a win-win software process.
   - Establish a realistic plan.
   - Use the plan to control the project.
   - Identify and manage your win-lose and lose-lose risks.
   - Keep people involved.

3. Structure a win-win software product.
   - Match product to end-users' and maintainers' win conditions.

Source: Adapted from "Theory-W Software Project Management: Principles and Examples" (Boehm and Ross 1989).

The steps in Table 37-2 are described in the following sections.

Step 1: Establish Win-Win Preconditions

In Theory-W, the first step you take is to establish objectives for the project that will allow everyone to win. The word "preconditions" in this case is used to mean "entrance criteria": if you can't figure out how to make everyone a winner, don't even begin the project.

To complete step 1, you need to understand how people want to win, establish reasonable expectations on the parts of all stakeholders, match people's tasks to their win conditions, and provide a supportive environment.

Understand how people want to win. Before you try to understand how people want to win, be sure to identify all the key people. Projects have failed because a key stakeholder—subcontractor, marketing department, user group, or product-support group—was not included.

Put yourself into other stakeholders' shoes to understand what they need to win. Understand that what your customers, marketers, and end-users need is likely to be different from what you need. Of these groups, the group that's arguably the most important to understand—and the one that's often the most under-represented—is your customers. Work extra hard to understand your customers' win conditions.

Theory-W works well even if one of the stakeholders is an S.O.B. who is determined to take advantage of you or the other stakeholders. The purpose of Theory-W is to make everyone a winner. If you can't structure the project so that everyone wins, you don't do the project at all. If you can get a win with the S.O.B. involved, fine. If not, don't do the project—there's no point in doing it if you're going to emerge a loser. When you use Theory-W with an S.O.B. on the other side of the bargaining table, you might come out a little worse than you would if Mr. Rogers were on the other side of the table. The S.O.B. might get more than his or her fair share, but that's OK as long as the rest of you can still meet your win conditions.

Establish reasonable expectations. The second sub-step in establishing win-win preconditions is to establish reasonable expectations. There's not much you can do to set up a win-win project if your customer wants the moon and wants it in 6 weeks.

CROSS-REFERENCE
For tips on negotiating mismatches in schedule expectations, see Section 9.2, "Beating Schedule Pressure."

If you find that some parties have unreasonable expectations, bring the stakeholders together to identify expectations and resolve mismatches. If the customer insists on a delivered product within 6 weeks and the developers are convinced that they can't do it in less than 6 months, you have a mismatch. Unless you can align the customers' and developers' expectations, one of those parties will emerge from the project as a loser, and the project itself will fail.

Here are some ways you can help to bring people's expectations into line with reality:

- Have people look at issues from one another's viewpoints.

CROSS-REFERENCE
For tables of the shortest possible schedules for projects of various sizes and kinds, see Section 8.6, "Ballpark Schedule Estimates."

- Relate people's expectations to experience. Refer to historical benchmarks or the judgment of experts to define what is realistic and what is not. If your customer or boss wants you to develop a product in less than the shortest time that your organization has ever developed a similar size product, that expectation is probably unrealistic. If they want you to develop a product in less time than anyone in your industry has ever developed a product of that size before, that's definitely unrealistic. Use historical benchmarks to reign in unrealistic expectations for schedule, functionality, cost, and other product or project attributes.

- Relate people's expectations to well-calibrated models. If your organization hasn't collected data on its experience, or if people don't take that data seriously, refer to the results of a software-estimation model. This can be especially effective because it allows the stakeholders to adjust the parameters of the project in real time and see how it's likely to affect the outcome of the project.

Match people's tasks to their win conditions. Many times people have no influence over the aspects of the project that will allow them to win. That's demotivating and sets the project up to fail.

Instead, assign people's tasks so that they can achieve their own win conditions. Here are some examples of how you could do that:

- Make the people who will maintain the code responsible for reviewing and approving it during its initial development.
- Put developers in charge of estimating the time required for tasks they will ultimately perform.
- Put end-users in charge of reviewing early storyboards or prototypes of the software for usability issues.
- Give developers the explicit goal of creating designs that they can implement quickly and reliably.
- Put customers in charge of identifying features to include and features to exclude in order to make the schedule as short as possible.
- Put customers in charge of tracking project status.

The common theme here is that you need to search for creative win-win situations. Some of those situations will require you to structure the project in unusual ways, but that's fine. Your project will be all the more successful for it.

Provide an environment that supports the project's goals. The kind of environment that you'll need will depend on each stakeholder's point of view. For developers, it usually means providing training, modern hardware, and modern software tools. For customers, it might require training in modern programming practices and using a lifecycle model that provides tangible signs of progress.

Step 2: Structure a Win-Win Software Process

The second main step in Theory-W is to create a software process that will make everyone a winner. To do that, you need to establish a realistic process plan, use the plan to control the project, identify and manage your win-lose or lose-lose risks, and keep people involved.

Establish a realistic plan. Planning is key to the success of the Theory-W approach. The plan maps out the road to achieving win-win results. It records the mutual commitment of the project stakeholders to a set of win-win conditions and to all the implications of agreeing to achieve them.

If you completed Step 1, you will have established reasonable expectations. Remember that the establishment of reasonable expectations is a precondition to starting the project. If you couldn't establish reasonable expectations, don't proceed with the project. Reasonable expectations make the job of planning immensely easier because you can create a realistic plan. You don't have to wrestle against unrealistic expectations in every paragraph and every sentence.

Use the plan to control the project. Once you've created the plan, it's imperative that you follow the plan. Too many plans become shelfware. If you find that you're not following the plan, either correct the project so that you are following the plan or revise the plan so that you can follow it. The plan provides a framework for detecting shortfalls from the win-win conditions and taking corrective action; if you don't follow the plan, you probably won't achieve a win-win outcome.

Identify and manage your win-lose and lose-lose risks. Risk management is a key aspect of the Theory-W approach, and the six basic risk-management steps from Chapter 5, "Risk Management," apply. For each of the stakeholders' win conditions, you should identify a risk of not achieving their win conditions. Then monitor that risk along with the other risks to your project.

Keep people involved. Theory-W is a people-oriented process, and it's important to keep all the stakeholders involved throughout the project. Stakeholders will care more about their own win conditions than anyone else will, and keeping the stakeholders involved in reviews, planning, progress monitoring, feature-change negotiations, and other activities will help to achieve a win-win outcome.

Step 3: Structure a Win-Win Software Product

In addition to structuring the process for success, Theory-W has you structure the product for success. This includes both the external aspects of the product, which will be visible to end-users, and the internal aspects of the product, which will be visible to developers and maintainers. From the end-user's point of view, the product will be a success if it's easy to learn, easy to use, and reliable. From the maintainer's point of view, the product should be well-documented, programmed with good style, and easily modifiable.

Kinds of Projects That Can Use Theory-W

Although Theory-W Management is most useful when you apply it from the start of a project, you can begin to apply it during any phase. If you've experienced difficult relations with a customer, you might conduct a win-win analysis to uncover the potential win-lose or lose-lose conditions that are the source of the difficulties. Theory-W can help you to keep a successful project running smoothly, and it can help to rescue a project that's in trouble.

Theory-W works best when it's championed by an upper-level manager or someone high enough to use it with customers and all other stakeholders. If it's not possible to obtain upper-level support, you can still use it at the technical-lead or individual-developer level to provide insight into why the other stakeholders in the project act the way they do.

There is no limit to the size or kind of project that can use Theory-W. It does not require much overhead, so it's suitable for small projects. Larger projects will have more stakeholders and more complicated win conditions, and identifying and creating the win-win conditions on those projects becomes all the more important. Theory-W is as well-suited to maintenance as it is to new development, and it is as well-suited to shrink-wrap software as it is to business or systems software. The specific stakeholders change, but the value of meeting their win conditions does not.

The Manager's Role

The manager's role in Theory-W is different from the manager's role in some other management theories. In other theories, the manager plays a role of boss, coach, or facilitator. In Theory-W, the manager manages more than his or her direct reports: he or she also manages stakeholder relationships and goals. In this schema, the manager is a negotiator with responsibility for creating project solutions that make everyone a winner.

Beyond that, the manager is also a goal-setter and a monitor of progress toward goals. On an ongoing basis, the manager seeks out day-to-day win-lose or lose-lose conflicts, confronts them, and changes them into win-win situations.

37.2   Managing the Risks of Theory-W Management

CROSS-REFERENCE
These techniques are the same as the techniques you use for risk monitoring. For details, see Chapter 5, "Risk Management."

There are no risks particular to the practice of Theory-W Management itself. Theory-W Management elevates the possibility that any stakeholder might become a loser to the level of a risk, and that creates two generic risks to a Theory-W project.

One of the parties starts to slip into a lose condition. When one of the parties starts to slip into a lose condition, the most appropriate reaction is to conduct a win-win analysis. When problems arise, it's easy to make knee-jerk corrections that create win-lose or lose-lose results. But it's usually possible to follow the Theory-W steps to create a corrective action that will either keep everyone winning or minimize losses compared to other possible actions.

Stakeholders are permitted to redefine their win conditions as the project progresses. Here's an example. The customers might originally have defined a delivery date of May 1 as one of their win conditions. As the project progresses, you might discover that you can't possibly deliver the project until June 1, creating a potential lose condition. At that point, the customers might decide that they can still salvage a win from any delivery date before July 1, and that puts the project back on a win-win footing.

A lose condition becomes unavoidable. The premise of Theory-W project management is that making everyone a winner is a sufficient and *necessary* condition for a project's success. If you discover that the project is certain to fail, shut it down as quickly as possible.

37.3   Side Effects of Theory-W Management

Depending on the stakeholders' win conditions, Theory-W can provide broad advantages that are more far-reaching than schedule efficiency. It can provide improved usability, maintainability, customer satisfaction, and team morale.

Theory-W also provides an excellent basis for tailoring out-of-the-box software methodologies to a specific project. Many methodologies deal less with the "why" than with the "what." In Theory-W, the "why" is the need to create wins for all stakeholders. When you document the stakeholders' specific win conditions in the project plan, you have a permanent record of the "why." That provides valuable information for when you go to tailor future methodologies to specific circumstances. It can also help you to determine how much of any particular methodology is enough for your project.

37.4   Theory-W Management's Interactions with Other Practices

Theory-W project management is particularly well-suited for use with the Spiral Lifecycle Model (Section 7.3, "Spiral," and Chapter 35). You can identify stakeholders' win conditions for each iteration of the spiral at the beginning of the iteration. Stakeholders can then modify their win conditions during each iteration, which will support high levels of satisfaction throughout the project.

Theory-W is useful during schedule negotiations (Section 9.2). Rather than focusing on the traditional three-months-no-six-I-say-four-no-five-OK-four-and-a-half style of negotiating, you can make it clear that, unless both parties stand to win by doing the project, the party that stands to lose has no rational basis for playing the game.

37.5 The Bottom Line on Theory-W Management

No quantitative data is available on the extent of schedule reductions resulting from Theory-W's use, but it seems apparent that Theory-W reduces schedule risk and can improve perceived development speed. In test cases, Theory-W has performed well (Boehm et al. 1995).

37.6 Keys to Success in Using Theory-W Management

Here are the keys to using Theory-W Management successfully:

- Understand how people want to win.
- Establish reasonable expectations on the parts of all stakeholders.
- Match people's tasks to their win conditions.
- Provide an environment that supports the project's goals.
- Establish a realistic plan.
- Use the plan to control the project.
- Identify and manage the win-lose and lose-lose risks.
- Keep people involved.
- Match product to end-users' and maintainers' win conditions.

Further Reading

Boehm, Barry, and Rony Ross. "Theory-W Software Project Management: Principles and Examples," *IEEE Transactions on Software Engineering,* July 1989. This paper spells out Theory-W. It's loaded with insights into successful negotiating principles and customer-relations psychology. It contains an excellent case study that describes a typical software project and analyzes how Theory-W could be applied to it.

38

Throwaway Prototyping

With Throwaway Prototyping, code is developed to explore factors critical to the system's success, and then that code is thrown away. The prototyping implementation uses programming languages or development practices or both that are much faster than the target language and practices. The user interface is prototyped far more commonly than any other part of the system, but other parts of some systems can also benefit from being prototyped. When used as a requirements-specification aid, the Throwaway Prototyping practice can accelerate projects based on traditional lifecycle models, such as DoD projects. It can be initiated at either a management or technical level.

Efficacy

Potential reduction from nominal schedule:	Fair
Improvement in progress visibility:	None
Effect on schedule risk:	Decreased Risk
Chance of first-time success:	Excellent
Chance of long-term success:	Excellent

Major Risks

- Keeping a throwaway prototype
- Inefficient use of prototyping time
- Unrealistic schedule and budget expectations

Major Interactions and Trade-Offs

None

The Throwaway Prototyping practice derives its development-speed benefit from the fact that it is often possible to explore individual requirements, design, and implementation options using languages and practices that allow for more rapid development than the ultimate implementation language and practices do. Here are some examples:

- You need to compare approximately how long it will take to store and retrieve 10,000 records using several different DBMSs, so you write throwaway code to exercise the DBMSs and to compare their performance.

- Your end-users can't decide between two user-interface styles, so you mock up two user interfaces using interface-building tools and give the users a "live" demo without ever writing a line of code.

- You want to check the feasibility of communicating with another application before basing your future design decisions on that ability, so you write test code to verify that such communication is possible. The test code contains no error checking and doesn't handle any exceptions, and you throw it away as soon as you've verified that you can communicate the way you need to.

You can employ Throwaway Prototyping at any time in a project—to clarify requirements, to decide an architectural issue, to compare design or implementation options, or to test a performance optimization.

38.1 Using Throwaway Prototyping

Throwaway Prototyping can be used by any of the project's personnel. Individual project participants can realize some benefit by prototyping risky areas within their individual areas of responsibility. Here is a list of areas that can benefit from being prototyped and suggestions about how to develop prototypes in those areas cheaply:

CROSS-REFERENCE
For more on user-interface prototyping, see Chapter 42, "User-Interface Prototyping."

- *User interface*—Prototype using a prototyping tool or visual programming language, or build a Hollywood facade in the target programming language.

- *Report formats*—Prototype using a word processor or report formatting tool.

- *Graph formats*—Prototype using a drawing tool or graphics library.

- *Database organization*—Prototype using a database design language, 4GL, or CASE tool.

- *Database performance*—Prototype using a database design language, 4GL, or CASE tool.

- *Accuracy and implementation of complex calculations*—Prototype using a spreadsheet or math-oriented language such as APL.

- *Time-critical parts of real-time systems*—Prototype using a small test program in the target programming language.

- *Performance of interactive systems*—Prototype using a small test program in the target programming language.

- *Feasibility of parts of the system that are pushing the state-of-the-art or with which the development staff has no experience*—Prototype using a visual programming language, small test program in the target programming language, or math-oriented language—whatever is appropriate.

As you can see, it can be profitable to prototype many areas of a program. However, if you understand your program well, don't prototype just for the sake of prototyping.

38.2 Managing the Risks of Throwaway Prototyping

Throwaway Prototyping is usually successful. Nonetheless, you should address several risks when planning a project that will use it.

CLASSIC MISTAKE

Keeping a throwaway prototype. One of the key problems in developing a throwaway prototype is that the prototype might not get thrown away. Managers often decide after the prototype has been developed that it will cost too much to "redo" the system and insist on evolving the prototype into the final product (Gordon and Bieman 1995).

Avoid this trap! Delivering a throwaway can result in poor design, poor maintainability, and poor performance. If you plan to develop a throwaway prototype, be sure that managers and technical staff both commit to throwing it away. Be sure that everyone understands that you are creating disposable software that isn't robust enough to be put into production or strong enough to serve as a foundation for the final product. You are not creating real software.

If you think that you might evolve the prototype rather than throw it away, plan from the outset to use an evolutionary approach so that the prototype's design and implementation will support full development.

As for the objection that throwing away the prototype costs too much, done right, the reason you create a throwaway prototype is that it is cheaper to develop a throwaway prototype, learn lessons the cheap way, and then implement the real code with fewer mistakes than it is not to create the throwaway prototype in the first place. If you can think of some other method that will be more cost effective in a specific situation, use that instead. Otherwise, far from creating extra costs, Throwaway Prototyping is the most cost-effective practice available.

CROSS-REFERENCE
For more on using prototyping time effectively, see "Inefficient use of prototyping time" in Section 20.2.

Inefficient use of prototyping time. As with Evolutionary Prototyping, projects often waste time during Throwaway Prototyping and unnecessarily lengthen the development schedule. Although prototyping is by nature an exploratory process, that does not mean that it has to be an open-ended process.

Monitor prototyping activities carefully. Treat each throwaway prototype as an experiment. Develop a hypothesis such as, "A disk-based merge-sort will sort 10,000 records in less than 30 seconds." Then be sure that the prototyping activity stays focused on proving or disproving the hypothesis. Don't let it stray off into related areas, and make sure that the prototyping stops as soon as the hypothesis has been proved or disproved.

CROSS-REFERENCE
For more on creating realistic schedule and budget expectations, see "Unrealistic schedule and budget expectations" in Section 20.2.

Unrealistic schedule and budget expectations. As with other kinds of prototyping, when users, managers, or marketers see rapid progress on a prototype, they sometimes make unrealistic assumptions about how quickly the final product can be developed. The time required to move from a throwaway-prototype implementation to implementation in the target language is sometimes grossly underestimated.

The best way to combat this risk is to estimate the development of the prototype and the development of the final product as separate projects.

38.3   Side Effects of Throwaway Prototyping

In addition to its rapid-development benefits, Throwaway Prototyping produces many side effects, most of which are beneficial. Prototyping tends to:

- Reduce project risk (since you explore risky implementation areas early)
- Improve maintainability
- Provide resistance to creeping requirements
- Provide a good opportunity to train inexperienced programmers since the code they write will be thrown away anyway

38.4 Throwaway Prototyping's Interactions with Other Practices

You can use prototyping in one form or another on most kinds of projects regardless of what other practices are used. Even in projects in which you can't use full-scale Evolutionary Prototyping (Chapter 21), you can still often use Throwaway Prototyping to explore key risk areas.

38.5 The Bottom Line on Throwaway Prototyping

The greatest schedule benefit of Throwaway Prototyping arises from its risk-reduction potency. It might not shorten a schedule at all, but by exploring high-risk areas early, it reduces schedule volatility. Any direct schedule benefits from Throwaway Prototyping depend on what specific area of a product is prototyped.

Steven J. Andriole has run his own requirements-modeling and prototyping business since 1980 and is the author of *Rapid Application Prototyping* (Andriole 1992). He says that the main lesson he's learned in his business is that the Throwaway Prototyping practice, when used to clarify requirements, "is *always* cost effective and *always* improves specifications" (his emphasis) (Andriole 1994).

38.6 Keys to Success in Using Throwaway Prototyping

Here are the keys to using the Throwaway Prototyping practice successfully:

- Choose your prototyping language or environment based on how quickly it will allow you to create throwaway code.
- Be sure that both management and technical staffs are committed to throwing away the throwaway prototype.
- Focus prototyping efforts on areas that are poorly understood.
- Treat prototyping activities as scientific experiments, and monitor and control them carefully.

Further Reading

For further reading on prototyping, see Chapter 21, "Evolutionary Prototyping."

39

Timebox Development

Timebox Development is a construction-time practice that helps to infuse a development team with a sense of urgency and helps to keep the project's focus on the most important features. The Timebox Development practice produces its schedule savings through redefining the product to fit the schedule rather than redefining the schedule to fit the project. It is most applicable to in-house business software, but it can be adapted for use on specific parts of custom and shrink-wrap projects. The success of timeboxing depends on using it only on appropriate kinds of projects and on management's and end-users' willingness to cut features rather than stretch the schedule.

S
U
M
M
A
R
Y

Efficacy

Potential reduction from nominal schedule:	Excellent
Improvement in progress visibility:	None
Effect on schedule risk:	Decreased Risk
Chance of first-time success:	Good
Chance of long-term success:	Excellent

Major Risks

- Attempting to timebox unsuitable work products
- Sacrificing quality instead of features

Major Interactions and Trade-Offs

- Depends on the use of Evolutionary Prototyping
- Trades feature-set control for development-time control
- Often combined with JAD, CASE tools, and Evolutionary Prototyping on RAD projects
- Can be combined with Evolutionary Delivery when timing of deliveries matters more than contents

It's amazing how much you can get done the day before you leave for a vacation. You can pick up the dry cleaning, pay the bills, stop the mail and the newspaper, buy new travel clothes, pack, buy film, and drop off a key with the neighbors. Just as amazing are all the things that you don't do the day before you leave. You don't seem to need to spend quite as long in the shower that morning or as long reading the newspaper that night. You might have many other things that you would like to do that day, but suddenly some of those day-to-day priorities slip down a notch.

Timebox Development is a means of harnessing the same sense of urgency that accompanies preparing for a vacation except that it usually accompanies preparing to work hard instead! When you follow the Timebox Development practice, you specify a maximum amount of time that you will spend constructing a software system. You can develop as much as you want or whatever kind of system you want, but you have to constrain that development to a fixed amount of time. This sense of urgency produces several results that support rapid development.

CROSS-REFERENCE
For more on trading off resources and product attributes for schedule gains, see Section 6.6, "Development-Speed Trade-Offs."

It emphasizes the priority of the schedule. By making the schedule *absolutely fixed*, you stress that the schedule is of utmost importance. The time limit, or "timebox," is so important that it overrides all other considerations. If the project scope conflicts with the time limit, you reduce the scope to fit the time limit. The time limit itself is not allowed to change.

CLASSIC MISTAKE

It avoids the 90-90 problem. Many projects get to the point where they are 90 percent complete and then stay at that point for months or even years. Many projects spend an undue amount of time in sinkholes that don't move the project forward but that consume huge amounts of resources. You build a small version first, and you build it quickly so that you can get on to version 2. Rather than building a feature-rich first version, it's often more efficient to get a basic version working, learn from the experience, and build a second version after that.

It clarifies feature priorities. Projects can expend a disproportionate amount of time quibbling about features that make little difference in a product's utility. "Should we spend an extra 4 weeks implementing full-color print-preview, or is black-and-white good enough? Should the 3D sculpting on our buttons be one pixel wide or two? Should our code editor reopen text files in the exact location they were last used or at the top of the file?" Rather than spending time arguing about whether to include features of "very low" priority or only "moderately low priority," tight time constraints focus attention on the top end of the priority list.

CROSS-REFERENCE
For details on the way that
gold-plating can occur
unintentionally, see "Unclear
or Impossible Goals"
in Section 14.2.

It limits developer gold-plating. Within the bounds of what was specified, you can often implement a particular feature in several ways. There is often a 2-day, 2-week, and 2-month version of the same feature. In the absence of the clarifying presence of a development timebox, developers are left to choose an implementation based on their own goals for quality, usability, or level of interest in the feature's design and implementation. Timeboxing makes it clear that if there is a 2-day version of a feature, that is what you want.

HARD DATA

It controls feature creep. Feature creep is generally a function of time and averages about 1 percent per month on most projects (Jones 1994). Timebox Development helps to control feature creep in two ways. First, if you shorten the development cycle, you reduce the amount of time people have to lobby for new features. Second, some feature creep on long projects arises from changing market conditions or changes in the operational environment in which the computer system will be deployed. By cutting development time, you reduce the amount that the market or the operational environment can change and thus the need for corresponding changes in your software.

CROSS-REFERENCE
For more on motivation, see
Chapter 11, "Motivation."

It helps to motivate developers and end-users. People like to feel that the work they're doing is important, and a sense of urgency can contribute to that feeling of importance. A sense of urgency can be a strong motivator.

39.1 Using Timebox Development

Timebox Development is a construction-phase practice. Developers implement the most-essential features first and the less-essential features as time permits. The system grows like an onion with the essential features at the core and the other features in the outer layers. Figure 39-1 on the next page illustrates the timebox process.

CROSS-REFERENCE
For details on this kind of
prototyping, see Chapter 21,
"Evolutionary Prototyping."

Construction in Timebox Development consists of developing a prototype and evolving it into the final working system. Timeboxing usually includes significant end-user involvement and ongoing reviews of the developing system.

Timeboxes usually last from 60 to 120 days. Shorter periods are usually not sufficient to develop significant systems. Longer periods do not create the sense of urgency that creates the timebox's clear focus. Projects that are too big for development in a 120-day timebox can sometimes be divided into multiple timebox projects, each of which can be developed within 60 to 120 days.

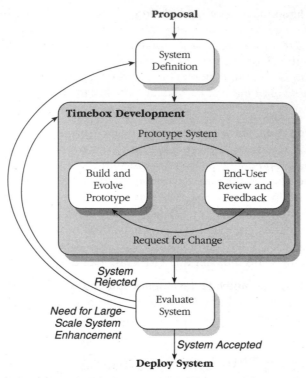

Figure 39-1. *Timebox Development cycle. Timebox Development consists of constructing and evolving an Evolutionary Prototype with frequent end-user interaction.*

After the construction phase, the system is evaluated and you choose from three options:

- Accept the system and put it into production.
- Reject the system because of a construction failure. It might have insufficient quality, or the development team might not have been able to implement the minimum amount of functionality needed for the core system. If that happens, the organization can launch a new Timebox Development effort.
- Reject the system because it does not meet the needs of the organization that built it. A perfectly legitimate outcome of a timebox development is for the team to develop the core system that was identified before Timebox Development began, but for end-users to conclude that the system is not what they wanted. In that case, work begins anew at the system-definition stage, as shown in Figure 39-1.

The people who evaluate the system include the executive sponsor, one or more key users, and a QA or maintenance representative. Technical support and auditing personnel can also be involved in the evaluation.

Regardless of the outcome, it is critical to the long-term success of timeboxing that the timebox not be extended. The end-date for the timebox is not a *due date*. It's a *deadline*. It needs to be clear to the timebox team that whatever they have completed at the end of the timebox is what will be either put into operation or rejected. If the organization has a history of extending its timebox deadlines, developers won't take the deadline seriously and the practice will lose much of its value.

Entrance Criteria for Timebox Development

Timeboxing is not suited for all kinds of development. Here are some guidelines you can use to be sure it is suitable for your project.

Prioritized list of features. Before timebox construction can begin, the functions and design framework of the system need to be defined. The end-users or customers need to have prioritized the system's features so that developers know which are essential and which are optional. They should have defined a minimal core feature set that you are sure you can implement within the timebox time frame. If this prioritization cannot be done, the system is not well-suited to timebox development.

CROSS-REFERENCE
For more on motivation and setting realistic goals, see "Goal Setting" in Section 11.2 and Section 43.1, "Using Voluntary Overtime."

Realistic schedule estimate created by the timebox team. An estimate for the timebox construction should be created by the development team. The construction team needs to estimate both how much time they need (usually 60 to 120 days) and how much functionality they think they can implement within that period. From a motivation point of view, it is essential that the team create its own estimate. Timeboxing is an ambitious practice, and it won't succeed if developers are simply presented with an impossible combination of schedule and functionality goals.

CROSS-REFERENCE
For more on languages that support rapid code generation, see Chapter 31, "Rapid-Development Languages (RDLs)."

Right kind of project. Timeboxing is best suited for in-house business software (IS software). Timeboxing is an evolutionary prototyping practice and should be built with rapid-development languages, CASE tools, or other tools that support extremely rapid code generation. Highly custom applications that require hand-coding are usually not appropriate projects for timebox development. Before beginning a timebox project, verify that you can build the project with the available tool set and staff.

Sufficient end-user involvement. As with other prototyping-based activities, the success of Timebox Development depends on good feedback from end-users. If you can't get adequate end-user involvement, don't use a timebox.

The Timebox Team

CROSS-REFERENCE
For more on effective team-work, see Chapter 12, "Teamwork."

A timebox-development team can consist of from one to five people. The full "timebox team" also includes end-users who have been designated to assist the construction team. These end-users are often dedicated full-time to their role of supporting the construction team.

The timebox team needs to be skilled in developing systems with the rapid-development software that will be used. There is no time to learn new software on a timebox project.

The timebox team needs to be highly motivated. The urgency created by the timebox development practice itself will provide some of the motivation. The ability to achieve a level of productivity rare within the organization should provide the rest.

Although my understanding of developer motivation makes me wary of his advice, James Martin recommends that motivation on a timebox project also include the following (Martin 1991):

- Tell developers that they will be judged by whether they create a system that is in fact accepted. Point out that most timebox efforts succeed and that they shouldn't distinguish themselves by being one of the rare failures.

- Tell developers that success will be rewarded and that their efforts are visible to upper management. Follow through on the rewards.

- Tell developers that if they succeed, you'll hold a major victory celebration. Follow through on the celebration.

Don't use Martin's advice verbatim without first thinking through how the issues discussed in Chapter 11, "Motivation," apply within your environment.

Variations on Timebox Development

Timeboxing is usually applied to the design and construction phase of entire business systems. It is generally not well-suited to the development of shrink-wrap software products because of the long development times needed. But timeboxing can be quite useful as a strategy for developing parts of software systems—live user-interface prototypes or throwaway prototypes on a shrink-wrap software project. Timeboxes for prototypes are much shorter than the time recommended for information systems, perhaps on the order of 6 to 12 days rather than 60 to 120. The development team will have to define a timebox that makes sense for the specific prototype they're building.

You can use timeboxing on a variety of implementation activities—software construction, help-screen generation, user-documentation, throwaway prototypes, training-course development, and so on.

39.2 Managing the Risks of Timebox Development

Here are some of the problems with timeboxing.

HARD DATA

FURTHER READING
For a different point of view on timeboxing upstream activities, see "Timeboxing" (Zahniser 1995).

CROSS-REFERENCE
For more on the effects of conflicting goals, see "Goal Setting" in Section 11.2. For more on the effects of low quality, see Section 4.3, "Quality-Assurance Fundamentals."

Attempting to timebox unsuitable work products. I don't recommend using timeboxes for upstream activities (or beginning-of-the-food-chain activities) such as project planning, requirements analysis, or design—because work on those activities has large downstream implications. A $100 mistake in requirements analysis can cost as much as $20,000 to correct later (Boehm and Papaccio 1988). The software-project graveyard is filled with the bones of project managers who tried to shorten upstream activities and wound up delivering software late because small upstream defects produced large downstream costs. Time "saved" early in the project is usually a false economy.

Timeboxing is effective on activities at the end of the development food-chain because the penalty for poor-quality work is limited to throwing away the timebox work and doing it over. Other work isn't affected.

Sacrificing quality instead of features. If your customer isn't committed to the timebox practice of cutting features instead of quality, don't use a timebox. Developers have a hard time meeting conflicting goals, and if the customer insists on a tight schedule, high quality, and lots of features, developers won't be able to meet all three objectives at once. Quality will suffer.

Once quality begins to suffer, the schedule will suffer too. The team will produce feature-complete software by the timebox deadline, but the quality will be so poor that it will take several more weeks to bring the product up to an acceptable level of quality.

With true timeboxing, the software is either accepted or thrown away at the timebox deadline. That makes it clear that the quality level must be acceptable at all times. The success of timeboxing depends on being able to meet tight schedules by limiting the product's scope, not its quality.

39.3 Side Effects of Timebox Development

Timebox Development's influence is limited to shortening development schedules. It does not typically have any influence—positive or negative—on product quality, usability, functionality, or other product attributes.

39.4   Timebox Development's Interactions with Other Practices

Timebox Development is a specific kind of design-to-schedule practice (Section 7.7). It is an essential part of RAD, which means that it is often combined with JAD (Chapter 24), CASE tools, and Evolutionary Prototyping (Chapter 21). Because Timebox Development calls for an unusual degree of commitment on the part of the development team, it is also important that each team member be Signed Up (Chapter 34) for the project.

FURTHER READING
The milestone process that Microsoft uses could be considered to be a modified timebox approach. For details, see *Microsoft Secrets* (Cusumano and Selby 1995).

Timeboxes can also be combined with Evolutionary Delivery (Chapter 20) if you need to define each delivery cycle more by the time you complete it than by the exact functionality you deliver. Similarly, shrink-wrap and other kinds of projects can use timeboxes as part of a staged, internal-delivery approach. Delivering the software at well-defined intervals helps to track the progress and quality of the evolving product. Most projects that use timeboxes in this way won't be willing to throw away work that isn't completed by the deadline, so they won't be using pure timeboxes. But they can still realize some of timebox development's motivational, prioritization, and feature-creep benefits.

39.5   The Bottom Line on Timebox Development

HARD DATA

Timebox Development has been found to produce extraordinary productivity at DuPont, where it was initially developed. DuPont averages about 80 function points per person month with timeboxing, compared to 15 to 25 with other methodologies (Martin 1991). Moreover, timebox development entails little risk. System evaluation and possible rejection is an explicit part of the practice, but after its first few years of use, DuPont had not rejected a single system developed with timeboxing. Scott Shultz, who created the methodology at DuPont, says that "[a]ll applications were completed in less time than it would have taken just to write the specifications for [an application in] Cobol or Fortran" (Shultz in Martin 1991).

39.6   Keys to Success in Using Timebox Development

Here are the keys to success in using timeboxing:

- Use timeboxing only with projects that you can complete within the timebox time frame (usually from 60 to 120 days).

- Be sure that end-users and management have agreed to a core feature set that the timebox construction team believes it can implement within the timebox time frame. Be sure that features have been prioritized, and that you can drop some of them from the product if needed to meet the schedule.

- Be sure that the timebox team is signed up for the ambitious timebox project. Provide any motivational support needed.

- Keep the quality of the software high throughout the timebox.

- If you need to, cut features to make the timebox deadline. Don't extend a timebox deadline.

Further Reading

Martin, James. *Rapid Application Development*. New York: Macmillan Publishing Company, 1991. Chapter 11 discusses timebox development specifically. The rest of the book explains the RAD context within which Martin suggests using timeboxes.

40

Tools Group

The Tools Group practice sets up a group that's responsible for gathering intelligence about, evaluating, coordinating the use of, and disseminating new tools within an organization. A Tools Group allows for a reduced amount of trial and error and minimizes the number of development groups that will be handicapped by the use of inadequate software tools. Virtually any organization that has more than one software project running at a time can set up a Tools Group, though in some cases the "group" might consist of a single person working only part time.

S
U
M
M
A
R
Y

Efficacy

Potential reduction from nominal schedule:	Good
Improvement in progress visibility:	None
Effect on schedule risk:	Decreased Risk
Chance of first-time success:	Good
Chance of long-term success:	Very Good

Major Risks

- Bureaucratic overcontrol of information about and deployment of new tools.

Major Interactions and Trade-Offs

- The same basic structure can be used by software-reuse and software-engineering process groups.

For more on tools groups, see "Tools Group" in Section 15.3.

41

Top-10 Risks List

The Top-10 Risks List is a simple tool that helps to monitor a software project's risks. The list consists of the 10 most serious risks to a project ranked from 1 to 10, each risk's status, and the plan for addressing each risk. The act of updating and reviewing the Top-10 Risks List each week raises awareness of risks and contributes to timely resolution of them.

Efficacy

Potential reduction from nominal schedule:	None
Improvement in progress visibility:	Very Good
Effect on schedule risk:	Decreased Risk
Chance of first-time success:	Excellent
Chance of long-term success:	Excellent

Major Risks

None

Major Interactions and Trade-Offs

- Can be used in combination with virtually any other practice.

For more on top-10 risks lists, see "Top-10 Risks List" in Section 5.5.

42

User-Interface Prototyping

In User-Interface Prototyping, the user interface is developed quickly to explore the user-interface design and the system's requirements. Sometimes a special-purpose prototyping language is used; other times prototyping is done in the target programming language. User-interface prototypes are either thrown away or evolved into the final product. Making the right choice about whether to evolve the prototype or throw it away is one key to success. Other keys to success include involving end-users appropriately, keeping initial prototype implementations as simple as possible, and using experienced developers.

S
U
M
M
A
R
Y

Efficacy

Potential reduction from nominal schedule:	Good
Improvement in progress visibility:	Fair
Effect on schedule risk:	Decreased Risk
Chance of first-time success:	Excellent
Chance of long-term success:	Excellent

Major Risks

- Prototype polishing
- Risks of Evolutionary Prototyping or Throwaway Prototyping, depending on whether the user-interface prototype is evolved or thrown away

Major Interactions and Trade-Offs

- Draws from either Evolutionary Prototyping or Throwaway Prototyping

Developers have found that putting a live prototype in front of a system's users is a more effective means of eliciting user feedback than a paper specification is. User-Interface Prototyping supports rapid development in several ways.

Reduced risk. Without prototyping, if the user interface is found to be unsatisfactory, the only options available are to discard the bad user interface and start over or to live with the bad user interface in spite of its problems. In either case, you don't discover the inadequacy of the user interface until late in the development cycle, and the cost of not discovering the mistake is high.

If you prototype the user interface early in the development cycle using development tools that are well-suited to the task, such as visual programming languages, you can develop different user-interface designs quickly, test them with users, and modify them until you find an acceptable design. You incur the costs up front, and you make the different user-interface design attempts using relatively inexpensive implementations in a visual programming language rather than relatively expensive implementations in the target language.

User-Interface Prototyping is probably best suited to business-software projects in which developers can have frequent, informal interactions with end-users. But it is also well suited to commercial, shrink-wrap, and systems projects as long as you can get end-users involved. The user interaction for these kinds of projects will generally need to be more structured and formal.

CROSS-REFERENCE
This benefit can be offset by the risk of feature creep. For details, see Section 14.2, "Mid-Project: Feature-Creep Control."

Smaller systems. One of the unexpected effects of User-Interface Prototyping is that it tends to lead to smaller systems. The features that developers think users want are not always the same as the features that users themselves want. Sometimes users will insist on having a feature that looks good on paper but works poorly in the live system. User-Interface Prototyping can weed out those features early in the project, thus making it easier to trim the feature set and reduce development time.

Less complex systems. Developers are drawn to complexity. For example, developers sometimes focus on the most complicated areas of a system because those areas are the most challenging and therefore the most interesting to them. End-users, however, often aren't interested in complexity in the same way that developers are; indeed, they frequently shrink from complexity. The most complex parts of the program—the parts that are most difficult to implement—are often the parts least desired by end-users, who are often willing to trade feature-richness for simplicity and better usability. Prototyping can identify the complex features that the users don't even care about.

Reduction in creeping requirements. Developers who have used User-Interface Prototyping have discovered that it reduces feature creep, the requirements that are added after you initially specify the system. With prototyping, users have a better initial understanding of the system than they would otherwise have, and so they request fewer changes.

Improved visibility. Developing a live prototype early in the project provides managers and customers with a tangible sign of progress earlier than traditional development methods do.

Demonstration Prototyping

A variation on User-Interface Prototyping is Demonstration Prototyping in which you develop a user-interface prototype during the proposal stage for a software product. A demonstration prototype provides a more vivid demonstration of a product concept than paper documents or viewfoil-based presentations do, and its goal is to increase the level of management or customer support for a product.

There isn't any inherent technical difference between User-Interface Prototyping and Demonstration Prototyping, but they are developed for different purposes, used differently, and produce different benefits. You develop a user-interface prototype to get feedback about a product's feature set or user-interface design, and that provides the benefits described in this chapter. A demonstration prototype can be a useful aid to obtaining funding for a project, but it won't produce development-speed benefits unless, in addition to its proposal duty, it's put to use in the ways described in this chapter.

42.1 Using User-Interface Prototyping

User-Interface Prototyping is most suitable as a strategy on new projects. You can use it to flesh out the feature set itself or just to design the user interface.

Throwaway or Evolve

Both evolutionary and throwaway prototypes are evolved in response to changes in the feature set or user-interface design. You'll generally want to keep the prototype flexible so that you can refine it in response to user feedback. Once you've explored the system's functionality with the users, the prototype can serve as a live requirements specification for the visible aspects of the program.

At some point, you begin building the real system, and at that point you either throw away the user-interface prototype and begin building the real system or you begin evolving the user-interface prototype into production code. The first decision you make with User-Interface Prototyping is whether to build a throwaway prototype or one that you will eventually evolve into production code—an evolutionary prototype. You need to make that decision at the time that you *begin* building the prototype, not the time that you begin building the real system.

One rule of thumb is: If you know a lot about requirements and have had relatively few conflicts about priorities and trade-offs, use the Evolutionary Prototyping approach. Otherwise there will be too many changes, in which case you should use the Throwaway Prototyping approach to explore requirements and user-interface designs.

Another guideline is that, on small systems, Evolutionary Prototyping is preferable because the overhead of creating a throwaway prototype makes it economically undesirable. On medium and large systems, you can use either Throwaway Prototyping or Evolutionary Prototyping successfully.

You can also prototype the main system using Evolutionary Prototyping and prototype the riskiest parts with Throwaway Prototyping before beginning full-scale development of those parts.

Choosing a Prototyping Language

CROSS-REFERENCE
For risks and benefits associated with prototyping languages, see Chapter 31, "Rapid-Development Languages (RDLs)."

If you plan to throw away the user-interface prototype, you might decide to use a special-purpose prototyping language. The main consideration in choosing a language in this case is how quickly you can develop the user interface. You don't even have to use a prototyping language. One company made screen shots of the product's screens, blew them up to giant size, and posted them on the walls of a conference room. Then they held an "art show," and had people walk through the "art gallery" and write their comments directly on the screen shots. When you use screen shots like this, they end up being covered with comments. People can proceed at their own pace, come and go according to their own schedules, respond to other written comments. This can be a useful practice.

If you plan to evolve the user-interface prototype into the final system, the most important consideration in choosing a language is determining how well the prototyping language supports the entire growth envelope of the system. Some user-interface–oriented languages offer strong support for user-interface development but weaker support for development of database, graphics, communications, report formatting, and other program areas, which can consume at least as much time as developing the user interface does. Choose a language based on its support for end-to-end product development, not just support for the user interface.

Hollywood Facade

Another key to success is remembering that you are prototyping, not developing the real system. All your prototyping work stands a chance of being thrown away if your users don't like it. Until you know for sure whether any part of the system is in or out, try to put 100 percent of your effort into the visible parts of the system. Don't spend time on parts the user can't see. Treat the prototype as a Hollywood movie facade—it looks real from certain angles, but aside from its looks, it's nothing like the real thing.

The more smoke and mirrors, the better. If the prototype is supposed to display color graphics, don't implement color graphics support in code even if it's relatively easy to do so. Instead, try to find an even easier way to display prebuilt color graphics. Create the graphics using an off-the-shelf drawing program, and load each prebuilt graphic at the appropriate time. The prototype should provide end-users with the look and feel of the program. It doesn't actually have to work. If it does work, you've probably spent more time than you needed to.

Calculations don't have to calculate: Simply show the same results every time, or switch back and forth between two sets of results. Reformatting doesn't have to reformat anything; simply swap one canned screen shot for another. The Print button doesn't have to perform printing; simply copy a preexisting print file to the printer. Data conversion from the old version of the product doesn't have to convert data; simply put up the wait cursor and then display predefined output. Have your group brainstorm about creative ways to provide the desired look and feel while writing the least amount of code possible.

Keep entry-level programmers away from prototyping. During prototyping, developers need to have a well-developed sense of how *little* they can do to explore the areas of risk that the prototype is intended to explore.

End-User Feedback and Involvement

Although User-Interface Prototyping usually improves software usability, that doesn't necessarily translate into improved user satisfaction. Inappropriate kinds of user involvement sometimes worsen user satisfaction.

You must involve end-users. You won't realize the benefits of prototyping if only developers and middle management are involved. Let the users test-drive the user-interface prototype. This will clarify the requirements, help to reveal the actual requirements of the program, improve the match between the software and the users' needs, and improve the product's overall usability.

Control access to the prototype. Unrealistically high user expectations are usually fueled by too much or too little access to the prototype. Tell the users that the purpose of showing them the prototype is to clarify the requirements. You might want to limit their use of the prototype to a demonstration of certain sequences of screen shots and operations, using the prototype more as a visual aid than as an interactive software program.

Be aware that customers don't always know what they're looking at when they see a prototype. I once developed a prototype for an analytical application in Microsoft Windows that generated graphical outputs. In the prototype, I used canned graphics so that no matter what numbers the user input, the same canned graphic would always appear. Since the canned graphics could be generated instantly, I put in a 2-second delay to create the impression that the prototype was doing the database access and number crunching that the real application would have to do.

Even with the 2-second delay, users were delighted at how quickly the prototype generated its graphics. The first time I demonstrated the prototype, several users argued with each other about why the Windows prototype was so much faster than the Microsoft MS-DOS product it was replacing. One user argued that it was because Windows graphics were faster than DOS graphics. Another argued that it was because the prototype must have had only a miniature database instead of the full-scale database. Another argued that it was because the new program was using a different math library than the old program. It didn't seem to occur to anyone that the prototype was truly just smoke and mirrors, that nothing was really going on behind the scenes, and that the graphics were actually taking longer to generate than they should have taken.

If you do a good job of prototyping the look and feel of your product, your users are likely to be overwhelmed by a live software demonstration. They will be so impressed that they won't think about whether the prototype includes all the functionality they want. If you're using the prototype to elicit user requirements, be sure that users study the prototype carefully enough to criticize it. Explain some of the design trade-offs you've made, and be sure that they understand the trade-offs and agree to them. Develop a checklist so that you can conduct a structured interview with users who use the prototype. Be sure that they look at everything you want them to look at.

Once you do get meaningful feedback from your users, evolve the prototype enough to confirm that you understand what they told you. One of the most effective ways of showing that you have heard and understood their comments is to show them an updated prototype that accounts for their feedback. In addition to building good relations with users, this helps to catch any miscommunications; it gives the user a chance to say, "No, that's not what I meant."

The Finished Product

Creating a Hollywood facade is a great prototyping strategy, but a product can't live on smoke and mirrors forever. At some point you have to decide how to move from the prototype to the finished product. At that point you have three options:

- Discard the prototype and implement the real product from the ground up.
- Fix the bugs in the prototype and ship it.
- Use throwaway prototypes for the first version of each feature and evolutionary prototypes for later versions. Implement the first version of each feature by optimizing the use of smoke and mirrors. Once a go decision has been made for a feature, throw out the prototype code, implement the real code, and evolve the real code from there.

You can also use different approaches for the user interface and the rest of the system. It's possible to prototype the user interface but develop the rest of the system using a traditional approach.

42.2 Managing the Risks of User-Interface Prototyping

User-Interface Prototyping is usually successful. It will have many of the same risks as either Throwaway Prototyping or Evolutionary Prototyping, depending on whether you develop the user-interface prototype as a throwaway or as an evolutionary prototype.

CROSS-REFERENCE
For more details on the risks of Throwaway Prototyping, see Section 38.2, "Managing the Risks of Throwaway Prototyping."

If you develop the user-interface prototype as a throwaway, beware of these risks:

- Keeping a throwaway prototype
- Inefficient use of prototyping time
- Unrealistic schedule and budget expectations

CROSS-REFERENCE
For more details on the risks of Evolutionary Prototyping, see Section 21.2, "Managing the Risks of Evolutionary Prototyping."

If you develop the user-interface prototype as part of an evolutionary prototype, beware of these risks:

- Unrealistic schedule and budget expectations
- Diminished project control
- Poor end-user or customer feedback
- Poor product performance
- Unrealistic performance expectations
- Poor design

- Poor maintainability
- Feature creep
- Inefficient use of prototyping time

42.3 Side Effects of User-Interface Prototyping

In addition to its rapid-development benefits, User-Interface Prototyping produces many side effects, most of which are beneficial. It leads to:

- More enthusiastic end-user and customer participation in requirements activities and improved feedback on the system's requirements
- Improved morale of end-users, customers, and developers
- Reduced project risk because the risky user-interface area is explored early
- Improved ease of use
- Better matches between software products and end-user needs
- Early feedback on whether end-users will accept the final system
- Decreased number of features
- Cooperation rather than antagonism between developers and their customers and end-users

42.4 User-Interface Prototyping's Interactions with Other Practices

HARD DATA

The User-Interface Prototyping practice is an effective remedy for feature creep when used with other practices. One study found that the combination of prototyping and JAD (Chapter 24) was capable of keeping creeping requirements below 5 percent. Average projects experience levels closer to 25 percent (Jones 1994).

User-Interface Prototyping interacts with either Throwaway Prototyping (Chapter 38) or Evolutionary Prototyping (Chapter 21), depending on which kind of user-interface prototype you develop.

Setting clear goals and objectives ("Goal Setting" in Section 11.2) or using Miniature Milestones (Chapter 27) to monitor progress are important aids to keeping prototyping efforts focused.

42.5 The Bottom Line on User-Interface Prototyping

The main benefit of User-Interface Prototyping per se is that it reduces the risk of developing an unacceptable user interface and having to rework it later. Beyond that, the benefits of User-Interface Prototyping depend on whether you use Throwaway Prototyping or Evolutionary Prototyping.

HARD DATA

In case studies, Evolutionary Prototyping has decreased development effort dramatically, from 45 to 80 percent (Gordon and Bieman 1995). On the other hand, Throwaway Prototyping is more a risk-reduction practice than an out-and-out timesaving practice. It helps keep schedules under control more than it helps reduce them.

42.6 Keys to Success in Using User-Interface Prototyping

Here are the keys to success with User-Interface Prototyping:

- Decide at the beginning of the project whether to evolve the prototype or throw it away. Be sure that both management and technical staffs are committed to the course of action that has been selected.

- Strive for creative Hollywood facade implementations of prototyped features that aren't yet definitely in the product, regardless of whether you're using Evolutionary Prototyping or Throwaway Prototyping.

- Involve end-users, actively solicit their feedback, and limit their interaction with the prototype to controlled settings.

In addition to these recommendations, be sure to follow the recommendations for either Throwaway Prototyping or Evolutionary Prototyping, depending on which form of User-Interface Prototyping you develop.

Further Reading

For further reading on prototyping, see Chapter 21, "Evolutionary Prototyping."

43

Voluntary Overtime

Voluntary Overtime is the practice of providing developers with meaningful work and with other contributors to internal motivation so that they will want to work more than they're required to. The extra hours provide a direct productivity boost, and the extra motivation gives developers an edge that transfers to their regular work hours. Moderate, voluntary overtime can be used in virtually any environment, but its applicability is limited by the fact that both it and excessive, mandatory overtime are already in widespread use.

**S
U
M
M
A
R
Y**

Efficacy

Potential reduction from nominal schedule:	Good
Improvement in progress visibility:	None
Effect on schedule risk:	Increased Risk
Chance of first-time success:	Fair
Chance of long-term success:	Very Good

Major Risks

- Schedule penalties resulting from excessive schedule pressure and excessive overtime
- Reduced capacity to respond to emergency need for still more hours

Major Interactions and Trade-Offs

- Requires use of sincere and nonmanipulative motivational practices
- Usually required as support for Miniature Milestones, incremental lifecycle models, Timebox Development—any development practices that make use of frequent deadlines

Too much overtime and schedule pressure can damage a development schedule, but a little overtime can increase the amount of work accomplished each week and improve motivation. An extra 4 to 8 hours a week increases output by 10 to 20 percent or more. A light-handed request to work a little overtime emphasizes that a project is important. Developers, like other people, want to feel important, and they work harder when they do.

43.1 Using Voluntary Overtime

Overtime is misused more often than it's used effectively, so keep the following guidelines in mind if you want to get more than 40 productive hours per week out of your team members.

CROSS-REFERENCE
For more on the damaging effects of excessive schedule pressure, see "Excessive Schedule Pressure" in Section 9.1.

Use a developer-pull approach rather than a leader-push approach. Trying to motivate developers can be like trying to push on a rope—you'd be better off pulling on the other end. Gerald Weinberg points out that one of the best known results of motivation research is that increasing the driving force first increases performance to a maximum—and then drives it to zero (Weinberg 1971). He says that the rapid falloff in performance is especially observable in complex tasks such as software development: "Pressing the programmer for rapid elimination of a bug may turn out to be the worst possible strategy—but it is by far the most common."

When motivation is low, it also doesn't matter how much time people spend at the office. You won't get 40 hours of work out of them. They'll put in time just to keep up appearances or to avoid feeling bad about not meeting their deadlines.

As Figure 43-1 suggests, developer motivation with average schedule pressure is already high. A nudge is all you need to achieve maximum performance. Additional pressure causes a falloff in performance.

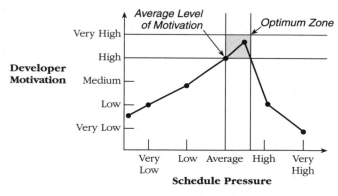

Figure 43-1. *Optimum zone for schedule pressure. A nudge is all that's needed to achieve the highest possible motivation. Source: Adapted from* Applied Software Measurement *(Jones 1991).*

It's OK to ask for a little overtime; just don't ask very hard.

CROSS-REFERENCE
For more on developer
motivation, see
Chapter 11, "Motivation."

Developers are naturally self-motivated, so the key to getting them to work overtime is to tap into their naturally high self-motivation. Create conditions that will make them want to work extra instead of forcing them to. Generally speaking, the top five ways to motivate developers are:

- *Achievement*—Give developers an opportunity to achieve something significant.
- *Possibility for growth*—Set up the project so that developers can grow both personally and professionally.
- *Work itself*—Assign tasks in such a way that developers find the work to be meaningful, feel responsible for the outcome, and can see the outcome.
- *Personal life*—Show developers that you respect their outside interests.
- *Technical-supervision opportunity*—Provide each developer with the opportunity to provide technical leadership in some area.

CROSS-REFERENCE
For more on creating high-
performance teams, see
Chapter 12, "Teamwork."

One of the most effective ways to motivate developers is to infuse the entire development team with excitement. Set a clear vision for what the team is supposed to achieve. Help the team develop a sense of team identity. And let the team know that results count more than hard work.

The importance of a results focus is one of the main reasons that leader-push overtime doesn't work. A focus on the number of hours a person spends at the office puts the emphasis on style rather than substance. On a rapid-development project, you need to focus on how much work is getting done. If people are meeting their deadlines and motivation is high, it doesn't matter whether they're in the office 50 hours or 25.

Don't require overtime; it will produce less total output. Here is one of the possible objections to Figure 43-1:

> "Sure, motivation decreases as you crank up the overtime. But the developers will be working more hours, so on balance the extra time will more than make up for the loss in motivation. Their total output will still be greater."

To understand the flaw in this argument, understand these three points:

- Most studies have shown that motivation is a stronger influence on productivity than any other factor (Boehm 1981)
- Pushing developers when they are already motivated causes a sharp decline in motivation (Weinberg 1971)
- The average developer is already working at close to the maximum level of motivation (Jones 1991)

The problem with pressing for more overtime than developers want to work is that when motivation begins to drop, it doesn't just affect the 10 or 20 overtime hours: it affects the 10 or 20 overtime hours *plus* the 40 regular hours. When you press for overtime, you lose productivity in motivation faster than you gain it in overtime. Figure 43-2 shows the relationship between schedule pressure/hours worked, total output, and developer motivation.

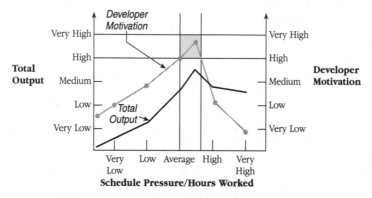

Figure 43-2. *Relationship between schedule pressure/hours worked, total output, and developer motivation. If you apply more than a hint of overtime pressure, motivation will drop sharply. Because you lose output faster in motivation than you gain it in extra hours, total output drops too.*

As the figure shows, the total output peaks at the same number of hours per week as developer motivation. Because motivation is the strongest influence on productivity, as motivation drops off, total output drops off too. It doesn't drop off as sharply because the drop in motivation is partially offset by the increased number of hours worked.

CLASSIC MISTAKE

The implication of Figure 43-2 is startling: Beyond the number of hours that the average developer will work voluntarily, you will reduce total output if you push for more overtime. It doesn't matter what your reasons are or how good they are unless your developers find them as persuasive as you do. If they don't buy your reasons, their motivation will drop and more overtime will result in less progress.

We all know of circumstances in which managers push so hard for overtime that developers work 60 hours a week or more, and sometimes in those circumstances more hours truly does result in more output. The reason for this is that once motivation hits rock bottom, it becomes possible to improve total output by demanding more overtime. The motivation can't get any worse and the hours go up, so the developers produce more total output.

In Figure 43-2, that would be a part of the graph that's not shown, the area to the right of very high schedule pressure. The problem with that practice is that it's penny-wise and pound-foolish. The overzealous manager who insists on that much overtime would gain far more by backing off a lot than by pushing for a little more.

Don't ask a developer to work more overtime than he or she wants to work. Developers are like cats. If you push them in one direction, you can't predict which way they'll go except that they won't go in the direction they're pushed. If you need to get more done, come up with a different solution.

The specific number of hours per week that's correlated with maximum output varies among projects. Some highly motivated developers hit their maximum output in a 35-hour workweek. A few might be able to work as many as 80. Typical developers in the U.S. probably achieve maximum output between 44 and 48 hours. Because it's difficult to know how many hours worked result in optimal output for a specific developer, the key to maximum output is to aim for the highest possible motivation regardless of how much or how little overtime that implies.

CROSS-REFERENCE
For more on bringing projects under control, see Chapter 16, "Project Recovery."

Don't use overtime to try to bring a project under control. When a project is perceived to be out of control, requiring developers to work more overtime is one of the most common things managers and team leads do to bring the project under control. But overtime is, in itself, a sign that a project is out of control. Projects that are under control do not require developers to work overtime. Some developers might work overtime because they are highly interested in their project, but they do not need to work overtime to meet their deadlines.

Ask for an amount of overtime that you can actually get. Opinions vary about how much time programmers can spend working. John Boddie, author of *Crunch Mode*, says that once the project gets rolling, you should expect members of the team to be putting in at least 60 hours a week and up to 100 hours a week for a few weeks at a time (Boddie 1987). On the other hand, Microsoft veteran Steve Maguire argues that people who work that many hours tend to sandwich personal tasks into their workdays. They take longer lunches, exercise, run errands, pay bills, read computer magazines—in other words, they do a lot of things at work that they would do on their own time if they were working only 8 hours a day. Maguire concludes that people who spend 12 hours a day at the office rarely actually work more than 8 hours, although he acknowledges that a self-motivated person will occasionally work more (Maguire 1994). Other experts have also concluded that you can't expect to average much more than 8 hours per day (Metzger 1981, Mills in Metzger 1981, DeMarco and Lister 1987, Brady and DeMarco 1994).

I don't know what effect schedule pressure has on the amount of time people spend working. I have often seen what Maguire describes. I have seen people work 50 hours per week for months at a time. I have occasionally seen people work as much as Boddie describes, although only for a week or two at a time.

FURTHER READING
For more on using this kind of feedback to manage a software project, see *Quality Software Management, Vol. 1: Systems Thinking* (Weinberg 1992), especially Chapter 6, "Feedback Effects."

If you're asking developers to work voluntary overtime, watch how much time they actually spend working. If lunches start to drag on and people start to arrive late at meetings because they have been running errands, you have asked for more overtime than the developers are willing to give you. Back off. You're driving developer motivation out of Figure 43-1's optimum zone.

An alternative to simply backing off is allowing the developers to cut back to 40 hours per week while you insist that they actually work each and every one of those 40 hours. That position is inherently fair and reasonable on a rapid-development project, and I think it often produces more real work hours than asking for overtime does.

After months of increasing stress, initial enthusiasm has become grim exhaustion and finally bitter cynicism. In the aftermath, these people develop a harder attitude toward spending their heart's blood on a project.

Ruth Wiener

Beware of too much overtime, regardless of the reason. By far the greatest problem associated with moderate overtime is its tendency to drift into excessive overtime. That's a systemic problem with any kind of overtime, voluntary or mandatory. It doesn't seem to matter whether the pressure to work massive overtime comes from within or without, excessive overtime and the excessive schedule pressure that accompanies it lead to the following schedule problems:

- Increased number of defects
- Increased incentive to take unwise risks
- Reduced creativity
- Increased burnout
- Increased turnover
- Reduced time for self-education and organizational improvement
- Reduced productivity

Help developers pace themselves. Even if no one is forcing developers to work too much overtime, they can sometimes force themselves to work too much. When that pressure comes from within, it doesn't have a motivational penalty, but it will likely have an effectiveness penalty.

Have you ever watched sprinters run the 100-meter dash? When they're done, their chests heave, their skin is blotchy, and sometimes they're even sick. If runners were to begin a marathon at that pace, they wouldn't finish.

In track and field events, distance runners pay an average-speed penalty for top performance over longer distances. As Figure 43-3 shows, the world-record holder in the marathon runs only about half as fast as the world-record holder in the 100-meter run.

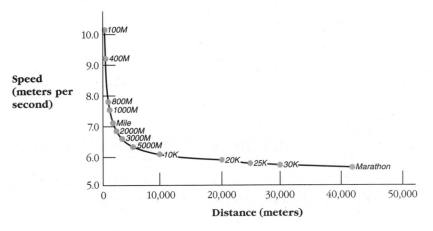

Figure 43-3. *Average speed of world-record holders in running events of various distances. As with running events, software developers should pace themselves differently on long and short projects.*

FURTHER READING
For details on the effect of program size on a development project, see Chapter 21 in *Code Complete* (McConnell 1993).

Likewise, sprinting for a few weeks is not an effective way to begin a major software-development project. Developers working on a 100,000-lines-of-code project are not as fast as developers working on a 5,000-lines-of-code project. There is more interaction with other developers because there are more people on the team, and there is much more integration work. The effect is that per-developer productivity on projects of different sizes varies similarly to runner's speeds at different distances, even when you have world-class developers.

You might be able to plan on 6- or 7-day weeks if you can sprint to a deadline a few weeks away. But if the deadline is 6 months away, you'd better be on the verge of discovering a cure for cancer or protecting the Earth from attack by space aliens to ask for that kind of sacrifice. Otherwise, that kind of sprint will just be a prelude to burnout, high turnover, and a longer schedule.

43.2   Managing the Risks of Voluntary Overtime

Most of the risks associated with moderate overtime are associated with excessive overtime and schedule pressure. Those risks have been discussed in the previous section. Here is one more.

Reduced capacity to respond to emergency need for still more hours. Scheduling overtime taps into your reserves. If you plan to complete your project by working 40 hours per week, you can ask for overtime when you run into trouble. You can probably ask for it without worrying whether you'll hurt motivation. But on a project in which everyone is already working overtime, you can't ask for more without hurting motivation and reducing productivity, which means that you actually don't have any room to maneuver.

To avoid this problem, use moderate overtime only as a corrective measure. Don't plan from the outset of a project to have developers work more than their nominal schedules. If you do run into trouble, you'll be able to tap into reserves and put the project back on track.

43.3 Side Effects of Voluntary Overtime

Moderate overtime has no side effects on quality, usability, functionality, or other product or project characteristics.

43.4 Voluntary Overtime's Interactions with Other Practices

Used poorly, requests to work overtime can lead to excessive schedule pressure (see "Excessive Schedule Pressure" in Section 9.1) and all its problems.

Because developer-pull overtime (rather than leader-push overtime) is the only way to be successful in using overtime, it's intertwined with motivational practices (Chapter 11), including Signing Up (Chapter 34) and teamwork (Chapter 12).

Moderate overtime is usually also needed to support Miniature Milestones (Chapter 27), Timebox Development (Chapter 39), Evolutionary Delivery (Chapter 20), Evolutionary Prototyping (Chapter 21), and other development practices that make use of frequent deadlines.

43.5 The Bottom Line on Voluntary Overtime

HARD DATA

If the average developer spends 40 hours per week at the office, some research indicates that only about 30 of those hours are productive (Jones 1991). When that developer is asked to voluntarily work a moderate amount of overtime, say 10 percent, two things happen. First, the developer spends

4 more hours per week at the office, which by itself increases productive hours from 30 to 33, if the proportion of productive hours to work hours is held constant. Second, the developer attaches a greater sense of urgency to the job at hand and can often find ways to increase the number of hours worked per day from 6 to 6.5 or more. Thus, overall, the productive hours have increased from 30 to 35.5, which is an 18-percent increase in output for a 10-percent increase in hours spent at the office.

The bottom line on Voluntary Overtime is that a slight increase in hours worked per week beyond the nominal, say 10 to 20 percent, will usually result in a disproportionately large increase in productivity.

For projects that start to use Voluntary Overtime during construction or testing, overtime can help to shorten a project's overall schedule by 10 or 15 percent (Jones 1991), but beyond that the motivational penalties come into play and additional schedule reductions through overtime are not possible.

Unfortunately for many organizations, Voluntary Overtime is a best practice that is already in widespread use or is already preempted by excessive, mandatory overtime. The average developer in the U.S. already works 48 to 50 hours per week (Jones 1991, Krantz 1995). Similar situations exist in Canada and Japan. This situation raises the interesting possibility that the average organization might actually increase total output by reducing overtime below its current level.

43.6 Keys to Success in Using Voluntary Overtime

Here are the keys to success in using Voluntary Overtime:

- Use a developer-pull approach rather than a leader-push approach.
- Tap into developer motivations such as achievement, possibility for growth, work itself, personal life, and technical-supervision opportunity to increase the amount of voluntary overtime that developers want to work.
- Ask for an amount of overtime that you can actually get.
- Beware of developers working too much overtime, regardless of the reason.

Further Reading

DeMarco, Tom, and Timothy Lister. *Peopleware: Productive Projects and Teams*. New York: Dorset House, 1987. Chapter 3 directly describes problems related to excessive overtime, and much of the rest of the book discusses the topic in various guises.

Maguire, Steve. *Debugging the Development Process*. Redmond, Wash.: Microsoft Press, 1994. Chapter 8 explores weaknesses in the arguments most commonly given for requiring lots of overtime.

Weinberg, Gerald M. *Quality Software Management, Volume 1: Systems Thinking*. New York: Dorset House, 1992. Chapters 16 and 17 discuss what happens to developers and leaders when they are under stress and what to do about it.

Jones, Capers. *Assessment and Control of Software Risks*. Englewood Cliffs, N.J.: Yourdon Press, 1994. Chapter 13 describes some of the problems associated with excessive overtime.

Bibliography

Albrecht, Allan J. 1979. "Measuring Application Development Productivity." *Proceedings of the Joint SHARE/GUIDE/IBM Application Development Symposium,* October: 83–92.

Albrecht, A., and J. Gaffney. 1983. "Software Function, Source Lines of Code, and Development Effort Prediction: A Software Science Validation." *IEEE Transactions on Software Engineering,* SE-9 (6): 639–648.

Andriole, Stephen J. 1992. *Rapid Application Prototyping.* Mass.: QED Information Systems.

Andriole, Stephen J. 1994. "Fast, Cheap Requirements: Prototype or Else!" *IEEE Software,* March: 85–87.

August, Judy. 1991. *Joint Application Design.* Englewood Cliffs, N.J.: Yourdon Press.

Augustine, Norman R. 1979. "Augustine's Laws and Major System Development Programs." *Defense Systems Management Review:* 50–76. Cited in Boehm 1981.

Babich, W. 1986. *Software Configuration Management.* Reading, Mass.: Addison-Wesley.

Bach, James. 1995. "Enough About Process: What We Need Are Heroes." *IEEE Software,* March: 96–98.

Baker, F. Terry. 1972. "Chief Programmer Team Management of Production Programming." *IBM Systems Journal,* vol. 11, no. 1: 56–73.

Baker, F. Terry, and Harlan D. Mills. 1973. "Chief Programmer Teams." *Datamation,* vol. 19, no. 12 (December): 58–61.

Basili, Victor R., and Albert J. Turner. 1975. "Iterative Enhancement: A Practical Technique for Software Development." *IEEE Transactions on Software Engineering* SE-1, no. 4 (December): 390–396.

Basili, Victor R., and David M. Weiss. 1984. "A Methodology for Collecting Valid Software Engineering Data." *IEEE Transactions on Software Engineering* SE-10, no. 6 (November): 728–738.

Basili, Victor R., Richard W. Selby, and David H. Hutchens. 1986. "Experimentation in Software Engineering." *IEEE Transactions on Software Engineering* SE-12, no. 7 (July): 733–743.

Basili, Victor R., and Frank McGarry. 1995. "The Experience Factory: How to Build and Run One." *Tutorial M1, 17th International Conference on Software Engineering, Seattle, Washington, April 24.*

Baumert, John. 1995. "SEPG Spotlights Maturing Software Industry." *IEEE Software,* September: 103–104.

Bayer, Sam, and Jim Highsmith. 1994. "RADical Software Development." *American Programmer,* June: 35–42.

Beardsley, Wayne. 1995. Private communication: November 17.

Bentley, Jon. 1986. *Programming Pearls.* Reading, Mass.: Addison-Wesley.

Bentley, Jon. 1988. *More Programming Pearls: Confessions of a Coder.* Reading, Mass.: Addison-Wesley.

Bersoff, Edward H., and Alan M. Davis. 1991. "Impacts of Life Cycle Models on Software Configuration Management." *Communications of the ACM,* vol. 34, no. 8 (August): 104–118.

Bersoff, Edward H., et al. 1980. *Software Configuration Management.* Englewood Cliffs, N.J.: Prentice Hall.

Boddie, John. 1987. *Crunch Mode.* New York: Yourdon Press.

Boehm, Barry W. 1981. *Software Engineering Economics.* Englewood Cliffs, N.J.: Prentice Hall.

Boehm, Barry W. 1987a. "Improving Software Productivity." *IEEE Computer,* September: 43–57.

Boehm, Barry W. 1987b. "Industrial Software Metrics Top 10 List." *IEEE Software,* vol. 4, no. 9 (September): 84–85.

Boehm, Barry W. 1988. "A Spiral Model of Software Development and Enhancement." *Computer,* May: 61–72.

Boehm, Barry W. 1991. "Software Risk Management: Principles and Practices." *IEEE Software,* January: 32–41.

Boehm, Barry W., ed. 1989. *Software Risk Management.* Washington, D.C.: IEEE Computer Society Press.

Boehm, Barry W., et al. 1984. "A Software Development Environment for Improving Productivity." *Computer,* 17 (6): 30–44.

Boehm, Barry, et al. 1995. "Cost Models for Future Software Life Cycle Processes: COCOMO 2.0." *Annals of Software Engineering, Special Volume on Software Process and Product Measurement,* J.D. Arthur and S.M. Henry, eds. Amsterdam: J.C. Baltzer AG, Science Publishers.

Boehm, Barry W., T. E. Gray, and T. Seewaldt. 1984. "Prototyping Versus Specifying: A Multiproject Experiment." *IEEE Transactions on Software Engineering* SE-10 (May): 290–303. (Also in Jones 1986b.)

Boehm, Barry, and F. C. Belz. 1988. "Applying Process Programming to the Spiral Model." *Proceedings of the 4th International Software Process Workshop,* May.

Boehm, Barry W., and Philip N. Papaccio. 1988. "Understanding and Controlling Software Costs." *IEEE Transactions on Software Engineering,* vol. 14, no. 10 (October): 1462–1477.

Boehm, Barry, and Rony Ross. 1989. "Theory-W Software Project Management: Principles and Examples," *IEEE Transactions on Software Engineering* SE-15 (July): 902–916.

Booch, Grady. 1994. *Object Oriented Analysis and Design: With Applications,* 2d ed. Redwood City, Calif.: Benjamin/Cummings.

Brady, Sheila, and Tom DeMarco. 1994. "Management-Aided Software Engineering." *IEEE Software,* November: 25–32.

Brodman, Judith G., and Donna L. Johnson. 1995. "Return on Investment (ROI) from Software Process Improvement as Measured by US Industry." *Software Process,* August: 36–47.

Brooks, Frederick P., Jr. 1975. *The Mythical Man-Month.* Reading, Mass.: Addison-Wesley.

Brooks, Frederick P., Jr. 1987. "No Silver Bullets—Essence and Accidents of Software Engineering." *Computer,* April: 10–19.

Brooks, Frederick P., Jr. 1995. *The Mythical Man-Month, Anniversary Edition.* Reading, Mass.: Addison-Wesley.

Brooks, Ruven. 1977. "Towards a Theory of the Cognitive Processes in Computer Programming." *International Journal of Man-Machine Studies,* vol. 9: 737–751.

Bugsy. 1991. TriStar Pictures. Produced by Mark Johnson, Barry Levinson, and Warren Beatty and directed by Barry Levinson.

Burlton, Roger. 1992. "Managing a RAD Project: Critical Factors for Success." *American Programmer,* December: 22–29.

Bylinsky, Gene. 1967. "Help Wanted: 50,000 programmers." *Fortune,* March: 141ff.

Card, David N. 1987. "A Software Technology Evaluation Program." *Information and Software Technology,* vol. 29, no. 6 (July/August): 291–300.

Card, David, and Ed Comer. 1994. "Why Do So Many Reuse Programs Fail?" *IEEE Software,* September: 114–115.

Carnegie Mellon University/Software Engineering Institute. 1995. *The Capability Maturity Model: Guidelines for Improving the Software Process.* Reading, Mass.: Addison-Wesley.

Carroll, Paul B. 1990. "Creating New Software Was Agonizing Task for Mitch Kapor Firm." *The Wall Street Journal,* May 11: A1, A5

Chow, Tsun S., ed. 1985. *Tutorial: Software Quality Assurance: A Practical Approach.* Silver Spring, Md.: IEEE Computer Society Press.

Coad, Peter, and Edward Yourdon. 1991. *Object-Oriented Design.* Englewood Cliffs, N.J.: Yourdon Press.

Connell, John, and Linda Shafer. 1995. *Object-Oriented Rapid Prototyping.* Englewood Cliffs, N.J.: Yourdon Press.

Constantine, Larry L. 1990b. "Objects, Functions, and Program Extensibility." *Computer Language,* January: 34–56.

Constantine, Larry L. 1995a. *Constantine on Peopleware.* Englewood Cliffs, N.J.: Yourdon Press.

Constantine, Larry. 1995b. "Under Pressure." *Software Development,* October: 111–112.

Constantine, Larry. 1996. "Re: Architecture." *Software Development,* January: 87–88.

Conte, S. D., H. E. Dunsmore, and V. Y. Shen. 1986. *Software Engineering Metrics and Models.* Menlo Park, Calif.: Benjamin/Cummings.

Costello, Scott H. 1984. "Software Engineering Under Deadline Pressure." *ACM Sigsoft Software Engineering Notes,* 9:5 October: 15–19.

Curtis, Bill. 1981. "Substantiating Programmer Variability." *Proceedings of the IEEE,* vol. 69, no. 7 (July): 846.

Curtis, Bill. 1990. "Managing the Real Leverage in Software Productivity and Quality." *American Programmer,* vol. 3, nos. 7-8 (July-August): 4–14.

Curtis, Bill. 1994. "A Mature View of the CMM." *American Programmer,* September: 19–28.

Curtis, Bill, et al. 1986. "Software Psychology: The Need for an Interdisciplinary Program." *Proceedings of the IEEE,* vol. 74, no. 8 (August): 1092–1106.

Cusumano, Michael, and Richard Selby. 1995. *Microsoft Secrets: How the World's Most Powerful Software Company Creates Technology, Shapes Markets, and Manages People.* New York: Free Press.

Davis, Alan M. 1994. "Rewards of Taking the Path Less Traveled." *IEEE Software,* July: 100–101, 103.

Dedene, Guido, and Jean-Pierre De Vreese. 1995. "Realities of Off-Shore Reengineering." *IEEE Software,* January: 35–45.

DeGrace, Peter, and Leslie Stahl. 1990. *Wicked Problems, Righteous Solutions.* Englewood Cliffs, N.J.: Yourdon Press.

DeMarco, Tom. 1979. *Structured Analysis and Systems Specification: Tools and Techniques.* Englewood Cliffs, N.J.: Prentice Hall.

DeMarco, Tom. 1982. *Controlling Software Projects.* New York: Yourdon Press.

DeMarco, Tom, and Timothy Lister. 1985. "Programmer Performance and the Effects of the Workplace." *Proceedings of the 8th International Conference on Software Engineering.* Washington, D.C.: IEEE Computer Society Press, 268–272.

DeMarco, Tom, and Timothy Lister. 1987. *Peopleware: Productive Projects and Teams.* New York: Dorset House.

DeMarco, Tom, and Timothy Lister. 1989. "Software Development: State of the Art vs. State of the Practice." *Proceedings of the 11th International Conference on Software Engineering:* 271–275.

Dreger, Brian. 1989. *Function Point Analysis.* Englewood Cliffs, N.J.: Prentice Hall.

Dunn, Robert H. 1984. *Software Defect Removal.* New York: McGraw-Hill.

Dyer, W. G. 1987. *Teambuilding.* Reading, Mass.: Addison-Wesley.

Emery, Fred, and Merrelyn Emery. 1975. *Participative Design—Work and Community.* Canberra: Center for Continuing Education, Australian National University.

Fagan, M. E. 1976. "Design and Code Inspections to Reduce Errors in Program Development." *IBM Systems Journal,* vol. 15, no. 3: 182–211.

Fagan, M. E. 1986. "Advances in Software Inspections." *IEEE Transactions on Software Engineering,* July: 744–751.

Fisher, Roger, and William Ury. 1981. *Getting to Yes*. New York: Penguin Books.

Fitz-enz, Jac. 1978. "Who is the DP Professional?" *Datamation,* September: 124–129.

Frakes, William B., and Christopher J. Fox. 1995. "Sixteen Questions about Software Reuse." *Communications of the ACM,* vol. 38, no. 6 (June): 75–87.

Freedman, Daniel P., and Gerald M. Weinberg. 1990. *Handbook of Walkthroughs, Inspections and Technical Reviews,* 3d ed. New York: Dorset House.

Freeman, Peter, and Anthony I. Wasserman, eds. 1983. *Tutorial on Software Design Techniques,* 4th ed. Silver Spring, Md.: IEEE Computer Society Press.

Freeman, Peter, ed. 1987. *Tutorial: Software Reusability.* Washington, D.C.: IEEE Computer Society Press.

Gause, Donald C., and Gerald Weinberg. 1989. *Exploring Requirements: Quality Before Design.* New York: Dorset House.

Gibbs, W. Wayt. 1994. "Software's Chronic Crisis." *Scientific American,* September: 86–95.

Gilb, Tom. 1988. *Principles of Software Engineering Management.* Wokingham, England: Addison-Wesley.

Gilb, Tom, and Dorothy Graham. 1993. *Software Inspection.* Wokingham, England: Addison-Wesley.

Glass, Robert L. 1992. *Building Quality Software.* Englewood Cliffs, N.J.: Prentice Hall.

Glass, Robert L. 1993. "Software Principles Emphasize Counterintuitive Findings." *Software Practitioner,* Mar/Apr: 10.

Glass, Robert L. 1994a. *Software Creativity.* Englewood Cliffs, N.J.: Prentice Hall PTR.

Glass, Robert L. 1994b. "Object-Orientation is Least Successful Technology." *Software Practitioner,* January: 1.

Glass, Robert L. 1994c. "IS Field: Stress Up, Satisfaction Down." *Software Practitioner,* November: 1, 3

Glass, Robert L. 1995. "What are the Realities of Software Productivity/Quality Improvements:" *Software Practitioner,* November: 1, 4–9.

Gordon, V. Scott, and James M. Bieman. 1995. "Rapid Prototyping: Lessons Learned." *IEEE Software,* January: 85–95.

Grady, Robert B. 1992. *Practical Software Metrics for Project Management and Process Improvement.* Englewood Cliffs, N.J.: Prentice Hall PTR.

Grady, Robert B., and Deborah L. Caswell. 1987. *Software Metrics: Establishing a Company-Wide Program.* Englewood Cliffs, N.J.: Prentice Hall.

Grove, Andrew S. 1983. *High Output Management.* New York: Random House.

Hackman, J. Richard, and Greg R. Oldham. 1980. *Work Redesign.* Reading, Mass.: Addison-Wesley.

Hall, Tracy, and Norman Fenton. 1994. "What do Developers Really Think About Software Metrics?" *Fifth International Conference on Applications of Software Measurement,* November 6–10, La Jolla, Calif., Software Quality Engineering: 721–729.

Hatley, Derek J., and Imtiaz A. Pirbhai. 1988. *Strategies for Real-Time System Specification.* New York: Dorset House Publishing.

Heckel, Paul. 1991. *The Elements of Friendly Software Design.* New York: Warner Books.

Henry, Emmanuel, and Benoît Faller. 1995. "Large-Scale Industrial Reuse to Reduce Cost and Cycle Time." *IEEE Software,* September: 47–53.

Herbsleb, James, et al. 1994. "Software Process Improvement: State of the Payoff." *American Programmer,* September: 2–12.

Herzberg, Frederick. 1987. "One More Time: How Do You Motivate Employees?" *Harvard Business Review,* September-October: 109–120.

Hetzel, Bill. 1988. *The Complete Guide to Software Testing,* 2nd ed. Wellesley, Mass.: QED Information Systems.

Hetzel, Bill. 1993. *Making Software Measurement Work: Building an Effective Measurement Program.* New York: John Wiley & Sons.

Humphrey, Watts S. 1989. *Managing the Software Process.* Reading, Mass.: Addison-Wesley.

Humphrey, Watts S. 1995. *A Discipline for Software Engineering.* Reading, Mass.: Addison-Wesley.

Iansiti, Marco. 1994. "Microsoft Corporation: Office Business Unit," Harvard Business School Case Study 9-691-033, revised May 31. Boston: Harvard Business School.

Jones, Capers. 1986a. *Programming Productivity.* New York: McGraw-Hill.

Jones, Capers, ed. 1986b. *Tutorial: Programming Productivity: Issues for the Eighties,* 2nd ed. Los Angeles: IEEE Computer Society Press.

Jones, Capers. 1991. *Applied Software Measurement: Assuring Productivity and Quality.* New York: McGraw-Hill.

Jones, Capers. 1994. *Assessment and Control of Software Risks.* Englewood Cliffs, N.J.: Yourdon Press.

Jones, Capers. 1994b. "Revitalizing Software Project Management." *American Programmer,* June: 3–12.

Jones, Capers. 1995a. "Software Productivity Research Programming Languages Table," 7th ed. March 1995. Burlington, Mass.: Software Productivity Research. (The full table can be accessed on the Internet at http://www.spr.com/library/langtbl.htm.)

Jones, Capers. 1995b. "Patterns of Large Software Systems: Failure and Success." *IEEE Software,* March: 86–87.

Jones, Capers. 1995c. "Determining Software Schedules." *IEEE Software,* February: 73–75.

Jones, Capers. 1995d. "Why Is Technology Transfer So Hard?" *IEEE Computer,* June: 86–87.

Joos, Rebecca. 1994. "Software Reuse at Motorola," *IEEE Software,* September: 42–47.

Karten, Naomi. 1994. *Managing Expectations.* New York: Dorset House.

Katzenbach, Jon, and Douglas Smith. 1993. *The Wisdom of Teams.* Boston: Harvard Business School Press.

Kemerer, C. F. 1987. "An Empirical Validation of Software Cost Estimation Models." *Communications of the ACM,* 30 (5): 416–429.

Kerr, James, and Richard Hunter. 1994. *Inside RAD: How to Build Fully Functional Computer Systems in 90 Days or Less.* New York: McGraw-Hill. (Includes an interview with Scott Scholz, among other things.)

Kidder, Tracy. 1981. *The Soul of a New Machine.* Boston: Atlantic Monthly/ Little Brown.

Kitson, David H., and Stephen Masters. 1993. "An Analysis of SEI Software Process Assessment Results, 1987–1991." In *Proceedings of the Fifteenth International Conference on Software Engineering:* 68–77. Washington, D.C.: IEEE Computer Society Press.

Klepper, Robert, and Douglas Bock. 1995. "Third and Fourth Generation Language Productivity Differences." *Communications of the ACM,* vol. 38, no. 9 (September): 69–79.

Kohen, Eliyezer. 1995. Private communication: June 24.

Kohn, Alfie. 1993. "Why Incentive Plans Cannot Work," *Harvard Business Review,* September/October: 54–63.

Korson, Timothy D., and Vijay K. Vaishnavi. 1986. "An Empirical Study of Modularity on Program Modifiability." In Soloway and Iyengar 1986: 168–186.

Krantz, Les. 1995. *The National Business Employment Weekly Jobs Rated Almanac.* New York: John Wiley & Sons.

Lakhanpal, B. 1993. "Understanding the Factors Influencing the Performance of Software Development Groups: An Exploratory Group-Level Analysis." *Information and Software Technology,* 35 (8): 468–473.

Laranjeira, Luiz A. 1990. "Software Size Estimation of Object-Oriented Systems." *IEEE Transactions on Software Engineering,* May.

Larson, Carl E., and Frank M. J. LaFasto. 1989. *Teamwork: What Must Go Right; What Can Go Wrong.* Newbury Park, Calif.: Sage.

Lederer, Albert L., and Jayesh Prasad. 1992. "Nine Management Guidelines for Better Cost Estimating." *Communications of the ACM,* February: 51–59.

Lyons, Michael L. 1985. "The DP Psyche." *Datamation,* August 15: 103–109.

Maguire, Steve. 1993. *Writing Solid Code.* Redmond, Wash.: Microsoft Press.

Maguire, Steve. 1994. *Debugging the Development Process.* Redmond, Wash.: Microsoft Press.

Marciniak, John J., and Donald J. Reifer. 1990. *Software Acquisition Management.* New York: John Wiley & Sons.

Marcotty, Michael. 1991. *Software Implementation.* New York: Prentice Hall.

Martin, James. 1991. *Rapid Application Development.* New York: Macmillan.

McCarthy, Jim. 1995a. *Dynamics of Software Development.* Redmond, Wash.: Microsoft Press.

McCarthy, Jim. 1995b. "Managing Software Milestones at Microsoft." *American Programmer,* February: 28–37.

McCarthy, Jim. 1995c. "21 Rules of Thumb for Delivering Quality Software on Time." (Available on audiotape or videotape.) Conference Copy (717) 775-0580 (Session 04, Conf. #698D).

McConnell, Steve. 1993. *Code Complete.* Redmond, Wash.: Microsoft Press.

McCue, Gerald M. 1978. "IBM's Santa Teresa Laboratory—Architectural Design for Program Development." *IBM Systems Journal,* vol. 17, no. 1: 4–25.

McGarry, Frank, Sharon Waligora, and Tim McDermott. 1989. "Experiences in the Software Engineering Laboratory (SEL) Applying Software Measurement." *Proceedings of the Fourteenth Annual Software Engineering Workshop, November 29.* Greenbelt, Md.: Goddard Space Flight Center, document SEL-89-007.

Metzger, Philip W. 1981. *Managing a Programming Project,* 2d ed. Englewood Cliffs, N.J.: Prentice Hall.

Millington, Don, and Jennifer Stapleton. 1995. "Developing a RAD Standard." *IEEE Software,* September: 54–55.

Mills, Harlan D. 1983. *Software Productivity.* Boston, Mass.: Little, Brown. 71–81.

Myers, Glenford J. 1978. "A Controlled Experiment in Program Testing and Code Walkthroughs/Inspections." *Communications of the ACM,* vol. 21, no. 9: 760–768.

Myers, Glenford J. 1979. *The Art of Software Testing.* New York: John Wiley & Sons.

Myers, Ware. 1992. "Good Software Practices Pay Off—Or Do They?" *IEEE Software,* March: 96–97.

Naisbitt, John. 1982. *Megatrends.* New York: Warner Books.

Naisbitt, John, and Patricia Aburdene. 1985. *Reinventing the Corporation.* New York: Warner Books.

NASA. 1990. *Manager's Handbook for Software Development,* revision 1. Document number SEL-84-101. Greenbelt, Md.: Goddard Space Flight Center, NASA.

NASA. 1994. *Software Measurement Guidebook.* Document number SEL-94-002. Greenbelt, Md.: Goddard Space Flight Center, NASA.

O'Brien, Larry. 1995. "The Ten Commandments of Tool Selection." *Software Development,* November: 38–43.

O'Grady, Frank. 1990. "A Rude Awakening." *American Programmer,* July/August: 44–49.

Olsen, Neil C. 1995. "Survival of the Fastest: Improving Service Velocity." *IEEE Software,* September: 28–38.

Page-Jones, Meilir. 1988. *The Practical Guide to Structured Systems Design.* Englewood Cliffs, N.J.: Yourdon Press.

Parnas, David L. 1972. "On the Criteria to Be Used in Decomposing Systems into Modules." *Communications of the ACM,* vol. 5, no. 12 (December): 1053–1058.

Parnas, David L. 1976. "On the Design and Development of Program Families." *IEEE Transactions on Software Engineering* SE-2, 1 (March): 1–9.

Parnas, David L. 1979. "Designing Software for Ease of Extension and Contraction." *IEEE Transactions on Software Engineering* SE-5 (March): 128–138.

Parnas, David L., Paul C. Clements, and D. M. Weiss. 1985. "The Modular Structure of Complex Systems." *IEEE Transactions on Software Engineering,* March: 259–266.

Parsons, H. M. 1974. "What Happened at Hawthorne." *Science,* vol. 183 (March 8): 922–32.

Paulk, M. C., et al. 1993. *Key Practices of the Capability Maturity Model, Version 1.1,* Software Engineering Institute, CMU/SEI-93-TR-25, February.

Perry, Dewayne E., Nancy A. Staudenmayer, and Lawrence G. Votta. 1994. "People, Organizations, and Process Improvement." *IEEE Software,* July: 36–45.

Peters, Chris. 1995. "Microsoft Tech Ed '95." March 27.

Peters, Tom. 1987. *Thriving on Chaos: Handbook for a Management Revolution.* New York: Alfred A. Knopf.

Peters, Tom. 1988. "Letter to the Editor." *Inc.* magazine, April: 80.

Peters, Tomas J., and Robert H. Waterman, Jr. 1982. *In Search of Excellence.* New York: Warner Books.

Pfleeger, Shari Lawrence. 1994a. "Applications of Software Measurement '93: A Report from an Observer." *Software Practitioner,* March: 9–10.

Pfleeger, Shari Lawrence. 1994b. "Attendance Down, Practitioner Value Up at ICSE (May, in Sorrento, Italy). *Software Practitioner,* November: 9–11.

Pietrasanta, Alfred M. 1990. "Alfred M. Pietrasanta on Improving the Software Process." *Software Engineering: Tools, Techniques, Practices,* vol. 1, no. 1 (May/June): 29–34.

Pietrasanta, Alfred M. 1991a. "A Strategy for Software Process Improvement." *Ninth Annual Pacific Northwest Software Quality Conference, October 7–8, Oregon Convention Center, Portland, Ore.*

Plauger, P.J. 1993a. *Programming on Purpose: Essays on Software Design.* Englewood Cliffs, N.J.: Prentice Hall PTR.

Plauger, P.J. 1993b. *Programming on Purpose II: Essays on Software People.* Englewood Cliffs, N.J.: Prentice Hall PTR.

Pressman, Roger S. 1988. *Making Software Engineering Happen: A Guide for Instituting the Technology.* Englewood Cliffs, N.J.: Prentice Hall.

Pressman, Roger S. 1992. *Software Engineering: A Practitioner's Approach,* 3d ed. New York: McGraw-Hill.

Pressman, Roger S. 1993. *A Manager's Guide to Software Engineering.* New York: McGraw-Hill.

Putnam, Lawrence H. 1994. "The Economic Value of Moving Up the SEI Scale." *Managing System Development,* July: 1–6.

Putnam, Lawrence H., and Ware Myers. 1992. *Measures for Excellence: Reliable Software On Time, Within Budget.* Englewood Cliffs, N.J.: Yourdon Press.

Raytheon Electronic Systems. 1995. *Advertisement, IEEE Software,* September: back cover.

Rich, Charles, and Richard C. Waters. 1988. "Automatic Programming: Myths and Prospects." *IEEE Computer,* August.

Rifkin, Stan, and Charles Cox. 1991. "Measurement in Practice." Report CMU/SEI-91-TR-16, Pittsburgh: Software Engineering Institute.

Rothfeder, Jeffrey. 1988. "It's Late, Costly, Incompetent—But Try Firing a Computer System." *Business Week,* November 7: 164–165.

Rush, Gary. 1985. "The Fast Way to Define System Requirements." *Computerworld,* October 7.

Russell, Glen W. 1991. "Experience with Inspection in Ultralarge-Scale Developments." *IEEE Software,* vol. 8, no. 1 (January): 25–31.

Sackman, H., W. J. Erikson, and E. E. Grant. 1968. "Exploratory Experimental Studies Comparing Online and Offline Programming Performance." *Communications of the ACM,* vol. 11, no. 1 (January): 3–11.

Saiedian, Hossein, and Scott Hamilton. 1995. "Case Studies of Hughes and Raytheon's CMM Efforts." *IEEE Computer,* January: 20–21.

Scherr, Allen. 1989. "Managing for Breakthroughs in Productivity." *Human Resources Management,* vol. 28, no. 3 (Fall): 403–424.

Scholtz, et al. 1994. "Object-Oriented Programming: the Promise and the Reality." *Software Practitioner,* January: 1, 4–7.

Sherman, Roger. 1995a. "Balancing Product-Unit Autonomy and Corporate Uniformity." *IEEE Software,* January: 110–111.

Sims, James. 1995. "A Blend of Technical and Mediation Skills Sparks Creative Problem-Solving." *IEEE Software,* September: 92–95.

Smith, P.G., and D.G. Reinertsen. 1991. *Developing Products in Half the Time.* New York: Van Nostrand Reinhold.

Sommerville, Ian. 1996. *Software Engineering,* 6th ed. Reading, Mass.: Addison-Wesley.

Standish Group, The. 1994. "Charting the Seas of Information Technology." Dennis, Mass.: The Standish Group.

Symons, Charles. 1991. *Software Sizing and Estimating: Mk II FPA (Function Point Analysis).* Chichester: John Wiley & Sons.

Tesch, Deborah B., Gary Klein, and Marion G. Sobol. 1995. "Information System Professionals' Attitudes." *Journal of Systems and Software,* January: 39–47.

Thayer, Richard H., ed. 1990. *Tutorial: Software Engineering Project Management.* Los Alamitos, Calif.: IEEE Computer Society Press.

Thomsett, Rob. 1990. "Effective Project Teams: A Dilemma, A Model, A Solution." *American Programmer,* July-August: 25–35.

Thomsett, Rob. 1993. *Third Wave Project Management.* Englewood Cliffs, N.J.: Yourdon Press.

Thomsett, Rob. 1994. "When the Rubber Hits the Road: A Guide to Implementing Self-Managing Teams." *American Programmer,* December: 37–45.

Thomsett, Rob. 1995. "Project Pathology: A Study of Project Failures." *American Programmer,* July: 8–16.

Townsend, Robert. 1970. *Up the Organization.* New York: Alfred A. Knopf.

Tracz, Will. 1995. *Confessions of a Used Program Salesman.* Reading, Mass.: Addison-Wesley.

Udell, John. 1994. "Component Software." *Byte* magazine, May: 45–55.

Valett, J., and F. E. McGarry. 1989. "A Summary of Software Measurement Experiences in the Software Engineering Laboratory." *Journal of Systems and Software,* 9 (2): 137–148.

van Genuchten, Michiel. 1991. "Why is Software Late? An Empirical Study of Reasons for Delay in Software Development." *IEEE Transactions on Software Engineering,* vol. 17, no. 6 (June): 582–590.

Vosburgh, J. B., et al. 1984. "Productivity Factors and Programming Environments." *Proceedings of the 7th International Conference on Software Engineering,* Los Alamitos, Calif.: IEEE Computer Society: 143–152.

Weinberg, Gerald M. 1971. *The Psychology of Computer Programming.* New York: Van Nostrand Reinhold.

Weinberg, Gerald. 1982. *Becoming a Technical Leader*. New York: Dorset House.

Weinberg, Gerald M. 1992. *Quality Software Management, Volume 1: Systems Thinking*. New York: Dorset House.

Weinberg, Gerald M. 1993. *Quality Software Management, Volume 2: First-Order Measurement*. New York: Dorset House.

Weinberg, Gerald M. 1994. *Quality Software Management, Volume 3: Congruent Action*. New York: Dorset House.

Weinberg, Gerald M., and Edward L. Schulman. 1974. "Goals and Performance in Computer Programming." *Human Factors,* vol. 16, no. 1 (February): 70–77.

Whitaker, Ken. 1994. *Managing Software Maniacs*. New York: John Wiley & Sons.

Wiener, Lauren Ruth. 1993. *Digital Woes: Why We Should Not Depend on Software*. Reading, Mass.: Addison-Wesley.

Wirth, Niklaus. 1995. "A Plea for Lean Software." *IEEE Computer,* February: 64–68.

Witness. 1985. Paramount Pictures. Produced by Edward S. Feldman and directed by Peter Weir.

Wood, Jane, and Denise Silver. 1995. *Joint Application Development,* 2nd ed. New York: John Wiley & Sons.

Yourdon, Edward. 1982, ed. *Writings of the Revolution: Selected Readings on Software Engineering*. New York: Yourdon Press.

Yourdon, Edward. 1989a. *Modern Structured Analysis*. New York: Yourdon Press.

Yourdon, Edward. 1989b. *Structured Walk-Throughs,* 4th ed. New York: Yourdon Press.

Yourdon, Edward. 1992. *Decline & Fall of the American Programmer*. Englewood Cliffs, N.J.: Yourdon Press.

Yourdon, Edward, and Constantine, Larry L. 1979. *Structured Design: Fundamentals of a Discipline of Computer Program and Systems Design*. Englewood Cliffs, N.J.: Yourdon Press.

Yourdon, Edward, ed. 1979. *Classics in Software Engineering*. Englewood Cliffs, N.J.: Yourdon Press.

Zachary, Pascal. 1994. *Showstopper! The Breakneck Race to Create Windows NT and the Next Generation at Microsoft.* New York: Free Press.

Zahniser, Rick. 1995. "Controlling Software Projects with Timeboxing." *Software Development,* March.

Zawacki, Robert A. 1993. "Key Issues in Human Resources Management." *Information Systems Management,* Winter: 72–75.

Zelkowitz, et al. 1984. "Software Engineering Practice in the US and Japan." *IEEE Computer,* June: 57–66.

Index

About the Author

Steve McConnell is chief software engineer at Construx Software Builders, Inc., a Seattle-area software-construction firm. He is the author of *Code Complete*, editor of *IEEE Software*'s "Best Practices" column, and an active developer. His primary focus has been on the development of mass-distribution shrink-wrap software, which has led him to consulting engagements with many companies in the Puget Sound area, including Microsoft Corporation.

Steve earned a Bachelor's degree from Whitman College in Walla Walla, Washington, and a master's degree in software engineering from Seattle University. He is a member of the IEEE Computer Society and the ACM.

Steve lives in Bellevue, Washington, with his English Springer Spaniel, Odie; Bearded Collie, Daisy; and elementary-school-teacher wife, Tammy.

If you have any comments or questions about this book, please contact Steve care of Microsoft Press, on the Internet at stevemcc@construx.com, or at his website at http://www.construx.com/stevemcc.

The manuscript for this book was prepared using Microsoft Word 6.0 for Windows and submitted to Microsoft Press in electronic form. Galleys were prepared using Microsoft Word 7.0 for Windows. Pages were composed by ArtSource, Inc., using Adobe PageMaker 6.01 for Windows, with text type in Garamond and display type in Helvetica Bold. Composed pages were delivered to the printer as electronic prepress files.

Cover Graphic Designer
Greg Hickman

Cover Photo Illustration
Todd Daman, DamanStudio

Cover Photo Credit
Burgum Boorman, Tony Stone Images

Interior Graphic Designers
Kim Eggleston and Peggy Herman

Interior Illustrations
Mark Monlux

Interior Graphic Artist
Michael Victor

Composition and Layout
ArtSource, Inc.